1001 ROAD TRIPS
YOU MUST EXPERIENCE BEFORE YOU DIE

1001 ROAD TRIPS
YOU MUST EXPERIENCE BEFORE YOU DIE

GENERAL EDITOR
DARRYL SLEATH

FOREWORD
CHARLEY BOORMAN

◉ Mountain road along Gorges du Nan in Vercors, Isère, France.

CASSELL
ILLUSTRATED

First published in Great Britain in 2017 by Cassell Illustrated
An imprint of Octopus Publishing Group Limited
Carmelite House, 50 Victoria Embankment
London EC4Y 0DZ
www.octopusbooks.co.uk

An Hachette UK Company
www.hachette.co.uk

This edition published in 2018

ISBN-13: 978-1-78840-093-0

A CIP catalogue record for this book is available from the British Library.

This book was designed and produced by
White Lion Publishing
The Old Brewery
6 Blundell Street
London N7 9BH

Senior Editor   Carol King
Editors   Rebecca Gee, Fiona Plowman,
     Dorothy Stannard
Designer   Damian Jaques
Picture Researcher   Isabel Tinkler
Editorial Assistant   Jack Phillips
Production Manager   Anna Pauletti
Editorial Director   Ruth Patrick
Publisher   Philip Cooper

Printed in China

Contents

Foreword | Charley Boorman

I was delighted to write the foreword to this book because the idea of the 'road' or 'road trips' resonates so strongly with me. Just the thought of being on the move stirs up a deep-seated emotion that cuts to the heart of who I am. Travelling with no real thought of the destination – it's all about the journey. Long before I was old enough to ride my first motorbike, I would stand in the garden at my parents' house in Ireland listening to the rasp and crackle of dirt bikes tearing through the green lanes on the other side of the river. A few years later I was riding those lanes myself, with visions of being a motorbike racer and that ambition came to fruition in 2006 with the Paris–Dakar Rally. On the old course in Africa – one of the most dangerous anyone can take undertake – you're up against the elements and vagaries of the desert and that presents challenges that are hard to imagine. The Dakar Rally no longer takes place in Africa due to concerns about security – it's in South America these days and I'd love to try it again.

I still ride in Africa, though – indeed, one of the tours I run takes in the Sani Pass, which is one of the many great roads discussed in this book. It is 9km (5.5 miles) of highland switchback that links South Africa with Lesotho and is dominated by a massively imposing section of the Great Escarpment known as Drakensberg. After a cup of hot chocolate at the highest pub in Africa, we'd be on the bikes negotiating a really treacherous section that's littered with smashed-up vehicles that didn't make it – at least not rubber side down.

When Ewan McGregor and I rode around the world, the road dominated every day of our lives, whether it was alpine tarmac like the Combe Laval (again featured here), which people drive just to take in the breathtaking views, or the Kolyma Highway that links the town of Magadan with Nizhny Bestyakh in Siberia. The Kolyma Highway is known as the Road of Bones because part of the foundation is formed from the skeletons of gulag labourers forced to build it under the oppression of Joseph Stalin.

Roads and road trips worm their way into the psyche and some have been immortalized on screen: *Two-Lane Blacktop* (1971) with James Taylor and Warren Oates, for example, or the iconic *Easy Rider* (1969) in which Peter Fonda and Dennis Hopper ride from California to New Orleans on a couple of chopped Harleys. Before *Long Way Down* in 2007, I was lucky enough to ride a section of the Pacific Highway with Fonda, and that's as good a tarmac ride as there is. There are others across North America, of course: Route 66 and the Cabot Trail, for example. I rode part of the Cabot when I travelled across Canada in the TV series *Extreme Frontiers*. It's a loop around Nova Scotia that takes in a plethora of different communities with historic ties to Acadians,

Scots, and Irish. That's a really atmospheric ride, particularly when the mist rolls in off the Atlantic. Such a rugged landscape – it's spooky almost and puts you in mind of the hardships faced by the very first settlers who landed. The road trips in this book cover the globe and I've been fortunate enough to ride many of them, though the Irohazaka, or 'Winding Road', in Japan managed to evade me. That's an unbelievably twisty mountain road where young guys go to drift their Nissans. Another place I've yet to lay rubber down is South America, but that's something I intend to rectify.

Right now it's racing season and that always gets my blood pumping because some roads are also race tracks. I suppose the most iconic is the Isle of Man and I've been to the TT more times than I can remember. I've never actually raced there, but I have worked a pit crew and the buzz is like nothing I've ever experienced. Back in 2008 I rode the circuit with King of the Mountain John McGuinness, who held the lap record until it was finally eclipsed by Michael Dunlop. Whether you're a biker or not, the island is worth a visit just to take in those 60.72km (37.73 miles) that have played host to two-wheel racing for more than a century.

Anyway, enough already – after a year with a metal frame on my leg, I'm back on a bike and, having read this book, it's time to grab a crash helmet and go.

June 2017

Introduction | Darryl Sleath

My lifelong love of the road trip began as a child growing up in suburban middle England when my two brothers and I were packed into the back of the family Ford Cortina ready for our annual summer getaway to somewhere by the sea in Wales. For me the journey was the most exciting part of the holiday, watching the countryside change from the flat arable lands of the English East Midlands to rugged and dramatic coastal landscapes out west; despite the inevitable squabbles for elbow room, and burning bare legs on searing vinyl seats, it was that sense of anticipation that inspired this young automotive adventurer.

However, it wasn't until my university exchange year at the University of Northern Colorado that I experienced my first epic road trip, travelling more than 2,092km (1,300 miles) in a non-stop caffeine-fuelled sprint to Matamoros in Mexico for the famous college spring break. Sure, flying would have been quicker – but then I would not have been schooled in the joys of The Doors (from 'Strange Days' through 'L.A. Woman') by my American co-passengers, for which I will always be thankful, or forged lifelong friendships in those long hours on the road. I would not have experienced the wonderful melancholy emptiness of New Mexico's Great Plains, the kindness of strangers in small-town America during our numerous breakdowns or eaten ridiculous quantities of meat at The Big Texan Steak Ranch in Amarillo. As a geography undergraduate, who until then had never driven outside the UK, it was an invaluable life-changing lesson in the sheer vastness of the USA and just how little of the planet I had seen. Aged just 19, I made it my mission from that point on to grasp every road-tripping opportunity that came my way.

Working as a motoring journalist, I've been lucky enough to get paid for driving many of the fabulous roads included in this volume; I've explored France in a press fleet Maserati Quattroporte making films about forgotten Formula One circuits; raced to the tip of Scotland in an Aston Martin Vanquish; and toured southern Ireland in a beautiful Morgan V6 Roadster. However, it's not always about the car; my proudest road-trip achievement has to be an ill-advised reliability test, among a convoy of British jalopies, driving a 1.1-litre Austin Metro to Casablanca in Morocco. The plucky little motor didn't miss a beat on this transcontinental escapade into North Africa, and yet, it was swapped on the return leg for a round of tea and cakes with a delighted Gibraltarian waiter before flying home.

There are an estimated 64 million km (40 million miles) of highway, dirt track, ice road, tunnel, and bridges swathed around the globe; this book strives to inspire like-minded explorers to sample some of the most extreme, breathtaking and extraordinary journeys our planet has to offer. The featured road trips vary in length and severity, from a trans-global motorcycling challenge following the tyre tracks of Ewan McGregor and Charley Boorman's *Long Way Round* (2004) TV series to a short blast around Monaco's Formula One street circuit; many are easy well-signposted tours on smooth tarmac, while others will need nerves of steel, a seriously capable vehicle and very good health insurance before you even think of tackling them.

Pooling the collective road-tripping experiences from a team of well-travelled writers we have included a broad mix of the most spectacular, exhilarating and rewarding drives from every country on the planet that was feasibly accessible at the time of publication. But, of course, the global road network is ever-changing; new passes are forged across mountains, engineers bridge the once-uncrossable chasms and scenic tourist routes open up in developing holiday destinations.

Each fact-packed entry provides information about distances, start and finish points, potential hazards, inclines, road surfaces and, in most cases, map links to assist in the planning of some unforgettable road trips. Although a small number of the more extreme undertakings are only possible at certain times of the year, with special permits, or with specialist vehicles, the majority are accessible to the ordinary motorist and rider.

Road trips are placed within one of three categories: Scenic, Adventure and Culture. The first theme is obvious enough; these explore some of the most dramatic, imposing, and visually impressive regions of the world that can be accessed by motorized vehicle, from the towering red-rock Mesa of Utah's Monument Valley, to Alpine tourist routes through high-altitude meadows and snowcapped peaks, from palm-fringed coastal roads of the Caribbean to the volcanic wilderness of Iceland. Narrowing down the shortlist of those to include and which to omit within this theme was an extremely tricky task; especially in the Alps, Scandinavia and across the USA, where hundreds of official scenic drives have been carefully conceived and signposted by government agencies keen to encourage vehicular tourism. To squeeze in a few extra ones, we've sometimes included references to other scenic routes nearby, tempting side roads, must-see stop-offs and interesting detours should you wish to embellish the Scenic itineraries.

The Adventure theme road trips hope to inspire travellers looking for more extreme challenges, long-distance explorations or high-octane thrills. Intrepid types will be stirred by the mere name of some routes included: Ecuador's Avenue of the Volcanoes, Trampolín del Diablo (Devil's Trampoline) in Columbia and, of course,

Bolivia's infamous Road of Death to list just a few macabre-sounding highlights. It is within this category that we find some of the more perilous expeditions that require a good head for heights, a confident driver and occasionally the assistance of a good local guide to ensure safe passage and points of interest are not missed en route. When I was whittling down the list of white-knuckle rides to include in this theme, New Zealand's spectacular Skippers Canyon Road and the cliff-clinging Shafer Canyon Trail in Utah were two vertiginous Adventure challenges that really grabbed my attention and now sit near the very top of my personal road-tripping bucket list (just below the Bolivian salt roads of Salar de Uyuni in No. 1 spot). Road trips with high-octane credentials have also been included under this theme, encouraging motorsport fans to tackle historic hill-climbing venues such as Mont Ventoux in southern France, legendary road circuits including Germany's notorious Nürburgring and the demanding Isle of Man TT Mountain Course.

Journeys of discovery that follow routes of some historical significance, important social reference or simply offer the best whistle-stop tour of a region have been grouped under the broad theme of Culture. These might include road trips inspired by music, such as Mississippi's Blues Highway, road movies – from Steven Spielberg's terrifying cult classic *Duel* (1971) to the comedy-drama *Little Miss Sunshine* (2006) – and numerous works of literature from authors such as Jack Kerouac and the drug-fuelled exploits of Hunter S. Thompson. We've also endeavoured to include routes of political and military import such the Ho Chi Minh Trail in Vietnam, the Lewis and Clark Trail Highway, the fabulous Route Napoléon through Provence and the confusingly named Harriet Tubman Byway, commemorating the secret escape routes through Maryland used by freedom-seeking African-American slaves.

We also introduce a number of motoring and motorcycling pioneers within the Culture theme, including Erwin 'Cannonball' Baker who in 1914 rode his Indian V-Twin across the USA in a record-breaking eleven days. But arguably the most important character in this book is Bertha Benz (wife of Karl Benz who had patented the first self-propelled automobile in 1886). In 1888, she embarked on the world's first road trip when she drove her husband's prototype Motorwagen No. 3, without his knowledge and with their two young sons onboard, from Mannheim in southern Germany to her mother's home in Pforzheim, picking up the solvent-based fuel from village pharmacists and improvising repairs along the way. This landmark 106-km- (66-mile) long journey is now commemorated with an official tourist route. Of course, the motorcar has had a massive impact on culture in general. At the dawn of the 20th century it was still an extravagant indulgence, and cars were fragile playthings owned by a privileged handful of super-rich enthusiasts. Today, there are an estimated two billion motor vehicles traversing planet Earth. Motorized transport has reshaped the world we live in. People now have the opportunity to dwell, work and explore almost anywhere their imaginations can take them. This newfound mobility has allowed cities to expand, trade to flourish and given mankind an unprecedented freedom of movement. In the 1840s it took American pioneers up to six months to travel the 3,490-km- (2,170-mile) long Oregon Trail from Independence, Missouri, out west; today, driving on modern tarmac interstate, you could make that journey in little more than a week.

To some folks those two billion automobiles, motorcycles, trucks, off-roaders, camper vans, RVs, buses plus a myriad of other types of vehicle, are simply convenient machines that help make the world we live in feel considerably smaller. To others, cars and bikes have been elevated to the ranks of modern art; they've become status symbols, a chance to show off one's wealth and tastes. But, to the true automotive adventurer, just the sight of a dog-eared key fob or battered motorcycle helmet represents much more than that: it's a world of possibilities, the chance to see new horizons, to choose your own path, meet new characters and expand one's mind.

Note: The road trips within have been carefully organized geographically by continent, country and state or region, from west to east and north to south across the globe for ease of reference. You will also find an index by country on page 12 and an index by distance on page 950 to help with the planning of your two- or four-wheeled escapades. Around three-quarters of the road trips featured here are accompanied by specially commissioned digital route outlines that can be explored with Google Maps. Others include links to official websites dedicated to that particular road or region, or useful guides produced by third parties with specialist knowledge of that itinerary. Please note that digital maps are only intended as a quick reference locator guide to whet your appetite for some amazing automotive adventures, rather than detailed and accurate route maps. Journeys suggested in this present volume should be only undertaken with due diligence. Check ahead with official highway authorities when possible and with your government's foreign travel advice website where necessary. Prepare your vehicle appropriately, drive/ride within your limits and always check the weather forecast. Enjoy yourself, stay safe and, as the old truckers' saying goes: 'Keep the shiny side up and the greasy side down.'

Index of Drives by Country

Index of Drives by Country

Index of Drives by Country

Index of Drives by Country

The Americas

◐ Drive through Canyonlands
National Park in Utah, USA.

Denali Highway Alaska, USA

Start Cantwell   **End** Paxson   **Distance** 217km (135 miles)
Type Scenic   **Info** goo.gl/KksONU

Opened in 1957, the Denali Highway – officially Alaska Route 8 – took more than 320km (200 miles) off the previous land journey between Cantwell and Paxson, but it is no easy drive. The first 3km (2 miles) heading east are paved, and so too are the last 33km (21 miles), but in between the road is gravel, a surface that conspires with the sub-Arctic climate to make the journey hazardous even during the short season (late May to early October) when the road is open. Weather conditions can change in moments, and consequently most rental companies forbid customers to use this road at any time.

The highway crosses numerous rivers, notably the Maclaren, a tributary of the Susitna, and passes over Maclaren Summit; at 1,245m (4,086ft) above sea level, it's the second-highest road in Alaska. (The highest is on the Dalton Highway through the Atigun Pass.)

The route has few amenities, but there are some well-equipped campgrounds, notably at Tangle Lakes, a base for the Delta River canoe trail. This is hunting territory, so big game tend to give the area a wide berth; nevertheless, grizzly bear sightings are not uncommon. The road also crosses the path of a herd of caribou – an estimated 36,000 head – that migrate in late autumn and early spring. **JP**

❶ The Denali Highway is a route through a wilderness.

Seward Highway Alaska, USA

Start Seward   **End** Anchorage   **Distance** 204km (127 miles)
Type Scenic   **Info** goo.gl/HK5euy

It's difficult to find a drive in Alaska that isn't scenic, but with its remarkable range of features – meadows and mountains, forests and fjords – the Seward Highway is hard to beat. It was completed in 1951 to link the state capital, Anchorage, with the small but hugely important fishing port of Seward, whose city motto is 'Alaska Starts Here'.

The scenery starts as soon as you leave from the highway's Mile 0 and drive past Resurrection Bay, a monumental fjord surrounded by mountains. Here you will see not only kayaks and fishing boats, but you should also look out for whales, seals and otters. The name of the first main town you pass through also tells you what other wildlife you might spot around here: Bear Creek. Farther north is another clue, since the road weaves through Moose Pass.

Farther north still the highway reaches another dramatic waterscape, Turnagain Arm, and passes through the ruins of the town of Portage, which disappeared during an earthquake in 1964 on Good Friday. The road then follows the northern shore of the lake almost all the way to Anchorage. On this section you will see signs for features such as the Bird Point Scenic Overlook and the Beluga Point Lookout, before you reach the last stretch of the highway. **MG**

❶ Some of the spectacular scenery along the route.

Chiniak Highway
Alaska, USA

Start Kodiak
End Cape Chiniak
Distance 71 km (44 miles)
Type Scenic
Info goo.gl/KKoi5l

It is hard to go anywhere in Alaska and not have a breathtaking scenic drive of some sort, but this route along the shoreline on Kodiak Island is especially impressive. Kodiak is the second-largest island in the United States (after Hawaii), and this itinerary gives you some of its majestic mountainous scenery on one side and almost constant sea views on the other.

The drive starts in the island's main town, Kodiak, which is the transport hub for the Alaskan mainland. It takes you across a couple of bridges, at the second of which, over the Russian River, you have a chance in late summer to see spawning salmon and perhaps even Kodiak brown bears attempting to catch them.

Soon after, where the road sweeps around the bay, you will see on your left the site of a World War II submarine dock. Over the next headland, look for signs for Happy Beach, a good place to pull over and enjoy the seashore – a mix of stones and black sand. On the opposite side of the bay, Mayflower Beach will offer you another temptation to stop.

Eventually, a scattering of huts and houses indicates you're reaching the final tiny settlement, Chiniak, which makes Kodiak look like New York City. You can drive on as far as Cape Chiniak, where a last short hike will take you to one of the best views of the whole drive. **MG**

❶ The flat and treeless south of Kodiak gradually gives way to the forested and mountainous northern region.

Parks Highway

Alaska, USA

Start Anchorage
End Fairbanks
Distance 576 km (358 miles)
Type Scenic
Info goo.gl/CulE6p

When you answer the question 'Where did you go on holiday?' with a nonchalant 'Oh, I just drove along the Parks Highway in Alaska', it is fair to assume that the questioner will be impressed by your courageous pioneering spirit.

However, the great thing about this highway across the United States' most northern state is that it is easy to travel by motorbike, car or RV. Those wide-eyed friends back home probably won't know that it's a well-maintained, high-quality highway that is open all year round.

Yes, it crosses some fearsome terrain, including a bridge 77m (254ft) above a creek on the Hurricane Gulch, and the lookout spot from which you can see the United States' tallest peak, Mt Denali, 6,190m (20,310ft) above sea level. But it is also the main route between Alaska's two biggest cities, Anchorage and Fairbanks, and it runs alongside the railroad for much of its length, so you won't be twisting around hairpin bends or climbing scary gradients, but you will get plenty of amazing views of forests, lakes, rivers and, of course, snowy mountains. It's also the best way to reach many of the world's finest ski areas and activity centres.

But beware: If you turn off the main road, even for a few miles, you can suddenly find yourself in wilderness ... And in winter, the road conditions will deter you from travelling too far. **SH**

❶ The Parks Highway takes a sweet and easy course through some of the world's most challenging terrain.

James W. Dalton Highway
Alaska, USA

Start Livengood
End Deadhorse
Distance 666km (414 miles)
Type Adventure
Info goo.gl/AupqXt

The James Dalton Highway often crops up on Internet compendiums of 'Most Dangerous Roads', often in the top five. It's an isolated road that starts at Livengood, near Fairbanks, and runs up to Deadhorse, just a few miles from the Arctic Ocean.

The road – named after James Dalton, who pioneered oil exploration in Alaska – was built as a supply route during the construction of the Trans-Alaska Pipeline in the 1970s. As well as extreme weather, there are some testing climbs and descents. At its highest point, it's more than 1,400m (4,700 ft) above sea level.

Although the road surface is unsealed in parts, it is traversed by some massive commercial vehicles that give little quarter to cars and motorcycles; since 2009 it has regularly starred in the History Channel's *Ice Road Truckers*, and, in 2011, it appeared on BBC TV's *World's Most Dangerous Roads* TV series.

For an ominous 666km (414 miles), The Dalton runs through one of the most isolated areas of the United States, with only three settlements along its entire length (total population at time of publication of the present volume: 57). That means there are few places to stop for fuel (which is ironic given that this is Alaskan oil country), food or medical attention if things go wrong. One final thing to beware of: you might want to keep a beady eye out for polar bears, too. **JI**

❶ Not all of the James Dalton Highway is sealed like this; parts of it are dirt track.

Richardson Highway
Alaska, USA

Start Valdez
End Fairbanks
Distance 600km (370 miles)
Type Adventure
Map goo.gl/5NyMmD

Fairbanks is the second-largest city in Alaska, after Anchorage. One of the challenges to its original development was its location, several hundred miles from the nearest port, Valdez. The two were connected by a proper road for the first time in 1910, when the Richardson Highway became the first major road to be built in Alaska. It was constructed as an army project and named after the general in charge, Wilds P. Richardson.

The road is still in good condition, give or take routine wear and tear, and is a full day's drive (longer with stops), starting with views over the Chugach Mountains and passing close to Valdez Glacier Lake. A short diversion allows you to see the glacier and icebergs on the lake, though there are many other outstanding sights along the way.

Two separate stretches of the road have been designated State Scenic Byways, and its highest point is about halfway along, where you drive through the Isabel Pass, 1,000m (3,280ft) above sea level, from where there are breathtaking views of glaciers and ice-carved landscapes. Just beyond is the startling and aptly named Rainbow Ridge, where rocks of various compositions paint the slopes in a kaleidoscope of colours.

It's impossible to highlight every feature of this remarkable and lengthy drive. Little can properly prepare you. Just drive it. **MG**

❶ Even the flat sections of the Richardson Highway are enlivened by stunning mountain scenery.

Pasagshak Bay Road
Alaska, USA

Start Olds River Inn
End Olds River Inn
Distance 27km (17 miles)
Type Adventure
Info goo.gl/9djWTO

If you want to drive Pasagshak Bay Road, you must first get yourself to the second-largest island in the United States. Kodiak Island is separated from southern Alaska by the Shelikof Strait. It is a verdant place, dubbed the Emerald Isle by locals, with 160km (100 miles) of paved and gravel roads that extend from the city of Kodiak into the wilderness, where 3,500 Kodiak bears feed on salmon.

Kodiak Island is one vast wilderness, but the nicely paved Pasagshak Bay Road – an out-and-back spur off Chiniak Highway, beginning at the Olds River Inn – will take you out to the inlet after which it is named. This is a favourite spot for barbecues and whale watching. If you come in November or December to the causeway over Lake Rose Tead, you might see hundreds of bald eagles feeding on sockeye salmon. The Pacific Spaceport Complex – Alaska, a rocket test and launch site owned by the Alaska Aerospace Corporation, is next, and the end of the road is Fossil Beach, reached via an unimproved 4WD-only road with the very real prospect of finding prehistoric relics embedded in its cliffs.

This is just a snapshot of the sort of terrain through which Pasagshak Bay Road runs. I bet you're already inquiring about car ferries. **BDS**

◐ Pasagshak Bay and the village of Pasagshak.

Haines Highway
USA/Canada

Start Haines, Alaska, USA
End Haines Junction, Yukon, Canada
Distance 238 km (148 miles)
Type Scenic
Map goo.gl/ZzK5PO

The journey ahead seems rather mild when you arrive at Haines. You'll be at sea level, with an airport and a picturesque cruise-ship harbour. The main street has busy stores and restaurants, and you'll find museums of history, native heritage, the salmon industry and local crafts. In the summer it can get warm and sunny down by the ocean. It's still flat as you follow the Chilkat River out of town on the Haines Highway, passing a nature reserve for bald eagles. A little farther you can stop at a Tlingit Native American village for heritage tours.

But after crossing into Canada, you start to climb into tall glaciated mountains. The views are memorable as the road rises to Haines Summit at 1,070m (3,510ft) above sea level. You'll pass waterfalls, tree-lined lakes and an extensive range of challenging hiking trails. You'll also see warnings about grizzly bears.

The two-lane paved road is open all year, but check weather reports. In winter it can get severe up here. There are no rest stops either, so fill up with fuel, food and drinks before you set out.

Finally, the road descends to link with the Alaska Highway at Haines Junction, a tiny, remote village of just 240 habitations where winter temperatures can fall as low as -48°C (-54°F). There's not much to do here, but the village does have fuel, food and beds for the night. **SH**

Golden Circle
Canada/USA

The town of Bennett, next to Bennett Lake, one of the many lakes in the Yukon.

Start Whitehorse, Yukon, Canada
End Whitehorse, Yukon, Canada
Distance 601km (373 miles)
Type Adventure
Info goo.gl/V2yMbX

You get a feeling for the emptiness of the Yukon in Canada when you learn that its only city, Whitehorse, has a population of less than 30,000, and this in an area that's larger than the US state of California. This road trip loops through wondrous scenery, incorporating mountains, ocean, rainforests and even sand dunes.

Heading west from Whitehorse, the drive takes in part of the Alaska Highway, the momentous 2,232-km- (1,387-mile) long road that was built in 1942 to connect Alaska with the 48 contiguous US states via Canada. As you head towards the first major stop, Haines Junction, you have mountains to the left and right, and straight ahead the Kluane mountain range, containing Canada's highest peak, Mt Logan, 5,959m (19,551ft) tall.

Turn south at Haines Junction, and join the spectacular Haines Highway past lakes and through fishing villages, still with the glorious mountains all around. It reaches the coast at the town of Haines, Alaska, which stands between the Chilkoot and Chilkat Inlets of the Pacific Ocean. Crossing the Chilkoot Inlet, the route returns north to Whitehorse, winding between snow-covered peaks and past more lakes. At Carcross you will find the sand dunes, described as the smallest desert in the world. It is just one more remarkable feature of what is a remarkable road trip. **MG**

Pacific Marine Circle Route
British Columbia, Canada

Start Victoria
End Victoria
Distance 255km (158 miles)
Type Scenic
Info goo.gl/MTYMfF

This trip can take anything from one to four days, depending on how much time you have to spend on it. Part of the drive is on backcountry roads, so it is best to have a 4x4 that can handle rugged terrain. This route starts and ends on the southern tip of the island at Victoria, and takes in some of the most breathtaking coastal scenery Vancouver Island has to offer. Head north on the Trans-Canada Highway (Highway 1), and then west on Highway 41 to the picturesque seaside town of Sooke. Continue up the west coast to Port Renfrew, which is a good base for hiking, whale watching and fishing.

From there, head northeast to Lake Cowichan, which is where the driving fun starts, because this part of the journey is on backcountry logging roads that were paved only recently. Yet any bumps you may encounter will be worth it, since the views across the large, freshwater lake to the forested hillsides are outstanding examples of what makes the outdoors great.

The next leg of the journey is east to Duncan, Canada's smallest city, famous for its 80 totem poles. As you drive south back to Victoria, stop off at some of the wineries between the towns of Cobble Hill and Mill Bay. British Columbia is known for its ice wines, which are especially popular in desserts. From here, complete the circle by heading back to Victoria via Malahat. **CK**

❶ This causeway on the outskirts of Victoria marks the start and finish of the trip.

Sea-to-Sky Highway Route British Columbia, Canada

Start Vancouver   End Whistler   Distance 163km (101 miles)
Type Scenic   Info goo.gl/3DkscU

The Sea-to-Sky Highway Route is an apt nickname for Canada's Highway 99, which gives panoramas of the sea, rivers and lakes while climbing inland in a landscape of steely gray granite cliffs, glaciers, sub-alpine meadows, glistening snow-capped mountains and cascading waterfalls. Heading out north across Vancouver Harbour over the Lions Gate Bridge with its view to The Lions mountain peaks whets the appetite for what lies ahead.

A short detour west to Horseshoe Bay makes for an excellent stop to eat before continuing. Look out for the Shannon Falls, with cliffs that rise 335m (1,099ft) above the highway. It's worth stopping at the park here to walk the easy trail to a viewpoint with dramatic vistas of the Stawamus Chief granite monolith. Alternatively, take the lazy option – a ride on the Sea-to-Sky Gondola, just outside the ocean-front town of Squamish, that offers spectacular views of the Howe Sound fjord.

From here, it's 58km (36 miles) north to Whistler, perhaps the most spectacular part of the journey, covering the backcountry Garibaldi Provincial Park with an essential stop at Alexander Falls. If it's winter, keep an eye out for bald eagles, since between November and February annually, they feed on salmon in the Squamish River. CK

❶ A typical section of Highway 99.

Chilcotin–Bella Coola Highway British Columbia, Canada

Start Bella Coola   **End** Williams Lake   **Distance** 454km (282 miles)
Type Adventure   **Map** goo.gl/gBECN4

The sign reads: 'Steep Grades Ahead. Brakes Adjusted?' And you'd better check them. The Chilcotin–Bella Coola Highway, aka 'The Freedom Road', links the communities of North Bentinck Arm and Bella Coola to Williams Lake via the desolate Chilcotin Plateau and the Coast Mountains, with its 18 per cent gradients and 11km (7 miles) of switchbacks. The sparsely populated route traverses cliffs unprotected by guardrails, and bisects the arid canyons of the Fraser River, with grizzlies and black bears in the forests and bald eagles overhead.

Construction began in 1953 and has been ongoing ever since. Bridges have been upgraded, and most of the old gravel and sand surfaces are now paved. Most, that is, except the final white-knuckle descent, 1,830m (6,000ft) from the Coast Mountains down to Bella Coola itself; still a dirt road just as it was when first dynamited out of the rock face. Known simply as 'The Hill', it contains almost all the highway's still-unpaved surface, including a perfectly frightening section through Tweedsmuir Provincial Park that is still a single-lane road with no guardrails; a truly wild ride. People who drive it coming from the east swear they'll never go back. So bad, in fact, it's held back the local tourism industry. Sounds like a challenge, doesn't it? **BDS**

❶ The highway through the Bella Coola Valley.

Yoho Valley Road
British Columbia, Canada

Start Field
End Whiskey Jack Hostel
Distance 16.8km (10.4 miles)
Type Adventure
Map goo.gl/UqNJFi

Construction of the Yoho Valley Road began in 1904, and took five years to complete; the increased tourist traffic had some rather unintended consequences, leading as it did to the discovery of the Burgess Shale Formation, one of the world's most famous fossil deposits. That's not the only surprise. The highway also has two diabolical switchback sections.

Switchbacks are a necessary and often fun ingredient of any mountain ascent or descent, but the two between the 6.1 and 6.5 km markers on the Yoho Valley Road have the steepest reverse angles you'll ever come upon – these are fine for most drivers, but if you're in an RV, they will be among the toughest tests of nerves you'll ever face.

The road takes you along the impressively carved Yoho Valley on the western slopes of the Continental Divide, past hanging glaciers, granite peaks and plunging waterfalls. Open from late June to mid-October, it gives access to Kicking Horse Campground and most of the valley's great natural features, including the junction of the Yoho and Kicking Horse Rivers. At the road's end is the serene and seriously laid-back Whiskey Jack Hostel, the trailhead for a wealth of hikes in summer and ice climbs in winter, and the always popular trail to the base of the 383-m (1,260-ft) Takakkaw Falls, Canada's second-highest waterfall. **BDS**

Gray Creek Pass
British Columbia, Canada

Start Crawford Bay
End Kimberley
Distance 129km (80 miles)
Type Adventure
Map goo.gl/bgFN74

It has the highest rate of climb of any section of the Trans Canada Trail, a 16 pecent gradient on a seasonal, dirt-and-gravel off-road track that follows a now-abandoned overhead powerline corridor built in the 1950s. Long mooted as a hoped-for shortcut between east and west Kootenay, the trail was destined never to realize its potential, due to a series of budgetary cutbacks that prevented it from being paved. The road over Gray Creek Pass was, however, later partially upgraded, albeit only to 'backroad status', and it was finally opened to road traffic in July 1990.

It gains 1,524m (5,000ft) in just over 16km (10 miles) from Kootenay Lake to the pass, which is steep, narrow and rocky. Weather forecasts can be obtained at the historic Gray Creek Cabin on Kootenay Lake, built in 1913 to supply the area's pioneering loggers and prospectors. It officially opens every year on 1 July, but only after typically heavy snows are safely ploughed by graders, and generally remains open to the end of October. On a typical summer weekend, more than 200 vehicles take on this exhilarating off-road challenge.

Stop near the top and have a picnic on scenic Oliver Lake before beginning the long descent around St Mary Lake to Kimberley on the trail that British Columbia guidebooks describe as 'BC's most important backroad'. **BDS**

Coquihalla/Highway Thru Hell
British Columbia, Canada

Start Kelowna
End Vancouver
Distance 406km (252 miles)
Type Culture
Map goo.gl/JqOGeF

Welcome to the Coquihalla Highway in British Columbia, better known as the Highway Thru Hell, which since 2012 has been the star of a Canadian reality TV show of the same name. In the freezing depths of winter, this is one brutally tough road, mixing engine-straining climbs, brake-burning descents, black ice, blizzards and perilous drops on either side.

The Coquihalla Highway is part of the 524-km- (326-mile) long Highway 5A that runs north–south between Vancouver and Edmonton, Alberta. Its width varies between four and six lanes, and most of the surface is of a very high standard; a thoroughly modern tarmac highway. But wait until you near Coquihalla Summit. On this 200-km- (124-mile) long section, there are hundreds of accidents each year. The mountain pass is 1,200m (4,000ft) above sea level, and in winter the weather really closes in: snowstorms and fog reduce visibility to almost zero, the road surface becomes treacherously slippery with slush and ice and temperatures can drop to -30°C (-22°F).

Drivers are warned to fill up with petrol before they head off and to make sure they have warm clothing with them in case they get stuck. Good brakes and appropriate tyres are essential. In winter the 'Coq' is a hell of a road trip, on what's been dubbed 'one of the worst roads in North America'. JI

● Yak Peak and Zopkios Ridge, seen from British Columbia's Highway 5A, the Coquihalla Highway.

Revelstoke and Lake Louise British Columbia to Alberta, Canada

Start Revelstoke, British Columbia   **End** Lake Louise, Alberta   **Distance** 227km (141 miles)
Type Scenic   **Map** goo.gl/OUNE4n

This spectacular trip through the Rockies, via a short section of the Trans-Canada Highway, takes in forests, mountains, glaciers and lakes. There is also the chance to see moose, deer, elk and, near Lake Louise, grizzly bears. During the winter months, sections of the highway may be closed for several hours by avalanches or heavy snowfalls. This is also a route that will test mountain driving skills, since the highway narrows with steep drop-offs at the side. The reward is the truly fabulous views.

From Revelstoke, the highway continues through Rogers Pass, and then swiftly into the Rocky Mountain Trench. From there, the stretch of road between Donald and Golden is marked by a floodplain before climbing once more up the Kicking Horse River on a curving road flanked by forests of spruce, pine, firs and aspen. The highway then follows the Bow River towards Lake Louise, an eye-catching pale green lake that sits at the centre of Banff National Park.

Although this trip can be done in a few hours, it is worth building in extra time if the weather is clement. Drivers will feel dwarfed by the sheer scale of the Rockies. It's hard not to feel staggered by the breadth of the range and how the mountains' colours and shapes seem to alter in the sunlight. **CK**

❶ Revelstoke Lake is a dam on the Columbia River.

Trans-Canada Highway British Columbia to Newfoundland, Canada

Start Victoria, British Columbia   **End** St John's, Newfoundland   **Distance** 8,030km (4,990 miles)
Type Adventure   **Info** goo.gl/KAzNvD

In 1942 it finally become possible, via a long chain of mostly minor interconnected roads, to drive from one side of Canada to the other, although it was another four years before two motorists, Kenneth MacGillivray and Alex Macfarlane, become the first to do it. The Trans-Canada Highway (TCH) came later; 1971 was its year of completion. There were countless obstacles apart from its daunting length: the swamps of northern Ontario; the mountains of British Columbia; and on Prince Edward Island, the road base had to be shipped across Northumberland Strait from New Brunswick.

There are now alternatives to the TCH's Route 1, primarily the northerly option along Route 16 (the Yellowhead Highway). Adventurous travellers will undoubtedly be tempted by scenic detours along the way, and the TCH's dedicated website has a useful road trip planner feature.

The national parks of Lake Louise, Fundy and Gross Morne, and the scoured, glacial grasslands of Saskatchewan, plus 3,500 other points of interest along its route, mean that you had best explore the TCH when you're on a gap year or a grand retirement tour – because on this road trip, weeks have a habit of becoming months as brief stopovers become long stays. **BDS**

❶ The Trans-Canada Highway through Rogers Pass.

Waterfall Highway
Northwest Territories, Canada

Start Twin Falls Gorge Territorial Park
End Fort Simpson
Distance 836 km (520 miles)
Type Scenic
Map goo.gl/mXI8vQ

A long, but generally undemanding, drive along well-made roads parallel to the Mackenzie River enables travellers to take in some of North America's greatest natural wonders. The first of these are the two magnificent cascades – the Alexandra Falls and the Louise Waterfall – that are just over 2km (1 mile) apart near the parking lot at the starting point of this road trip.

About two hours' drive to the west is the Lady Evelyn Falls Territorial Park, which has well-marked hiking trails along the banks of the aptly named Trout River. The next stop is Redknife River, where visitors can fish for pike and arctic salmon.

The Sambaa Deh Falls Territorial Park is a popular park and campground located at the junction of Highway 1 and the Trout River. It features the eponymous cascade and Coral Falls, whose waters carry prehistoric fossils that originated in the Arctic.

This road trip ends at Fort Simpson, which stands on an island at the confluence of the Mackenzie and Liard Rivers. Originally a trading post for the Hudson's Bay Company, it is only since 1971 that the settlement has been accessible by road. There are summer excursions from here into the Nahanni National Park Reserve, where the Virginia Falls are twice the height of those at Niagara and, because of their remoteness, have only about 1 per cent of the visitors. **JP**

Tibbitt Winter Ice Road
Nunavut/NWT, Canada

Start Jericho Diamond Project, Contwoyto, Nunavut
End Tibbitt Lake, Northwest Territories
Distance 595 km (370 miles)
Type Adventure
Info goo.gl/qlFVgp

Ever since 1982, an ice road has been constructed each winter to service the mines and exploration trips in Canada's Northwest Territories and Nunavut. The road takes around six weeks to put in place and is in operation from the last week of January, for an average of 67 days each year. It varies in length from 400km (250 miles) up to 600km (370 miles), depending on the conditions. As such, it is the longest heavy-haul ice road in the world. About 85 per cent of it is built over frozen lakes; the rest of it runs over 64 land bridges.

The road, which is wide enough to avoid blockages during blizzards and allow opposing trucks to pass, is kept free of snow, since its removal allows the ice to freeze thicker and faster. Once the road is completed, holes are drilled to check the depth of the ice: if it needs to be thickened, water trucks add a new, quick-freezing layer. The road enforces strict speed limits, with a maximum speed of 60 kph (37 mph). Trucks travel in convoys of up to four for safety.

Obviously, this is not a road for the fainthearted, although its safety record is outstanding. For those tempted, take a VHF radio to communicate with the truckers, who share information about the current state of the road. **SA**

➲ The world's longest heavy-haul ice road.

Icefields Parkway
Alberta, Canada

Start Banff
End Jasper
Distance 232km (144 miles)
Type Scenic
Info goo.gl/fPqMt0

● The Athabasca Falls are among the wonders of nature on or just off the Icefields Parkway.

The Icefields Parkway is a spectacular scenic drive in the Canadian Rocky Mountain Parks – a UNESCO World Heritage Site – and through an imposing landscape of waterfalls, turquoise-blue lakes, thick pine forest and 200 square kilometres (80 square miles) of glaciers and ice fields.

A permit is needed to drive the Icefields Parkway (Highway 93), which you can collect in Banff, and a strict speed limit of 90 kph (55 mph) is enforced throughout the area. However, drive anywhere close to that speed, and you'll most likely miss the rich local wildlife; many keen-eyed drivers have spotted grizzly bears, elk, moose, and caribou feeding at the fringes of the parkway.

After 34km (21 miles) it's well worth a rest stop at Bow Lake for a good look at the imposing Crowfoot Glacier as it teeters from the mountainside. Looking west, Bow Glacier Falls tumbles nearly 120m (400ft) from a hanging valley above the lake. For drivers and riders wanting to stretch their legs (or experience the world's most extreme ice-cold power shower), a short waymarked trail leads to the base of the cascade.

Frequently listed among the world's most rewarding scenic drives, there are very few other road trips that manage to combine easy vehicular access for nature-loving riders and motorists with such jaw-dropping panoramas. **DIS**

Lake Minnewanka Scenic Drive
Alberta, Canada

Start Banff Avenue interchange with Highway 1
End Banff Avenue interchange with Highway 1
Distance 24km (14.9 miles)
Type Scenic
Info goo.gl/rAIvrO

Lake Minnewanka – its name meaning 'water of the spirits' in the local Nakoda language – is a glacial formation in Banff National Park approximately 5km (3 miles) northeast of Banff itself. At 21km (13 miles) long and 142m (466ft) deep, it is the longest and one of the deepest of the lakes in the mountain parks of the Rockies.

What you see, however, is nothing like the lake as nature intended. The construction of dams for hydroelectricity in 1912 and 1941 raised the depth of the lake by almost 30m (100ft), and thus engulfed the village of Minnewanka Landing. The presence of this submerged former settlement makes the lake popular with scuba divers.

To get to the lake, start at the Banff Avenue interchange with Highway 1 (the Trans-Canada Highway). From here on, the road is known as Lake Minnewanka Scenic Drive. As you head east, a spur road takes you down to the small Johnson Lake. Stay on the main drive, however, and you will pass the picturesque Two Jack Lake before reaching the dam at the western end of Lake Minnewanka itself. The best way to explore this beautiful expanse of fresh water is to take a boat trip. From here, the drive loops back west on itself, although this route is often closed by snowfalls between November and April. It is worth driving along, if only to see the abandoned coal-mining town of Bankhead. **SA**

❶ Storm clouds hang threateningly above the road along the shores of Lake Minnewanka.

Alberta Highway 40 – Kananaskis Trail Segment
Alberta, Canada

Start Highway 541
End Trans-Canada Highway
Distance 105km (65 miles)
Type Adventure
Info goo.gl/kP1pnk

Alberta's Highway 40 stretches for hundreds of miles up the western side of the province, close to the border with British Columbia. It's a beautiful though confusing road to drive, with its four main segments disconnected from one another and masquerading under different names and road numbers. However, its second section, the Kananaskis Trail, is self-contained and a delight to explore.

The trail begins on Highway 541 and then heads north over Highwood Pass, the highest paved pass in Canada and one of the most spectacular. Be warned, though, that the pass is closed each year from December to June to protect wildlife. The trail then advances through the Peter Lougheed Provincial Park, one of the largest provincial parks in Alberta and named after the long-serving provincial premier who was in office from 1971 to 1985, and then on to the Spray Valley Provincial Park.

It is possible to camp in both parks and watch the varied wildlife, including grizzly bears, black bears, elks, cougars, lynxes and the odd mountain goat. Nicknamed Alberta's Mountain Playground, there is plenty to sidetrack energetic outdoor enthusiasts in Kananaskis Country, from white-water rafting and mountain biking to fly-fishing and hiking trails. This road trip ends at the junction with Highway 1 (the Trans-Canada Highway), one of the longest national highways in the world. **SA**

🛈 The spectacular Kananaskis Valley is in the front ranges of the Rocky Mountains.

Riverhurst Ice Crossing
Saskatchewan, Canada

Start Riverhurst
End Lucky Lake
Distance 2.1km (1.3 miles)
Type Adventure
Map goo.gl/if8EQv

In 1967 the Gardner and Qu'Appelle Dams across two rivers in southern Saskatchewan were finally closed, and the vast Lake Diefenbaker filled up behind them. At 225km (140 miles) long and a maximum depth of 66m (217ft), the new lake severed existing communications, and a cable ferry was introduced to carry traffic on the SK-42 between Riverhurst on the east bank and Lucky Lake on the west.

However, Saskatchewan is famous for its bitter winters, so during the coldest months the ferry rests and the Ministry of Highways and Infrastructure lays an ice road across this spur of the lake.

Most other ice roads lie in the north of the province, making this southerly example a particularly accessible treat. In the absence of the kind of formal markings that might be expected on a conventional road, a degree of common sense is required to stay on course to the opposite bank. Speeds on the ice are limited to 50 kph (31 mph) and the maximum permitted load is 4,536kg (10,000lb). The other (no doubt unsurprising) restriction is that it is forbidden by provincial law to drive on an ice road before its official opening and the lake is properly frozen. If you are planning a road trip to this neck of the woods, then check ahead; the local Highway Hotline will advise you if the ice road is open. **SA**

Prairies Historical Tour
Saskatchewan, Canada

Start Regina
End Regina
Distance 925km (575 miles)
Type Culture
Map goo.gl/dqauAL

Some Canadians affect disdain for Saskatchewan, which seems grossly unfair, considering that it is the nation's breadbasket. While the southern half of the province has much to offer the road tripper, the north is largely under water, with lakes almost too numerous to mention.

A good starting and ending point to explore this inland prairie is the provincial capital of Regina, home to the Royal Canadian Mounted Police Heritage Centre. From there, take the Trans-Canada Highway west to Moose Jaw, a bootleg paradise during US Prohibition times with its infamous smuggling tunnels. Then head north up Highway 2 via the Buffalo Pound Provincial Park, where the buffalo still roam, around to Craven and the Last Mountain House Provincial Historic Park, a former Hudson's Bay Company post where you can re-enact the life of a 19th-century fur trader. Highway 1 will take you to the Western Development Museum in Yorkton, where you can learn about the prairie settlers. From there, head south down Highways 47 and 247 along the Qu'Appelle River and on via Highway 9 to Whitewood, where Old George's Authentic Collectables is a mansion of eccentric antiques. It is then a short hop down Highway 9 to Cannington Manor and its English country village before heading west at Carlyle along Highways 13, 35 and 33 back to Regina. **SA**

Parks Route
Manitoba, Canada

Start Brandon
End Brandon
Distance 869km (540 miles)
Type Scenic
Info goo.gl/BUZdtZ

This tour is a great stress buster. Relax, kick back and take in the beauty of this rich agricultural region, with its seemingly never-ending vistas, undulating prairies and attractive parks. There is much to see and do – many are the museums dedicated to rural life and the history of the early settlers. But that's not what the trip is about. It's about slowing down time. Space seems infinite, population is sparse and the skies are enormous.

Begin by heading south from bustling Brandon. At Souris make a brief stop to be swayed about on Canada's longest single-span suspension footbridge, then continue to the beautiful Turtle Mountain Provincial Park with its natural woodland, some 200 lakes and the chance to hear loons calling. Nearby is Canada's International Peace Garden, in which the 150,000 bulbs planted each year cause a riot of colour between May and August. Morden is a good stopover, and the Canadian Fossil Discovery Centre and the Pembina Threshermen's Museum (vintage farm equipment) are both worth visiting. The Fort la Reine Museum, near Portage la Prairie, is good, too. Spruce Woods Provincial Park offers wildflower meadows in the Assiniboine River delta.

The highlight of the trip is Riding Mountain National Park with enchanting lakes and mountains, wooded trails and wildlife – bears, wolves, bison and elk. Wasagaming is a good place to stay. **DK**

❶ The International Peace Garden straddles the border between Canada and the United States.

Wapusk Trail
Manitoba to Ontario, Canada

Start Gillam, Manitoba
End Peawanuk, Ontario
Distance 752km (467 miles)
Type Adventure
Info goo.gl/Pd2XyV

The trail starts at Gillam, Manitoba, one of the most northerly places in the world that can be reached by road year round. From there it proceeds southeastwards parallel to the shore of Hudson Bay.

The route can be undertaken only between January and March because it's an ice trail – the longest of its kind in the world. For the rest of the year the terrain is muskeg – boggy marsh that is neither land nor water, but an inhospitable halfway house between solid and liquid, impassable by any form of surface transportation. Beneath it lie permafrost and some of the world's most extensive deposits of peat.

There is plentiful wildlife along the way, including arctic foxes, caribou and polar bears – *wapusk* is the Cree word for the great furry white carnivore, *Ursus maritimus*.

By the New Year, these bears are mainly to be seen in the distance, basking in the tundra on the edges of the bay. But it's never completely safe on the trail itself, so a guide is essential for anyone brave enough to undertake this itinerary.

Peawanuk – the name means 'flintstone' in Cree – was built after the town of Winisk was washed away in 1986 by a flood. From there, another winter road leads to Fort Severn, Ontario; for nine months of the year, the place is accessible only by air. **JP**

Highway 60 Corridor
Ontario, Canada

Start Algonquin Park–West Gate
End Algonquin Park–West Gate
Distance 55.7km (34.6 miles)
Type Scenic
Info goo.gl/ZkkTlw

The oldest provincial park in Canada, the Algonquin covers some 7,653 sq km (2,955 sq miles). Its proximity to both Toronto and Ottawa makes it a popular destination for city dwellers and tourists alike. Geographically, the park forms part of the border between Northern and Southern Ontario, between northern coniferous and southern deciduous forests. As such, its widely varying trees and environments support a range of plant and animal species and make the park an important centre for wildlife research.

Highway 60 cuts through the south of the park and is one of the best ways to explore and enjoy this wonderful natural resource. The road runs alongside several attractive lakes and gives access to the many backpacking trails, as well as to the Algonquin Logging Museum, for this is the only park in Ontario in which industrial tree felling is permitted.

The best fun is to turn up in August or early September, when you can join park staff on a 'wolf howl' expedition and attempt to make contact with nearby packs by imitating their calls. You can't get a lot more back to nature than that. Look out, too, for moose and deer wandering across the road. Access to the park is free, although you will require a visitor's permit to use any of the trails, campgrounds or visitor centres – the benefits are much greater than the cost. **SA**

Thousand Islands Parkway Ontario, Canada

Start Gananoque   **End** Butternet Bay   **Distance** 39.1km (24.3 miles)
Type Scenic   **Info** goo.gl/p8rZsa

The so-called Thousand Islands is, in fact, an archipelago of 1,864 islands in the St Lawrence River as it emerges from the northeast corner of Lake Ontario. The islands stretch downstream from Kingston, Ontario, for about 80km (50 miles) and lie between the Canadian province of Ontario and the US state of New York. Some of these islands are more than 100 sq km (40 sq miles) in area, while others bear just a single isolated residence or are nothing more than uninhabited lumps of rock.

The best way to view the islands is from the parkway that runs along the northern shore of the St Lawrence. At the start point on the outskirts of Gananoque, the road splits from Highway 410 and heads northeast across the edge of the Canadian Shield – the massive, U-shaped, almost circular section of exposed Precambrian rock that forms the bedrock of much of eastern North America. At about the midpoint of the suggested itinerary, the parkway interchanges with Highway 137 and the Canadian approach to the Thousand Islands Bridge across the river to New York state. Continue driving through Rockport, a port since the late 1700s and now the major Thousand Islands cruise centre, before merging back at Butternut Bay onto the eastbound Highway 401. **SA**

❶ A few of the Thousand Islands.

St Lawrence River Scenic Route Quebec, Canada

Start Baie-Saint-Paul   End La Malbaie   Distance 47km (29 miles)
Type Scenic   Map goo.gl/m8an5T

The smooth road surface presents few challenges, but Route 362 through this predominantly Francophone part of Quebec Province is more than worthwhile for the scenery alone. It runs along the north shore of the St Lawrence, and the river is in sight for much of the journey.

Baie-Saint-Paul sits prettily at the mouth of the Gouffre River. It was here in 1984 that Cirque du Soleil was founded as a performing troupe of acrobats and trapeze artists; it is now the biggest theatrical production company in the world.

Two wayside villages are worthy stopovers. From the centre of the first of them, Les Éboulements, a steep road leading down to the riverbank was used

in 2008 for the world-record fastest street luge run – 157.41 kph (97.81 mph). Saint-Irénée is also pretty, and both places have numerous shops, pubs and beaches.

La Malbaie is set on the waterfront in a natural amphitheatre between the promontories of Saint-Fidèle and Pointe-au-Pic. Originally a fishing port, it became a holiday resort for Americans because it's within easy reach of the United States, and its bars stayed open throughout Prohibition (1920–33).

Another good trip along the St.Lawrence corridor is the Navigators' Route out of Quebec. JP

❶ Looking east on the north shore of the St Lawrence.

Circuit Trois-Rivières
Quebec, Canada

Start Avenue Gilles-Villeneuve
End Avenue Gilles-Villeneuve
Distance 2.4km (1.49 miles)
Type Culture
Info goo.gl/j6zPaV

On a street circuit in Trois-Rivières, situated approximately midway between Montreal and Quebec City, you can drive in the fat, slick tyre tracks of your motorsport heroes.

The circuit was created in the mid-1960s by a group of racing enthusiasts who wanted to replicate what they had seen on the streets of Monaco, home to one of Formula One's most iconic races. The first race was held in 1967, within the grounds of an exhibition centre, with little more than hay bales to protect spectators from stray race cars. Since then the circuit has been upgraded, and its route and length altered, but it remains one of the most exciting street circuits in the world, currently hosting both the NASCAR Pinty's Series and the FIA World Rallycross Championship.

Starting on the Avenue Gilles Villeneuve, named after Canada's most famous F1 driver, the circuit heads anticlockwise around some spectacular turns, the most famous being the Porte Duplessis archway, after which drivers take a sharp left-hand turn. There are two long straights to test your speed, and enough corners to test your skills . . . as long as the traffic cops aren't looking.

Time your visit according to the circuit's calendar; the Grand Prix campground to the north of the track is a friendly and lively place to stop on a race weekend, and there are also hotels and inns. **SA**

🛈 Competitors in the Formula Tour 1600 race in 2015 offering racing fans a show full of action.

Route des Saveurs
Quebec, Canada

Start Baie-Saint-Paul
End La Malbaie
Distance 48km (30 miles)
Type Culture
Map goo.gl/Rbze6v

This route parallel to the St Lawrence River is tailor made for gastronomes: it passes no fewer than 23 top-quality food producers and 16 of the finest restaurants in Canada.

Start in Baie-Saint-Paul at Les Volières, a farm that breeds rabbits, guinea fowl, quail and pheasants. From here Route 138 passes a microbrewery, an organic butcher and numerous local cheese makers. Between these dairies, comparisons are odious, but the consensus is that the pick of an outstanding bunch is La Maison d'Affinage Maurice Dufour, which produces Le Migneron, an award-winning soft cheese, and Le Ciel de Charlevoix, a smooth blue number.

Just 4.5km (2.5 miles) off the highway at Saint-Urbain is an emu farm, the largest such establishment outside Australia. Back on the main drag are bakeries, chocolate makers, cider orchards, a honey farm and a fish processing factory.

Those who prefer their food on the plate are spoilt for choice. Special mention must be made of Le Mouton Noir (The Black Sheep), which serves walleye (a pike perch), buffalo and caribou, all garnished with local produce, and Le Charlevoix, the most opulent of five restaurants at the Fairmont Le Manoir Richelieu Hotel. Budget travellers congregate at Le Saint-Pub, a bistro with its own microbrewery, at 2 rue Racine, Baie-Saint-Paul. **JP**

Viking Trail Newfoundland and Labrador, Canada

Start Deer Lake
End St Anthony
Distance 489km (304 miles)
Type Adventure
Info goo.gl/137B38

Anyone who suggests that North American history stretches back only a few hundred years needs to be pointed in the direction of the Viking Trail. Your car becomes the closest thing to a time machine as the route takes you back through some of the most important historical sites on Newfoundland island.

Shortly after setting off from the intersection of Routes 1 and 430, on good smooth tarmac, you'll pass by the agricultural community of Cormack, created by veterans of World War II. Head back on Route 430 and you'll arrive at Gros Morne National Park – the first of two UNESCO World Heritage Sites on the route – renowned for its staggering natural beauty and its geological history.

Other stopovers on the route include the former economic capital of Newfoundland, Woody Point; the coastal lowlands and plains around Rocky Harbour; and the ancient aboriginal burial grounds of the Port au Choix National Historic Site, which were rediscovered in 1967.

The Viking settlement that gives this route its name is the second UNESCO World Heritage Site: L'Anse aux Meadows National Historic Site. It was originally established in 986 CE by a Viking trader, Bjarni Herjólfsson, and the modern-day site pays tribute to him and the other early settlers by re-creating their dwellings to give a glimpse back through time. **TW**

Irish Loop
Newfoundland and Labrador, Canada

Start St John's
End St John's
Distance 312km (194 miles)
Type Culture
Info goo.gl/syfql9

Take a tour through Canada's rich history and head deep into the hinterlands that were home to Irish and British settlers in the state of Newfoundland, and where their influence can still be seen and heard to this day.

Set off, as many of those first immigrants would have done, from St John's on the easternmost point of the Avalon Peninsula, overlooking the bay.

Taking Route 10 and heading toward Kilbride and Bay Bulls, you'll be passing through the rolling green hills that are still farmed by descendants of the Irish settlers who arrived here in the 19th century. Bay Bulls is one of several vantage points on the loop where you can indulge in a spot of whale watching, since the creatures often choose to feed here among the bay's icebergs.

Continue from there to La Manche Provincial Park, which is situated in a river valley and is home to a wide array of wildlife, stunning waterfalls and the abandoned settlement after which it is named. Farther along Route 10 you will reach Ferryland, where the old lighthouse (which offers delicious picnics) is a well-known landmark of this historic Irish settlement.

The final leg of this long road trip heads south through the small fishing towns of Aquaforte and Renews-Cappahayden before turning west to Trepassey, and from there back to St John's. **TW**

❶ A humpback whale breaches the surface off the coast of Newfoundland.

Fundy Coastal Drive
New Brunswick, Canada

Start St. Stephen
End Aulac
Distance 378km (235 miles)
Type Scenic
Map goo.gl/CdwspH

The Bay of Fundy is a spectacular natural wonder, with the world's most extreme tidal ranges. As the sea rises and falls twice a day, by as much as 16m (53ft), you are greeted by ever-changing coastal scenery as you drive along it.

Starting at Aulac, the location of the Fort Beauséjour National Historic Site, you first head inland to the town of Moncton. Nearby is Magnetic Hill, which mysteriously seems to drag cars uphill (but don't worry, it's an optical illusion). Heading south back to the Bay of Fundy, your next port of call is Hopewell Rocks park; just 40 minutes from Moncton, it's one of the best places to appreciate and learn more about the bay's enormous tides. It has an excellent interpretation centre, a walking trail to the 'ocean floor' at low tide and a range of refreshments at the High Tide Café.

The many lighthouses, lookouts, beaches and picnic spots along the way are all beautiful in their own right, but Fundy National Park is exceptional. The park, which encompasses the popular tourist town of Alma, stretches over 207 sq km (80 sq miles) and features 25 waterfalls, miles of peaceful walks and a host of wildlife.

There are other interesting towns to explore en route, including St John's, where you'll find the famous Reversing Falls, and Sussex, with its beautiful covered bridges. **TW**

❶ Boats at low tide in Westport on Brier Island, visible from the coastal drive across the Bay of Fundy.

Acadian Coastal Drive

New Brunswick, Canada

Start Dalhousie
End Aulac
Distance 338km (210 miles)
Type Scenic
Info goo.gl/wjLXW2

This road trip explores one of Canada's most beautiful maritime provinces, New Brunswick, home to the Acadian culture. The Acadians are the descendants of French settlers who went to North America from 1604 onwards. The French influence is apparent in the architecture and cuisine found en route on roads that border the Atlantic coast. Although it is possible to do this drive in a day without undue difficulty, the temptations of hearty traditional dishes such as chicken tricot, fine, sandy beaches and the perfect photo opportunities provided by picturesque white lighthouses, painted weatherboard houses and small fishing villages mean that it is probably best to take it slowly over a few days.

The Acadian Coastal Drive runs north–south along New Brunswick's east coast and is easy to follow, being marked by red signs sporting a white starfish. Heading south on Route 134 by Chaleur Bay, there are plenty of places to stop and sample fresh seafood. If time is not an issue, keep an eye out for a detour to see the oldest operating wooden lighthouse in New Brunswick at the tip of the island of Miscou, and check out Le Pays de la Sagouine, a reproduction of a Prohibition-era fishing village. One of the best places for a stopover is Bouctouche, to see one of the last great sand dunes on the northeastern coast of North America. **CK**

Appalachian Range Route

New Brunswick, Canada

Start Charlo
End Perth-Andover
Distance 291km (181 miles)
Type Scenic
Map goo.gl/EoQ3Yh

The Appalachian Mountains stretch for almost 3,200km (2,000 miles) between the northernmost tip of Newfoundland and the US state of Alabama.

This road trip through the range tackles the first part of the route, and starts in Charlo, in the northern tip of New Brunswick in Canada. Start by leaving Charlo and head towards the first, and largest, city on the Range Route – Campbellton. Avoid the quicker, main Route 11 and take the smaller 134 as it hugs the waterline of Chaleur Bay.

Campbellton is where you will find Sugarloaf Mountain, the first of the Appalachian Range peaks. There are multiple trails to the top, where you can enjoy stunning views over the bay. In the winter, strap on your skis for a quicker way back down.

Head away from Campbellton on Route 17 before turning east at Saint-Quentin, a small town famed for its maple syrup. This leads towards Mt Carleton, the tallest mountain in New Brunswick at 817m (2,680ft) above sea level, and Mt.Carleton Provincial Park – a perennially popular and outstandingly beautiful spot for hiking, mountain biking and other energetic outdoor pursuits. The views out over the Restigouche River make the climb well worth the effort.

Continue on from here down to Perth-Andover, which is divided by the St John River – Perth on the east bank and Andover on the west. **TW**

Evangeline Trail
Nova Scotia, Canada

Start Yarmouth
End Mt Uniacke
Distance 299km (186 miles)
Type Scenic
Map goo.gl/HCvP62

The Evangeline Trail, which extends along the west coast of Nova Scotia on the Bay of Fundy, follows approximately the same course as the track first laid down by the now-defunct Dominion Atlantic Railway in the early 1900s.

The chief charm of this itinerary is the natural wonder of the Bay of Fundy tides, whose range is so great that deepwater harbours are left high and dry and extensive areas of ocean floor exposed twice daily. One of the consequences is that travellers' proximity to the shoreline depends largely on when they travel: at low tide, the sea can be miles away; at high tide, the waves may be breaking against the side of their vehicles.

The trail along Highway 1 connects a string of historic French, Scottish and Irish settlements. It begins in the south in Yarmouth, with its wide tree-lined streets and grand mansions, then proceeds to Digby, famous for having one of the world's largest scallop fleets. It bisects the apple orchards of the Annapolis Valley and the town of Annapolis Royal – first a French settlement, then British, and attacked more often than any other town in North America – before reaching its northern terminus at Mt Uniacke.

This is a spectacular journey that combines timeless natural wonders with relics of the earliest European settlements in the New World. **BDS**

❶ Delaps Cove, with the sea temporarily off in the distance – but the rock pools hint at its imminent return.

Lighthouse Route
Nova Scotia, Canada

Start Halifax
End Cape Forchu Lightstation
Distance 484km (301 miles)
Type Scenic
Map goo.gl/VwTqU9

There are 160 lighthouses on Nova Scotia's 13,300km (8,264 miles) of coastline, and this enthralling route passes more than 50 of them. The trip connects the island's maritime past with the present day, passing some of its most famous lights, its prettiest towns and its most weathered, salty villages, from which fishermen still set out each day in traditional wooden dories (flat-bottomed boats), echoing the days of the Grand Banks of Newfoundland schooners.

Not far out of Halifax, the provincial capital, on NS-333 you pass one of the route's star attractions, Peggy's Point Lighthouse, at the eastern entrance to St Margaret's Bay (SMB). Stick with SMB before joining Highway 103 to the sailing hub of Chester, with its grand mansions overlooking Mahone Bay, then continue to the UNESCO World Heritage town of Lunenburg and Liverpool harbour's timber-clad Fort Point Lighthouse.

Farther south, visit Shelburne's historic waterfront and on no account miss the Dory Shop, which has built more than 50,000 dories since it first opened in 1880. The final waymarker, on a finger of land beyond Yarmouth Bar, is the beautifully preserved red-and-white 'apple core' Cape Forchu Lightstation, which was opened in 1840. **BDS**

➲ Peggy's Cove, Nova Scotia.

Sunrise Trail
Nova Scotia, Canada

Start Amherst
End Auld's Cove
Distance 280km (174 miles)
Type Scenic
Info goo.gl/97kaXz

As its website proudly boasts, the Sunrise Trail offers 'Gently rolling farmlands that create a quilt of emerald green fields that meets the sparkling blue waters of the Northumberland Strait. Country roads wind along sandy shores with their bright red bluffs and tidal saltmarshes that are vibrant with life.'

From Amherst, a stop on the Montreal–Halifax railroad, Highway 366 leads to the coast at Tidnish and then east along the northern coast of Nova Scotia, within sight of Prince Edward Island. Some 30km (19 miles) down the road is Pugwash, a village whose global significance is out of all proportion to its tiny size: it is the venue for the Nobel Prize-winning international conferences on science and world affairs – which is why it styles itself 'Home of the Thinkers.'

A turning between Pugwash and Tatamagouche leads to Malagash, the site of Canada's first rock salt mine, now an industrial history museum. Pictou has a historic port with an outstanding attraction in *Hector*, the tall ship that in 1773 brought the first European immigrants from old Scotland to the place they named Nova Scotia ('New Scotland'). The Scottish theme continues on the other side of Pictou Harbour, where New Glasgow sprang up in the 19th century, and at Antigonish, the venue for the biggest Highland Games festivals in the world outside the home nation. **JP**

Cabot Trail
Nova Scotia, Canada

Start Baddeck
End Baddeck
Distance 298km (185 miles)
Type Scenic
Info goo.gl/UDIIW

When you drive the Cabot Trail, one of the world's finest coastal drives, be sure to bring your walking shoes, because meddlesome trails are going to play havoc with your itinerary. There are bog trails, coastal trails and trails through forests of old-growth hardwoods; there are trails around old beaver ponds and past disused gold mines.

Completed in 1932, the Cabot Trail is a loop drive around the northern tip of this temperate Atlantic island, connecting eight different communities, from Acadian French to Irish and Scottish outposts. A good place to start is Baddeck – then head north along the rugged Atlantic coast on steep oceanside cliffs through St Anns to Ingonish Beach, before detouring to the historic resort town of White Point, where there are opportunities to kayak the tranquil waters of Aspy Bay.

Continue through Cape Breton Highlands National Park's landscape of cliffs, canyons and wildflower-filled plateaus to Pleasant Bay on the west coast, overlooking the Gulf of St Lawrence. From here, head south to the Acadian village of Chéticamp, where you can take a whale-spotting tour or simply rest up and listen to Scottish fiddle music. A final inland sweep through the farmlands of the Margaree River Valley and the 'inland sea' of Bras d'Or Lake, a UNESCO Biosphere Reserve, returns you to the picturesque village of Baddeck. **BDS**

❶ The Cabot Trail near Chéticamp.
❷ A view of the highway from a biker's head cam.

Bras d'Or Lakes Scenic Drive
Nova Scotia, Canada

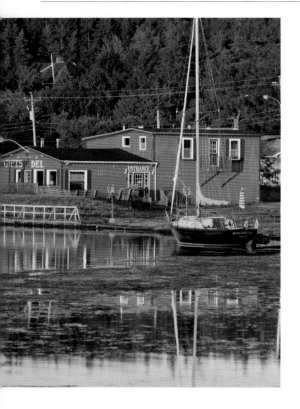

Start Whycocomagh
End Whycocomagh
Distance 290km (180 miles)
Type Scenic
Info goo.gl/iTMGXV

Bras d'Or Lake fills up the centre of Cape Breton Island in the Canadian province of Nova Scotia. The etymology of its name is disputed, coming either from the French *bras d'or* meaning 'arm of gold', referring to the sun's rays reflected on the water, or from *bras d'eau*, meaning 'arm of water'. Circling the 100-km- (60-mile) long lake is a scenic drive that can be started and ended at any point along the shore, but most travellers choose Whycocomagh, a small town in the northwest corner. From there, head west along Highway 105 and turn left at Iron Mines to Orangedale, where the Orangedale Railway Station Museum has some nostalgic exhibits. The proposed itinerary then proceeds along the Marble Mountain Road, past some delightful coves and inlets teeming with wildlife. At St Peter's, cross over the canal that links the lake to the Atlantic Ocean. The next section of the road runs along the south shore of the lake. Just before Iona, a road branching off leads to the picturesque Boisdale Hills and the easternmost end of the lake. Back at Iona, it is a short haul across the Washabuck Peninsula back to the starting point.

This is an easy drive that will take a full day to explore properly. Motorists and bikers are well catered for, with strategically placed rest areas, viewpoints and overlooks at which to pause and drink it all in. **SA**

○ A sailboat reflected in the water at Groves Point, one of the villages along the route.

International Selkirk Loop
USA/Canada

Start Newport, Washington, USA
End Newport, Washington, USA
Distance 451km (280 miles)
Type Scenic
Info goo.gl/c6M9TK

This major circular trail through the snowcapped Selkirk Mountains straddles the border between the United States and Canada. It is an acclaimed tourist driving route blessed with constant views of lakes, forests and mountains.

Indeed, much of the route follows rivers and lakes that were once the main transport routes in this wild area. One of the highlights of this road trip is a ferry ride across Kootenay Lake, the longest free ferry ride in North America.

The travelling is punctuated by visiting charming small towns dating back to the days of fur-trapping pioneers and gold prospectors. The modern road is wide, of good quality, well signed and lined throughout with excellent travel facilities, including hotels, restaurants and visitor attractions. The recommended starting point is at Newport, the most southerly town on the route, but the itinerary is circular, so you can start anywhere.

This road trip can incorporate any of several marked detours or breaks to tackle mapped hiking trails. At Schweitzer Mountain Resort, there's a chance to take a cable car to the 1,951-m- (6,400-ft) high summit for amazing views of the surrounding countryside. On Kootenay Lake you'll pass the strangest sight of the route: the Glass House, which a mortuary worker built for himself using half a million used bottles of embalming fluid. **SH**

❶ The banks of Slocan Lake are among British Columbia's most popular cycling routes.

The Cascade Loop Washington, USA

Start Everett **End** Everett **Distance** 708km (440 miles)
Type Scenic **Info** goo.gl/8ESRZp

This road trip could be dashed off in a day, but sensible folk will allow at least three days to savour all the mountains, forests, islands and river valleys.

The city of Everett is a popular starting point on a clockwise loop towards Mukilteo on the WA-526 to catch the ferry over to Whidbey Island. From there the road cuts north past freshwater lakes and unspoiled beaches toward Deception Pass, and several bridge crossings to the smaller islands, before picking up Highway 20 heading east inland past Burlington and the gateway to North Cascades National Park. From there you can pick up guidebooks and the free permits required for overnight camping, if needed.

You'll now be scooting along the fabled North Cascades Highway through jaw-dropping scenery peppered with picturesque bodies of water, including Diablo, Picture and Ross Lakes. Through the Methrow Valley you eventually reach Winthrop, a popular rendezvous for mountain bikers and hikers.

At Wenatchee, the Stevens Pass (Highway 2) brings you back west via the Bavarian village of Leavenworth and the spectacular Tumwater Canyon. It's then a long and wonderful drive on US 2 through the Alpine Lakes Wilderness and Snohomish River Valley back to Puget Sound. **DIS**

❶ Mt Shuksan, seen from the highway.

Chuckanut Drive Washington, USA

Start Burlington   **End** Bellingham   **Distance** 34km (21 miles)
Type Scenic   **Info** goo.gl/WVOMwr

This exceptional drive is regarded as Washington's version of the Big Sur – and the comparison is by no means unrealistic. This coastal road – roughly midway between Vancouver and Seattle – hugs the cliffs of Chuckanut Mountain above Puget Sound. The narrow two-lane highway winds around the cliffs with sharp drops to sandy beaches and terrific sea views out across the Sound, to the San Juan Islands and even to Vancouver Island.

Starting out from Burlington, the road is nothing special – mostly near sea level – but from Blanchard on, that all changes. Things quickly get mighty twisty and clifflike, as Washington's Cascade Range reaches right down to the Pacific Ocean.

Halfway along the route is Larrabee State Park; this is perhaps the best place to take a break, stretch the legs and admire the sea. The end point, Bellingham, is the northernmost city in the contiguous United States.

The weather will be a big factor in deciding when to attempt this route, which is all about the sea views. Poor weather – rain and low cloud – will greatly reduce the scenic joy. On good days, Chuckanut Drive is a route popular with classic car clubs; just check the weather forecast before you put your convertible's roof down. **DK**

❶ Part of the route goes through the Skagit Valley.

Mountains to Sound Washington, USA

Start Ellensburg   **End** Seattle   **Distance** 172km (107 miles)
Type Scenic   **Info** goo.gl/lmEaym

Any trip that takes you through something that sounds as strange as the Snoqualmie Pass has got to be good. And it sure is. Beginning in the high mountains of Washington State, this interstate route runs downhill to Seattle and the Pacific Ocean by way of snowcapped mountains, ski villages, beautiful volcanic lakes and cute historic towns – and ends with a spot of island hopping.

After you leave Ellensburg, it's not long before you are winding through steep mountains. Then the route runs alongside Keechelus Lake before traversing Snoqualmie Pass, in which there are ski resorts and a visitor centre. Farther on, the highway skirts the Alpine Lakes Wilderness, a vast, heavily glaciated area with great hiking opportunities. A little farther along the route lies the town of North Bend, an excellent place to browse the attractive shops and wander through the historic downtown district. Here, fans of the ABC TV series *Twin Peaks* will recognize Twede's Café and will probably just have to sample its cherry pie. The route then skips across Lake Washington; as you near Seattle by crossing the bridges, look behind to see a great view of Mt Rainier and the Cascades. Seasonal note: the whole route is open year round, but in winter some sections may require cars to use snow chains. **DK**

❶ Snoqualmie Falls on the Snoqualmie River.

Around Mt Rainier Washington, USA

Start Enumclaw   End Enumclaw   Distance 237km (147 miles)
Type Scenic   Map goo.gl/iUpBhE

Mt Rainier is the highest peak in the state of Washington. More than that, it is the most prominent mountain in the contiguous United States, and also has more glaciers on it than any other, with 25 in total.

This circular drive around the great landmark allows travellers to see it from almost every angle – assuming, of course, that they come at the right time of year: this is a road trip for the summer and early autumn only, because the road regularly closes from November to June because of snowfalls.

Beginning and ending in the small city of Enumclaw on Highway 410, you can drive around in either direction. Going clockwise you start out

on good roads through forested land to Federation Forest State Park. Then drive on to the town of Greenwater, where you should make sure your fuel tank is full before swinging south into the spectacular Mt Rainier National Park.

Photographers should stop at Suntop Lookout and take the side trip to Paradise for the finest overlooks of the mountain. The route then loops around the west side of the mountain, through a mix of rich forests, canyons, waterfalls and crystal-clear lakes, before looping back to Enumclaw via the scenic Orville Road and Pioneer Way. **MG**

① Sunset over Mt Rainier.

Chinook Scenic Byway Washington, USA

Start Enumclaw   **End** Naches   **Distance** 156km (97 miles)
Type Scenic   **Info** goo.gl/ddxYsA

Washington's White River flows out of the Emmons Glacier on Mt Rainier. The first part of this Scenic Byway follows the watercourse, picking it up near the city of Enumclaw. The route, which is along State Route 410, takes you east out of town into typical Washington forests.

Eventually, the road enters Mt Rainier National Park, providing wonderful views of the summit. It may look beautiful, but remember that it is still an active volcano – a sleeping giant whose behaviour is closely monitored. There are at least a dozen smaller scenic detours within the park, including the wonderful Cayuse Pass, Carbon River and Sunrise Road.

The byway leaves the national park through the Chinook Pass, which frequently closes because of snowfalls, making this trip impossible between November and May. In the summer, though, look for the pull-off for the short walk to Tipsoo Lake, which is, with Mt Rainier in the background, an unmissable photo opportunity.

Beyond here, the Scenic Byway descends through forests and turns south to end in the lumber town of Naches. If you're looking for somewhere to stay overnight, continue on to Yakima, about 24km (15 miles) farther east. **MG**

➊ In the shadow of Mt Rainier.

Lake Washington Shoreline Drive Washington, USA

Start Seward Park   **End** Washington Park Arboretum   **Distance** 13km (8 miles)
Type Scenic   **Map** goo.gl/0gcI1o

Seattle is famous for its old restored waterfront facing west into Elliott Bay and Puget Sound, but it also has another, less developed, waterfront facing east onto Lake Washington. This route runs alongside this stretch of water from one fabulous park to another.

You'll start at the southern end, in Seward Park, in the Columbia City district. This little peninsula is covered by wooded parkland jutting out into the lake opposite Mercer Island. Don't expect to be able to drive around it – there are 4km (3 miles) of cycle and footpaths if you want to explore the lakeshore here. It's worth the trek to see the attractive waterside homes along the trees of Mercer Island

and, in the distance, the snowy summit of Mt Rainier, 4,392m (14,411ft) above sea level.

From Seward, head north, with the ducks, boats and views of the lake on your right. Then follow Lake Washington Boulevard through parks with beaches, lifeguards and several picnic areas. With swimming platforms and cafés, Madison Park Beach is probably the best of the lot.

Finally, you'll reach Washington Park Arboretum, a hidden gem on the shores of Lake Washington, where you can lose yourself in forests and gardens of more than 40,000 waterside trees and shrubs. **SH**

❶ The Seattle Japanese Garden in the Arboretum.

Spirit Lake Memorial Highway Washington, USA

Start Castle Rock   End Johnston Ridge Observatory   Distance 82km (51 miles)
Type Culture   Info goo.gl/pNLGPG

On 18 May 1980, the deadliest and most destructive volcanic event in US history occurred when Mt St Helens, in Washington State's Cascade Range, erupted so catastrophically that its summit was reduced by more than 396m (1,300ft). Spirit Lake, itself formed by pyroclastic flows from the mountain 4,000 years ago, received the full impact of the lateral blast and the ensuing avalanche of debris. Thousands of trees were ripped from the landscape and thrown into the lake.

Today the devastation wrought by the eruption can be seen close up by following the Spirit Lake Memorial Highway from the town of Castle Rock into the volcanic blast zone. After 8km (5 miles) on WA-504, you'll pass a visitor centre before continuing along a course roughly parallel to that of the north fork of the Toutle River, which has now largely reverted to its usual form after having been turned into a vast mudflow during the eruption.

At Milepost 24, the mountain is suddenly before you, and it remains an intimidating sight. Your goal is the Johnson Ridge Observatory at the end of WA-540, from where you can see the mountain's lava dome, crater, pumice plain and a landscape that could have been created yesterday: tree trunks several feet thick, snapped like matchsticks. **BDS**

➊ Mt St Helens from Johnston Ridge Observatory.

Lewis and Clark Trail Highway Washington, USA

Start Clarkston   End Cape Disappointment   Distance 735km (457 miles)
Type Culture   Map goo.gl/DyO2pR

In 1803, US President Thomas Jefferson effectively doubled the size of the United States by purchasing the Louisiana Territory from France. In order to find out exactly what he had bought, Jefferson commissioned Captain Meriwether Lewis and Second Lieutenant William Clark to explore and map the area. The expedition, including a number of US Army volunteers, set out from Camp Wood near St Louis in May 1804 and eventually, in November 1805, reached the mouth of the Columbia River on the Pacific coast.

Adventurous souls can attempt to drive along their entire route, but a more practical suggestion is to follow their course across what is now Washington State. Starting on the eastern border at Clarkston, the route heads along US 12 via the Tri-Cities (Richland, Kennewick and Pasco) before heading south down US 730 to Plymouth, from where Route 14 then heads west along the northern bank of the irresistibly photogenic Columbia River. At Vancouver, US 5 and then Route 4 take you northwest until a short hop along the 401 brings you to Cape Disappointment. Here the Lewis and Clark Interpretive Center will help you to understand the historical significance of what you have just driven along. SA

❶ Looking down on Clarkston, Washington.

Cascade Lakes Scenic Byway
Oregon, USA

● Mt Bachelor is in full view throughout the greater part of this fantastic itinerary.

Start Bend
End Odell Lake
Distance 106km (66 miles)
Type Scenic
Info goo.gl/ExpjLv

The Cascade Lakes are a collection of twelve lakes and two reservoirs on the eastern side of the Cascade Range in central Oregon, and unsurprisingly, there's a fabulously scenic route running through the area. It's much more than a drive from lake to lake, though, as it goes through thick forests where there are many hiking trails and also gives good views of Mt Bachelor, 2,764m (9,068ft) above sea level. There are other peaks, too, including several of the volcanoes whose activity created these lakes.

In 1998 this route was designated a National Scenic Byway. It begins in the city of Bend, the largest community in central Oregon, where a visit to the High Desert Museum would be a good preparation for the country the drive will take you through. Heading west out of town towards Todd Lake, you're immediately passing pine-covered mountain slopes. Rest stops along this section give great views and photo opportunities.

Soon after is Devil's Lake (according to legend, a man-eating creature lurks in its deeps), where the byway swings south towards Elk Lake, a picturesque body of emerald-green water popular with canoeists. Fly fisherman can be seen casting from the shores of Little Lava Lake, Crescent Lake and finally Odell Lake, where this pond-hopping scenic road trip finally ends. **MG**

Hells Canyon Scenic Byway
Oregon, USA

Start Baker City
End La Grande
Distance 317km (197 miles)
Type Scenic
Info goo.gl/kLqI3w

This is a road trip full of vertigo-inspiring views. Heading east from Baker City – an old mining centre on the Union Pacific Railroad and the setting for the Western musical movie *Paint Your Wagon* (1969) – the first notable wayside settlement is the tiny village of Halfway, so named, fairly randomly, for its geographical position relative to La Pine and Cornucopia – the latter, once the site of a gold mine, is now a ghost town.

Around 53km (33 miles) north of Halfway is a vista that, once seen, will never be forgotten: a Hells Canyon lookout atop North America's deepest river gorge, the floor of which is 2,436m (7,993ft) below you. Carved out over six million years by the mighty Snake River on the Oregon–Idaho border, this place would normally be an end in itself. Here, however, in the midst of Hells Canyon National Recreation Area, it's only the beginning.

The National Scenic Byway gives access not only to Hells Canyon, but also to the majestic Wallowa Mountains, an 'Old West' world of cattle drives and ranches, lush valleys and pine-scented mountain air. A network of paved state and forest highways, the route encircles the range. It is generally well serviced, but there are stretches of up to 128km (80 miles) without petrol or amenities in a region sometimes known as 'Little Switzerland'. Journey's end, La Grande, is another former mining town. **BDS**

Rogue–Umpqua Scenic Byway
Oregon, USA

Start Medford
End Roseburg
Distance 275km (171 miles)
Type Scenic
Map goo.gl/KHLDWe

This trip makes a dramatic and beautiful loop through the Southern Cascade Range in southern Oregon, following the routes of two rivers: the Rogue and the Umpqua. These are wild rivers, with white water, deep gorges and spectacular waterfalls.

The trip is particularly beautiful in late spring, when there is still lots of snow in the higher areas. Recent (geologically) volcanic activity has produced many of the trip's best features, beginning at the Rogue River Gorge Viewpoint as the river cuts through basalt lava. Also worthwhile is a side trip to the two dramatic volcanic pinnacles known as Rabbit Ears.

Nearby are the splendid National Creek Falls. Beyond that the route skirts the delightful Diamond Lake, where the resort is a good place to break your journey. From there the route follows the steep descent of the Umpqua River, and you will likely see fully dressed-up anglers casting for prized summer steelhead, a hardy sort of sea trout.

After the town of Clearwater is the Steamboat Inn, to which hungry fishermen go for fine dining, to glean tips on the best lures and to swap tall tales about the ones that got away. Before reaching Roseburg, there is one final photo opportunity at Colliding Rivers, a spectacular white-water maelstrom at the confluence of the North Umpqua and Little Rivers. **DK**

Oregon Pacific Coast Highway
Oregon, USA

Start Brookings
End Portland
Distance 637km (396 miles)
Type Scenic
Map goo.gl/aJmW9w

US Highway 101 is famous for its Californian run along Big Sur, but less well known is its northern section, which extends all the way along the Oregon coastline to the Canadian border – less well known, but even more memorable.

Heading north from the Californian border near Brookings, there are hints of the great things to come – fabulous cliff views to the sea, and picturesque islands from the overlooks at Cape Sebastian State Scenic Corridor.

First stop is Bandon. Take the loop road and marvel at the rock stacks on the beach and in the sea. Proceed to Newport, and a stopover in this charming fishing town. Check out the basking seals, right there on the harbour deck. Here too is the excellent Oregon Coast Aquarium, with everything from sea otters to sea anemones.

Over the impressive Yaquina Bay Bridge are yet more beautiful coastline stretches and long sandy beaches. Perhaps another stop is needed to tour what is inexplicably the Oregon coast's top tourist attraction: the Tillamook Cheese Factory.

Finally, at the laid-back seaside resort of Cannon Beach, turn inland, via Klootchy Creek Park, with its giant Sitka spruce trees, to arrive in the charming, eco-friendly city of Portland, which is now most famous for its welcoming microbreweries and independent coffeehouses. DK

◓ The Pacific from Highway 101 near Tillamook.
❶ Seal Rock Beach, south of Newport.

Historic Columbia River Highway Oregon, USA

Start Troutdale   **End** The Dalles   **Distance** 119km (74 miles)
Type Culture   **Info** goo.gl/MFcsGa

The Historic Columbia River Highway was the first planned Scenic Byway in the United States. It was begun in 1913 and completed eight years later. It is that most wonderful and rare type of road, one of the lucky few that owes its existence not merely to bulldozers, engineers and blind necessity, but also to those who worked in the more 'refined' spheres of endeavour – architects, stonemasons, landscapers. As if the beauty of the mighty Columbia River that runs alongside it was not enough, the constructors have added to it by creating a monument to the art of road building – a road that has few rivals anywhere.

Oregon's first tarmacked road owes its existence in large part to engineer and landscape architect Samuel C. Lancaster, who made sure that the glory of the road would be both reflected in and enhanced by its tunnels, bridges and viaducts. Modelled on the water-hugging Axenstrasse freeway in Switzerland, everything you see on this road is seductively beautiful. There are the majestic arches of Dry Canyon Creek Bridge and Benson Footbridge in front of the Multnomah Falls. And, perhaps most precious of all, the stone-walled seating areas and the ornately arched masonry and concrete barriers built by local stonemasons to keep cars from tumbling over its edges. **BDS**

❶ Multnomah Falls.

Volcanic Legacy Scenic Byway Oregon to California, USA

Start Chemult, Oregon **End** Lake Almanor, California **Distance** 804km (500 miles)
Type Culture **Info** goo.gl/EXg938

This is a geologist's road trip of a lifetime that allows vulcanologists to get up close and personal with at least four major volcanoes and a handful of equally impressive smaller ones in just a few days. The byway itself is one of only twenty stretches across the United States to be designated an 'All-American Road' because of its geological importance.

Heading out west on Oregon Route 62, your first tectonic treat is Rim Drive, a scenic loop around Crater Lake, a tranquil body of fresh water that filled the magma chamber of Mt Mazama after it imploded in around 5677 BCE. Farther south, the Upper Klamath National Wildlife Refuge sits on the shores of the Upper Klamath Lake.

Volcanic highlights along the California section include Lava Beds National Monument and Medicine Lake Volcano, the largest in the Cascade Ranges. Black basalt waterfalls line the route, including the McCloud River Falls and Burney Falls.

A final loop around Lake Almanor signals the southern terminus of this journey, but the geothermal features of the Lassen Volcanic National Park nearby are well worth the additional excursion. With hiking trails to sulphurous springs, steaming gas vents and thumping mud pots, it's a fascinating place to stretch your legs at the end of the trip. **TW**

➊ Crater Lake from the side of the byway.

Pacific Coast Highway
California, USA

Start Monterey
End Morro Bay
Distance 200km (124 miles)
Type Scenic
Info goo.gl/dMiIhL

Running a close second to the fabled Route 66, the Pacific Coast Highway (PCH) is one of the most iconic US road trips.

Envisaged as part of a more ambitious plan to link Mexico and Canada, California's portion of Highway 1 clings to its rugged western seaboard for 1,500km (930 miles) from its border with Oregon down to San Diego.

The finest section is the coastal stretch between the old Spanish capital of Monterey and the picturesque haven of Morro Bay – a route National Geographic placed at number one in its Top 10 Motorcycle Rides in the USA.

From the fashionable art galleries, broad beaches and quaintly painted cottages of Carmel, the PCH winds south for 145km (90 miles) through Big Sur – world famous for its dramatic coastline and towering redwood forests – and traverses sea cliffs on wide spandrel bridges. Highway 1 is broad and well surfaced, perfect for leisurely cruising on a good day, but watch out for the notorious sea mists.

Passing through San Simeon and Cambria, the PCH eventually drops through oak-covered hills toward Morro Bay; famed for its seafood restaurants, this is the perfect place to refuel after experiencing one of the world's greatest scenic road trips. **DIS**

● Bixby Creek Bridge on the Big Sur coast.

Lombard Street and Vermont Street
California, USA

Start Corner of Hyde and Lombard Streets, San Francisco
End Vermont Street, San Francisco
Distance 6km (3.7 miles)
Type Scenic
Map goo.gl/i3twcJ

Can an itinerary that covers just one urban block, and a short block at that, rightly be categorized as a road trip? When it is one of the most distinctive thoroughfares in one of the world's greatest cities, then the answer to that question just has to be in the affirmative.

San Francisco's famously crooked road between Hyde and Leavenworth in the neighbourhood of Russian Hill, the so-called 'crookedest street in the world', was built in 1922 to reduce the 27 per cent incline, which was much too steep for the automobiles of the time.

Paved with red bricks and bordered by sumptuous displays of flowering plants and shrubs, this serpentine street first became a tourist destination in the 1950s. Today, its eight tight switchbacks take up to 350 vehicles an hour during peak times.

Lombard Street has appeared in many TV shows and movies, including *Bullitt* (1968), and is said to be the inspiration for Windy Street in the *Grand Theft Auto* video game. But you won't be hitting it fast. With a speed limit of 8 kph (5 mph), this is one very crooked street that is designed to keep leadfoots honest. Even so, eight hairpin bends in the middle of a city . . . That really is an adventure. Vermont Street, the second crookedest in the city, is just 5km (3 miles) drive to the south. **BDS**

❶ This aerial view shows the curves but not the incline: together, they make an unforgettable combination.

Banning to Idyllwild
California, USA

Start Banning
End Idyllwild
Distance 50km (31 miles)
Type Scenic
Map goo.gl/6Rs5EN

It takes only a matter of minutes to escape the suburban gridlock of Banning and start climbing up into the mountains to the south of the town.

Almost immediately the road starts winding its way upwards through a series of switchbacks. Slowly the houses and buildings are replaced by the wilderness of the San Bernadino National Forest, with the roadsides dominated by a wide variety of pine trees. Officially called State Route 243, it also appears on maps under its alternative name of 'Esperanza Firefighters Memorial Highway', as a tribute to five firefighters who died in October 2006 while tackling a wildfire.

The route is easy to follow, passing alongside the Mt San Jacinto State Park, with its three mountain peaks towering more than 3,300m (10,000ft) above sea level, and several viewpoints offering stunning panoramas over western Riverside and southern San Bernardino counties.

Idyllwild is flanked by Tahquitz Peak and Suicide Rock, which are famous with climbers, while the surrounding area is ideal for outdoor enthusiasts, with hiking and horse riding in abundance. Once voted LA's Best Mountain Getaway, Idyllwild has a thriving cultural scene that makes it popular with artists, musicians and actors. It's also a great place for celebrity spotting, since many Hollywood A-listers have homes near here. **TW**

Shores of Lake Tahoe
California/Nevada, USA

Start Tahoe City, California
End Tahoe City, California
Distance 124km (77 miles)
Type Scenic
Map goo.gl/dHqw5S

The start and finish point shown here is arbitrary, but Tahoe City is closest to San Francisco. The road does not remain in sight of the water throughout its length, and is in places more than a mile away; however, this makes its frequent returns to the lakefront all the more dramatic, and there are plenty of stopover points from where one can admire the views at leisure.

On a clockwise circuit, the first landmark is beyond the California state line in Nevada: Incline Village, a place of luxury homes for the super-rich. Next comes Glenbrook, the first settlement on the lakefront and originally the site of a timber yard.

South Lake Tahoe is a ribbon development along the waterfront that straddles the state line as the road turns back into California: the whole town is geared to tourism, but because of state laws only the Nevada section has casinos.

Emerald Bay on the western shore is flanked by a state park in which the highlights are Eagle Falls and Vikingsholm, the latter a mansion now open to the public. This section of the route is closed in winter: the rest of the perimeter road is open year round, weather permitting.

The last big town before completing the circuit is Tahoma, the venue for the cross-country skiing and biathlon events at the 1960 Winter Olympics in Squaw Valley. **JP**

Big Sur's Old Coast Road
California, USA

Start Bixby Creek Bridge
End Pfeiffer Beach
Distance 28.8km (17.9 miles)
Type Scenic
Map goo.gl/wPYfxO

Once described by the *New York Times* as the 'most stunning meeting of land and sea in the world', the wonders of Big Sur are often only glimpsed by road trippers from the 145km (90 miles) of smooth, scenic tarmac – part of California's Pacific Coast Highway – that skirt its southern fringes. Prior to the arrival of this highway, the only way to traverse Big Sur's rugged creek beds and towering redwood forests was the twisting inland trail now known as the Old Coast Road.

Starting just north of the magnificent single-span Bixby Creek Bridge, the wide dirt road heads east into thick woodland parallel to Bixby Creek. Climbing steeply above the tree line, you crest the 'boulder pastures' as the views open up to reveal the wild rugged coastline far below. On the steep descent back to the Pacific Coast Highway are several challenging switchbacks and vertiginous narrow stretches on which you will be praying not to meet oncoming road trippers.

Although the Old Coast Road is in generally good condition, a 4x4 with good ground clearance is strongly recommended; surfaces are slippery and littered with rocks and tree branches. After this challenging off-piste excursion, you will likely be ready for a cooling dip at Pfeiffer Beach, a gorgeous crescent-shaped patch of sand nestled into the craggy cliffs. **DIS**

❶ The wildlife that populates the route includes deer, coyotes, wild boars and even mountain lions.

Joshua Tree National Park
California, USA

Start Palm Springs
End Cottonwood Visitor Center
Distance 156km (97 miles)
Type Adventure
Map goo.gl/sGyZo4

It is easy to forget when you are in the middle of glitzy Palm Springs that a whole world of desert adventure awaits on the other side of Interstate 10. Take exit 117 (you have to be driving west to east to access it), and head into one of the most unusual national parks in the United States: Joshua Tree National Park.

The Joshua tree (*Yucca brevifolia*) that gives the park its name is found in many places in the American southwest, but nowhere more so than in this park, where the intense concentration of the plants in places gives the landscape an otherworldly feel. There is much more to the park than acres of trees, however. Joshua Tree also has some startling rock formations, such as Arch Rock, which is just off the road and provides a dramatic 9.1-m- (30-ft) tall backdrop for photographs.

More of the park's remarkable geological features can be seen on Geology Tour Road, a short detour heading south off this route that requires a 4x4 for part of the way. The dirt road circuit runs for 29km (18 miles), with 16 features to stop at and explore marked on the special driving map that you can access online or pick up at the start of the trip. The detour takes about two hours. After enjoying this trip and the rest of Joshua Tree National Park, Palm Springs is going to seem pretty tame when you return. **MG**

❶ The park is a vast, otherworldly wilderness where the Colorado and Mojave deserts meet.

Bullitt Car Chase California, USA

Start Potrero and Army Streets, San Francisco   **End** Guadalupe Canyon Parkway and North Hill Drive, San Francisco
Distance 64km (40 miles)   **Type** Culture   **Map** goo.gl/JVMIpy

The 1968 movie *Bullitt*, starring Steve McQueen and Robert Vaughn, included a high-speed pursuit through the streets of San Francisco that has become renowned as one of the greatest chase scenes in cinema history. While it's inadvisable to try to emulate that famous pursuit, you can still have the thrill of driving in the same places seen in the film. Watching the movie before your road trip will also give you an appreciation not only of the skills of the drivers but also of director Peter Yates, who stitched scenes together from all over the city to give the impression of a continuous chase.

It actually took three weeks to produce about eleven minutes of screen time. McQueen liked to do his own stunts, but 90 per cent of the chase scenes in *Bullitt* were actually driven by the great stunt driver Bill Hickman. Heavy editing led to some continuity errors, such as cars being visibly damaged before the collision that supposedly caused it, and a rather convoluted route.

The movie sections are highlighted on the map shared here, and can easily be pieced together to make a fabulous morning's road trip through downtown Frisco, preferably to the soulful soundtracks of Lalo Schifrin and ideally in a dark green 1968 Ford Mustang GT Fastback. **MG**

❶ A still from the car chase in *Bullitt*.

Highway 49 – The Gold Rush Trail California/Nevada, USA

Start Oakhurst, California **End** Reno, Nevada **Distance** 480km (298 miles)
Type Culture **Info** goo.gl/qt9aXS

This trip through the western foothills of the Sierra Mountains presents dramatic landscapes steeped in the history of the California Gold Rush. After the discovery of gold in the mid-19th century, some 300,000 migrants from across the globe arrived on the West Coast seeking their fortune. And the billions of dollars of precious metal they unearthed there laid the foundations of the modern state of California. The historical mining communities of Chinese Camp, Jamestown, Sonora and Angels Camp are all worth stopping at en route. In Jamestown there is the Sierra Railroad steam railway and a vineyard, and you can try your luck panning for gold.

The route winds into the mountains, through San Andreas, Drytown, Diamond Springs, Gold Flat and Sebastopol. A little beyond the halfway point is Coloma, where, in 1848, gold was first discovered. Here, the Marshall Gold Discovery State Historic Park includes one of the many mining ghost towns in this part of California. After Nevada City, the route swings east and the spectacular mountain scenery intensifies as the road cuts through the High Sierras, dropping down, eventually, on the eastern side to desert and the gambling town of Reno. Here, you may lose any gold you discovered earlier. DK

🛈 There may really be gold at the end of this rainbow.

Duel – Sierra Highway
California, USA

Start Sylmar
End Santa Clara
Distance 119km (74 miles)
Type Culture
Map goo.gl/7THOaB

The movie *Duel* (1971) was to the business trip what *Jaws* was to swimming. A middle-aged salesman, David Mann, is driving his red Plymouth Valiant through the desert on a lonely California road. He passes a brutish-looking Peterbilt 281 tanker truck, which then overtakes and deliberately slows down in front of him. Mann passes it again and speeds off, leaving the truck in his wake. While he is refuelling at a petrol station, the tanker pulls in. When Mann leaves the station, the anonymous driver follows. The deadly game of cat and mouse begins again.

Directed by Steven Spielberg on a shoestring budget, *Duel* was shot over just 13 days and based on a short story in *Playboy* magazine. This gripping thriller was filmed on California's Sierra Highway (Route 14) and nearby Soledad Canyon Road among the rolling peaks of the San Gabriel Mountains. This lovely old highway was once the main link between Los Angeles and the High Desert. Now almost entirely bypassed by freeways, landmarks from the movie remain, including the tunnel on Soledad Canyon Road, the Crown Valley railway crossing and Chuck's Cafe (now a French restaurant, Le Chêne).

And if you should spy a 1955 'Needlenose' Peterbilt bearing down on you in your rear view mirror, don't worry: in reality the truck's top speed was only 119 kph (74 mph). **BDS**

❶ Dennis Weaver starred as David Mann in Steven Spielberg's first full-length TV movie.

Gone in 60 Seconds
California, USA

Start 600 E Ocean Boulevard, Los Angeles
End Vincent Thomas Bridge, Los Angeles
Distance 93km (58 miles)
Type Culture
Map goo.gl/CXIVgd

This is one of Hollywood's greatest movie car chases, featuring police cars colliding with wrecking balls and skidding into garbage trucks, and a hero escaping by jumping his Mustang over a huge line of traffic. Filming famously left an expensive trail of wrecked vehicles in its wake. It is to be hoped that your Los Angeles road trip following the locations of the final car chase won't be quite as destructive.

The 2000 movie, a remake of the 1974 cult classic, cast Nicolas Cage as a legendary car thief who set out to steal fifty beautiful classic vehicles in a single night. The final target was a customized 1967 Ford Mustang Fastback (more precisely a Shelby GT500 nicknamed Eleanor) from an apartment block in Long Beach.

Police start chasing, and Cage takes a route north through Compton to Downtown Los Angeles. You'll find it easier to follow than the police did.

The Mustang loses the chasing cars for a while. Cage then stalls and tries to restart, attracting the attention of a passing squad car. Soon the chase is on again, this time heading south via Gardena and Carson to the Vincent Thomas Bridge.

You'll be able to drive across the bridge admiring the views of the southern Los Angeles waterfront – and if you can do the trip in a 1960s 'Pony car', then that would make this already fabulous road trip even more authentic and special. **SH**

James Dean Memorial Road Trip California, USA

Start Los Angeles
End James Dean Memorial Junction
Distance 298km (185 miles)
Type Culture
Map goo.gl/XLu811

As well as being one of the finest and most exciting young actors of his generation, James Dean was developing a parallel career as a race car driver at the time of his death, at the age of 24. In what turned out to be his last drive, on 30 September 1955, he was on his way from Los Angeles to compete in an event at Salinas. He had just finished filming *Rebel Without a Cause*, during which the studio had barred him from racing, and he was now itching to get behind the wheel of his new Porsche 550 Spyder, nicknamed 'Little Bastard'.

Dean set out from downtown Los Angeles accompanied by his mechanic, Rolf Wütherich, who had suggested Dean drive the car to the races in order to 'break it in'. His route takes you out from Los Angeles through the suburb of Van Nuys to join Interstate 5. Even before the route leaves the sprawling Los Angeles conurbation, the mountains are clearly visible in the distance, and they soon come into an attractive close-up.

Leave the main highway at Exit 221, where Dean was pulled over by a traffic cop and given a speeding ticket. From there you're on quieter two-lane roads through agricultural lands till you reach the fateful spot where Dean's Porsche ploughed into a black Ford that was turning in front of him. It was a tragic end to the promising young actor's all-too-short life. **MG**

Mulholland Drive and Highway   California, USA

Start Hollywood Bowl Overlook
End Pacific Coast Highway
Distance 85km (53 miles)
Type Culture
Map goo.gl/SLxfp9

Named in honour of Los Angeles's pioneering Irish-born civil engineer William Mulholland, these two interconnecting roads are among California's most famous thoroughfares, celebrated in both film and song. Ironically, not all of Mulholland Drive can be driven; a short, unsurfaced section nicknamed 'Dirt Mulholland' requires a little detour to the north. Nevertheless, there remains no finer way to traverse the famous Santa Monica Mountains.

Our road trip begins at the Hollywood Bowl Overlook, with its legendary vista over the downtown skyline and the Hollywood Sign. From there a wonderfully serpentine stretch of tarmac winds towards Encino Hills Drive – this is said to be Jay Leno's favourite Sunday-morning drive.

You pick up the route heading west, past some of the most lavish and expensive real estate on the planet, before it forks southwest onto Mulholland Highway. Passing through Los Angeles's rural fringes, this road was built in the 1920s to 'take Angelenos from the city to the ocean'. The highway is popular with bikers and performance car owners, especially the 3-km- (2-mile) long segment known as 'the Snake', which concludes with a spectacular 180-degree switchback at Edwards Corner. In the 1960s this road was one of Steve McQueen's favourite haunts a place he'd visit to clear his head and 'stretch the legs' of his Triumph TR6 Trophy motorcycles. DIS

Napa and Sonoma Wine Country Loop   California, USA

Start Napa
End Novato
Distance 134km (83.5 miles)
Type Culture
Map goo.gl/1FGCPF

Heading north out of Napa, the wine capital of California, this road trip is an easy – and easy-on-the-eye – drive through some of the most appealing country scenery in the United States. It's a very popular drive, so summer weekends are best avoided, especially if you plan to call in at some of the wineries to enjoy the tours and the tastings.

As you pass through pleasant little places like Yountville and St Helena, countless signs for wineries beckon and you'll see hillsides covered in the pleasingly symmetrical rows of grapevines. It isn't dramatic scenery, but very relaxing, with some wooded, rural stretches. In the small city of Calistoga it's worth a slight diversion to see the geyser known as Old Faithful of California, which erupts roughly every 45 minutes, though more frequently after rainfall.

The road crosses wooded hills into the neighbouring Sonoma Valley and heads south along Petrified Forest Road towards more vineyards and wineries. As in Napa there are also hot spring, enabling you to enjoy some water with your wine.

As a change from wineries, the road trip passes through Petaluma, with a collection of impressively preserved historic buildings, and ends in the city of Novato, whose attractions include several museums and plenty of restaurants where you can enjoy some more Napa and Sonoma wines. MG

49-Mile Drive
California, USA

Start Polk Street opposite City Hall, San Francisco
End Polk Street opposite City Hall, San Francisco
Distance 74.5km (46.3 miles)
Type Culture
Info goo.gl/i3g8QU

It won't get you to every sight that the City by the Bay has to offer, but if you have time for only one driving route in San Francisco, this is the one you need to make. Created by the Downtown Association of San Francisco in 1938 to show the place off to the thousands of visitors projected to arrive for the 1939 Golden Gate International Exposition, the route remains every bit as relevant today as it was then.

With a course altered frequently over the years to mirror the city's growth, 49-Mile Drive's distinctive blue-and-white seagull signs currently take you to Japantown, Union Square, Chinatown, exclusive Nob Hill, Lake Merced, the Marina District, the Financial District, the Presidio, Golden Gate Park, the Mission Dolores, and Twin Peaks, then along the Pacific Ocean past Ocean Beach to wonderful Baker Beach, with the Golden Gate Bridge towering magnificently before you.

City Hall is the suggested start and finish point, but since this is a circular itinerary you can begin and end anywhere. The route is named in honour of the Miner 49ers of the Californian Gold Rush, and corresponds to the city's area: 127 sq km (49 square miles). One of the first people to drive it was US President Franklin D. Roosevelt. The seagull signs, first introduced in 1955, might vary from scarce to abundant, but the landmarks are guaranteed to come thick and fast. **BDS**

❶ The Golden Gate Bridge from Baker Beach on the edge of the Pacific Ocean.

Sideways **Wine Trail** California, USA

Start Santa Barbara   **End** Santa Maria   **Distance** 161km (100 miles)
Type Culture   **Info** goo.gl/nCNyZ8

The 2004 comedy movie *Sideways* followed Miles (Paul Giamatti) and Jack (Thomas Haden Church) on a road trip through Santa Barbara's wine country. It spawned a *Sideways* industry, and you'll still find *Sideways* guides to the region. One of the locations on this route changed its name to the Sideways Inn.

Following the exact route taken in the film isn't easy, since the two friends are supposed to live in San Diego, but the film was all shot in Santa Barbara, where your trip begins. From here it's a pleasant drive north along a stretch of the Pacific Coast Highway to Gaviota State Park Beach, where the scene showing the men gazing out at the Pacific was shot. The route then heads inland towards wine country, the ocean views giving way to vineyards as the road goes into the hills. The trip takes in the small city of Buellton, where the duo stayed at the Windmill Days Inn and dined at the Hitching Post II. They also visited Solvang, with its unusual Danish-style architecture, while the wineries where they did their tastings included Kalyra, Foxen and Fess Parker.

This journey ends in Santa Maria, which stood in for San Diego in the scene where Miles has to drink an expensive wine from a paper cup. It was filmed in the Orcutt Burgers, if you want to visit, although they don't serve wine. **MG**

❶ Jack (left) and Miles enjoy wine and friendship.

Steinbeck Country California, USA

Start Monterey   End San Juan Bautista   Distance 82km (51 miles)
Type Culture   Map goo.gl/dCnkEK

John Steinbeck was born in Salinas and the surrounding area inspired him throughout his life. This road trip begins in Monterey, which features frequently in his novels, especially *Cannery Row* (1945). Today, where there were fish processing buildings there are now expensive hotels. Fans will want to see the one notable place that remains: the little shack of a laboratory where Steinbeck's close friend marine biologist Ed Ricketts worked.

From Cannery Row it's a short drive north alongside the sand dunes and beaches before turning inland towards Salinas. You soon see the Salinas Valley, a flat expanse of land that is one of the main agricultural producers in California. So many vegetables are grown here that it's been nicknamed 'The salad bowl of America'. For Steinbeck fans, it's the setting for *Of Mice and Men* (1937) and *East of Eden* (1952).

Breaking the journey in Salinas, the big attraction is the National Steinbeck Center, though if you're visiting in the middle of the day you can have lunch in the Steinbeck House, where the author was born and grew up.

The final part of the drive goes up to Fremont Peak State Park, from the summit of which there are great views over the valley. MG

ⓞ Sunset from the top of Fremont Peak State Park.

Sunset Boulevard California, USA

Start Downtown Los Angeles   End Pacific Coast Highway, Los Angeles   Distance 38km (23.6 miles)
Type Culture   Map goo.gl/ByhJz4

Is there a more iconic road name? This simple urban street is so deeply ingrained in popular Western culture that it makes a superb mini road trip.

In full arm-out-the-window, radio-on mode, you'll feel like you're an extra in 100 movies and TV shows as you cruise along in the slow-moving traffic through Beverly Hills and Hollywood.

Probably the coolest section of the Boulevard is Sunset Strip, where the road passes through the gritty West Hollywood area amid huge colourful billboards, neon signage and some of the best-known hangouts in the world.

Look out for the Rainbow Bar and Grill, favoured watering hole of stars through the ages, from Marilyn Monroe to Lemmy of Motörhead. Nearby is the Viper Room, once owned by Johnny Depp, and the Whisky a Go Go and Troubadour clubs, which helped to launch acts like The Doors, The Eagles and Guns N' Roses.

You'll pass the sites of pioneering movie studios, music stores where top musicians buy their guitars and restaurants with long lists of famous customers. You won't be able to stop yourself scanning the sidewalks for off-duty stars, and you'll see buses full of holidaymakers doing the same thing on guided tours to see celebrity homes. **SH**

❶ The Whisky a Go Go nightclub on Sunset Strip.

El Mirage California, USA

Start El Mirage OHV End El Mirage OHV Distance 9.7km (6 miles)
Type Culture Info goo.gl/uLk34y

Just 160km (100 miles) northeast of Los Angeles, El Mirage was once the place where California's pre-war hot-rodders went to blow off steam. The parched, flat lake bed in the middle of the Mojave Desert drew less interest from the traffic cops than illegal street races, and eventually evolved into the location for time trials under official jurisdiction.

The atmosphere here is much lower key than at Utah's Bonneville Salt Flats, perhaps because its drag strip is only two-thirds of the length. Yet on arriving at El Mirage's Dry Lake Off-Highway Vehicle Recreation Area (OHV), you'll still have some 9,700 hectares (24,000 acres) of bone-dry lake bed to explore. There's no official speed limit, but local police drop by from time to time to see that everyone is playing nicely and that they have all bought the appropriate permits from the ticket machine. Check ahead before visiting, because the OHV is frequently closed after heavy rain.

Time your visit to coincide with one of the weekend race meets held between May and November, when many supporters camp out in the desert overnight. Don't worry if you don't know the difference between a lakester, a streamliner, a hot rod and a belly tanker; regular speed freaks will be only too happy to explain. DIS

❶ El Mirage dry lake bed in the Mojave Desert.

Death Valley Highway
California, USA

Start Death Valley Junction
End Olancha
Distance 377km (234 miles)
Type Adventure
Map goo.gl/Of4KIi

With an average annual rainfall of only 60mm (2.3 in) and temperatures nudging 49°C (120°F), Death Valley is perhaps the most extreme natural environment on Earth accessible to the automotive adventurer. It is also vast, covering 13,650 sq km (5,270 square miles), with more than 480km (300 miles) of highway, the same amount of dirt roads and several hundred off-road trails of varying grades. If you are short on time, Death Valley Scenic Byway runs east to west for 130km (81 miles) through some of the park's most spectacular desert landscapes, with the snowcapped Sierra Nevada mountains dominating the backdrop.

Travelling west, the first stopover is Zabriskie Point, offering fabulous views over the vibrant landscape. Farther along, just before Furnace Creek and the park's official visitor centre, there is a must-do detour to the desolate salt flats at Badwater Basin (the lowest point in North America) and the surreal jagged landscape of Devil's Golf Course. On the return leg, off Badwater Road, is a scenic loop known as Artist's Drive through wonderful multi-hued desert hills. At Beatty Junction, intrepid explorers with reasonable ground clearance take another detour north to the gold mining ghost town of Rhyolite – probably the best preserved of the hundreds that litter Death Valley – before looping back via the stunning Titus Canyon. **DIS**

◓ Death Valley Highway runs through a 'land of extremes'.
❶ The wildly eroded desert badlands of Zabriskie Point.

Fear and Loathing
California/Nevada, USA

Start Los Angeles, California
End Las Vegas, Nevada
Distance 501km (311 miles)
Type Culture
Map goo.gl/MLmzVL

Hunter S. Thompson's novel *Fear and Loathing in Las Vegas: A Savage Journey to the Heart of the American Dream* (1972) was based on two trips the author made from Los Angeles to Las Vegas via Red Rock Canyon in Nevada. It's a road trip that links two of the busiest and most characterful cities in the United States through some of the country's remotest desert landscapes.

When you head east from the Pacific coast, it at first seems as if you'll never get clear of the urban sprawl of Los Angeles. Eventually, though, you will be into the San Gabriel Mountains (part of the Transverse Ranges) and out on the other side. Desert plains then open before you, with cacti instead of chain stores lining the road. The dry bed of Jean Lake, home to the legendary Mint 400 desert bike race that Thompson was sent to report on, is, of course, a must-see en route, too.

As you approach journey's end, the high-rise hotels of the Las Vegas Strip start to appear on the distant horizon. On the to-do list for fans of the book (or the film adaptation of 1998, directed by Terry Gilliam) will be Circus Circus and the Flamingo Casino. Arriving by road this way, after experiencing the extreme desert conditions, is indeed a surreal experience that makes you realize that, no matter whether you like it, fear it or loathe it, Las Vegas is indubitably a remarkable city. **MG**

UFO Trail California to New Mexico, USA

Start San Diego Comic-Con, California
End Roswell UFO Museum, New Mexico
Distance 2,854km (1,773 miles)
Type Culture
Map goo.gl/x6oaly

For Graeme and Clive, two English sci-fi geeks, this was supposed to be the road trip of a lifetime. In the film comedy *Paul* (2011), the unlikely heroes, played by Simon Pegg and Nick Frost, head out east at the end of San Diego's Comic-Con entertainment convention in a rented RV towards Roswell, New Mexico, stopping off at a number of mysterious places made famous by conspiracy theorists, alien hunters, UFO spotters and science-fiction movies.

Most of these locations are clustered around Rachel, Nevada, and along State Route 375, aka 'The Extraterrestrial Highway'. This proposed itinerary largely follows the route taken in the movie.

First stop is Vasquez Rocks Natural Area Park, California, which was used as a location in numerous episodes of the original *Star Trek* TV series. The route then turns south to the notorious 'Black Mailbox' just outside Alamo, Nevada, where UFO spotters regularly congregate, and there are reputedly two to three sightings every week.

Next up on this tour of alien hot spots are the towns of Camp Verde and Apache Junction, both of which have claimed several spaceship sightings since the 1950s. This road trip caters mainly to ufologists, but it is also good for lovers of solitude and desert scenery. **DIS**

➲ Something in the air near Rachel, Nevada.

Easy Rider California to Louisiana, USA

Start Ballarat, California   **End** Krotz Springs, Louisiana   **Distance** 4,303km (2,674 miles)
Type Culture   **Map** goo.gl/J3tdbL

The coolest film of 1969 was *Easy Rider*, starring Peter Fonda and Dennis Hopper as two Harley-chopper-riding, drug-dealing hippies crossing the United States in the face of small-town redneck bigotry. It is a cult classic among bikers, but this road trip works just as well by car.

You'll start where the duo's journey began, in the ghost town of Ballarat in Death Valley. Fonda stuffed the receipts of a big drug deal into his petrol tank, threw away his watch and set off with Hopper east on Route 66.

This is classic US motor-touring country and there are plenty of retro diners along the way for you and your fellow time-travellers to stop off and enjoy. To follow the route, you'll have to dip in and out of the remaining sections of Route 66 and modern replacement highways.

The Arizona landscapes are among the main highlights, particularly the huge rock formations of Monument Valley. Other movie locations include the old jail where the pair were locked up overnight (in Las Vegas) and the pool (Manby Hot Springs, New Mexico) where they skinny dip with two girls.

Finally you'll head for a quiet stretch of US Route 105 to the west of Baton Rouge, where the heroes are shot dead by a truck driver. **SH**

❶ In the tyre tracks of Fonda and Hopper.

Salmon River Scenic Byway Idaho/Montana, USA

Start Stanley, Idaho **End** Darby, Montana **Distance** 312km (194 miles)
Type Scenic **Map** goo.gl/xbFXDG

This acclaimed route through outback territory crosses some of the best landscapes in Idaho and Montana. You'll drive from the jagged Sawtooth Mountains, down through volcanic desert canyons, and end in the heavily forested Bitterroot Valley.

Catch the flavour of this rugged corner of North America by following the Salmon, Idaho's biggest river, through forested gorges where it churns in stretches of furious white water. Along the way you'll learn more about the history of local mining, fur-trapping and Native American culture.

Deer, elk, moose and otters are all local residents, but most of all try to spot the fish that gave the river its name. Once there were so many salmon

here that, according to local legend, it was possible to walk across the river on their backs. Now you may have to visit the spawning site at Indian Riffles to be sure of seeing any at all.

The road passes logging forests and ghost towns that were abandoned after a brief 19th-century gold rush. The route ends in the evocatively named Lost Trail Pass, 2,132m (6,995ft) up in the Montana mountain range.

Along the way there are plenty of spots where great hiking trails lead off from the route and several places for relaxing soaks in hot springs. **SH**

➊ Hells Canyon on the Salmon River.

Sawtooth Range Scenic Drive Idaho, USA

Start Shoshone   **End** Stanley   **Distance** 203km (126 miles)
Type Scenic   **Map** goo.gl/FMh3XI

From Ernest Hemingway's favourite landscapes to Clint Eastwood's regular ski haunt, the highlights of this route have attracted A-list stars for decades.

Hemingway liked the Sawtooth Range so much that he chose to be buried in the town of Ketchum. Nearby is the Spa at Sun Valley, to which the rich and famous, from Clark Gable and Errol Flynn to Demi Moore, have come to enjoy the upmarket shops, ski lodges and hotels.

Towns along the route may be chic and affluent, but the drive is a meander through the wilds. The road climbs high into the Sawtooth Mountains, past beautiful salmon and trout streams, hot natural bathing springs and lava tube caves.

Start in the heart of Idaho's Magic Valley at the old railroad town of Shoshone, where underground volcanic caverns stay icily cold throughout summer. Then follow lakes, forests and hills towards the jagged snowy pinnacles of the Sawtooth range dominating the horizon ahead.

Pass through 1860s' gold-rush areas and explore deep, wooded river gorges. In the summer there are hot natural pools and sandy beaches for bathing. You can swim at the biggest, Redfish Lake, while gazing up at the peak of Mt Heyburn, 3,139m (10,229ft) high. **SH**

❶ Redfish Lake with Mt Heyburn.

Northwest Passage Scenic Byway Idaho, USA

Start Lewiston   **End** Lolo Pass   **Distance** 279km (173 miles)
Type Culture   **Map** goo.gl/mzqLrI

Follow in the footsteps of early 19th-century pioneers Meriwether Lewis and William Clark, the earliest pioneering European explorers of the northwestern United States.

More than 200 years after they battled through the uncharted rivers, canyons and mountains of Idaho, their route was designated an official US Scenic Byway. This means it's judged to be one of the most attractive roads in the United States.

Along the way, you will traverse the Nez Perce Reservation and see many of the landmarks of that people's brief war against the US Army.

The region's highland scenery is much the same as it was when Lewis and Clark trekked through it, but modern travellers have the benefit of US Highway 12, which makes progress much easier.

There are many visitor centres at which to learn more about the hardships that Lewis and Clark faced. At Canoe Camp, for example, the expedition spent days carving new canoes from pine trees to paddle west on the Clearwater River. In contrast, you'll be able to cruise past this site on a multi-lane road.

The road then follows the path along which Lewis and Clark were guided on foot by a Native American through deep snow to the summit of the Lolo Pass, at 1,595m (5,233ft) above sea level. **SH**

➊ Lochsa River in Clearwater National Forest.

Las Vegas Strip Byway
Nevada, USA

Start Frank Sinatra Drive
End Fremont Street
Distance 10.5km (6.5 miles)
Type Scenic
Info goo.gl/2FcLB

This is a scenic road trip like no other, a neon drive along the iconic Las Vegas Strip – famous from innumerable movies, including *Ocean's Eleven* (two versions: 1960 and 2001), *Diamonds Are Forever* (1971) and *Jason Bourne* (2016). Depending on traffic, it takes less than ten minutes to complete. But what a ten minutes; you'll want to do a U-turn and see it all the other way, then do it all again. It's important to see it at night, when all the neon displays are on. Better yet, hit it at the magic hour, just after dusk.

The route begins at Frank Sinatra Drive, near the airport, and ends at Fremont Street in the 'historic' district. The Strip – properly, South Las Vegas Boulevard – is a modern absurdity, from the Bellagio Hotel's operatic fountain display to the one-half-scale copy of the Eiffel Tower; from the canals, gondolas and fake Doge's Palace at the Venetian; from the Treasure Island's pirate show to the 350-m- (1,100-ft) tall Stratosphere Tower.

Interwoven with all the glitz are older, more traditional Vegas sites like Harrah's, Caesars Palace, and the Flamingo. It's recommended to do this trip after having crossed the desert to get there. It is only then that the sheer improbability of it all becomes fully apparent. How can this place exist? The answer lies in a combination of advantageous legislation and the love of money. **DK**

◓ The Las Vegas Strip.
❶ The mountains on the western approach to the city.

Valley of Fire Highway
Nevada, USA

Start Crystal
End Northshore Road
Distance 38km (23.6 miles)
Type Scenic
Map goo.gl/CRJT4z

Deep in the Mojave Desert, northeast of Las Vegas, you'll find a road leading into an apparent wilderness. Head out of the city for 40km (25 miles) on Interstate 15, arrow-straight across the flat desert plain, before turning right onto one of Nevada's most dramatic roads.

The Valley of Fire Highway leads across more parched dusty desert towards the mountains. Whatever you're driving, you'll enjoy the sweeping curves and undulations. The highway loops around the Valley of Fire State Park, and you can make it into a circuit by rejoining Interstate 15 farther on.

Soon the road enters the State Park, where the landscape becomes dotted with vibrant red sandstone formations eroded into spectacular shapes. This almost alien landscape is a favourite of Hollywood's location scouts: the Mars scenes from *Total Recall* (2012) were almost entirely shot here.

Take a break at the visitor centre to discover the geology behind the sights. From here, hiking trails branch off into the canyons. The best one leads to a cliff covered with Native American paintings.

The road now gets narrower and twistier as it squeezes between blood-red cliffs and boulders. Here you will see swirls, stripes, arches and towers of surreal rock. However keen a driver or biker you may be, it is almost impossible not to keep stopping to take photographs. **SH**

Red Rock Canyon Loop
Nevada, USA

Start 3205 NV-159
End 3205 NV-159
Distance 21km (13 miles)
Type Scenic
Info goo.gl/JWYjq

Just a few miles west of the glitzy show town of Las Vegas you'll find the unlikely location for a memorable drive through a geological marvel.

The Red Rock Canyon Loop is a vividly coloured rocky area that forms a National Conservation Area in Nevada's Mojave Desert.

There are plenty of hikes, climbs and tours of the area, but this route concentrates on the Red Rock road trip. That has been made very easy with a 20-km- (13-mile) long loop of one-way paved road. The bad news is that there's a fee to drive around it; the good news is that it's only a few dollars.

The Conservation Area loop is full of parking lots and walking routes if you feel inspired to explore farther afield. There's a visitor centre that explains the geology behind the colours and formations, and, inevitably, a gift shop selling souvenir plates and baseball caps.

Forget the commercialism of the downtown area; this route is a great antidote to the human-made excesses of Vegas. You will see arid desert dotted with great sandstone cliffs thousands of feet high. Polychromatic mineral deposits dramatically stain the exposed rock surfaces in stripes of red, orange and brown. These natural wonders may be less flashy than the light shows on the Strip, but they have been around a good while longer: 190 million years, according to geologists. **SH**

Route 50 – The Loneliest Road
Nevada, USA

Start Ely
End Fernley
Distance 459km (285 miles)
Type Adventure
Map goo.gl/5aR8We

No other road in the United States has such a beguiling label. In 1986, when *LIFE* magazine gave Route 50 in Nevada the title 'the loneliest road in America', it was jumped upon by the state's tourism authority, who could spot a marketing opportunity when they saw one. Certainly, there is something about this road's lure of desolation that has a particular pull on the human spirit. You will find no Route 66-style kitsch here. This is true abandonment, the sort of road you drive when you have left the family behind. From the town of Ely in the east across the barrenness of central Nevada to Fernley in the west, Route 50 passes nine towns, a handful of petrol stations, a couple of abandoned mining camps, the occasional forlorn-looking coyote and very little else.

The road takes you across the Great Basin, the United States' largest closed drainage basin with no rivers and no outlet to the oceans beyond. The speedometer creeps upwards; it is easily done on the featureless smooth tarmac. There is Austin, which likes to call itself a 'living ghost town', and Eureka, with its incongruous-looking opera house. There are no chain restaurants, no tourist traps. Everywhere about you just desert, mountains and a road. And signs like: 'Welcome to Middlegate. The middle of nowhere. Elevation 4,600 feet. Population 17 (Formerly 18)'. **BDS**

❶ A stretch of the 'loneliest road in America', between Fallon and Austin, Nevada.

Silver State Classic Challenge
Nevada, USA

Start Lund
End Hiko
Distance 145km (90 miles)
Type Culture
Info goo.gl/aSiSeN

This is an all-American road trip with a twist, combining the vast, open, high desert highways of Nevada with an opportunity to dip your toe in the high-octane world of competitive motorsports.

Running twice a year, in May and September, the Silver State Classic Challenge is a 145-km (90-mile) time trial along a closed section of Route 318 between Lund and Hiko. After registration in Las Vegas the pre-event party moves to race HQ in Ely for the traditional cocktail mixer, attended by veteran racers, celebrity drivers and nervous novices alike.

In the most competitive class, pro-drivers in 1000+ brake horse-power machines come to set new Public Highway Land Speed Records nudging 338 kph (210 mph). However, there are novice classes open to any law-abiding licence holder aged over 18 years old with a standard road car. Rather than a flat-out drag race, the skill in the newcomer classes is maintaining a constant speed of between 150 and 240 kph (95 and 150 mph) to cross the 90-mile marker at precise target times. While much of the route is arrow straight there are more technical sections to keep drivers focused, including a tricky 4.8-km- (3-mile) long canyon road nicknamed 'The Narrows'. In a world wrapped up in health and safety restrictions, the Silver State Classic seems like a leftover from a bygone era. Do it while you still can. **DIS**

● A section of the route at sunrise – the best time to make the trip, before the day heats up.

Dead Horse Point Scenic Byway
Utah, USA

Start Crescent Junction
End Grand View Point Overlook
Distance 109km (68 miles)
Type Scenic
Map goo.gl/d235me

Dead Horse Point Scenic Byway, on Utah's SR-313, runs for 56km (35 miles) through magnificent red rock canyon country. Its macabre moniker comes from cowboy times, when the area served as a huge natural corral for herding wild mustangs, many of which died from exposure in this harsh, arid environment. Today, it is better known as the film location where the dramatic final scenes of Ridley Scott's *Thelma & Louise* (1991) were shot.

After winding along smooth, sweeping tarmac above russet sandstone cliffs for 14,5km (9 miles), you reach the fork to Dead Horse Point. The road teeters 610m (2,000ft) above the Colorado River as it snakes through Canyonlands National Park.

After the obligatory selfies, head back up SR-313 through desert scrub, past towering buttes and crumbling rock pinnacles, towards the Island in the Sky and this road trip's finish point atop a massive 457-m- (500-ft) high mesa (giant table of rock) at Grand View Point Outlook.

Armed with a tourist map from the park's visitor centres, you can expand this itinerary and explore dozens of scenic backroads and hair-raising jeep trails. Those with off-road machines – plus some nerves of steel and a good head for heights – might even consider tackling the awesome Shafer Canyon Trail, which snakes down the cliff walls to the Colorado River below. **DIS**

❶ The approaches to Dead Horse Point are no less spectacular than the summit itself.

Bicentennial Highway Utah, USA

Start Blanding   End Hanksville   Distance 202km (126 miles)
Type Scenic   Info goo.gl/PQusCC

Opened in 1976 for the 200th anniversary of US independence, this highway offers mountains and canyons, desert and natural rock bridges.

Before starting the drive in Blanding, visit the Edge of the Cedars State Park Museum, an archaeological site that was once home to the Ancestral Puebloan people who lived across much of the southwest United States. As soon as you leave Blanding you're into a flat and open desert landscape, but heading for the mountains that will accompany you for much of the way, and where the road snakes to seek a way through.

Watch for a right turn and a slight diversion to the Natural Bridges National Monument. The ancestors of modern Puebloans lived here from about 700 CE until 1300 CE. In among the wondrous rock formations are three natural bridges, including the Sipapu Bridge, one of the world's largest formations of this type.

The road later crosses the Colorado River in the delightfully named Leprechaun Canyon, and then passes through more of Utah's archetypal red rock countryside to wind up in the small town of Hanksville, where you might want to fill up at Hollow Mountain, a petrol station that's carved out of the rocks. **MG**

❶ The Bicentennial Highway in Glen Canyon.

Flaming Gorge National Scenic Byway Utah, USA

Start Flaming Gorge Dam Visitor Center   End Manila   Distance 72km (44.7 miles)
Type Scenic   Map goo.gl/OMSTkb

When construction of the Flaming Gorge Dam began in 1958, only rutted mule tracks traversed the eastern Uinta mountain range. The 153-m- (502-ft) high dam across the Green River eventually improved access and led to smooth modern highways that helped develop this magnificent region into one of Utah's premier outdoor recreation destinations along the shores of the 17,000-hectare (42,000-acre) freshwater reservoir.

Start at the visitor centre at Flaming Gorge Dam to get some perspective on this colossal engineering achievement. Free dam tours can be enjoyed all year round. Then head southwest on Highway 191 through woodlands to Camperworld-Pine Forest Park before meeting Highway 44 at Greendale Junction. Just to the west is a short detour to Red Canyon Visitor Center, perched high above the flooded Green River, where park staff are often on hand to point out nesting raptors or grazing bighorn sheep. Returning to Highway 44 you weave west through forested valleys, nestled between Dowd Mountain and Windy Ridge, to Sheep Creek Geological Loop, a 16-km- (10-mile) long mix of tarmac and gravel through the Uinta Crest Fault that reveals weird rock formations in the cliff sides. The trip ends in the quiet town of Manila. **DIS**

❶ The Flaming Gorge National Recreation Area.

Utah's Scenic Byway 12
Utah, USA

Start Panguitch
End Torrey
Distance 200km (124 miles)
Type Scenic
Info goo.gl/HwIU8

It's a drive through time as much as space. So don't rush. Remember, it takes time to drain ancient sea beds, to erode and carve out variegated buttes and mesas. It takes time to reduce mountains of Navajo sandstone to tiny, rounded nodules using nothing but wind and rain. It takes time for ice and gravity to create Bryce Canyon's Hoodoos. So when you drive through it all on Utah's Scenic Byway 12, note the speed limit. Then halve it. Nothing's ever been in a rush here.

In a book full of great drives, this is one of the greatest. Red Canyon in Dixie National Forest, Grand Staircase-Escalante, Kodachrome Basin State Park, Capitol Reef National Park – this road gets you to them all. It passes through or close by everything from the grand beauty of Boulder Mountain to tiny unheralded slot canyons like Spooky Gulch and the incredible Hogsback.

Caution is needed throughout. You will be overwhelmed by a vortex of panoramas and won't resist the urge to be pulled into them. You will want to leave this byway and drive its numerous country roads with inviting names like Hell's Backbone. But be sure your vehicle can cope – high-clearance 4x4s are necessary for some side roads – and do not rely on your GPS. Trust only your sense of adventure, which got you this far . . . and should see you safely home again. **BDS**

❶ Some of the amazing rock formations that line the side of Scenic Byway 12.

Kolob Terrace Road
Utah, USA

Start Virgin
End Lava Point Overlook
Distance 33.8km (21 miles)
Type Scenic
Info goo.gl/rligLf

Kolob Terrace Road is a ribbon of red-topped tarmac that threads its way through the rugged beauty of Zion National Park in southwestern Utah. From the small town of Virgin, the road climbs steadily to heights of more than 2,500m (8,000ft) above sea level towards Kolob Reservoir.

Even in the best of weather the road is wind-battered; it should be avoided when it's dark or raining, and it's impassable in winter. The best time to make the trip is between June and October, when the going is easiest and the scenery is at its best. Outside of these times, snowfall often closes the area and 4x4s are recommended.

This scenic drive is popular with nature lovers, especially birdwatchers, and adventurous hikers accessing the various trailheads along the route. One particular favourite is Zion's Subway, which is a narrow, tunnel-like slot canyon up the North Fork Park of the Virgin River. Permits are required and are limited to 80 visitors per day. Various other trails head into the scrubby green parkland and up to the spectacular rock pinnacles that line the Kolob Terrace Road.

Back on the road, continue to Lava Point, the summit of the ride, from which one can survey Cedar Breaks National Monument, the dramatic Pink Cliffs and the steep gorge at Zion's Narrows. There is a basic campground nearby. **DS**

❶ It's just as well the driving is easy, because it's hard to concentrate on the road when the scenery is this great.

Moki Dugway
Utah, USA

Start Fry Canyon
End Mexican Hat
Distance 93km (58 miles)
Type Adventure
Info goo.gl/Ol1pxS

Cut into the side of Cedar Mesa plateau by the mining company Texas Zinc Minerals in 1958 to transport uranium mined in Fry Canyon to a mill in Mexican Hat, Moki Dugway is a 4.8-km- (3-mile) long series of loose-surfaced switchbacks, part of the otherwise paved Utah State Route 261 in San Juan County. Up or down, this section of the suggested trip is a wild drive. On the mesa top, another road (level, but lacking even a gravel base) takes you to Muley Point overlook, a coveted picnic spot with views over the canyons of the San Juan River.

Having once starred on the Discovery Channel's *Hell Roads* television show, Moki Dugway is one for confident drivers only. There are no guardrails, and it is recommended you don't drive it if your vehicle is longer than 8.4m (28ft) or heavier than 4,500kg (10,000lb). But don't be intimidated. Don't concern yourself that this sinewy gravel thread drops 335m (1,100ft) in 4.5km (2.8 miles). Worry instead about giving yourself enough time to admire the jaw-dropping views around you, and don't miss pulling into its well-placed overlooks.

Certainly there is more caution required if you are heading down the Dugway's 11 per cent gradient rather than up it, but either way this wonderful road is an unmissable, down-to-earth attraction, a road that was literally 'dug out' of the American West. **BDS**

Shafer Canyon Trail
Utah, USA

Start Moab
End Shafer Canyon Road
Distance 10km (6.2 miles)
Type Adventure
Map goo.gl/JiqhZI

Originally built during the 1950s by the US Atomic Energy Commission, who prospected this region for uranium during the height of the Cold War arms race, the remaining access roads, which seem to cling to the canyon walls, are now traversed by thrill-seeking off-road adventurers.

Relentless serpentine switchbacks wind down from the Island in the Sky Road: to one side there are sheer red sandstone cliff faces filling your field of vision, and to the other breathtaking vistas across the Canyonlands National Park, without any pesky guardrails to spoil the wonderful view. As the road levels off at the base of the mesa, grab a well-earned breather to let your nerves settle and the brakes cool. At the end of the trail, you have the option to explore the ancient Potash Road, famed for its prehistoric artwork and petroglyphs. Adventurers looking for serious off-road challenges can also pick up the White Rim Road near here.

Although the route has tricky loose surfaces, steep gradients, sandy washes and deeply rutted sections, it is not seen as technically demanding. No special permits are required. Nevertheless, a 4x4 with low-range gearing and decent ground clearance is the smart option. Park authorities also suggest you carry additional supplies, fuel and water in case of an emergency. Most importantly, don't forget your camera. **DIS**

White Rim Trail
Utah, USA

Start Potash Road, Moab
End Mineral Canyon Road, Moab
Distance 116km (72 miles)
Type Adventure
Map goo.gl/8q6zlE

Utah is riddled with Scenic Byways – the envy of most other states – but every year hard-core adventurers looking for a real off-road challenge are drawn to this remote place. The route runs on a thin layer of White Rim sandstone perched below the Island in the Sky mesa, an enormous tabletop formation in Southern Utah. Combining sheer drops, steep inclines and deeply rutted desert trails, the road is only accessible by capable 4x4s with high ground clearance.

In order to preserve the wildness experience, a maximum of 50 permits are issued to motorized vehicles each day, and visitors can only stop overnight at one of the ten official campgrounds along the route. It usually takes two days to complete the trip, but longer if you are distracted by the numerous side roads, walking trails and hidden slot canyons. Photographers are spoiled for subject matter in this desolate natural wonderland, but the huge sandstone Mesa Arch is a favourite.

Although rated as 'moderate', White Rim Road has some tricky sections: Murphy's Hog Back, the Mineral Bottom switchbacks and the treacherous climb up Hardscrabble Hill. But the key to a successful road trip here is preparation and patience: be aware that there is no potable water available along the way and calling the tow truck will cost you more than $1,000. **DIS**

❶ The horseshoe-shaped route skirts the edge of red rock canyons.

Bonneville Speedway
Utah, USA

Start Wendover
End Wendover
Distance 64km (40 miles)
Type Culture
Info goo.gl/mOmDUu

Two hours west of Salt Lake City on Interstate 80 are Utah's remarkable Bonneville Salt Flats. The speedway is a 16-km- (10-mile) long run marked out along the ground each summer, which attracts racers and spectators each August from all over the continent to compete in the famous Speed Week drag races. The event's high-octane atmosphere was beautifully captured in the 2005 film *The World's Fastest Indian*, which is essential pre-trip viewing.

There have been motorsports here for almost as long as there have been cars and motorbikes, but it was the fierce Anglo-American rivalry for the land speed record – which began with Sir Malcolm Campbell's Blue Bird's 484.620 kph (310.129 mph) in 1935 – that cemented Bonneville's status as the Cradle of Speed.

If the flats aren't being used for racing or filming car ads, then you pretty much have the run of the place to yourself. But beware: stray off the course, and you risk driving into areas where the salt crust is thin and may break under the weight of a vehicle, rendering you stuck and requiring an expensive tow. The salt can be anything from about 1.5m (5ft) to 2.5cm (1in) thick. The surface can also become surprisingly gloopy with less than half the grip of tarmac. MG

➲ Bonneville Salt Flats during Speed Week.

Trail of the Ancients
Utah/Colorado, USA

Start Bluff, Utah
End Durango, Colorado
Distance 301km (187 miles)
Type Culture
Map goo.gl/YrXwJu

This is a journey to the four corners of the United States – the only point where four states meet together, a crossroads between Arizona, Utah, Colorado and New Mexico. The reason to be in this remote region and drive this route is to visit a truly remarkable concentration of ancient historical sites. All the archaeology along the route – and there is a lot – relates to the Anasazi, the Ancestral Pueblo civilization that existed in this region between 200 and 1300 CE. This was a sophisticated agriculture-based community, and its ancient inhabitants built complex clusters of cliff dwellings, the well-preserved remains of which will be seen on this trip.

Leaving Bluff, there are four main sites. The first ruins, a group of oddly shaped stone towers, are at Hovenweep National Monument. Just outside Pleasant View is Lowry Pueblo, constructed around 1060, which housed as many as 100 inhabitants. The Anasazi Heritage Center in Dolores is where all the decorated pottery and other artefacts recovered from the various sites can be seen. Then – leaving the best until last – Mesa Verde National Park is a UNESCO World Heritage Site with hundreds of cliff dwellings. Be sure to take the loop road drive and to take in at least some of the guided tours of the main sites – Cliff Palace, Balcony House and Long House. This road trip ends at Durango, terminus of a narrow-gauge steam railroad. **DK**

Monument Valley
Arizona/Utah, USA

Start Kayenta, Arizona
End Bluff, Utah
Distance 122km (76 miles)
Type Scenic
Info goo.gl/xkPR6a

It's hard to think of a natural skyline that is more readily identifiable than that of Monument Valley. The desert silhouette of the giant sandstone buttes is almost instantly recognizable, immortalized in countless Western movies. It's the archetypal landscape of the Great American West. And the best thing is you can actually drive it – out there among the towering rock stacks. Monument Valley is not big – just 13 sq km (5 square miles) in area – but as a road trip it packs a hugely memorable punch. It's not the easiest place to get to. Straddling the Arizona–Utah border in the Four Corners region, the valley lies within the semi-autonomous Native American territory of the Navajo Nation.

At the entrance to the valley's access road off Highway 163 is a visitor centre where you can buy the necessary ticket before setting off along this otherworldly 27-km- (17-mile) long loop of dirt road through and around the Mitten Buttes, the tallest of which is nearly 300m (1,000ft) high. Despite being unpaved, the road quality is good – doable in a sedan, though easier in an SUV. Because of the light, the best time to see Monument Valley is near either dawn or dusk. If you want to do this, then Kayenta is the best place to stay overnight before or after the journey. **DK**

➲ Sunrise over Monument Valley.

Grand Canyon Scenic Loop
Arizona, USA

Start Flagstaff
End Flagstaff
Distance 351km (218 miles)
Type Scenic
Map goo.gl/cuOAtZ

There are several ways to explore the magnificent Grand Canyon, including flying over it by helicopter or travelling up the Colorado River in a boat, but by far the best option is to take a well-planned road trip. In fact, when driving, the Grand Canyon almost sneaks up on you. Suddenly, there it is: vast and deep and improbable. It is advisable to make this at least a two-day trip. That way it is possible to park and stay the night at one of a number of hotels in Grand Canyon Village (not Tusayan), which are all within walking distance from the canyon's rim. Get up early and see the sun rise over the canyon, when deep shadows make it highly dramatic. Maybe even surprise some wild deer; there are a lot about.

This scenic loop begins in Flagstaff, on Route 66, then heads north to the canyon rim through beautiful, densely forested landscape. After Grand Canyon Village the route follows the edge of the canyon for some 15km (10 miles), and there are several viewing points, which will demand a stop. The route then veers away from the canyon and returns to Flagstaff. Several other attractions in the area are worth a detour, such as two archaeological sites with 12th-century cliff dwellings of Ancestral Pueblo tribes at Wupatki National Monument and Walnut Canyon National Monument. DK

⊖ Navahopi Road running towards the Grand Canyon.

Red Rock Scenic Byway
Arizona, USA

Start Sedona
End Interstate 17
Distance 24km (14.9 miles)
Type Scenic
Info goo.gl/mGbJGb

It is strange to think that travellers who journeyed through Red Rock Country in the Sedona region of Arizona a few million years ago would not have been making their trip by road. At one time this whole region was home to a prehistoric sea, which left behind the iron ore that gives the rocks their distinctive red colour.

The Red Rock Scenic Byway (also known as Arizona State Route 179) cuts right through this unusual landscape, approximately 160km (100 miles) north of Phoenix, with its giant towers of jagged red rock that are almost Martian-like in appearance. In 2005 the unique landscape and geology earned the route its designation as an All-American Road, a coveted title that signifies to the travelling public that this is a road that is 'a destination unto itself'.

Recently resurfaced, the road is now suitable for all types of vehicle. Along its short meander through the Coconino National Forest are some fascinating human-made sights, such as the Chapel of the Holy Cross, which was built into one of the red rock mesas. There is also Bell Rock Vista, always popular with photographers, with its wonderful views over the valley. The Red Rock Scenic Byway is only a few miles long, but it is easy to spend a whole day stopping to admire the scenery and exploring the local hiking trails. JI

Globe to Show Low
Arizona, USA

Start Globe
End Show Low
Distance 142km (88 miles)
Type Scenic
Map goo.gl/SXbaPS

This route takes the traveller from hot, arid semi-desert to cool, clear mountain scenery in a relatively short distance, passing en route rich relics of at least three groups of pre-Columbian inhabitants of what is now the United States. From Globe, an old stagecoach town situated approximately 144km (90 miles) east of Phoenix, the Arizona state capital, the northbound Highway 60 passes through Tonto National Forest on its way to the heart of Apache territory. At the San Carlos Apache Reservation, there is a culture centre lodgings and a casino. The road then descends 600m (2,000ft) in a series of hairpin bends into Salt River Canyon, where the rock art at Hieroglyphic Point attests to human habitation from 1,000 years BCE. There is a great deal to see and do in this astonishingly beautiful valley: white-water rafting, for example, is particularly popular.

Beyond the canyon, the road climbs steeply through scenery that is first dominated by cacti and later by pine trees; in the distance are the peaks of the White Mountains. Journey's end, Show Low, is deep in Navajo territory; it reputedly got its unusual name from a legendary game of poker that was played there during the 19th century. The town is 664m (2,835ft) higher than Globe, so any travellers who have not brought warm clothing have made a serious mistake. **JP**

❶ The sun rises across Fool Hollow Lake State Park, near Show Low, Arizona.

Apache Trail
Arizona, USA

Start Apache Junction
End Theodore Roosevelt Lake
Distance 71km (44 miles)
Type Adventure
Info goo.gl/WXaqpj

Apache Trail in Arizona is steeped in US history. Originally, it was used by the Apache Native Americans to travel through the Superstition Mountains, and later it became a stagecoach trail. In those days it was just a dirt track, but today it is tarmac for most of its length. One thing that has not changed much over time is the landscape. To the north is Four Peaks Wilderness Area, while south of the route is Superstition Wilderness Area. And don't assume that the term 'wilderness' is a marketing gimmick; it really is just desert and scrub.

The trail starts at Apache Junction and runs northeast for 71km (44 miles) to Theodore Roosevelt Lake, and is officially designated State Route 88. Although there are some straight sections along the way, there are plenty of tight bends thrown into the mix to make the trip more interesting. All around the landscape is like something out of a Western movie (given this is Arizona, that is no surprise). There is a lot of sand, rock and cactus in the wilderness, but also Salt River, Canyon Lake and Apache Lake. Apache Trail is narrow and twisty, and in the later stages the road is unsurfaced. There are also some steep drops along the route, unguarded by safety barriers. It is not a road trip to take on in a large or low-slung vehicle, but with the right set of wheels it is a great way to experience a legendary US drive. JI

❶ Many people like the Apache Trail best in spring, when the terrain is at its greenest.

Route 66 – West   Arizona/California,USA

Start Lupton, Arizona   **End** Santa Monica Pier, Santa Monica, California   **Distance** 1,144km (711 miles)
Type Culture   **Maps** goo.gl/s6FsRy and goo.gl/WzQ6Pq

This section of Route 66 – the classic all-American 3,600-km- (2,200-mile) long route from Chicago to Los Angeles – stretches from the desert landscapes of Arizona to the Pacific Ocean at Santa Monica Pier in California. After the coming of the interstate highways in the 1960s, this historical migration route was nearly lost. However, it was kept alive through the efforts of road-trip fans and devotees of nostalgic small-town US life. Today the route is probably more famous than it has ever been.

This segment of 'The Mother Road' starts in Lupton. Soon the route passes through the fascinating Painted Desert and Petrified Forest National Parks, before arriving in Flagstaff. This place has embraced Route 66 culture enthusiastically and is also a jumping-off point for visiting the Grand Canyon. Other time-warp stops include Seligman, Kingman, Newberry Springs (home to the Bagdad Café) and Barstow. After this the route proceeds into the Greater Los Angeles Metropolitan Area, San Bernardino and Pasadena, skims the centre of LA itself, turns onto Santa Monica Boulevard, and passes through West Hollywood and Beverly Hills before arriving, at last, at the seafront in Santa Monica. Santa Monica Pier is the official Route 66 western end point. **DK**

❶ Amboy, California, near the Mojave National Preserve.

The Ultimate American Road Trip Forty-Eight States, USA

Start Grand Canyon, Arizona   **End** Hoover Dam, Nevada   **Distance** 22,046km (13,699 miles)
Type Culture   **Info** goo.gl/pZA9UJ

For many the perfect road trip is all about the journey; for others it's about the places you discover along the way. If you fall into the latter camp and are looking for the ultimate trans-American adventure, then this could be the one for you.

In 2016 computer scientist Randal Olson was challenged to create the perfect US road trip. The rules were simple: all 48 contiguous US states must be visited by car in the shortest time possible, stopping off at 50 of the country's most important landmarks, buildings and parks. Using a complex set of computer algorithms, Olson eventually came up with an incredible road trip that could be travelled in just 224 hours.

Classic all-American stopovers include the White House, Mt Rushmore and the Statue of Liberty, as well as the country's finest natural wonders, such as Yellowstone National Park and the Grand Canyon. History buffs are also catered to, with pit stops at the Alamo, the home of Abraham Lincoln and Graceland Mansion in Memphis, Tennessee.

Olson said: 'The result was an epic itinerary with a mix of inner city exploration, must-see historical sites and beautiful natural landscapes … A path that would minimize our time spent driving and maximize our time spent enjoying the landmarks.' **DIS**

❶ Computer algorithms created the perfect US road trip.

Going-to-the-Sun Road Montana, USA

Start West Glacier   **End** St Mary   **Distance** 80km (50 miles)
Type Scenic   **Map** goo.gl/9RoKIl

This gloriously scenic drive through grizzly country takes place within Glacier National Park. After 11 years of construction work, it was opened in 1932, and it was worth the wait.

The trip begins in tiny West Glacier, where a few hundred people live near the western entrance to the national park. First, the road crosses the Middle Fork Flathead River before plunging into forests, then swinging right and leading to the shores of Lake McDonald. This is the largest lake in the park, and the road clings to its southern shore for almost the whole of its 16-km (10 mile) length. The lake's far shore is approximately 1.6km (1 mile) away. After leaving the lake, the road follows the course of McDonald Creek, which feeds the lake, as it winds its way through more forests. Mountain slopes rise high to the side and more mountains are glimpsed ahead. Soon the road rises and the views keep getting better. Should you be tempted to stop and go for a walk, remember that Glacier National Park has one of the largest grizzly bear populations in the lower 48 states of the United States. Finally descending, the road skirts another lake, St Mary Lake, and ends in the little town of St Mary, at the eastern end of the park, where a rustic café serves home-cooked dishes. **MG**

❶ Sunrise lights mountains on Going-to-the-Sun Road.

Nebraska – The Movie   Montana to Nebraska, USA

Start Billings, Montana   **End** Lincoln, Nebraska   **Distance** 1,555km (966 miles)
Type Culture   **Map** goo.gl/wuk8Dw

The road-trip movie *Nebraska* (2013) tells the story of Woody Grant (Bruce Dern), who drives to Lincoln, Nebraska, with his son David (Will Forte) in the mistaken belief that he has won $1 million in a sweepstake. This route takes you through key places from the movie, but bear in mind that the director took some artistic liberties with geographical facts.

The journey begins in the Grants' home city of Billings, Montana, a historic place and an old railroad town, now one of the centres of the US oil industry. The route heads out east on Interstate 90, taking you through the vast grasslands and undulating hills of southern Montana and into the Crow Reservation. An essential stop is at the site of the 1876 Battle of the Little Bighorn. The scenery then gets a little more diverse, with the Wolf Mountains to the east and, farther on as you cross into Wyoming, the Bighorn National Forest to the west.

In the movie the Grants stopped at Sheridan, Wyoming, to refuel their Subaru automobile. The bar, petrol station and motel here look exactly as they did in the movie. After a visit to Mt Rushmore, the route continues east past the Badlands National Park before long, flat stretches take you through the Nebraska farmlands, across the pretty Platte River and south to Lincoln. **MG**

❶ Bruce Dern (left) and Will Forte star in *Nebraska*.

Glacier National Park to Yellowstone National Park
Montana/Wyoming, USA

Start Glacier National Park, Montana
End Yellowstone National Park, Wyoming
Distance 766km (476 miles)
Type Scenic
Map goo.gl/qzyHYN

This spectacular north–south road trip across mountainous Montana links two of the United States' great national parks. To the north are Glacier National Park and the Lewis and Livingston mountain ranges, whereas to the south, Yellowstone – the world's first national park – has spectacular geysers and waterfalls. Between the two, the route goes through the foothills of the Rocky Mountains, with snowy peaks to the right and views across the grasses of the Great Plains to the left. Other highlights of this road trip include the 113-km- (70-mile) long stretch designated the Kings Hill Scenic Byway, which runs between Belt and the pretty Victorian town of White Sulphur Springs.

The Lewis and Clark National Forest celebrates the pioneering mapping expedition of more than 200 years ago, and this road trip covers many of the landscapes that the intrepid team visited. Today, the forest is a popular ski area in the winter, whereas summer visitors enjoy hiking, fishing and picnics. On the way to Yellowstone, look out for the Devil's Slide, a strange streak of red rock plunging down a 38-m- (125-ft) tall cliff face. The final leg of the journey, on Highway 89, crosses into Wyoming and leads through deep canyons, dark forests and fast mountain rivers that are ideal venues for white-water rafters. But don't get lost in the woods... This is prime grizzly bear territory. **SH**

❶ Bison migrate across the foothills.

➋ A colourful geyser in Yellowstone National Park.

Beartooth Highway
Montana/Wyoming, USA

Start Red Lodge, Montana
End Yellowstone National Park, Wyoming
Distance 109km (68 miles)
Type Scenic
Info goo.gl/T2OoX6

The Beartooth Highway has been hailed 'the most beautiful drive in America', and it is extremely popular with road-tripping bikers. It starts in Red Lodge at an elevation of 1,697m (5,568ft), and travellers are treated to uninterrupted mountain scenery all the way to the northeast entrance of Yellowstone National Park. At these heights winters are fierce, so plan to make the drive between May and October. The Beartooth Pass itself, which is approximately 48km (30 miles) out of Red Lodge, is at 3,337m (10,947ft), and the extra height is gained through the ascent of a spectacular series of switchbacks whose mountain views – for those not watching the road – will take your breath away.

The switchbacks continue down the other side, with open and expansive views to distant mountain peaks. In total, there are some 20 peaks that are more than 3,658m (12,000ft) in height. The route passes deep pine forests, waterfalls and unspoiled glacial lakes, and for many the phrase 'the most beautiful drive in America' is not hyperbole but simply an accurate description. Sadly, high-altitude road trips often mean seasonal road closures. However, when snow forces the Beartooth Highway to close to automobiles, it is still possible to make the trip by snowmobile. **MG**

➲ Breathtaking scenery as far as the eye can see.

Grand Teton Loop
Wyoming, USA

Start Craig Thomas Discovery and Visitor Center
End Craig Thomas Discovery and Visitor Center
Distance 71km (44 miles)
Type Scenic
Info goo.gl/OXuRGr

Grand Teton National Park, in northwest Wyoming, is one of the United States' greatest natural treasures. It is crisscrossed by fabulous scenic roads, which give unrivalled access for adventurers seeking jaw-dropping mountain vistas, tranquil glacial lakes and abundant forest teeming with wildlife.

It is easy to spend a day exploring the park's byways, but most visitors start with the scenic loop drive, during which handy shoulders on the roadside allow drivers to stop, take photographs and observe the park's rich fauna and flora without holding up other road users. Throughout the circuit, rangers have installed boards with information about the landscape's key features, unique geology and diverse local wildlife. Take your time and you will be rewarded with stunning views; lungfuls of fresh mountain air; and glimpses of moose, bison, elk and, if you are very lucky, bald eagles.

Three memorable detours include the road to Snake River Overlook, photographed by Ansel Adams in the 1940s, and the Jenny Lake Scenic Drive, which skirts the picturesque eastern shoreline and summer meadows teeming with wildflowers. The third and most challenging sideshow, however, is the Signal Mountain Summit Road, which climbs 242m (800ft) to reach panoramic viewpoints over the magnificent snow-dusted Teton Range, Jackson Lake and Jackson Hole. **DIS**

Bighorn Scenic Byway
Wyoming, USA

Start Sheridan
End Greybull
Distance 151km (94 miles)
Type Scenic
Map goo.gl/PEZTfH

This route bookends a trip through the Bighorn National Forest with two stretches of grassy rangelands. Start in Sheridan, which prides itself on its mix of New West culture and Old West hospitality. On Tuesday evenings, there is country music in the park. After about ten minutes' drive north, take the left turn west onto Highway 14, the Bighorn Scenic Byway. Before long, as the road begins to climb into the Bighorn Mountains of the national forest area, the landscape changes from grasslands, first to rolling hills and sub-alpine meadows and then to forest and dramatic craggy limestone peaks. It is a huge, wild, unspoiled area that is ideal for picnicking, camping and exploring in relative solitude – the nearest big city, Denver, Colorado, is 800km (500 miles) away.

Granite Pass marks the highest point, at an elevation of 2,752m (9,033ft) above sea level. After that, the descent passes into the picturesque Shell Canyon, where a stop to view the impressive 36.5-m- (120-ft) tall Shell Falls is pretty much obligatory between May and September. Nearby, Shell Creek was the site of an infamous 1905 grazing rights war between cattle and bighorn sheep farmers. Greybull, the small town at the route's conclusion, is an interesting commercial hub where the Museum of Flight and Aerial Firefighting is well worth a visit. **DK**

Cloud Peak Skyway Scenic Byway
Wyoming, USA

Start Buffalo
End Ten Sleep
Distance 102km (63.6 miles)
Type Adventure
Info goo.gl/ydCJvm

Cloud Peak Skyway is, at its simplest, an easy paved drive, with gentle gradients, through the southern tip of Bighorn National Forest, one of the oldest protected forests in the United States covering a massive 4,4982 sq km (1,731 square miles). The drive also offers views of the Bighorn Mountains and many opportunities to stop, take hikes and watch wildlife. However, it is possible to spice things up with numerous side roads and off-road trails tempting adventurous drivers deeper into the wilds, including the 56-km- (35-mile) long unpaved Red Gulch/Alkali National Back Country Byway, which cuts through steep canyons to reach the Red Gulch Dinosaur Tracksite and its impressive fossilized footprints.

The backbone of this road trip is US Route 16; the Cloud Peak Skyway section starts in the small city of Buffalo, still an agricultural town and a popular base for tourists exploring the area. Driving west, you soon leave the town behind and are headed for the mountains and forest. At first the landscape is flat, although Buffalo stands at an elevation of 1,416m (4,646ft). Not for long, though, as the road rises gently and the landscape becomes increasingly wooded and more dramatic. There are excellent views of the forest, and the highlights come when you reach Powder River Pass, Meadowlark Lake and eventually Ten Sleep Canyon before the historic little town of Ten Sleep. **MG**

❶ A springtime view of the road through the evocatively named Ten Sleep Canyon.

Yellowstone's Grand Loop Road
Wyoming, USA

Start Mammoth Springs
End Mammoth Springs
Distance 229km (142 miles)
Type Scenic
Info goo.gl/NvWbj4

Yellowstone was the first national park in the world. It is a glorious area of Rocky Mountain landscapes with the additional attractions of geysers, waterfalls and lakes. The best way to see the park is to drive – and the only route that takes it all in is the Grand Loop Road.

It's a well-designed figure of eight linking all five park entrances with the main sights, so you can see all the best bits without retracing your path.

You'll travel alongside Yellowstone Lake, which is really the flooded caldera of an active volcano, and the most famous of the park's hundreds of geysers, Old Faithful, which puts on its water show every 91 minutes. Look out, too, for impressively deep river canyons, cooled lava flows, petrified forests and 290 major waterfalls, the highest of which cascades 94m (308ft).

The road is good, but there's a speed limit of just over 70 kph (45 mph) in the park. It's meant to protect wildlife – wolves and grizzly bears often wander across the road.

The most dangerous animal in Yellowstone, however, is neither of those. Park authorities warn you to remain in your vehicle if you encounter this unpredictable and dangerous creature that can run three times faster than any human. Surprisingly, perhaps, the animal that has injured more visitors than any other is the bison. **SH**

❶ This itinerary passes close to Lower Falls, the biggest waterfall in the park.

San Juan Skyway
Colorado, USA

Start Durango
End Durango
Distance 375km (233 miles)
Type Scenic
Info goo.gl/pXmuJz

Colorado is blessed with 26 National Scenic and Historic Byways, but if you are going to explore only one of them, then make sure that it is the fabulous San Juan Skyway, a route justly lauded for its 'dazzling multi-hued' views over some of the finest mountains and forests in North America.

Heading west from the old frontier town of Durango via Cortez, the road loops through the heart of the San Juan Mountains, paralleling the old narrow-gauge railroad, turning northeast along the banks of the Dolores River through forested box canyons to Telluride. Once the hub of the region's silver mining activities, the pretty town of Telluride is better known today for its music festivals and world-class ski areas.

Adventurous types can explore the Alpine Loop National Back Country Byway, a network of four-wheel-drive trails through thick pine forests and eerie ghost towns, just south of Bear Creek. However, the highlight of this road trip is the cliff-clinging stretch between Silverton and Ouray, known as the Million Dollar Highway. Legend has it that it cost that amount of money per mile to hack out this road from the granite canyon walls. With scary drop-offs, it is a severely testing, white-knuckle ride that weaves around rock spurs and into the magnificent Uncompahgre Gorge before heading back to the starting point in Durango. **DIS**

❶ Along the Million Dollar Highway between Silverton and Ouray.

Rim Rock Drive Colorado, USA

Start Fruita   End Grand Junction   Distance 50km (31 miles)
Type Scenic   Map goo.gl/Y35wki

Although the start and finish points are only 14.5km (9 miles) apart, this road trip is in no hurry to finish, as it meanders for 50km (31 miles) through Colorado National Monument along the upper rims of a series of canyons, from the town of Fruita in the west to Grand Junction in the east. The entire road was constructed by a team of 800 men as part of a public works program during the Great Depression in the 1930s. It was designed for 'maximum scenic impact', using the accepted National Park Service rustic style – nothing more than basic tools, human strength and explosives to create an impressive roadway and three tunnels through solid rock. Today, the road is runway-smooth, gradients are gentle and scenic shoulders are around every bend.

Lauded by many as 'one of the grandest scenic drives in the American West', Rim Rock Drive passes through dramatic red rock canyons, towering flat-topped mesas and deserts peppered with juniper. It's a road trip popular with nature lovers (look out for golden eagles, bighorn sheep and Hopi chipmunks) and hikers striking out from its 14 waymarked trails. Spend some time at the Saddlehorn Visitor Center to learn more about this amazing place that's thought to be more than two billion years old. **DIS**

❶ Sunrise over Colorado National Monument.

Trail Ridge Road Colorado, USA

Start Estes Park   End Granby   Distance 101.3km (63 miles)
Type Scenic   Map goo.gl/4BDu3A

From beneath the snowy peaks of Colorado's Estes Park begins the wonderful Trail Ridge Road, part of Route 34; when it was opened in 1932, the press described it as a 'scenic wonder road of the world'.

Starting from the east gate, the first leg is strung between a series of peaks on a spur of the Rocky Mountains between Fall River and Big Thompson River. This spectacular high-level road climbs gently (never more than 7 per cent by design) towards the Alpine Visitor Center through forests of limber pine, sub-alpine fir and spruce, and six large, looping switchbacks. Most of these bends are also furnished with commodious shoulders that offer majestic panoramas from the comfort of your car.

One-quarter of this route is above the tree line, snaking across barren alpine tundra to 3,713m (12,183ft). Winds up here can be savage and temperatures significantly colder than at the starting point. From then on, the route descends southwards past Grand Lake, a tree-ringed picnic spot with a nearby lodge that offers weary travellers hearty meals and tall, cool drinks. The final descent to the valley floor loops through a series of switchbacks towards lush flowering meadows in springtime. Granby, a smart little town popular with energetic outdoor types, is this trip's terminus. **DIS**

❶ Trail Ridge Road in a blizzard.

Colorado River Headwater Byway
Colorado, USA

Start Grand Lake
End Bond
Distance 116km (72 miles)
Type Scenic
Map goo.gl/jD2Si1

The mighty Colorado River is an icon of the North American landscape, flowing from the Rocky Mountain National Park to the Gulf of California and cutting its way through the magnificent Grand Canyon. This spectacular drive shadows the river back towards its source.

Start in the town of Grand Lake, a popular spot with locals and tourists alike. Head south, passing the stretch of water that gives the place its name. Two bigger, human-made, lakes follow – Shadow Mountain Lake and Lake Granby. The road then crosses the river as you head up to Granby, 2,400m (8,000ft) above sea level, before once again crossing the Colorado.

From there on, the road twists and turns as it follows the river, partly along the Trail Ridge Road, another fantastic drivers' route once traversed by horse-drawn stagecoaches. There are plenty of places to stop along the way: Hot Sulphur Springs, where you can take an invigorating, steamy soak, is one example. Another place worth visiting is the old silver-mining settlement of Kremmling, in striking distance of three national parks and noted for its fishing, white-water rafting and kayaking.

With excellent tarmac road surfaces throughout, this is a relatively easy scenic drive. Its southern end point is near the town of Bond, originally a stop on the never-finished Denver and Salt Lake Railroad. JI

❶ Even the mightiest rivers start out as gentle streams: this is one of the sources of the Colorado River.

Top of the Rockies Scenic Byway
Colorado, USA

Start Aspen
End Leadville
Distance 299km (186 miles)
Type Scenic
Map goo.gl/mOipfe

This long-distance Scenic Byway, high in the Rockies, rarely dipping below 2,750m (9,000ft), offers great access to the many hiking, mountain biking and off-road 4x4 trails that branch off from it. The byway's fringes teem with wildlife, including bighorn sheep, elk and red foxes, while its rivers and lakes offer some of the finest fishing in the United States.

From the winter sport mecca of Aspen on Highway 82, head east towards Twin Lakes. Better known as Independence Pass, this lovely stretch of road, nestled between snowcapped mountain peaks, was once voted one of 'America's Prettiest Fall Drives' by *Forbes* magazine.

Turning north on Route 24, proceed towards the quintessential mountain town of Leadville. Now famed for its splendid Victorian architecture, this was once the seedy social centre of Colorado's gold-mining boom, sporting nearly 100 saloons, gambling dens, dance halls and brothels.

Here the byway forks: left through Tennessee Pass past the ghost town of Gilman towards Vail; right on CO-91 towards the lovely holiday resort of Copper Mountain. Both roads are gorgeous, so it's best that you turn this itinerary into a loop via the I-70 and return to Leadville. Check out the Pastime Bar and Café, the last surviving saloon on State Street, which is now a top-quality restaurant. **DIS**

❶ Independence Pass through Mountain Boy Gulch in the San Isabel National Forest.

Pikes Peak Highway
Colorado, USA

Start Cascade
End Pikes Peak summit
Distance 30.6km (19 miles)
Type Adventure
Info goo.gl/HeUEd2

The huge granite monolith that is Pikes Peak is proudly known to many as 'America's Mountain', and since 1916 it has been home to one of the country's greatest motorsports spectacles, Pikes Peak International Hill Climb (PPIHC). Every year, on the weekend closest to 4 July, some of the world's best race-car drivers descend on this picturesque corner of Pike National Forest to tackle the infamous sliver of tarmac as it weaves its way through 156 demanding turns on a 1,440-m- (4,720-ft) tall rise to the summit.

The PPIHC's popularity soared after the award-winning short film *Climb Dance* (1989) astounded audiences by capturing the record-breaking ascent of Finnish rally driver Ari Vatanen. But the good news is that, outside of race weekend, Pikes Peak Highway is a public road. The first half is spectacularly scenic, but after Glen Cove, things start to get more serious. Above the tree line, there are perilous drops beyond the narrow scrubby shoulders; the names of its trickier sections – Ragged Edge, Devil's Playground and Bottomless Pit – won't fill you with confidence either. As you gasp the final few yards to the highway's end at 4,300m (14,110ft) above sea level, you will be left awestruck by two things: the phenomenal panoramas and the astonishing bravery of the men and women that compete in the PPIHC each season. **DIS**

❶ Where the road meets the sky with no land in between on the Pikes Peak International Hill Climb.

Gold Belt Tour Scenic Byway Colorado, USA

Start Florence
End Florence
Distance 183km (114 miles)
Type Culture
Info goo.gl/iq3ye4

This circular drive linking some of the old mining towns that sprang up during the Colorado Gold Rush combines scenery, history (19th century and prehistoric) and characterful urban settlements. It is a glorious ride in any season, but the best time is in autumn, when the aspens turn yellow and the mountains are crowned with crisp, fresh snow.

From Florence (though the drive is just as good in reverse from Florissant), head west on Freeway 50, bypassing Cañon City, and turn right onto County Road 9 after 16km (10 miles). A right fork after another 14km (8.6 miles) leads on to High Park Road, an easy ride through rolling ranchlands dotted with isolated miners' shacks. Joining Teller County Road 1, the route passes the unmistakable Dome Rock before winding into the little town of Florissant. On the outskirts of town, Florissant Fossil Beds National Monument has petrified redwood stumps and the fossils of plants and insects trapped in mudstones and shales 34 million years ago.

Return via Cripple Creek, hub of the mining area, where a fork offers two routes back to Florence. The Shelf Road, partially unpaved, wiggles along a ledge on the canyon wall. It is narrow and dusty, with many drops but plenty of passing places. Alternatively, take Phantom Canyon Road (also unpaved), which has high wooden bridges and two hand-cut tunnels. **DIS**

Turquoise Trail New Mexico, USA

Start Tijeras
End Santa Fe
Distance 80km (50 miles)
Type Scenic
Info goo.gl/DoFyvG

New Mexico's Turquoise Trail takes its name from the semi-precious gemstone that was first mined in the region by the Ancestral Pueblo people as early as 900 CE and later traded along the route that linked Albuquerque and Santa Fe. It was such a valuable commodity that railroads were eventually built to transport the turquoise back east.

Many people start the drive from Albuquerque, because that is where most visitors stay, but technically this National Scenic Byway begins in the small village of Tijeras. From here it heads north, with views of wooded hills soon appearing. Farther north the hills become higher and more frequent, and when you reach Sandia Park to the west, the 3,255m (10,678ft) of Sandia Crest becomes visible. For a detour, it is possible to drive or take the tramway to the summit for exhilarating views.

The road continues northwards through the gold-mining town of Golden and the coal-mining town of Madrid, which now has a thriving artistic community where visitors can stop to browse the galleries. Tiny Cerrillos was once one of the main gem-mining areas, and today it hosts the Turquoise Mining Museum. North of here, the mountains remain on the horizon as you enter the final leg back to Santa Fe, one of the loveliest places in New Mexico and the perfect spot to pick up a turquoise souvenir of this memorable road trip. **MG**

Billy the Kid Trail
New Mexico, USA

Start Ruidoso
End Ruidoso Downs
Distance 136km (84.5 miles)
Type Culture
Map goo.gl/MQUNXR

Unlike some trails that merely commemorate historical figures, this trail was actually used by William Bonney, better known as Billy the Kid, during the Lincoln County War (1878), a dispute between two rival factions for control of cattle and trade that involved lawmakers and criminals on both sides – a clear example showing that in, the Old West, it wasn't always a clear-cut case of good guys versus bad guys.

This circular trail begins in Ruidoso, a town in the Lincoln National Forest that is home to a casino, a racehorse track and the Hubbard Museum of the American West. The last named is worth visiting before setting off, for some background to the story.

Leaving town you'll see ahead the Sierra Blanca range, which rises to 3,652m (11,981ft), the highest point in southern New Mexico. The trail then turns south, through wooded hills, with additional mountain ranges to the west, before heading northwest through the heart of Lincoln County. An essential stop en route is the Lincoln State Monument, a collection of original buildings including the Lincoln County Courthouse from which Billy the Kid escaped after his arrest.

The trail finally returns through a typical New Mexico desert landscape to Ruidoso Downs, a popular haunt with local gamblers at its casino and racehorse track. **MG**

❶ The Sierra Blanca peak in the Sacramento Mountains of southern New Mexico.

Trail of the Mountain Spirits New Mexico, USA

Start Silver City
End Silver City
Distance 118km (73.3 miles)
Type Culture
Info goo.gl/pK9xjK

This National Scenic Byway takes drivers through the southwestern corner of New Mexico that was traditionally home to Native Americans. However it starts and ends in Silver City, whose boom as a mining town ensured that the white man soon made his mark on this landscape. The area around here had been known first to the Spaniards as a source of copper, but when silver was discovered in 1870, Silver City was born. Before leaving town, visit the Silver City Museum to learn of the region's colourful history.

The byway heads north into the Gila Wilderness Area and the Pinos Altos Mountains and through the town of Pinos Altos (Tall Pines), which stands at 2,137m (7,011ft) above sea level on the Continental Divide. Continuing north, the backroad heads through thousands of such trees, with many narrow twists, and eventually passes a left turn that offers an optional detour of approximately 29km (18 miles) to the pre-Columbian relics at Gila Cliff Dwellings National Monument.

Here the main route swings east, skirts the edge of the Gila National Forest, the sixth largest in the United States, and passes Lake Roberts before turning south through the tiny towns of Mimbres and San Lorenzo, and finally heading back west to Silver City through the open valleys that the Apaches once called home. **MG**

Geronimo Trail Scenic Byway New Mexico, USA

Start Beaverhead
End San Lorenzo
Distance 240km (149 miles)
Type Culture
Info goo.gl/C7Aeu6

One of the most powerful and feared Apache chiefs, Geronimo waged a long war against the US authorities in the late 19th century, much of it in this part of New Mexico and neighbouring Arizona. Driving this National Scenic Byway not only provides you with breathtaking scenery, it also offers an insight into these historic conflicts that helped to shape the American West and the United States of today.

The road trip starts in Beaverhead, in the Gila National Forest, a vast area of some 11,000 sq km (4,250 square miles). Before arriving at San Lorenzo, on the far side of the forest, the route provides several side-trip opportunities. It passes through the towns of Winston, Cuchillo and Chloride before heading south and running for a while parallel to the busy Interstate 25 highway.

Among the many unmissable stopovers en route is the delightfully named spa town of Truth or Consequences, which is home to the Geronimo Trail Scenic Byway Visitor Center and the Geronimo Springs Museum. A visit to these two places will provide the necessary background information on the history, culture and landscapes of this area.

The road then heads back west and climbs to 2,438m (8,000ft) through the Emory Pass, from which there are unrivalled views of the pine-covered mountains all around. **MG**

Little Miss Sunshine New Mexico to California, USA

Start Albuquerque, New Mexico   End Ventura Beach, California   Distance 1,509km (938 miles)
Type Culture   Map goo.gl/WX6gkc

Lauded as one of the best feel-good road movies of all time, *Little Miss Sunshine* (2006) was produced on a shoestring budget and won two Academy Awards. Fans of the film now follow in the tyre tracks of the Hoover family's problematic Volkswagen T2 Microbus on their own road trips from Albuquerque, New Mexico, to Redondo Beach, California, the location of the fictional titular beauty pageant.

The filmmakers took quite a few geographical liberties with locations on the way, but to get into the spirit of the movie you should start in Albuquerque and head west through the New Mexico desert. Interstate 40 takes you through the kind of flat and barren landscapes that were featured in the film, and into Arizona, which is where most of the filming actually took place.

There you'll see flat-topped mesas, familiar from Westerns, and pass through some of the towns in the film, including Flagstaff. However, it would require a considerable detour from there to Scottsdale, where many of the scenes were filmed in the evocative red rock landscape around Sedona.

Most of the identifiable film locations are in California, and require a wiggling drive through Los Angeles and then northwest to the Crowne Plaza Ventura Beach Hotel. MG

❶ The family pile into their temperamental VW bus.

Guadalupe Mountain Drive New Mexico/Texas, USA

Start Whites City, New Mexico   End Whites City, New Mexico   Distance 650km (404 miles)
Type Scenic   Info goo.gl/AZKxi4

Surrounded by the Chihuahuan Desert, the Guadalupe Mountains are a mix of salt flats, pine- and juniper-filled grasslands and alpine uplands of ponderosa pine, Douglas fir and aspen. Their highest point, 910m (3,00ft) above the surrounding desert, is 2,667-m- (8,751-ft) high Guadalupe Peak, one of North America's most recognizable mountains. There's also a trail, accessed via US 62 to the mountain's southeast, that can get the most intrepid travellers all the way to its summit.

For most people, though, the network of US highways that surround these mountains are the real lure, providing access to the varied landscapes that encircle this isolated range. US 70 takes you past White Sands National Monument, a vast expanse of dunes composed of gypsum crystals, and through Alamogordo, with its International Space Hall of Fame, before joining US 54 to the Three Rivers Petroglyph Site.

The Guadalupe Mountains are also the site of the world's premier example of an exposed marine fossil reef – the 265-million-year-old Capitan Reef – once submerged beneath the ancient Delaware Sea and now the 330-m- (1,000-ft) tall cliffs of El Capitan, long hidden but now in plain view, one of the United States' greatest geological wonders. **BDS**

❶ The highway to Guadalupe Mountains National Park.

Mt Rushmore and the Badlands South Dakota, USA

Start Junction of Interstate 90 and South Dakota Highway 240   **End** Custer   **Distance** 225km (140 miles)
Type Scenic   **Map** goo.gl/R4WEYq

Remember Cary Grant and Eva Marie Saint scrambling over the Mt Rushmore National Monument in Alfred Hitchcock's film *North by Northwest* (1959)? This huge memorial to four well-known US presidents is the star attraction of this route, bookended by two thrilling drives through some of the most unforgiving and ornery scenery.

Just after the start is the Ben Reifel Visitor Center, gateway to the wilderness of the Badlands National Park and a desolate and memorable section of road. Sedimentary rock rarely gets this exciting, with contorted rock formations and spectacular fossil beds. After, perhaps, a stopover at Rapid City, the route continues to Mt Rushmore where the monumental faces of four US presidents – George Washington, Thomas Jefferson, Theodore Roosevelt and Abraham Lincoln – are carved 18m (60ft) or so high out of the granite cliff. If gravel road excursions are your thing, then the Sage Creek Rim Road is an interesting detour from the town of Scenic.

Afterwards, the route winds up through the mountains (stop at Norbeck Overlook for a great view back to Mt Rushmore) and follows a marvellous twisty road past natural granite spires. The trip ends with another natural wonder: Custer State Park. **DK**

❶ **The memorial was sculpted by Gutzon Borglum.**

Black Hills Needles Highway South Dakota, USA

Start Custer   **End** Hill City   **Distance** 31km (19 miles)
Type Scenic   **Map** goo.gl/ClLJkU

In the early decades of the 20th century, a raft of solid granite upthrusts in the Harney Range – now affectionately referred to as 'needles' – were so imposing, so daunting, that they discouraged road building in the central mountainous area of South Dakota's Black Hills for many years. Then along came the governor of South Dakota, Peter Norbeck, whose dedication to the creation of a scenic highway through the mountains he loved knew no bounds. Norbeck marked out the entire route on foot and on horseback, and in 1919 construction began. At every great view that Norbeck encountered, he told his engineer, Scovel Johnson, 'Run the road here'.

Completed in 1922, the Needles Highway lies wholly within the must-see Custer State Park, long-time home to 1,500 free-roaming bison. Closed throughout winter, the highway is a memorable drive through forests of spruce and pine, as well as birch- and aspen-fringed meadows. It also has three fabulous tunnels blasted through solid granite, including the 2.5-m- (8.3-ft) wide Needles Eye Tunnel. Mostly, though, it is the towering spires of granite that create the thrills, rocks that crystallized under ground eons ago and then 'punched' their way to the surface. **BDS**

❶ The needles have made the area popular with climbers.

Native American Scenic Byway South Dakota, USA

Start Chief Standing Bear Memorial Bridge   End Kenel   Distance 771km (479 miles)
Type Culture   Info goo.gl/ThTuyH

Chief Standing Bear was a Native American who fought a landmark case in 1879 in the courts in Omaha, Nebraska, to establish that Native Americans were 'persons within the meaning of the law'. This drive begins on the bridge named in his honour, which crosses the Missouri River and marks the Nebraska–South Dakota border.

The Scenic Byway follows the course of the river north to the border with North Dakota. (Variations on the route continue into that neighbouring state, if you wish to extend the drive.)

Leaving the wide Missouri behind – and it really is wide here – the road heads north through the fairly flat landscape to the town of Mitchell, then west a short way on Interstate 40 to meet the river again. It follows the east bank with lovely views across the water to the tree-filled west bank before entering the Crow Creek Reservation and arriving in Fort Laramie. This is a small town, but the largest on the reservation.

The road then zigzags up through South Dakota and the hypnotically monotonous flatlands of the prairies. The Missouri, though, more than makes up for the flatness of the land, with gorgeous views of it as you cross and recross it before ending the trip just short of the state line. MG

❶ The Missouri River in South Dakota.

Sturgis Rally Black Hills Loop South Dakota, USA

Start Sturgis   End Sturgis   Distance 406km (252 miles)
Type Culture   Map goo.gl/EZMMCv

In the first week of August every year, the population of Sturgis in Meade County explodes from around 6,000 to more than 700,000 for a ten-day gathering of motorcycling enthusiasts from all over the world. There are races, burnouts, bike unveilings, celebrity appearances, tattooists, gear shops, hog roasts, and concerts at the Full Throttle Saloon, the world's biggest biker bar, covering 12 hectares (30 acres).

Once the hangovers have subsided, most visitors just want to meet up with their buddies to get out and ride the magnificent Black Hills of South Dakota.

This popular round trip can be linked up with two other itineraries in this present volume: Needles Highway, and Mt Rushmore and the Badlands.

Heading west towards Spearfish, the twisty US 14A loops back east through the gold-rush town of Deadwood, once the home of Wild Bill Hickcok. Nearby, at the Broken Boot Gold Mine, you can have a go at gold panning for yourself.

Farther south is the colossal Crazy Horse Memorial rock carving: begun in 1948, it's still a work in progress. US 18 via Hot Springs brings you back north past Mt Rushmore to Rapid City, the hub of gold-mining activity in the late 1800s. It's then just a fast blast on Interstate 90 back to Sturgis in time for another hard night's partying. **DIS**

❶ Bear Butte between Sturgis and Rapid City.

Frontier Military Historic Byway Kansas, USA

Start Fort Leavenworth   End Fort Blair   Distance 270km (168 miles)
Type Culture   Info goo.gl/HGOIT6

At one end of this road trip is Fort Leavenworth, built in 1827 to protect pioneers on the Santa Fe Trail, and a focal point of the westward expansion of the United States. At the other is Fort Blair, first garrisoned in 1842 to safeguard the town of Fort Scott and to be a base for patrols of the eastern fringe of the so-called 'Permanent Indian Frontier'.

The north–south trail that once connected these two outposts is now followed, as best it can be, by the Frontier Military Historic Byway, which links not only the state's significant pioneering sites but also areas in which there were bitter confrontations between pro- and anti-slavery forces during the Bleeding Kansas civil war of 1854 to 1861.

Must-see stops along the way include the site of the Battle of Mine Creek, the second-largest cavalry engagement of the American Civil War (1861–65), and Fort Scott National Historic Site, which consists of 20 historic buildings, a parade ground and an expanse of carefully restored tall grass prairie. The state's first designated byway, now redesignated a Historic Byway, is also blooming, thanks to a government-sponsored initiative to line it with wildflowers. These add a colourful flourish to the many museums, homesteads, riverfronts, waterfalls and wildlife areas of eastern Kansas. **BDS**

❶ Fort Larned on the Santa Fe Trail.

Cherokee Hills Byway Oklahoma, USA

Start Gore   End West Siloam Springs   Distance 136km (84.5 miles)
Type Culture   Map goo.gl/Ll5urR

The Cherokee Hills were, of course, named after the Cherokee Nation, whose capital Tahlequah is halfway along this byway, which cuts through some of eastern Oklahoma's most impressive landscapes. It's an attractive part of the world, but a tragic story for the Cherokee tribes who were made to march several hundred miles along the Trail of Tears to be forcibly settled here. It's a story you'll hear frequently in places along this drive.

The route begins by exiting Interstate 40 near the town of Gore, the 'Trout Capital of America', at the centre of some prime fishing waters, most notably the Illinois River and the Tenkiller Ferry Lake. The drive takes you past the lake on tree-lined rural roads, finally crossing over the wide expanse of water at the Cherokee Landing State Park.

Take a break in Tahlequah to learn about the history of the area and the Native American people, and peruse the arts and crafts that are on sale here. The road continues north, more or less following the Illinois River, before swinging east to end up in West Siloam Springs on the Oklahoma–Arkansas border. Before you get there, though, take a slight detour into the Natural Falls State Park, where you'll find hiking trails through thick woodland and one of the tallest waterfalls in Oklahoma. MG

➊ The Natural Falls are a rewarding diversion.

Route 66 – Central
Oklahoma to Arizona, USA

Start Tulsa, Oklahoma
End Lupton, Arizona
Distance 1,333km (828 miles)
Type Culture
Maps goo.gl/CiHVFL and goo.gl/XYaEr1

This is the middle section of the classic 3,600-km (2,200-mile) route from Chicago, Illinois, to Los Angeles, California. Also known as 'The Mother Road' or 'The Main Street of America', it's where, musically, you get your kicks. Following a vigorous heritage campaign, the route is now renavigable and has morphed into a motorized mythological Americana, redolent with nostalgia. Modern-day pilgrims of leisure travel the route in search of old-time petrol stops, lunch spots and motels.

This segment begins in Oklahoma, clips Texas, passes all through New Mexico and ends at Lupton, just inside Arizona. This heartlands-of-America section is all good, getting dustier and more desertlike as it goes. By the time you reach New Mexico, you are properly in the land of mesas and dry gulches. The scenery is terrific, the diners, petrol stations and small-town main streets all seemingly stranded in time. The names of the places en route are enough to make one enthusiastic for the trip. Some of the most interesting stops include Tulsa, Chandler, Bethany, Calumet, Hydro, Clinton, Sayre, McLean, Amarillo, Vega, Albuquerque, Laguna, Grants and Gallup. Many of these places have their own radio stations. Tune in and listen as Middle America unfolds before you. **DK**

➲ One of the many traditional diners that line the road.

El Camino del Rio
Texas, USA

Start Presidio
End Lajitas
Distance 80km (50 miles)
Type Scenic
Map goo.gl/dPaqVh

El Camino del Rio follows the Rio Grande along the United States–Mexico border through various canyons and the Big Bend Ranch State Park, the largest state park in Texas. Driving the route west to east, the starting point is Presidio, a border town and the location of the park's headquarters. There it is possible to pick up information about the fascinating and historic lands that lie ahead.

Presidio is only a small town and you quickly find yourself in open country, with hills on the horizon and Mexico somewhere off to the right. As the road starts to rise, imposing mountains come into view, and eventually the route heads through the surprisingly green Tapado Canyon. Shortly after comes a stretch of the road that is known as the 'Big Hill', which has one of the steepest inclines in Texas. It is not advisable to make the climb if you are driving a motor home or other heavy vehicle, but the view from the top of the Colorado Canyon has been described as one of the best panoramas in the United States.

The road then turns with the Rio Grande's meanders until it reaches the Old West town of Lajitas, where General John J. 'Black Jack' Pershing first built a military outpost to protect settlers from the raiding parties of Mexican revolutionary, Pancho Villa. It is now home to shopping boutiques, equestrian centres and golf courses. **MG**

San Marcos to Guadalupe River State Park Texas, USA

Start San Marcos
End Guadalupe River State Park
Distance 82km (51 miles)
Type Scenic
Map goo.gl/8yJxb1

This relaxing trip along wide, well-made highways starts in San Marcos, a city that was founded on agriculture and ranching, and at the end of the 19th century became the seat of Southwest Texas State University. The main tourist attraction here is Aquarena Springs at the headwaters of the San Marcos River, where there are hanging gardens, an underwater theatre and a network of caves.

Mew Braunfels, 29km (18 miles) southwest along Highway 35, lies at the confluence of the Comal and Guadalupe Rivers. Originally settled by immigrants from Prussia, this city retains a Germanic air year round, not only for the duration of its Wurstfest, 'the ten-day salute to the sausage; that starts on the first Friday of November each year.

Leaving the main highway the route goes west for 48km (30 miles) to Guadalupe River State Park, which has something for almost everyone. At the water's edge there are canoes to rent, places to fish and designated swimming areas. In the depths of the park there are hiking and equestrian trails, picnic spots and campsites. Nature lovers will find a wide range of trees, including bald cypress, Ashe juniper and mesquite, and numerous animal species: white-tailed deer are almost ubiquitous, and there are also armadillos, raccoons and skunks. Among the birds is the endangered golden-cheeked warbler, aka the Texas goldfinch. **JP**

Twisted Sisters Ranch Road Loop
Texas, USA

Start Leakey
End Leakey
Distance 233km (145 miles)
Type Scenic
Map goo.gl/qitfpM

In the United States ranch roads (or farm-to-market roads) are paved secondary roads that connect rural or agricultural areas to nearby towns or distribution hubs. The first ranch road in Texas, just 9km (6 miles) long, was completed in 1937, and highways of the same type have since proliferated to such an extent that they now account for more than half of the state's total paved-road network.

This version of the Twisted Sisters Ranch Road Loop, so named because of its many curves – one 24-km- (15-mile) long stretch has 65 bends – starts on the RR-337 outside Leakey and passes over typical hill country to Little Dry Frio Creek Valley. The bends and rises will try to throw you from your seat, so take it easy here (be on the lookout, too, for white-tailed deer). Take Highway 41 for 22km (14 miles) to the RR-335, a thrilling series of up-and-over hills but with fewer bends than the previous stretch, then top up with petrol at Camp Wood before returning to Leakey on the RR-337 for the second eastern loop, including a must-do detour at Vanderpool to the excellent Lone Star Motorcycle Museum, with its extensive collection of classic American and British bikes.

The Twisted Sisters' figure-of-eight loop remains a two-wheeled magnet because of its roller-coaster-like bends, its smooth surfaces and its seriously invigorating paucity of traffic. **BDS**

❶ One of many commendable eateries in Leakey, the start and finish of this road trip.

Texas Forts Trail

Texas, USA

Start Abilene
End Abilene
Distance 1,046km (650 miles)
Type Culture
Info goo.gl/bXlyAb

In the mid-19th century, Texas, the Lone Star State, was on the US frontier, but this was an age of territorial expansion. Pressing ever-farther into the territories of the Kiowa, Kiowa Apaches and Comanche, a line of forts linking settled lands and 'wild'country was established to provide protection for a westbound stream of pioneers. By the time Native American resistance in Texas came to an end in 1879, Texas had 44 major army posts and more than 100 military camps, with buildings made from trees and rocks felled and quarried by the soldiers themselves.

Part of the award-winning Texas Heritage Trails Program, the Texas Forts Trail in West Central Texas comprises eight forts – Belknap, Richardson, Chadbourne, Griffin, Concho (home of the Buffalo Soldiers), McKavett, Mason and Phantom Hill – and one presidio (a Spanish-built fortified settlement): San Luis de Las Amarillas.

This proposed itinerary does not always take the most direct route from fort to fort, detouring instead to soak up some Central Texas scenery, including seven state parks and more than 20 lakes. A 1.047-km- (650-mile) long drive through 29 counties, the Texas Forts Trail brings you face to face with some of the American West's best-preserved military frontier outposts. Check out the dedicated website listed above. **BDS**

JFK Assassination Tour

Texas, USA

Start Hilton Hotel, Fort Worth
End Rose Hill Cemetery, Fort Worth
Distance 122km (76 miles)
Type Culture
Map goo.gl/lYo4Ku

Rather than a ghoulish tour of a tragic murder scene, this road trip is an educational experience that will help those who make it better understand events that led up to a pivotal moment in modern history: the 22 November 1963 assassination of US President John F. Kennedy (JFK).

Feel free to take the route in any order; this trip is roughly chronological, so it doesn't make much geographic sense.

Start at the Hilton in Fort Worth, where JFK spent his last night. There's a commemorative plaque inside. Then drive east to Dallas on the famous motorcade route. Dealey Plaza and the grassy knoll are popular tourist attractions today; you'll find an 'X' painted in the road on the exact spot where the President was shot.

Nearby is the Sixth Floor Museum in what was then the Texas School Book Depository. This is where Lee Harvey Oswald fired the fatal shots. Look out at the haunting view he had over the plaza.

The president was rushed to Parklands Hospital, where he died. Another plaque marks the spot at the hospital. Oswald hid in the Texas Theater, where he was cornered and arrested. He was then shot and killed by Jack Ruby at the former municipal building on South Harwood, before being buried at Rose Hill Park in Fort Worth. It's hard to find the small gravestone with the one-word legend:'Oswald'. **SH**

North Shore Scenic Drive
Minnesota, USA

Start Duluth
End Grand Portage
Distance 229km (142 miles)
Type Scenic
Map goo.gl/8YrMdI

Minnesota's North Shore Scenic Drive parallels the majestic shoreline of Lake Superior, the world's largest freshwater lake, with every possible vista you could wish a lakeside drive to have: waterfalls; fabulous cliffs; seemingly endless trailheads; forests of pine, aspen and birch; historic towns. And always by your side, that endless expanse of blue, containing 10 per cent of the world's fresh water.

The options for detours on this drive are mind-numbing in their scope. You can head into the Superior National Forest, kayak in Boundary Waters Canoe Area Wilderness, or along the Lake Superior State Water Trail, which will take you past some of the lake's towering escarpments. Fish in its rivers and streams, go for a walk along the cobbled beach of Sugarloaf Cove, or hike one of the trails around Split Rock Lighthouse for the sort of views that only lighthouses provide. The drive, the most popular of the state's 20-plus Scenic Byways, will take you through no fewer than seven state parks.

It starts in Duluth and continues north on State Highway 61, ending at the Canadian border. The state's only designated All-American Road is part drive, part time-warp, a journey along a B-and-B-studded shoreline that has never seen a railroad, where pioneers first arrived in the 1670s and their descendants still live along the edge of a veritable inland sea. **BDS**

❶ Winter on the shore of Lake Superior – the water is frozen solid, but the highway is ice free.

Minnesota Great River Road Minnesota, USA

Start Itasca State Park   **End** Iowa state line   **Distance** 925km (575 miles)
Type Culture   **Info** goo.gl/wOPmID

Travelling down the Mississippi River is a great way to tour Minnesota, the North Star State. Begin this trip at the Mary Gibbs Mississippi Headwaters Center in Itasca State Park, where you can walk across the start of the mighty 3,200-km- (2,000-mile) long waterway on a few stepping stones.

Minnesota is also known as the Land of 10,000 Lakes, and you'll soon start spotting some of them as you head east through lush pine forests to Grand Rapids. The spectacular chain of lakes along this stretch of road used to form a water highway for Native American canoes.

Then the route turns south, through rich farmland, to reach the bustle of the Twin Cities of Minneapolis and St Paul. This is a big conurbation, but you'll still find 116km (72 miles) of protected waterfront parks and historic sites to explore, and perhaps take a ride on a period steamboat.

Approaching the Iowa state line, the landscape changes again amid the Mississippi Bluffs – rocky cliffs rising to 150m (50ft) above the banks.

The best place to see these magnificent geological formations is in John A. Latch State Park, where three prominent neighbouring bluffs were named by passing steamboat captains as Mt Faith, Mt Hope and Mt Charity. **SH**

❶ The Mississippi River from atop the bluffs.

After Robert M. Pirsig Minnesota to California, USA

Start Minneapolis, Minnesota   End San Francisco, California   Distance 3,862km (2,400 miles)
Type Culture   Map goo.gl/kMOCNY

In 1974, *Zen and the Art of Motorcycle Maintenance* became an unlikely bestseller that combined an account of a 17-day road trip with lengthy philosophical discussions and sections on the author's personal history, told largely in the third person. There were precious few tips on how to actually fix a bike. Rejected by 121 publishers, the work went on to sell more than five million copies.

Author Robert M. Pirsig set off from his home in Minneapolis on his 1964 Honda SuperHawk with his son Chris for a parent–child bonding trip after some traumatic experiences in his own life. Unlike many literary road trips, Pirsig's route is noted accurately and relatively easy to follow.

It first heads northwest across flat Minnesota farmland before turning west near Fargo and into North Dakota, where it passes through seemingly endless cornfields. Gradually the terrain begins to undulate, as the route heads into Montana and the Rocky Mountains lie ahead.

In Idaho the road goes through several national forests. Turning south through Oregon brings even more spectacular landscapes before the road reaches the Pacific Ocean at Crescent City. The California coast is then followed across the Golden Gate Bridge into San Francisco. **MG**

❶ Dawn over the Pacific at Crescent City.

Western Skies Scenic Byway Iowa, USA

Start Stuart
End Missouri Valley
Distance 225km (140 miles)
Type Scenic
Map goo.gl/nU5rMD

In the prairies of the Midwest, the best views are often of the open skies, which the pancake-flat landscape dramatically emphasizes. The Western Skies Scenic Byway leaves the busy Interstate 80 at Stuart, a small city that dates back to the 1860s. Immediately, you are on a gently undulating rural road, typical of this part of the world, with farmland all around and only the occasional building.

From Panora, the route heads west through some of the farmland that fuels the region's economy. There is little variation – in summer, there is field after field of sweet corn – and certainly no outstanding features, but the fact that the scenery is repetitive and undramatic makes for a tranquil and atmospheric road trip. At Kimballton, take a detour south to Elk Horn, whose few hundred inhabitants celebrate their Scandinavian ancestry in the Museum of Danish America. Return to Kimballton and continue west to Harlan, where the Scenic Byway goes in two different directions. One route runs north and then west to Woodbine, before going south again to join up with the other route, which heads west from Harlan. The loop via Woodbine adds 47.3km (29.4 miles) to the journey. Both legs of the road trip follow the final southwards stretch through seemingly endless fields of maize to the city of Missouri Valley and the end of the Western Skies Scenic Byway. **MG**

The Straight Story Iowa/Wisconsin, USA

Start Laurens, Iowa
End Blue River, Wisconsin
Distance 394km (245 miles)
Type Culture
Map goo.gl/k1Mg8u

In 1994 Alvin Straight, a 73-year-old retired labourer from Laurens, Iowa, no longer able to drive a car, rode his 1966 John Deere 110 lawnmower east to Wisconsin to visit his brother Henry, who had suffered a stroke. Towing a 3-m- (10-ft) long trailer, his vehicle broke down in West Bend, Iowa; and in Charles City, Iowa, Alvin ran out of money, and camped there until his next social security payment arrived. Breaking down again 3km (2 miles) from his brother's home, it took him a total of six weeks driving ten hours a day to make the 384-km- (240-mile) long trip to Blue River, Wisconsin, at a top speed of 8 kph (5 mph).

In 1999 a film about Alvin's journey, starring Richard W. Farnsworth and Sissy Spacek and directed by David Lynch, was released to critical acclaim and Academy Award nominations.

Retracing Alvin's journey today is easy enough to do, but just driving this typical Midwestern route – north on Highway 15, then on to Highway 18 – simply won't do. There are lessons here. Old notions have changed. Roads, once seen only as symbols of modernity and progress, have pulled families apart. Here they pull you forwards in a return to familial things. Alvin's road trip represents not rebellion, solitude or freedom, but community, connectedness and reunion. Road trips can also be the means by which you come home. **BDS**

Hermann Wine Trail
Missouri, USA

Start Hermann
End New Haven
Distance 32km (20 miles)
Type Culture
Info goo.gl/mgbPyn

The seven family-owned wineries along the banks of the Missouri River between Hermann and New Haven, east of the state capital, owe their existence to Gottfried Duden, a German explorer who settled in 1824 in the region. Duden fell in love with the Missouri River, often likening it to the Rhine in his native land. Inspired by Duden, Germans by the thousands began emigrating to the surrounding area in the 1830s, and it was not long before they started planting vineyards. The German-speaking town of Hermann was founded in 1837, and by 1904 the surrounding area was producing more than 11.3 million litres (3 million gallons) of wine a year.

The wineries – Adam Puchta, Bias, Dierberg, Hermannhof, OakGlenn, Röbller and Stone Hill – can all be visited in a single day on this route. The trail also plays host to several themed annual events, including a Chocolate Wine Trail (February) and a Wild Bacon Wine Trail (May).

Each winery is distinctive: Adam Puchta, founded in 1855, is the oldest US farm winery in continuous ownership by a single family; Stone Hill has cavernous underground cellars; Hermannhof's stone cellars and brick superstructures mean that there is not only wine here, but also plenty of history in a state that was, prior to Prohibition, the second-largest wine producer in the United States. **BDS**

❶ The Stone Hill winery was established in 1847, ten years after Hermann, the town in which it is located.

Scenic 7 Byway
Arkansas, USA

Start Bull Shoals Lake, Diamond City
End Louisiana state line near El Dorado
Distance 467km (290 miles)
Type Scenic
Info goo.gl/4JxB2y

The Scenic 7 Byway – dedicated in 1994 and the first highway of its type in the state of Arkansas – often features in Top Ten lists of the most beautiful scenic drives in the United States. Well, when you have the Ozark and Ouachita Mountains, the state's lush West Gulf Coastal Plain, dense forests, rolling farmlands and dazzling geological formations all around you, why wouldn't it?

Leaving Diamond City, it won't be long until you're in the 4,700 sq km (1,800 square miles) of the Ozark National Forest. Be sure to stop at the Ozark Café, a state landmark since it first opened its doors in 1909, and take a tour of the 'living' Blanchard Springs Caverns along the Dripstone Trail.

From there the road continues south, down into the Arkansas River Valley, before entering the Ouachita Mountains, once as high as the Rocky Mountains (before erosion set in) and still the highest heights between the Rockies and the Appalachians. It is here you will find Hot Springs, a spa town since the 1830s with its famous Bathhouse Row, which is one of North America's most architecturally eclectic streets.

The drive ends near El Dorado, a lovely area of lowland hills, river valleys and thick forests of pine and bottomland hardwoods. By the time you arrive there, you will understand full well why they call Arkansas 'The Natural State'. **BDS**

❶ A typically gentle stretch of Scenic Highway 7 through Ouachita National Forest.

Talimena National Scenic Byway
Arkansas/Oklahoma, USA

Start Mena, Arkansas
End Talimena, Oklahoma
Distance 87km (54 miles)
Type Scenic
Info goo.gl/WGIQxF

The Ouachita National Forest spreads over more than 7,300 sq km (2,800 square miles) across the Arkansas–Oklahoma border, an expanse of forests and lakes renowned not only for their panoramic mountain views, but also for the clarity of the waters in the countless rivers and streams. The Talimena National Scenic Byway, established as a National Forest Scenic Byway in 1989, takes you along the ridge lines of the Ouachita's Winding Stair Mountains and Rich Mountain, at 817m (2,681ft) Arkansas's second-highest peak, immersing you in a region of old-growth forests that have never been logged and remain rich in wildlife.

Originally constructed from 1964 to 1969 to connect two trucking routes, this road takes you through foliage so dense that it hugs the highway's edges and at times almost threatens to hem you in. A favourite motorcycle route, the byway was also built to highlight the beauty of one of the highest mountain ranges between the Rockies and the Appalachians.

There are steep mountain roads here, with some sections having 13 per cent gradients. There are sharp curves, sudden inclines aplenty and no shortage of turnouts. Historic points of interest abound as well, including early pioneer homes and Native American museums on what is Arkansas's and Oklahoma's No. 1 rated Scenic Byway. **BDS**

❶ The trees start closing in on this early section of the proposed route.

Thelma & Louise
Arkansas to Arizona, USA

Start Little Rock, Arkansas
End Grand Canyon, Arizona
Distance 2,414km (1,500 miles)
Type Culture
Map goo.gl/bN11df

This Academy Award-winning road movie centres on two friends, Thelma Dickinson (Geena Davis) and Louise Sawyer (Susan Sarandon), who set out for a two-day road trip in a classic 1966 Ford Thunderbird convertible. Heading north from Little Rock, Arkansas, to the Ozark Mountains, the trip takes a darker turn after Louise shoots a lecherous local and would-be rapist in the parking lot of a sleazy honky-tonk bar.

Rather than spending the rest of their lives in jail, the pair decide to make a run for the Mexican border; on Louise's insistence that they avoid Texas, the pair flee west along Interstate 44 through the vast open plains of Oklahoma and the sunbaked landscapes of the American Southwest. The film, directed by Ridley Scott, has become a cult classic, and has also inspired adventurers to retrace the screenplay's original route from Arkansas to Arizona.

Although the route is entirely doable, as it propels the tragic pair westward, many parts were actually shot around Bakersfield, California. However, some of the films most powerful scenes, such as the long, lonely ride along US 163 through Utah's majestic Monument Valley, just couldn't be faked.

Thelma and Louise are eventually cornered by the police just 90m (100 yards) from the Grand Canyon; unwilling to submit to arrest, the two embrace before Louise floors the throttle and launches the T-Bird over the edge of the precipice. **DIS**

◐ Sunrise with the view from Hunts Mesa in Monument Valley, south of the border between Utah and Arizona.

❶ Geena Davis (left) and Susan Sarandon (right) play a housewife and a waitress, respectively, on the run.

Lake Pontchartrain Causeway Louisiana, USA

Start Lewisburg **End** Metairie **Distance** 42km (26 miles)
Type Adventure **Map** goo.gl/EIlbX2

This was the world's longest bridge over water until 2011, when it lost its title to the Jiaozhou Bay Bridge, although the US structure still has the longest aggregate spans continuously over water – the Chinese bridge has intermediate stages on *terra firma*. But for those who have driven the 38-km (24-mile) length of the Lake Pontchartrain Causeway, it will always remain their favourite.

Most bridges lift you up and take you away from the world. This one does not. Because Lake Pontchartrain is so shallow – with an average depth of only 4.5m (15ft) – this was built as a low-level trestle bridge. This means that the roadway is dead flat, and seems almost to rest on the surface of the

lake. The effect of traversing it is peculiar and slightly mesmeric: half an hour's drive time, in a perfect straight line. Of course, there is water that sparkles all around, but ahead only a thin strip of tarmac disappearing to a vanishing point.

The first two-lane bridge was built in 1956 at a cost of $30.7 million. For those on the north shore of the lake, it cut some 50 minutes off their commute time into New Orleans. It was such a success that another two lanes were added in 1969, as an entirely separate parallel structure. This road trip is a journey like no other. **DK**

❶ Heading south over the bridge towards New Orleans.

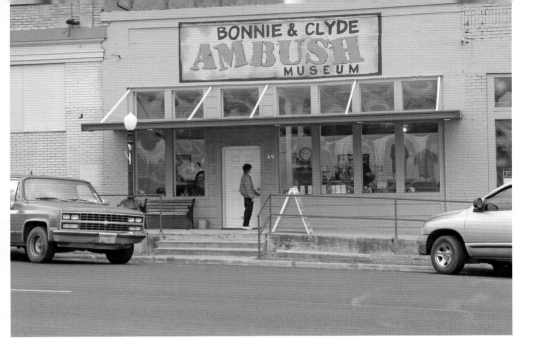

Last Ride of Bonnie and Clyde Louisiana, USA

Start Gibsland   End Memorial on Highway 154   Distance 13km (8 miles)

Type Culture   Map goo.gl/uV5Ha5

Bank robbers and killers Bonnie Parker and Clyde Barrow are widely regarded as the world's first celebrity criminals. This road trip retraces the tragic couple's final joyride in their stolen gray Ford V8.

The journey begins at the Bonnie & Clyde Ambush Museum in Gibsland; the larger of the town's dedicated museums, this was once the location of Ma Cranfield's Café, where the pair stopped for breakfast on that fateful morning. The proudest exhibits include Bonnie's red hat, one of Clyde's Remington shotguns, and his favourite weapon, a Browning semi-automatic rifle.

In the early hours of 23 May 1934, Bonnie and Clyde headed south along Louisiana's Highway 154 towards Sailes, unaware that four heavily armed lawmen were lying in wait 13km (8 miles) out of town. On hearing the distinctive rumble of the Ford's flathead V8, the posse opened fire, putting 130 rounds into the car, killing the couple outright.

Time your visit to coincide with the weekend closest to the anniversary of their deaths to join Gibsland's annual Bonnie and Clyde Festival, a light-hearted gathering that concludes with a well-attended road trip along broad, tree-lined rural highways to the ambush point, which is currently marked with a stone roadside memorial. DIS

❶ The starting point in Gibsland.

Louisiana Bayou Byway
Louisiana, USA

Start New Orleans
End Lafayette
Distance 249km (155 miles)
Type Culture
Map goo.gl/cGOLCc

North America's greatest river, the Mississippi, empties into the Gulf of Mexico at the Atchafalaya Basin, creating a vast jungle of cypress swamplands and sleepy bayous. The area's unique mix of white, African American, Cajun and Creole peoples – originally arriving variously as exiles, like the Arcadian Cajuns, as slaves for the sugar plantations, or freely to work on the oil rigs – has created a special culture, way of life, music and cuisine. This jaunt tours the heart of the region, through a string of small towns and settlements stretched out along the Bayou Teche waterway.

Leaving New Orleans, head south first to Morgan City, the main port of the region, and then along the banks of the bayou, through Franklin, Jeanerette, New Iberia and St Martinville to Lafayette. It's a fascinating drive through arcades of live oaks with Spanish moss, past grand neoclassical plantation houses – notably Oaklawn Manor in Franklin, open to the public – and through charming historic small towns. The pace of life is quite leisurely here, so make this a relaxed drive. Take a look at the monument to the USS *Diana*, a Confederate gunboat captured by the Union during the American Civil War (1861–65), and the ancient Evangeline Oak in St Martinville. And maybe stop for a lunch of fried shrimp or a po'boy in New Iberia, at Victor's or at Bon Creole. **DK**

Mississippi Blues Highway
Tennessee/Mississippi, USA

Start Memphis, Tennessee
End Vicksburg, Mississippi
Distance 393km (244 miles)
Type Culture
Map goo.gl/AzQTFj

Today, blues has been commercialized and its origins as the music of oppressed black people has been at least partly airbrushed out of history. Not entirely, though: US Route 61, better known as 'The Blues Highway', helps to keep the story straight. Once part of the seasonal route migrant workers undertook from the plantations in the South to the factories of the North, this road hugs backroads close to the Mississippi River, passing cotton fields where blues singers once toiled and near which plantation owners built imposing mansions in the period before the American Civil War (1861–65).

Heading southwest out of Memphis, head into the Mississippi Delta, the swampy, sweltering landscape of Mark Twain. You pass through arcades of live oaks, draped with Spanish moss. Here you will still see some of the juke joints that gave the delta blues its voice. At the northern extent of the trip are two of the blues' most sacred sites – the music clubs of Nelson Street in Greenville, and the Clarksdale's Delta Blues Museum near the famous crossroads where Robert Johnson reputedly sold his soul to the Devil.

Although the Mississippi Blues Highway ends in the city of Vicksburg, your musical road trip doesn't have to end there; US 61 carries on into Louisiana, through Baton Rouge and on to the home of jazz in the steamy clubs of New Orleans. **DK**

Natchez Trace Parkway
Mississippi to Tennessee, USA

Start Natchez, Mississippi
End Nashville, Tennessee
Distance 715km (444 miles)
Type Culture
Info goo.gl/kHwvEp

This route is one of the specially constructed National Scenic Drives managed by the US National Park Service. It has a limited number of entry and exit points along its route, and there is a maximum speed limit of 80 kph (50 mph) throughout. The idea is to take it slow and easy, stopping at as many of the 90 or so waymarked points of interest along the way as may take your fancy. There are designated rest stops and picnic sites, and the traveller is transported from the hurly-burly of normal life into something quite other – natural, and incalculably more peaceful.

The scenery is great: woodlands, waterfalls, river crossings and rolling grassland. The parkway route follows as closely as it can what remains of a forest walking trail used by ancient woodland tribes and then by Native Americans as a long-distance trading route between the Mississippi and central Tennessee. Parts of the original trail can be seen at Milemarker (MM) 41.5. There are spectacular archaeological sites, dating from the early part of the first millennium CE: Emerald Mound (MM 10.3); Bynum Mound and Village (MM 232.4); and Pharr Mounds (MM 286). Take a look, too, at Mt Locust (MM 15.5), the only surviving 18th-century inn on the old trail; the impressive cypress swamps at MM 122; and Birdsong Hollow (MM 438.2), one of the most popular points to rest up and unwind. **DK**

❶ Natchez Trace Parkway Bridge over Highway 96 in Franklin, Tennessee.

Door County Coastal Byway
Wisconsin, USA

Start Sturgeon Bay
End Sturgeon Bay
Distance 129km (80.3 miles)
Type Scenic
Info goo.gl/zZUIaa

Wisconsin's Door Peninsula juts out northwards to separate Lake Michigan from Green Bay and provide sweeping views over the state's agricultural hinterland. It also offers less typical coastal vistas and winding stretches of road that push through dense yet attractive forests.

Door County Coastal Byway starts about halfway along the peninsula, just north of Sturgeon Bay, where the strip of land begins to narrow like the tip of a finger. From there, visitors can travel clockwise or anticlockwise, as both roads meet up again at Sister Bay before a drive north to the very tip of the peninsula via the smooth, wide tarmac of Highway 57. Either way, the route travels through flat Midwestern farmland and past plenty of fields of sweet corn, for which the region is known. Both directions lead to appealing small towns, and eventually to coastal views, with those across Lake Michigan especially impressive.

The popular tourist village of Sister Bay makes a good stop for a break, to see the boats bobbing in the harbour on the historic waterfront. Beyond Sister Bay, it is Green Bay that comes into view, before the two bodies of water meet near the pretty little towns of Gills Rock and Northport at the top of the Door Peninsula. From there it is a scenic drive south along Highway 42 back to the starting point near Sturgeon Bay. **MG**

❶ The road winds like a snake through a mixture of aspen, oak and pine trees.

Northwoods
Wisconsin, USA

Start Marinette
End Park Falls
Distance 312km (194 miles)
Type Scenic
Map goo.gl/ktz21u

There are some places that no one ever goes to because they are unpleasant or dangerous. There are others that are lovely but get missed out on because there's too much going on elsewhere. The Northwoods region is firmly in the latter category: few visitors to Chicago break sufficiently far out of the city's gravitational pull to make it all this way, but those who do so will be richly rewarded.

This itinerary is just one of many that are possible across the area. It starts on the shores of Green Bay, an arm of Lake Michigan: Marinette styles itself 'The Waterfall Capital of Wisconsin'.

Just over 160km (100 miles) inland, at the confluence of the Prairie and Wisconsin Rivers, lies the city of Merrill, near the centre of which is a huge park, formerly a Chippewa (Ojibwe) encampment, with modern facilities for biking, boating, camping, fishing, hiking and swimming.

The evocatively named city of Tomahawk lies on a bend in the Wisconsin River. This is the southern end of the 22-km- (14-mile) long Hiawatha Trail walkway along the abandoned track bed of the Milwaukee Road railroad.

Park Falls is a small town straddling the North Fork of the Flambeau River. Many tourists use it as a base for canoeing, fishing and white-water rafting before either going back the way they came or carrying on north to Duluth, Minnesota, on Lake Superior. JP

❶ There is more to Marinette than waterfalls – this is the town's tribute to its logging industry.

Great River Road
Illinois, USA

Start East Dubuque
End Cairo
Distance 885km (550 miles)
Type Culture
Map goo.gl/jVCzXk

Meander down the western border of Illinois, along the banks of the Mississippi River, for a snapshot of America's history in one drive. It's well marked: just follow the signs shaped like a ship's wheel with a river steamboat in the centre.

This is the Illinois portion of the Great River Road, which accompanies the Mississippi for more than 3,200km (2,000 miles) through ten states all the way to the Gulf of Mexico.

Start in the northwest corner of Illinois and head south, with the river on your right. This is a different type of Illinois from the familiar image of Chicago's skyscrapers along Lake Michigan. You'll drive through what was once the leafy heartland of Native Americans, French colonialists and escaping slaves. Today it's rolling farmland dotted with red-painted barns and homesteads.

Through these fertile floodplains and sleepy farming communities, the route's highlights include a complex of prehistoric Native American burial mounds at Cahokia (a UNESCO World Heritage Site) and a string of historic towns that date back to the early European settlers. You find spots to learn about the American Civil War, too. And as if to emphasize how this route encapsulates much of the story of the United States, one of the wildlife highlights could be a sighting of the national bird, the bald eagle, in the bluffs along the river. **SH**

The Blues Brothers Chicago Road Trip Illinois, USA

Start Joliet
End Downtown Chicago
Distance 209km (130 miles)
Type Culture
Map goo.gl/2L3I8K

This route follows the course of the 'Mission from God' undertaken by the Blues Brothers – Jake and Elwood (John Belushi and Dan Aykroyd) – in the classic 1980 road movie. It begins at the gates of Joliet Correctional Center, from which Jake is released into the dubious care of his brother, and ends in Daley Plaza in downtown Chicago, where the duo remarkably manage to fend off angry neo-Nazis, pretty much the entire Chicago Police Department and the National Guard.

From Joliet prison (tours available), the itinerary heads first to Lake Michigan at Calumet, where the Bluesmobile jumped the 95th Street Bridge. From there it continues to the Pilgrim Baptist Church (gospel choir scene), South Shore Cultural Center (Palace Hotel Ballroom) and through Jackson Park (where the Nazis rally). On to Shelly's Loan & Jewelry (Ray's Music Store), Maxwell Street Market (at 807, the site of the former Lyon's Deli, where Aretha Franklin sang 'Think'), and Wrigley Field, where the Nazis are sent. Sadly, Chez Paul, the expensive restaurant at 660 North Rush Street where Jake disgraces himself, has long since closed its doors. The route continues to the disappointingly loungeless Quality Inn at O'Hare (Murph and the Magic Tones) and the West Wind Motel, where Twiggy is left waiting. Finally, the home run, the climactic chase along Lower Wacker Drive, to the end of the road at City Hall. **DK**

Stagecoach Trail
Illinois, USA

Start Lena
End Galena
Distance 61km (38 miles)
Type Culture
Map goo.gl/NHZf5h

Hitch up your wagon and head out on this picturesque short drive across the American Midwest. It follows the wheel tracks of an old stagecoach route that twists and turns through the rolling hills of northwest Illinois.

The gentle gradients and sweeping bends are probably much better for automobiles and bikes than for stagecoaches, although many of the wide-open landscapes have changed little, if at all, in the intervening century and a half.

You'll pass old staging posts; now saloons, stores or taverns. You won't be changing your horses, of course, but you can certainly feed the driver and passengers. Some of the local businesses have embraced the historic atmosphere and now offer tourists short rides in their own stagecoaches during the summer.

Ancient towns along the route appear as if in a time warp, with main streets of wooden facades and fabric awnings. Near the town of Scales Mound you can climb the highest hill in Illinois. It won't take long: Charles Mound is only 376m (1,235ft) high.

Visiting Galena at the end of the journey is like stepping inside a living museum. Around 85 per cent of the buildings are on the National Register of Historic Places, including the museum home of President Ulysses S. Grant and a main street full of genteel antique shops. **SH**

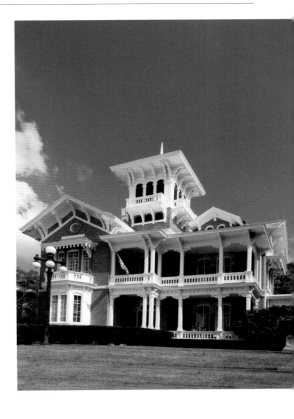

❶ Now a museum, the Belvedere Mansion is one of the finest old buildings in Galena.

Route 66 – East
Illinois to Oklahoma, USA

Start Chicago, Illinois
End Tulsa, Oklahoma
Distance 1,152km (716 miles)
Type Culture
Maps goo.gl/NhY54k and goo.gl/ogmLyL

Celebrated in song, literature and countless road movies, Route 66 is the most mythologized road in the whole of North America. Stretching from the industrial northeast in Chicago and ending out west in the land of opportunity and sunshine in Los Angeles, California, the route covers a total of 3,600km (2,200 miles).

Part of the great inter-war building program, the route was established in 1926, and in 1938, it was fully paved. For the next 25 years, east to west, it became a major migration path for people seeking prosperity and a better quality of life. Traffic brought commerce, and the road developed its own ecosystem of motels, stores, even music spots. Largely bypassed after the completion of the interstate highways in the late 1950s and 1960s, Route 66 was officially declassified in 1985, by which time most of the route markers had been removed.

Today, after a hard-fought heritage campaign, it is again possible to travel 'The Mother Road'. This leg starts at the 'Begin Route 66' marker on East Adams Street in downtown Chicago, and heads out west through Joliet and on through Missouri and (briefly) Kansas to Tulsa, Oklahoma.

Highlights include the Dixie Truck Stop in McLean (a culinary institution for more than 75 years) St Louis, Devils Elbow, Rolla, Springfield, Carthage, Riverton and Foyil. **DK**

🛈 Now a walkway, the Chain of Rocks Bridge carried the original Route 66 over the Mississippi near St Louis.

Shores of Lake Michigan
Michigan, USA

Start New Buffalo
End Mackinaw City
Distance 678km (421 miles)
Type Scenic
Map goo.gl/Ydft4t

Far from the urban sprawl and post-industrial wastes of Detroit, travelling up the east coast of Lake Michigan is like taking a coastal drive in a quiet rural backwater. The lake stretches away to the left like a sea, while waves batter sandy beaches and rocky headlands next to the road. In fact, this route can be bracing and beautiful in equal measure. In winter, for example, the weather can be very challenging, and a windy day in Saugatuck Dunes State Park can leave you feeling sandblasted. However, cruise the leafy lanes inland, and there are relaxing treats to be found, such as the chic boutiques and restaurants of the quaint inland town of Saugatuck. North of Petoskey, the lakeside road enters what locals call the 'Tunnel of Trees', winding prettily through thick, overhanging woods to Harbor Springs. At Sleeping Bear Dunes National Lakeshore, visitors can work out by climbing mountainous sand slopes reaching up to 137m (450ft) high. Farther north, the drive enters the renowned Mackinac Island State Park, which spreads onto a pretty wooded island.

This is a road trip full of small harbours; extensive woodlands; and a maze of inlets, islands and rivers. The liveliest spot along the route is Traverse City, where things really hot up for July's National Cherry Festival. Look out for cherry-festooned parades and pie-eating contests. **SH**

❶ The Holland Harbor Light, usually known as 'Big Red', is one of many attractions along this route.

Woodward Avenue Automotive Heritage Trail Michigan, USA

Start Detroit **End** Pontiac **Distance** 43.5km (27 miles)
Type Culture **Info** goo.gl/Rz9arU

Woodward Avenue links two of the United States' great motoring cities. It begins in Motor City itself, Detroit, and ends in Pontiac, renowned for being the home of General Motors and for providing the name of a popular US automotive brand. Pontiac produced cars for or 84 years, until 2010, when the very last one, a white G6 sedan, rolled off the line. Before leaving Detroit, take time to visit some of the city's museums to learn about its automotive fame; car enthusiasts should not miss Ford Piquette Avenue Plant. This is where the Ford Model T was built, and although it is no longer a working factory, it remains the oldest car factory building in the world that is still open to the public.

Heading out of Detroit, Woodward Avenue takes you northwest through some of the city's oldest suburbs along what was originally a Native American route, the Saginaw Trail. Watch out for the 50 historical markers that indicate places of interest. Woodward Avenue is also home to Highland Park Ford Plant, where in 1913 Henry Ford built the first motor car assembly line. The best time to see Woodward Avenue is on the third Saturday in August, when hundreds of hot rods drive up and down, attracting a million spectators to the Woodward Dream Cruise. MG

❶ Pontiac GTO convertible at Woodward Dream Cruise.

Wabash River Scenic Byway Indiana, USA

Start Prophetstown State Park   End Ross Camp   Distance 31km (19.3 miles)
Type Scenic   Map goo.gl/tGKhlu

This drive follows the course of the Wabash River, mostly on the appropriately named River Road. Short but totally delightful, it begins at the entrance to Prophetstown State Park, which tourists should explore in as much detail as they have time for. The eponymous prophet was a Native American spiritual leader, and the park contains a recreated Native American settlement and the Farm at Prophetstown, a living farm that is maintained as it would have been in the 1920s.

Initially, River Road goes past woodland and farmland, but eventually the Wabash River comes into view through the trees on the left. The Wabash is Indiana's state river and stretches for 810km

(503 miles), so this drive runs alongside only a tiny portion of it. After following the river for a while, visitors reach the city of West Lafayette, renowned for being the home of Purdue University, with its sister city of Lafayette on the far side of the river.

After a short urban stretch, River Road emerges again through woodland to rejoin the course of the river. It changes its name twice – first to Base Line Road and later to Division Road – and then a zigzag turn takes the route to its journey's end at Ross Camp, with a campground, a wedding chapel and hiking trails among its facilities. MG

❶ The railroad bridge at West Lafayette.

Hocking Hills Scenic Byway Ohio, USA

Start Rockbridge   **End** South Bloomingville   **Distance** 51.5km (32 miles)
Type Scenic   **Info** goo.gl/OHSCyz

The Midwestern state of Ohio is known for its flat plains of farmland, but this route explores a special area of hills, caves and rock formations southeast of Columbus: Hocking Hills State Park, covering 162 hectares (400 acres) of forest, lakes, waterfalls and gorges. The road trip, mainly along Highway 374, tours the best of the scenery and the most interesting sights. It is particularly popular with local bikers because the smooth, curving road is great to ride swiftly through the forests.

Visitors will find the best landscape views by stopping and taking foot trails from the roadside. Highlights include the marked path around Cantwell Cliffs, where there is a notorious cleft known as Fat Woman's Squeeze. Nearby is the Rock House, a natural cave with window-like openings that, over the centuries, have been home to Native American Indians, outlaws and bootleggers. Farther on, Conkle's Hollow is a 60-m- (200-ft) deep gorge through the trees, leading to a beautiful waterfall. And the region's most popular sight is Old Man's Cave, a natural rock formation amid more picturesque waterfalls. If you are feeling very brave, the region is renowned for zip-line tours of the canopy and there are several commercial operators along the route. **SH**

❶ Morning along Iselboro Road in Hocking Hills.

Amish Country's Scenic Byway Ohio, USA

Start Sugarcreek   End Sugarcreek   Distance 116km (72 miles)
Type Culture   Info goo.gl/BH5PLm

The Amish people are a traditional Christian fellowship of Swiss origins who live a simple, rural way of life that emphasizes sustainability, humility, self-composure, self-sufficiency and community spirit. This complex winding route loops through an area of Amish communities to create a fascinating road trip across the midwestern state of Ohio. It offers a way of exploring the culture and lifestyle of Amish Country amid miles of tranquil, rolling, green farmland. You will pass old wooden churches, whitewashed schoolhouses and neat farmsteads and be able to stop at hotels and inns where you can sample Amish home cooking. The Amish people largely avoid modern conveniences, so expect to see them travelling by horse and buggy as you motor past. Along the roadside you may find Amish farmers, complete with broad-brimmed hats and beards, selling fresh produce from wicker baskets. Best of all would be stumbling upon a barn-raising ceremony, in which a whole community comes together to build a wooden barn for one of its members.

As a road trip it's a relaxing experience: the roads are smooth, wide and well-maintained, and the traffic is light. But as a cultural experience, Amish Country's Scenic Byway is a real eye-opener. **SH**

❶ Amish countryside around Sugarcreek.

Rain Man Road Trip
Ohio to California, USA

Start Cincinnati, Ohio
End Los Angeles, California
Distance 4,796km (2,980 miles)
Type Culture
Map goo.gl/CpGqyo

In the Academy Award–winning movie *Rain Man* (1988), unlikely brothers drove 4,800km (nearly 3,000 miles) across the United States in their 1949 Buick Roadmaster convertible. It is a journey of discovery that is hard to replicate perfectly, partly because the autistic Raymond (Dustin Hoffman) refused to travel on interstates after witnessing a road accident. For this trip, driving on the backroads will depend on how much time you have. But the route does its best to revisit key locations and recapture the atmosphere of the movie.

Leaving Ohio, much of the early part of the trip is through the flat landscapes of the American Midwest and past plenty of cornfields. In the equally flat Oklahoma, an essential stop is El Reno, where the scene in which Charlie (Tom Cruise) realizes Raymond is the Rain Man from his childhood was filmed. The dilapidated petrol station where the pair later stop is in Cogar to the south.

The journey continues west, through the Texas Panhandle and New Mexico before the cacti-filled deserts and mesa mountains of Arizona's cowboy country, which characterized the movie, start to appear. From Kingman, there is a detour to Las Vegas, where brash neon lights clash with the desert all around, before heading southwest to Los Angeles. It is an unforgettable drive, inspired by an unforgettable film. MG

🛈 A convertible Buick – the perfect choice of car for this road trip – cruises through El Reno on Route 66.

Duncan Hines Scenic Byway Kentucky, USA

Start Bowling Green
End Bowling Green
Distance 138km (86 miles)
Type Culture
Info goo.gl/K7BXFZ

There is more to Kentucky than bourbon, chicken and horse racing, and this scenic byway will reveal some of the state's other hidden treasures. It begins and ends in one of Kentucky's loveliest small towns, Bowling Green, where the author and gourmet Duncan Hines was born. He is well known to US travellers thanks to the Duncan Hines food brand that lives on, but he was also an early pioneer of restaurant ratings, helping travellers to make an informed choice when dining out.

The drive starts at the 1940 house that was the author's home and office. However, motor enthusiasts will soon want to stop at the National Corvette Museum on the edge of town, and book a walking plant tour to see the Corvette assembly line in action, building the much-loved all-American sports car. The route then heads out through lush, green farmland to, by way of contrast, Mammoth Cave National Park. You have to take a ferry across Green River to get there, and once there, you will find the world's longest known cave system.

The road trip continues through more of the beautifully undulating Kentucky countryside, passing historic mansions and quaint little towns, before looping back to Bowling Green, where you might want to try the world-famous bourbon, perhaps on a tour of the award-winning Corsair Distillery. This is Kentucky, after all. MG

Kentucky Bourbon Trail Kentucky, USA

Start Louisville
End Lexington
Distance Variable
Type Culture
Info goo.gl/J8VdLc

The beginnings of bourbon in the state of Kentucky can be traced back almost to the state's settlement in the 1700s, when a number of farmers began to convert corn and various other grains into whiskey in order to make them more transportable over the state's rugged terrain and to prevent excess amounts of grain from rotting. In Bourbon County, they shipped their product down the Ohio and Mississippi Rivers to New Orleans; during the journey, it mellowed and turned amber inside oaken barrels. Declared a product of the United States by Congress in 1964, all-American bourbon is the nation's 'Official Native Spirit', and 95 per cent of it comes from Kentucky.

Driving Kentucky's Bourbon Trail, first launched in 1999, isn't anything like driving a wine trail. It is a journey into the heart and soul of the United States. Jim Beam, Four Roses and Wild Turkey are just some of the distilleries that can be reached on beautiful winding rural roads, and other distilleries not on the official tour are worth a visit, too, such as Barton 1792 Distillery in Bardstown.

Currently, nine distilleries between Louisville and Lexington participate in the Kentucky Bourbon Trail, but the myriad alternate routes you can take, visiting as many or as few as you'd like, are legion. Take it easy, get someone else to do the driving for a change and let the 'spirit' guide you. BDS

Lincoln Heritage Scenic Byway Kentucky, USA

Start Hodgenville
End Danville
Distance 120km (75 miles)
Type Culture
Map goo.gl/Ltm16b

There are four essential ingredients to Kentucky's Lincoln Heritage Scenic Byway: the Civil War, religion, bourbon and the nation's revered sixteenth president. Beginning in Hodgenville, at Abraham Lincoln Birthplace National Historic Park, the first stop is the town of Trappist, and the Abbey of Gethsemani, the United States' oldest operating monastery. Bardstown, the bourbon capital of the world and once voted the United States' most beautiful town, is next. Bardstown's Civil War Museum of the Western Theatre has one of the finest collections of Union and Confederate uniforms in the nation. Then the distilleries beckon. Heaven Hill, Maker's Mark and a tiny detour to Jim Beam American Stillhouse cannot and must not be missed. (The Kentucky Bourbon Trail, with its nine distilleries, is also a must-do.)

Continuing on the byway brings you to Springfield and Lincoln Homestead State Park, the original home of Lincoln's mother and a replica of his father's cabin and blacksmith shop. Next is Perryville. In 1973 the entire town of Perryville was placed on the National Register of Historic Places, and the Perryville Battlefield State Historic Site honours the largest Civil War battle fought on Kentucky soil. The journey on one of the United States' shortest byways ends in Danville, where the US Constitution was first drafted and signed. **BDS**

Music Lovers' Road Trip Tennessee to Louisiana, USA

Start Nashville, Tennessee
End New Orleans, Louisiana
Distance 978km (608 miles)
Type Culture
Map goo.gl/QJhTSj

For anyone with an interest in the extraordinary North American music legacy of the 20th century – blues, jazz, gospel, country, soul and rock and roll – this is the definitive road trip. Interstate 40, better known as the Music Highway, links Nashville with Memphis before heading south on Interstate 55 to the birthplace of jazz, New Orleans. You could hop on a plane to visit these places, but to really feel the music you have to be there, with your feet on the ground, absorbing the backroads and landscape that produced it.

Don't be afraid to slip off the fast interstates to explore the roads less travelled; only then can you begin to understand the forces that propelled these great popular musical movements – in the hard-scrabble Tennessee farms, the mill town industrial centres, and the cotton plantations. Whole books have been written about this route, but suffice to say, this is the South, with all the contradictions that it implies: beautiful and difficult, rich and poor, black and white. Wherever you stop, you will find opportunities to hear great live music. Be sure to visit: Nashville – Music Row and the Grand Ole Opry; Memphis – Graceland, Sun Studio, Stax Records and Beale Street; and New Orleans – the French Quarter, Bourbon Street and Louis Armstrong Park. But remember: wherever you travel, turn that radio up loud. **DK**

Cherohala Skyway
Tennessee/North Carolina, USA

Start Tellico Plains, Tennessee
End Robbinsville, North Carolina
Distance 82.1km (51 miles)
Type Scenic
Map goo.gl/H7KxhK

This National Scenic Byway goes through two national forests as it crosses from Tennessee into North Carolina. Its name is a manufactured word derived from the two forests: 'Chero' is from Cherokee National Forest, which is mostly in eastern Tennessee, and 'hala' from Nantahala, a river and a National Forest in North Carolina.

The route begins in Tellico Plains. It is advisable to pick up some information from Cherohala Skyway Visitor Center near the very start of the road, and to make sure that you have a full tank of petrol, since there is nowhere to buy fuel on the way. Immediately, the road plunges straight into the Cherokee National Forest and runs alongside the Tellico River, where fishermen can be seen trying to catch some of the trout for which the river is well known. The skyway then twists its way upwards as the trees get denser. As you cross the state line at Unicoi Crest, stop for a magnificent view of the Tellico River Valley. Once over the state line, the trees continue as before, the dense forest earning its Cherokee name 'Nantahala'. This word means 'the land of the noonday sun', since it is only when the sun is overhead that it penetrates the treetops. Don't worry, though – there are plenty of scenic views as the road wriggles its way down to Robbinsville, which will be familiar to viewers of the Discovery Channel's TV show *Moonshiners*. **MG**

❶ At its highest point (Haw Knob), Cherohala Skyway is more than 5,400 feet (1,646 m) above sea level.

Tail of the Dragon at Deals Gap
Tennessee to North Carolina, USA

Start Tabcat Bridge, Tennessee
End Fugitive Bridge, North Carolina
Distance 17.7km (11 miles)
Type Adventure
Map goo.gl/k8Xc6V

Championed by many as the greatest motorcycling road in North America, the Tail of the Dragon snakes around 318 corners in only 17.7km (11 miles) of smooth, two-lane tarmac. With no intersecting junctions, driveways, roadside distractions or heavy traffic, the road has a distinctive race-circuit feel about it, which is what attracts swarms of keen motorcyclists and sports-car drivers from across the United States every weekend.

Rising and falling over 366m (1,200ft), this wonderfully serpentine stretch of Highway 129 threads through the dense northern hardwood forests of the Great Smoky Mountains. The route concludes near Fugitive Bridge, so named for the Harrison Ford movie that had been filmed nearby. However, this hallowed road's starring role was in the gearheads' cult classic *Two-Lane Blacktop* (1971).

With blind crests, off-camber black spots, long drops beyond narrow verges and few safety barriers, it is a beast of a road that claims several victims every year. A poignant reminder of this fact are the multi-coloured shards of shattered motorbikes hung from the Tree of Shame near Deals Gap Motorcycle Resort, a macabre arboreal tribute to the sports bike riders who, since 1981, have been bitten by the Dragon. Treat this road trip with the utmost respect; you don't want to see pieces of your prized machine hanging from that tree. **DIS**

❶ Although most visitors come for the adrenaline rush, the Tail of the Dragon is also known as a scenic drive.

Alabama's Coastal Connection Scenic Byway
Alabama, USA

Start Grand Bay
End Mobile
Distance 209km (130 miles)
Type Scenic
Info goo.gl/bdpxSk

Alabama's Coastal Connection website proudly boasts: 'Beautiful beaches, authentic downtowns, wildlife preserves, historic sites and the freshest seafood you'll ever put in your mouth are all yours to enjoy on Alabama's Gulf Coast.'

After you head off from Grand Bay, near Grand Bay National Wildlife Refuge and its maritime forest, take the road southeast towards the bay, but stop off in Bayou La Batre before you reach the coast. Known as the seafood capital of Alabama, the town offers a selection of authentic and well-respected restaurants. Continue down to the 4.8-km (3-mile) bridge that crosses the water to Dauphin Island, and if time is on your side, take a break here to explore further. The entire island is a bird sanctuary, with walking trails and numerous lookouts from which to watch the birds that use this location as a migratory stopover. By the ferry port, on the eastern end of the island, sits Fort Gaines, a stronghold established in 1821 that played a vital role in the American Civil War (1861–65).

Head along the spit and past the 2,800-hectare (7,000-acre) Bon Secour National Wildlife Refuge, the Gulf State Park and Orange Beach before turning north towards Foley. Head west again to skirt Weeks Bay and pick up the road towards Fairhope. Hug the coast all the way north before turning west to the city of Mobile. TW

❶ Among the many habitats at Bon Secour National Wildlife Refuge are freshwater swamps.

Selma to Montgomery March Byway Alabama, USA

Start Selma   **End** Montgomery   **Distance** 84km (52.1 miles)
Type Culture   **Map** goo.gl/ZsOx5w

The Selma to Montgomery March Byway is more than a road trip. It marks a turning point in modern US history. In 1965 the Rev. Dr Martin Luther King Jr led a march from Selma to protest against the strict rules on voter registration that disenfranchised most African Americans.

On 7 March they attempted to cross the Edmund Pettus Bridge, which would take them towards Montgomery, the state capital. They were beaten back by Alabama State Police, on what became known as 'Bloody Sunday'.

But later that month another march was allowed over the bridge. This time the demonstrators made it to Montgomery, spending their nights en route sleeping in the fields of farmers who supported their cause. Eventually they reached the state capitol, but were not permitted to present a petition to the governor.

This drive starts at Brown Chapel African Methodist Episcopal (AME) Church in Selma, which was the marchers' HQ. It crosses the Edmund Pettus Bridge and goes past the same fields where the marchers slept. It ends at the capitol itself.

The road is just an ordinary stretch of US highway that will take you around an hour to cover. But this is an itinerary of real historical significance. JI

➊ The state capitol in Montgomery, Alabama.

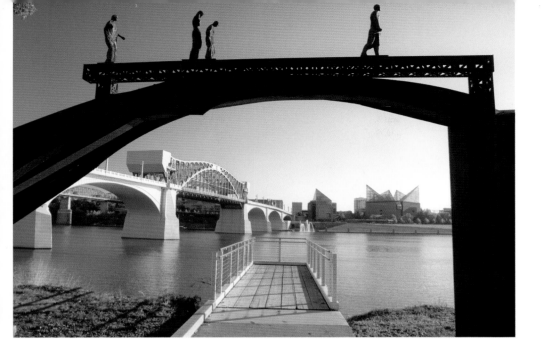

Trail of Tears Alabama to Oklahoma, USA

Start Bridgeport, Alabama   End Tahlequah, Oklahoma   Distance 1,030km (640 miles)
Type Culture   Info goo.gl/JxiQmf

There is no single Trail of Tears, because the phrase commemorates the many Native Americans from all over the southeastern United States who were forcibly removed from their land in the 1830s and made to walk hundred of miles to be resettled in what became Indian Territory in Oklahoma.

This particular route is chosen because it is the itinerary followed on the third Saturday of every September by the Trail of Tears Commemorative Motorcycle Ride. It starts at Bridgeport near Chattanooga, which was one of the main settlements for the Cherokee Nation, and then heads south, for much of its course along the banks of the Tennessee River.

The road crosses several wide offshoots of the river, but follows it all the way to Florence, where a short diversion leads to Tom's Wall. This is one man's commemoration of the walk his great-grandmother made, in both directions, since on arrival she turned around and walked back home again.

Through Tennessee and into Arkansas, the landscape remains heavily wooded, but flatter, and follows the course of the Arkansas River. It later turns north through thick forest, then west again into Oklahoma to the Native Americans' new enforced home MG

❶ Memorial on the riverbank at Chattanooga.

Driving the Adirondacks New York, USA

Start Lake Placid   End Lake Placid   Distance 195km (121 miles)
Type Scenic   Map goo.gl/sciEa6

Traversing the Adirondacks of upstate New York, this circular route merges a number of smaller scenic drives suggested by Lake Placid's Regional Office of Sustainable Tourism, through mountains, coastline and freshwater lakes.

From Lake Placid, host of the 1932 and 1980 Winter Olympics, your clockwise loop heads first to the picturesque shoreside village of Saranac Lake; voted Best Small Town in New York State, it was once home to author Robert Louis Stevenson.

On a winding Route 18A, cross the forested foothills of McKenzie Mountain to Santa's Workshop, in the hamlet of North Pole, from where an interesting scenic detour up the Whiteface Veterans Memorial Highway offers great views back over the Olympic Village. For a change of pace, there is also a scenic railway that leaves from near here.

A long leg east arrives at the magical Ausable Chasm, a sandstone gorge whose river empties into nearby Lake Champlain, before an hour-long scenic coastal drive via Essex and Westport. From there another 50-minute drive wings you west on the pretty and twisty Route 9-N via Elizabethtown to Lake Placid, through an area known as Pleasant Valley. The autumn, or 'leaf-peeper season' as some folks call it, is the best time to visit if you can. DIS

❶ The Ausable River gorge.

Catskill Mountains Scenic Route 30 New York, USA

Start Hancock End Grand Gorge Distance 114km (71 miles)
Type Scenic Map goo.gl/APOHXO

More the remnants of an eroded plateau than true mountains, the Catskills in the southeastern corner of New York State were nevertheless the first swathe of wilderness to capture the imagination of the early settlers. Today they are crisscrossed by numerous scenic drives, including routes along the Upper Delaware River, the Durham Valley and a network of backroads connecting mid-19th-century timber bridges. This is one such route, along the east branch of the Delaware River.

Hancock lies at the western edge of Catskill Park, a 283,000-hectare (700,000-acre) wilderness with bobcats, minks and a black bear population that still numbers in the hundreds. The road to Grand Gorge passes through the towns of Colchester, Middletown and Roxbury, but it's easy to take detours, to become contentedly lost in the region's meandering roads. Spend a day at the confluence of the east and west branches of the Delaware River; visit the summer home of essayist and naturalist John Burroughs in Roxbury; detour on NY23A at Palenville to access the trailhead to Kaaterskill Falls, at 79m (260ft) in height, the tallest two-tiered waterfall in New York. Other scenic itineraries are also possible through a sparsely populated area of one of the most populous US states. **BDS**

❶ The Catskills in the autumn.

Lake Placid Ironman Oval
New York, USA

Start Lake Placid
End Lake Placid
Distance 90km (56 miles)
Type Culture
Map goo.gl/un3bES

Lake Placid in the Adirondack Mountains of upstate New York was home to both the 1932 and 1980 Winter Olympics. Its athletic activities continue every summer with the infamous Ironman triathlon, the second oldest Ironman event in the United States (the oldest is the World Championship in Hawaii). On a single day each July, about 2,500 athletes swim two circuits of Mirror Lake , then cycle two loops of an 89-km- (56-mile) long course around the Sentinel Range Wilderness Area before running a marathon – the full 42.195km (26.219 miles) – through a village and around the lake.

Road trippers might find all this a bit too strenuous to undertake, but a leisurely cruise in an automobile or on a motorbike around most of the cycle loop gives a great insight into this gruelling event and fine views of the scenery surrounding this famous sporting venue.

The route starts at the James B. Sheffield Olympic Skating Rink in the centre of Lake Placid. From there you take Route 73 south out of town, past the Olympic Ski Jumping Complex and the Cascade Lakes, and then down the wonderfully steep Keene Hill. At Keene, turn left up Route 9N and head north to Jay, where the Ironmen turn left onto Route 86 to Wilmington and back to Lake Placid. Our loop is a little longer, more scenic and considerably less physically demanding. **SA**

New York Guided Night Tour New York, USA

Start Manhattan
End Manhattan
Distance 29km (18 miles)
Type Culture
Info goo.gl/ZunSep

New York is the city that never sleeps. Just as well, then, that it's also the city that's got more nighttime sightseeing tours than anywhere else. There are many tours and even more transport options – you can go by bus, car, taxi, minibus, stretch limo, even Humvee. Though perhaps not the most exotic choice, the best way to see the bright lights is by open-top bus. After all, the whole point is to be able to look up from the urban canyons of Manhattan to the illuminated vanishing points of the skyscrapers far above. Most of these tours offer a hop-on, hop-off ticket, and this is the best kind. It means you can break your journey to marvel at Times Square, the frenetic centre of Manhattan. Take time out to ride to the 100th-floor observation deck of New York's newest skyscraper, One World Trade Center, with spectacular views both uptown and across the bay to New Jersey.

Must-see spectacles from the bus include Broadway, the Empire State Building, the Chrysler Building, Radio City Music Hall, the Flatiron Building, Rockefeller Center and Trump Tower. Get a tour that crosses Brooklyn Bridge. As well as being an illuminated thing of beauty in its own right, from Brooklyn you'll get the best views back across the East River to the Manhattan skyline. **DK**

➲ Times Square, New York.

Great Lakes Seaway Trail New York/Pennsylvania, USA

Start Massena, New York **End** Erie, Pennsylvania **Distance** 834km (518 miles)
Type Culture **Info** goo.gl/VQq71j

Long before there was a designated scenic byway along the St Lawrence Seaway, those in the know were in motoring heaven exploring their own networks of scenic roads all around the region. How could they not? With the St Lawrence River's Thousand Islands area (1,864, actually) to the north shores of the St Lawrence Seaway, with its locks, canals and navigable, boat-filled channels (completed in 1959 to connect the Atlantic Ocean to the Great Lakes), and the thundering beauty of Niagara Falls at the southern tip of Niagara Gorge, it should come as no surprise. This is one scenic drive that was popular long before it became officially recognized.

The Great Lakes Seaway Trail, established in 1978, has a stop at the Seaway International Bridge connecting the United States to Canada across the St Lawrence River, and from there runs south along the shoreline of Lake Ontario. The route was not extended to Niagara Falls and Lake Erie until 1984, but now runs all the way to the Ohio state line in Erie County, Pennsylvania.

The drive provides great views over Lakes Erie and Ontario, as well as 29 lighthouses and many sites from the War of 1812. The road is gentle; the traffic, light; and the scenery, gorgeous. **BDS**

❶ The US side of Niagara Falls.

Road Trip – **The Movie** New York to Texas, USA

Start Ithaca, New York   End Austin, Texas   Distance 2,868km (1,782 miles)
Type Culture   Map goo.gl/XieyWl

It was perhaps inevitable that one day there would be a road movie called *Road Trip*, and it arrived with this 2000 US comedy. Four guys in college in Ithaca, New York, have to race to Austin, Texas, to retrieve a sex tape mistakenly sent by one of them, Rubin, to the girlfriend of Josh, another of the four. Naturally, they have to get there before the girl sees the tape.

The usual cinematographic sleight of hand means that you couldn't replicate the trip shown in the movie: some scenes were filmed in Georgia, which is not the way you would go if time is of the essence, while another was shot in California, which is definitely out of the way.

The theoretical route heads south from Ithaca, through the rolling farmlands of Pennsylvania, past forests and state parks. Passing through Maryland, the itinerary then heads west into Tennessee, picking up Interstate 40, as the friends visit Knoxville, downtown Nashville (where the guys are filmed singing 'I Wanna Rock') and Memphis.

The next leg goes through the woods and farmland of Arkansas, before the route swings south, traversing the seemingly endless outskirts of Dallas and on to the music city of Austin, which is definitely a good place to end a road trip. **MG**

❶ The four college friends hit a problem.

Cannonball Run
New York to California, USA

Start New York, New York
End Los Angeles, California
Distance 4,506km (2,800 miles)
Type Culture
Info goo.gl/jhWynV

Many folks of a certain age will know something of the Cannonball Run from the classic 1981 road trip comedy. The star-packed cast included Burt Reynolds, Jackie Chan, Roger Moore and the Ferrari-driving Catholic priests played by Sammy Davis Jr and Dean Martin, who set out on a cross-country race from Connecticut to California. The script was loosely based on the original Cannonball, which first ran in 1971, conceived by two motoring journalists as a way of celebrating the US highway system that had made such epic road trips possible, and as a protest against tightening traffic laws which the pair believed were taking the fun out of motoring. The name was inspired by the automotive adventurer, Erwin 'Cannonball' Baker who, in 1914, first made this road trip.

The only rules of the Cannonball were to leave the Red Ball Garage in New York City (subsequently, Darien, Connecticut, as per the movie) in the early hours of the morning and drive to the Portofino Inn in Redondo Beach, California, as quickly as possible.

The final run took place in April 1979, when Dave Heinz and Dave Yarborough drove a Jaguar XJS in a record time of 32 hours 51 minutes at an average speed of 140 kph (87 mph). The Cannonball has continued, off and on, in various guises over the years, but not under the auspices of the originators of the run. **MG**

❶ The urban freeways of Los Angeles are the final stage of the Cannonball Run.

On the Road – Jack Kerouac
New York to California, USA

Start New York, New York
End San Francisco, California
Distance 4,989km (3,100 miles)
Type Culture
Info goo.gl/0uxQBi

Published in 1957, *On the Road* is a seminal road-trip tome hailed as the defining work of the Beat Generation. It recounts author Jack Kerouac's adventures against a backdrop of a melancholy postwar America, jazz music and poetry. Written in a three-week Benzedrine-fuelled surge of creativity on a single scroll of paper 36m (120ft) long, *On the Road* loosely chronicles Kerouac's time travelling across the United States between 1947 and 1950 with his friend Neal Cassady (thinly disguised as the characters Sal Paradise and Dean Moriarty) in a quest for self-enlightenment.

In the first, and best-known, journey, Sal sets out from New York for California with just $50 in his pocket and the 'stupid hearthside idea that it would be wonderful to follow one great red line across America'.

There are eventful stopovers in Chicago, Des Moines, Cheyenne and Denver. To aid travellers who wish to follow in the two men's tyre tracks, Kerouac aficionados have picked the text apart to best guess that 1947 route, and created an excellent interactive map linking extracts from *On the Road* to modern-day locations. In San Francisco, you can learn more about the Beats on the guided Kerouac tour.

Kerouac's dying wish to have *On the Road* made into a movie came true in 2012, in a production by Francis Ford Coppola. **DIS**

❶ Giants of the Beat Generation, Neal Cassady (left) with Jack Kerouac in 1952.

Travels with Charley
New York and more, USA

Start Sag Harbor, New York
End Sag Harbor, New York
Distance 15,710km (9,762 miles)
Type Culture
Map goo.gl/VOudmW

It's impossible to re-create the exact journey John Steinbeck made 'in search of America', described in his book *Travels with Charley* (1962). It's known, for instance, that some of the book is fiction rather than fact and that the author interrupted the journey on a few occasions to meet up with his wife, staying in well-appointed hotels not mentioned in the book. Nevertheless, it would be a fascinating trip to make in the spirit of the book, broadly following the same route around the perimeter of the United States.

On 23 September 1960, Steinbeck took his motor home and standard poodle, Charley, leaving his home in the fishing village of Sag Harbor on Long Island, New York. The route started with several ferries north to Connecticut, to avoid the New York traffic, and from there he visited his son at school in Deerfield, Massachusetts.

The route heads north into New Hampshire, with beautiful autumn colours. His onward journey went through the flat Midwest, into Montana, where an impulse took him to Yellowstone National Park. Travelling south along the Pacific Coast Highway gave him a chance to see the giant redwoods before visiting Monterey County, where he grew up.

Seeming to tire of his trip, Steinbeck raced through the southwest and the south, then north back to his home in Sag Harbor. For anyone with time, this is one of the great American road trips. **MG**

Lake Champlain Island Hop
New York/Vermont, USA

Start Champlain, New York
End Colchester, Vermont
Distance 77km (48 miles)
Type Scenic
Map goo.gl/jMKREO

This road trip packs a lot of terrific landscapes, or more accurately waterscapes, into its short run as it island hops across Lake Champlain, North America's sixth-largest freshwater lake. En route it passes over spectacular bridges and alongside picturesque beaches. If visitors are really lucky, they may even glimpse 'Champ', the lake's elusive cousin of 'Nessie', Scotland's Loch Ness monster.

Leaving eastwards from Champlain in upstate New York quickly brings up the first of many bridges, as the road crosses the lake for the first time into Vermont. Here, at Alburg Dunes State Park, there are unspoiled beaches and wild dunes, which are good for bird- and even moose-watching. After crossing onto North Hero Island, continue heading south, where the route traverses the lake again via a drawbridge to Grand Isle, giving fine views across the water as far as the Adirondack Mountains. Here, visitors will see signs to Hyde Log Cabin, which was built by pioneers in 1783 and is thought to be the oldest such structure in the United States. Grand Isle State Park is a fine spot to take a break and to absorb the excellent views. Then, after the last bridge crossing, it is back to the mainland. One final stop before the journey's end at Colchester is Sand Bar State Park. It is great for shallow-water swimming from clean sandy beaches – the perfect end to an outstanding road trip. **DK**

Vermont's Main Street
Vermont, USA

Start Brattleboro
End Newport
Distance 354km (220 miles)
Type Scenic
Map goo.gl/QUPuoz

It is difficult to imagine a more delightfully scenic road trip than this one. New England is well known for its picture-book villages nestling in gently rolling, densely wooded hills. This route along what is known as Vermont's Main Street navigates through the greatest hits of this scenery, beginning at the state's fourth-largest town, Brattleboro, and continuing north through the Green Mountains, right to the Canadian border.

On leaving Brattleboro, head west to Highway 100, then travel north through the gentle, hilly terrain. A short distance later a five-minute detour will lead to the enchanting wooden Scott Covered Bridge, which provides a superb photo opportunity. Take a break from all this captivating countryside in Weston, a quaint town with interesting eateries, galleries and antique shops. Onwards towards Ludlow and Killington, and the road heads into the skiing areas, where it becomes mountainous and richly forested. After Rochester the woodland breaks briefly and the landscape turns to pastureland and soft grassy slopes. Around Warren, in the Mad River Valley, there are eight more historic covered bridges to view. And it is impossible to pass Waterbury without going on a tour of Ben & Jerry's ice-cream factory. All along the route there are impossibly cute villages, of which Stowe, at the northern end, is an exquisite example. DK

❶ In autumn, the trees lining the route display in almost-luminous red, orange and gold.

Quintessential New England
New Hampshire, USA

Start Sanbornville
End Conway
Distance 58km (36 miles)
Type Scenic
Info goo.gl/BwhM6h

Could these be the world's loveliest hills, lakes and trees? This stretch of New Hampshire is so wonderful, it feels as though it is not real. However, the gently winding Highway 153 is genuine enough. The route is a simple way of taking a tour through the classic New England landscape of pretty rolling hills; clear blue lakes; and unspoiled deciduous woodland dotted with white clapboard homesteads and picket fences. You can stop at a farm shop to buy homemade honey and to admire the collection of old farm implements, or pull in at a leafy village café for the local speciality – some delicious, creamy, clam chowder.

It is best to keep the revs low and enjoy a leisurely saunter along smooth and spacious highways. Experience trundling through old forests and spotting glittering ponds where herons patiently wait for fish. Arrive in a small country town where an 18th-century wooden candy store is the busiest retail outlet on Main Street. And then take a short detour to Eaton to see its little white church nestling in among the trees. It is proud to be 'New England's most photographed church'. The whole route looks like a Christmas card in winter snow, and in spring you will feel inspired by the flowers and buzzing wildlife. Be warned: in autumn, the stupendous leaf colours may leave you with a permanent blissful gaze. **SH**

Mt Washington Auto Road
New Hampshire, USA

Start Jackson
End Jackson
Distance 12.2km (7.6 miles)
Type Adventure
Map goo.gl/TgHJ1W

Mt Washington is the United States' highest peak east of the Mississippi. At 1,917m (6,288ft) its particularly prominent summit experiences notorious climatic extremes. For example, it holds the record for northern hemisphere wind speeds: 372 kph (231 mph). The peak is battered by hurricane force winds for 110 days a year, and temperatures as low as -51°C (-59°F) have been recorded there.

The toll road climbs from State Highway 16 to the summit, ascending 1,408m (4,618ft) at a piston-straining average gradient of 11.6 per cent. Yet this steep, unguarded mountain climb was originally a genteel 19th-century coach road to transport curious tourists to the top. Other period relics include a cog railway.

This inhospitable spot is still a tourist attraction. Some walk and a few visitors try to cycle. Many cannot face the drive and take a guided coach tour instead. Some tours continue even when the road is impassable in winter, using snowcat buses. In the summer, however, it is a relatively easy drive to the top. Amazingly, visitors can occasionally experience lovely weather and beautiful clear views. The record temperature at the summit is a balmy 22°C (72°F). **SH**

➲ A serious adventure best tackled in summer.

Old King's Highway Massachusetts, USA

Start Bourne   End Provincetown   Distance 105km (65 miles)
Type Scenic   Info goo.gl/hnEAMT

Cape Cod has long been the go-to New England seaside retreat for upmarket New Yorkers who are drawn to its remoteness, windswept beaches and wild sandy dunes. It is a narrow 97-km- (60-mile) long raised-arm spit of land, jutting out into the North Atlantic, strange of geography and packed with history. The most direct route along its length is Highway 6, but this whizzes past everything you might want to see. So take the Old King's Highway instead and meander through the historic towns of Sandwich, Barnstable, Yarmouth, Dennis and Truro before reaching the far pointy end at Provincetown. There are old shingle-clad wooden houses galore, historic lighthouses and unspoiled coves and beaches all along the coast. Antique stores and art galleries, too, and fine places to stop for refreshments; seafood is always on the menu.

The section through Barnstable is on the National Register of Historic Places. To the south is Hyannis, renowned for its association with the Kennedy presidential family and now the site of the John F. Kennedy Hyannis Museum. In the town of Dennis, Scargo Tower on Scargo Hill gives panoramic views from the highest point on the peninsula. In Provincetown, don't miss the monument to the *Mayflower* Pilgrims who, in 1620, landed there. **DK**

❶ The Pilgrim Monument at Provincetown.

Martha's Vineyard *Jaws* Movie Tour Massachusetts, USA

Start Edgartown   **End** Chilmark   **Distance** 51km (31.7 miles)
Type Culture   **Map** goo.gl/E4c6vG

It's always a delight to drive around Martha's Vineyard, whether you have a purpose in mind or not – except, of course, when everyone else has the same idea. So try to plan this trip outside of high season, before the tourists swarm. This itinerary takes in several locations from Steven Spielberg's Academy Award–winning movie *Jaws* (1975), which was shot here in the previous summer.

South Beach State Park features in the movie's opening scene, in which a young woman becomes the shark's first victim. It's a lovely, long stretch of beach and perfectly safe for swimming … honestly. From there it's a short drive north past open fields and under vast empty skies to Edgartown, one of the two original towns on Martha's Vineyard, dating back to 1642 and home to the Chappy Ferry.

On the coastal road to Oak Bluffs you drive along a narrow causeway where the Joseph Sylvia State Beach was the scene of another attack in the film. The American Legion Memorial Bridge is now known as the Jaws Bridge because of its prominence in the movie. From Oak Bluffs you can meander down the coast or inland, since any number of roads will take you to the western tip of Martha's Vineyard and the historic Gay Head Lighthouse, which also features in the screen thriller. **MG**

❶ Menemsha Harbor on Martha's Vineyard.

Mohawk Native American Trail
Massachusetts, USA

Start Athol
End Williamstown
Distance 109km (67.7 miles)
Type Culture
Map goo.gl/tMFhmg

For thousands of years this was a Native American Indian trail through the woods, hills and rivers of Massachusetts. It twisted across the Berkshire Ranges between the Connecticut and Hudson River Valleys.

A century ago the route was deemed so useful that it was paved, and it then became one of the United States' first scenic driving routes. Today it's part of State Highways 2 and 2A and considered one of the most scenic routes in New England.

You'll discover that this is still a road dedicated to Native American heritage. The signage features native symbols, and one of the route's highlights is the impressive bronze Hail to the Sunrise Statue. This depicts a Mohawk Indian raising his arms to the east in a traditional ceremony in honour of the Great Spirit. Native peoples throughout North America contributed to this monument in Mohawk Park, alongside the trail.

Farther into the hills, the road curves through Mohawk Trail State Forest, where there are many original Indian side trails for walkers to explore. Among the network of rivers are plenty of spots for swimming or trout fishing. Keep your eyes peeled: the state forest is renowned for its black bears.

Of course, the Mohawk Trail is at its best in the autumn, when it becomes a great place for viewing the famous New England leaf colours. **SH**

❶ The Hail to the Sunrise Statue of a Mohawk Indian in Charlemont. It was sculpted in 1932 by Joseph Pollia.

Revolutionary Road Tour
Massachusetts, USA

Start Pittsfield
End Boston
Distance 270km (168 miles)
Type Culture
Map goo.gl/euDGSP

If you're a student of America's Revolutionary War, there are several historic drives you can take that showcase the Patriots' struggle against the British. There's Route 5 through New York, which includes Fort Ontario at Oswego where, on 25 July 1777, the British began their invasion. There's Route 9 through New York, which includes the state capital of Albany, the target of so many British assaults throughout that year. But if you really want to follow in the footsteps of America's greatest early heroes, men like Henry Knox and Paul Revere, you can't ignore Massachusetts's Route 20.

There are several detours on this route, but beginning at Pittsfield, where Knox tried to organize transportation for British cannons captured at Fort Ticonderoga, you bisect the beautiful Berkshire Mountains before arriving at Sudbury's Wayside Inn, site of patriot gatherings and later immortalized in Henry Wadsworth Longfellow's *Tales of a Wayside Inn* (1863). The war's first military engagements at Lexington and Concord follow as you drive the aptly named 'Battle Road', and then comes Bunker Hill, a tactical British victory during the Siege of Boston. Now walk the Freedom Trail through Charlestown and the North End, visit Paul Revere's House, Faneuil Hall, Old South Meeting House and the Granary Burying Ground, and then reflect on your history-filled day in the midst of Boston Common. **BDS**

❶ The home of American Revolutionary Captain William Smith, between Lexington and Concord.

Oregon National Historic Trail Massachusetts to Oregon, USA

Start Plymouth, Massachusetts **End** Oregon City, Oregon **Distance** 5,310km (3,300 miles)
Type Culture **Info** goo.gl/7atwnS

In the first decades of America's westward expansion, no trail symbolized the aspirations of the nation more than the Oregon Trail. From the Missouri River, west to Oregon, 400,000 pioneers, their families, ranchers, miners and dreamers followed the trail and its numerous shortcuts and offshoots in search of new lives. Their journeys can now be retraced by car along an array of connecting highways from Plymouth, Massachusetts.

This road trip will take you through Boston, Concord, New York, along the Mohawk Trail (the nation's first Scenic Byway), and up into New York's Adirondack wilderness. Picking up US 20, you pass through Buffalo and enter Ohio along the southern shores of Lake Erie. Next you go through Indiana, and Illinois, leading up to Chicago. Still on US 20, you cross the Mississippi River into Iowa, then Nebraska, South Dakota and central Wyoming. Make a detour on US 287 to the Grand Teton Mountains before hitting Yellowstone Park. Idaho is next, then the Snake River, and at last you're in Oregon.

The journey is long and demanding, even if you stop, which you will because between Missouri and Oregon alone there are more than 125 designated historic sites. So you might want to plan this one for your gap year. **BDS**

❶ **Bison grazing below the Grand Teton Mountains.**

Acadia All-American Road Maine, USA

Start Ellsworth   End Bar Harbor   Distance 33km (20.5 miles)
Type Scenic   Map goo.gl/lAOVkO

A looping drive around Maine's largest island, Mt Desert Island, is the highlight of this tour through part of the Acadia National Park. It begins in the popular tourist town of Ellsworth, noted for its many historical buildings and an unusual attraction: the Telephone Museum.

From here, the route heads south through Maine's rural wooded landscape to Trenton, beyond which the road crosses the Mt Desert Narrows to the hillier landscape of Mt Desert Island. At 280 sq klm (108 square miles), it is the sixth-largest island in the contiguous United States. The road then sweeps east through woodland until it emerges at the coast just north of the Acadia National Park

Visitor Center at Hulls. Make a stop here for background information and maps.

A right turn leads into the park and on to Park Loop Road. This is a delightful drive, partly through woodland, with many scenic views, hiking trails and sea views. A twisting section along the south and then the east coasts is exhilarating, before it delivers you into one of the island's four towns, Bar Harbor, where hotels and restaurants serving freshly caught lobster await. Here, you can decide whether to return and take the Mt Desert Island drive or save it for another day. **MG**

❶ The rugged coastline on Schoodic Peninsula.

Mt Desert Island Maine, USA

Start Trenton   End Trenton   Distance 59.7km (37.1 miles)
Type Scenic   Map goo.gl/rT827I

Mt Desert Island has so much to offer that there are two options for scenic drives included in this book; the other is the Acadia All-American Road. They are best tackled on different days, since you are sure to want to stop regularly and take time to enjoy the wonderful coastal scenery, beaches and roadside craft shops.

This journey starts in the small town of Trenton, from where you cross over to Mt Desert Island. The unusual name is an Anglicized version of the one originally given by a French explorer: Île des Monts Déserts. It means 'island of the bare mountains', as the mountain peaks are some of the few places not covered by trees. The route loops around the western half of the island, going straight ahead on a wooded country road through small rural communities. After several miles the first glimpse of water comes into view. When the road loops around the southern end of this part of the island, you can take a small detour to see Bass Harbor Head Lighthouse, which is now a private residence. The road turns back north to drive around Bass Harbor, then past Seal Cove Pond and through thick woodland again – with occasional ocean glimpses – before crossing back to Trenton and the mainland. MG

❶ Park Loop Road winds through Acadia National Park.

Atlantic Highway 1 Maine, USA

Start Brunswick   End Calais   Distance 385km (239 miles)
Type Scenic   Map goo.gl/WFPv9T

California is famous for its Pacific Coast Highway, but the east coast of the United States has the no less impressive Atlantic Highway 1, the pass through the state of Maine, which has led to it being dubbed Maine's Big Sur. The road does not need comparing to anything else, though, as this rugged coast has a beauty uniquely its own.

The name of the Atlantic Highway goes back to its creation in 1911, when it ran all the way from the Canadian border to the very southern tip of Florida. The longest north-to-south road in the United States, it is officially known today as US Route 1.

The most scenic stretch can be driven by joining the highway in the small city of Brunswick, where visitors can enjoy a number of museums before setting off north to Calais, on the Canadian border. You no sooner leave town than you are crossing over or driving alongside water, past lakes, and through woodland, with the Atlantic Ocean appearing as a companion from time to time. There are small harbour towns where you can break the journey and enjoy some of the freshest seafood imaginable, with lighthouses, state parks and other attractions tempting you to stop. Another companion is the US–Canada border, which runs alongside part of the final stretch of this road. **MG**

🄸 Portland Head Light on the shores of Cape Elizabeth.

Old Canada Road Scenic Byway
Maine, USA

Start Solon
End Sandy Bay Township
Distance 126km (78 miles)
Type Scenic
Info goo.gl/QMssl3

Similar to the Atlantic Highway along the Maine coast, Old Canada Road Scenic Byway takes visitors deep into northern Maine, all the way up to the Canadian border. It is an historic trail, now officially known by the less inspiring title, US Route 201.

The road trip begins in the tiny village of Solon and passes a series of beautiful, old clapboard houses. Before long, however, it leads into thick woodland, following the course of the Kennebec River. The journey used to be made by the Abenaki Native Americans, who at one time were spread all over New England, and utilized this trail for trading purposes. Soon after a dot on the map called the Forks, the road follows the Dead River for a while before swinging north and plunging into even denser forests. Keep an eye out for the stopping places that lead to walking trails because these remote woodlands are thick with wildlife, including, unfortunately, incessant mosquitoes in high summer. Settlements are few and far between, so try to stop at the pretty little communities of Bingham and Moscow on the shores of Wyman Lake.

When you are not driving through forests, you are gazing at spectacular mountain views, which get better as you progress, beckoned on by the Canadian mountains on the horizon. By the end of the journey, the label 'scenic byway' will seem somewhat of an understatement. **MG**

Connecticut Coast
Connecticut, USA

Start Mystic
End Bridgeport
Distance 121km (75 miles)
Type Scenic
Map goo.gl/2ITZyd

Before embarking on this coastal drive, take a detour to Mystic Seaport in the town of Mystic. It is the United States' largest maritime museum, and its exhibits reveal why this coast is so special and describe the town's history as a seaport. If you are interested in sea life, you might also want to take in the Mystic Aquarium and learn about the sea creatures around this coast, which include the magnificent beluga whale.

After heading west from Mystic on Interstate 95 and crossing the Connecticut River, be sure to leave the main road behind and weave your way down along the coastal roads. You may need to go back to Interstate 95 from time to time to cross the various bodies of water, but do not stay on it for convenience because this road trip is all about the journey, not the fastest route.

Sticking to the coast takes you through pretty little fishing towns such as Niantic and Sound View Beach, with some leafy inland stretches, too. There are also plenty of diversions to tempt you to take a break, such as Rocky Neck State Park, where you can explore the salt marshes and white-sand beaches. In addition, there are wildlife refuges and other attractions, including the Henry Whitfield State Museum. Although the coast here is in no way rugged, it has a timeless beauty and shows coastal Connecticut at its absolute best. **MG**

Litchfield Hills Loop
Connecticut, USA

Start New Milford
End New Milford
Distance 122km (76 miles)
Type Scenic
Map goo.gl/9nciy6

This varied drive through Connecticut hills takes in state parks, woodland, historic houses, lakes, covered bridges and more. It begins in the attractive small town of New Milford, which in 2007 celebrated its tricentenary. From here the road heads out through idyllic suburbs and woodland to Mt Tom State Park, where the Mt Tom Tower offers fantastic views as far as Long Island Sound and the Catskills in New York State.

A short diversion allows a visit to Litchfield, one of Connecticut's most historic towns, before journeying on through Mohawk State Forest and circling around Mohawk Mountain. More quiet rural roads run through farmland to Seven Falls State Park, although the number of falls varies with the rainfall. If you want to stretch your legs, then Macedonia Brook State Park offers a choice of hiking trails, some of which provide additional, impressive views of the Catskills.

The route then leads to the town of Kent, which dates back to the 1730s. Just beyond the town, there is Bull's Bridge across the Housatonic River, one of only two covered bridges in the state that still allows vehicles to drive through. Beyond here, Lake Waramaug State Park offers a final opportunity for some recreation before looping back through more idyllic rural communities to New Milford. **MG**

❶ One of a series of waterfalls and cascades at Kent Falls State Park, Connecticut.

In the Wake of F. Scott Fitzgerald Connecticut to Alabama, USA

Start Westport, Connecticut   End Montgomery, Alabama   Distance 1,819km (1,130 miles)
Type Culture   Map goo.gl/tfow0m

The Cruise of the Rolling Junk (1924) is F. Scott Fitzgerald's account of the lengthy road trip he undertook, seemingly on impulse, to take his wife, Zelda, from their home in Connecticut back to the Alabama of her childhood. The couple made the journey in 1920, shortly after the publication of Fitzgerald's first novel, *This Side of Paradise*.

Leaving their home behind in the coastal colonial town of Westport, the Fitzgeralds drove their second-hand Marmon 34 touring car through Connecticut's rural landscape. Anyone making the same journey today should remember that the roads back in the 1920s were not the smooth-surfaced highways there are now. There were a lot

of rough tracks; as a consequence, the Fitzgeralds' car was even junkier at the end of the trip than it had been at the beginning.

The route passes through the big cities of New York, Philadelphia and Washington, D.C., before drivers get their first glimpse of the south when reaching Virginia. The landscape then becomes lusher, the culture and the accents change, and woodland and farmland start to predominate. It's a land where the Fitzgeralds find peaches, Zelda's longing for which inspired the journey in the first place. MG

❶ The Fitzgerald Museum, Montgomery.

Newport Loop Ocean Drive Rhode Island, USA

Start Newport   End Newport   Distance 22km (13.5 miles)
Type Culture   Map goo.gl/VW3CmE

Newport is a wealthy place and has been ever since the Vanderbilts and the Astors built fabulous, lavish mansions there during the so-called gilded age at the end of the 19th century, when the riches of the top industrialists and plantation owners seemed to have no limit. On this circular coastal route you can visit many of their sumptuous creations, now open to the public. The Breakers mansion is probably the most popular. The Elms, too. But you won't have time to see them all, so you must choose. High Victorian, neoclassical, Gothic revival, Italianate: it's all here, grander and more overblown than you probably imagined. You can even see their luxury cars at the Audrain Automobile Museum.

Today, lots of modern-day moneyed folk still have their private mansions here, too. The people who inhabit these houses do not wish to be discreet about their circumstances; this area is all about ostentation, with a profusion of neo-Greco-Roman architecture and, in some places, fully operational miniature cannons to be fired off on important national days. Do the tour, then perhaps take a break to look out over the sea at Fort Adams State Park. If, after that, you fancy a total change of mood, 15 minutes' drive north the slightly mad Green Animals Topiary Garden is just what you need. DK

❶ Castle Hill Lighthouse and Newport Bridge.

Brandywine Pennsylvania/Delaware, USA

Start Chadds Ford, Pennsylvania   **End** Dover, Delaware   **Distance** 109km (68 miles)
Type Scenic   **Info** goo.gl/jQ3ZrW

This delightful trip through rolling hills and along the banks of the Brandywine River offers some of the finest formal gardens, a good deal of military history and spectacular wildlife.

Start the journey at Brandywine Battlefield Park, the site of the military confrontation in 1777 between US and British forces that culminated in the British capture of Philadelphia. Next is a quartet of stately homes and gardens, all at one time belonging to the wealthy Du Pont family: Longwood Gardens; the Winterthur Museum, Garden and Library; the Mount Cuba Center; and Nemours Mansion and Garden. Of these, Longwood Gardens is one of the greatest formal gardens in the United States.

Farther south, the Delaware Art Museum has an excellent collection of British Pre-Raphaelite paintings. From there the landscape changes, and there are fine views of the Delaware River. The river's military importance resulted in the construction of Fort Delaware, a spectacular Civil War fortress built on an island, accessible from Delaware City by short ferry ride. The area is also a haven for wildlife, and the 19.3-km- (12-mile) long drive around the Bombay Hook National Wildlife Refuge is a chance to see migratory birds, blue herons and beavers. The trip ends at Dover, Delaware's second-largest city. **DK**

❶ The wetland habitat of the Leipsic River.

Amish Country Scenic Loop Pennsylvania, USA

Start Lancaster   End Lancaster   Distance 161km (100 miles)
Type Culture   Map goo.gl/8WM7EN

The Amish people, or Pennsylvania Dutch, are renowned for not accepting modern technology. Their heartland is in Pennsylvania and neighbouring Ohio. They live in peaceful, rural communities, and this drive takes you through rustic terrain, where you are sure to see Amish people in horse-drawn buggies. Indeed, there are special lanes for them on many roads. Note that the Amish prefer not to have their photos taken.

The route begins and ends in Lancaster. Founded in 1734, this city has the oldest continually operating farmers' market in the United States: its building (opened in 1889) is a sales outlet for traditional Amish arts and crafts.

Heading east out of town takes you into the flat but fertile countryside, with a photo opportunity as you pass through the unusually named village of Intercourse. Scenes from the Peter Weir film *Witness* (1985), starring Harrison Ford, set in the Amish community, were shot around here.

Farther on you'll see some of the area's many covered bridges, several chocolate museums and pretzel factories, and a wolf sanctuary. The route returns to Lancaster through more of the relaxed countryside that makes it easy to understand why the Amish settled here. MG

❶ Amish children in Lancaster County, Pennsylvania.

Kittatinny Ridge Loop
New Jersey, USA

Start Delaware Water Gap
End Newton
Distance 121km (75.2 miles)
Type Scenic
Info goo.gl/Au79om

This drive begins at the point where New Jersey meets Pennsylvania, and the Delaware River flows through a gap in the Appalachian Mountains. It partly follows the river, on the New Jersey side, along the Old Mine Road, although this is closed in the winter. A line of trees separates road from river, with the thick woodland of Worthington State Forest climbing up hillsides along the route.

The river and road then split, and the road continues alongside the Walpack Fish and Wildlife Management Area, which is popular for its hiking trails, hunting and fishing, and through Walpack Township. When the road goes under Interstate 84, take a sharp turn to head south through the vast High Point State Park. Here, you will find the highest point in New Jersey, the rather obviously named High Point, at an elevation of 550m (1,803ft).

The heavily wooded park is a delightful reminder of just how scenic parts of New Jersey can be, and it is a perfect place to go leaf-peeping in the autumn. South of the park, the route skirts around the Bear Swamp Wildlife Management Area and alongside several lakes, before winding up in the town of Newton, which dates back to the middle of the 18th century. Do not miss the historic Old Newton Burial Ground, which also dates back to that time. **MG**

❶ The panoramic view from Delaware Water Gap is simply stunning at dusk.

Clinton Road
New Jersey, USA

Start West Milford
End Newfoundland
Distance 20km (12.4 miles)
Type Culture
Map goo.gl/1XcItN

Almost no one lives along this stretch of innocuous-looking tarmac, and when you hear some of the bone-chilling stories about it, you'll understand why – for many believe that New Jersey's Clinton Road is the United States' most haunted highway.

This narrow two-lane road, with dark woodland on both sides and no lighting, is certainly spooky. In fact, if there weren't already so many stories about, it you'd probably want to invent some. One of the rumours about the road is that it's where the hitmen, gangsters and hoodlums of New York dispose of their victims. In reality, there's only one recorded case of that actually happening – but then maybe all the other bodies have simply not been discovered yet?

Other things to watch out for are phantom headlights that come towards you though there is no vehicle behind them, and, of course, there are the run-of-the-mill ghost stories of shadowy men on wraithlike horses. The adjacent woods are also said to contain meeting places for secret societies of satanists, witches and the Ku Klux Klan, although sceptics have wondered whether anyone would hold secret meetings in a place that is famous for secret meetings.

Whatever your feelings about the supernatural, if you're in the area, you have to drive Clinton Road on a dark, foggy night for the full experience. **MG**

Baltimore's Historic Charles Street
Maryland, USA

Start Charles Street
End Charles Street
Distance 17.7km (11 miles)
Type Culture
Info goo.gl/oQbSmy

Apart from a few small twists, Charles Street is a Scenic Byway that runs north to south in an almost straight line through the heart of downtown Baltimore, ending up near the Patapsco River. It's one of only four US Scenic Byways that traverse a predominantly urban location.

It is a street that's as old as the city itself, and since Baltimore has more public monuments than any other US city, it is not surprising that many of them are along Charles Street in the downtown area. It's a thoroughfare that tells the city's story and is lined with museums, and passes through several historic neighbourhoods.

One feature that's impossible to miss is the Washington Monument, a massive 54.46m (178ft 8in) high, and worth climbing, if you can, for the expansive city views from the top. Nearby is the Walters Art Museum, which has works by Manet, Monet and Turner, among others.

A ten-minute drive north is the Baltimore Museum of Art, one of the finest collections in the United States, which includes works by Picasso, Renoir, Manet, Degas, Gaugin and Van Gogh, and the largest public collection of works by Matisse anywhere in the world. Close by are the Sherwood Gardens, best seen in the spring, when thousands of colourful tulips come out, a reminder that Baltimore is more than just a big city. **MG**

Chesapeake Wine Trail
Maryland, USA

Start Baltimore
End Ocean Pines
Distance 377km (234 miles)
Type Culture
Info goo.gl/zAaB37 **Map** goo.gl/ZZiXtZ

The Chesapeake Wine Trail has many highways and byways – there are several possible detours, but every one of them has the same aim: to take in as many as possible of the wineries on the Delmarva Peninsula. The itinerary suggested here is the greater part of a day's drive, with only a few stops; with as many as most people will want to make, it may occupy several days. For those who have neither time nor stamina to complete the whole journey, round trips from Baltimore are almost as good as going the whole way to Ocean Pines.

Before setting off it would be useful to check the opening hours of any wineries you want to visit, since not all of them are open to the public, and some are open only on weekends.

Head northeast out of Baltimore, and you soon leave the city behind and enter the rural heartland of Maryland. The trail then turns south on the far side of Chesapeake Bay. It's not a dramatic landscape – nothing like the Napa Valley in California – being mostly flat, but on sunny days in spring, summer or autumn, it's a thoroughly pleasant place to be. And precisely because it's not Napa, which is often overrun with tourists from all over the world, the winemakers of Maryland generally have more time for visitors and seem genuinely pleased to welcome travellers who have taken the trouble to come and see their vineyards. **MG**

Harriet Tubman Byway
Maryland/Delaware, USA

Start Bucktown, Maryland
End Bucktown, Maryland
Distance 201km (125 miles)
Type Culture
Info goo.gl/Muf8oZ

Harriet Tubman was born in Maryland in 1822 to slave parents, the middle child of nine enslaved siblings. She grew up to be an abolitionist, humanitarian and one of America's greatest inspirations. Escaping from slavery in 1849, she established her own Underground Railroad, the term given to a vast network of escape routes using roads, waterways and safe houses utilized by African Americans fleeing the South to freedom in the North. To celebrate her life, a self-guided driving tour visiting sites in Delaware's Kent and New Castle Counties, and Dorchester and Caroline Counties in Maryland, has been established, to take you where Harriet Tubman lived, worked, worshipped and agonized as she helped countless souls in their quest to escape oppression.

This officially designated Scenic Byway passes through Blackwater National Wildlife Refuge, where Tubman worked as a child, and Linchester Mill on Hunting Creek, an important crossing point for freedom seekers. It takes you down rural roads and through the forests and marshes along the shores of Chesapeake and Delaware Bays to places like Bucktown Village Store, where she was almost killed by a white overseer. By 1860 Harriet Tubman had become a symbol of hope, known to many by the nickname Moses – because she had led so many souls out of slavery to freedom. **BDS**

Journey Through Hallowed Ground National Scenic Byway Pennsylvania to Virginia, USA

Start Gettysburg, Pennsylvania
End Monticello, Virginia
Distance 290km (180 miles)
Type Culture
Info goo.gl/D1lCho

On this road trip through three states on the US eastern seaboard, you'll pass through dozens of historic villages, battlefields, plantation mansions and national parks.

The route was an important transport link during the War of Independence (1775–83) and a key battleground during the American Civil War (1861–65). So it's an excellent way of learning about the history of the nation.

You'll pass the homes of nine former presidents, including Thomas Jefferson's house at Monticello, which is a UNESCO World Heritage Site. The Civil War battles of Manassas, Gettysburg, Antietam and Appomattox happened along the route of the byway, too. And landmark events like the Declaration of Independence, the Emancipation Proclamation, the Gettysburg Address and the Marshall Plan occurred along the trail.

It's not all about events from dusty history books, though, as the route meanders through a glorious countryside of orchards, vineyards and farms dotted with charming old rural towns like Frederick, Culpeper and Madison. And if that is not enough to entertain you on the journey, there are 13 national parks within the Journey through Hallowed Ground Heritage Area offering a multitude of opportunities for picnics, walks, rides, and adventure sports. SH

❶ Civil War re-enactment societies often operate along this historic route.

The National Road
Maryland to Illinois, USA

Start Cumberland, Maryland
End Vandalia, Illinois
Distance 1,326km (824 miles)
Type Culture
Map goo.gl/o2P1NL

Transportation was a major problem for the new union of American states more than 200 years ago. Ohio had just joined – but there wasn't a reliable way of getting to and from it.

Most roads were mule tracks and paths cut through forests. So the East Coast authorities devised the first-ever road that would be paid for by the federal government.

It was a massive project that passed through the states of West Virginia, Pennsylvania, Maryland, Ohio, Indiana and Illinois. It aimed to reach the Ohio River, but eventually, money ran out, and it ground to a halt around Vandalia after 20 years of building, still 96km (60 miles) short of its target.

Today, it offers a magical road trip across the country – a tapestry of farming homesteads and small, half-forgotten townships across the rural United States. You can see how the road acted as a corridor, with small farming communities growing up along its sides. On the way, you'll pass historic landmarks that are part of the story of the road itself, like toll-houses, coaching inns and mileposts.

One of the great highlights of this itinerary may be seen at the Casselman River in Maryland. There, the road passes over an elegant stone arch whose 15-m- (48-ft) long span made it, at the time of its completion in 1814, the widest single-span stone bridge in the world. **SH**

Mountain Maryland Scenic Byway Maryland, USA

Start Keysers Ridge
End Cumberland
Distance 311km (193 miles)
Type Scenic
Info goo.gl/Z8zpcX

In a state famous for its 13,000km (8,000 miles) of stunning shoreline, the Mountain Maryland Scenic Byway may come as a surprise. Winding across the western Appalachians, this byway begins at 910m (2,894ft) above sea level on Keysers Ridge. Descending west on Interstate 68 brings you first to Friendsville (famed for its vineyards and white-water rafting on the nearby Youghiogheny River) and then on US 219, to McHenry, home to the Deep Creek Lake State Park, before the lakeshore roads lead you to the charming historic town of Oakland. Find time to explore this popular Main Street community, with its quaint Victorian architecture, boutique stores and antique shops.

The second leg of the byway is a network of roads rather than a simple linear route. Take the itinerary through Swanton and the ancient swamplands of the Allegheny Highlands to Grantsville, before looping back on the Big Run Road through Savage River State Forest, a popular outdoor playground with hikers and anglers. The byway's smooth tarmac meanders south to Westernport before picking up MD 36 heading east, passing the 19th-century ironworks of Lonaconing and the historic town of Frostburg, through the Cumberland Narrows and into downtown Cumberland, well known for its sidewalk festivals and summer street markets. **DIS**

Coal Heritage Trail
West Virginia, USA

Start Bluefield
End Fayetteville
Distance 114km (71 miles)
Type Culture
Info goo.gl/CE5MoR

The Appalachian Mountains of West Virginia are noted above all for their majestic beauty, but as the demand for coal boomed in the 19th century they also saw a population explosion as large numbers of European immigrants were recruited to unearth the region's 'black diamonds'. That industrial heritage is commemorated in this Coal Heritage Trail, one of the most popular Scenic Byways in the United States.

The trail begins in the city of Bluefield, which was a small and insignificant place until bituminous coal was discovered beneath it in what turned out to be the largest deposit of its kind in the world. The Coal Rush was on.

The route heads northwest to Bramwell, where there is a museum that outlines the history of the Coal Rush and which was itself the centre of numerous mining activities. It's hard to believe now, but this speck on the map, where just a few hundred people live, once had more millionaires per head than anywhere else in the United States.

The route winds north through heavily wooded hills, with various memorials and murals about the coal industry, and ends in Fayetteville, another former coal boomtown that's now a delightfully laid-back place, popular with tourists. Today, it is the great outdoors and not the underground mines that bring people and money to this region. **MG**

❶ The Coal Camp Cabin at Beckley Exhibition Coal and Youth Museum is one of the highlights of this route.

Skyline Drive
Virginia, USA

Start Front Royal
End Rockfish Gap
Distance 172km (107 miles)
Type Scenic
Info goo.gl/ZDkpxb

This is one of the oldest and prettiest of the United States' gentle purpose-built scenic drives, running north to south through the length of the beautiful Shenandoah National Park, which offers 80,000 hectares (200,000 acres) of rampant nature. The Skyline Drive is the only public route through the park, and apart from the start and end, there are only two other access points, so you need to pack everything you need for a day trip, such as outdoor gear and provisions. This is particularly important if you want to break the trip with a short hike into the wilderness, perhaps to one of the many waterfalls.

Driving, there is a 55kph (35 mph) speed limit in place, to help protect jaywalking wildlife. Of course, the wildlife is one of the primary reasons – apart from the peace and solitude – why you are there: the chance of glimpsing black bears, deer, wild turkeys and other animals. There are many terrific views, too, out across the densely wooded Shenandoah Valley – so many, in fact, that there are 75 designated scenic overlook points along the road where you can stop to take a photograph.

At its southern end the Skyline Drive connects with the Blue Ridge Parkway, which continues on through the Appalachians. It is worth noting that the park has an entry fee; the route is open year round, except for rare autumn evening closures for hunting. **DK**

❶ The Skyline Drive curves through the mountainscape and is particularly impressive in autumn

Colonial Parkway
Virginia, USA

Start Jamestown
End Yorktown
Distance 37km (23 miles)
Type Culture
Info goo.gl/iFSvXz

The Colonial Parkway is a smooth 40-minute drive that links Virginia's famous historical triangle: Jamestown, Williamsburg and Yorktown.

These three towns are a 200-year mini-history lesson in the English colonial experience in North America: Jamestown, the site of the first British colony on the continent in the early 1600s; the colonial grandeur of Williamsburg's historic district; and the site of the pivotal British defeat to the American Revolutionary forces following the 1781 siege of Yorktown.

The parkway is a wonder of sensitive engineering. Like other US parkways, it has limited access points and a strict speed limit – in this case, 70 kph (45 mph). Once embarked upon the route, you are separated from urban life and free to focus on the scenic and historical delights, which are numerous. You will, of course, take time at the main way-stops (there are entry fees at all three).

In Historic Jamestowne you can see the site of the original 1607 James Fort. In Williamsburg, Colonial Williamsburg is a living-history museum with more than 90 preserved 18th-century buildings and many hundreds of reconstructions. At the road's eastern end is the site of the siege and surrender of the British forces under General Cornwallis to George Washington and the French army during the American Revolutionary War. DK

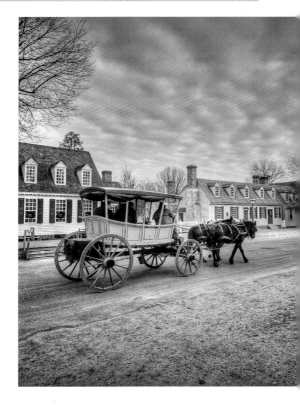

❶ A horse-drawn carriage ride back in time through the living-history museum of Colonial Williamsburg.

George Washington Memorial Parkway Virginia/D.C., USA

Start Mt. Vernon, Virginia   **End** Langley, Virginia   **Distance** 43km (27 miles)
Type Culture   **Info** goo.gl/ZKTv5z

The George Washington (GW) Memorial Parkway is not a conventional scenic drive – it runs through the urban centre of Washington, D.C. – but it delivers classic views across the Potomac River to the Capitol. Despite being a purpose-built recreational road, the GW Parkway is pretty busy. It's a commuter route and one of the fastest ways to and from Washington Dulles International Airport. In rush hours, it gets really clogged up. You can drive it in either direction, of course, but the roadways divide at Lady Bird Johnson Park, opposite the National Mall on the banks of the Potomac, and it is the northbound roadway that provides the better views.

Start in the south of the city at Mt Vernon, site of George Washington's tomb and his plantation home, then head northeast to Jones Point, from which there are impressive views across the Potomac. Next come the Woodrow Wilson Memorial Bridge and the Jones Point Lighthouse. Beyond the airport you get views across to the Lincoln Memorial and the Washington Monument. At Lady Bird Johnson Park, it's just a short detour left to Arlington Cemetery, with the Tomb of the Unknown Soldier, the Robert E. Lee Memorial and the grave of President John F. Kennedy. Your journey ends outside the CIA's Langley HQ. **DK**

❶ The CIA buildings in Langley, Virginia.

Blue Ridge Parkway Virginia/North Carolina, USA

Start Rockfish Gap, Virginia   End Chimney Rock, North Carolina   Distance 587km (365 miles)
Type Scenic   Info goo.gl/aJ2iv9

In the United States, when a road is given the designation 'parkway', you know you're in for a treat. Parkways, an idea put forth in the late 19th century by Frederick Olmsted, designer of New York's Central Park, were originally 'pleasure roads' to link cities with parks in their suburbs. The definition has since broadened. Now parkways are called 'linear parks', unsullied by billboards and bordered only by nature. And the Blue Ridge Parkway – lined with beech, elm, hickory, maple and chestnut trees – is the longest parkway of them all.

First proposed in the 1920s, and largely completed in 1966, the road many call 'America's Favourite Country Road' travels along the Blue Ridge, part of the Appalachian Mountain chain, through Virginia and North Carolina. There are 26 tunnels, many of which can be closed from November to April; more than 160 bridges; and six viaducts. Especially popular with bikers, the superb Diamondback and Tail of the Dragon are two not-to-be-missed detours just off the parkway.

The founders of the Blue Ridge Parkway fully achieved their stated aim to create a road unlike any other, to sculpt a glorious drive that would 'link the notches, the hollows, the promontories and the knobs of these two Appalachian states'. **BDS**

❶ Chimney Rock in the park of the same name.

Newfound Gap North Carolina/Tennessee, USA

Start Cherokee, North Carolina **End** Gatlinburg, Tennessee **Distance** 58km (36 miles)
Type Scenic **Map** goo.gl/xLSltK

The old road crossed the Great Smoky Mountains at a spot called Indian Gap until a Swiss geographer discovered an easier and lower pass nearby. A good-quality road was built through this new pass in 1932, and it became known as Newfound Gap. Today, the Newfound Gap Road is one of the United States' most acclaimed scenic drives, twisting through the Great Smoky Mountains National Park on the border of North Carolina and Tennessee. It is a well-known tourist landmark, and the road is kept open throughout the year with snowploughs, except during the most severe winter storms.

Driving along the route, you will climb some 900m (3,000ft) through the woods. The highlights of this steep and winding road include overhanging canopies of deciduous trees; bubbling creeks and waterfalls; misty views across rolling hills and mountains; and spotting eagles, elks and bears. There are plenty of marked walking trails leading from the visitor centres, campsites and car parks. A popular short detour takes you to Clingmans Dome Road, another paved park road, which leads to a parking spot high in the mountains. From here, a steep paved path rises up to Clingmans Dome, the highest peak in the region at a lofty 2,025m (6,643ft), where there is a 360-degree view. **SH**

❶ The Great Smoky Mountains seen from the road.

Diamondback Loop North Carolina, USA

Start Little Switzerland   End Little Switzerland   Distance 62km (38.5 miles)
Type Scenic   Map goo.gl/BjinIU

The Diamondback Loop was once little known outside North Carolina's biking fraternity, but today it is seen as the bonus track road for those who come to this area to tackle the legendary Tail of the Dragon and the Blue Ridge Parkway.

Forming a rough diamond shape, the route heads in a clockwise loop from the charming alpinesque settlement of Little Switzerland. From the outset, you get straight into the action with a long, tortuous descent through forests of pine, sugar maple and beech before the sweeping curves and faster highways turn due south. The most exciting part of the route from Lake Tahoma packs nearly 200 bends and switchbacks into a mere 19.3km (12 miles) of road as it climbs through the lush green woodland on steep runway-smooth roads – with gradients nudging 15 per cent in places – ascending to a height of 1,056m (3,466ft) and a noticeably cooler clime.

Take particular care through the switchbacks that motorcyclists have coined the Devil's Whip. It is from here that you get a taste of the fabled Blue Ridge Parkway as you close the loop heading back northeast. The Diamondback Motorcycle Lodge is a great place for a stopover and conveniently close to the hospitable Switzerland Inn. DIS

❶ The sign says it all: switchbacks ahead.

Outer Banks National Scenic Byway   North Carolina, USA

Start Whalebone Junction   End Beaufort   Distance 222km (138 miles)
Type Scenic   Info goo.gl/EfQh45

The barrier islands that protect the coast of North Carolina, guarding the mainland from fierce Atlantic squalls, were formed between 3,500 and 5,000 years ago. There are nine of them – Currituck Banks, Bodie Island, Pea Island, Hatteras Island, Ocracoke Island, Portsmouth Island, Core Banks, Shackleford Banks and Bogue Banks.

They have survived a gradual rise in sea levels by slowly migrating landwards, as much as 80km (50 miles) since their formation. They may look fragile, but they are tough natural sea defences, and together they comprise the Outer Banks, an American landfall rich in birdlife, marshlands, dunes and tales of pirates and ghosts that rose up

from beyond shifting sands out of sunken ships in the so-called Graveyard of the Atlantic.

The William B. Umstead Bridge first brought the mainland's US Route 64 to Whalebone Junction in 1955, and now a series of bridges and car ferries takes you through the Outer Banks' wildlife refuges, past beaches and the nation's tallest brick lighthouse (Cape Hatteras). Visit the site where the Wright Brothers made their first controlled powered airplane flight near Kitty Hawk, and see the 21 communities on the salty road that runs flat and straight through a bygone world. **BDS**

❶ Bodie Island Lighthouse on the Outer Banks.

Cullasaja River Gorge North Carolina, USA

Start Franklin   End Highlands   Distance 31.4km (19.5 miles)
Type Adventure   Map goo.gl/3y6pBp

This is one of North Carolina's favourite driving roads, with several narrow sections and lots of sweeping bends: a real treat for any keen biker or motorist cutting through the beautiful Nantahala National Forest. Also known for part of its length as the Waterfall Byway, Cullasaja River Gorge naturally follows the route of Cullasaja River, which rushes spectacularly over several large waterfalls. There is also a Mountain Waters Scenic Byway, which overlaps part of the route.

Setting off from the historic city of Franklin, whose roots go back to 1799, the route runs south through the hilly and wooded North Carolina countryside as it winds and follows the Cullasaja River. Rocky cliffs stand on one side of the road and a wooded valley on the other. It is into this valley that the Cullasaja Falls plunge 76.2m (250ft), the longest drop of any of the falls along the route. Unfortunately, it is only possible to catch brief glimpses of them. There is only one small stopover, and even then it is a dangerous walk along the road to try to get a slightly better view.

Before reaching Highlands, try to visit the Dry Falls, which are so called because they rush over an overhanging cliff, which means that you can walk behind them without getting wet. MG

🛈 Cullasaja Falls is the most dramatic cascade en route.

Daniel Boone Memorial Trail North Carolina, USA

Start Salisbury
End Boone
Distance 285km (177 miles)
Type Culture
Map goo.gl/KIRff2

The frontiersman and explorer Daniel Boone was one of the first US heroes, and he travelled particularly widely in this part of the United States, especially in Kentucky, Virginia and North Carolina. There are several trails – official and unofficial, driving and hiking – that link places associated with him, and this route enables visitors to see most of them in a scenic one-day road trip.

The drive begins in the historic town of Salisbury, where the Rowan Museum offers some Daniel Boone background. North of here, through undulating woodland, is Boone's Cave Park, where the explorer's family used to go fishing in the 1750s. The route takes in some delightful rural backroads, with stops at places such as Historic Bethabara Park. This is an open-air museum, not solely dedicated to Boone, but showing what life was like here in his day. The tour also visits Joppa Cemetery, where Boone's parents are buried; the site of Fort Dobbs, where the family sought protection during the Cherokee War; and Hickory Ridge Living History Museum, another vivid re-creation of the tough life folks lived in those pioneer times.

Virginia to the north is equally proud of its Boone associations. If you want extend this road trip, sticking with the same central theme, then the official Daniel Boone Heritage Trail begins at the state line just north of Kingsport. **MG**

Cherokee Foothills Scenic Highway South Carolina, USA

Start Fair Play
End Gaffney
Distance 193km (120 miles)
Type Scenic
Map goo.gl/8gPWEW

The Cherokee Foothills Scenic Highway is a great way of avoiding Interstate 85, since it takes a scenic route through farmland, peach orchards, lakes, waterfalls, hills and several quaint and quiet villages, all against the picturesque backdrop of the southern edge of the Blue Ridge Mountains. As the name suggests, this was once a Cherokee trail, a trading route for Native Americans, linking Tennessee with the port of Charleston in South Carolina, and later used by European fur traders.

If travelling northeast, leave Interstate 85 at exit 1, after visiting South Carolina Welcome Center to pick up essential literature and information about the route. Immediately you will pass Lake Hartwell State Park and find yourself driving through thick woodland, before crossing Lake Keowee, which is actually a human-made reservoir. Soon after, take the time to visit Keowee-Toxaway State Park, if you can, to view the blue wall of hills known as Jocassee Gorges.

There are no major tourist towns along this route, only rural settlements such as Cleveland, Campobello and Chesnee, which are all the more interesting thanks to their unapologetic authenticity. The route comes to its conclusion in another small town, Gaffney, which is a perfect example of the delights that can be found only when you venture off the busy interstates. **MG**

Ashley River Road
South Carolina, USA

Start West Oaks
End Mount Pleasant
Distance 22km (13.4 miles)
Type Culture
Map goo.gl/yTs1h1

This is a road trip that delivers exactly what you would expect to see in the Deep South: plantation houses and long sections of road lined with oak trees draped in Spanish moss and forming a living ceiling above your head.

The Ashley River Road is one of the shortest Scenic Byways in the United States, but it still manages to pack a lot in. The official stretch designated as a Scenic Byway is only 17.7km (11 miles) long, but the full length of the road follows the course of the Ashley River as it flows into historic Charleston Harbor. You can drive the route in either direction, depending on whether you are entering or leaving Charleston. Either way, it is an easy two-lane tarmac road for most of the way, and although the trip is relatively short it can take you all day if you plan to visit the plantation homes that are open to visitors. Along this stretch of road, there were once 20 such grand houses. The three that remain are Drayton Hall, Middleton Place and Magnolia Plantation and Gardens, with Drayton Hall being the only home to have survived intact from when it was first occupied in the 1750s.

At Middleton Place, alongside the opulent house and stunning gardens, visitors can also tour the Plantation Stableyards, where costumed interpreters explain how the enslaved African plantation workers once lived. **MG**

❶ Drayton Hall in Charleston, built by John Drayton, is an outstanding example of Palladian architecture.

Ocmulgee–Piedmont Scenic Byway Georgia, USA

Start Juliette   End Gray   Distance 34km (21 miles)
Type Scenic   Map goo.gl/N6jUOH

There is a lot of history packed into this short drive known as the Ocmulgee-Piedmont Scenic Byway. From end to end, without stopping, it would take little more than an hour, but most people want to take much longer than that. The route presents a neatly condensed history of the region from the 17th century to the present day.

For example, 200 years before the birth of the United States, this was an important trade route used by the indigenous population: the Muscogee. In Piedmont National Wildlife Refuge, the remains of buildings constructed by early European settlers can be seen. And a 9.6-km- (6-mile) long detour through the refuge offers visitors a chance to see endangered species of birds, pine forests, creeks and wetland habitats. In 1864, during the Civil War, the opposing forces met along the line of the route at the Battle of Sunshine Church. In addition, Jarrell Plantation, now a State Historic Site, shows visitors what life was like in a cotton plantation at the start of the 20th century.

Finally, the city of Juliette, across the Ocmulgee River, was the setting for the film *Fried Green Tomatoes* (1991). Here, the WhistleStop Café is a memorable place to refuel at the end of this road trip through Georgia's rich history. DK

❶ Opry House music hall in Juliette.

Cohutta Chattahoochee Scenic Byway Georgia, USA

Start Cohutta   **End** Ellijay   **Distance** 90.1km (56 miles)
Type Culture   **Map** goo.gl/kaEdv6

The name of this Scenic Byway confirms that there is a Native American influence around here, and it is but one of the attractions of this exceptional drive. In addition, the route offers nature lovers marvellous mountain views and two national forests, which are best driven in the autumn, when the changing colours add an extra dimension.

The drive starts in the small town of Cohutta, whose name is a Cherokee word meaning 'mountains that hold the sky'. 'Chattahoochee' is a Muskogean word that roughly translates as 'stream with pictured rocks', referring to nearby hieroglyphics. The route follows the edge of the national forest, with a convenient stopping point about halfway along in the quaint town of Chatsworth. From here, you can make a slight diversion east into Fort Mountain State Park or west to the Chief Vann House Historic Site. James Vann was a Cherokee chief who also became a wealthy businessman and the first Cherokee to live in a brick house.

The road continues on and skirts around the southern edge of the national forest before ending in Ellijay, the apple capital of Georgia. Don't miss the chance to drive along Apple Orchard Alley, where you can taste wonderful varieties of apple that you will hardly ever find on supermarket shelves. **MG**

❶ Chattahoochee River is often misty as the sun rises.

Smokey and the Bandit Challenge Georgia to Texas, USA

Start Atlanta, Georgia   **End** Texarkana, Texas   **Distance** 1,131km (703 miles)
Type Culture   **Map** goo.gl/YWesef

Obviously, a challenge is a challenge: from Georgia to Texas, to pick up the beers and back again, all in 28 hours. Burt Reynolds made the trip (with ten minutes to spare) in the movie *Smokey and the Bandit* (1977), and even managed to pick up Sally Field along the way.

Before setting off on this crazy odyssey, take a short detour to visit the main locations from the film, just to get your head in the right place. The movie begins and ends at Lakewood Fairgrounds – Jonesboro stood in for Texarkana – and the spectacular Trans-Am bridge jump – the remains of the bridge can still be seen – was on the Flint River. Having done that, it's time for the trip to begin.

These days, with improved road conditions, it is far more feasible than it was in 1977 to make the return trip in 28 hours. Even so, it is likely that you may want to do the journey in one direction only and take your time along the way.

Regardless of the movie, it is such a great route to drive, cutting a great swathe across Middle America through four of the southern states. The trip is like an Americana roll call: Waco, Birmingham, Tuscaloosa, Jackson, Vicksburg, Monroe and Shreveport. And of course, be careful to stick to the speed restrictions in order to avoid any fines. **DK**

❶ Burt Reynolds as Bo Darville, the 'Bandit'.

Florida Keys Scenic Highway Florida, USA

Start Miami   End Key West   Distance 267km (166 miles)
Type Culture   Info goo.gl/5vPbJV

Drive this gorgeous route to get some idea of what it is like to go island hopping in the Caribbean. You will skip across the turquoise tropical sea, taking in the gentle arc of 43 small coral and limestone islands known as 'Keys' at the tip of the Florida peninsula. It's a joyous journey across a sequence of long, low bridges that seem to float above the surface of the water. You will also enjoy extensive seascapes of mangroves, palms and pelicans as you cruise on a smooth, wide highway.

Head south from the shiny skyscrapers and Art Deco embellishments of Miami, taking Highway 1 onto the first island, Key Largo. Then follow the road all the way down to the last island, Key West. This southernmost point of the contiguous 48 US states is a popular if windy destination for water sports and visiting Sloppy Joe's Bar, an old haunt of novelist Ernest Hemingway. Look out for glamorous, expensive beachside homes and reflect on the fact that you're now closer to Cuba than to the US mainland – Cuban influence is plain to see in the culture here, along with that of the Bahamas, an archipelago in the Caribbean that is even closer to the US mainland. Altogether there are 84 bridges on this trip, the longest of which extends for 11km (7 miles) across the Gulf of Mexico. SH

❶ Florida Highway 1 stretches into the Gulf of Mexico.

Big Bend Scenic Byway
Florida, USA

Start Tallahassee
End Tallahassee
Distance 354km (220 miles)
Type Scenic
Info goo.gl/Lc5JIM

Florida's western panhandle is a world away from the crowds, neon and theme parks of South Beach and Orlando. And what a blessing that is. A pioneering land still characterized by wet prairies, flatwoods, bottomland forests and strand swamps covering hundreds of acres, it has the United States' largest remaining swathe of longleaf pine. There are tidal creeks, coastal marshes, 300-year-old dwarf cypresses and 300 species of bird. And running through it all, connecting the area's nine state parks and three state forests, is the Big Bend Scenic Byway.

The bend, where Florida's Gulf Coast curves to the southwest, is explored via a coastal and inland forest drive – a two-day loop that combines a complex mix of highways and backroads, but thankfully, the dedicated website (referenced above) has an excellent route guide.

Along the coastal trail, first mapped by the conquering Spanish in 1528, are three 18th-century lighthouses; a 16th-century Spanish fort; numerous fishing villages; marshes, coastal sand dunes and vast offshore sea grass beds. The forest trail drops in elevation from 70m (230ft) to sea level and follows an ancient sea bed through the hardwood Apalachicola National Forest, whose wetlands and floodplains are accessed on a well-maintained byway that takes the traveller deep into the heart of 'Old Florida'. **BDS**

A1A Scenic and Historic Coastal Byway Florida, USA

Start Ponte Vedra Beach
End Port Orange
Distance 130 km (81 miles)
Type Culture
Map goo.gl/qSP1y9

You might think a road trip along the Florida coast would be all about the beaches, azure-blue waters and smart resort towns. But this stunning coastal highway, on the main route down Florida's Atlantic coast, also has some surprising human and natural history to stimulate your mind, as well as a strong motorsport heritage.

Officially starting in the resort of Ponte Vedra Beach, the route soon has you driving a dream of a road along a narrow spit of land, with Atlantic beaches on one side and the Guana River on the other. Beyond the river is the protected Guana River Wildlife Management Area. To discover more about the wildlife of Florida's coast, stop towards the southern end and cross the river to visit Guana Tolomato Matanzas National Estuarine Research Reserve. There are pelicans, manatees, porpoises and alligators, among the many creatures that live here, and you can also learn about the conservation work taking place along this coastline.

Where the road crosses back over the Tolomato River you will see Castillo de San Marcos National Monument, a 1672 Spanish fort. However, the highlight for motorsport fans along this route will be Daytona Beach, the home of NASCAR and the famous Bike Week in early March, which draws nearly half million people. It seems this road trip has a little something for everyone. **MG**

Seven Mile Bridge
Florida, USA

Start Marathon
End Little Duck Key
Distance 12km (7.5 miles)
Type Culture
Map goo.gl/OLtHqW

No matter how many years pass, if you have driven Florida's Seven Mile Bridge, you will never forget what it felt like. One of the longest overwater bridges in the world when it was completed in 1982, it replaced the original Seven Mile Bridge, built and completed in 1912 by oil tycoon Henry Flagler. The new bridge runs parallel to the old one, linking Knight's Key in the Middle Keys with Little Duck Key in the Lower Keys, an intrinsic part of the southernmost section of US Highway 1, the road that binds the Florida Keys together. Unlike the old bridge, it bypasses Pigeon Key.

A pre-cast, pre-stressed, segmented box girder bridge, the new Seven Mile Bridge has a whopping 440 spans that rise in a gentle arc near to its centre to reach a height of 20m (65ft) above the water, in order to allow for the passage of boats. And although its precise length is 10.9km (6.79 miles), which makes it shorter than the original bridge, the new model is far closer to the water. To look either side of you as you drive and see nothing but water is an unusual and invigorating sensation. (The trip's additional overall distance is accounted for by the approach roads on either side.)

If you want to extend this short discovery road trip into a much longer scenic tour, then the Florida Keys Scenic Highway runs for 177km (110 miles), linking 43 all the way to Key West. **BDS**

❶ An aerial view of a section of the Seven Mile Bridge in Florida Keys.

Old Spanish Trail
Florida to California, USA

Start St Augustine, Florida
End San Diego, California
Distance 4,426km (2,750 miles)
Type Culture
Info goo.gl/IFA7u3

In the early days of the United States' motoring history, many years before there was widespread automobile ownership, an entrenched love of the road trip, or even a Route 66, the Old Spanish Trail began its journey across the south of the nation, from St Augustine, Florida, to San Diego, California. Begun in 1915 and officially opened in 1929, the road featured a surface that was an ad-hoc mix of asphalt, concrete, dirt-red earth, hand-laid bricks and even timber planks. It was claimed that the route followed centuries-old trails once trod by Spanish conquistadors, which is, perhaps, the reason why it is now proving quite a labour of love to resurrect. The trail was never marked out by the conquistadors, and most of it is now missing, which is why it is referred to as 'America's Ghost Highway'.

Fortunately, an all-volunteer organization – Old Spanish Trail Centennial Celebration Association (OST100) – is planning to bring back the road's glory days, first conceived 100 years ago and laden with a heavy dose of mystique ever since. They are asking farmers, and anyone old enough to remember, just where the old road may have run before it was consumed by Interstate 10. It is possible, although far from easy, to drive it now. But if ever a highway needed a grassroots campaign, it is this one: the nation's very first Mother Road 'thru the lands of America's ancient history'. **BDS**

Kuhio Highway
Kauai, Hawaii, USA

Start Princeville
End Lihue
Distance 54km (33.5 miles)
Type Scenic
Map goo.gl/pdSgmM

This delightfully scenic road trip takes in around one-quarter of the coast of Kauai, a small, almost circular, Hawaiian island in the Pacific Ocean some 112km (70 miles) northwest of Oahu. Some of the vistas may be familiar to moviegoers who saw Steven Spielberg's *Jurassic Park* (1993), parts of which were shot on location here. One exceptionally good vantage point is close to the start point at the Hanalei Valley Lookout.

From Princeville, where there is a modern development of luxury holiday homes, the road – also known and signposted as Highway 56 – proceeds to Anahola, close to the ancient surfing area of Kanahawale.

Farther along the coast, Kealia has a long sandy beach that is great for walking and cycling, but it's not as tranquil as it may seem: there are strong currents close to the shore, and fierce winds may blow in without warning off the ocean, so bathing and water sports should be undertaken with care. The next point of interest is Wailua, a small community divided in two by Nounou Mountain. This 366-m- (1,200-ft) long ridge is also known as the Sleeping Giant, because of its imagined resemblance to a reclining human figure. The trip ends at Lihue, the island's chief port and business centere where there is a wide range of retail outlets, hotels and eateries. **JP**

Diamond Head to Makapuu Point
Oahu, Hawaii, USA

Start Diamond Head, Honolulu
End Makapuu Point, Waimanalo
Distance 24.1km (15 miles)
Type Scenic
Map goo.gl/7NQBy9

If you complete the road trip from Diamond Head to Makapuu Point without getting out of the car, then you are missing a treat. Before starting the journey, set off on foot up the 1.3-km- (0.8-mile) long trail to the peak of the volcanic tuff cone of the Diamond Head State Monument, which sits atop the hill with views out over the ocean below and towards Waikiki and the state capital of Honolulu to the northwest. Down in the bay take the opportunity to enjoy some snorkelling or scuba diving in clear waters that are teeming with aquatic life.

Coastal Route 72 offers additional breathtaking scenery. One of the highlights en route is Halona Blowhole, which showcases the forces of nature that have shaped the island landscape. The power of the ocean is also on display at Sandy Beach, where the world-famous waves regularly draw experienced surfers.

Signalling the end point of the road trip is the lighthouse perched atop Makapuu Point. Make the short hike up to the lookout, which dates back to 1909, and keep an eye open for the migratory humpback whales that can be spotted offshore from around May to November. If you want to extend the road trip, continue north on Route 72 and west on Route 61, before looping back through the rocky volcanic interior to Honolulu and Diamond Head. **TW**

❶ A view of the lighthouse at Makapuu Point from the beach on windward Oahu.

Pali Highway
Oahu, Hawaii, USA

Start Honolulu
End Kailua
Distance 34km (21 miles)
Type Scenic
Map goo.gl/HJZWQ6

This is the most direct route from Hawaii's capital to the opposite side of the Big Island, and it can be covered in less than half an hour, but the wayside scenery is too beautiful to pass by with no more than a cursory glance: this magnificently diverse terrain demands contemplation and study.

Setting off from downtown Honolulu, the Pali Highway – known officially as Hawaii Route 61 – rises up over the mountains of the Ko'olau Range, through the Nu'uanu Pali Tunnels and down past the Kawainui Marsh to the outskirts of Kailua. Driving nonstop in a rush, the 16-km- (10-mile) long route may take as little as 20 minutes, but the views from the top will beg you to stop, get out of the car and spend much longer at the peak, just soaking in the vistas.

The Old Pali Highway – which went straight over the peak of the mountain, a place with strong spiritual connections – has been replaced by a modern road tunnel. Visitors can still walk the old route, though, and even drive along a short section to reach the Nu'uanu Pali, or lookout. From there the traveller can admire the breathtaking views out over the Pacific Ocean and across the mountains on the island interior. This is just one of several lookout points on the route, each with its own charms, offering idyllic panoramas stretching far across the water. **TW**

❶ Typical scenery along the Pali Highway as it sweeps across the verdant Ko'olau Range.

Kamehameha V Highway
Molokai, Hawaii, USA

Start Ho'olehua
End Kaunakakai
Distance 60km (37.5 miles)
Type Scenic
Map goo.gl/fjOzYA

Molokai, the fifth-largest of the Hawaiian Islands, lies east of Oahu and northwest of Maui. It is 61km (38 miles) long and 16km (10 miles) across at its widest point. Its north coast is almost entirely cliff lined and unreachable by road. The south, however, has beaches and is accessible along a single highway named after Kamehameha V who, from 1863 to 1872, was king of Hawaii.

The Kalaupapa Peninsula, part of Palaau State Park, was the site of a leper colony where sufferers from what is now known as Hansen's disease were kept in isolation. It was here that 19th-century Belgian priest Joseph de Veuster devoted his life to the care of victims, until he succumbed to the illness himself. Better known as Father Damien, he was canonized in 2009 by the Roman Catholic Church; the colony is now a place of pilgrimage.

The highway is a switchback and, exposed to the wild Pacific, can be scarily windy – moreover, the ocean not infrequently submerges the tarmac. At the end of the road, however, is one of the few sheltered parts of the whole island: Halawa has two swimming beaches, Kawili and Kamalaea. The former is rocky and can be hit by riptides, but the latter is sheltered and sandy. The beach park is great for fishing and all kinds of water sports, especially surfing and bodyboarding: the waves here are particularly well shaped. **JP**

❶ Road signs on the Kamehameha V Highway capture the spirit of the North Shore's surf spots.

Road to Hana
Maui, Hawaii, USA

Start Kahului
End Hana
Distance 82km (51 miles)
Type Scenic
Map goo.gl/7l7liA

Maui's famous Hana Highway hugs the island's coastline, winding through 620 bends and 59, mostly single-lane, bridges. On one side, intrepid explorers gaze across the wild, azure-blue Pacific; on the other, luxuriant jungle rises upwards, thick with bamboo, exotic fruit and tropical flowers.

With many single-track sections, and sheer drop-offs to the sea below, this is not a scenic drive for the fainthearted and has a strict 40 kph (25 mph) speed limit. However, with so much breathtaking natural beauty on view, this is not a journey to rush. Mile markers direct visitors to popular tourist attractions, including the Lower Puohokamos Falls (near mile marker 10), plummeting 40m (130ft) into a crystal-clear plunge pool. At mile marker 32 is Wai'anapanapa State Park (the name means 'glistening waters'), which has some of the most dramatic coastal scenery in all of Maui, with black-sand beaches, natural sea arches and turquoise waters, all of which are set against a backdrop of verdant green forests.

With so many sites of great botanical interest, swimming holes, waymarked trails and commanding viewpoints, Hana Highway deserves at least a whole day. Although it is one of the shorter scenic road trips featured in this book, it is achingly beautiful and an absolutely essential bucket-list entry for every true automotive adventurer. **DIS**

❶ The Hana Highway crosses waterfalls . . .

❷ . . . and twists through tropical forests.

Kahekili Highway Maui, Hawaii, USA

Start Kapalua   End Kahakuloa   Distance 22km (14 miles)
Type Scenic   Info goo.gl/4rmIGd

The west–to–east itinerary is preferable to the same route in the opposite direction, because this way the car is farther from the cliff's edge. It's a route of extreme beauty and peril in almost equal measure and, rather predictably, it has been dubbed by some travel bloggers as Maui's 'Road of Death'!

After Kapalua, once voted 'America's Best Beach', your first stop is at Honolua Bay, a protected marine reserve where visitors can snorkel when the sea is calm, surf when the water is up or just sit and watch the breakers. The next highlight is the Nakalele Blowhole, a hole in the cliff top through which forced seawater may shoot some 30m (100ft) into the air.

Between milestones 40 and 41 is the head of the Ohai Loop Trail, a short walk around the headland and a good spot for whale watching. Next come the Olivine Pools – dried lava deposits that fill and empty with the tides. At Kahakuloa there is an unmissable banana bread shop; beyond the village is a headland, 197m (646ft) high, where the etymology of the highway's name finally becomes clear: Kahekili II, supreme ruler of Maui in the 18th century, was said to have dived every morning before breakfast off a ledge 60m (200ft) above the water. **JP**

❶ The scenery is better than the road surface.

Hamakua Heritage Corridor Drive Hawaii, Hawaii, USA

Start Hilo   **End** Waipi'o Valley Overlook   **Distance** 72.4km (45 miles)
Type Scenic   **Info** goo.gl/zKPBuh

The northeast coast of Hawaii's Big Island receives more than 200cm (80in) of rainfall a year, a rate of precipitation that makes for lush waterfall-draped sea cliffs, moss-laden bridges and a rainforest that is home to more than 5,000 species of flora.

The Hamakua Heritage Corridor Drive takes you through it all, along a coastline formed and uplifted by two of Hawaii's most spectacular volcanoes – Mauna Kea, 4,207m (13,803ft) above sea level, and Kohala, 1,670m (5,480ft) high. You will span ravines with names like Maulua, Laupahoehoe and Ka'awali'i and pass by numerous tempting side roads to waterfalls and black-sand beaches bookmarked by craggy volcanic promontories.

Must-see detours along the way include a drive on Highway 220 to the 134-m- (442-ft) high Akaka Falls. Grab a herbal brew at Mauna Kea Tea farm before pressing on past once-thriving sugar plantation communities such as tiny, all-but-forgotten Pepeekepo. And when you arrive in Honoka'a, population around 2,000, don't stop, but carry on to the lookout over the Waipi'o Valley and be awestruck by the scale of Hawaii's most beautiful gorge, once the political and religious heart of the island and the home of its royalty – the Big Island's very own Valley of the Kings. **BDS**

❶ The road runs along the tops of cliffs like these.

Hawaii Belt Road
Hawaii, Hawaii, USA

Start Hilo
End Hilo
Distance 412km (256 miles)
Type Scenic
Map goo.gl/neHDnf

It may look like a dot on a map of the Pacific, but don't be deceived; the biggest island of the Hawaii group can offer an excellent long day's road trip. Locals call it 'The Big Island' or 'TBI'. After New Zealand, it is the biggest island between Australia and the United States and covers more than 10,000 sq km (4,000 square miles). The trip is a mix of local Routes 11, 19 and 190, plus a few others. Most people call it the Māmalahoa Highway or the Hawaii Belt Road.

En route you will be skirting around the biggest mountain in the islands: Mauna Kea is 4,207m (13,803ft) high. Locals claim that if measured from its base under the ocean, Mauna Kea is much taller than Everest. If you fancy a detour, there is a road to the top, but it rises so steeply that visitors can experience altitude sickness. You will see numerous views of Mauna Kea along the way – plus lots of sea views – but driving around the coast of TBI will also take you through macadamia orchards, coffee plantations, fishing villages and international beach resorts while you spot waterfalls, sugarcane fields and misty eucalyptus woods. It's warm and tropical, and the air smells of flowers.

Before you get too comfortable, though, note the memorial you pass at Wailoa Bridge: the 1960 Hilo Clock here has its hands frozen at the moment a killer tsunami hit the island. **SH**

❶ A view of Mauna Kea from the gravel access road. Only 4x4s should be used to attempt it.

Kau Scenic Byway
Hawaii, Hawaii, USA

Start Kailua-Kona
End Hawaii Volcanoes National Park
Distance 132km (82 miles)
Type Scenic
Info goo.gl/omfzwf

The Kau Scenic Byway provides the traveller with a great deal to look at, but is partly a misnomer because it runs for much of its course along Highway 11, a busy main road. Nevertheless, its rewards are fantastic and varied. The route follows a course around the base of Mauna Loa which, at 4,169m (13,677ft), is the world's largest volcano. It is not only big; it is active, too, and among the highlights of the journey are the transitions from established terrain with lush vegetation to the recently deposited lava flows.

In addition, the settlement of Naalehu is worth a brief stopover. It's sheltered in a valley from Mauna Loa's main flow and has the distinction of being the most southerly town in the United States. As the highway turns east near the southern tip of the island, there are distant views of Kilauea, Hawaii's other great volcano, 1,247m (4,091ft) high. Also visible are the Ninole Hills, basalt formations that pre-date the volcanoes.

Routes through the National Park may change when they are covered with slow-moving lava from one of the island's many actively eruptive sites. This is a scenic road trip of wildly different landscapes: some of the park is lush tropical rain forest; other areas, such as the dried lava fields of the Kau Desert, are barren wastelands in which plant life has yet to establish itself. JP

❶ Black sand and tropical vegetation are typical of the terrain along this route.

Chain of Craters Road
Hawaii, Hawaii, USA

Start Kīlauea Visitor Center
End Holei Sea Arch
Distance 35.2km (21.9 miles)
Type Adventure
Map goo.gl/sllEvW

Chain of Craters Road runs through the verdant and desolate Hawaii Volcanoes National Park. It begins at an altitude of 1,127m (3,700ft) in the rainforests along Mount Kīlauea's eastern rift zone, passes through a primaeval lava-filled landscape of fissures, smoking vents and cinder cones, and ends prematurely at sea level just past the Holei Sea Arch. The road was cut off by lava flows in 2003, as intermittent flows of molten rock found their way to the coast and solidified in spectacular fashion as they hit the cooling waters of the Pacific Ocean, making Hawaii's Big Island even bigger.

The pit craters that give the road its name – Lua Manu, Puhimau, Ko'oko'olau, Hi'iaka, Pauahi and Nāpau – were formed when lava drained from underground lava tubes, thereby resulting in voids and dramatic surface collapses. There are abundant petroglyphs, too, including the Pu'u Loa petroglyph field with over 15,000 drawings. Be sure to check the daily advisory posted by the US Geological Survey before heading out on the road and its various detours, but do not be deterred. The road was opened in 1928 to Makaopuhi Crater, extended in 1965, partly buried under lava flows in 1969, realigned and reopened in 1979, and since 1986 constantly reburied under fresh flows. There is barely a road anywhere whose course has been more determined by Mother Nature. **BDS**

❶ Chain of Craters Road gets blocked by lava flowing across its path and solidifying.

Royal Footsteps Along the Kona Coast
Hawaii, Hawaii, USA

Start Kailua-Kona
End Keauhou
Distance 10km (6.2 miles)
Type Culture
Map goo.gl/GqpjTb

This short road trip along Ali'i Drive on the Kona coast is a fascinating journey through 700 years of Hawaiian history and its royal and cultural traditions. That's just over a century a mile.

The starting point is at Kailua-Kona, where the Hulihee Palace is a mansion that was once the home of Hawaiian royalty. More recently, it was the residence of the governor; today, it is a furniture museum run by the Daughters of Hawai'i, an organization that aims to 'perpetuate the memory and spirit of old Hawaii and of historic facts, and to preserve the traditional nomenclature and correct pronunciation of the Hawaiian language'.

The next place of note along the route is Kahaluu, where the surfing beaches were once the exclusive preserve of Polynesian royalty but are now open to anyone who can afford the equipment. Kahaluu also boasts the island's oldest Christian church and several heiau – temples of the island's pre-Christian polytheistic religions. At the southern end of the road, Keauhou lies on a bay that has culture and recreation in equal abundance: ancient temples and fishponds, and modern centres for snorkelling, diving and kayaking. By day there are sometimes opportunities to see green sea turtles (*Chelonia mydas*) basking in shallow rock pools; at night there are boat trips to observe manta rays feeding on plankton in the bay. **JP**

❶ Wooden images of gods guard the Hale o Keawe heiau at Pu'uhonua o Hōnaunau National Historical Park.

Gulf of California Coast
Baja California, Mexico

Start La Paz
End San Evaristo
Distance 129km (80 miles)
Type Scenic
Map goo.gl/Rqe6fF

Baja California is the strip of Mexico that drops down from the US state of California. It is a largely untamed area of cactus desert; sand dunes; and long, wild beaches.

This road trip takes you through one of the most scenic parts of the Baja coast – along its eastern side, facing the Gulf of California and the mainland of Mexico rather than the side that fronts the Pacific Ocean. You'll start in the capital of the Baja province, La Paz, an old port built up around a Spanish colonial square and often the finish line of the famous Baja 1000 off-road races. The route heads west, then north out of the town along the coast and beaches. It is paved all the way, although you may find road edges crumbling away in the heat. Take care: some of these craters are marked; others are not.

The road rises and falls over headlands and outcrops as it sweeps through a dry landscape of rocks and sand, with the sparkling blue sea on your right and the islands of Espirito Santo and Partida on the horizon. Expect to find empty beaches and few signs of human habitation. You will discover that the road becomes narrower and sandier the farther north you go. By the time you arrive at the tiny beach settlement of San Evaristo, you will almost certainly be whipping up a cloud of dust in your wake. **SH**

❶ The Gulf of California coastline near San Evaristo, with the Isla San José in the right of the photograph.

La Rumorosa
Baja California, Mexico

Start Mexicali
End Mexicali
Distance 196km (122 miles)
Type Adventure
Map goo.gl/CbsjMz

If you believed all the articles written in the press about La Rumorosa, you would never come here. 'Drive into it and never return', says one. 'A fright, a myth, a graveyard', says another. The route is known as the Ghost Highway, where the spirits of those killed on it haunt the drivers of today, and also as the enigmatic Whispering Woman. Separate hype from reality, though, and what is left? You have a road with some serious gradients, steep drop-offs and always the wind – *las colas del diablo* (the devil's tails) – which howls its way through the rusted red cliffs of the Sierra de Juárez.

Originally, there was only one treacherous two-way road, but in the face of a mounting death toll, a second was added, running roughly parallel, to provide two two-lane roads, one running uphill and the other heading down. Depending on which direction you choose to drive the route, you will gain or lose 1,220m (4,000ft) on the precipitous Cantú Grade, with its hazy views over the Colorado Desert, and up to 20°C (69°F).

Once genuinely dangerous, La Rumorosa has been tamed somewhat, but it is no less thrilling. Drive it, and you will always smile when you hear the words of the celebrated Baja poet Jorge Ortega, who described these landscapes as 'places where the wind converses with man in the silent language of dust and light'. **BDS**

❶ This lonely road trip is always a challenge, but even more so when the fierce winds blow in bad weather.

Mexico Federal Highway 1
Baja California, Mexico

Start Tijuana
End Cabo San Lucas
Distance 1,685km (1,047 miles)
Type Adventure
Map goo.gl/QUWjkW

Mexico's Federal Highway 1 on the sun-drenched Baja California Peninsula is not blessed with an abundance of road signs, and what few guardrails there are seem to have been installed as an afterthought. The road is in a constant state of repair, full of blind corners and devoid of hard shoulders. Roadside shrines are all too common. And worst of all, there are the topes: speed bumps placed nowhere in particular in a forlorn effort to slow down traffic on a road that seems to have been built for speed.

Survive all this, as you surely will, and this road will take you deep into the idealized Old Mexico of your dreams. From Tijuana in the north to the marlin-filled waters of Cabo San Lucas – once home to Ernest Hemingway and John Steinbeck, and the southernmost point of the world's second-longest peninsula – this road trip never ceases to inspire its visitors. Mexico's Federal Highway 1 kisses both sides of Baja California – east along the Sea of Cortez and west down the Pacific – and crosses the desolate Sierra de la Asamblea with its tortuous mountain roads.

Get out of your car as often as you can to admire the desert landscapes that surround you. This road is not designed to encourage spontaneous exits, so make an effort to pull over and admire the sights of this ethereal, untamed peninsula. **BDS**

El Espinazo del Diablo
Sinaloa/Durango, Mexico

Start Mazatlán, Sinaloa
End Victoria de Durango, Durango
Distance 319km (198 miles)
Type Adventure
Map goo.gl/Gv4Plh

El Espinazo del Diablo (the Devil's Backbone) is a suitably vivid name for a mountain pass that stands between the Pacific coast and Victoria de Durango, or City of Durango, the state capital of Durango. The whole drive extends for about 319km (198 miles), although the Devil's Backbone stretch of it lasts – thankfully for nervous drivers – only about 10km (6.2 miles). You can also avoid it completely if you stay on Highway 400, which tunnels through the mountains, rather than Highway 40, which goes up and around them. Either way you will be rewarded with wonderful views of the dramatic and lushly green mountains.

The first stretch of the drive is flat and unexciting, and you will wonder what the fuss is about as the mountains are merely a speck on the horizon. But you soon leave the industrial towns behind and drive through verdant farmland as the road rises towards the mountains. When you start getting into the mountains, you will recognize the challenge that lies ahead. Around you are the Sierra Madre Occidental mountains, and the road clings to their slopes, sometimes with sheer cliffs on one side and nerve-racking drops on the other. The highway zigzags around numerous hairpin bends and crosses deep ravines. The road is well maintained and reasonably safe, if you take it carefully: you just have to hope that other drivers do the same. **MG**

Carretera a Urique
Chihuahua, Mexico

Start Cerocahui
End Urique
Distance 38km (23.6 miles)
Type Adventure
Map goo.gl/YgrdSN

The charming village of Urique is an increasingly popular destination with a growing band of adventurous travellers, and it has been described as one of the most welcoming places in northern Mexico. This old mining town sits in a deep valley and is used as a base for keen hikers; it even has its own ultramarathon. The only problem with Urique is getting there.

The road to the village takes you down the side of a vast canyon, the Barranca de Urique, more than 1.9km (1 mile) deep. Its surface is unfinished, so you have the joy of loose gravel and dirt beneath your wheels, and there are more than 100 tight turns to negotiate. Many of these are either blind corners or switchbacks – some of the latter are blind. If you are wondering whether there are any safety barriers, well there aren't any. Only the nervous need barriers and nervous drivers do not use the road to Urique. In other words there is nothing between you and a long drop from the edge, apart from some frantic praying and your own driving skill. Furthermore, there are precious few passing points, but this does not deter truck and bus drivers from taking the route, possibly because they know that car drivers will have to back up out of their way.

As this a mountain area, weather conditions can vary considerably, so it is a good idea to check the forecast before you set off. **JI**

❶ Towering cliffs covered with vegetation line the dirt track down to the village at the bottom of the canyon.

Autopista Durango–Mazatlán
Durango/Sinaloa, Mexico

Start Durango, Durango
End Mazatlán, Sinaloa
Distance 248km (154 miles)
Type Scenic
Map goo.gl/PGKaOX

El Espinazo del Diablo (the Devil's Backbone) – a section of the old main road between Durango and the Pacific coast at Mazatlán – is famous for its high altitudes, twisting corners and tight curves. As its traffic increased, the road became increasingly impractical, and so a replacement was built: Highway 40, opened to traffic in 2013, is nothing less than a marvel of engineering.

Starting in inland Durango, 1,880m (6,168ft) above sea level, the new construction bumps across the western Sierra Madre, rising in places to nearly 2,745m (9,000ft). During the winter, there is always a danger of ice, and the road can be closed at any time due to snow. Along its length, it goes through 61 tunnels, of which the Túnel el Sinaloense is the longest at 2.7km (1.7 miles). More impressive are the 115 bridges, most notably the Puente Baluarte. This beautiful construction crosses a deep river valley 403m (1,322ft) below it and is the highest cable-stayed bridge in the world, the third-highest bridge in the world and the highest bridge in the Americas. Its majestic 1,124-m- (3,687-ft) long span should be taken slowly so that you can best enjoy the commanding views.

After a roller-coaster ride, the road eventually drops to the Pacific Ocean coast at Mazatlán, whose name in the Aztec Nahuatl language rather wonderfully means 'place of deer'. **SA**

❶ Construction of the Puente Baluarte began in 2008; at the end of 2013 it was opened to traffic.

Ruta Tepehuana
Durango/Nayarit, Mexico

Start Victoria de Durango, Durango
End San Juan Peyotán, Nayarit
Distance 288km (179 miles)
Type Adventure
Map goo.gl/thDMZu

Wherever you have high elevations, you can be guaranteed a spectacular driving route, particularly when you are passing through the heart of Mexico's mighty Sierra Madre mountains. Ruta Tepehuana can be a very lonely drive at times, but its canyon drop-offs of up to 2km (1.2 miles) are as impressive as anything you will find north of the border. Add to that an impressive variety of biomes, including painted and cactus deserts, and forests of pine and oak, and suddenly you know that you are experiencing one of Mexico's truly great drives.

Ruta Tepehuana, also known as Camino a Huazamota, is a spectacular road that continues to build an enviable reputation among automotive adventurers. It is littered with switchbacks and has a fearsome reputation for high winds; rarely will your speedometer rise above 64 kph (40 mph). Don't drive it at night if you can avoid it, because many sections, particularly along the canyons, do not have guardrails, and mobile-phone reception is minimal. Fog is another frequent hazard, and the area is also known for its drug-trafficking activities. Ascents and descents are measured in the hundreds of feet and can be seriously tough on brakes. Road markings are occasionally absent, too, which means that you need to be careful in the face of oncoming traffic. Although potholes are numerous, for the most part, the surface is good. **BDS**

❶ As soon as they leave Durango, travellers encounter scenery like this in the Sierra Madre mountains.

Michoacán Coastal Road
Michoacán, Mexico

Start Playa Arenas Blancas
End Solera de Agua
Distance 84km (52 miles)
Type Scenic
Map goo.gl/xeEin9

Here is a chance to explore the fabulous Pacific coastline of the state of Michoacán in southwest Mexico. Federal Highway 200 runs down the country's sunny west coast from Nayarit to the Guatemala border for around 2,000km (1,250 miles).

This road trip follows an 83-km- (50-mile) long section, away from the cities and along a quiet stretch of shore. It is as undeveloped and wild as any coast in Mexico, but there is a good, smooth, wide tarmac surface. You will follow the ocean on one side and the green hills and thick forests on the other. Between lush verges of coconut palms, mango trees and banana plantations, there are glimpses of long, empty beaches. On the far side of the headlands are tempting little restaurants and bars overlooking the waves. Some of these undiscovered beaches are pounded by huge ocean breakers; others are sheltered sand alongside a pretty river mouth. A few have a scattering of shacks and traders; most are empty.

Start at the gorgeous sandy cove of Playa Arenas Blancas, with its rocky islands and a few houses set among the lush vegetation behind the beach. Head east with the sea on your right. You can't get lost. Eventually you reach the leafy village of Solera de Agua. From there you could drive on to the busy port of Lázaro Cárdenas or head inland to the elegant city of Uruapan. **SH**

La Carrera Panamericana
Chiapas to Chihuahua, Mexico

Start Tuxtla Gutiérrez, Chiapas
End Ciudad Juárez, Chihuahua
Distance 3,219km (2,000 miles)
Type Culture
Map goo.gl/2TV1ot

Mexico's La Carrera Panamericana may have only been staged five times, but it is listed in motorsport annals as one of the greatest road races. It was also one of the deadliest; between 1950 and 1954, it amassed 27 driver and spectator fatalities.

The cross-country dash from the border with Guatemala to the US border at Ciudad Juárez was first hosted to celebrate the completion of Mexico's portion of the Pan-American Highway. The route incorporated everything from 3,048-m (10,000-ft) mountain ascents to flat-out drag races across desert plains; Mexico's newest road cut through tropical forests, passed ancient Mayan ruins and linked some of Mexico's largest inland settlements. During its heyday, 65 aircraft and nearly 45,000 marshals, medics, and soldiers supported the 100 or so competing cars. In 1952 a Mercedes-Benz works team set a course record of 18 hours 51minutes at an incredible average speed of 166 kph (103 mph).

A leisurely modern-day road trip is best done with plenty of time allowed for breaks, detours and sightseeing. For a motorsport enthusiast, there is no better way to explore the Mexican hinterlands than driving point to point via Puebla, León, Durango and Chihuahua between the Sierra Madre mountain ranges. **DIS**

➲ A crash at La Carrera Panamericana in the 1950s.

Carretera a Punta Allen
Quintana Roo, Mexico

Start Tulum
End Punta Allen
Distance 54km (33.5 miles)
Type Scenic
Map goo.gl/QjtFn1

Without a boat, the only way to reach the village of Punta Allen is down this rough track. The itinerary proposed here is a rugged and demanding driving adventure, but the reward for completing it is the laid-back, end-of-the-line atmosphere of the sleepy fishing village at journey's end, on the point of a long, sandy peninsula.

Mexico's southern Yucatán region juts out into the Caribbean Sea. Tulum, on the east coast facing the Cayman Islands, is a popular resort, with fabulous beaches and Mayan remains. Head south along the shore beyond the tourist buses and souvenir shops, however, and you'll discover a very different atmosphere. Route 15 is an unpaved track leading into the sparsely populated Sian Ka'an Biosphere, a vast UNESCO World Heritage Site full of Mayan archaeological relics and important protected environments, including a section of coral reef, tropical forests and mangroves. You may spot some of the amazing wildlife along this route, including tapirs, flamingoes, crocodiles, howler monkeys and, if you are extremely lucky, jaguars.

The beaches, lagoons and jungle views are spectacular, but take care with the journey – there are axle-breaking potholes and ruts, areas of sand to sink into and, after rain, slippery muddy sections. If it's dry, you can make it in a rental car; if it's wet, using a 4x4 would be best. **SH**

❶ The *castillo* at the ancient fortress city of Tulum was built overlooking the waters of the Caribbean.

Cozumel Island Loop
Cozumel, Mexico

Start San Miguel
End San Miguel
Distance 66km (41 miles)
Type Scenic
Map goo.gl/y1WOX1

Cozumel lies approximately 10 miles (16 km) off the east coast of the Yucatán Peninsula. At 46km (29 miles) long and averaging 14km (9 miles) in width, it is Mexico's largest Caribbean island. It gets its name from the Mayan *ah cuzamil peten*, which means 'island of swallows'. The land, formed from limestone and almost totally flat – the highest point is only 15m (49ft) above sea level – and is covered by mangrove forests. Deep cenotes (sinkholes), formed by water eroding the soft limestone, punctuate the ground; only qualified divers are allowed to enter them.

The best way to explore this fascinating island is by rental car along the loop road that sweeps around the southern half of the island though the Punta Sur national park. From the island's main town of San Miguel, you can go around in either direction; the remote east coast features some fabulously sandy beaches where you will want to enjoy the sun and drink at the beach bar; the west coast is lined with reefs teeming with fish and corals. Along the route, you are likely to see some exotic wildlife, including large orange iguanas and saltwater crocodiles. If you are on the island at the end of April, take a detour off the western side of the loop to visit the inland town of El Cedral, complete with Mayan ruins, where the annual festival includes rodeos, traditional music and feasting. **SA**

❶ One of the highlights of this trip is the Mayan ruins at San Gervasio.

Carretera Central Pinar del Río to Guatánamo, Cuba

Start La Fe, Pinar del Río
End Baracoa, Guatánamo
Distance 1,443km (897 miles)
Type Adventure
Map goo.gl/pN3hxK

Initiated at the request of US shipping magnate Henry J. Kaiser in 1927, Carretera Central opened in 1931 and stretches the length of the nation. It was originally designed to be 6m (20ft) wide and surfaced with stone and bituminous cement. Armies of Cuban labourers reshaped the local geography to create a flowing highway with minimal gradients and curvature, requiring deep cuts through mountains and heavy fill over porous depressions. They reinforced crossings for the nation's oxcarts and built hundreds of bridges. Finished with typical Cuban efficiency, a year ahead of schedule, it was a triumph of civil engineering. In the 1940s Americans put their cars on ferries from Key West and Miami just to come and drive it.

Over time many sections have been bypassed by modern highways, but the road continues to connect most of the island's major cities. Largely an inland road, it brushes by the coast in only three places and remains a vital link to more than 16,000km (10,000 miles) of the Cuban road network.

Cuba, of course, is famed for its old US cars, survivors from the 1940s and 1950s. To do this road trip in style, rent your own classic Ford Thunderbird, Chevy Bel Air or similar from one of the rental companies based in Havana. **BDS**

❍ The road provides an outlet to rural parts of Cuba.

Havana Loops
Havana, Cuba

Start Havana
End Havana
Distance 1,551km (964 miles)
Type Adventure
Info goo.gl/PpJZLb

At one time, planning a road trip around the Caribbean island of Cuba was a bit of a major administrative undertaking. Public transport was decrepit and filthy, and the paperwork required to rent a car was more convoluted than a multinational trade and armaments agreement. Thankfully, things are finally changing.

Due to the length of this road trip, it is advisable to rent a modern four-wheel drive vehicle; this Caribbean adventure heads out of Havana on a large figure-of-eight circuit. Highway 1 brings you to your first port of call, Playa Rancho Luna, a wonderful little-known beach of soft white sand, before swinging north to the Jardines del Rey island chain, home to a colony of pink flamingos, beautiful lagoons and coral reefs. The charming 16th-century city of Camagüey is the turnaround point. Its labyrinth of narrow, winding alleys and dead ends was thought to be a way of entrapping pirate raiders and slaying them from above. The return loop passes the tobacco town of Trinidad before cruising the long northern coast back to the capital.

Hitchhiking is a way of life for many rural folk; if you speak a little Spanish, then picking up a passenger can be a great way to discover more about the real Cuba. If you are a biker, there are tour companies that will rent you a motorcycle and set up a very similar travel itinerary to this trip. **DIS**

Grand Bahama Jeep Safari Grand Bahama Island, Bahamas

Start Freeport   End Freeport   Distance 70km (43.5 miles)
Type Adventure   Map goo.gl/aspKHq

Some Bahamian island tours are a gentle, albeit scenic, saunter between golden beaches along the Atlantic coastline. Not so here; this popular safari route sets forth on an expedition deep into the thickly vegetated interior, far off the beaten track. To get the most out of this tour, most people rent experienced local guides and a Jeep Wrangler, and head out in convoy in search of the island's most historic and idyllic beauty spots. Each jeep is equipped with CB radio to avoid any navigational mishaps and so guides can point out sights of interest en route.

It is steady going on the rutted forest trails, but it is a great slow-paced way to savour the island's forests, dominated by Bahamian pine trees and home to rock iguanas, West Indian woodpeckers, the Bahama yellowthroat and the buffy flower bat. It may only be a short excursion, but there is no better way to explore the island's hidden gems, away from the crowded beach resorts.

Emerging from the trees, the route heads over Casuarina Bridge, which crosses the Grand Lucayan Waterway: the stretch of water that divides the island into two. From there, head down to the private Junkanoo Beach Club, before visiting the tropical and idyllic Garden of the Groves. **TW**

❶ Mangrove wetland in Lucayan National Park.

Discover Nassau New Providence, Bahamas

Start Montagu Beach, Nassau   **End** Albany, Nassau   **Distance** 42km (26 miles)
Type Culture   **Map** goo.gl/ItQfhq

This drive along the northern and western coasts of New Providence island passes some of the finest beaches and most expensive real estate in the world. Plenty of bus tours follow a similar itinerary, but for those who prefer independent travel, start your road trip at Montagu Beach, overlooked by a fort built in 1741 by the British. From there, drive west through downtown Nassau, past Cable Beach, to Old Fort Bay via a duck pond that is also a regular hangout for turtles.

Gambier is famous in the history of rock music as the site of Compass Point Studios, founded in 1977 by Chris Blackwell of Island Records. Chief among the memorable albums recorded here was *Back in Black* (1980) by AC/DC. The place closed in the 1990s but remains a nostalgic landmark.

Out on the westernmost tip of the island is the setting for a love scene in *Thunderball* (1965), one of several locations in the Bahamas used in the James Bond movie franchise. Also nearby in Clifton Bay is Jaws Beach, named for its appearance in *Jaws: The Revenge* (1987), the fourth and final shark shocker. At journey's end, Albany House is a pink beachfront manor house that played the home of the villain in the 2006 remake of *Casino Royale*, Daniel Craig's first outing as Bond. **JP**

❶ A coral reef in the turquoise waters of Nassau.

Pirate Route
Surrey and more, Jamaica

Start Port Royal, Kingston
End Port Royal, Kingston
Distance 674km (419 miles)
Type Culture
Map goo.gl/fWV3Fm

Jamaica is renowned today for athletes, rum and reggae, as well as for its beautiful beaches. But for much of its history it was also famous for its pirates. Lying astride the main shipping route used by the Spanish to take home gold from their American empire during the 16th and 17th centuries, the island provided a perfect base from which pirates could plunder the treasure ships. There are no longer any pirates in these waters, but the memories of them linger around the coastline, as this circular tour of the island makes clear.

From Port Royal on the south coast, you start in the port to which Captain Henry Morgan returned in 1668 after looting the Spanish treasure stronghold on Portobelo in Panama. Head west to Spanish Town, the island's former capital, where John 'Calico Jack' Rackham was tried for piracy. From there, continue farther westward and then north via Bloody Bay to Montego Bay, where a fort on Round Hill guarded the land from marauding buccaneers. On the way back along the north coast, you pass the Firefly estate that belonged to 20-century British playwright Sir Noël Coward. His composing room looks out over a gun-slit pirate cabin that once sheltered Morgan. The last scenic leg of the route, past sugarcane fields and around the eastern coast, brings you back to Port Royal, once hailed as the 'wickedest city in Christendom'. **SA**

➊ Sculpture of Sir Noël Coward in the grounds of Firefly.
➋ Rodney's Monument Memorial in Spanish Town.

Samaná Highway National District to Samaná, Dominican Republic

Start Santo Domingo, National District End Las Terrenas, Samaná Distance 158km (98 miles)
Type Scenic Map goo.gl/3P7JRm

This smooth road is the safest and most scenic way to travel from Santo Domingo – the capital of the Dominican Republic, and the main point of entry into the country – to the booming tourist hubs of Samaná Province. Passing azure-blue ocean and lush tropical jungle, this blissful drive along the D-7 is interrupted only by toll booths.

Opened on 1 June 2009, at a cost of $150 million, the Samaná Highway crosses 12 bridges and links the cities of Monte Plata and Arenoso, Los Haitises National Park and – at the far eastern tip, via Boulevard Turístico del Atlántico (Route 133) – the Atlantic coast at Las Terrenas. Once a British slavers' port, Las Terrenas became a busy fishing village before transforming itself into a popular tourist destination, no doubt helped by this highway, which has reduced travelling time from the airport from four and a half arduous hours along the treacherous D-1 and mountainous backroads to just two thoroughly pleasant ones.

Near Las Terrenas, Playa Bonita is a popular surfing beach with a wide range of good-quality hotels and restaurants along its seafront. If you want a little more solitude, then drive a bit farther out of town towards the beautiful, palm-fringed sands of Playa Moron. **DIS**

❶ A stunning waterfall in El Limón.

Panoramic Route Mayagüez to Maunabo, Puerto Rico

Start Mayagüez, Mayagüez   End Maunabo, Maunabo   Distance 241km (150 miles)
Type Scenic   Map goo.gl/mmFbt3

The lush, tropical Caribbean island of Puerto Rico is only 180km (110 miles) long and 65km (40 miles) wide. The proposed itinerary – officially La Ruta Panorámica Luis Muñoz Marin, after Puerto Rico's first elected governor – was developed in the 1970s as an early attempt to attract US tourists. It worked. The route winds through the peaks, gorges and foothills of the central range of mountains on more than 40 different local roads. It was a multimillion-dollar project that involved building scores of viewing points and rest stops.

Today it is one of the foremost tourist attractions in Puerto Rico and is regarded as one of the best driving routes in the whole of the Caribbean. You will travel from one palm-fringed coast to the other, through a backwoods of humid rainforest, sleepy hillside villages, old plantations and high mountain landscapes reaching an altitude of 1,200m (4,000ft). Look out along the way for exotic wildflowers, banana trees and swimming lakes. The travel is slow, the road undulating and twisty, and you can expect sudden torrential downpours that make driving tricky.

Locals may sometimes pass you at ridiculous speeds, but most sensible visitors will struggle to get into top gear anywhere along the route. **SH**

❶ The historic fire station at Ponce.

Discover Bermuda Loop Pembroke and more, Bermuda

Start Hamilton, Pembroke   End Hamilton   Distance 93km (57.8 miles)
Type Culture   Map goo.gl/8ebQ6O

The name Bermuda implies a single island but, in fact, this British Atlantic territory contains 181 islands, of which eight are populated. The islands were formed from the high points of the rim of what was once a massive underwater volcano, now sunken beneath the waves.

Trips around the island usually start in Hamilton on Main Island. It might be the island's capital, and its main financial centre and port, but it boasts a population just over a thousand, all of whom are probably on first-name terms. From Hamilton, head south and west along the long, curving peninsula that wraps itself around the Great Sound. Horseshoe Bay is ridiculously photogenic, while Gibb's Hill Lighthouse is well worth a visit to see the views from the hill. Following the curve, you cross over Somerset Bridge, the smallest drawbridge in the world, before reaching the end of the peninsula and the historic Royal Naval Dockyard. From here, you need to retrace your steps to the northeast of the island and the UNESCO World Heritage Site that is St George's, the island's former capital, established in 1616 and the oldest continuously inhabited English town in the New World. A gentle drive back along the north shore, and a hop across the island, brings you back to Hamilton. **SA**

❶ View of Tucker's Town Bay in St George's.

Fig Tree Drive St Paul to St Mary, Antigua and Barbuda

Start Jonas Road, Swetes, St Paul   **End** Old Road, St Mary   **Distance** 8km (5 miles)
Type Scenic   **Map** goo.gl/AVAumg

With a circumference of only 87km (54 miles), Antigua is a small island, so no matter where you stay it is easy to get to Jonas Road in the flat, central farmland. From there, Fig Tree Drive winds up through sleepy villages and rainforest canopies over the volcanic mountains of the southwest corner. The road can be muddy and rutted after rain, so try not to be too distracted by the views of Falmouth Harbour and the island's highest point, 402-m- (1,319-ft) high Mount Obama (formerly Boggy Peak, but renamed in 2009 in honour of the forty-fourth president of the United States).

Expect to get up close to big old mango trees and large flapping leaves of bananas, which are called 'figs' on Antigua – hence the road name. Pass tall swaying palms and lush roadside verges and remember to check out some of the colourful roadside stalls that sell fresh local ginger, guavas, pineapples and passion fruit.

After the crest of Fig Tree Hill, the road winds down to meet the coast at Old Road, and if you have now caught the mood for Antiguan exploration, you can continue along the coast to Jolly Harbour, passing secluded luxury resorts and quiet beaches. After completing the proposed route, you may loop back through Jennings to where you started. **SH**

❶ Fig Tree Studio Art Gallery.

Route de la Traversée Basse-Terre, Guadeloupe

Start Pointe-Noire   **End** Petit-Bourg   **Distance** 41km (25.5 miles)
Type Scenic   **Map** goo.gl/95oEdb

The main island of Guadeloupe – a French overseas territory in the Lesser Antilles chain in the Caribbean Sea – is divided in two by the Salée River which, in spite of its name, is a narrow sea channel. To the east of the passage is Grande-Terre (Big Land), and to the west Basse-Terre (Low Land). The latter is also misleadingly named because it contains the island's highest point, the Soufrière volcano, 1,467m (4,813ft) above sea level.

Basse-Terre is densely forested throughout, with verdant expanses of chestnut, mahogany, fig trees, ferns and philodendrons. A good way to explore this region is on the Route de la Traversée, which extends east to west across the island.

The main N-2 road from Pointe-Noire heads south before the Route de la Traversée splits off through tropical rainforest at the northern end of Guadeloupe National Park. It is an exhilarating and tortuous route, but local drivers show little respect for speed limits. And be aware also that as the road passes through the forest, its well-maintained surface often becomes wet and very slippery. At its eastern end, this scenic road drops down through Barbotteau before joining the main N-1, where a right turn takes you into Petit-Bourg on the island's east coast. **SA**

❶ A view from Route de la Traversée.

Dr Nicholas Liverpool Highway St George, Dominica

Start Roseau   **End** Morne Trois Pitons National Park   **Distance** 97km (60 miles)
Type Adventure   **Map** goo.gl/RByOa3

The Caribbean island of Dominica has some of the world's best-preserved tropical rain forest, which has been designated as a World Heritage Site for its unique flora and fauna. If rainforest is nature's wonderland, then this is a road trip through a land of enchantment. Dominica is geologically very much the new kid on the block. It is mountainous, still geothermally active, and has hot springs and nine active volcanoes (although thankfully no eruptions for more than 300 years).

This drive along the newly refurbished former Pond Case Road, now renamed (after a recent president) Dr Nicholas Liverpool Highway, starts at the island's main airport, then cuts diagonally through the whole island and across the hilly central section between the Northern and Central Forest Reserves. The road is good, but the going is wet, this place gets a lot of precipitation.

At the end of the road, the laid-back capital, Roseau, retains its historic charm, with a mix of 18th-century Creole and 19th-century colonial French architecture. The route continues into Morne Trois Pitons National Park, where you can take a short hike to boiling mud ponds and geysers and also swim right up to a waterfall at the shimmering green Emerald Pool. **DK**

❶ The Boiling Lake in Morne Trois Pitons National Park.

Route de la Trace
Martinique, French West Indies

Start Fort-de-France
End Le Morne-Rouge
Distance 26km (16.1 miles)
Type Culture
Map goo.gl/ye4GgY

Most people will visit the French Caribbean island of Martinique for its glorious beaches, thus missing the equally glorious countryside of the interior. The best way to avoid this lapse of judgment is by heading up the twisting Route de la Trace from the capital, Fort-de-France, to Le Morne-Rouge in the north of the island.

The road, technically the N-3, follows a route first cut by the Jesuits, who arrived in 1640 on Martinique. Islanders allege that its twists and turns are due to the Jesuits' fondness for rum. A few minutes up the road is the village of Balata, which features a scaled-down replica of the Sacré-Coeur in Paris, likewise standing on an impressive hill. A little farther on is Jardin de Balata, a mature botanical garden in the rainforest. From here, the road continues to climb, reaching a height of 600m (1,968ft) before dropping down to La Revière de l'Alma, where a river runs through a ridiculously verdant gorge. Continuing north, the road sweeps through banana plantations and nurseries of flowers before reaching Le Morne-Rouge, at 450m (1,476ft) the highest town on the island.

For those with an adventurous spirit, continue the trip on the D-39 road, which leads up to the slopes of the volcanic Mount Pelée, from where there is an arduous two-hour slog up the south face to the summit. **SA**

❶ Built between 1924 and 1925, the Sacré-Coeur de Balata is set high in the hills.

Castries to Marigot Bay and Sulphur Springs
Castries to Soufrière, St Lucia

Start Castries, Castries
End Sulphur Springs, Soufrière
Distance 50km (31 miles)
Type Adventure
Map goo.gl/tcSBcL

The West Indian island of St Lucia has had a checkered history ever since France signed a treaty in 1660 with the native Caribs. England seized the island from 1663 to 1667, and from then on the two nations vied for control, each ruling the island seven times until 1814, when the British finally grabbed the prize. As a result, the island boasts a rich and mixed cultural heritage.

Any road trip on St Lucia must start at Castries, the island's capital, founded by the French in 1650 as Carénage ('safe anchorage') and then renamed Castries after the French marquis who in 1756 commanded the island. From here, you can rent a car; the best option is a small jeep because you will appreciate this type of vehicle when you hit the backroads. From Castries, it is a short but beautiful drive south down the west coast and past the cruise ship terminal to Marigot Bay, which was described by US writer James A. Michener as 'the most beautiful bay in the Caribbean'.

Tempting bars and restaurants line its shores, making the bay an idyllic destination to take a break. However, the best bit of the adventure is yet to start. The real reason for this road trip is the thrilling section of viciously winding roads heading south past Canaries to Sulphur Springs, southeast of Soufrière. You did tick the 'collision damage waiver' box, didn't you? **SA**

❶ Locals and tourists flock to Castries Market for fruits, vegetables and handicrafts.

Leeward Highway
St Vincent and the Grenadines

Start Kingstown, St. George
End Richmond Beach, St. David
Distance 40km (24.8 miles)
Type Scenic
Map goo.gl/OTDKYO

The strong winds that buffet the West Indian island of St Vincent blow in from the Atlantic and hit its rugged east coast. However, the west coast is the sheltered side, a beautiful stretch of rocky cliffs, small pretty bays and sandy beaches. The best way to explore this enchanting coastline is along the scenic Leeward Highway, starting in the nation's capital, Kingstown, a bustling agricultural and tourist centre founded in 1722 by the French. In around 1793, British navigator William Bligh, commander of HMS *Bounty* before its famous mutiny, brought some seeds of the breadfruit tree from Tahiti to plant here.

From Kingstown, the tarmac road heads north, climbing slowly into the foothills past numerous villages, black-sand beaches and coconut plantations. Carib Rock features a carved face dating back to 600, while a Carib stone altar and more rock carvings can be seen at Barrouallie. After 35km (22 miles) the road gently winds down, through lush, green forests, to the black sands of Richmond Beach. The warm sea will beckon swimmers, but cast your eyes upwards to La Soufrière; at 1,234m (4,049ft) high, the island's highest peak and still an active volcano. Regular tours depart from the beach for the Falls of Baleine, a picturesque 18-m- (59-ft) high waterfall on the northwestern tip of the island, accessible only by boat. **SA**

North Coast Road
St George, Trinidad and Tobago

Start Port of Spain
End Maracas Beach, Maracas Bay Village
Distance 14km (8.7 miles)
Type Scenic
Info goo.gl/crW4Vg

In 1940 the United States obtained two naval bases on Trinidad from the West Indian island's British rulers in return for providing destroyers to a nation fighting for survival in World War II. In compensation for seizing the entire peninsula of Chaguaramas, in the northwest of the island (to build one of the bases, thus depriving its residents of sea bathing), the Americans built a new road up from the nation's capital, Port of Spain.

The road twists and turns along 300-m- (984-ft) high cliffs and through tunnels of rainforest, but it remains to this day one of the island's smoothest thoroughfares, and is sometimes known as the American Road, in honour of its constructors. The views from the highway are extensive and breathtaking – to Port of Spain and then across the Maraval Valley to the tiny spice centre of Paramin, and the dramatic sweep of the Caribbean far below. The mineral springs that pour across the road provide chilled water to drink, but to refresh yourself properly, stop to sample the roadside treats of coconut fudge, spicy tamarind balls and *kurma* (fried dough coated in ginger) sold by local street vendors. You'll then be in the mood for a swim at the beautiful Maracas Beach, safely sheltered at the head of a deep bay. **SA**

➲ The coast of Trinidad at sunset.

Hummingbird Highway
Cayo/Stann Creek, Belize

Start Belmopan, Cayo
End Dangriga, Stann Creek
Distance 87km (54 miles)
Type Scenic
Map goo.gl/IiF8XR

With a population of only 16,000, Belmopan is the smallest national capital in the Americas. It stands near the Belize River among rainforest and jungle in the foothills of the mountains. Roads in Belize are often pretty rough, but the main route from Belmopan to the coast is smoothly paved along its length, and thankfully draws the heavy traffic away from this sublime, scenic highway heading southeast. This well-known route, winding to the coastal town of Dangriga, has been dubbed the Hummingbird Highway, and you should see plenty of the tiny colourful hovering birds along the way.

Hummingbird Highway is one of the few roads through the mountains and jungle here; Belize maps have large blank spaces often labelled 'Unknown', and tracks are noted as 'Seasonal'. Yet this route is an amiable cruise through valleys between lush mountains. Much of the land alongside the road is taken up by fruit farms, and wildlife from the jungle beyond the orchards often wanders across the highway with no regard for motor vehicles. The most prized sightings are jaguars. These rare, solitary big cats are concentrated in an area to the south of the highway. Other natural highlights include marching columns of cutter ants, toucans in the treetops and grazing tapirs. **SH**

◓ The idyllic coastline at Dangriga.

Mayan Ruins Tour
La Libertad/Santa Ana, El Salvador

Start Joya de Ceren, La Libertad
End Santa Ana Volcano, Santa Ana
Distance 111km (69 miles)
Type Scenic
Map goo.gl/lZYKRc

The Maya of Central America developed one of the world's great civilizations. Starting in around 750, they built a series of vast stone cities replete with monumental temples and splendid palaces.

The modern remnants of Mayan constructions lie partly hidden in the jungles of El Salvador and some neighbouring countries. A good place to start any tour of them is at Joya de Ceren, in the centre of El Salvador. This Mayan village was buried by a volcanic eruption some 1,400 years ago and unearthed in 1976 – it's El Salvador's Pompeii. Its remarkable preservation under the ash gives a wonderful insight into what life was like as a Maya. Close by are the ruins of San Andrés, although many of its pyramid temples are still covered in thick jungle growth.

From there, drive west across the country to the Tazumal ruins at Chalchuapa, with all its pyramid temples facing west. The ruins also include a court on which the Maya played an early version of modern handball.

If you want to break away from this well-trodden tourist route and explore the wild and dynamic landscape, then head south from El Congo on the RN 10N around Lago de Coatepeque – a crater lake that was a sacred site of the ancient Maya – up the switchbacks that climb the lower slopes of the revered Santa Ana Volcano. **SA**

Discover Nicaragua
León to Granada, Nicaragua

Start León, León
End Granada, Granada
Distance 134km (83 miles)
Type Culture
Map goo.gl/qOHiHP

Nicaragua is not on many tourists' radars, but the historic towns of León and Granada are two good reasons why it should be. Both are 16th-century Spanish colonial towns packed with history and fine architecture, the road in between offering a snapshot of Nicaragua past and present. León, the second-largest city after the capital, Managua, is remarkable for being the home of 17 different Roman Catholic orders, each with its own churches. Many of these are in the Baroque style, as is the main cathedral. The city was once the capital of Nicaragua, although the more conservative governments of the 19th century preferred Granada. In 1858 as a compromise, Managua, halfway between the two, became the capital.

The road out of León takes you along the south shore of Lake Xolotlán (Lake Managua) and around the outskirts of Managua to the active Masaya volcano, situated in Nicaragua's first national park. From here you head to Granada on the west shore of the Lake Nicaragua. Granada was founded in 1524 by the conquistador Francisco Hernández de Córdoba and is the oldest city in the Americas. Today, the city is renowned for its fine dining, with all the food locally sourced – another good reason to set your radar towards Nicaragua. **SA**

➲ **Masaya volcano constantly emits sulphur dioxide.**

Discover Costa Rica
Puntarenas/San José, Costa Rica

Start Malpais, Puntarenas
End San Isidro del General, San José
Distance 310km (192 miles)
Type Adventure
Map goo.gl/LkayBQ

This trip passes alongside some of the most beautiful and unspoiled surfing beaches on the whole American Pacific coast, but they are not the only attraction among the route's abundant charms. The starting point, Malpais, is a fishing village whose distance from the beaten track has attracted Western superstars in search of privacy. Movie actor Mel Gibson and model Gisele Bündchen are among the rich and famous who have purpose-built mansions here overlooking the ocean. At Naranjo the road runs out, and there is a car ferry across the calm and shallow Gulf of Nicoya. The hour-long sea crossing passes close to several small islands inhabited only by birds.

After landing at Caldera, the port of Puntarenas, the road runs southwards along shores and cliff tops through Jaco, a resort named after the US oil tycoon who founded it, and Quepos, the regional nightlife centre. At Dominical, the itinerary leads inland into the hills, where there are many great views and one essential stop at Nauyaca Waterfalls, a two-tiered cascade in a forested setting.

The road trip ends at San Isidro del General, a regional transportation hub on the Pan-American Highway. Few travellers linger here, so in an effort to attract them the local tourist board promotes the town as the birthplace of the most beautiful people in Costa Rica. **JP**

Cerro de la Muerte
San José/Cartago, Costa Rica

Start Cañón, San José
End Cerro de la Muerte, Cartago
Distance 32km (19.9 miles)
Type Adventure
Map goo.gl/tVkJsG

This side excursion off the Pan-American Highway is not for the fainthearted traveller. Anyone who has journeyed this far through Central America will already realize that the Talamanca Mountains are hardly a relaxing drive. Even though the main road reaches 3,000m (9,800ft) shortly before the turn-off, it still gives you little preparation for the enormous challenge ahead: the final twisting ascent to the top of the impressive Cerro de la Muerte (Mountain of Death).

A junction at signpost Km 89 in Cañón turns onto a dirt track that leads to the summit at 3,491m (11,453ft). On a clear day, it is easy to see the forest of phone poles on the peak, but the trouble is that there are not many clear days, or at least, whole clear days. The steep ascent is best started at dawn, while the temperature is still below freezing, before the sun becomes oppressively hot and the wind whips up and the fog rolls in.

The landscape on the final approach is peat bogs and marshy grasses. At the summit you will find a panorama of Valle del General, and beyond that the Pacific Ocean. It is an amazing view that recalls the English poet John Keats's description of the moment in the 16th century when the Spanish conquistador Hernán Cortés and his men first saw the same sight in neighbouring Panama and 'look'd at each other with a wild surmise'. **JP**

Coffee Lovers' Loop
Cartago, Costa Rica

Start Orosí
End Orosí
Distance 36km (22.4 miles)
Type Culture
Map goo.gl/F8TJlY

This circular trip begins around 32km (20 miles) south of San José, the capital of Costa Rica, in Orosí, a small valley town with the nation's oldest Roman Catholic church, built in 1743. The real wonders begin in the surrounding countryside, where the rainforest melds seamlessly with sugarcane and coffee plantations. These are miracles of ecofriendliness: perhaps·nowhere else on Earth is the hub of a nation's economy in such unspoiled surroundings.

On an anticlockwise circuit of the loop, the road twists and turns before straightening out along the banks of Lake Cachí, formed by the damming of the Reventazón River for a hydroelectric power plant. Beyond the head of the dam, the road passes through the village of Ujarrás before reaching a turning to Finca Cristina. This is by no means the only coffee plantation that offers tours (they nearly all do), but this is one of the most highly regarded: for a modest fee, visitors not only get to learn about (and taste) the coffee, but they also pass through groves abounding with colourful birds and flora. The three-hour package ends with an opportunity to bathe in thermal hot springs. The return leg of the journey to Orosí goes through Paraíso, where the botanical gardens are full of orchids and bromeliads that attract hosts of exotic birds, especially between February and April. **JP**

❶ Orosí is one of the small, tranquil towns in the picturesque Orosí Valley.

Panama Canal Drive
Panamá/Colón, Panama

Start Balboa, Panamá
End Colón, Colón
Distance 103km (64 miles)
Type Culture
Map goo.gl/iqgRwz

One must-see sight on any visit to Panama is its canal, a breathtaking piece of engineering opened at considerable cost in 1914. The canal was built as a shortcut for ships to cross the Americas rather than sail around dangerous Cape Horn to the far south. It wasn't built with cars in mind, but don't let that stop you from driving along its banks.

The best place to start is at Balboa on the southern Pacific end of the canal. From here, head up the northeast bank of the canal to the Miraflores locks and on to the Pedro Miguel locks, which lift up the ships into the central Gatun Lake. Here, you can watch the powerful tugs positioning ships in the canal. Day trips are available to take visitors out on the canal itself. The road then continues up the Gaillard Cut to Gamboa, which is approached over a bridge also carrying a canal-side railway. Here, the canal opens up into the Gatun Lake, formed when the Chagres River was dammed to build the canal. Unfortunately, no roads line its shores – although the railway runs across the middle – so you are forced to retreat south from Gamboa and head inland along Highway 3 to the Caribbean city of Colón, close to where the Gatun locks return the ships to sea level as they head out into the Caribbean beyond. **SA**

❍ The beltway offers impressive views of the canal.

Trampolín del Diablo
Putumayo, Colombia

Start Mocoa
End San Francisco
Distance 70km (43.2 miles)
Type Adventure
Map goo.gl/VZFFcO

Any road that goes by the name of Trampolín del Diablo (Devil's Trampoline), or its even scarier alternative Adiós mi Vida (Good-bye my Life), is certainly one to be wary of. And with good reason, for the Trampolín del Diablo in Puntumayo province is one of the most dangerous roads in the world. Estimates vary about the number of lives lost along the route, but around 300 people died when part of the road collapsed in 1989; in 2011 some 500 travellers died from accidents alone.

This hazardous road was built quickly by the Colombian government in the 1930s to transport soldiers across the country when war unexpectedly broke out with Peru over disputed lands in the Amazon basin. The road hugs the steep Andes mountainsides and zigzags alarmingly around 100 hairpin bends and through numerous narrow passes. Steep precipices and sheer cliffs add to the drama. In poor weather the road can get very muddy and slippery after rain, while heavy mists can severely reduce visibility. Even in good weather, this road is unsuitable for buses and heavy trucks.

Although the route is slowly improving, with safety barriers now fitted along its most perilous sections, this is a hard-core road trip that will need some serious preparation. Even 4x4s can find the going difficult, so take your time and postpone your trip if bad weather is forecast. **SA**

Natural Pool Jeep Safari
Oranjestad/Santa Cruz, Aruba

Start Oranjestad, Oranjestad
End Natural Pool, Santa Cruz
Distance 12.9km (8 miles)
Type Adventure
Info goo.gl/cXOVDp

The island of Aruba off the coast of Venezuela is a constitutional possession of the Netherlands and part of the so-called 'Dutch Caribbean'. A land of low rainfall, it has a cacti-strewn, rocky landscape with thorny shrubs and extensive scrublands, not the sort of environment that springs to mind when you think 'tropical'. However, it goes to show that you can find great road trips in the unlikeliest of places.

Natural Pool is a circular depression and popular swimming hole enclosed by volcanic rocks located on a deserted stretch of Aruba's isolated windward coast. Its surrounding wall of rock protects it from the rough and unpredictable ocean swells beyond, and swimming and snorkelling there is an experience worth the considerable effort required to reach it. The journey can be a dirty, dusty ride, particularly if there haven't been any recent rains. Don't forget to dress appropriately and take water.

This is 4x4 terrain only, not accessible by an ordinary car. The route is unmarked and potentially disorienting, with a final jagged and nerve-jangling descent to the pool. Some car rental agencies insist that you sign a waiver saying that you won't drive the vehicle there yourself, even if you are adept at off-road driving. Take their advice: seek out a tour operator who offers guided tours, sit back and – just this once – let the experts do the driving. **BDS**

❶ The Natural Pool is not accessible by ordinary car, yet the dusty ride is worth it for the views.

Christoffel National Park
Curaçao, Netherlands Antilles

Start Barber
End Westpunt
Distance 21km (13.1 miles)
Type Scenic
Info goo.gl/NnR9lq

Christoffelpark is the largest national park on the Dutch West Indian island of Curaçao. It lies near the northwest tip of the island and contains a huge variety of local floral and fauna, including the rare native barn owl (*palabrua*) and the Curaçao white-tailed deer, of which there are thought to be only around 250 remaining, so watch your speed. The park also includes the historic Savonet Plantation, one of the earliest plantations on the island, where you can view the main house, storerooms, wells and dams, as well as an excellent museum. Access to the park is roughly midway along the road between Barber and Wespunt.

There are two main routes to explore. The 9-km- (5.6-mile) long Savonet Plantation and North Coast Route heads past fields and the former irrigation works of the plantation to the north coast of the island, where there are caves with ancient Indian drawings as well as some interesting rock formations. The 12-km- (7.5-mile) long Mountain Route includes the ruins of Landhouse Zorgvlied and affords views over Christoffel and Shete Boka National Parks. A shorter mountain route leads directly to the foot of Christoffelberg, from where it is possible to clamber for two hours up through the semiarid landscape to the top. The third route – the 5-km- (3-mile) long Orchid Trail – is closed to cars but accessible by pickup trucks on special request. **SA**

❶ At 375m (1,230ft), Christoffelberg is the highest point on the island.

Parque Nacional Sierra Nevada Scenic Drive
Mérida, Venezuela

Start Mérida
End Laguna Mucubají
Distance 85km (52.8 miles)
Type Scenic
Map goo.gl/Xa59qL

In Venezuela's Northern Andes, nestled between the states of Mérida and Barinas in the west of the country, lies a wonderful national park, set up in 1952 to protect its rich and diverse mix of bird and animal life, including the spectacle bears, pumas, lynx and the endangered Andean condor. Very few roads probe far into the Parque Nacional Sierra Nevada, but there is one fabulous stretch of tarmac that whisks you by its northern fringes on the Carretera Trasandina.

Before you head off, though, you should get an overview of the area by taking a trip on the famous Mérida cable car (the highest and second-longest in the world) that travels for 12.5km (7.7 miles), at altitudes of up to 4,765m (15,633ft), to the barren rocky slopes of Pico Espejo.

Back on terra firma, your road trip heads east on Troncal 7 towards the village of Tabay. As the road begins to wind up into the Andean foothills, the smooth-flowing tarmac clings to the contours, bounded by white concrete pillars, cleverly designed to allow travellers uninterrupted views over the magnificent rugged hilltops and thick cloud forests unfurling below. The trout-filled Laguna Mucubají, a spectacular kettle lake glacial formation, awaits you at this scenic road trip's eastern terminus – a fabulous end point for a memorable road journey. **DIS**

🛈 A winding road in the spectacular mountains of Sierra Nevada National Park.

Trans-Andean Highway
Lara/Táchira, Venezuela

Start Agua Viva, Lara
End San Cristóbal, Táchira
Distance 615km (382 miles)
Type Adventure
Map goo.gl/WupEB5

This road runs parallel to, and partly through, the Cordillera de Mérida, the northeastern arm of the mighty Andes mountain range. It was built during the administration of President Juan Vicente Gómez, who forced prison convicts to carry out much of the manual labour.

The highest point is reached near Collado del Cóndor at a dizzying 4,118m (13,511ft) above sea level. This summit is marked with a bronze statue of a condor, part of a memorial to the achievements of Simón Bolívar and his liberation army, who drove the Spanish out of South America. There is also a small chapel, a café and a gift shop, the last of which may seem an undesirable intrusion of commercialism in such wild surroundings, but anyone who makes it up here will almost certainly want a tangible memento of the great ascent.

This is an exhilarating section of the Trans-Andean Highway to drive, with innumerable curves and switchbacks, especially the long descent after the pass. Road surfaces are generally good, but the changeable mountain climate is a constant hazard, and safety barriers are few and far between. Past the grand city of Mérida, it is one final push towards San Cristóbal at the western end of this road trip. An important commercial centre, it is the capital of the Venezuelan state of Táchira, a region famed for its fine coffee. **JP**

❶ For a section of the trip, the Trans-Andean Highway runs through Sierra de la Culata National Park.

Avenue of the Volcanoes Pichincha to Tungurahua, Ecuador

Start Quito, Pichincha   End Baños de Agua Santa, Tungurahua   Distance 193km (120 miles)
Type Adventure   Map goo.gl/s32Lhg

Part of the Pan-American Highway, this route runs through the centre of Ecuador. It is 2,000–3,000m (6,500–10,000ft) above sea level, but because of its proximity to the equator the roadside scenery is green and cultivated. In the distance enormous Andean peaks are in plain sight, including the active volcanoes Antisana and Tungurahua.

The road out of Quito is slow, and it takes about three hours to travel the 90km (56 miles) to the next big town, Saquisilí, whose early morning market deals in everything from meat – on and off the hoof – to herbal medicines. The next stop could be Salcedo, which claims to produce the world's best ice cream. Pillaro, about 145km (90 miles) from

Quito, is close to Llanganates National Park, which straddles the Andes and has a desertlike western zone and a lush eastern zone with vegetation so dense that it can be explored only on foot.

Beyond Pelileo (famous for blue jeans) is Baños de Agua Santa, from where footpaths lead to waterfalls on the Río Pastaza and hot springs on the slopes of Tungurahua. Less than 2km (1 mile) out of town, but three hours on foot, the Swing at the End of the World offers incredible views over the Andes, but in the absence of safety nets or harnesses it is one only for adrenaline junkies. **JP**

❶ Volcanic ash strata in a gully through Chimborazo.

Cotopaxi Volcan Road Cotopaxi, Ecuador

Start El Chaupi   **End** Cotopaxi   **Distance** 43km (26.7 miles)
Type Adventure   **Map** goo.gl/xmKOSx

The starting point of this road trip, which is short but tough, lies at the end of a 7-km- (4.3-mile) long cobbled lane off the E-35 highway. El Chaupi is a small village with astounding views of the surrounding Andes. On the western side are the Ilinizas twin volcanic peaks, but this route heads east, back across the main highway and on to a steep ascent to as close as it is sensible to get to the summit of Cotopaxi.

One of the world's highest volcanoes, at 5,911m (19,393ft), and perhaps the most shapely, with an almost perfectly symmetrical cone, Cotopaxi is highly active, and the path across its upper slopes may have to change according to the latest lava flows or pyroclastic rock falls. Its largest 20th-century eruption created two lahars (mud torrents) that extended for more than 100km (60 miles) – one to the Pacific Ocean, the other to the Amazon River. Even the recommended route is full of potholes, so off-track diversions are inevitable. The greatest care should be taken when crossing dry riverbeds. In fine weather they look like leading examples of desertification, but the slightest rainfall on higher ground can turn them into raging torrents: flash floods are a major cause of death and injury in these parts. **JP**

❶ A view of Cotopaxi volcano across the national park.

Carretera de Yungay
Ancash, Peru

Start Yungay
End Yanama
Distance 69km (43 miles)
Type Scenic
Map goo.gl/oV4xtU

It's a stunning sight: two sparkling blue lakes stand side by side, surrounded by almost vertical rock faces leading to snowcapped mountains.

The only trouble is getting there. The Llanganuco Lakes stand high in the Peruvian Cordillera Blanca at the foot of Peru's highest mountain. That means that these stretches of water are a dizzying 3,850m (12,630ft) above the sea. The route from the nearest settlement, Yungay, is around 25km (16 miles), but it is along a rough, dangerous, and stony track.

The official name of the road – Ruta 106 – makes it sound much grander than it really is, which is in places not much more than a footpath. Nevertheless, if you want to see the lakes, this is the only way you can reach them.

The driving challenge includes hairpin bends on steep gradients on a surface resembling sand and gravel. There are unguarded drops of hundreds of feet, and sheer cliffs with frequent rockfalls. As you climb, the air becomes thinner, so breathing difficulties and altitude sickness can hamper progress. The consolation is that the higher you rise, the more spectacular the views over Peru's Parque Nacional Huascarán.

The 106 continues beyond the lakes to the village of Yanama, but it's a long way east before the next paved road, so the best course is to return to the starting point the way you came. **SH**

❶ The Llanganuco Lakes on the Santa Cruz trek in Huascarán National Park.

Chacas to Shilla
Ancash, Peru

Start Chacas
End Shilla
Distance 68km (42 miles)
Type Scenic
Map goo.gl/fRqCl3

Right, you have a choice here. There is a perfectly boast-worthy, gasp-inducing route on offer that does not include danger of death at any moment. And there's another route that does.

So you could tackle the fabled AN 107 over the Andes. You will conquer one of the highest roads in the Americas, a route once described as one of the world's most dangerous. Except that since then, Peruvian authorities have improved it greatly. It's now a neatly paved two-lane highway with a 1.3-km- (1-mile) long tunnel under the highest section. You'll still get amazing views of the snowy Cordillera Blanca mountains and have to tackle the notorious '1,000 Curves' section, which is actually 46 hairpin bends in a short stretch.

But you'll always have this nagging doubt. Could you have made it over the original pass? What was it like to travel on the unpaved Punta Olimpica that twisted over the mountain at 4,900m (16,076ft)?

Well, if you fancy it, it's still there. Of course, it hasn't been maintained even to its original poor standard since the new tunnel opened underneath. So now it's definitely one of the most spectacular, and terrifying, journeys in this book. The narrow and steep gravel-and-mud track has monstrous unguarded drops, and it is littered with huge potholes, ruts and boulders that have tumbled down the slopes. It's your choice. **SH**

❶ Terrain such as this is typical of the high-altitude Huascarán National Park.

Carretera del Cañon del Pato Ancash, Peru

Start Yungay
End Calipuy National Reservation
Distance 122km (76 miles)
Type Adventure
Map goo.gl/Cfawp1

There are very many striking things about Carretera del Cañon del Pato (Road to Duck Canyon), but at the top of the list are the tunnels. There are more than 40 of them on this challenging route through northern Peru; almost all are wide enough for only one vehicle to pass through at a time. They have been hand cut out of the mountain rock, and the walls are jagged and rough, with an otherworldly feel, resembling something you might expect to find in a Tolkien novel.

Elsewhere, the rest of the landscape is similarly fantastic and makes you feel as though you might be on another planet. The rocky canyon walls that hem you in are relentlessly bleak and unforgiving, only broken up by the odd ghost town or battered road bridge. Beneath you, the road surface is gravel: gray and dusty. Nevertheless, there is a definite rugged beauty about this road trip.

Carretera del Cañon del Pato rises to a height of 2km (1.25 miles) above sea level, and as it climbs, so the roadway narrows. In places, you are on a tight track with a sheer drop to one side. When bad weather comes in, the surface deteriorates rapidly, and there can be flash floods. It is a truly dangerous drive, but one that is certain to bring out the real adventurer in you. JI

◔ An SUV on the Cañon del Pato road.

Ticlio Pass
Lima, Peru

Start Lima
End La Oroya
Distance 185km (115 miles)
Type Adventure
Map goo.gl/Y5T8cR

● The average gradient of this mountain pass is a gentle 3.5 per cent, but watch out for the heavy trucks.

In Peru, the main carretera central, Ruta 22A, starts on the Pacific coast at Lima and then heads up across the Cordillera Central of the Peruvian Andes to the densely populated city of La Oroya. On its way it goes through the Ticlio Pass, also called the Abra Anticona. At its highest, the pass is 4,818m (15,807ft) above sea level and is often, but erroneously, referred to as the highest paved road in South America. At one time, however, it did have the highest railway junction in the world: the Ferrocarril Central Andino railway came this way, servicing the lead and zinc mines at La Oroya and Morococha, until a new tunnel built at a lower elevation took it through the heart of a nearby mountain.

Driving through the mountain pass is a hair-raising experience. The high altitude means that the road is often covered with snow, so appropriate tyres and chains are recommended. More urgently, large boulders sometimes crash down from the mountains above, and landslides are common. In addition, one previous visitor complained of suicidal wild llamas darting into the road. A llama in full charge is always to be avoided. The road is narrow and twisting, with sequences of hairpin bends and precipitous drops to keep drivers awake and aware. However, for the beautiful rural landscape and breathtaking views of the Andes, this is a road trip well worth the effort. **SA**

Hiram Bingham Highway
Cusco, Peru

Start Aguas Calientes
End Machu Picchu
Distance 9km (5.6 miles)
Type Adventure
Map goo.gl/M1r8kV

Once you have travelled all the way to the Peruvian mountains, you will be faced with a choice. In order to reach the ruins of the famous Incan city of Machu Picchu, you can either trek up a steep mountain path for an hour or take a quick road trip aboard a tourist bus to the top.

Before you leap onto the bus, it is useful to know a little about the mountain road. It was built in 1948 and was named after the US explorer and politician Hiram Bingham, who discovered the site and opened the route to tourists. More than 65 years later, the road is a narrow crumbling track of dirt and gravel. At first it follows a river through thick rainforest, then begins a steep climb up to 2,430m (7,970ft) above sea level via a series of 14 savagely sharp hairpin bends. Rock slides and floods sometimes make the route completely impassable. In addition, fog, torrential rain and even snow are regular events. The only vehicles that are allowed to drive on the road are the ramshackle fleet of 22 shuttle buses carrying tourists, who pay heavily for the ride. The bus operators are supposed to maintain the road in return.

Passengers discover that Hiram Bingham Highway is very narrow with crumbling edges. Buses have to back up to let one another pass. The views from your seat on the bus will be wonderful. Your sense of well-being may not. **SH**

❶ The 550-year-old citadel of Machu Picchu sits between two peaks of the Andean mountains.

Cotahuasi Canyon Arequipa, Peru

Start Cotahuasi   **End** Puica   **Distance** 35km (21.7 miles)
Type Adventure   **Map** goo.gl/AXkWrP

Almost twice as deep as the Grand Canyon in Arizona, the Cotahuasi is a startling slice of planet Earth. Slipped between two massifs, it plunges 3,535m (11,598ft) in places and has 12 ecosystems, encompassing fertile terraces of quinoa, vines and lemon trees, and plateaus of bare rock or cacti forest. The Cotahuasi River grinds along the bottom while a road noses up and down the canyon walls, occasionally forking off to tiny settlements. The Inca used the canyon to take fish from the coast to Cusco; you need a 4x4 these days.

Cotahuasi, a demanding 368-km- (228-mile) long journey from Arequipa, is the springboard for exploring the canyon. From here, the easier option is to drive north along the south side, largely along the valley floor, stopping for a soak in the thermal springs in Lucha. Switchbacks and views climax around Puica, where tributary gorges converge on the canyon. For a more testing driving experience, head downstream from Cotahuasi toward Quechualla, the deepest part of the canyon, where the route runs out. It is a rough ride with many drop-dead corners, but it is also rewarding, with waterfalls, pre-Incan tombs and candelabra cacti. Keep your nerve and don't get distracted – even if you spot an Andean condor wheeling overhead. **DS**

❶ The road is just a track in places.

Acceso a La Rinconada Puno, Peru

Start Puno   End La Rinconada   Distance 177km (110 miles)
Type Adventure   Map goo.gl/Iyi932

La Rinconada is the highest human settlement in the world. The remote Peruvian mining town stands at 5,100m (16,732ft) above sea level in the Andes near the Bolivian border. Yet, it is no beauty spot. The chilly windswept settlement consists of largely makeshift shacks clinging to a steep mountainside. There is not a tree in sight. Gold-miners' children play on garbage dumps and along impassable, muddy streets. There is no plumbing or sewers. The air is so thin that newcomers can barely breathe, and visitors are susceptible to altitude sickness.

Despite this, there is an appeal to driving up the rough track to reach La Rinconada. It is amazing to see how people adapt to living in harsh conditions.

The surrounding mountains look spectacular from this height, but the average temperature is barely above freezing. Because of the mining processes, the town is now heavily polluted with mercury.

Most visitors start down at the port of Puno on Lake Titicaca. From here it is about 200km (110 miles) up to La Rinconada. At first, it is a beautiful journey through Titicaca National Reserve, on smooth, flat roads. After Huatasani, roads become harsher and you will end up climbing on a dangerously crude gravel-and-dirt track to this 21st-century gold-rush town. **SH**

❶ The miners live in shacks near the glacier.

Trans-Amazonian Highway
Paraíba to Amazonas, Brazil

Start Taperoá, Paraíba
End Lábrea, Amazonas
Distance 4,049km (2,516 miles)
Type Adventure
Map goo.gl/MkZrw5

This highway is a remarkable feat of engineering, but it is destroying a rainforest. A corridor linking seven Brazilian states, it began in the 1970s as a dirt track and is now in the ongoing and extra laborious process of being paved. Nothing has been permitted to stand in its way. It cuts through the reserves of indigenous peoples and has resulted in land clearing, deforestation and rampant soil erosion on a scale that can hardly be quantified. Built as part of an ambitious but deeply flawed resettlement program designed to boost economic growth, no other road in the world has been the cause of so much ecological havoc.

Its still-unpaved, dusty surfaces, as fine as talcum powder in places, turn glue-like whenever it rains – which is frequently in an equatorial rainforest. This renders the road unusable for approximately half of every year, but the project is still beloved by speculators and ranchers – although despised by almost everyone else.

Of course, driving the length of the Trans-Amazonian highway would be a heavenly road trip and one hell of an adventure, but innumerable negative factors make it difficult to recommend this route wholeheartedly. As Andrew 'Freddie' Flintoff, the former England cricketer, said after cycling almost 1,200km (750 miles) of it in 2014: 'This road has a lot to answer for.' **BDS**

The highway bisects the Amazonian rainforest.

Rodovia Presidente Dutra
Rio de Janeiro, Brazil

Start Rio de Janeiro
End Itatiaia National Park
Distance 208km (129 miles)
Type Culture
Map goo.gl/9jhsNI

This is an easy road trip of discovery linking two of Brazil's most popular attractions, Rio de Janeiro and Itatiaia National Park. Most of the journey follows the excellent BR 116 highway that links Brazil's two main cities, Rio and São Paulo. It is also one of the longest and most important of the state highways, running from the north coast down to the border of Uruguay. For this trip you will be travelling on the section known as 'Rodovia Presidente Dutra', after a politician in the 1950s.

Leave behind the colourful city of Rio by heading north from Sugarloaf Mountain, with the shore of Guanabara Bay on your right and the Christ the Redeemer statue on Corcovado Mountain on your left. The highway will take you past the city's main airport, Antonio Carlos Jobim International, to meet the BR 116 in the northern suburbs. It takes a while to escape the sprawl of Rio, but watch for the moment that prominent green mountains start appearing on the horizon.

The route cruises through lush countryside with rolling hills and climbs through long, easy curves higher into the mountains, passing lakes, forests and rivers. At the town of Itatiaia, leave the highway for a smaller paved road heading into the park, which is a beautiful protected area of mountains and rainforests. Look out for monkeys, sloths and more than 400 species of tropical birds. **SH**

Rio–Niterói Bridge
Rio de Janeiro, Brazil

Start Rio de Janeiro
End Niterói
Distance 13.4km (8.3 miles)
Type Adventure
Map goo.gl/yNGCHb

This box-girder structure is the longest bridge in the southern hemisphere and the sixth-longest of any kind in the world at just under 13.3km (8.3 miles) across. Although the six-year creation project was completed in 1974, the idea for a bridge was first conceived in 1875, almost a century earlier. It now saves a journey of more than 100km (62 miles) skirting the bay to the north.

Its little-used official name is the President Costa e Silva Bridge, in honour of the Brazilian politician who originally ordered its construction. However, this crossing will be better known to fans of *The Fast and the Furious* movie franchise, since it featured in the fifth film of the series, *Fast Five* (2011), starring alongside Vin Diesel and Paul Walker during the climactic high-octane police chase.

To enjoy the impressive box-girder bridge at a more leisurely pace, start in the city of Niterói (calling first at the impressive Oscar Niemeyer-designed Niterói Contemporary Art Museum). This way you will get to enjoy some of Rio's more striking landmarks – such as the world-famous statue of Christ the Redeemer and the natural wonder of Sugarloaf Mountain – on the horizon as you approach. A slightly more leisurely return to your start point, after you've sampled the delights of Rio, could be by one of the nearby ferry links across Guanabara Bay. **TW**

Rodovia Graciosa
Paraná, Brazil

Start Portal da Graciosa
End Antonina
Distance 39km (24.2 miles)
Type Scenic
Map goo.gl/Elnk71

Rodovia Graciosa (Graciosa Trail) is the official, rather grand, name for an old mule route in the rainforest of Paraná in southern Brazil. This historic road winds through the mountainous jungle of Pico do Marumbi State Park. Stretches of the road are beautiful, twisting up through colourful vegetation and banks of exotic flowers, past babbling streams and pretty waterfalls. It is possible to stop and take photographs of moss-covered stone bridges and panoramic views of misty green mountains from frequent lookout points. Official resting places and cafés appear sporadically en route. Often you can still see the original mule track running alongside the road.

Beware that some parts of the trail can be quite hazardous. It is often wet, and some stretches are very slippery, with uneven cobblestones on steep climbs. Sharp hairpin bends and prolific rainforest plants intruding into the road mean that drivers need to keep on their toes.

When the Trail was built in the 17th century, it was the only route from the city of Curitiba to the coast. It was very remote, and even in 1873, when its surface was paved, it was the only road in Paraná, and remained unique in the state for the following 50 years. **TW**

⬅ This road is cobblestones throughout its length.

Santa Catarina Coastal Drive Santa Catarina, Brazil

Start Blumenau   **End** Praia do Rosa   **Distance** 365km (227 miles)
Type Scenic   **Map** goo.gl/UD4Y6n

The Brazilian state of Santa Catarina boasts 563km (350 miles) of spectacular Atlantic coastline, dotted with seafront resorts ranging from quaint fishing villages to surfing centres and vibrant party towns, and this road trip gives the automotive adventurer a little taste of all of that variety.

The route begins in Blumenau, which was founded by German settlers who brought their distinctive alpine architecture and love of beer to South America – the Blumenau Oktoberfest is one of Brazil's biggest street festivals, second only to Carnival in Rio de Janeiro. From here, head east to Balneário Camboriú, with its lively bars, hotel-fringed beaches and vibrant nightclub district.

The route then runs south to the state capital of Florianópolis, on Santa Catarina Island. With 60 beaches, this is one of Brazil's most desirable locations for second-home owners. Farther south the pace of life slows as the old coastal road leads to two of Brazil's best-loved surf resorts. Guarda do Embaú is a pretty, laid-back bohemian village of around 400 residents, with surf shops, boutiques, seafood restaurants and artists' studios. Praia do Rosa is a trendier hangout – popular with Brazil's A-listers and famous as a yoga retreat, it's a maze of cobbled streets on a bluff above golden sands. **DIS**

❶ Balneário Camboriú is a Copacabana with less hype.

Rodovia Daniel Brüning Santa Catarina, Brazil

Start SC 390 in São Joaquim   End Lauro Müller   Distance 62km (38.5 miles)
Type Scenic   Map goo.gl/3csibF

Daniel Brüning was the first mayor of Braço do Norte and a highly respected politician. However, rather incongruously, the road that bears his name in Santa Catarina province in southeast Brazil is absolutely ludicrous, in a magnificent sort of way. Photographs cannot do justice to this zigzag of hairpin bends along the mountainside. With more than 250 corners to navigate, this is a test for any driver; but thankfully, the road surfaces are all good, and there are sturdy guardrails throughout.

The SC 390 road begins north of Bom Jardim da Serra and, at first, is fairly well behaved. It is only when it reaches the Serra do Rio do Rastro that it seriously messes around. From there on, the twists and turns really kick in, until you arrive at the bottom at Lauro Müller. The descent is rapid, a total of 1,460m (4,790ft) to near sea level, past spectacular waterfalls and lakes, through canyons, and around hillsides covered with luxurious vegetation.

The Brazilian summer is the best time to drive this road, since in winter thick, incoming sea fog shrouds the view and snow can make the road impassable. Mist remains a problem throughout the year and localized subsidence can cause delays. But don't let such trivial problems put you off; this is the scenic drive of a lifetime. **SA**

❶ This road is as twisty as Daniel Brüning was straight.

Serra do Corvo Branco
Santa Catarina, Brazil

Start Urubici
End Braço do Norte
Distance 74km (46 miles)
Type Scenic
Map goo.gl/CKgWj4

The SC 370 that crosses the Serra do Corvo Branco (Road of the White Crow Mountains) to the coast in southeast Brazil does not look much on the map, but it packs a considerable punch in real life. It starts inland at Urubici, a regional tourist centre, and for 30km (18.6 miles) is little more than a dirt track that climbs up through fields along the Canoas River Valley before taking to the hills. At this point it starts to rise and fall more steeply up and down the mountainsides, at one stage gaining 1,470m (4,800ft) in only 5km (3.1 miles). The road is full of hairpin bends, steep ascents and equally steep descents, with some breathtaking cliffs along the sides of the road.

The views all the way are unforgettable. At the top of the mountain is the largest vertical cut through solid rock of any in Brazil, measuring an impressive 90m (295ft). From this point onwards the road begins its steady descent, again with more than tight curves and vast cliffs to keep you fully concentrated. Viewing points on most of the curves are protruding platforms from which you can take in the mountain scenery all around. Just after the tiny settlement of Igreja, the road becomes the 475 and descends through Grão-Pará before ending up in the centre of Braço do Norte. From there it's only half an hour's drive to the beaches of the Atlantic Ocean coast. **SA**

❶ Road cuttings normally obstruct the view, but this one is a spectacle in itself.

Serra do Rio do Rastro Road
Santa Catarina, Brazil

Start Bom Jardim da Serra
End Lauro Müller
Distance 24km (14.9 miles)
Type Adventure
Map goo.gl/MsZq6j

Winding through the dense, green, cloud- and mist-filled upper valleys of the Serra do Rio do Rastro mountain range in the southeast state of Santa Catarina in Brazil, this road appears on aerial photographs like some tarmac-skinned jungle python. Tenaciously clinging to the mountainsides, it has such a dense repetition of hairpin bends that you have to see it to believe it; they are turns that will have your hands forever working the steering wheel – over and over.

Starting at the Mensageiro da Montanha Café and Restaurante in Bom Jardim da Serra, the road trip passes teeming waterfalls and vantage points over lakes, canyons and forest canopies, along one of the more outrageous zigzag routes on the planet. It descends from 1,460m (4,790ft) to sea level in just over 12,8km (8 miles), connecting the Brazilian plateau to the coastal plain via 250 corners.

Built in 1903 and well lit thanks to three modern propellor-style windmills, the Serra do Rio do Rastro is in a temperate zone where heavy fogs are common in winter, and snowfalls can close its summit. The best time to drive it is summer, when on a clear day you can see the Atlantic Ocean. Even then, caution is required: there is little wriggle room should you miscalculate, and it is easy to be mesmerized by the many precipitous drop-offs to the valleys far below. **BDS**

❶ This crazy road is certainly not one to be tackled by novice drivers.

La Paz to Zongo
La Paz, Bolivia

Start La Paz
End Zongo
Distance 70km (43.5 miles)
Type Scenic
Map goo.gl/hFdBZs

La Paz is the national capital of Bolivia, but Sucre is the nation's constitutional and judicial capital. One title that La Paz holds undisputedly alone is that of the world's highest capital. At 3,650m (11,975ft), it has its own subtropical highland climate, producing rainy summers and dry winters. It sits in a bowl-like depression surrounded by snowcapped mountains, notably the triple-peaked Illimani, the highest point of which is an additional 2,400m (8,000ft) above the city, 6,438m (21,122ft) above sea level.

Splendid as the city is, it is always nice to head out of town into the surrounding countryside. One such route is up to the remote Hotel Mollinedo in the Zongo River Valley. La Paz has a wonderfully complex road system, but basically you want to be on Ruta Nacional 3 and follow that until it sweeps around in a big loop and heads west out of the city. At this point you make a sharp right back on yourself and head up Ruta Nacional 41, for much of its length known as the Avenida Chacaltaya, as it passes close to Chacaltaya mountain to its east. The road then gets increasingly rural, with long straight sections suddenly interrupted by series of hairpin bends. Just before journey's end at Zongo you pass the Hotel Mollinedo, a charming multi-coloured structure, whose bar will warmly welcome you. **SA**

➲ The world's highest ski resort is on Chacaltaya.

South Yungas Road
La Paz, Bolivia

Start Coripata
End Coripata
Distance 121km (75 miles)
Type Adventure
Map goo.gl/RWq4di

The North Yungas 'Road of Death' has been frequently nominated the most treacherous road trip in the world; this road, its slightly longer, southern brother, is little better. For reasons that will become clear, there are a few rules of the road to be followed when driving on the infamous South Yungas Road, at one time the only connection between the Bolivian capital of La Paz and Chulumani town. Firstly, the vehicle that is heading uphill always has right of way, because it is difficult to stop and reverse downhill on such rough, slippery terrain. Secondly, where the road is wide enough, cars are meant to change their positions on the road so that each can judge how far away they are from either the cliff's edge or the mountainside. Unfortunately, this is one of those roads that has no guardrails, and there are numerous places to loose your tyre grip and cascade over the edge.

The circular loop is popular with mountain bikers and follows the steep-sided valley of the Río Unduavi and links with Roads 40 and 25. Crossing the river depends on the season and your vehicle, but South Yungas Road is no longer a continuous route on official road maps, in an attempt to divert traffic to the newer and much safer road to Chulumani. Nevertheless, a little imaginative route planning will get you to the hair-raising highlights of this incredible road. **SA**

❶ The surface shown here is typical of the quality of the road throughout its course.

Camino a Caranavi–Coroico Canyon
La Paz, Bolivia

Start Coroico
End Caranavi
Distance 77.1km (47.9 miles)
Type Adventure
Map goo.gl/XOzco3

It would be true to say that visitors do not go to Bolivia to enjoy its fabulously smooth road surfaces and safety-conscious highways. Despite this, nothing can quite prepare you for the dangers of the 77.2-km- (47.9-mile) long track from Coroico to Caranavi. This is the road from hell, a gravel-and-dirt track bordered by crumbling cliffs to one side and a massive river canyon on the other, all without any substantial guardrails to keep you safe.

The journey starts in Coroico and confusingly heads south before a sharp hairpin bend redirects the road northwards along the Coroico canyon. From here onwards, the road weaves its way along the wooded mountainsides of the high-humidity Yungas forests. Signs advise motorists to drive to the left, which means that those driving north almost have two wheels hanging off the side of the road. Oncoming heavy trucks and buses provide much terror and excitement as they try to squeeze past you.

The mountainous slopes are very steep and the climate often rainy, so landslides are common, made worse by loggers felling trees and deforesting the slopes. At first, the road is around 150m (490ft) above the river below, but as the canyon narrows to the north, the road dips to about 10m (33ft) above the river. By the time you make it to Caranavi, you will be in need of refreshment. **SA**

❶ This dangerous high mountain road lies between La Paz and Coroico, near La Cumbre Pass.

Cerro Chacaltaya
La Paz, Bolivia

Start La Paz
End Chacaltaya
Distance 30km (18.6 miles)
Type Adventure
Map goo.gl/Dsp7Fl

On top of Cerro Chacaltaya in the Cordillera Real of the Bolivian Andes is a disused ski station. It once held the honour of being the highest lift-served ski station in the world, and was a thriving winter sport destination until 2009, when the glacier on which it depended melted, thus closing the resort. Luckily, the narrow road to the station remains open for the more intrepid automotive adventurers to explore.

Starting in the northern suburbs of the Bolivian capital of La Paz, Avenida Chacaltaya slowly climbs up north, entering the Zongo River Valley, until it reaches the base camp of Mt Huayna Potosí. After approximately 5km (3 miles), the side road takes a turn to the left. Initially, the gradient is not particularly steep, but it increases for the last 5km (3 miles) until it reaches the ski station.

For those with some energy to spare – don't forget that at this point you are 5,260m (17,257ft) above sea level and the air is thin – you can scramble up a path to the top of Cerro Chacaltaya itself. The views from the summit are spectacular, not only of the surrounding mountains, but also toward the visible tip of Lake Titicaca in the west. It goes without saying that you should not travel up this pass in bad weather, as snowfalls, avalanches and landslides are persistent hazards. **SA**

● **The impressive switchbacks of Cerro Chacaltaya.**

Collpani Pass
La Paz, Bolivia

Start ES Cruce Luribay petrol station
End Collpani
Distance 43km (26.7 miles)
Type Adventure
Map goo.gl/eabW2R

On the many lists of roads in the world with the most hairpin bends, one road always features. Collpani Pass is not especially long, but it does have 52 savage switchbacks packed into one 9.6-km- (6-mile) long stretch, which will keep even the most experienced drivers busy at the steering wheel. In addition to those making the road trip by car, this route is equally popular with South America's touring motorcyclists and hard-core road cyclists testing their mettle on the lung-bursting ascent.

The pass is in the mountainous La Paz Department of western Bolivia, southwest of the capital. Approach it from La Paz, along Autovía La Paz–Oruro, and then take a left turn at ES Cruce Luribay petrol station, just past the small town of Lahuachaca. From here the gravel road climbs up alongside a largely dry riverbed, past the village of Kollpa Khuchu Belén. It then rises through some scrubby landscape until it goes up a long, stony valley and across swaths of bare rock to reach the foot of the pass. From here onwards it is sharp hairpin bends all the way: an initial set of 11 followed by an awe-inspiring 33 more, with a few stragglers waiting to surprise you at the top. Note that there are some very steep sections – with gradients up to 15 per cent – but the views from the stopping point near the road's crest are breathtaking; this is a road trip not to be missed. **SA**

North Yungas Road
La Paz, Bolivia

Start Highway 3
End Coroica
Distance 44km (27.3 miles)
Type Adventure
Map goo.gl/cEEdGM

Built by prisoners of war in the 1930s through thickly forested Andean foothills, Bolivia's 'Road of Death' is universally acknowledged to be the scariest road on the planet; a notoriety that has seen it star on television in the BBC's *Top Gear* and featured on *World's Most Dangerous Roads*.

Heading out on this cliff-skimming road, it is not unusual to see local drivers sitting deep in prayer before they start their engines – an estimated 300 travellers lose their lives on this route every year. Tiptoeing along precipitous mountain tracks, there are drops of more than 610m (2,000ft) and virtually no guardrails for protection. Furthermore, North Yungas Road is so narrow that there is barely enough space for two cars to pass, let alone trucks and buses. Weirdly, this is the only road in Bolivia where vehicles pass on the left, so drivers can lean out and check that their wheels are not dangling in thin air.

There is no good time of year to attempt this road trip: in winter, torrential rain, mudslides and fog make this deadly road even deadlier; in summer, rockfalls and impenetrable dust clouds add to the horror. Nevertheless, it is reckoned that some 25,000 thrill-seeking tourists strike out on the North Yungas Road each year. Not all of them come back. **DIS**

➲   In short, this road trip is absolutely terrifying.

Carretera de Tupiza a Quiriza Potosí, Bolivia

Start Tupiza
End Quiriza
Distance 65km (40.4 miles)
Type Adventure
Map goo.gl/Aj2Hef

If wild adventures and off-road exploits are your things, this is the road trip for you. Situated high up in the Andes in the western La Paz Department of Bolivia, the dirt track from Tupiza to Quiriza is consistently more than 3,100m (10,170ft) above sea level, and often much higher. The countryside is wild and remote, the road little more than a sandy, loose-surfaced track with the occasional dry riverbed to cross, so chains and snow tyres can be needed at any time. When driving along this track, come fully prepared for every eventuality.

The road starts in Tupiza, a small city in the far south of Bolivia, nestling in the Tupiza River Valley between dramatic red sandstone cliffs. It is believed that the notorious but celebrated bank robbers Butch Cassidy and the Sundance Kid met their bloody ends at the hands of the Bolivian army northwest of here, and day trips by jeep or on horseback can be arranged to visit the memorial site. From there the road heads south along the valley and then west into the hills, its red surface cutting and carving its way through the equally red and gray hillsides. This is dramatic scenery, with no habitation along the way. On a good day you will not pass another vehicle, which is some people's idea of heaven. **SA**

● The Cordillera de Chichas near Tupiza.

Paso del Condor Desert Road Potosí, Bolivia

Start Laguna Blanca
End Laguna Colorada
Distance 89km (55.3 miles)
Type Adventure
Map goo.gl/sQaZyW

For reasons that are not entirely clear, the barren valley of the Potosí Department of southwest Bolivia is known to many as Salvador Dalí Desert. Rumour has it that it got this name because it resembles the landscapes of the surrealist's best-known paintings, especially the melted clocks of *The Persistence of Memory* (1931). The strange wind-sculpted rocks of the Piedras de Dalí rock formations off to the east are also very similar to Dalí's more outrageous creations. From flamingo-filled lakes to conical volcanoes, the area certainly has a surreal quality about it, and the loose-surfaced road across its high desert is not to be missed.

The track starts at the barren salt lake of Laguna Blanca, next to the more colourful Laguna Verde, and then heads north and northeast over the pass to Aguas Termales de Polques. As it does so, it rises to 4,730m (15,518ft) above sea level. The road itself is largely flat and consists of sand and gravel; the landscape around it is eerily empty, with just the distant views towards the many nearby volcanoes, including Mt Nelly and Mt Juriques. Since this remote pass is almost completely devoid of people, you should come fully prepared for every eventuality. A 4x4 is necessary, and your speed should be kept sensibly low. This is a road to enjoy at your leisure, for its scenery is truly magnificent and you can usually enjoy it in splendid solitude. **SA**

Salar de Uyuni
Antonio Quijarro, Bolivia

Start Uyuni
End Isla Incahuasi
Distance 97km (60 miles)
Type Adventure
Map goo.gl/LQwEjD

By the lucky few who have already explored Bolivia's Salar de Uyuni, the world's largest salt flat is universally described as the journey of a lifetime. However, some of its secrets are not easily found, and at 10,582 sq km (4,086 square miles) in area, it is not without its dangers; the knowledge of a good local guide is essential to get the most out of this amazing road trip.

Most visitors employ a driver with a 4x4, but if you have a motorcycle licence there are guides who will rent you everything you need, including well-prepared off-road motorbikes. Tours often begin on the fringes of Uyuni town at the bizarre train cemetery, an eerie graveyard of rusting steam locomotives. From here, it's an 29-km- (18-mile) long surfaced road past Colchani, a salt-processing town, to the unique and impressive Hotel de Sal Luna Salada, an exclusive hotel built entirely from salt: walls, furniture, sculptures – the whole lot.

But the highlight of this trip is undoubtedly the salt road to the 'island' of Incahuasi; if it weren't for the searing heat, you might think that the surface of the lake was dusted with snow. After 60km (37 miles), you arrive at a large and incongruous outcrop. Covering 25 hectares (61 acres), and dotted with gigantic cacti, hidden among the rocks are unusual and fragile aquatic fossils and coral-like creatures. It's a truly magical place. **DIS**

❶ The lack of identifiable features at Salar de Uyuni makes it easy to become disoriented.

Ruta 11
Arica y Parinacota, Chile

Start Arica
End Chungara
Distance 203km (126 miles)
Type Adventure
Map goo.gl/4X7fmv

This itinerary begins without fanfare on the western slopes of the Andes in the town of Arica. A scenic enough spot, for sure, but nothing like as impressive as what is to come. Few roads in the world take you on the sort of journey this one does, from near sea level to more than 4,480m (14,700ft) into the clouds of Lauca National Park, and the Bolivian border. It's a seven-hour out-and-back drive, so it's worth taking your time and planning ahead for an overnight stop.

First, see the Lluta Valley's extraordinary pre-Columbian Lluta Geoglyphs, a series of figures carved into an otherwise barren hillside. To the west of Arica, at Poconchile, you'll see the road begin to rise. In almost no time you're at 2,000m (6,500ft), with candelabra cacti growing in a rain-starved desert. Then spend the night at Putre, taking time to acclimatize to the thinness of the air at 3,500m (11,480ft) above sea level. The next morning, take a detour to bathe in the waters of Termas de Las Cuevas, which reputedly slow the aging process.

Heading east on Ruta 11, continue on your ear-popping ascent into the splendour of Lauca National Park, which begins just above Putre and continues to the Bolivian border, a Global Biosphere Reserve with lovely Lake Chungara at the foot of the Payachata twin volcanoes in the dry-climate majesty of the famed Altiplano. **BDS**

❶ A relatively flat stretch of the road – but look what is up ahead.

Ruta 5 Arica y Parinacota to Los Lagos, Chile

Start Arica, Arica y Parinacota   **End** Puerto Montt, Los Lagos   **Distance** 3,066km (1,905 miles)
Type Adventure   **Map** goo.gl/OQX7rc

Part of the Pan-American Highway, Ruta 5 is Chile's longest road and the country's only continuous north-to-south highway. A two-lane paved road from the Atacama Desert on the Peruvian border south to La Serena, it becomes a four-lane freeway from La Serena to Puerto Montt, where it connects to the Isla Grande de Chiloé by ferry. On its way, it crosses several east-to-west highways connecting the Pacific coast to Argentina. Avoiding all towns except the capital, Santiago, it looks like an easy drive. But don't be fooled. With its notoriously strong winds and horizons so broad they threaten to swallow you whole, Ruta 5 bisects vast expanses of featureless grey desert on open roads that seem to make speedometers creep upwards. Fatigue, speed and the flat roads of an Andean desert can be a deadly combination.

Every 48km (30 miles) or so, on alternate sides of the highway, are rest areas with petrol, showers and drinking water – essential infrastructures on a road that is the backbone of Chile's transportation system. There are four impressive tunnels along the route, ranging in length from 298m (978ft) to 2,543 m (8,343ft). The freeway sections carry tolls, and it becomes the six-lane Autopista Central as it passes through Santiago. **BDS**

❶ A broad road down a very narrow country.

South Pacific Coastal Road Tarapacá/Antofagasta, Chile

Start Iquique, Tarapacá   End Antofagasta, Antofagasta   Distance 418km (260 miles)
Type Scenic   Map goo.gl/atoDRi

This road trip is a relaxing cruise down the west coast of South America along part of Chile's scenic Ruta 1, between the old colonial port of Iquique and the modern skyscrapers of Antofagasta. The road is smooth and wide all the way, and passes some extraordinarily remote landscapes that feature salt flats, geysers, sand dunes and volcanoes. Look out for weirdly shaped rock formations and beautiful pink mountains sweeping down to the shores of the Pacific Ocean.

During the entire time you'll have the Atacama Desert on the inland side. This arid region is the world's driest place. There are parts of the Atacama where some scientists believe it has never rained.

Less attractively, also en route is Tocopilla, a heavily industrialized port and mining centre that need not detain you, especially in view of the fact that the city is prone to severe earthquakes. Instead, thriving Antofagasta makes a better place to explore. Thanks to an economic boom, Chile's second city has become prosperous, with parks, shops, high-rise apartments and sandy beaches all attractively well maintained. Look out, too, for the city's iconic sight: the massive modern sculpture on the desert outskirts that marks the exact latitude of the Tropic of Capricorn. SA

❶ The port of Iquique.

Atacama Desert Highway
Antofagasta, Chile

Start Tocopilla
End Calama
Distance 156km (97 miles)
Type Scenic
Map goo.gl/iRMD8Z

Between the Pacific and the Andes stands the driest place on Earth, without plants, shade or inhabitants: the Atacama Desert. This is a road trip right across that unforgiving area. Motoring along the Atacama Desert Highway (Ruta 24), you will pass through a dramatic dusty landscape of desert sands, volcanic remains and mysterious salt flats.

The road runs east from the industrial port of Tocopilla through the heart of the desert to Calama, one of the world's driest cities. You can leave the roof of the soft-top down: the average annual rainfall here is less than 5mm (1/4in). Beyond Calama the land rises up into the heights of the Andes, but the city itself is worth visiting for the obvious signs of copper mining wealth. There are copper statues and wall etchings everywhere. The city's cathedral even has a copper spire.

Note that Ruta 24 won't test your cornering skills. It will be more of a challenge to your powers of staying awake. It's straight and often flat for miles as it arrows across the bare desert. This barren, scorched panorama is memorable in its own way, however. If it seems like driving across the surface of Mars, you won't be the first to make that comparison: this patch of desert is used to test surface vehicles for NASA's Mars expeditions. **SH**

➲ Typical wayside terrain along the highway.

Chungungo to Conay
Coquimbo/Atacama, Chile

Start Chungungo, Coquimbo
End Conay, Alto del Carmen, Atacama
Distance 253km (157 miles)
Type Scenic
Map goo.gl/h9dYua

The highlights of Chungungo are its historic iron ore mines and the sea otters that gambol along the Pacific shoreline. From the coast, head eastwards inland until you reach the intersection with Highway 5, the Pan-American Highway, and then turn left.

With the Andes to the right, follow the main road northwards for 80km (50 miles), then take the exit to Vallenar – the name is a corruption of Ballenary, the birthplace in County Sligo, Ireland, of Ambrose O'Higgins, who founded the city in 1789 and was father of Bernardo O'Higgins, the first head of state of independent Chile.

From here the road twists and turns through more than 30 hairpin bends and rises sharply into the mountains. The highest point is 3,573m (11,700ft) above sea level – since drivers may have been on the shore only a couple of hours previously, it is perhaps unsurprising that altitude sickness is a serious danger here: ill effects commonly start to be felt above 2,500m (8,000ft). There is also plenty of snow, which often closes the road: the trip should be undertaken only during southern summers.

Chollay, the penultimate settlement on the route, is a pleasant mountain village where goatherds tend their flocks among peach and walnut orchards. Conay, the end of the itinerary, has all the same attractions but better facilities and onward connections. **JP**

Paso de Los Caracoles
Chile/Argentina

Start Parada Caracoles, Valparaíso, Chile
End Las Cuevas, Mendoza, Argentina
Distance 17km (10.6 miles)
Type Adventure
Map goo.gl/EeoubP

Let's clear up any confusion right now about the name of this South American mountain pass. It's officially known as 'El Paso Internacional Los Libertadores', 'international' in that it carries heavy traffic between the Chilean capital of Santiago and the Mendoza region of Argentina. It is also known as 'El Paso del Cristo Redentor' on account of the huge statue of Christ the Redeemer of the Andes placed in 1904 on the Argentinian side of the border. Locals, however, sensibly call it Paso de Los Caracoles, or 'Snails' Pass', on account of the speed that you will be crawling up its slopes, negotiating endless hairpin bends.

The approach from the Chilean side is steep, before the road suddenly begins to climb up what looks like an almost vertical series of 19 switchbacks. At the top, at 3,207m (10,521ft) above sea level, the road disappears into the 3,080-m- (10,105-ft) long Túnel Cristo Redentor, where Chile Route 60 turns into Argentina Route 7 as it crosses the international border. From here onwards, it is a far more gentle glide downhill to the city of Mendoza for a stiff drink and a welcome lie-down.

The actual statue of Christ is higher up the mountain, where the road struggled up another 632-m- (2,072-ft) high ascent and an additional series of 65 switchbacks before the relief tunnel was built. Thank goodness for civil engineers. **SA**

Carretera Austral
Los Lagos/Aysén, Chile

Start Puerto Montt, Los Lagos
End Villa O'Higgins, Aysén
Distance 1,223km (760 miles)
Type Adventure
Map goo.gl/3pYm65

It must be flattering to have a road named after you, especially if it is one that winds its way through a mind-blowing landscape of mountains, snow and lakes. But if, like General Augusto Pinochet, you are the leader of a military dictatorship, you cannot be surprised if people reject the name at the earliest opportunity. So it was with Carretera General Augusto Pinochet, which runs through Chilean Patagonia. It was built in the 1970s and 1980s, during the dictator's time as Chilean leader, and was unofficially named after him. However, in the post-Pinochet world, it was renamed Carretera Austral.

The road itself carves its way through southern Chile, to provide better access to a remote part of the country for military reasons. It is mostly gravel, and conditions on it can vary. A 4x4 is suggested, if not essential, as potholes pockmark the unfinished surface in some stretches. The landscape around you varies enormously, from snowcapped mountains and lush forests to vast South American lakes and even glaciers. It is a remote area, so you need to travel well equipped, but you will be rewarded with beautiful views. There are some steep climbs and descents along this trip, and plenty of bends and switchbacks to keep you on your toes. Thankfully, there are regular camping spots dotted along the road, so you can take your time and enjoy the ride. JI

❶ The surface varies as the road winds its way through the mountains, and some sections are dirt and gravel.

Ruta 265
Aysén, Chile

Start Puerta Guadal
End Chile Chico
Distance 106km (66 miles)
Type Scenic
Map goo.gl/QqaYyj

This trip along the southern shore of General Carrera Lake – known in neighbouring Argentina as Lake Buenos Aires – starts from Puerto Guadal, a village that, according to the *Lonely Planet* travel guides, 'appears to hold siesta at all hours'.

From there the road is never boring and seldom entirely safe. The lake on the left, framed by the Andes mountain range, is a picture-perfect paradise for trout and salmon fishing; on the right are the remains of long-abandoned gold and silver mines. However, there are few barriers to prevent the unwary from toppling off the road, which runs for long stretches along frighteningly narrow ledges high above the water.

Also dangerous are other drivers: so far away from police speed cameras, this is prime territory for people who would prefer to be in Formula One.

As the road nears Argentina, the surface improves – the dirt track that it has been for much of the route thus far is replaced by smooth tarmac. The weather gets better, too, as the traveller enters a warm microclimate that makes a welcome contrast to much of the rest of Patagonia, which is best known for its almost relentless winds.

Although Chile Chico is right on the border, many travellers prefer to enter Argentina at Puerto Ingeniero Ibáñez, which is two hours away by ferry on the northern side of the lake. **JP**

❶ The Marble Chapel: a rock formation on the lake. The road runs along the cliff top.

Cuesta del Lipán – National Route 52
Jujuy, Argentina

Start Purmamarca
End Salinas Grandes
Distance 65km (40.4 miles)
Type Scenic
Map goo.gl/qmDRIC

Nine out of ten visitors to Jujuy Province in the northwest of Argentina come from Latin America. For most other people, the region remains the unknown mountainous world of the Altiplano, an arid, semi-desert, high-altitude plateau. This is the land of the Cuesta del Lipán (Lipán Slope), where a section of National Route 52 begins in the pre-Hispanic town of Purmamarca; against the backdrop of the Cerro de los Siete Colores (Hill of Seven Colours), the route heads upward for the next 34km (21 miles).

The 1,980-m- (6,500-ft) high elevation gain from Purmamarca is a continuous ascent along a road as beautiful as it is dangerous – a tarmacked zigzag highway that reaches its summit at the Abra de Potrerillos, 4,170m (13,680ft) above sea level, before leaving the hairpin bends behind and descending to the Salinas Grandes, vast salt flats that extend over 525 sq km (200 square miles).

A viewpoint near Abra de Potrerillos allows travellers to stop and marvel at the chain of switchbacks they have just negotiated on a road that began centuries ago as little more than a mule trail. It was widened and upgraded in the 1970s to become a dirt road, and in 2000 began to be sealed. Ironically, though, little has changed. Cuesta del Lipán remains a harmonious imprint of humanity upon the contours of nature. **BDS**

 Cuesta del Lipán is part of an important road link between Argentina and Chile.

Carretera de Iruya
Jujuy/Salta, Argentina

Start Humahuaca, Jujuy
End Iruya, Salta
Distance 74km (46 miles)
Type Adventure
Map goo.gl/sa5mJl

Welcome to the wilds of northwest Argentina, where you may hop on a daily bus, expecting a normal ride to the next town, but end up tackling a route like this instead. Whether you're driving yourself or are someone else's passenger, you'll find that the first section is no problem. The RN 9 is a normal two-lane stretch of tarmac. Of course you notice that jagged mountains dominate the horizon to the north, but although they're beautiful they are of no urgent concern. That all changes, however, when suddenly you veer off the road. There's no road sign at the junction – just a dirt track leading into those mountains. This is the RP 13, and its bends and gradients are tricky propositions in wet weather – and it can and does rain around here, copiously and often.

This is a route full of dramatic mountain vistas, particularly the deep gorges towards the end of the trip. The road climbs over a 4,100-m- (13,500-ft) high pass before making a steep 2,800-m (9,300-ft) descent to Iruya, a hillside village with adobe houses. The most obvious photo opportunity here is the picturesque old cottages around the church square with a backdrop of looming mountains. Foreign visitors will also want to capture the local people on film – many of them are the descendants of Incan Indians – but note that it is forbidden by law to photograph them without their permission. **SH**

❶ One of the easier sections of the road to Iruya in the Andean foothills.

Fiambalá to Copiapó
Argentina/Chile

Start Fiambalá, Catamarca, Argentina
End Copiapó, Atacama, Chile
Distance 481km (299 miles)
Type Adventure
Map goo.gl/eg3jlC

This remote, high-desert Andean pass takes you through a dry, volcanic landscape connecting the Argentine province of Catamarca with Copiapó on Chile's arid coastal plain. With a maximum elevation of 4,726m (15,505ft) above sea level, it is almost 1,340m (4,400ft) higher than Europe's highest road, Pico del Veleta in Spain. So high, in fact, that you will need to keep a check on yourself and any passengers for signs of altitude sickness.

If you come in summer, you will miss the flesh-freezing temperatures common to winter, but there is always the wind – the dreaded *viento blanco* (white wind) whips up out of nowhere and blows across this road with unrelenting brutality. The scenery, however, will have you forgetting all about that. At 6,893m (22,614ft), the stratovolcano Ojos del Salado, the world's highest active volcano and the western hemisphere's second-highest mountain, is close by. If you have a 4x4, you can get even closer. There are also the desolate salt flats of Chile's Salar de Maricunga and the volcanic massif Nevado Tres Cruces.

On the Argentine side, the route is paved, but beyond the border it becomes an unpaved road on the descent towards Copiapó. This is where it gets really dangerous, because as the road deteriorates, the background scenery becomes more magnificent and more distracting. **BDS**

❶ The point at which the road crosses the Argentina–Chile frontier.

Lenguas del Cochuna
Tucumán, Argentina

Start Yunka Suma
End Alpachiri
Distance 45km (28 miles)
Type Scenic
Map goo.gl/5a2W1S

Some of the road trips described in the present volume follow an almost straight line on the map. This route, by contrast, appears on paper as a convoluted wiggle of lines. You'll find it in Argentina's northwestern Tucumán Province, which is in general one of the country's most developed regions, but which here on the RN 15 through the Campo de los Alisos National Park reveals a different, rural aspect. This protected area of rainforest contains important Incan remains but very little evidence of modern civilization.

The Lenguas del Cochuna stretch of road lies between the remote villages of Yunka Suma and Alpachiri, in a beautiful area of deep, lush, green valleys surrounded by steep-sided forested hills and mountains that are often swathed in clouds.

The most squiggly section on the map is purely a track of mud and gravel leading through rainforests to climb from the valley floor up one of the mountain sides. The track is narrow and slippery, especially after rain, which is frequent. In just 6km (4 miles), you'll have to tackle no less than 31 hairpin bends that have no guards against sheer drops of hundreds of feet.

Amazingly, you can now follow this wild itinerary using Google Street View – and if that company's camera car can make it up the road, you should be able to do so, too. **SH**

Tunnels of Taninga
Córdoba, Argentina

Start Taninga
End El Cadillo
Distance 52km (32.3 miles)
Type Adventure
Map goo.gl/S9Tw05

It won't jump out at you from the pages of any guidebooks, but if you ever find yourself near the village of Taninga in the Córdoba region of Argentina, there's a nicely graded gravel road – or *un ripio*, as locals call any highway with such a surface – that heads up from its outskirts into the surrounding mountains. It's not the only one that fans out from this remote town, but you'll have no trouble finding it. Just ask anyone the way to *los túneles* ('the tunnels') – they'll know at once exactly what you're talking about.

These five tunnels, as well as several lovely bridges, were designed and built in the foothills of the Sierras Chicas in the 1930s by Don Juan Breggia, an Italian immigrant, in an effort to keep the town of Taninga connected to the Argentine capital, Buenos Aires. It's a road of blind curves, switchbacks and a rare 'pigtail' – a road bridge that loops back over itself.

Dug into a rocky mountainside, where the Sierras fall abruptly to the vast plain of La Rioja below, this road has almost negligible traffic, and consequently there are plenty of opportunities to get out of your car and examine the exquisite masonry of the tunnels up close. Proceed with caution, though: a smattering of feeble wooden guardrails and crumbling knee-high walls on the highest stretches offer little room for error. **BDS**

Trans-Andean Highway
Argentina/Chile

Start Mendoza, Argentina
End Santiago, Chile
Distance 364km (226 miles)
Type Scenic
Map goo.gl/LmsJKW

Argentina's classic National Route Seven crosses the country from east to west. Starting in the capital, Buenos Aires, it travels up into the Andes to cross the border into Chile, where it becomes the CH 60 and CH-57 down the far side of the mountains into the capital Santiago or onwards to the Pacific Ocean port of Valparaiso.

The whole route is an adventurous road trip, but this scenic drive covers only a small section. It's the stretch from the wine-growing city of Mendoza, over the Andes, close to the snowy peak of South America's highest mountain, Aconcagua, 6,962m (22,841ft) above sea level.

Most of the road is excellent, with smooth tarmac and good signage. There are often tricky sections where maintenance work is happening or when there's a buildup of freight traffic. Watch out, too, for some serious hairpin bends.

At the Chilean frontier, 3,832m (12,572ft) above sea level, a landmark statue, Christ the Redeemer of the Andes, marks the start of Los Libertadores International Pass. There's a tunnel between the two nations, so you are underground when you go through the border checkpoints.

Generally, the route is a safe and easy chance to see the scenery of the high Andes, but it can be tricky in winter. Check official weather reports and ignore local rumours. **SH**

❶ The coast-to-coast highway winds its way through the jagged peaks of the Andes.

9 de Julio Avenue Buenos Aires, Argentina

Start Presidente Arturo Illia 212, Retiro   End Ruta Nacional 205, Avellaneda   Distance 8km (5 miles)
Type Culture   Map goo.gl/rSzxEX

The 9 de Julio Avenue in Buenos Aires is the widest street in the world: it spans a city block and is 16 lanes wide. Although this route is short in length, it could take almost any amount of time, depending on the traffic congestion in what is the Argentine capital's busiest north-to-south thoroughfare.

The avenue is named after Argentina's Independence Day, and that is reflected in the major historical monuments along the route.

From the Presidente Arturo Illia expressway (a toll road), head south onto 9 de Julio Avenue. The first building of note is the opera house, Teatro Colón, which was built in 1908 to signal to the world that Buenos Aires was a city of culture. Ahead in the distance is a 67-m- (220-ft) high obelisk. The white structure stands on the central reservation in the Plaza de la República, at the intersection with Corrientes. Ever since its completion in 1936, this place has been a venue for public gatherings of all sorts – national celebrations and political protests. Continue straight ahead to Agenda de Mayo avenue, keeping a lookout for the statue of Don Quixote, the hero of Miguel de Cervantes's 1605 novel. The road is surrounded by greenery on both sides as it continues to a bridge that crosses the Matanza River and ends at Ruta Nacional 25. **CK**

❶ The avenue and the obelisk.

Che Guevara's *The Motorcycle Diaries* Argentina and more

Start San Francisco, Santa Fe, Argentina   End Buenos Aires, Argentina   Distance 18,864km (11,722 miles)
Type Culture   Info goo.gl/s4B9pD

In 1952, medical student Che Guevara and his pal Alberto Granado took a break from college for a nine-month motorbike tour of South America.

Retracing their route today takes considerable determination. From their university town, they went first to Buenos Aires and then rode through the Andes, the Amazon rainforest and the Atacama Desert. The entire journey took in six countries – Argentina, Chile, Peru, Colombia, Venezuela and the United States. Whichever way you tackle such a huge distance, it is highly likely to be a life-changing trip. And so it was for Che, who famously was inspired by the poverty he saw to become a committed revolutionary.

The website referenced here gives the full itinerary, but it would be unrealistic to attempt it all, and the penultimate leg, which took the young men from Caracas, Venezuela, to Miami, Florida, can only really be undertaken by air.

Che wrote a memoir about the trip, *Diarios de Motocicleta* (*The Motorcycle Diaries*), which was made into a film in 2004 directed by Brazilian Walter Salles and starring Mexican actor Gael García Bernal as Che. Rodrigo de la Serna, the Argentine who plays Granado, is in real life a cousin of Guevara, who was killed in 1967 in Bolivia. **SH**

❶ A still from the 2004 movie.

Valdés Peninsula
Chubut, Argentina

Start Puerto Madryn
End Punta Pardelas
Distance 315km (196 miles)
Type Scenic
Map goo.gl/sdBqbU

This itinerary is a road circuit around the Valdés Peninsula, a flat, windy promontory in southern Argentina. It's a warm, dry area of Patagonia bisected by long, straight roads across huge, empty landscapes dotted with occasional sheep. If you're lucky, you may spot the ostrichlike rhea that lives in the grasses here.

There's a desolate and melancholy beauty to this landscape; between the endless stretches of straight, smooth, gravel highways are the strange salt lakes, some of which are among the lowest spots of South America, at 40m (130ft) below sea level. But the main reason that road trippers venture to the Valdés Peninsula is because it is one of the best places in the world to observe penguins. There are colonies of hundreds of thousands of them here, some more than half a mile away from the water. You are also likely to see elephant seals and sea lions. Perhaps best of all, you can sometimes catch one of the most exciting natural scenes in the world: huge orcas deliberately beaching themselves trying to catch seals.

Take local advice about which are the best current wildlife-spotting places along the shore of the peninsula. There are plenty of guides and boat trips available. The sea life on the Valdés Peninsula is so special that the whole area has been designated a UNESCO World Heritage Site. SH

Ruta Provincial 31
Chubut, Argentina

Start Junction for RN 25 and RP 31
End Estancia la Concepción
Distance 89km (55 miles)
Type Scenic
Map goo.gl/6tbCpi

In the middle of a vast, flat, arid plain, you'll turn off the smooth tarmac of RN 25 in southern Argentina onto an unpaved track heading south. The new road is flat, straight and featureless, like a drag-racing strip. For miles you'll speed through the dusty savanna without needing to adjust your steering wheel or handlebars. Don't nod off, though, because suddenly you'll be required to negotiate a bend, then another, and the now-paved road starts dropping down through rock arches and rugged canyons. After all that, you reach the spectacular Florentino Ameghino hydroelectric dam. You drive right across the top of this landmark, named after a local naturalist. It's a good place to stop for photos. On one side the waters lead back into flooded rocky gorges; on the other there's a village in a valley.

The road winds through crude rock tunnels into a series of exciting twists and turns between red rock formations. Now it seems as if you're in Arizona, sweeping between jagged rock cliffs and huge stone pillars amid the gorges of the upper Chubut River. Eventually, you'll climb back up onto a high sierra for another session of long, straight, flat mile-crunching. Then suddenly you reach the RN 3 at Estancia La Concepción, and this surreal driving adventure is over. SH

⊙ The lake behind the dam on the Chubut River.

Ruta Nacional 40
Santa Cruz to Jujuy, Argentina

Start Punta Loyola, Santa Cruz
End La Quiaca, Jujuy
Distance 5,024km (3,122 miles)
Type Adventure
Info goo.gl/WlhkLk

How's this for a nice little road trip? Argentina's longest highway – and one of the world's longest roads – is the glorious Ruta Internacional 40. It runs for more than 5,000km (3,500 miles) from the southern tip of the country – one of the closest points in South America to Antarctica – to the Bolivian border in the high Andes.

A road journey of that length is going to be a major expedition, so expect to encounter a long list of sights and experiences as you travel the entire length of Argentina. For example, your highlights might include seeing the prehistoric hand paintings at the UNESCO World Heritage Site Cueva de las Manos or the 47 glaciers in Los Glaciares National Park. You'll also have the chance to visit the colourful rocks and mountains of the Calchaquí Valleys and Argentina's wine capital, Mendoza. La Cuarenta, as the locals call it, follows the eastern edge of the Andes throughout its length, so there are always great views.

Much of the road is now paved, and there are plans in place to complete the job in order to boost trade and tourist traffic. To Argentines, the route's symbolic significance is similar to that of Route 66 across the United States: it is the subject of countless myths and songs, and the kind of journey that many South Americans have thought about or plan to make one day. **SH**

❶ The road near Monte Fitz Roy in the Southern Patagonian Ice Field.

Ruta 3, Tierra del Fuego
Ushuaia, Argentina

Start Argentina–Chile border
End Ushuaia
Distance 399km (248 miles)
Type Adventure
Map goo.gl/KHkrKO

Driving south on the world's most southerly paved road, Argentina's Ruta 3 from Buenos Aires, there are two major barriers on the approaches to Tierra del Fuego. One is human-made (a border crossing into Chile), the other natural (the Strait of Magellan). Once across the water, you re-enter Argentina where the road reverts to Ruta 3 for the final push to Ushuaia, the world's southernmost city, through the bleak, dangerous and lonely hinterlands of the rugged archipelago.

The Tierra del Fuego section of Ruta 3 begins as a narrow and poorly maintained gravel road, but improves the farther south it goes. The weather here is changeable in the extreme, with the region's subpolar climate, bringing harsh winds and frequent snowfalls during the southern winter between April and September. In the warmer months, however, it offers a unique road trip experience through a landscape of stark beauty and desolate solitude.

The midpoint of this itinerary is the provincial capital, Río Grande, where there is accommodation to suit all budgets. Taking a 4x4 will increase your options if you want to stay overnight in one of the surrounding estancias, many of which lie off the main road along rough, unpaved tracks. Otherwise keep driving. Never miss an opportunity to fill up your petrol tank and make sure in advance that there are no road closures. **BDS**

Discover Uruguay
Maldonado/Rocha, Uruguay

Start Punta del Este, Maldonado
End Punta del Diablo, Rocha
Distance 193km (120 miles)
Type Adventure
Map goo.gl/aYY2zr

This is an adventure trail between two seaside resorts that could not be more different in character. You'll start at Punta del Este, which is one of Uruguay's – and South America's – flashiest seaside cities. Its apartment blocks and luxury villas stand on an idyllic sandy peninsula at the mouth of La Plata River, to the east of the capital, Montevideo. Among the expensive yachts, chic restaurants and beautiful people, the highlights of Punta del Este include a landmark statue of five fingers protruding from the sandy beach, and a Monte Carlo-like racing circuit through the city streets. You won't be racing, but you will head east along the shore.

As much as you can, follow Route 10, calling at beaches such as El Caracol and La Paloma. Gradually you'll see Uruguay transform from the Riviera into a South American equivalent of the US Wild West. The highway becomes a rutted dirt track in places, and the resorts become less glossy and more suited to laid-back surfers. At some points you will have to take detours inland to get around lagoons or river mouths. Route 10 is not a continuous highway. By the time you reach Punta del Diablo you'll probably have a bandana around your head and a tie-dyed T-shirt. Relax and enjoy a more bohemian experience here among the driftwood bonfires and makeshift beach bars of this colony of backpackers and artists. **SH**

Europe

Experience the spectacular high road of the Transalpina in Romania.

Route 622 Westfjords, Iceland

Start Thingeyri **End** Fossdalur **Distance** 37km (23 miles)
Type Adventure **Map** goo.gl/lrPYS3

This is a road trip for the intrepid around the edge of a remote headland between two fjords – Dyrafjördur and Arnafjördur – in the far northwest of Iceland. Even in good weather, Route 622 is passable only by robust 4x4s with high wheel clearance. However, as might be expected at this latitude, the weather is seldom good: from the land side, there is a constant danger of falling rocks; the sea side is uncomfortably close, and the tide washes away the track at least a couple of times each year. The road is closed more often than it's open (the best time to try it is in spring), and the only way to find out its current status in advance is to ask at the petrol station in Thingeyri.

To make matters worse, the skies might be clear and the road open at the outset, but there is no telling what might happen in the hour needed to complete the journey: storms blow up suddenly in these parts; even a small amount of rainfall makes the track slippery, and over the edge lies nothing but ocean.

Route 622 is sometimes known as 'The Dream Road', but usually only by people who have never driven it or those with a strong sense of irony. But nightmares are survivable, and this one is exciting at the time and entertaining to look back on. **JP**

❶ Along the route near Thingeyri.

Route 61 Westfjords, Iceland

Start Hólmavík   End Ísafjördur   Distance 220km (137 miles)
Type Adventure   Map goo.gl/aCPnC6

The south of Iceland is challenging enough for most tourists, but this part of the far northwest of the island makes Reykjavik and the Golden Circle (Thingvellir, Gullfoss and Geysir) seem almost manicured and soigné. Only one in ten visitors makes it this far, and thus for nature-loving road-trippers it's unmissable.

Route 61 between Hólmavík and Ísafjördur takes the only course available to it, hugging tight to the coast for the greater part of its length. And since the sea forms five fjords that eat deep into the landmass around here, that means plenty of wiggling and numerous tight hairpin bends. Almost the only relief from zigzagging comes on the bridge across

the mouth of Mjólfjordur, the second of the inlets, but it's there that you'll probably feel the iciest blasts of the winds that blow in off Isafjardardjúp, the sea lane that opens out into the North Atlantic Ocean only 64km (40 miles) below the Arctic Circle.

Conditions along Route 61 are seldom balmy, but the best time to drive it is between 10 and 29 June, when daytime temperatures soar to 10°C (50 °F) and there is 24-hour daylight – this is the Land of the Midnight Sun.

Ísafjördur is the site of the oldest house in Iceland. Built in 1734, it is now a folk museum. **JP**

❶ The austere beauty of Ísafjördur.

Golden Circle Capital Region/Southern Region, Iceland

Start Reykjavik **End** Reykjavik **Distance** 319km (198 miles)
Type Scenic **Map** goo.gl/8rhrG8

The Golden Circle is a popular day trip over smooth, well-maintained highway. The loop passes some of Iceland's must-see natural and historic attractions. The foremost of the latter is Thingvellir National Park, site of the first Icelandic parliament and more recently a film location for TV's *Game of Thrones*.

The geological highlights soon follow. A walkable trail passes along the dividing line between the North American and Eurasian plates – the Mid-Atlantic Ridge – plates that are still being dragged apart. This is the only place on Earth where such formations have risen above the surface.

At Haukadalur, geothermal delights await, including the Strokkur geyser, which erupts every few minutes spouting scalding water 30m (100ft) into the air, and from there to Gullfoss, where two waterfalls combine to cascade over three giant steps of solidified lava at the rate of 140 cubic metres (30,000 gallons) per second.

Also worth a stop en route is the Kerid volcanic crater, ringed with mosses and vibrant red and green mineralized soils. It takes five minutes to hike down from the rim to the crater's lake, and this is well worth doing. This short road trip into Iceland's southern uplands provides a fabulous introduction to this remarkable land of fire and ice. **BDS**

❶ Part of the Gullfoss waterfalls.

Iceland's Ring Road Capital Region and more, Iceland

Start Reykjavik   **End** Reykjavik   **Distance** 1,286km (799 miles)
Type Adventure   **Map** goo.gl/qHroMI

There are so many natural wonders on this round trip that you'll be skimping it if you try to do it in less than a week; ten days are needed to do it full justice.

Leaving the capital, the well-maintained tarmac of Route 1 leads east to Seljalandsfoss, a picturesque waterfall that you can walk behind, between the cascade and the cliff. The next stop is Vik, where there is the first of many beaches of black, volcanic sand.

At Jökulsárlón the road crosses a short metal bridge, on the north side of which is a small bay that is packed year round with icebergs that have calved from the glacier on the landward shore. Watch and listen to them as they roll around almost within reach and jostle each other to reach the exit to the sea.

At the fishing port of Höfn there are spectacular views of Vatnajökull, the nation's largest glacier. The next section of the trip crosses bleak ash fields created by recent volcanic activity before reaching the banks of Myvatn, a shallow lake – maximum depth 2.5m (8ft) – famed for its enormous populations of ducks and midges.

Next comes Iceland's second city, Akureyri, which boasts the world's most northerly eighteen-hole golf course. Beyond Laugarbakki, the road turns back inland; from here the going is easy back to the starting point at Reykjavik. **JP**

➊ At Jökulsárlón you can almost touch the icebergs.

Kaldidalsvegur Southern Region/Western Region, Iceland

Start Thingvellir, Southern Region   End Husafell, Western Region   Distance 70km (43.5 miles)
Type Adventure   Map goo.gl/8y855e

Iceland's Kaldidalsvegur – officially Highway 550 – is shorter than most of the other roads across the interior of this surprisingly temperate country, but it is its very brevity, and its proximity to the capital, Reykjavik, that make it so popular.

Kaldidalsvegur is a well-maintained gravel road, ideal for any 4x4 (or high-clearance 2WD) and a good place to learn what it's like to drive off-road here. Highway 550 – sometimes nicknamed the 'Highlands for Beginners' – has no unbridged streams or other nasty surprises, just a long, flat trail of loose and compacted stones. Once comfortable here, the country's frozen heart – the Central Highlands, crisscrossed by a network of designated

4x4-only F roads – will start to beckon. Highway 550 begins to the north of Thingvellir, site of the nation's first parliament established in 930, and heads north, past the small glacier volcano of Thorisjokull and the shield volcano of Ok before reaching the farming estate of Husafell. And while driving Iceland's sealed Route 1, its famed Ring Road, is something everyone must do, nothing makes the hairs on the back of your neck stand up quite like leaving it behind and finding yourself crunching and sometimes sliding along a tantalizing expanse of Icelandic gravel. **BDS**

❶ The Hvita River from the side of Kaldidalsvegur.

Old Road to Sumba Suðuroy Island, Faroe Islands

Start Lopra   **End** Sumba   **Distance** 11km (6.8 miles)
Type Scenic   **Map** goo.gl/uVwxLP

The Faroe Islands sit between Norway and Iceland, their scenery like a smaller-scale version of both. The southernmost island, Suðuroy, has a hilly interior that rises to 610m (2,000ft), and this old road takes drivers on a switchback ride up and across the island. Note that it can be dangerous in winter, and is not to be driven during the extreme weather conditions of which the Faroes have plenty.

Although tarmacked, it is a single-track road for much of its length, with occasional passing places, so it is not for those who don't like backing up – not that you're likely to meet much traffic on it. There is an alternative route between Lopra and Sumba through a road tunnel, the Sumbatunnellen, but this ragged old road is for those who like a challenge and prefer the scenic route up and over.

After leaving Lopra, the road soon starts to climb, twist and turn, and takes you into an area so peaceful and quiet that it makes Lopra, with its population of fewer than 100, seem like a thriving metropolis. An essential stop – you won't miss it, the road passes very close – is at Beinisvørð. This is the highest sea cliff on the island, at 470m (1,542ft). Those with vertigo may prefer to find one of the several spots on the island where you can see it from the sides or looking up. **MG**

❶ The cliffs midway between Lopra and Sumba.

Senja National Tourist Route Northern Norway, Norway

Start Gryllefjord
End Botnhamn
Distance 101km (63 miles)
Type Scenic
Info goo.gl/m9XOjC

The island of Senja lies off the north coast of Norway, near Tromso. It covers a vast 1,586 sq km (612 square miles), yet only has 7,800 inhabitants. So don't expect traffic jams.

The sheltered south coast is a gentle, green place with lush fields and rounded hills. The north is different: it faces the open Arctic seas, and wave-battered fjords have torn the coastline into long fingers of steep-sided rock. Among the jagged sea mountains you'll discover fishing villages clinging to the shore.

The views are stupendous. At Bergsbotn they have built a wooden viewing platform high on the slopes overlooking the fjord. Nearby Ersfjord's white sand beach is great for bracing walks. But don't expect to go swimming.

At the fishing village on Husoy Island, reached by a tunnel, wooden houses are tied to the rocks with cables to stop them from being torn away by the fierce winds.

Senja's north coast is one long sequence of distracting views, but reaching it takes a bit of planning. There's a bridge to the mainland in the south and local ferries to both end points. Best of all, try linking the drive with the Hurtigruten (the Fast One), Norway's coastal express car ferry. **SH**

● Ersfjord from Senja.

Andøya National Tourist Route
Northern Norway, Norway

Start Andenes
End Akneskrysset
Distance 58km (36 miles)
Type Scenic
Info goo.gl/hLU5Lf

The surprising thing about driving in northern Norway is that, despite the inhospitable climate, the roads are quite normal. Temperatures can be incredibly cold, but you often pass people doing normal things, like cycling or walking the dogs.

So a super-scenic stretch like this route along the coast of Andøya, one of the Vesteralen Islands, can give you a snapshot of what life is like almost 300km (200 miles) inside the Arctic Circle, between Narvik and Tromsø.

The scenery is wild, but the roads are smooth and well signed, and there are numerous stylish cafés along the way.

This is one of the finest coastlines in the world, so expect magnificent views of white sand beaches, rugged mountains rising up from a sea peppered with islands and tiny fishing villages clinging to the shore.

Locals say that the water here is so full of nutrients that there's a 95 per cent chance of seeing whales. Other highlights could be a show by the Northern Lights or a visit to a space exploration museum: Andøya is the launch site for Norway's blossoming space program.

In summer a car ferry links Andenes with the island of Senja, where you can continue exploring along another spectacular Norwegian National Tourist Route. **SH**

❶ A trip along the coastline of west Andøya offers magnificent views of long, white, sandy beaches.

Varanger National Tourist Route

Northern Norway, Norway

Start Varangabotn
End Hamningberg
Distance 159km (99 miles)
Type Scenic
Info goo.gl/VCjVUm

Traversing the very top of Europe, this road snakes along the coastline of the far northeastern point of Norway, near its border with Russia.

As might be expected given its proximity to the North Pole, this route is open only between May and November – for the rest of the year, it is covered with snow and in constant darkness. Even in the summer months it's a bleak, challenging place, but one that you will never forget – never warm, rarely pretty, but always captivating.

You'll start in the comparative sophistication of Varangerbotn, a tiny town sheltered at the head of the Varanga Fjord. People travel from miles around to the shops, bars and garage here. Amid jagged cliffs and icy winds, it feels like the end of the world – and in some ways it is.

The road gets narrower and the landscape less hospitable as you drive out along the fjord shore. At times plants have just given up and the scenery seems more lunar than earthly. Watch out for sections of exposed road with no safety barriers.

After such a journey perhaps it's fitting to arrive at Hamningberg and find that it is a ghost town, an abandoned fishing village where old grass-topped wooden houses stare blankly out across a sandy beach into the Arctic Ocean. You'll do the same, braced against the chill, before turning round and heading back to civilization. **SH**

❶ The closer you get to Hamningberg, the more the landscape resembles that of the Moon.

Havøysund National Tourist Route
Northern Norway, Norway

Start Kokelv
End Havøysund
Distance 66km (41 miles)
Type Scenic
Info goo.gl/tSpxNN

Plenty of people see the coast of Norway from the deck of a cruise ship, but the way to get the full flavour of the place is on a road trip. This one, inside the Arctic Circle, takes just a couple of hours and is a mere taster compared to the Helgelands Kysten National Tourist Route or the Atlantic Road, but it still packs a visual punch – verdant fjords, fantastic road furniture (viewpoints, rest areas, bridges) and wildlife. In winter, you may see the Northern Lights; in summer, expect the Midnight Sun. If you are lucky, you may see reindeer, seals and sea eagles.

Heading out from the scattered community of Kokelv, the 889 wiggles north through the jagged landscape, dipping within inches of the water in places, then twisting around rocky outcrops. After 14km (9 miles), Lillefjord offers the first architectural feature – a curling white shelter leading to a 'love bench' overlooking the beach. If you miss this one, Snefjord, 18km (11 miles) farther on, has wooden shelters that enclose their occupants like cabinets, protecting them from whipping Arctic winds. The quaint fishing community of Havøysund, 38km (23 miles) later, marks the end of this road trip. The cluster of red, yellow and blue houses, loosely gathered around a church with a wooden steeple, includes places to eat and stay. It is also a stop on the Hurtigruten (the Fast One), a ferry-cum-cruise ship that hops along the coast. **DS**

E69 Northern tip of Europe
Northern Norway, Norway

Start Olderfjord
End North Cape
Distance 111km (69 miles)
Type Adventure
Info goo.gl/ApK6Md

The E69 begins at Olderfjord on Porsangerfjord, one of Norway's largest fjords; skirting its shoreline, beneath its barren hills of fractured rock and mica schist-encrusted cliffs, it is populated with little more than a scattering of *rorbu*, traditional fishermen's huts. It may not be the world's northernmost bitumous road (roads on Svalbard and Greenland are at higher latitudes), but it's the most northerly road that connects to other international highways. Good news indeed if you're wanting to get to the E69's ultimate destination: Mageroya Island's North Cape, just 2,100km (1,305 miles) from the North Pole.

Once accessible only by ferry, Mageroya is a tundra-covered, treeless landscape with 300-m (1,000-ft) cliffs overlooking the Atlantic Ocean and the Barents Sea. To get there you'll pass through five tunnels, including the spectacular 6.9-km- (4.3-mile) long North Cape Tunnel, one of the country's longest undersea tunnels with 9–10 per cent gradients at either end, connecting Mageroya to the mainland.

The goal of many who drive the E69 is to see the midnight sun, fog permitting, which shines here from mid-May to the end of July. And maybe even make the 16-km- (10-mile) long hike to the northerly tip of mainland Europe at Knivskjellodden. **BDS**

➔ The long and winding road to the North Cape.

Mo i Rana to the Arctic Raceway

Northern Norway, Norway

Start Mo i Rana
End Storforshei
Distance 25.7km (16 miles)
Type Adventure
Info goo.gl/jvNvG6

Mo i Rana in northern Norway is often referred to as the Gateway to the Arctic. Most road trippers converge here to pick up the E12 and the 910-km-(570-mile) long Blue Highway Tourist Route that winds southeast to Helsinki, Finland.

However, if you prefer road trip kicks of a slightly higher octane, then there is a little-known place just half an hour's drive to the north of Mo i Rana.

The 3.75-km- (2.33-mile) long Arctic Raceway circuit opened in 1995 on the site of a disused iron-ore quarry. Its intricate looping layout, with 31m (102ft) of elevation change, was designed primarily for motorcycles, but for many years it also held rounds of the Swedish Touring Car Championship. With constant summer daylight – this is the Land of the Midnight Sun – it has been the go-to circuit for Scandinavian 24-hour endurance races. However, because it is a good 13-hour drive from Oslo, it remains a low-key venue.

To get there, follow the E6 highway north from Mo i Rana through thick pine forests before picking up the road signs from the village of Storforshei, just 30km (19 miles) below the Arctic Circle. On days when there is no official event on the circuit, visitors can drop in and, for a reasonably modest fee, have a thrash around the world's most northerly racetrack. **DIS**

Helgelands Kysten National Route

Northern Norway, Norway

Start Holm
End Godøystraumen
Distance 433km (269 miles)
Type Adventure
Info goo.gl/iJkEww

The longest of Norway's 18 National Routes, the FV17 allows motorists to explore the Helgelands, a rocky web of thousands of islands, islets and skerries, the larger ones strung together by bridges and causeways or linked by ferries. This grand drive north includes six ferry crossings (book in advance), beginning with a hop from Holm to Vennesund. The route crosses the Arctic Circle just before Jetvic.

Architecturally designed rest areas – clean, crisp and minimalist – are dotted throughout the route, and invite road trippers to stop and probe the Norwegian tradition of *allemansätten* (every man's right). Don't miss the Enbrageen Glacier (pull in at the rest area at Braset for the best view); the mountain chain known as the Seven Sisters, rising sharply above the coastal strandflat south of Sandnessjøen; or the long beach at Storvika. At Horn, you can take a ferry to the UNESCO World Heritage Site of Vega, an archipelago of some 6,500 islands and skerries that has been a centre for the production of eiderdown since the 9th century.

If tracing the intricate indentations of the fjords becomes too time-consuming, you can bypass sections of the route by transferring to the E6 freeway, which remains inland. This cuts through the Saltfjellet Svarisen National Park before reaching the village of Godøystraumen. **DS**

Nordkalotten
(Cap of the North)
Norway/Sweden

Start Narvik, Northern Norway, Norway
End Kiruna, Lapland, Sweden
Distance 179km (111 miles)
Type Adventure
Map goo.gl/syvphK

The Nordkalotten (Cap of the North) route is the section of the E10 highway that connects Narvik on the Norwegian coast with Kiruna, the northernmost city in Sweden. Prior to the completion of this road in 1984, the only connection between the two cities was by train. This is a journey through one of Europe's last areas of true wilderness, a preserved landscape of Nordic fell in northern Lapland.

Almost half your time will be spent driving along the southern shoreline of the beautiful, 70-km- (43-mile) long Tornetrask, a glacial remnant and Sweden's second-deepest lake and, at 200km (125 miles) above the Arctic Circle, one of Scandinavia's most popular locations to view the Northern Lights. Surrounded by mountain peaks as high as 1,700m (5,580ft), this is as serene a drive as one can possibly have, often with little or no traffic to distract wandering eyes.

South from Tornetrask is Abisko National Park, a small 7,700-hectare (19,000-acre) park established in 1909 that hosts a trailhead to one of Sweden's most popular hiking routes, the Kungsleden (King's Trail). From the road you can also see Lapporten, Sweden's renowned U-shaped valley bookmarked by identical twin peaks – the legendary gate to Lapland – that will have you looking for a trail to take you right into the heart of the region. **BDS**

❶ Lapporten (Lappish Gate) is a gap between the mountains in Abisko National Park.

The Blue Highway
Norway to Russia

Start Mo i Rana, Norway
End Pudozh, Russia
Distance 1,790km (1,112 miles)
Type Adventure
Map goo.gl/dFoOfR

The concept of the Blue Highway, a tourist route linking Norway, Sweden and Finland, was hatched during the Cold War (1947–91). After the collapse of communism, Russia opened its border at Vyartsilya, and in 2000 the route was extended to Pudozh on Lake Onega in Russian Karelia. The tag 'Blue' alludes to the fact that the road runs alongside a succession of lakes and rivers through some of the finest Nordic scenery, brushing the southern fringes of Lapland; the road is also a celebration of Karelian culture.

The route begins at Mo i Rana, in Helgeland, near the Arctic Circle in Norway, and follows the E12 to the Swedish border at Storuman. Continuing on the Swedish portion of the E12, it heads southeast, passing lakes and forests to the port of Umeå, from which it's a short ferry ride through the heavenly Kvarken archipelago to the Finnish town of Vaasa. From there, the route (now on roads 16, 77 and 9) leads to Finland's Lakeland – a lacy labyrinth of land and water that forms the largest lake district in Europe. There is plenty to detain you here – delightful wooden cottages (with saunas) to rent, kayaking among the skerries and little churches with wooden belfries. Niirala, on the Russian border, is the gateway to the final stretch of the journey, a 500-km (300-mile) drive to Pudozh in the republic of Karelia. **DS**

Hardanger National Tourist Route
Western Norway, Norway

Start Granvin
End Låtefossen waterfall
Distance 158km (98.2 miles)
Type Scenic
Info goo.gl/XNvU6S

This itinerary starts in Granvin, a small town of a few hundred citizens, which stands between the Granvinsvatnet lake and the Granvin fjord. It's the only part of western Norway in which you'll find spruce forests, and scenically the whole area is an absolute gem of nature.

The first part of the journey hugs the western side of the fjord, whose steep wooded slopes rise up on either side of the water. This is awe-inspiring enough, but then you discover that the Granvin fjord leads into the Hardangerfjord, the fourth-longest fjord in the world, and from here the drive just gets better. It doesn't cover the whole length of the fjord, which leads all the way to the Atlantic Ocean, going only as far as the village of Tørvikbygd, where the fjord narrows slightly, and from which there's a ferry that takes you across the water to the village of Jondal, from where an onward drive heads up the eastern side of Hardangerfjord.

At Utne another ferry takes you across the waters where the Sørfjorden and Eidfjorden meet and join into both the Granvin fjord and the Hardangerfjord. This itinerary ends at the Låtefossen waterfall, where two separate cascades tumble down the hillside and meet in the middle to end in a single giant torrent. **MG**

● Låtefossen sprays the road as it falls into the fjord.

Sognefjellet National Tourist Route Western Norway, Norway

Start Gaupne, Sogn og Fjordane   End Lom, Oppland   Distance 108km (67 miles)
Type Scenic   Info goo.gl/usDq8j

Northern Europe's highest mountain pass road is best seen in May, when it re-opens after the long dark winter. The route runs between huge banks of snow and frozen lakes with white mountains all around, but the road is as clear and safe as any stretch of summertime highway. It twists up to a pass at 1,430m (4,692ft) in the heart of Norway's wild Jotunheimen National Park. This rugged area of central Norway is home to the country's highest peaks. Look out for photogenic panoramas with waterfalls plunging down the sides of mountains into fjords below, or a pretty traditional wooden stave church against a backdrop of thick forest. One of the most photographed spots is the modern square stone sculpture at the Storevasskrysset rest area, surrounded by bleak high-altitude wilderness. At Nedre Oscarhaug, there is a viewing point with a useful glass panel through which you can look to see all the mountain peaks labelled.

Historically, the R55 across Sognefjellet was a vital way of getting inland from the coastal fjords to the fertile farming valleys of eastern Norway. Today, it is a popular tourist route, both for the scenery and for the access to energetic and typically Norwegian mountain activities, which range from glacier hiking to ice climbing. **SH**

❶ The road undulates along the mountainside.

Lysebotn Road Western Norway/Southern Norway, Norway

Start Lysebotn, Western Norway   **End** Sinnes, Southern Norway   **Distance** 45km (28 miles)
Type Adventure   **Map** goo.gl/3EPOLW

Truly great motoring adventures should ideally mix incredible views with elevation changes, flowing straights, switchbacks and tunnels. Lysebotn Road, running above and alongside the dramatic Lysefjorden, has all these ingredients and something more: a hairpinned 1,103-m- (3,619-ft) long tunnel.

This roughly cut borehole deep in the heart of the Lysefjorden's towering granite mountains is one of 27 hairpin bends on a road that was completed in 1984 to serve the Tjodan hydroelectric power station.

The road, which is open only between late May and early September, descends from Andersvatn Lake at 932m (3,057ft) to fjord level over 32 sharp

corners and hairpin bends with an average gradient of more than 9 per cent on an alternating single and two-lane roller coaster. The views on the way down are stupendous, as the route hops through rocky outcrops, boulder-strewn mountain slopes, fjords and forests on super-smooth tarmac replete with safety barriers.

While in the area you should not miss the chance to hike to the top of the mighty 1,084-m- (3,556-ft) high Kjerag and stand on the Kjeragbolten, a giant boulder wedged into a high crevice. Do this, and Lysebotn Road suddenly won't seem so scary. **BDS**

🛈 Lysebotn lies at the end of the fjord.

Trollstigen National Tourist Route Western Norway, Norway

Start Andalsnes **End** Valldall **Distance** 106km (66 miles)
Type Adventure **Info** goo.gl/Pngw1D

Opened in July 1936 after eight years' construction, the Trollstigen (Troll's Road) high above Geirangerfjord has an average gradient of 10 per cent and the unforgettable Ornesvingen (Eagle's Road), the 11 hairpin bends on mountainside between sea level at the edge of the fjord and Stigrora, 858m (2,81ft) above.

Parts of an old packhorse trail – a bridlepath finished in 1913 – can still be seen, and the road takes you past some of Norway's most sublime waterfalls, including Dei Sju Systre, Friaren, Stigfossen and Brudesloret. Numerous viewing points allow you to take in the Gudbrandsjuvet Gorge and the Valldalen valley, and the Trollstigen mountain plateau provides views over the entire serpentine route. Today, it is the most popular of all Norway's National Tourist Routes: even though it is open only in the summer months, it still attracts more than 500,000 visitors each year.

Don't let anything deter you from experiencing this drive, which takes you close to the 1,0897-m- (3,600-ft) high Trollveggen (Troll Wall), Europe's highest vertical rock face. According to Norwegian legend, this a world where ugly, slow-witted trolls wander the hills and mountain trails, causing mischief to all who pass, as 'swallowers of the wheel'. **BDS**

❶ The road viewed from the summit.

Laerdal Tunnel Western Norway, Norway

Start Laerdalsøyri   **End** Laerdalsøyri   **Distance** 71.5km (44.4 miles)
Type Adventure   **Map** goo.gl/j7vixR

King Harald of Norway cut the ribbon at the opening of the world's longest road tunnel in November 2000. This 24.5-km- (15.2-mile) long tunnel carrying two lanes of the E16 between Laerdal and Aurland has created an important all-weather ferry-free road link between Bergen and Oslo.

To keep regular road users alert during the drive, the tunnel has been split up into four sections by creating three large 'mountain halls' at 6-km (4-mile) intervals. These huge caverns, complete with rest areas (and turnaround points for claustrophobics), are bathed in bright blue and golden lighting to create the illusion of driving into the sunrise and thus keep drivers' brains stimulated.

The old overland 'Snow Road' – now redesignated as the National Tourist Route Aurlandsfjellet – offers a breathtaking return trip over the 1,306-m- (4,285-ft) high mountain pass above the Laerdal Tunnel. Usually open between June and November, this 47-km- (29.2-mile) long stretch threads through desolate mountain landscapes, barren snowfields and lonely pine forest.

On this return leg, visitors should also make time to visit the award-winning Stegastein Lookout – a viewing platform jutting out from the mountainside over the Aurland Fjord. **DIS**

❶ Artificial sunshine effect in the Laerdal Tunnel.

The Atlantic Road
Western Norway, Norway

Start Vervang
End Kårvåg
Distance 8.4km (5.2 miles)
Type Adventure
Info goo.gl/O3fONS

With its eight breathtaking bridges combining panoramic views of mountains, sea and sky, this route has been compared to the back of a sea serpent as it arches up out of the ocean. This won't be the longest road trip on your bucket list, but it's certainly one of the most spectacular.

The Atlantic Road snakes from tiny island to tiny island along the western coast of Norway, starting in Vervang on the mainland and ending at Kårvåg on the island of Averøy.

Completed in 1989, the Atlantic Road has gained National Tourist Route Status, and on a clear day you may spot whales and seals close to the shore. However, the road really comes into its own when a storm sweeps across this exposed coast and motorists run the gauntlet as Atlantic rollers break across the causeway. Halfway along, the cantilevered Storseisundet Bridge rears up like an immense, tarmac-clad roller coaster, testing a driver's nerve in inclement weather.

Not only does this road provide a stunning drive across a magnificent archipelago, but there are also specially constructed fishing platforms alongside the Myrbaerholm Bridge where you can catch your own supper. What is more, you can combine the drive with a ferry trip to the quaint island of Haholmen, with its 18th-century fishing village and seafood restaurants. **DIS**

❶ Storseisundet Bridge is just one of the breathtaking sights along the Atlanterhavsveien.

Rondane National Tourist Route Eastern Norway, Norway

Start Enden
End Folldal
Distance 75km (46.6 miles)
Type Scenic
Info goo.gl/k6WftM

One of the most popular scenic drives in Norway, the Rondane National Tourist Route shows the Scandinavian landscape at its most spectacular, with views of lakes, mountains and forests. There are some human-made architectural delights along the way, too.

Starting in Enden, the route follows the eastern edge of Rondane National Park, which is an irresistibly tempting diversion. It is one of the few places in Europe where you might see herds of wild reindeer (most are now domesticated) and also roe deer and elk. Wolves and brown bear live here, too, but they are more elusive. In addition, you can enjoy the views of ten mountain peaks, each at more than 2,000m (6,562ft) above sea level. Rondeslottet is the highest, at 2,178m (7,146ft). This landscape inspired Norwegian author Henrik Ibsen in his play *Peer Gynt* (1867) and the Norwegian painter Harald Sohlberg.

Staying on the road, you will be rewarded with breathtaking views of Lake Atnsjøen from the swooping concrete viewing platforms at Sohlbergplassen. Beyond here, en route towards Folldal, there are endless glorious views of rivers, birch forests, lakes and heather-clad hillsides. To describe it as picture-postcard scenery does not do it justice. You need to get out, step into the postcard and breathe it all in. **MG**

Lysevegen Southern Norway/ Western Norway, Norway

Start Flatstølåna, Southern Norway
End Lysebotn, Western Norway
Distance 33km (20.5 miles)
Type Adventure
Map goo.gl/a2HnOx

It's one of the most extraordinary stretches of road in Europe. It will challenge and thrill everyone who tackles it. The Lysevegen is a seemingly endless zigzag down the sheer side of a deep fjord in southwest Norway.

The road involves 32 severe bends, steep gradients and excruciatingly narrow stretches where two cars cannot pass. The finale is a narrow tunnel that screws through almost a complete circle inside the rock before emerging at the sleepy fjordside village of Lysebotn. From there you can drive onto the ferry to Stavanger or drive back up the Lysevegen.

The village was cut off from the road network until 1984. The only way of reaching this end of the fjord was by boat. This special works road was built to move stone during the construction of a hydroelectric plant way up in the mountains.

Today the Lysevegen is a visitor attraction. You'll find online videos of rally drivers doing the whole thing in less than ten minutes. But it is best to allow rather longer for this journey, not least because of the speed limit – 80 kph (50 mph).

The Lysevegen is open only in summer, and even then you can be surrounded by tall snowdrifts. The final short, sharp descent is almost 1,000m (3,280ft) in a few miles. While passengers get eye-watering views, drivers get tired arms. **SH**

Marguerite Route
Denmark

Start Anywhere in Denmark
End Anywhere in Denmark
Distance 3,600km (2,237 miles)
Type Culture
Info goo.gl/mD6aah

Want to see everything that Denmark has to offer? And this means everything . . . Well, this self-drive tourist route is the complete answer. It's the creation of the Danish government as a way of linking up more than 1,000 of the country's attractions and sights, using its most picturesque roads. It's easy to follow, thanks to clear signs with a daisy symbol on a brown background, signifying the local flower that the route is named after.

You are allowed, of course, to do shorter sections of the route. You could, for example, arrive from England by ferry in Esbjerg and explore the wild beaches and dunes of the west coast. Then drive to discover Thy National Park, where pine forests lead down to the sea. Alternatively, you could fly into Copenhagen and hire a car or motorbike to tackle some of the great sights of Denmark's east coast, including the impressive castles at Kronborg (the notional setting of William Shakespeare's *Hamlet*), Frederiksborg and Holsteinborg.

No part of Denmark is untouched by the twists and turns of Marguerite. You could drive or ride down south to Funen Village, a whole community of half-timbered cottages unchanged since the days of Hans Christian Andersen; or head north, to Linholm Hoeje, Scandinavia's largest ancient burial ground, to see the impressive spot where 700 standing stones represent Viking graves. **SH**

Møns Klint Road
Zealand, Denmark

Start Vordingborg
End Geocentre Møns Klint, Borre
Distance 48km (29.8 miles)
Type Scenic
Map goo.gl/f9Rai7

After miles and miles of pancake-flat, tranquil countryside with distant ruler-straight horizons, it comes as something of a shock to get to the end of Møns Klint Road. Suddenly there are rolling hills covered with wild forests, leading to huge cliffs of white rock. It does not feel very Danish at all; particularly after such a pretty route following a smooth, open road through leafy villages, surrounded by vast grain fields under huge skies. Perhaps that is why the Møns area has become a popular destination for Danes on holiday.

Among the highlights are the chalk cliffs of Møns Klint, which are Denmark's highest. Down on the pebble beaches facing into the Baltic, these 120-m (400-ft) rock walls above certainly look imposing. Up on top, the paths through steep forests provide excellent viewing points from which to gaze at the views to the east. There is also a high-tech visitor centre with information on the geology of the area. From here, an impressive wooden staircase winds down through the woods to the beach.

It is a great area to explore by road; there are dozens of pretty lakes nestled among the woods. Look out for characterful half-timbered houses dotted through the trees, too. The hills here might be some of the highest in the country, but there is still no need to pack crampons. **SH**

Flatruetvägen
Jämtland, Sweden

Start Funäsdalen
End Åsarna
Distance 148km (92 miles)
Type Scenic
Map goo.gl/p1c34L

Everything in Sweden seems so well organized and safe. The roads are smooth, wide and clearly signed; the drivers courteous and careful. But even the Swedes cannot do anything about the weather. This means that this mountain pass, the highest road in Sweden, can be closed off at almost any time of the year because of its unpredictable conditions.

It is worth making the effort to reach it, though. From Funäsdalen Valley, climb through the Sami reindeer herders' village of Mittådalen and over the high and desolate Flatruet plateau at 975m (3,198ft). An impressive side valley leads to Ruandan, where you can park and walk a trail to see a collection of 4,000-year-old Stone Age paintings on huge slabs of rock. The route then drops down steeply into Ljungdalen Valley and to a pretty village deep in the cleft of the mountains. From here, the more energetic explorers hike off to visit Helags Glacier, Sweden's 'Holy Mountain'.

The road continues east across a memorable landscape: a largely uninhabited wilderness of tundra, swamp, forest and lakes. This is a long way from the stereotype of Swedish sophistication and design. Instead, it is lumberjack country. You will pass huge piles of felled timber waiting to be shipped away. Eventually, the road sweeps into the small lakeside town of Åsarna and the chance to return to civilization on the E45 highway. **SH**

❶ This route through central Sweden captures much of the essence of life in Scandinavia.

Vildmarksvägen (Wilderness Road)
Jämtland/Lapland, Sweden

● This section of the Wilderness Road across the Stekenjokk plateau is open only in the summer months.

Start Strömsund, Jämtland
End Vilhelmina, Lapland
Distance 364km (226 miles)
Type Adventure
Info goo.gl/7e31xe

The Vildmarksvägen (Wilderness Road) is one of the most dramatic drives in Scandinavia, and aptly named. The wilderness describes the scenery, although this doesn't necessarily imply that you won't see another soul on your road trip. This is a very popular drive, especially in summer, but if you're planning a winter trip, be aware that parts of the road will be closed, since the snow can be as much as 7m (23ft) deep.

The wilderness journey begins in the small town of Strömsund, but instead of taking the shortest route to journey's end at Vilhelmina, the Vildmarksvägen loops around to take in several of the remote communities in the surrounding region. Once out of Strömsund, you'll be driving through pine forests where you should watch out for brown bears, as this is where you'll find the largest population of them in the world. It's also home to lynx, polar foxes and wolverines.

You'll soon be driving alongside vast lakes, then heading towards the mountains around Gäddede and north to the town of Stora Blåsjön, which sits by a lake. There is a winter sports activity centre, if you fancy a stopover. More lakes and pine forests lead you eventually to Vilhelmina, whose lovely old town will seem positively cosy and welcoming after all the vast open expanses through which you have just driven. MG

Sweden's High Coast Road
Västernorrland, Sweden

Start Härnösand
End Örnköldsvik
Distance 105km (65 miles)
Type Scenic
Info goo.gl/7s9ACl

Sweden's High Coast reared up at the end of the last Ice Age when the continental ice sheet melted. The uplift pushed up islands and created high cliffs; at the same time, glaciers carved out deep inlets. Today, UNESCO recognizes this natural sculpture park as a Site of Universal Interest.

Around halfway between Stockholm and the Arctic Circle, the small town of Härnösand is the gateway to this coast. From there, the E4 heads north, crossing the High Coast Bridge, a Golden Gate lookalike, over Ångerman River after 25km (15 miles). The road then moves between coast and forest, with wide views over the islands in the Gulf of Bothnia from higher ground. There are little bays where you can stop for a swim, and mossy banks in the forests that are perfect for a rest; stop at one of the farm shops (*gårdsbutiker*) to pick up a Scandi picnic or to enjoy *fika* (coffee and cake).

A short distance beyond Docksta, 66km (41 miles) north of Härnösand, the immense eastern slope of Skuleberget rises to the left. Robbers once lurked in the caves here; today it is a paradise for hikers and rock climbers – on fine days you'll see many of the latter clamped to its front. From this point, the E4 skirts the Skuleskogen National Park, which showcases the unusual geology – including a giant crevice that you can walk through – before leaving the High Coast at Örnköldsvik. **DS**

○ The Skuleskogen National Park is known for its lakes, spruce forests and intriguing geological phenomena.

Lake Vänern Shoreline Drive Värmland, Sweden

Start Karlstad   End Karlstad   Distance 499km (310 miles)
Type Scenic   Info goo.gl/WLmTKS

More like a sea than a freshwater lake, Vänern is dotted with some 22,000 islands and islets, making it one of the most scenic lakes in Europe. Swedes come here to sail, kayak, spot birds, fish and forage; there are plenty of campsites and cafés set within the surrounding pines and spruce, as well as countless places to stop the car and take a bracing dip.

The main roads around the lake – the E18, 26 E20 444, and for most of the western side, the E45 – keep their distance from the shore for large sections of the journey, but plenty of smaller roads lead to the water's edge. At Sjötorp, the road crosses the Göta Canal, which leads to Vänern's twin, Lake Vättern.

Other highlights include the chunky 13th-century Läckö Castle near Lidköping, the fishing village of Spiken, where you can have a lunch of lake fish on the boardwalk or rent a boat to visit some of the islands, and the long sandy beach around Svalnas. A bridge a few miles south of Sjötorp crosses to the island of Torsö, the largest on the lake. It has several white wooden churches. The chief appeal of Vänern, however, is nature, so take the foot off the accelerator and stop frequently. The best time to visit is early spring, sometime between the last snowfall and the arrival of the mosquitoes. **DS**

❶ Tranquil Lake Vänern near Läckö Castle.

Swedish Scenic Odyssey Götaland, Sweden

Start Gothenburg   End Malmö   Distance 275km (171 miles)
Type Scenic   Map goo.gl/N7vB3o

The west coast of Sweden is the kind of place where visitors make sharp intakes of breath, both for the purity of the air and in appreciation of the landscape's beauty. It is a region of lakes, forests, farmland and the Kattegat Sea, the last of which sits between Sweden and Denmark. This drive between two of the country's major cities shows visitors some of the best of Sweden.

Gothenburg is a vibrant city that can be hard to leave behind, but the disappointment of heading south will soon be dissipated by the stunning scenery ahead. If time is tight, stick to the main road that links the city to Malmö, because this in itself is a delightful scenic drive. Better, though, is to get off the main highway and drive to some of the peaceful coastal communities, which offer expansive views up and down the coast and across the sea. There is no set route that will take you easily along the coast, but explore and experiment, returning to the main highway from time to time, then leaving it again when the opportunity arises.

By the time you get to Malmö, you might feel like you want to drive on forever. You can, if you like, head farther south then back up the east coast until you eventually run out of time and have to return to the real world. **MG**

❶ Sixteenth-century half-timbered house in Malmö.

Lake Vättern Circle Tour
Götaland, Sweden

Start Jönköping
End Jönköping
Distance 300km (186 miles)
Type Scenic
Info goo.gl/6Lx4zZ

On a map, Lake Vättern looks like a slender slip of water compared to its vast neighbour, Lake Vänern. However, at an impressive 135km (84 miles) long and 30km (19 miles) wide, it is Sweden's second-largest lake. A three-day circuit of the lake, a road trip of 300km (186 miles), allows enough time for exhilarating lake-hugging drives punctuated by gourmet lunches and invigorating swims. Try to make the trip outside school holidays, when motorhomes converge on the area, because the roads around the lake will be gloriously empty. A longer time frame means more time to potter around villages and to explore castles, or to get out on the water itself. The potential for fishing for salmon and Arctic char – a survivor from the last Ice Age, when Vättern was connected to the Baltic Sea – makes it a popular spot with anglers.

Jönköping, at the southern tip of the lake, is a good starting point. Heading anticlockwise, the E4 highway hugs the eastern shore for some 57km (35 miles), with the rest area at Brahehus Castle ruins providing a knockout view across the lake. At Ödeshög, the highway heads to Stockholm, so follow the meandering roads around the lake to historic Vadstena and Karlsborg and picturesque Hjo. Be sure to park in time for sunset each day. Nothing beats sitting on a lakeside pontoon watching the lake and sky turn gold. **DS**

❶ One of a pair of lighthouses that protect Hjo harbour on the western shore of Lake Vättern.

The Emigrant Trail
Blekinge to Kalmar, Sweden

Start Karlshamn, Blekinge
End Eriksmåla, Kalmar
Distance 92km (57.1 miles)
Type Culture
Map goo.gl/cOp9Sx

If you wanted to add to the Swedish Scenic Odyssey drive from Gothenburg to Malmö, you could carry on around the coast to Karlshamn and head inland on what has become known as 'The Emigrant Trail'. It's named for the mass emigration of an estimated 1.3 million Swedes who left their impoverished homeland in the early 19th century to try to find a better life, many of them in the United States.

Those emigrants would have made the journey in the other direction, heading for the coast and the ports, though today's visitors usually head the other way. There are many places where you'll learn more about that mass migration as you head north on Route 29 into Småland province, where the Kingdom of Crystal is not, as its name may suggest, a department store or a film location but an area that has been renowned for its startlingly original glassware since the 18th century.

The final leg of this itinerary, heading east from Lessebo, is a landscape of spectacular natural beauty, medieval forests and open spaces devoid of people. Picking up stories of the exodus en route, you will soon appreciate what a heart-rending decision it must have been for these people to leave their native land behind. If time allows, take the 26-km (16-mile) detour west to Växjö and its museum dedicated to the region's mass migration that began almost two hundred years ago. MG

❶ Rottnen, near Lessebo, is one of the many beautiful lakes along this historic route.

Øresund Bridge
Sweden/Denmark

Start Malmö, Sweden
End Copenhagen, Denmark
Distance 41km (25.5 miles)
Type Culture
Map goo.gl/6C7PLk

● The Øresund Bridge has reduced the journey time between Denmark and Sweden to 10 minutes.

The upper half of one woman and the lower half of another are on either side of the centreline of a bridge, the precise border between Sweden and Denmark. The gruesome double murder is investigated by two detectives, one Swedish, the other Danish. So begins the saga of *The Bridge*, an award-winning Swedish–Danish made-for-television crime drama that has been broadcast in more than 100 countries. But even without this unprecedented degree of publicity, the bridge in question – the 7,845-m- (25,738-ft) long Øresund Bridge over the Flinte Channel connecting Malmö in Sweden with Copenhagen, Denmark, opened in 2000 – would be worthy of your attention. Part bridge, part tunnel, it spans half the channel's width, from Sweden to the Danish island of Amager, before dropping beneath the waves at the artificial island of Peberholm to join the 4,050-m- (13,287-ft) long Drogden Tunnel for the remaining part of the journey into downtown Copenhagen.

A cable-stayed bridge, with the wires suspended from its two towers supporting the bridge deck below, it weighs 82,000 tons and has four lanes of traffic above and a double-track railway below. Driving over it and looking up at the two 204-m (669-ft) pylons supporting its 490-m (1,608-ft) span is a thrill not soon forgotten. Concrete and cabling never looked so sleek. **BDS**

Tenontie Road
Lapland, Finland

Start Karigasniemi
End Utsjoki
Distance 105km (65.2 miles)
Type Scenic
Map goo.gl/Ino8rn

Inside the Arctic Circle, Tenontie Road is often described as the most beautiful road in Finland. Running parallel to Norway's E6 highway, Route 970 follows the course of the salmon-filled Tenojoki River, which forms part of the border between the two countries. Not that national borders are paramount here. The valley is an ancient trading and herding route of the Sami, the indigenous people of northern Finland, Norway, Sweden and Russia. Sami villages lie along the valley and their reindeer graze the slopes.

Although this road trip can be made in a day, or even a long afternoon, the drive is worth savouring. In places, road and river cleave close; in others, the road climbs into the fells, providing balcony views of the river and its islands (some of which belong to Norway). The best lookout is at Nuvvus Aligas (Aligas means 'holy fell').

Light and colour fill the valley for much of the year. In summer, the sun does not set for 70 days; for three weeks in the autumn, or *ruska* season, the fells glow, as the leaves of bilberries and blueberries turn crimson and the aspen trees gold. Spring or autumn are the best times of year for the Aurora Borealis (Northern Lights), although the light show also occurs during the polar nights of midwinter, when the sun does not rise above the snowy horizon. **DS**

Northern Lights Route
Finland to Norway

Start Kemi, Lapland, Finland
End Tromsø, Northern Norway, Norway
Distance 647km (402 miles)
Type Scenic
Map goo.gl/3C7MbV

Most people are enchanted by the Northern Lights, and this exhilarating drive to Tromsø, the world's most northerly city, gives you every chance of seeing them. As with anything to do with nature, there are no guarantees, but it is a racing certainty that you will enjoy this magical journey through three Scandinavian countries.

The route starts in Kemi, where in winter you'll find the world's largest snow castle built in the harbour. There are several possible routes (this one is the most direct), with many north–south roads on the Finnish and Swedish sides of the border, but whichever way you choose you'll see the same forests, fields and wide-open skies as you proceed northwards parallel to the Torne River.

The whole area is packed with activity options year round and, because of the length of the drive, it makes sense to stop off en route to enjoy some of the hiking, skiing and white-water rafting on offer along the way.

By the time you reach the halfway point of this itinerary, in Muonio, you're inside the Arctic Circle, the Land of the Midnight Sun, surrounded by lakes and forests. The farther north you go, the greater the chances of seeing the Northern Lights, and once you're well inside Lapland they appear, on average, on alternate clear nights between September and March. **MG**

Lietvedentie Scenic Road
Southern Savonia, Finland

Start Puumala
End Mikkeli
Distance 71km (44.1 miles)
Type Scenic
Map goo.gl/THUj4O

The Lietvedentie between Puumala and Mikkeli leapfrogs through Lake Saimaa in the heart of Finland's Lake District, in places barely touching terra firma before flying over another bridge or human-made causeway. There are places to stop to appreciate the surroundings, including several attractive rest areas, but the pleasure is the drive itself and the mesmerizing sequence of water, islands, pine and spruce. Set before you like a tableau as you round a bend or crest a hill (although nothing is very high in Finland), the impressive scenery then gently dissolves into its separate parts as the road subsides, before building to a new crescendo and another view.

Tempting though it is to turn up the volume on the sound system and simply drive on and on, Mikkeli and Puumala are interesting start and finish points to explore. With its historic manor houses, some of which are now hotels and restaurants, and military barracks, Mikkeli reflects Finland's shifting relationship with Russia, a mere two hours away. Puumala, on the other hand, is a popular holiday village with boats, trails and a spectacular bridge. At Kuutinvuori, 10km (6 miles) before Puumala, look out for the ochre-coloured remnants of Stone Age rock art on the right-hand side of the road, just above the water line; a boat is required for closer examination. **DS**

❶ The bridge at Lietvesi, west of Puumala: much of this itinerary runs on highways on stilts above water.

Scandinavia's King's Road
Finland/Russia

Start Turku, Southwest Finland, Finland
End St Petersburg, Russia
Distance 550km (342 miles)
Type Adventure
Map goo.gl/bYcztx

One of the oldest touring routes in Europe, the King's Road began as a medieval mail route that stretched from Bergen on the North Sea coast of Norway to St Petersburg, Russia's main port on the Baltic. The drivable section that now runs across southern Finland and into Russia closely follows the trail once trodden by 13th-century Swedish royalty and nobility at a time when Finland was a vassal state of the Swedish empire, a trail that took plundering armies eastwards into Russia.

The road begins in Turku, Finland, and passes through a succession of rural villages with manor houses, guesthouses, taverns, inns and churches, many of which have been unchanged for centuries. Eventually it reaches the Finnish capital, Helsinki, and from there proceeds to Porvoo, Finland's best-preserved medieval town, and beyond Kotka there's a 32-km- (20-mile) long section through typically Finnish forests of birch and pine.

The roads are excellent, and you can't miss the signs, which are in both Swedish and Finnish and topped by a golden crown symbol. From the Finnish border to St Petersburg, the road designation changes to the M10, which is currently a two-lane highway but there are plans to increase it to six lanes. But it is the Finnish section of the road that most delights, providing deep insights into the nation's history and current way of life. **BDS**

🅞 The interior of Porvoo Cathedral. The city is around 50km (30 miles) east of Helsinki.

Turku Archipelago Trail
Southwest Finland

Start Turku
End Turku
Distance 232km (144 miles)
Type Culture
Map goo.gl/uQ6D8i

This road trip starts and ends at the mouth of the Aura River in Turku, the oldest city in Finland, founded in the 13th century. From here you can follow the proposed itinerary clockwise or anticlockwise: one way is much the same as the other. Whichever way you go, you'll soon be out into open farmland, under vast Scandinavian skies, and then driving into pine forests where you could start to believe there really are trolls and elves.

If you don't like retracing your footsteps, then plan to do this drive in June, July or August, since outside those months the closure of seasonal ferries means that you'll have to backtrack in places. But during the glorious Finnish summers you can drive and take ferries (mostly free) in a huge sweeping circle that takes you through forests and across the Baltic Sea from island to island.

The trail takes you over bridges from one island to the next, with occasional fun on the ferries, too, where you'll get a glimpse of the way of life of these island fishing and farming communities. Break the journey in Näsby to learn more at the Archipelago Museum, and factor in at least one overnight stop, perhaps in Nagu, to eat fresh fish in a harbourside restaurant. By the time you arrive back in Turku, you may wish it was a never-ending circle, and you may just be tempted to turn around and drive it again in the other direction. **MG**

Tallimäki Virojoki Road
Kymenlaakso, Finland

Start Hamina
End Virojoki
Distance 38km (23.6 miles)
Type Culture
Map goo.gl/DdA4jS

Connecting Hamina and Virolahti in southeast Finland, near the border with Russia, the Tallimäki to Virojoki Route 3513 is known by Finns as a 'museum road', a designation indicative of the historic importance and challenges of creating land routes through a country fragmented by water. It forms part of the Great Coastal Highway, also known as the King's Road, built in the 14th century between the medieval towns of Turku, Finland's first capital, and Vyborg, Finland's second-largest city until it became Russian in 1940. This well-surfaced road is perfect for motoring, often empty outside high summer, with great loops and tight twists through gently undulating fields and forests dotted with tiny villages and isolated farms. (Trucks heading for the Russian border prefer the fast E18 freeway to the north of the 3513.) The route nudges the Gulf of Finland in places, affording views over its islands and islets.

Several old stone bridges testify to the age of the route: look out for the double-span stone-vault bridge across the Salmenvirta River in Hamina, a circular town with old wooden houses and a 16th-century star-shaped fortress. Virojoki stands on the Salpa Line, a 1,200-km (750-mile) defence built during World War II to protect Finland from a Soviet invasion. This is commemorated at the Bunker Museum. **DS**

Giant's Causeway Coast
Antrim, Northern Ireland

Start Ballycastle
End Portrush
Distance 34.1km (21.2 miles)
Type Scenic
Map goo.gl/fhzyfZ

This stretch of the Antrim coast of Northern Ireland is an attractive coastal drive that takes in cliffs, beaches and headlands, with a short diversion to the unique Giant's Causeway, a UNESCO World Heritage Site. It begins in the appealing seaside resort of Ballycastle, from where you can see offshore Rathlin Island and, on the horizon, the Mull of Kintyre in Scotland. Rathlin Island remains in view as the road heads west, with hills on one side and the Sea of Moyle on the other.

Approximately 8km (5 miles) out of Ballycastle, it is worth taking a break to see the remarkable Carrick-a-Rede rope bridge, which links the mainland to the tiny island of Carrick-a-Rede. Used for centuries by salmon fishermen wishing to sail from the island, it provides an unsteady crossing over the churning waters.

A few miles farther on, there are several turnings off the main road to the Causeway Road, directly above the coast. All lead to the Giant's Causeway Visitor Centre, where you can get a close look at this remarkable natural feature, where an estimated 40,000 basalt columns march out from the coast and disappear under the sea. The road then runs through Bushmills, where the well-known distillery is located, and on to Portrush, another delightful little seaside resort at the western border of County Antrim. **MG**

❶ The dramatic landscape was created by volcanic activity some fifty to sixty million years ago.

Antrim Coast Road Antrim, Northern Ireland

Start Belfast   **End** Ballycastle   **Distance** 106km (66 miles)
Type Scenic   **Map** goo.gl/79iAFl

The coast of eastern Antrim, which includes the nine valleys known as the Glens of Antrim, is short in distance but makes a road trip that can easily stretch to an entire day if you want to explore its delights fully. Once the route from Belfast turns from motorway to main road, it starts hugging the shoreline of Belfast Lough and passes the historic town of Carrickfergus before reaching the seaside resort of Whitehead, oddly nicknamed 'the town with no streets'. You will discover why when you visit.) Once past Larne, the road runs next to the sea.

The village of Glenarm marks the starting point for the Glens of Antrim, and from here onwards there are plenty of opportunities to leave the coast road and head into the wooded hills to explore as many of the glens as you like. There are waterfalls and walking trails, archaeological sites, forests, gorges, picturesque villages and many other beautiful things to discover.

Returning to the coast road, the route ends in the appealing seaside town of Ballycastle. From here, it is possible to see Rathlin Island off the coast, and beyond that Scotland's Mull of Kintyre. This route can also be combined with the Giant's Causeway Coast drive, which covers Antrim's equally glorious northern coast. **MG**

❶ The Red Arch between Waterfoot and Cushendall.

Belfast Black Taxi Tours Antrim, Northern Ireland

Start Belfast   End Belfast   Distance 16km (10 miles)
Type Culture   Info goo.gl/nse9Yd

Belfast is now a thriving, modern European city, but it is also known for its turbulent past, with the period known as 'The Troubles' lasting for almost three decades until the Good Friday Agreement in 1998.

The best way learn more about The Troubles is from someone who lived and worked in the city during these dark times . . . and nobody likes to tell a good story more than a cab driver.

Several taxi companies offer tours of the major political landmarks across Belfast. Starting from the corner of Falls Road and Shankill Road, tours head to the Peaceline wall that divided loyalist and nationalist communities. Today it's plastered with graffiti and murals depicting political messages and the hopes and fears of people who lived through the conflict. Your black cab driver will explain the sad and hopeful stories behind the street art.

Crumlin Road Gaol and Court House also have fascinating stories to tell. Having been the scene of killings, bombings and several escape attempts, these Victorian buildings have played a major part in Irish political history. By the end of this hard-hitting history lesson, you'll be ready to unwind with a pint of the 'black stuff' (Guinness) at the perfect place: Crown Liquor Saloon, one of Northern Ireland's oldest and most beloved pubs. TW

❶ A black cab parked in the Republican Falls Road.

Dundrod Circuit
Antrim, Northern Ireland

Start Rushyhill
End Rushyhill
Distance 11.9km (7.4 miles)
Type Culture
Map goo.gl/qHACO6

The Emerald Isle has a rich motorsports heritage, with dozens of half-forgotten circuits for the curious automotive adventurer to rediscover. Northern Ireland's golden age of motor racing began in 1950 when a young Stirling Moss, on the eve of his twenty-first birthday, romped home in his Jaguar XK120 at the inaugural Ulster Tourist Trophy (TT) race at the Dundrod Circuit, a rough pentagon of country roads west of Belfast. In 1953 the motorcycling fraternity joined in the fun, with Dundrod becoming home to the Ulster Grand Prix.

Increasing safety concerns saw the last TT race here in 1955. But bikers are a different breed altogether: despite the obvious hazards along these narrow rural backroads, lined with trees, telegraph poles and barbed-wire fencing, the Ulster GP still runs to this day. As a top-flight racing venue, Dundrod is as raw and unforgiving as you can get; it's also the world's fastest motorcycle race circuit.

Begin your loop by heading clockwise from the makeshift pit complex near Rushyhill; a smattering of black-and-white curbstones waymark the course. It's a pleasant country drive for the most part, but blind crests, negative cambers and aging rippled tarmac will keep you focused even when driving within the current UK national speed limit of 112 kph (70 mph). At 216 kph (134 mph), the lap record, it must be terrifying. **DIS**

Game of Thrones
Antrim, Northern Ireland

Start Belfast
End Belfast
Distance 235km (146 miles)
Type Culture
Map goo.gl/U7MxAc

George R. R. Martin's *A Song of Ice and Fire* fantasy novels gained a huge new fan club when they formed the basis of the popular television series *Game of Thrones*. The novels are set in the fictional continents of Westeros and Essos, although the actual programmes are filmed in the Titanic Studios in Belfast, Northern Ireland, and on location in the province and elsewhere. Enterprising tourist operators in Northern Ireland have cashed in on their success by organizing film tours to visit the locations used in the series, but of course you don't need a bus to get the best out of this experience.

The best place to start is Belfast, taking in a tour of the studios before heading northwest to Carrickfergus Castle and then up the Antrim coast via Carnlough's harbour, featured in Season Six, and the Cushendun Caves. The best is yet to come at Carrick-a-Rede rope bridge, heavily featured in the series: you will need all your courage to cross it. From there, continue north to Larrybane, and then to the geologically extraordinary Giant's Causeway, Northern Ireland's Eighth Wonder of the World. Next visit the ruined Dunluce Castle and the Dark Hedges on the King's Road back to Belfast. End the day in front of the television watching the box set of you know what. **SA**

➲ The fictional King's Road is the real-life Dark Hedges.

Wild Atlantic Way
Donegal/Cork, Ireland

Start Inishowen Peninsula, Donegal
End Kinsale, Cork
Distance 2,575km (1,600 miles)
Type Scenic
Info goo.gl/3lVIOn

Stretching along Ireland's dramatic western seaboard, the Wild Atlantic Way passes through nine counties from the Inishowen Peninsula in County Donegal in the north to the pretty coastal town of Kinsale in County Cork. At approximately 2,575km (1,600 miles), it proudly claims to be the world's longest defined coastal touring route.

Few tourists visiting the west of Ireland take on the whole route, which is conveniently broken down into fourteen bite-sized sections for those looking to sample its delights. Intrepid adventurers intending to take on the full challenge should allow at least three weeks to do it properly; Ireland's rural roads are narrow and twisty, which makes it difficult to cover big distances. But this is not a road trip to be rushed anyway; that is not really the Irish way of doing things. In order to appreciate fully the spectacular landscapes, vibrant culture and rich local history, there are 157 discovery points and 1,000 visitor attractions flagged on the official route maps. Popular detours along the way include the Cliffs of Moher, the spectacular Dingle Peninsula and scenic drives around the Ring of Kerry.

Threading your way through enchanting coastal villages, stopping at thriving local pubs and enjoying spellbinding panoramas over the restless Atlantic Ocean, a road trip along the Wild Atlantic Way is an unforgettable experience. **DIS**

❶ One of several spectacular waterfalls along the way.
➲ The road hugs the coast along the Dingle Peninsula.

Lough Corrib Galway, Ireland

Start Galway City   **End** Galway City   **Distance** 140km (87 miles)
Type Scenic   **Info** goo.gl/mWElWX

The west coast of Ireland is renowned for its beauty and Lough Corrib is a particular gem. It has rugged moorland, World Heritage-listed nature reserves, bags of history, castles galore and as much angling as you might desire. Starting at the city of Galway, with the lough as its focus, this circular trip can be made in a day. The southern half is gentle and green, but beyond that, the landscape gives way to picturesque wild moorland and terrific mountain views north towards County Mayo. There are also great vistas over the lough itself from the top of the Hill of Doon near Oughterard.

The whole area has been fought over and defended for centuries, and the circuit is littered with fascinating medieval castles and other ruins. These include Aughnanure Castle (near Oughterard), Caislean-na-Circe (near Maum, home in the 16th century to Grace O'Malley, the pirate queen of Connemara), Ashford Castle (near Cong), the ruins of Ross Errilly Friary (near Headford, one of the best-preserved medieval monastic sites in Ireland) and Annaghdown Priory and Cathedral (founded in the 12th century). Lough Corrib also boasts many islands, reputedly one for each day of the year. There are too many to keep count as you make the trip, but you can certainly try. **DK**

❶ Lackavrea Mountain on the shore of Lough Corrib.

R115 Military Road Dublin/Wicklow, Ireland

Start Rathfarnham, Dublin   End Aghavannagh, Wicklow   Distance 59km (36.7 miles)
Type Culture   Map goo.gl/sWtsNs

In 1798 the republican Society of United Irishmen revolted against British rule in Ireland, taking advantage of Britain's distraction during the wars against republican France on the time-honoured Irish principle that 'England's difficulty is Ireland's opportunity'. he rebellion was brutally put down, but it exposed the lack of British military strength in Ireland. To remedy this lack, a new road was built across the spine of the Wicklow Mountains from the south of Dublin down into County Wicklow in order to assist British soldiers round up rebels who were still hiding out in the mountains. The road, built between 1800 and 1809, was one of the first purpose-built thoroughfares in Ireland. Its chief engineer, Alexander Taylor, was also responsible for building the four barracks that line the route and many other roads in Ireland. The road can be enjoyed today for its scenic views of the mountains and the old villages it passes through. It is now the R115 as far south as Laragh, from where it continues south as a local road to its end at Aghavannagh. For much of its route, its narrow path twists and turns across peat moors, the boggy ground causing the road to sag alarmingly in places. Snow and ice can close the road during winter, while spring floods can make the drive hazardous. **SA**

❶ White Hill in the Wicklow Mountains.

The Sally Gap
Road Wicklow, Ireland

Start Roundwood
End Blessington
Distance 30km (18.6 miles)
Type Culture
Map goo.gl/ARhIJA

The Wicklow Mountains to the south of Dublin are the largest upland area in Ireland, with 500 sq km (190 square miles) at more than 300m (1,000ft) above sea level. Lugnaquilla, the highest peak in the range, is 925m (3,035ft) – not high by global standards, but its verdant beauty is more than adequate compensation. Roads through the mountains are few and far between: the R759 Sally Gap and the R756 Wicklow Gap are the only two that cross the area from east to west. If these two are closed, you need to take M50 around the south of Dublin, which is often congested.

The Sally Gap Road begins at the R755 to the north of Roundwood in the east of County Wicklow. From there it heads northwest across the mountains to the N81 in the west of the county. Its highest point in the mountains is at Sally Gap (a corruption of the old Irish word for 'saddle'), where it crosses the R115 Military Road at an elevation of 503m (1,650ft). For most of its route, the road crosses peat moors amid the spectacular scenery of the Wicklow Mountains, passing alongside the deep corrie lake of Lough Tay below Luggala in the eastern hills and along the valley of the Liffey River on the descent to the N81.

This road trip is highly rewarding at any time of year, but it should be noted that snow and ice often block the road in winter. **SA**

Gordon Bennett
Route Carlow, Ireland

Start Ballyshannon Crossroads
End Ballyshannon Crossroads
Distance 167km (104 miles)
Type Culture
Info goo.gl/7xbdk

Gordon Bennett, Jr. (1841–1918) was a hard-drinking American millionaire playboy and heir to a publishing empire: his father founded *The New York Herald* newspaper. In 1900, after brawling with his fiancée's brother and urinating in a grand piano, Gordon was 'relocated' to Paris, where he witnessed one of the earliest French road races. Always keen to find new ways to promote his newspaper, he decided to sponsor the world's first international motor race.

After British racer Selwyn Edge won the 1902 race in his 6.4-litre Napier, it became Britain's duty to host the 1903 Gordon Bennett Cup. In rural southeast Ireland (which was then a part of the United Kingdom), a closed road circuit was laid out in a figure of eight that started at the Ballyshannon crossroads on today's N78 highway. The westerly anticlockwise loop turned through Kildare and Stradbally before heading east on a shorter clockwise loop via Castledermot and Carlow. The race, won by Belgian driver Camille Jenatzy, was a huge commercial success.

Today, the route is a pleasant country drive on smooth tarmac, waymarked with brown tourist signs. If possible, time your visit to mid-June, when the Gordon Bennett Classic sees a fabulous ensemble of vintage cars and motorcycles converging near Portlaoise for a scenic tour of this historic road circuit. **DIS**

Gap of Dunloe
Kerry, Ireland

Start Kate Kearney's Cottage, Killarney
End Lord Brandon's Cottage, Gearhameen
Distance 11km (7 miles)
Type Scenic
Info goo.gl/qwFJWz

The Gap of Dunloe is a narrow, winding and undulating road through rocky mountain terrain, but the biggest hazard for drivers is other tourists. Pick a quiet time of day or year to travel this route, otherwise you will be stuck behind walkers, vintage buses and pony-and-trap tours through the mountain pass. You could find yourself in first gear for an hour. It is definitely worth trying to get this classic scene to yourself. The short drive is full of all the poetic Celticness that you would want from a road trip in Ireland.

The scenery is uniformly spectacular as you weave between the aptly named Purple Mountain, 832m (2,730ft) high, and Macgillycuddy's Reeks, a range of mountains up to 1,038m (3,406ft) above sea level. Along the route there are five small lakes that, in true Irish tradition, all have mystical legends attached. There is also a tiny old stone bridge over the River Loe, lyrically known as the Wishing Bridge.

The start point of the proposed itinerary is at Kate Kearney's Cottage, a touristy bar and restaurant complex developed from an old stone homestead. At the end of the trip is Lord Brandon's Cottage, a Victorian hunting lodge that is now an outdoor café. In the summer, you can complete the scenic experience by taking a boat trip across the tree-lined lake alongside. **SH**

❶ A lone cyclist on the Gap of Dunloe route during a quiet time out of season.

Slea Head Loop Kerry, Ireland

Start Dingle   **End** Dingle   **Distance** 48km (30 miles)
Type Scenic   **Info** goo.gl/9cSHkY

The Dingle Peninsula is the northernmost of the three main Kerry peninsulas that jut out into the Atlantic Ocean. Dunmore Head is the westernmost point of Ireland. Slea Head lies on the south of the peninsula, facing across Dingle Bay with dramatic views of the now uninhibited Blasket Islands.

Starting in Dingle, the capital of the Kerry Gaeltacht Irish-speaking area, the R559 loop road runs around the edge of the entire peninsula, offering spectacular views of both land and sea. It is best to travel this loop in a clockwise direction, to avoid the large tour buses that clog up the roads during summer. This is an area of great historic interest, as shown by the beehive-shaped stone huts made by prehistoric settlers and the various early Christian sites. It is believed that St Brendan, who voyaged to America 1,000 years before Columbus, set sail from Cuas an Bhodaigh or Brandon Creek. As the road leaves the coast and heads south again to Dingle, it runs alongside the base of Mt Brandon, at 954m (3,130 ft) the second-highest mountain in Ireland. Pilgrims climb to the summit from here. And in case some of the scenery looks familiar, David Lean's *Ryan's Daughter* (1970) was filmed in these parts, as were parts of Ron Howard's *Far and Away* (1992). **SA**

❶ The Dingle Peninsula at sunset.

Ring of Kerry Kerry, Ireland

Start Killarney   End Killarney   Distance 172km (107 miles)
Type Scenic   Map goo.gl/Lhq7sQ

The road trip around the Iveragh Peninsula, known as the Ring of Kerry, is one of the most popular scenic drives in Ireland. It is a particular favourite with tour buses, too, which generally find it easier to drive in a clockwise direction. Motorists and bikers should, therefore, go anticlockwise to avoid being caught behind a slow vehicle on some of the narrow and winding roads.

The route begins in the lively town of Killarney and heads out past Lough Leane toward Killorglin, with views to the south of the mountain scenery, followed by views of the Atlantic to the north. The ocean panoramas get better as the road takes you west, past farms and through pretty little villages.

Eventually, it brings you to the peninsula's main town, Cahersiveen, although this has fewer than 1,500 inhabitants. It is a good place to stop for a walk, refreshments and some retail therapy.

From here, the Ring of Kerry heads south and then back towards Killarney along the southern edge of the Iveragh Peninsula, with the village of Sneem offering another chance to take a break. Approaching Kenmare, the route turns north and climbs up through craggy hills to Moll's Gap, and down again past the woods and lakes of Killarney National Park to return to Killarney town. **MG**

❶ Mountain scenery dominates the Ring of Kerry.

Conor Pass Kerry, Ireland

Start Dingle   **End** Brandon   **Distance** 19.7km (12.2 miles)
Type Scenic   **Map** goo.gl/Fmd3fE

This road trip proves that drives do not have to be long to be dramatic. It takes you from one side of the Dingle Peninsula to the other, on one of the highest tarmac mountain roads in Ireland. The route begins in the popular fishing and holiday village of Dingle, where attractions range from Fungie the dolphin (Dingle Harbour's most famous resident) to the Dingle Whiskey Distillery. From here, the R560 heads inland through the kind of gloriously green fields that give the Emerald Isle its name. Hills rise on either side and the houses peter out when the road begins its slow but steady climb. In places, as it skirts the sides of the hills, the highway becomes a single lane, before widening out again.

At the peak of the pass, which is at 456m (1,496ft) above sea level, a parking area is perfectly placed to allow motorized visitors a break and give them a chance to look back at the vistas they have passed and at those that lie ahead. In both directions the views are magnificent and will raise the spirits of anyone who travels this way. Once over the crest, the road narrows again to a single lane with occasional passing places, so Conor Pass is not for the nervous driver. Journey's end is the little village of Brandon, quieter than Dingle but no less charming a place to stay. **MG**

❶ View from the Conor Pass between Dingle and Tralee.

Healy Pass Cork/Kerry, Ireland

Start Adrigole, Cork   End R571 near Lauragh, Kerry   Distance 12km (7.5 miles)
Type Culture   Map goo.gl/WBCWlG

Between 1845 and 1849 the potato crop, the main food source of Ireland's rural poor, was struck by potato blight. The result was widespread famine, causing the deaths of up to one million Irish people and forcing another 1.5 million to emigrate.

The British government did little to alleviate the suffering, although its Board of Works did provide some much-needed employment by building new roads. One of these crossed the Caha Mountains of the Beara Peninsula between County Cork and County Kerry.

Starting in the sprawling village of Adrigole, the Healy Pass heads north across the peninsula and rises to 334m (1,095ft), giving amazing views of Bantry Bay and the Kenmare River, which in spite of its name is actually a bay. It's a wonderfully wild and scenic road, narrow and often bounded with low stone walls, that meanders with the contours of the landscape. But given its history, this is a highway that evokes mixed emotions.

The road then drops to Lauragh in County Kerry, where the gardens of Derreen House include exotic plants, trees, ferns and bamboo. If it's refreshment you need, head to the late Pete McCarthy's Bar in Castletownbere; as Ireland's answer to Bill Bryson, he's essential pre-trip reading. SA

❶ Near the summit of the Healy Pass.

Isle of Barra Ring Road
Outer Hebrides, Scotland

Start Castlebay
End Castlebay
Distance 29km (18 miles)
Type Scenic
Map goo.gl/nkS6XS

The Isle of Barra might not seem like a driver's paradise because it only has one classified road. However, this road – the A888 – loops the whole way around the island, offering uninterrupted views over the stark grassy mountainsides and vast gray oceans. It is impossible to get properly lost here, so it is nice to just freestyle this road trip, stopping when you choose to explore abandoned crofts, misty inlets and deserted white-sand beaches. Barra may be a wild and rugged isle, but it has an honest and melancholy beauty about it.

The route is a circuit so can be started at any point, but visitors to the island will have most likely arrived on the ferry at Castlebay, a five-hour voyage from mainland Scotland. Heading east, the smooth tarmac loop hugs close to the rocky coastline before cutting over the mountainous interior of the isle to the north. After your return leg via the west coast, try to find time to visit Kisimul Castle in Castlebay, an impregnable island fortress and ancestral home to the MacNeil clan since the 11th century.

Barra's main claim to fame is the Ealing comedy *Whisky Galore* (1949), which was filmed on the island. Another is Beach Airport located at the northern tip, which, as the name suggests, uses the beach for take-off and landing – the only airport in the world to do so. **TW**

Road to the Isles
Highland, Scotland

Start Fort William
End Mallaig
Distance 72km (44.7 miles)
Type Scenic
Map goo.gl/Pc82g7

Start your engine in the shadow of the United Kingdom's highest mountain, Ben Nevis – 1,344m (4,409ft) above sea level – and head west from Fort William. Cross the Caledonian Canal on top of Neptune's Staircase, a flight of locks. This is mapped as a main road, the A830, but don't expect a broad highway: it's winding and narrow in many places. However, this road trip is not for testing acceleration and cornering skills; it is all about the views.

Don't miss the great viaducts at Loch nan Uamh and Glenfinnan. The latter, with its 21 arches, curves elegantly around a cleft in the shores of Loch Shiel. Catch sight of one of the regular steam trains that cross it, and suddenly you will remember that it was used as a setting in the *Harry Potter* movies, featuring the Hogwarts Express.

Nearby is the monument that marks the spot where Bonnie Prince Charlie raised his standard in 1745 to begin the Jacobite rising, which ended in defeat at the Battle of Culloden. Farther on, look out for open sea, white-sand beaches and mountainous islands on the horizon. Mallaig may not be a picturesque finale, but it is a fascinating, bustling little fortress against the elements, full of fishermen and trucks heading for ferries to the Isle of Skye and smaller Hebridean outposts. **SH**

➲ A steam locomotive crosses the Glenfinnan Viaduct.

North Coast 500
Highland, Scotland

Start Inverness
End Inverness
Distance 803km (499 miles)
Type Scenic
Map goo.gl/gO7ikS

This drive is being promoted as the United Kingdom's answer to Route 66. The comparison is somewhat misleading, because this is a circular route through well-watered landscapes rather than parched desert. Although the likes of Ullapool and Thurso perhaps lack the romance of Flagstaff and Amarillo, this is a truly sensational trip offering scenery just as stunning and majestic as any you will find in the United States.

The circuit around the Scottish Highlands begins in the east at Inverness, takes in the very best of the intricately fretted and endlessly beautiful western coastline, crosses the dramatic bleak moorland of the northern coast, and reaches the United Kingdom's most northerly point, John O'Groats. The visitor centre here is a good place to stop for the obligatory 'signpost' photographs. North Coast 500 then heads south along the North Sea coast to return to the start. The main highlights are probably the western coastal leg through Wester Ross, which includes the treacherous Bealach na Bà pass to Applecross, and the shoreside sections along Loch Maree and Loch Broom. Sutherland and the north coast offer different delights: wild unspoiled wilderness and the possibility, if you are up early enough, of having your journey delayed as a stag holds up traffic while he waits for his harem to cross the road. A rare privilege to see. **DK**

❶ Bealach na Bà means 'Pass of the Cattle' in the Scottish Gaelic language.

Isle of Skye
Highland, Scotland

Start Kyle of Lochalsh
End Aird of Sleat
Distance 227km (141 miles)
Type Scenic
Map goo.gl/SdmZDS

The Isle of Skye is the largest and most northerly of the Inner Hebrides. It is a place of romance and mystery, of history and tragedy, and probably one of the most beautiful and awe-inspiring parts of Scotland. The centre is dominated by the Black Cuillin Hills, rising at Sgurr Alasdair to 992m (3,255 ft). From these these peaks radiate the island's many peninsulas, all of which have rich profusions of golden eagles and red deer.

The approach to the island is over the road bridge from the mainland at the Kyle of Lochalsh. The main A850 hugs the eastern coast up to Portree, the island's largest town, known for its attractive harbour. From there you can loop around the northern tip of the island on the Trotternish Peninsula. Romance greets you at Kilmuir, where Flora MacDonald, who helped Bonnie Prince Charlie to escape into exile after the defeat of his Jacobite rebellion at Culloden by the British in 1745, is buried. History, too, is evident in the many castles on the island and also in the villages abandoned after crofters were evicted from their lands – 30,000 between 1840 and 1880 – as their smallholdings were cleared for sheep farming. Keeping to the westernmost roads via Bracadale and Armadale takes you on a winding scenic route to the wild southern tip of Skye, with its magical views towards the isles of Rum and Eigg. **SA**

❶ Part of the main ridge of the Cuillin Hills, which form the backbone of Skye.

Heart of the Highlands
Highland, Scotland

Start Pitlochry
End Pitlochry
Distance 127km (79 miles)
Type Scenic
Map goo.gl/IF4jNj

The countryside of rural Perthshire is a Scottish delight, with Loch Tummel and Loch Rannoch surrounded by wooded hills and empty moors.

The best base from which to explore this area is Pitlochry, complete with whisky distilleries. This bustling tourist town is next to what looks like an ancient expanse of freshwater, but don't be fooled: Loch Faskally emerged only in 1950 as part of a hydroelectric scheme.

From Pitlochry, you head west and then north up the B8079 through the Pass of Killiecrankie, scene in 1689 of the first Jacobite military victory in their ultimately unsuccessful attempt to restore the Stuarts to the British throne, although their commander was promptly killed by a stray bullet in his moment of triumph. You then reach Blair Castle, a stately pile that in part dates back to 1269. The road next goes on a rural loop that brings you to Kinloch Rannoch and the eastern end of Loch Rannoch. Hug the north shore to the end, and then continue if you want to go up the hills to Rannoch Moor and its lonely railway station on the Glasgow to Fort William line.

The Black Wood of Rannoch that runs along the south side of the loch was once infested with whisky smugglers. As you drive west alongside Loch Tummel, pause at the Queen's View, where Victoria admired the beautiful loch scenery. **SA**

❶ Low-lying cloud disperses over Loch Faskally, a human-made lake.

Highland Perthshire
Highland, Scotland

Start Pitlochry
End Inverness
Distance 143km (89 miles)
Type Scenic
Map goo.gl/XZv7Tc

For a scenic snapshot of the Scottish Highlands, it is hard to beat the main road from Pitlochry to Inverness. With an early-morning start, all the classic ingredients of the Highlands – a famous salmon river, island-dotted lochs and heather-covered mountains – can be enjoyed before lunchtime, even with brief stops. However, there are plenty of reasons to linger on the drive north.

The first of these is a few miles off the main road, just outside Pitlochry. A left turn squeezes between the north shore of Loch Tummel and Tay Forest Park. It is worth following the footpath from the Forestry Commission parking lot to Queen's View, sweeping along the loch to Schiehallion, which is the highest peak in the area at 1,083m (3,553ft), but easy to climb. Back on the road, the grandeur of the Highlands builds as the route heads north through Cairngorms National Park. Blair Castle rises a short distance from the highway, 5km (3 miles) north of Killiecrankie. Climbing higher, the road joins the Spey River at the small town of Kingussie, beyond which there are several lochs. Loch an Eilein has a romantic ruined castle on an island.

Beyond Aviemore, the road veers west to Inverness, on the Moray Firth. The city is a springboard for other great drives – along the Great Glen to Fort William and around the northeast coast, for example. **DS**

❶ A narrow road winding through rolling green hills, heather and moorlands in Cairngorms National Park.

Invergarry to the Isle of Skye Highland, Scotland

Start Invergarry End Kyle of Lochalsh Distance 84km (52 miles)
Type Scenic Map goo.gl/mHJGJi

The Scottish Highlands are home to some stunning routes, easily among the best drives in the UK. Well-made roads, jaw-dropping scenery and challenging bends make a great combination. The road from Invergarry to the Isle of Skye is a fine example.

From Invergarry, head northwest. Almost at once you hit a series of wide, sweeping curves that hug the side of Loch Garry. This pretty much sets the tone for the rest of the journey. The road runs in a succession of fast curves and short straights past five sublimely beautiful lochs.

Eventually you reach Kyle of Lochalsh, a village dubbed the gateway to the Isle of Skye. From there you can see the bridge that will take you across the water to your final destination. The bridge was built in the 1990s (before then people had to cross by ferry), and these days is toll free. It takes you over the Inner Sound to Skye. Once on the island, there's a great scenic loop that is detailed elsewhere in the present volume.

The roads throughout are smooth, and the drive is generally safe, but in winter check the weather forecast before you set off. Highland conditions can change quickly, and you might find yourself facing snow, gales and high winds. In summer or spring, though, this trip is a delight. JI

❶ The Skye Bridge, viewed from the mainland.

Applecross Pass Highland, Scotland

Start Lochcarron   End Applecross   Distance 28km (17.4 miles)
Type Adventure   Map goo.gl/6yI2rG

Known to local people as Bealach na Bà (Pass of the Cattle), this challenging Scottish road follows the historic drovers' path over the mountains of the Applecross Peninsula in the West Scottish Highlands.

From Lochcarron, take the A896, then turn left on to the minor road to Applecross just before the Bealach Cafe. Here a warning sign, covered in tattered club stickers left by visiting bikers and cyclists, declares that this is not a route for the inexperienced, or for drivers of large vehicles. Rising from sea level to 626m (2,054ft), it is Scotland's third-highest motorable pass, and boasts the greatest ascent of any British road, with 20 per cent inclines in places.

The climb has a distinctly alpine feel about it, with tight, rock-lined switchbacks weaving to the head of the glen as the rugged Highlands close in ominously. Approaching the boulder-strewn summit, the road flattens out and straightens; a small gravel viewing area beckons you for a well-earned breather. On clear days, the vista across Applecross Bay and the Inner Sound towards the Isle of Skye is one you'll never forget.

The descent is less demanding, as it zigzags to the coast, giving you time to savour the views before lunch at the renowned Applecross Inn. **DIS**

❶ The twisting road around the peninsula.

The Shores of Loch Naver
Highland, Scotland

Start Altanharra
End Syre
Distance 19km (11.8 miles)
Type Adventure
Map goo.gl/nwIPSn

In the shadows of the lonely Ben Klibreck, a singular, isolated hill in the far north of Scotland towering over the local moors 962m (3,165ft) above sea level, the Naver River flows east through Loch Naver and then north to the coast at Bettyhill. The river is famous for its salmon, the loch for its beauty. There are remains of ancient settlements here that reveal its prehistoric heritage.

This fascinating and remote area can be explored along the B873 that runs east along the north side of the loch from Altanharra, whose hotel, opened in 1820, has long been popular with anglers. It is the salmon that draws the crowds, but the Naver once sported a prosperous pearl fishery. It is unlikely you will meet another car on your slow but challenging drive through this remote part of the Highlands. Although this road trip is short, it still needs to be broken into short, thoughtful segments so that the traveller can pause, drink in the wild landscapes and appreciate the solitude.

The narrow and undulating shoreside road – well surfaced but, at the time of publication of the present volume, fraying a little at the edges – concludes in the Naver Valley at the hamlet of Syre, where there is little to detain you. It is best to continue farther up the road to Bettyhill, where there are two pubs and a craft shop serving fish and chips at the weekend. **SA**

Cape Wrath Road
Highland, Scotland

Start Kyle of Durness
End Cape Wrath
Distance 18km (11 miles)
Type Adventure
Info goo.gl/emjc5p

Most people would consider John O'Groats to be the most northerly tip of mainland Britain, although more correctly nearby Dunnet Head takes that accolade. Often overlooked in this unseemly battle for northern honours is the majestic Cape Wrath, whose main claim to fame is that it is the most northwesterly point of the mainland. This is a place of stormy seas and howling gales, but its name is actually derived from the Old Norse *hvarf* ('turning point'), since Viking navigators used the headland as a navigation point around which they would turn their ships for plunder or for home.

On the edge of the cape an unmanned lighthouse, built in 1828 by the famed engineer Robert Stevenson, warns mariners to keep clear of the rocks below. A little way to the east of the headland are the Clò Mòr cliffs, at 281m (922ft) the highest sea cliffs in Britain and a seasonal home to countless thousands of breeding sea birds. Access to this area is by passenger ferry across the Kyle of Durness to the east. Having left your car behind on the other side of the water, you are forced to take the minibus that runs during the summer months only up the rough 18-km- (11-mile) long track to the lighthouse. As the British Ministry of Defence uses much of the local land as a firing range, your journey is likely to be interrupted by the sound of military ordnance. **SA**

Shores of Loch Ness
Highland, Scotland

Start Inverness
End Inverness
Distance 146km (91 miles)
Type Culture
Map goo.gl/ReC43G

Loch Ness, the ancestral home of the fearsome Chisholm and Fraser clans, is a place of remarkable natural beauty, with deep attenuated waters dissecting thickly forested hills. Once described by Britain's Automobile Association as 'the most energetic road in Scotland', this lakeside loop has long been popular with keen car drivers and motorcyclists alike. But, of course, it's the tall tales surrounding Loch Ness's so-far-undiscovered monster that draw the crowds, particularly during school summer holidays.

Heading out from Inverness on the A831 towards the Crask of Aigas, the route passes pretty deciduous woodland, lonely hill farms and the occasional grazing red deer. Beyond the village of Cannich, the road heads back to the lake shore, where the nearby ruined 13th-century stronghold of Urquhart Castle is worth a visit; so too is the Loch Ness Monster Exhibition at Drumnadrochit, which does a great job of keeping the local legend alive.

Hugging the scenic shoreline for the next 22.5km (14 miles), the A82 heads down to Fort Augustus, where the Caledonian Canal passes through an impressive flight of locks. The return leg goes northeast via the B852, a narrow tree-lined road along the water's edge. If time allows, stop by the lookout at Inverfarigaig; with great views across the loch, it's a popular vantage point. **DIS**

❶ Urquhart Castle is just one of the essential stops on the banks of the loch.

Forres to Alford
Moray/Aberdeenshire, Scotland

Start Forres, Moray
End Alford, Aberdeenshire
Distance 132km (82 miles)
Type Scenic
Map goo.gl/bwltW1

The Cairngorms National Park in the Highlands of Scotland is larger in area than the country of Luxembourg, and it is inhabited by considerably fewer people. On this road trip from Forres to Alford, you stand a very good chance of travelling a long distance without seeing another car or motorbike, so the road's wild beauty can be enjoyed in peace.

Set off from the small town of Forres on the Moray coast and head south towards Grantown-on-Spey, climbing sharply up the twisty road to Dava Moor. Once through the snow gates and over Dava Moor, head into the Cairngorms themselves. After Grantown-on-Spey, continue on the same road towards Tomintoul. At this point, the road rapidly opens out to give spectacular views on all sides, so this is a section to take slowly and to appreciate. Tomintoul itself is the highest village in Scotland, not far from one of Scotland's most popular ski areas, the Lecht. Soon after the ski centre, the road veers sharply to the right and plummets down like a roller coaster to Cock Bridge. The 16th-century Corgarff Castle, a former noble house later used as a military barracks, sits near the bridge, and it is open to the public. Pick up the route through the communities of Strathdon and past Glenkindie and Kildrummy Castle to Mossat alongside the River Don until Alford. **TW**

Speyside Malt Whisky Trail Moray, Scotland

Start Forres
End Grantown-on-Spey
Distance 108km (67.3 miles)
Type Culture
Map goo.gl/Uf3Biu

To whisky lovers, the Spey is the most famous river in the world. Speyside is where you will find Glen Grant, Glenfiddich and Glenlivet, among other distilleries, and this route provides the opportunity to visit several of them.

The drive begins in the historic town of Forres on the Moray Coast. Nearby is the Benromach Distillery, which dates back to 1898. From Forres it's worth a short detour south to the Dallas Dhu Historic Distillery, where whisky is no longer made but instead the buildings have been converted into a fascinating whisky museum, a perfect way to get some background before heading back through Forres and east to the town of Elgin and the Glen Moray Distillery.

The road then heads south to the Glen Grant Distillery in Rothes, beyond which you will get your first glimpse of the salmon-rich Spey. It's a delightfully scenic drive through farmland and past heather-clad hills.

The Malt Whisky Trail has more than just distillery visits to recommend it, however. It includes the Speyside Cooperage, where the art of barrel-making is demonstrated, and goes through Dufftown, where The Whisky Shop stocks more than 600 whiskies and whisky-related items. The journey ends in Grantown-on-Spey, where the historic cemetery of Inverallan is not to be missed. **MG**

Royal Deeside Victorian Heritage Trail
Aberdeenshire, Scotland

Start Aberdeen
End Braemar
Distance 122km (76 miles)
Type Culture
Info goo.gl/H8qwxO

Queen Victoria put Deeside on the map when she and her husband Prince Albert purchased Balmoral Castle in 1848, thereby establishing a royal connection that continues to this day. As a consequence, the drive west on the A93 from Aberdeen bristles with Scottish baronial castles and mansions, built either by the royals themselves or by Scottish nobles, often on the structural footprints of medieval tower houses.

Shaking off the city suburbs, this signposted ride begins with Drum Castle, the nearby Finzean Estate, which has a large Victorian art collection, and Crathes Castle, notable for its 19th-century arboretum. The scenery changes along the way from open water meadows flanking the lower reaches of the Dee River to brooding mountains rising sheer from the road and river just beyond Balmoral. If the estate that Victoria called 'my dear paradise in the Highlands' is closed (late August to March), visit the nearby village of Ballator, which grew up to serve Balmoral. It holds a Victoria Week in August every year.

The drive ends at Braemar, a town built around its castle on the confluence of the Dee and the Clunie Rivers. For a scenic extension, take the Old Military Road up through Glen Clunie to the Cairnwell Pass, which, at 670m (2,199ft) above sea level, is the highest main road in Britain. **DS**

❶ Crathes Castle was founded in 1323; the current buildings date from the 17th century.

Ardnamurchan Peninsula
Argyll and Bute, Scotland

Start Fort William
End Fort William
Distance 212km (132 miles)
Type Scenic
Map goo.gl/87AHYs

Fort William is a popular springboard for the Highlands, but head west instead of north or east to discover the Ardnamurchan Peninsula – an unspoiled backwater with crofting villages on the shore. It ends at the most westerly point on the Scottish mainland. Setting off in a clockwise direction from Fort William, take the main road alongside Loch Linnhe to Corran, where a ferry will deliver you and your vehicle to the opposite bank in about four minutes; a journey that adds to the impression of visiting a land apart. Head to Strontian, one-time hub of a thriving lead-mining industry, and continue around the northern shore of Loch Sunart to the peninsula proper, transferring to a single-track road at Salen to reach Kilchoan, the main community on the peninsula, after about 47km (29 miles). From here, short hops north lead to Ardnamurchan Point, topped by an Egyptian-style lighthouse (visitor centre, café and views to the Outer Hebrides), and Sanna, where white sand beaches peep like a petticoat from a skirt of black rocks and marram grass. Back on the main road, look out for Glenfinnan Viaduct, famously crossed by the Hogwarts Express train in the *Harry Potter* movies. From Glenfinnan, it is a straightforward run alongside Loch Eil back to Fort William. **DS**

➲ A stunning stretch of road near Loch Sunart.

Kintyre Peninsula
Argyll and Bute, Scotland

Start Tarbert
End Tarbert
Distance 183km (114 miles)
Type Scenic
Map goo.gl/Yruyvs

The geography of Scotland throws up some extraordinary places, but few are stranger than Kintyre. Hanging off the bottom of the Knapdale Peninsula, to which it is connected by only a narrow isthmus between two sea lochs at Tarbert, the Kintyre Peninsula extends south for 48km (30 miles) to the Mull of Kintyre. Nowhere more than 18km (11 miles) wide, Kintyre is a land of forests, sheep farms, small coastal settlements and only one town worthy of the name.

The route around the edge of Kintyre begins at Tarbert, from where the A83 heads down the west coast to Campbeltown, an ancient town known until 1667 as Kinlochkilkerran ('head of the loch by the church of Ciaran'). This is a centre of the whisky industry, producing some fine single malts from its three distilleries – Glen Scotia, Mitchell's Glengyle and Springbank.

From there, you might want to drive south to the Mull of Kintyre, immortalized by the 1977 global hit song, co-written by part-time local resident former Beatle Paul McCartney and Denny Laine, and performed by their band Wings. On a clear day, when the mist isn't rolling in from the sea, you can see the Antrim coast of Northern Ireland. Back on the loop road, head up the east coast along the narrow and twisty B842 and B8001 through woods and across river valleys back to Tarbert. **SA**

Isle of Mull Scenic Loop Argyll and Bute, Scotland

Start Craignure   **End** Craignure   **Distance** 196km (122 miles)
Type Scenic   **Map** goo.gl/RfPaIv

Getting to the Isle of Mull is a great trip in itself, with the Hebridean island only easily accessible by ferry from the west coast of Scotland. These ferries run regularly all year around; catch an early crossing to allow good time for your scenic island loop, starting from the port. The sparsity of roads on the Isle of Mull means there are only two options when leaving Craignure: clockwise or anticlockwise. Turn left and head clockwise and you soon arrive at the restored 13th-century castle at Duart, overlooking the bay.

At the mouth of Loch Beg comes the first and only major junction on the route, and it is well worth turning left and continuing to the most westerly point of the island, at Fionnphort. If you fancy taking the short ferry across to the Isle of Iona, you will have to leave your vehicle behind; only residents are allowed cars on the island.

Retrace your route back up the road and around the base of the unrelentingly steep mountain of Ben More. Continue up the west coast via Gruline and Kilninian before turning east past Loch Peallach to the island's largest town, Tobermory, with its brightly painted buildings. Fans of Scottish whisky will want to pay a visit to the town's eponymous distillery before heading back to the ferry. **TW**

❶ Single-track roads wind through unspoiled scenery.

Loch Fyne and Loch Awe Argyll and Bute, Scotland

Start Inveraray   End Inveraray   Distance 117km (73 miles)
Type Scenic   Map goo.gl/3a2ZD3

Championed by Britain's Automobile Association (AA), this popular scenic tour visits the shores of two beautiful Scottish lochs. Both are long and narrow, carved by long-gone glaciers and flanked by thick coniferous forest, but each has a very different character, because Loch Fyne contains sea water, while Loch Awe is freshwater.

The circuit begins at the imposing Inveraray Castle, ancestral home of the Dukes of Argyll. Heading north anticlockwise on the A819 through Glen Aray, you reach Loch Awe, famous for its game fishing and the Portsonachan Hotel, a time-honoured haunt with visiting anglers. The B840 along the southern shore is an absolute joy. The picture-perfect ivy-covered ruin on an islet near here was once the stronghold of the Campbell Clan that ruled these parts.

At the 16th-century Carnassarie Castle, the route heads south to the sailing haven of Crinan before turning southeast to Achnaba and back to Loch Fyne. You should visit the Auchindrain Folk Museum to learn about area's rich cultural history.

By this time you may have worked up an appetite – there's no shortage of eateries in the area and fresh-caught trout are always on the menu, along with a wide range of whiskies. DIS

❶ Glen Fyne adjacent to the loch of the same name.

Rest and Be Thankful Argyll and Bute, Scotland

Start Tarbet   End Rest and Be Thankful Viewpoint   Distance 13.2km (8.2 miles)
Type Culture   Map goo.gl/oYRB6b

Starting at Tarbet near Loch Lomond, the A83 road climbs near the shores of Loch Long through some of Scotland's finest mountain scenery.

Ascending through Glen Croe, peeping over the barriers into the valley below, you can glimpse running parallel the Old Military Road built by General George Wade during the Jacobite Rebellion. Driving livestock or marching armies up such a relentless steep pass to 245m (804ft) above sea level was no easy task; so much so that in 1753 soldiers erected a commemorative stone at the saddle inscribed with some sage advice to weary travellers: 'Rest and Be Thankful'. Heed their suggestion and admire this spectacular vista.

From 1906 to the late 1970s, there were regular hill-climbing events over a 1,303-m- (1,425-yard) long stretch of the old road. Many racing greats, including Scottish Formula One World Champion Jackie Stewart, honed their craft along this tortuous course. Until quite recently it was possible to bribe the landowner with a good bottle of whisky to open the gates and have a blast up it yourself. However, there are now interesting plans afoot to restore the circuit to its former glory and build a heritage centre nearby celebrating Scotland's numerous motorsport achievements. **DIS**

❶ The A83 through Glen Croe.

Skyfall Tour Argyll and Bute/Highland, Scotland

Start Loch Lomond, Argyll and Bute **End** Glencoe Village, Highland **Distance** 146km (91 miles)

Type Culture **Map** goo.gl/uec3uO

In the climactic scenes of this 2012 blockbuster you join 007 as he whisks away M, his MI6 superior, to his childhood home, Skyfall Lodge, a bleak, mist-shrouded estate in the Scottish Highlands. As they escape north, in Bond's prized Aston Martin DB5, you get to see some of the greatest driving roads that Scotland has to offer.

As with most movies, some artistic licence was taken with the screenplay's geography; the 'A9', quoted in the film as the most direct route to Skyfall, would have certainly been the A82, a spectacular stretch of road that runs from the shores of Loch Lomond through the wide rugged valleys of Glen Coe, where most of the film's aerial shots were taken.

The scene in which the Aston drives along a lonely Highland road fringed by pine forest was filmed between Bridge of Orchy and the Glen Coe ski area. Those 007 über-fans keen to find precise film locations might also wish to seek out the spot where Bond and M pull over to admire the mountains of Buachaille Etive Mòr by taking the single-track road to Glen Etive that leaves the A82 near the Kingshouse Hotel.

Skyfall Lodge itself is not part of this trip, because the estate was a plasterboard mock-up built in a disused army base in Surrey, England. **DIS**

❶ The bonnie bonnie banks of Loch Lomond.

The Old Military Road Perth and Kinross/Highland, Scotland

Start Blairgowrie, Perth and Kinross End Grantown-on-Spey, Highland Distance 129km (80 miles)
Type Culture   Map goo.gl/jLXaGv

It's the highest public road in Britain, crossing the Cairnwell Pass through the Cairngorm Mountains in northeast Scotland.

Normally it's a great, fast-cruising highway across a wide open landscape with little traffic. But the tourist board's marketing name for the journey, 'The Snow Roads Scenic Route', hints at the seasonal problems you can face here. You'll pass snow gates at Spittal of Glenshee, which close the road in the serious conditions that often occur between October and April. The gates are designed to prevent motorists getting stranded in snow overnight. So pay attention to weather reports before you tackle this route.

The summit is at 670m (2,199ft) near Glenshee, Scotland's biggest ski resort. The modern road bypasses a notorious stretch of hairpin bends here called The Devil's Elbow. Today the curves are much milder and the gradients less challenging.

The road is a roller coaster of dips and crests, mirroring the surrounding landscape, which rises in and falls in waves rather than jagged peaks. If they are not covered in snow, you will see these mountains form a harsh, treeless, tundra-like environment with piles of exposed rocks visble alongside the road. **SH**

❶ Heading north along the A93.

Moffat to Selkirk Dumfries and Galloway/Scottish Borders, Scotland

Start Moffat, Dumfries and Galloway   End Selkirk, Scottish Borders   Distance 56km (35 miles)
Type Scenic   Map goo.gl/hgmxsV

Routes in the Scottish Highlands are often named among the world's great driving roads, but this stretch in the Lowlands will demonstrate whether you and your car have got what it takes. You do not need to break the speed limit or take risks to tackle this bucking, twisting, weaving road as it swaggers diagonally over the desolate moor between two attractive Scottish border towns. Just drive swiftly and smoothly through the undulations and corners as the scenery sweeps up and down around you.

There is barely a house along the main road: only dry-stone walls and the bleak rolling hills of the Southern Uplands. It makes a memorable scenic alternative route for anyone travelling between England and Edinburgh. Leave the main road behind and enjoy dips, crests and bends instead; the road is mostly smooth, well-maintained tarmac. The scenic highlights include the stretch along the shore of St Mary's Loch, which legend holds has no bottom. Locals say it is the coldest loch in Scotland, and St Mary's is certainly the largest natural loch in the Lowland region. At the remote Gordon Arms Hotel, turn left for a scenic route to Edinburgh, go straight on for Selkirk, or take a right for an even more challenging drive across the hills to Lockerbie. SH

❶ Talla Reservoir at Tweedsmuir is en route to Edinburgh.

Jim Clark Memorial Rally
Scottish Borders, Scotland

Start Auchencrow
End Duns
Distance 22km (13.7 miles)
Type Culture
Map goo.gl/E7zDVC

Jim Clark was a Scottish farmer's son who proved to be a genius at the wheel of whatever class of car he sat in, from Aston Martins to NASCARs, Lotus GP racers to saloon-based rally cars. He was twice Formula One world champion, in 1963 and 1965 – titles he claimed through skill rather than naked aggression. After Clark was killed at Germany's Hochenheimring in 1968, his legions of admirers set about creating a fitting memorial to him.

For many years the Jim Clark Memorial Rally (JCMR) was held on private land in the Scottish Borders where the great champion grew up, but in 1996 permission was gained for what is currently Britain's only closed-road event.

Enthusiasts who have watched the annual rally will readily appreciate the amazingly varied and beautiful countryside the stages run through. To get a flavor of the JCMR, try the Edrom Stage, which heads west off the B6437 and into a warren of tiny country lanes towards Blanerne, Edrom and the marshes, before weaving north to the finishing line near Preston. However, motorsport fans will undoubtedly want to conclude their road trip at the Jim Clark Room in Duns. Among this intimate collection of photographs, race overalls and helmets is a coruscating collection of silverware and other trophies from the glittering, but all-too-short, career of Scotland's 'Gentleman Jim'. **DIS**

Isle of Man TT Course
Isle of Man

Start Douglas
End Douglas
Distance 60.7km (37.7 miles)
Type Culture
Info goo.gl/WnuGLm

Championed by motorcycling enthusiasts as the planet's last great road race, the Snaefell Mountain Course is a brutal high-speed circuit looping out from the capital Douglas over the mist-shrouded mountains of the island's interior, through sleepy villages and dozens of treacherous corners that are often renamed in memory of the riders who have been killed here.

The first motor race on the Isle of Man took place in 1904, but the motorcycling fraternity made it their own after the inaugural Tourist Trophy (TT) race of 1907. Come if you can during the manic TT Fortnight in late May when around 40,000 motorsport fans and 15,000 motorbikes flock to the island. Witnessing the very best riders charging around at average speeds in excess of 209 kph (130 mph) just inches away from solid walls and buildings, and getting airborne over narrow humpback bridges, is a mind-blowing spectacle.

Following the TT course is not difficult: black-and-white painted curbstones line much of the route. Although the course record holders can get around the circuit in less than 17 minutes you should allow a whole morning to do it properly, before heading back to Douglas for a leisurely lunch on the elegant Victorian promenade. **DIS**

➲ TT racers climbing towards Snaefell Mountain.

Along the Shores of Lake Windermere
Cumbria, England

Start Ambleside
End Ambleside
Distance 46km (28.5 miles)
Type Scenic
Map goo.gl/EiyvTJ

The lakes and mountains of Cumbria have inspired poets and artists for centuries, and this road trip offers a chance for drivers and bikers to enjoy those same landscapes. It is a circuit around the most popular lake in the heart of the Lake District National Park, starting and finishing in the pretty tourist town of Ambleside at the north end of Windermere. Try to avoid the crowds of the peak holiday period; the narrow, winding stretches quickly become jammed, and coaches fill the lakeside towns. Instead, find a quiet out-of-season day to enjoy the open roads, with time to take in the panoramas across England's largest lake and the hills and mountains beyond.

En route, there is a combination of standard rural roads and narrow country lanes with lots of sharp bends and hilly sections. Drive through neat villages, old forests and a patchwork of grassy pastures between tumbling dry-stone walls where rugged mountain sheep graze. The circuit is packed with attractions, too, from the quaint home of author Beatrix Potter – now owned by the National Trust – to the acclaimed fell walks in all directions. A fabulous driving detour is to head north on the A592 up into the dizzy heights of Kirkstone Pass at 454m (1,489ft). Pull over on a clear day and it feels like you can see the whole of the Lake District spread out below you. **SH**

❶ The road winds through the valley, with hills and snow-covered mountain peaks to either side.

The Roof of England
Cumbria/Northumberland, England

Start Penrith, Cumbria
End Haydon Bridge, Northumberland
Distance 60km (37.2 miles)
Type Scenic
Map goo.gl/HegNCl

The north of England has a downbeat reputation for being wet, gray and windy. However, it is home to some stunning scenery and many fantastic driving roads. The route from Penrith in Cumbria to Haydon Bridge in Northumberland is a fine example as it straddles the 'Roof of England', technically part of the North Pennine hills.

Head out of the town of Penrith and soon you will be in the English countryside, with dry-stone walls and rolling fields lining the route. Although the road is a only single lane each way, it is easy to make good progress. Nevertheless, the area is a mecca for weekend bikers and keen motorists, so it is a good idea to keep an eye out for over-enthusiastic visitors and hidden speed cameras.

At Langwathby village, cross the River Eden on a single-track metal bridge. Then continue on to Melmerby and out (and up) to Hartside Summit, where there is a popular biker's haunt, the Hartside Top Cafe, at 580m (1,900ft) above sea level, looking out over the Solway Firth to southern Scotland and England's highest peaks. It is certainly worth taking time to appreciate the view before the road takes you down into Alston, the highest market town in England. The last leg of the journey is a further descent, with a number of tight bends, to Haydon Bridge. Come rain or shine, this is a road trip to clear away the cobwebs. JI

❶ With a smooth road surface and views far ahead in the distance, Hartside Pass is a driver's dream.

The Northern Lakes and Mountains
Cumbria, England

Start Keswick
End Keswick
Distance 97km (60 miles)
Type Scenic
Map goo.gl/YptVCn

The Lake District occupies some 2,243 sq km (866 square miles) of northern England; it has been a National Park since 1951.

The northern half of this beautiful region is best explored from the old market town of Keswick, which has long been associated with such poets as Samuel Taylor Coleridge and Robert Southey. From there, head south down Borrowdale, past Derwentwater, and then west in an anticlockwise direction alongside Buttermere and Crummock Water. A short way farther east past High Lorton brings you to Braithwaite and the southern end of Bassenthwaite. In one of the potentially confusing anomalies of British English, Bassenthwaite is the only stretch of water in the area that is officially known as a lake: the others are all called 'meres', 'tarns' or 'waters'. On the eastern side of the lake lies Skiddaw, at 931m (3,054ft) England's sixth-highest peak, and reputedly the easiest of the Lake District peaks to climb.

At the northern end of Bassenthwaite, the empty country lanes take you northeast in a large scenic loop around the Uldale, Caldbeck and Lonscale Fells back south and west again to Keswick.

The roads of the Lake District get utterly choked with traffic during the high season. Don't let congestion spoil this lovely lakeside road trip – time your visit with care. **SA**

❶ Ashness Bridge and Derwentwater in Borrowdale near the town of Keswick.

Hardknott and Wrynose Passes
Cumbria, England

Start Ambleside
End Holmrook
Distance 27km (16.8 miles)
Type Scenic
Map goo.gl/IrJqdW

On the map it seems a simple rural drive from east to west in the scenic heart of the Lake District National Park. But brace yourself, for this route has been called 'Britain's most outrageous road'.

Signage hints at what's coming: 'Narrow road. Severe bends', it announces. By then it's too late. Stay focused and enjoy the experience.

Ultimately you'll pass to the south of Scafell Pike, at 978m (3,209ft) England's highest peak, to reach the remote lush beauty of the Eskdale Valley.

On the way, the scarily steep slopes and hairpin bends will have you reaching to change down when you're already in first gear. It's as narrow as a bridleway in places; gradients reach 33 per cent. Sometimes it's best not to look down as you weave between unguarded drops.

Then there's the weather. It's challenging enough on a sunny day. But that's rare in these mountains. Expect horizontal rain, buffeting side winds and slippery roads. It could be worse. The route is impassable in severe winter weather.

The reward for all that concentrated steering and gear-changing is access to a landscape of rare, savage beauty. Spot waterfalls, sheer rock faces and sudden stunning views. Dramatic terrain rises into the clouds on either side as Herdwick sheep wander imperiously in front of you. They know that it's the motorized vehicles that are the outsiders here. **SH**

❶ The steep west side of Wrynose Pass is one of the easiest parts of this itinerary.

The Trip Cumbria/Yorkshire, England

Start Grasmere, Cumbria   **End** The Yorke Arms, Yorkshire   **Distance** 222km (138 miles)
Type Culture   **Map** goo.gl/cbwIor

This drive follows the route of *The Trip*, the acclaimed film and BBC TV series of 2010 starring Steve Coogan and Rob Brydon. You can eat in the same celebrated restaurants, see the same inspiring views and even practise your Michael Caine impressions in the same locations.

This foodies' road trip has been retraced by countless fans of the show; it's also a lovely scenic driving route for anyone exploring the landscapes of England's Lake District and Yorkshire Dales – and you don't have to visit all the expensive restaurants and hotels that the actors did.

You'll start at Dove Cottage, once the home of the poet William Wordsworth. Head south to see the spectacular limestone pavement at Malham Cove, where Coogan's reverie was spoiled by an encounter with a boring amateur geological expert, and the atmospheric ruins of Bolton Abbey, where the duo argue about who likes it most.

The finale of your own version of *The Trip* will be the rolling green hills of Nidderdale in the Yorkshire Dales. Like Coogan and Brydon you can stay at the luxurious 18th-century coaching inn, The Yorke Arms . . . although you are not obliged to see who can do the best Peter Sellers impersonations while eating dinner. **SH**

❶ Bolton Abbey was destroyed by King Henry VIII.

By Hadrian's Wall Tyne and Wear to Cumbria, England

Start Wallsend, Tyne and Wear   **End** Bowness-on-Solway, Cumbria   **Distance** 126km (78 miles)
Type Scenic   **Map** goo.gl/OkW2Fa

The largest extant Roman artefact in the world still puzzles historians. Known as Hadrian's Wall, this line of ditches and stone walls punctuated by milecastles with a fort every five Roman miles – each mile measured by the left foot hitting the ground one thousand times while marching – is now a popular tourist attraction across the width of England, between the Tyne River on the North Sea and the Solway Firth and the Irish Sea.

Work began on the wall in 122 during the reign of Emperor Hadrian, but it is unclear whether the fortification was intended as a defensive measure against hostile ancient Britons to the north or whether it was merely a marker of the northern boundary of the Roman Empire. It may, alternatively, have been a protection against cattle rustlers, and a customs and immigration control. Whatever its purpose, long stretches of the wall have survived the centuries well. Road trippers can drive the length of it on the A69, B6318 and B6264. The rolling hills of the border region are simply splendid to drive through, but it's often hard to keep sight of the wall as it rises and dips over them, so stop often and explore on foot. Must-see places en route include Birdoswald Roman Fort and the Roman Army Museum at Vindolanda. **SA**

❶ No one knows the real purpose of Hadrian's Wall.

Alnwick to Lindisfarne
Northumberland, England

Start Alnwick Castle
End Lindisfarne
Distance 63km (39.1 miles)
Type Culture
Map goo.gl/sieub4

Magical coastal drives don't get a better start than this one, from the imposing grounds of Alnwick Castle, where Britain's most famous wizard flew his broomstick in the first *Harry Potter* film.

From here, past one of the world's oldest golf courses, the coastal road heads through the villages of Longhoughton and Craster, where the imposing ruin of Dunstanburgh Castle, home to John of Gaunt, looms on the horizon. Rejoin the B1339 and pass Embleton Tower, built in 1395 to defend the area from the Scots.

Pick up the B1340 to Bamburgh, and the second grand fortress of this road trip soon appears high above, clinging to the crags and looking out over the sand dunes towards Lindisfarne. A short spell on the A1 through rolling Northumberland farmland brings you to the 3-km- (2-mile) long drive across the tidal causeway to the island itself. Timing the tides correctly is absolutely crucial here; over the decades dozens of motorists have had to be rescued from the rapidly rising sea.

The Holy Island of Lindisfarne is equally famous for its medieval religious heritage and its picturesque 16th-century castle – the third and final grand fortress of this road trip – atop the island's highest rock outcrop. **TW**

● Lindisfarne Causeway partly covered by the tide.

Buttertubs Pass and the Yorkshire Dales
Yorkshire, England

Start Hawes
End Thwaite
Distance 11km (7 miles)
Type Scenic
Map goo.gl/tFj4zj

The rugged millstone grit-and-limestone hills and the verdant glacially carved valleys that make up the Yorkshire Dales are among Britain's most dramatic landscapes. Best of all, in the opinion of many people, is the scenery surrounding the road across Buttertubs Pass in the north of the county. Jeremy Clarkson of BBC TV's *Top Gear* once championed this stretch of tarmac as 'England's only truly spectacular road', and it is regularly used by motoring journalists testing new cars and by film crews looking for pretty backdrops.

Buttertubs is named for the 20-m- (66-ft) deep potholes of limestone formed in the rock face. Local farmers once used these holes as natural refrigerators to keep their butter cool during the summer months.

Starting in the small market town of Hawes at the head of Wensleydale, famous for its cheese, the road rises north up Fossdale through Simonstone and High Shaw to Abbotside Common on Stags Fell. To the left, the land rises to 714m (2,341ft) at Great Shunner Fell. You are now in Buttertubs Pass, from where the views are spectacular. A steep descent takes you down to Thwaite. It should be pointed out that this is also a great land for cyclists: the pass was the second of three 'King of the Mountains' climbs in Stage 1 of the 2014 Tour de France. So watch out for fast folk on two wheels. **SA**

🛈 Buttertubs Pass is photogenic year round, but quietest in winter.

Brontë Country
Yorkshire, England

Start Batley
End Top Withens
Distance 55km (34.2 miles)
Type Culture
Map goo.gl/wgMFzb

Discover part of Britain's literary heritage on a road trip that revolves around the personal lives and acclaimed works of the famed Brontë family.

You'll discover how the three Brontë sisters, Charlotte, Emily and Anne, produced some of the world's most famous and widely read novels from a sleepy little hamlet high on the windswept Yorkshire moors.

The highlight of the tour will be the Brontë family home at The Parsonage in Haworth, where their father was the vicar. Inside the house you can still see their furniture and possessions arranged as they were while Emily was producing *Wuthering Heights*, Charlotte was penning *Jane Eyre* and Anne was working on *The Tenant of Wildfell Hall*. Farther along Haworth's cobbled main street you'll see the family vault in the churchyard, as well as Brontë-themed gift shops and cafés.

The route includes the Victorian Red House Museum in Gomersal and the Elizabethan Oakwell Hall in Batley, which both featured as settings for Charlotte's novels. See the sisters' birthplace in Thornton and follow the trail up onto the moor to find Top Withens, the ruined farmhouse that supposedly served as the setting for Wuthering Heights. You can drive part of the way but you'll have to walk the final stretch over the moor ... just like the sisters used to do. **SH**

Vale of York
Yorkshire, England

Start York
End York
Distance 114km (71 miles)
Type Culture
Map goo.gl/qJWFrj

This route starts and finishes in York, one of Britain's most popular city-break destinations. York is full of historic attractions, including the Minster, The Shambles and the Roman Walls, and such contemporary delights as boutique shopping, restaurants and hotels. If you fancy a day's road trip out, this is a cracker.

Following this route you head north along the banks of the Ouse River via the stone cottages and traditional parish churches of villages like Shipton and Linton-on-Ouse. Then loop east across the rugged moor through pretty little country lanes to Easingwold at the foot of the Howardian Hills.

These hills form an Area of Outstanding Natural Beauty covering 204 sq km (79 square miles) of leafy, undulating countryside. The landscape is the main sight here, but look out too for Gilling Castle, a fortified manor house, and Hovingham Hall, a Palladian mansion featuring Britain's oldest cricket pitch. The highlight of the area is Castle Howard, one of Britain's finest stately homes, designed by architect and playwright John Vanbrugh.

You loop through the hills via the photogenic ruins of Sheriff Hutton Castle and Sutton Park, a grand Georgian country house and garden. Then you turn south through the more genteel Vale of York farmland, back to your starting point in the grand old city of York. **SH**

Holmes Chapel to Alderley Edge
Cheshire, England

Start Holmes Chapel
End Alderley Edge
Distance 16km (9.9 miles)
Type Scenic
Map goo.gl/B6iVrZ

Holmes Chapel and Alderley Edge form part of Cheshire's 'golden triangle' of leafy, affluent villages, sought-after by millionaire footballers, self-made entrepreneurs and media personalities from the urban sprawl of Manchester to the north. The conspicuous wealth of fellow road-users is easy to spot as you sweep along this lovely classic rural road, where overhanging trees, well-tended farmland and open, wide, sweeping bends make it a gorgeous route on a quiet sunny day.

The road's scenic highlight comes near the hamlet of Withington, when you start to glimpse something very incongruous through the roadside hedges. Soon the massive radio dishes of Jodrell Bank Observatory begin to dominate the western horizon. The largest of these astrophysicists' implements is more than 76m (250ft) high, the biggest of its kind in the world. Take a break from the drive to explore Jodrell Bank Discovery Centre and learn more about what the dishes do. There is a chance to enjoy dishes of a different kind at the smart café, which also offers close-up views of the telescopes.

The route's grand finale is the rustic panorama across Cheshire and the Peak District from the escarpment that gives Alderley Edge its name. The best viewing spots are reached from a smaller road – the B5087 – just to the east of the village. **SH**

❶ Alderley Edge is associated with myth and legend, and 'hermits' caves' can be found dug into the sandstone.

Snake Pass and Peak District Moors
Derbyshire, England

Start Glossop
End Snake Pass
Distance 76km (47 miles)
Type Scenic
Info goo.gl/YS9dEL

Britain is a crowded island, but this road trip takes you through the closest thing England has to wilderness. Even though the Peak District National Park is only 32km (20 miles) from Manchester and Sheffield, very few byways traverse its bleak moorlands. This exhilarating loop covers the finest roads the region has to offer.

Head out on the Devil's Elbow road from Glossop, with its 17th-century cottages and Victorian cotton mills, past numerous small reservoirs towards the charming old mill town of Holmfirth. For 37 years this was where the British sitcom *Last of the Summer Wine* was filmed.

After passing a handful of sleepy Pennine villages, the A57 enters open country on the wildest road in the High Peak, Snake Pass. Climbing to 512m (1,680ft), the Snake Road's sweeping bends and smooth tarmac are perennial magnets for bikers and car drivers. But beware, this road can bite back: it gets very slippery when the mountain mists descend, and adverse cambers and elevation changes frequently catch out the unwary and the over-confident.

Nicknamed the 'Oopnorthring', this is a route best saved for a balmy summer's evening when you can stop for a drink and swap road-tripping tales with like-minded drivers who gather at the Snake Pass Inn near the summit. **DIS**

❶ When viewed from Rowlee Pasture near Edale, it is easy to see how the road acquired its name.

Cat and Fiddle
Derbyshire/Cheshire, England

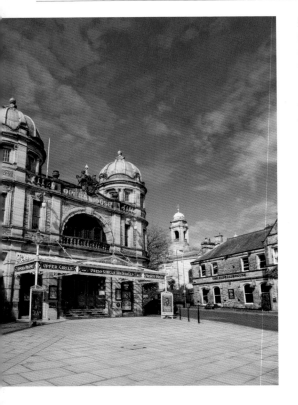

Start Buxton, Derbyshire
End Macclesfield, Cheshire
Distance 19km (11.8 miles)
Type Adventure
Map goo.gl/jGmHeC

This gloriously titled stretch of road takes its name from the public house that sits at its summit, high in the Peak District of northern England. But its quaint title belies its fearsome reputation. It is regarded by many as the most dangerous road in Britain. The tight, blind bends scattered along its length are the main reason for this, and it has been the scene of many traffic accidents over the years. But slowing down is no bad thing on a road like this, as you'll be rewarded by a stunning selection of views that reach out across the Derbyshire and Cheshire countryside, over the Macclesfield Forest and beyond.

Start on the A53 through the western outskirts of Buxton until a right turn onto the A54 at Ladmanlow, then head up on to the flat moorland of Goyt's Moss. Once past the pub, the road descends through yet more tight switchbacks until it reaches the market town of Macclesfield.

Although the road is still a major attraction for weekend bikers and sports car enthusiasts, the Cat and Fiddle's notoriety has resulted in a reduced, 80 kph (50 mph) speed limit, the introduction of speed cameras and regular patrols by unmarked police cars. Nevertheless, it is still a wonderful road to drive with a conveniently located pub nearby, the second-highest in England, overlooking the magnificent High Peak. **TW**

❶ The Opera House in Buxton.
↪ The Cat and Fiddle in winter.

Winnats Pass and the Peak District
Derbyshire, England

Start Grindleford
End Mapleton
Distance 47km (29 miles)
Type Culture
Map goo.gl/QQ7xfl

Starting out from the car park at the appropriately named Surprise View, the A6187 heads up to Hathersage through the wild, hilly heart of the Derbyshire countryside towards this road trip's scenic highlight, the spectacular Winnats Pass. It's not a high Alpine saddle, but a dramatic stretch of road winding up through a cleft between limestone cliffs, with prominent rocky outcrops looming above the road. It's intimidating and very narrow, and there are steep sections of up to 28 per cent gradients to watch out for.

The pass stands just to the west of the quaint village of Castleton, a classic tourist spot in the National Park. It's a great base for hikes, caving expeditions . . . or just exploring the large selection of tempting teashops.

After a short detour to the fascinating 'Plague Village' of Eyam and the pretty town of Bakewell (famous for its delicious tarts and puddings), the road trip ends at the charming little village of Mapleton in the Dove Valley at the southern edge of the National Park. Amid the old brick cottages and a quirky domed parish church here, you'll find yet more traditional teashops.

If you're hungry for more, this scenic road trip can easily be combined with the more challenging Snake Pass loop in the northern half of the Peak District National Park. **SH**

❶ The road ascends through Winnats Pass towards the summit at Mam Tor.

Midlands Tick Nottinghamshire/ Rutland, England

Start Bingham, Nottinghamshire
End Uppingham, Rutland
Distance 85km (52.8 miles)
Type Scenic
Map goo.gl/tEx36f

At the heart of England lies a fabulous little road trip that is not immediately obvious at first glance on a map. Instead of the usual point-to-point or circular loop, this drive is shaped like a written tick (√), hence the name.

Start at Bingham and head south on the Bingham Road via Langar, Harby and Eastwell, where you take a right turn at the crossroads. In addition to the rural scenery and quaint villages, keep an eye on the sky, as the route passes two old British Royal Air Force bases, so there is every chance a glider or two might fly overhead. Eventually you will come to Melton Mowbray, home of the world-famous pork pies. It is a pretty little market town and a good place to stop before the second leg of the trip. Once refreshed, head out to the villages of Great Dalby, Twyford and Tilton on the Hill, before you make your way all the way up through Sutton Bassett and Stockerston to the journey's end at Uppingham, an old market town now best known for its private school, founded in the 16th century.

The drive is largely fast straights and sweeping curves, with plenty of entertaining elevation changes over the final stretches. It is also pretty quiet, scenic and accessible, with the East Midlands countryside looking its best just before the summer harvests. **TW**

Horncastle to Louth
Lincolnshire, England

Start Horncastle
End Louth
Distance 23km (14 miles)
Type Scenic
Map goo.gl/ZniFVp

Even in a country not renowned for its mountains, Lincolnshire is notoriously flat. A gentle escarpment know as the Lincoln Cliff runs down the west of the county and proudly supports the glorious gothic edifice of Lincoln Cathedral, but with one other exception the rest of the county is almost as flat as a pool table. That exception is the Lincolnshire Wolds, a range of low chalk hills that wind gently through northeast Lincolnshire and rise no higher than 168m (551ft) above sea level at Wolds Top. It is over these lowland alps that the equally understated road from Horncastle to Louth makes its way.

The small town of Horncastle bills itself as the 'Gateway to the Wolds', while the barely larger Louth ups the ante by calling itself the 'Capital of the Wolds'. But they're not metropolises, and the A153 that connects them is no bustling highway, but a gentle amble past well-tended fields and through open countryside that is always pleasing to the eye, with wide expansive landscapes.

The road is popular with bikers heading to Cadwell Park Circuit, and has a good mix of long sweeping bends, tightening corners, elevation changes and long, fast straights to make it an interesting and rewarding drive. More importantly, it's a road that lets you enjoy the glorious English countryside at its very best. **SA**

Around the Norfolk Broads
Norfolk, England

Start Wroxham
End Wroxham
Distance 58km (36 miles)
Type Scenic
Map goo.gl/vGpHIY

Until the 1960s, it was generally assumed that the Broads were entirely natural lakes. Not so, said ecologist Dr Joyce Lambert, who proved that they are the remains of medieval peat excavations flooded when sea levels began to rise. Norwich Cathedral alone used 320,000 tons of this fossil fuel a year, hence the numerous wet holes in the ground that exist today. Covering an area of 303 sq km (117 square miles), most of which are in Norfolk, the Broads and their many interconnecting rivers are a wetland heaven for birds and fish, as well as a sailing delight for inshore mariners.

An anticlockwise tour of the Broads, starting and finishing at Wroxham on the Bure River, gives a good idea of what this strange watery world is all about. The route takes you past Ranworth and South Walsham Broads in the west, and back and forth across the long, thin Filby and Ormesby Broads in the east. Finally, you drive alongside Hickling Broad, the largest expanse of water in Norfolk and a National Nature Reserve. Between May and July you might glimpse the beautiful swallowtail, Britain's biggest and rarest butterfly. If wildlife and water do not appeal, rest assured that the area is teeming with pubs that serve car drivers as happily as anglers and mariners. **SA**

● Thatched boat houses floating on Hickling Broad.

The Elgar Route
Worcestershire, England

Start Lower Broadheath
End Lower Broadheath
Distance 71km (44 miles)
Type Culture
Map goo.gl/CEqoKp

Sir Edward Elgar (1857–1934), the best-known of all England's great composers, spent most of his life in the picturesque Malvern Hills, where the soft, rolling landscape is said to have been his main source of inspiration. As a keen cyclist, he often explored the local area; his favourite rides are retraced, in part, by this circular road trip, which also passes homesteads and civic buildings that played parts in Elgar's long and productive career.

Perhaps the most logical starting point is at the Elgar Birthplace Museum in Lower Broadheath, where you can learn more about the man; there is nowhere better to end than at St Wulstan's Church, where he lies buried.

The Elgar Route is a great way to explore this beautiful, little-known part of Worcestershire, even if you're not a classical music fan. Roads here are often narrow, but the route is well marked with brown tourist signposts.

Motoring buffs will enjoy a detour to the Morgan Motor Company, officially the world's oldest privately owned car manufacturer, which has been hand-building sports cars in Malvern since 1909. For a small fee, you can tour the factory or take a short passenger ride in one of their classic two-seaters; well-heeled road trippers, however, should hire a Morgan Roadster for the day to explore this pretty corner of England's rural southwest. **DIS**

Spa Northamptonshire/ Cambridgeshire, England

Start Higham Ferrers, Northamptonshire
End St Neots, Cambridgeshire
Distance 32km (20 miles)
Type Scenic
Map goo.gl/CJJiPF

Keen local drivers and bikers call this route 'Spa', after the challenging Formula One race circuit in Belgium. When a car company recently ran a poll to find the United Kingdom's best driving road, this was one of the winners.

Unfortunately, you cannot expect to be able to tackle this road like a Formula One driver. In addition to a number of sudden bends and concealed junctions, the road leads through several busy little villages such as Stonely and Kimbolton. And be warned: this route's challenging reputation lures enthusiastic drivers and riders, so hidden police speed traps are common.

You will find that this road trip sweeps across the softly rolling farmland on the edge of East Anglia between the A6 and the A1 highways. The gentle landscape here means big skies, distant views and great visibility. There are numerous twists and turns in the road, but you can usually see if hazards are waiting to surprise you around the corner. You will also find plenty of inspiring, long, empty stretches heading straight towards the horizon.

If you fancy a detour, Grafham Water reservoir is a short drive to the north at Dillington. It measures almost 4.8km (3 miles) across and is one of England's largest reservoirs. It is a popular place for picnics and hikes, with a nature reserve, visitor centre and waterside restaurant. **SH**

The Painters' Trail Suffolk/Essex, England

Start Sudbury, Suffolk
End Ipswich, Suffolk
Distance 54km (33.5 miles)
Type Culture
Map goo.gl/WCFSAk

This is a journey through some of the places that nurtured and inspired East Anglia's great landscape painters: Thomas Gainsborough and John Constable in the 18th century, and Alfred Munnings in the 19th and 20th.

The itinerary follows the lush, green banks of the Stour River, which forms the border with Essex, through farm meadows dotted with thatched, half-timbered cottages. Many scenes seem unchanged since the artists depicted them.

The highlight is Flatford Mill, near where Constable painted *The Hay Wain* (1821), one of Britain's best-loved rural scenes. Willy Lott's House and Bridge Cottage, which stand alongside the river here, are now National Trust attractions.

The starting point is Sudbury, a pretty market town founded by Saxons in the 8th century. Gainsborough's birthplace here is now a museum dedicated to his achievement. Constable went to school in Dedham, just over the county line in Essex, and later painted the village many times. You'll see one of his paintings in the church here, as well as Castle House, the home of Munnings, which is now a museum about his life and work.

By now you'll be itching to see more of these artists' paintings. An acclaimed collection of the work of all three of them is housed in Christchurch Mansion, a glorious Tudor palace in Ipswich. **SH**

Cotswold Escarpment
Gloucestershire/Wiltshire, England

Start Stroud, Gloucestershire
End Stroud, Gloucestershire
Distance 97km (60 miles)
Type Scenic
Map goo.gl/R4kJra

The Cotswold hills in the west of England rise gently from the water meadows of the upper Thames Valley to reach a peak of 330m (1,083ft) at Cleeve Hill near Cheltenham before plunging down the steep escarpment of the Cotswold Edge into the valley of the Severn, the longest river in Britain. The hills are of Jurassic limestone, a honey-coloured rock quarried for the golden stone used to build the local houses. The whole area, both rural and urban, is one of outstanding natural beauty, best enjoyed on a circular tour starting and finishing in the former mill town of Stroud.

Once out of the town at Dudbridge, the B4066 heads south along the escarpment, with startlingly good views westwards across the Severn Valley to the Forest of Dean and, on a good day, the Welsh mountains. The nearby Tyndale Monument commemorates the 16th-century Protestant martyr William Tyndale, the first man to translate the Bible into English. Along the way, you pass the home of the Dukes of Beaufort, Badminton House, after which the game of badminton was named. Across the M4 motorway and beyond Yatton Keynell, the route turns east and then north through Malmesbury, Tetbury and Avening, where an annual hog-roasting ceremony is held on Pig Face Sunday in mid-September. The road trip ends where it began, in Stroud. **SA**

① Cleeve Hill is the highest point in the Cotswolds, which extend for around 145km (90 miles).

Bodmin Moor and the North Cornish Coast

Cornwall, England

● This stretch of highway near Porteath is typical of the local terrain.

Start Wadebridge
End Wadebridge
Distance 121km (75 miles)
Type Scenic
Map goo.gl/VSlOrR

Unlike the genteel south coast, North Cornwall is a rugged, fascinating stretch of treacherous rocks with a few sandy coves. This road trip offers a great chance to see the best stretch of this inspiring Atlantic-facing shore and then loop back to your starting point via the secluded villages of Bodmin Moor. Start in the comparatively civilized town of Wadebridge, where a popular bike and walking trail leads along the River Camel to Padstow's seafood restaurants. Drive north to the windy surfers' beach at Polzeath and the pretty little fishing villages of Port Isaac and Port Gaverne before passing the massive crater of Delabole slate quarry and the locals' secret beach at Trebarwith Strand to reach Tintagel. It is worth running the gauntlet of gift shops to visit one of the United Kingdom's most exciting castles, reached via a bridge on to a tiny island.

At Boscastle there is a spectacular natural harbour like a mini fjord, while Crackington Haven, Widemouth Bay and Bude have sandy stretches to catch Atlantic rollers. Finally, turn back inland to explore the fringes of Bodmin Moor, with its wild ponies and windswept rocky outcrops called 'tors'. From Hallworthy, you will see the highest points of Rough Tor and Brown Willy on the southern horizon. You can't drive much closer, but it makes a great walk if the weather is good. **SH**

St Ives to St Just
Cornwall, England

Start St Ives
End St Just
Distance 25km (15.5 miles)
Type Scenic
Map goo.gl/Y7vXfM

Experience a drive through a part of Cornwall that is very different from the well-kept sandy beaches and chic boutique hotels of the popular resorts. This inspiring road twists across almost tree-less cliff tops, with rugged coastal views on one side and windswept moorland on the other. Look out for the crumbling towers and chimneys of disused mines, as well as mysterious Celtic stone circles. Great granite boulders litter the landscape, and cottages built from these rocks jut out into the road when you least expect them.

The narrowness of the road is emphasized by imposing mossy stone walls and sudden steep drops and rises. It creates one of the rawest and most memorable routes anywhere in the West Country. It is a totally involving route to ride or drive – but don't expect to reach top gear at any point.

Light relief comes at the hamlet of Zennor, where the path down to Gurnard's Head from the charming Tinners Arms is a bracing adventure, especially in the face of a serious Atlantic storm. The challenge ends in the granite town square of St Just, where ranks of miners' cottages surround a few pubs and shops patiently hoping for tourists. A tiny lane to the west leads out to a jagged viewpoint at Cape Cornwall that makes the famous headland of Land's End a few miles south seem soft and over-developed in comparison. **SH**

❶ The view from the road between Gurnard's Head and Zennor Head.

Poldark Country
Cornwall, England

Start Charlestown
End Lizard Point
Distance 124km (77 miles)
Type Culture
Map goo.gl/PTG3lf

Okay, you won't see Ross Poldark cutting the grass without his shirt – but this route captures the essence of both the hit BBC TV series based on Winston Graham's *Poldark* novels and the finest coastal scenery south Cornwall has to offer.

Start your journey in the pretty Georgian harbour village of Charlestown, a frequent location for the series. There is usually a big square-rigged sailing ship moored in the harbour to complete the period atmosphere. From here, head west via winding coastal lanes with amazing sea views and take the King Harry car ferry across the River Fal at Trelissick. Loop around Falmouth Harbour and the beautiful wooded Helford estuary to reach Poldark Mine in Wendron. This ancient tin mine is a World Heritage Site and served for many underground scenes in the show.

The sandy beach at Gunwalloe was the scene of a dramatic nighttime shipwreck in the series, while the big hotel overlooking nearby Mullion Cove accommodates the cast and crew during filming. The pretty coves at Kynance and Landewednack featured in the programme, too.

Finally, end your journey at the wonderfully rugged headland known as The Lizard. Forget the over-commercialized Land's End to the west; The Lizard is a more dramatic landscape and the UK's most southerly point. **SH**

❶ Tall ships in the harbour at Charlestown, Cornwall, part of *Poldark* was filmed around the quay.

LeJog
England/Scotland

Start Land's End, Cornwall, England
End John O'Groats, Highland, Scotland
Distance 1,347km (837 miles)
Type Culture
Map goo.gl/VoXmSX

Leaving the crowds of day-trippers behind, drive slowly out of the Land's End car park to embark on the longest road journey in Britain – from the country's southern end to its northern tip. It is, of course, pointless. You'll drive for many hours to reach a similar bleak, windswept cliff top at the other end of the British mainland. Yet the Land's End–John O'Groats journey – abbreviated to the acronym LeJog – is strangely compelling. This marathon of motorways and highways feels uniquely purposeful. It's like conquering the whole of the UK.

Walkers, cyclists, baby-carriage-pushers and fridge-carriers make the journey for charity, but everyone knows they are secretly chasing the bragging rights acquired by completing such a feat. Drivers or bikers can decide how long they want to take. They can do it in one long day, keeping to the route given here, or spread the journey over days or weeks by taking smaller roads and making diversions. (Note that the traditional route is slightly arbitrary anyway – Lizard Point is farther south than Land's End, and Dunnet Head is a few miles north of John O'Groats.)

You can, of course, do 'LeJog' from north to south instead, but the views of the Orkney Islands from John O'Groats make a more rewarding finale to the trip than the busy pay-and-display car park at Land's End. **SH**

Thomas Hardy's Wessex
Dorset, England

Start Dorchester
End Dorchester
Distance 114km (71 miles)
Type Culture
Map goo.gl/rO2TCL

Explore the wistful romantic scenery of writer Thomas Hardy's Wessex on this circular tour of his home county of Dorset. Hardy's classic novels, including *Tess of the d'Urbervilles*, *Jude the Obscure* and *Far from the Madding Crowd*, were set among its rolling farmland.

Hardy always changed the names of the places in his novels. Dorchester, the start of this route, is Hardy's Casterbridge. Today, it's a grand market town. You can visit Hardy's home, 'Max Gate', his grave at Stinsford Churchyard, a mile outside town, and see many of the writer's artefacts in the County Museum. Hardy's birthplace, a thatched cottage near Stinsford, is owned by the National Trust and open to the public.

From Dorchester, head west towards Bridport, 'Port Bredy' in Hardy's short story *Fellow Townsmen* and now popular with artists. There are good beaches nearby and an even bigger beach, famous for its fossils, at Charmouth, 12km (7 miles) to the west. From here, the route turns north through the Blackdown Hills to the bustling country towns of Axminster and Beaminster.

Before looping back to Dorchester, stop at Cerne Abbas, Hardy's Abbot's-Cernel in *The Woodlanders* and *Tess of the d'Urbervilles*. Carved into the chalk hill overlooking the village is a huge naked man, an extraordinary ancient fertility symbol. **SH**

Exmoor Coastal Road Somerset/Devon, England

Start Minehead, Somerset **End** Barnstaple, Devon **Distance** 66km (41 miles)
Type Scenic **Map** goo.gl/5iZb24

Rare is the road trip that has it all, but the road between Minehead and Barnstaple is not an average trip. It is usually a quiet area, but set an early alarm to appreciate this road at its ethereal best. When you set off west from Minehead, the first couple of miles are standard rural fare: wide tarmac with hedgerows. It is only when the route reaches the village of Porlock that you get the first real taste of why this is a must-do journey. The gradient kicks upwards violently, rising at an angle of 25 per cent in places, and climbing about 396m (1,300ft) in less than 3.2km (2 miles). From here, the countryside opens out on either side, with the fields and moorland stretching far away to the horizon all around. At times, the Bristol Channel is visible on the right-hand side. This continues for a little over 17.7km (11 miles), until the road sweeps down the less steep but still sharp Countisbury Hill to the twin gorge-side settlements of Lynton and Lynmouth.

Additional mountainlike climbs await inland when crossing Exmoor National Park, with a series of Alpinesque switchbacks thrown in to test driver and car alike. The final stretch to Barnstaple offers tight turns, some chicanelike narrow corners, sweeping straights and the odd sheep thrown in to keep you alert. **TW**

❶ Sheep roam the coastal road above Lynmouth.

Cheddar Gorge Somerset, England

Start Cheddar   End Wells   Distance 29km (18 miles)
Type Scenic   Map goo.gl/KArJNe

A road trip through this part of northern Somerset can offer some of the most picturesque glimpses of life in rural England: medieval cottages, pretty village churches and riots of flowers and greenery everywhere you look. However, this soft English landscape dramatically changes as you head eastwards on Cliff Road, from the village of Cheddar. Ahead lie a sinous 6.4km (4 miles) in the heart of Cheddar Gorge. The first sections of road through this ancient limestone gorge are demanding, with tight, twisty bends snaking between vertical rock walls towering 137m (450ft) above. The scenery is wondrous, especially late afternoon in summer when the evening sun penetrates the gorge and illuminates its dramatic geology. Once out of the gorge, mature deciduous trees replace the cliffs and boulders, rock-lined hairpins open out into sweeping curves and there is opportunity for more spirited driving through the Mendip Hills towards the historic town of Wells.

Getting the best out of this route is all about timing; half a million tourist visit each year and Cliff Road often gets clogged with tourist buses. To beat the crowds, plan your road trip for the crack of dawn and drive the gorge from both directions; you will get wildly differing perspectives. **DIS**

❶ The road twists through the gorge.

Historic Wiltshire and Stonehenge Wiltshire, England

Start Westonbirt   End Stonehenge   Distance 122km (76 miles)
Type Scenic   Map goo.gl/MZMhmr

Strictly speaking, this route begins in Gloucestershire, but the trees in the Westonbirt National Arboretum are only two minutes away from the Wiltshire border and they are just too wonderful to miss. From then on, the itinerary is a delightful toot through picture-perfect villages like Sherston, Castle Combe and Lacock. The last of these is owned by the National Trust and has resisted modern-day intrusions. Here, too, is Lacock Abbey, a grand country house that was once home to photography pioneer Henry Fox Talbot. There's a fascinating museum here tracing the early history of photography. After that the route includes two wonders of the early industrial age, both on the Kennet and Avon Canal: the impressive Caen Hill Locks, a flight of 16 locks at Devizes and, beyond the picturesque Pewsey Valley, the Crofton Beam Engines – amazing steam-powered water pumping machines, still in working order after more than 200 years.

The final section of this journey traverses the pretty rolling hills of the North Wessex Downs and ends with some altogether older history – the most famous and mysterious prehistoric monument in Europe, Stonehenge, which was built between 3000 and 1520 BCE. **DK**

❶ The megalithic stone circle at Stonehenge.

New Forest Loop Wiltshire/Hampshire, England

Start Winchester   End Winchester   Distance 119km (74 miles)
Type Scenic   Map goo.gl/g7Asg8

Heading out of Winchester, the county town of Hampshire and the former capital of England, this oval loop takes in two cathedral cities, a Roman villa and the wild, wooded landscape of the New Forest.

Driving clockwise brings you first to Romsey, a pretty country town with fine Norman and early English architecture on the banks of the River Test.

From Bramshaw to the west you catch fine views over the New Forest. Despite the name, this woodland has been managed by the Crown for centuries, firstly for hunting and later supplying mighty English oaks for Royal Navy shipbuilders.

Today, this national park is a hiker's paradise, with dozens of waymarked trails. Gearheads will enjoy a gander at the vintage steam engines at the Breamore Carriage Museum, while history buffs might prefer a quick visit to Rockbourne's Roman Villa; for children, Peppa Pig World trumps them all.

Beyond medieval Salisbury, with its magnificent cathedral, a twisty return leg east on the A36 sweeps through open heathlands. Pause for high tea on the lawns of Mottisfont Abbey, a National Trust property famous for its splendid grounds. History, engineering, theme parks, walks, ancient forest and rolling countryside: this road trip has something for everyone. DIS

❶ A road in the heart of the New Forest.

The Beaujolais Run
England to France

Start Goodwood, Chichester, West Sussex, England
End Beaujolais, Burgundy, France
Distance 805km (500 miles)
Type Adventure
Info goo.gl/FyzKXV

On the third Thursday of November, at 12:01 a.m., the year's Beaujolais Nouveau is released to the local markets. The wine is a *vin de primeur* – fermented and sold in the year in which it was harvested. Heavy marketing surrounds the event, but for a truly classy Beaujolais experience, nothing beats the annual Beaujolais Run.

This unique event began on 18 November 1970, when wine distributor Joseph Berkmann was dining with British MP and bon viveur Clement Freud at the Hotel Maritonnes in Romanèche-Thorins, in the heart of Beaujolais. A few bottles later, a challenge was laid down: who could get a case of the new Beaujolais to London first?

In 1973, this private battle between Berkmann and Freud was opened up by Alan Hall, a columnist for Britain's *Sunday Times*, who offered a bottle of champagne to the first person to deliver the new Beaujolais to his desk in London. Reinvented in 2006, the event now runs the reverse route as a navigational rally, with the winner's trophy going to the team that covers the shortest distance between checkpoints using a cunning combination of farm tracks and long-forgotten backroads.

The contest is open to anyone prepared to raise significant sums for charity. It attracts a glorious mix of modern supercars, high-end classics and vintage racecars. **SA**

Mongol Rally
England to Russia

Start Goodwood Race Circuit, West Sussex, England
End Ulan Ude, Siberia, Russia
Distance At least 8,700km (5,400 miles)
Type Adventure
Info goo.gl/dY7SQA

This is the original. The mother of all mad-cap, high-risk, banger rallies. The Adventurists, fans of epic journeys, ran their first Mongol Rally in 2004, with just a handful of entrants. Back then, the idea of this kind of 'adventure tourism' was comparatively new. A decade and more on, the annual rally now attracts hundreds of competitors and has spawned dozens of similar events all over the world. None can compare with the original, however. The basic idea: take a secondhand car of up to 1000cc – totally unsuitable for transcontinental adventuring – beef it up a little bit, and then drive it thousands of miles from England to the outer reaches of Mongolia and the finish line in Siberia.

There's not much more to it than that. The rally is not closely supervised. The whole idea is that you are pretty much left to your own devices. Any trouble you get into along the way is your problem, and yours to sort out.

How you get there is up to you. Several routes are favoured. Austria–Romania–Ukraine–Kazakhstan–Mongolia is one option, and Germany–Poland–lots-and-lots-of-Russia is another. In fact, the organizers even promote something called the 'un-route' since it 'forces you to be lost, to not know what's around the next corner, to embrace the unknown . . . find out what's there when you arrive, and unleash the unexpected'. **DK**

Isle of Wight Loop
Isle of Wight, England

Start Cowes
End Cowes
Distance 111km (69 miles)
Type Scenic
Map goo.gl/s2xG42

England's largest island lies about 6km (4 miles) off the south coast of Hampshire, separated from the mainland by the two arms of the River Solent. It is home to around 133,000 people and is famous as a yachting centre and for its annual rock music festival, which takes place in June.

Your road trip is an anticlockwise tour starting and ending at Cowes. Every year, Cowes plays host to the world's oldest yachting regatta, Cowes Week, and has been home to the Royal Yacht Squadron since 1815. From there, the route takes you west along the north coast of the island via the capital, Newport, to the multi-coloured sands of Alum Bay and the chalk stacks of The Needles.

On the southwest coast, you traverse the Military Road, built along with an artillery battery on the Needles in the early 1860s when England feared invasion by Emperor Louis Napoleon of France. Running from Freshwater to Chale, this stretch of road has been hailed as one of England's greatest scenic drives. Running over the cliff tops, bucking and weaving with the contours of the soft chalk landscape, the A3055 passes over a designated Area of Outstanding Natural Beauty that is slowly falling into the English Channel – see it while you still can. It's then a steady northeasterly trek to Shanklin and Ryde before heading west again to East Cowes. **SA**

❶ Alum Bay is near the westernmost point of the Isle of Wight and is famous for its polychromatic sands.

London to Cape Town Rally
England to South Africa

Start London, England
End Cape Town, South Africa
Distance 14,371km (8,930 miles)
Type Adventure
Info goo.gl/GNPhjl

Not so much a road trip, more the adventure of a lifetime, this drive from London to Cape Town is not for the fainthearted. The sheer logistics of getting a car from start to finish in one piece is enough to confound the most experienced drivers, while the contentious politics of many countries along the route are not to be taken lightly.

In 2012, this epic journey was undertaken by 48 vehicles taking part in a World Cup Rally in the spirit of similar adventures that took place in the 1970s. Its purpose was to raise funds to improve the lives of people living along the route. The schedule was strictly controlled, with daily time trials designed to urge the drivers forwards.

The rally first headed south through France to Italy, Greece, and then across the Mediterranean to Egypt, using ferries when necessary. It then headed south through Saudi Arabia and across the Red Sea to Sudan, avoiding conflict zones in North Africa. From there, the rally headed south through East Africa and across Zambia to Namibia and South Africa. On day 29, it reached Cape Town itself. Prizes were awarded for the overall winners and for the winners in five categories, including classic cars and 4x4 vehicles.

Feeling inspired? You will find more details and a full itinerary on the Endurance Rally Association's comprehensive website. **SA**

ⓘ A 1917 Crane-Simplex (left) and a 1927 Lagonda (right) at Jerash, Jordan, during the 1998 rally.

Long Way Round – Transglobal Adventure
England to USA

Start London, England
End New York, USA
Distance 32,187km (20,000 miles)
Type Adventure
Info goo.gl/6bAIyA

In 2004, movie star Ewan McGregor and the British writer/presenter Charley Boorman made a landmark TV series travelling this marathon route on a pair of BMW R1150 GS Adventure bikes. They rode from London to the east coast of Russia, flew to Alaska and then rode on to New York. If you've got at least three months to spare, their route would make a magnificent, life-changing road-trip.

The only sections not ridden by the duo were the Channel Tunnel, the Bering Strait and various impassable rivers in Siberia. They were escorted into New York by a mass of celebrating fellow bikers.

A lengthy global trip like this is not without hazards. McGregor and Boorman were followed everywhere by two off-roaders carrying a film crew, a security consultant and a doctor. You probably won't have those luxuries, so be prepared to tackle a wide range of hurdles.

The rigours of the terrain in Siberia meant both bikes needed repeated repairs, including welding. The pair also had to overcome accidents, which included petrol spraying into Ewan's eyes at a filling station, having a vehicle back up into their bikes while they were stationary and having a wallet stolen while jumping into hot springs for the cameras in Canada. Perhaps worst of all, after a particularly unfortunately placed mosquito bite, Ewan suffered a painfully swollen penis. SH

❶ Charley Boorman (left) and Ewan McGregor launched their motorbike adventure in London in 2004.

London by Classic Mini Cooper
London, England

Start London
End London
Distance 48km (30 miles)
Type Culture
Info goo.gl/FoYkuK

London is a vast and vibrant city with 50,000 streets, 30,000 eateries and 250 museums to explore. To discover its hidden gems, you'll need something compact and nimble to carve through its congested backstreets. There is nothing more quintessentially British for that job than a classic Mini Cooper.

The folk at smallcarBIGCITY have a fleet of eight restored Minis that can be rented for self-drive adventures or chauffeured guided tours. In about two hours, you should be able to tick off the major landmarks, including Buckingham Palace, St Paul's Cathedral and the Houses of Parliament, but, at the wheel of your tiny runabout, you have the freedom to tailor your urban road trip as you wish

Some of the capital's more offbeat treasures lie hidden away, down narrow back alleys – places only a Mini can reach. On a smallcarBIGCITY tour, you can zip through the back streets of Covent Garden, with its street art, or pay a visit to Victorian London's more nefarious neighbourhoods, such as the Cross Bones Graveyard, where the city's prostitutes used to be buried. There are also itineraries linked to England's fashion and music industries and route plans that provide insights into wartime London and the monarchy.

Classic Minis might be noisy, cramped, and uncomfortable, but there is no better, or more British, way to road-trip London. **DIS**

❶ Nippy and stylish, the Mini is the ideal vehicle for exploring London.

London to Brighton
London to Sussex, England

Start London Bridge, London
End Brighton, Sussex
Distance 174km (108 miles)
Type Culture
Map goo.gl/PCzOXm

The annual London to Brighton Veteran Car Run is said to be the oldest road event in the world. It was first held in 1896 and still gives participants an excuse to dust off the bodywork of their veteran vehicles and trundle between the two cities.

If you can't join the annual procession (usually held in early November), this journey is based on the route it takes. It is sprinkled with points of interest and passes through some of the best countryside in southeastern England.

Heading east from the north side of London Bridge, leave the capital via the modern tower blocks of Canary Wharf and the city's eastern suburbs. Cross the river on the graceful Queen Elizabeth II Bridge and head south to the attractive old towns of Sevenoaks, Tonbridge and Royal Tunbridge Wells. From here, the route becomes more rural, rising over the rolling hills of the High Weald towards the village of Battle, the site of the Battle of Hastings in 1066. An abbey commemorates the spot where Norman invader William the Conqueror defeated England's King Harold.

Brighton is a grand and vibrant seaside town. Serious motorsport fans should time this trip for early September, when the Brighton Speed Trials take place along the seafront. The quarter-mile drag races, first held in 1905, are thought to be the world's oldest surviving motor race. **SH**

London to Bath
London to Somerset, England

Start Kew, London
End Bath, Somerset
Distance 311km (193 miles)
Type Culture
Map goo.gl/ev2wGG

This quintessentially English road trip west from the capital to the thermal spa resort of Bath has been popular since Roman times. It passes through sweeping landscapes dotted with historic sights.

Start your engine in the leafy west-London suburb of Kew, home of the famous Royal Botanic Gardens and royal palace. A few miles west is one of the world's biggest royal fortresses, Windsor Castle, a home of British monarchs since William the Conqueror, 1,000 years ago. Continue west, via the elegant aristocratic mansion at Cliveden, the remains of a Roman walled town at Silchester and the crumbling medieval castle at Ludgershall. On a bleak hill on Salisbury Plain rises Stonehenge, the famous prehistoric stone circle; the visitor centre attempts to explain some of its mysteries.

A short drive away is the grand 18th-century mansion of Stourhead, set in fabulous lakeside gardens. This part of England is packed with history. A few miles farther west, you can explore the romantic ruins of Glastonbury Abbey and the poetic beauty of Glastonbury Tor, a nearby hill linked to the legends of King Arthur.

End your road trip in Georgian Bath. Highlights here include the Gothic abbey and the Roman Baths, although you'll want to tour the backstreets, too, to see the Georgian squares and terraces. The whole city is a World Heritage Site. **SH**

North Pembrokeshire Coast and Country Loop
Pembrokeshire, Wales

Start Fishguard
End Fishguard
Distance 78km (48.5 miles)
Type Scenic
Map goo.gl/2xHeJy

Fishguard in west Wales is best known today as the ferry port for Rosslare in Ireland, but it was also the site of the last successful invasion of England, by the French in 1797. Inexplicably, the invaders were said to have been startled by local women wearing Welsh costume, perhaps mistaking their tall black hats and red cloaks for uniformed British Grenadiers. One of the women, Jemima Nicholas, rounded up twelve French soldiers with a pitchfork and escorted them into the town, where she locked them up in St Mary's Church.

Fishguard is also an ideal base for exploring the rugged coast of northern Pembrokeshire and the Preseli Hills inland. The A487 takes you up past Newport, closely shadowing the Pembrokeshire Coastal Path that runs all along the seaside edge of the county. At the northernmost extremity of Pembrokeshire, the road heads inland along the Afon Teifi estuary and enters the adjacent county of Ceredigion (formerly Cardiganshire) before arriving at the town of Cardigan itself.

Passing the romantic ruined battlements of Cilgerran Castle, the route then heads southwest through the Preseli Hills, renowned for their many prehistoric sites and also as the source of the bluestones used to construct the inner circle of Stonehenge. At the Rosebush Reservoir the road turns right back to Fishguard. **SA**

❶ The round towers of Cilgerran Castle, a ruined 13th-century fortress built on the River Teifi.

Llanberis Pass
Gwynedd, Wales

Start Capel Curig
End Caernarfon
Distance 29km (18 miles)
Type Scenic
Map goo.gl/rK5eMp

Snowdonia National Park in North Wales is not just for hikers. It also has thrilling drives. Foremost of these is the A4086 Llanberis Pass, from the walkers' hub of Capel Curig, high in the Snowdon range, to sea level at Caernarfon. In places, the landscape is astonishingly bleak – scree-covered mountains that fall away to racing streams and isolated lakes – while in others it is a rolling Arcadia in emerald green. Perceptions very much hinge on the weather and season. It's hard to beat a crisp day in the autumn, when golden bracken and snowcapped peaks are offset by sapphire lakes and skies, tempting drivers to park the car and pull on their hiking boots.

From Capel Curig, the road sweeps west alongside the twin lakes of Llynnau Mymbyr, affording the most famous view of Snowdonia's highest peaks – with Mt Snowdon the tallest in the tiara at 1,085m (3,560ft) above sea level. Bearing right at Pen Y Gwryd, it follows the Pen-y-Pass to Llanberis. An old slate-mining town, situated between two lakes, this is the lower terminus of the Snowdon Mountain Railway and the site of the National Slate Museum. Vast terraces of slate quarries can be seen carved into the hillsides on the northern side of Llyn Padarn. From Llanberis, it is a short ride through the lush river valley to Caernarfon, whose dramatic castle was the setting for the investiture in 1969 of Charles, Prince of Wales. **DS**

❶ The bleak grandeur of the Llanberis Pass through the Snowdon mountain range.

Barmouth to Welshpool Gwynedd/Powys, Wales

Start Barmouth, Gwynedd   **End** Welshpool, Powys   **Distance** 76km (47.2 miles)
Type Scenic   **Map** goo.gl/A2Lvez

For many people, the centre of Wales is *terra incognita*, a land of mountains and sheep with few people and even fewer major roads, all of which makes this cross-country road trip from the west coast to the eastern border a particular delight.

Barmouth, a seaside town on the mouth of the River Mawddach, in the shadow of Snowdonia National Park, is an attractive start point. The A496 road heads east from here, with wooded hills on the left and the estuary to the right. If the tide is out, you will see oystercatchers and herons stalking the sandbanks.

After 16km (10 miles), the road reaches the market town of Dogellau, a popular centre for hiking. It is the last town before the route reaches Welshpool, and from here, the A470 and A458 head into the hills, crossing the largely sandstone Cambrian Mountains of central Wales. This area is so sparsely populated that it is known as the Desert of Wales, although it does contain the source of both the Severn and Wye Rivers, and there are many grazing sheep.

Journey's end is at Welshpool, only 6km (4 miles) from the English border. It was once known as Pool, but it changed its name in 1835 to avoid confusion with the English town of Poole in Dorset. **SA**

❶ Barmouth, tucked into the coastal cliffs.

Lap of Snowdon Loop Gwynedd/Powys, Wales

Start Caernarfon, Gwynedd   **End** Caernarfon, Gwynedd   **Distance** 55km (34.1 miles)
Type Scenic   **Map** goo.gl/XTYbAA

At 1,085m (3,560ft), Snowdon, or Yr Wyddfa to give it its Welsh name, is the highest mountain in Wales. It is also the busiest, as its summit can easily be reached by a number of well-trodden paths or by a rack-and-pinion mountain railway, a journey of 7.6km (4.7 miles). The name Snowdon comes from Old English for 'snow hill', while its Welsh name means 'the tumulus'.

Forming a rough triangle, this road trip scoots along the flat bottoms of three glaciated valleys bounded by rugged valley walls, which spring waterfalls after heavy rain. Starting in castle-topped Caernarfon on the Menai Strait, the A4085 takes you along the southern side of the mountain, past Llyn

Cwellyn and the Snowdon Ranger Hostel, from where the Ranger Path heads up to the peak.

At Beddgelert, a pretty Victorian town on the River Glaslyn, you turn left on to the A498, and in a few miles turn left again on to the A4086, which takes you along the northern side of the mountain and down the spectacular Llanberis Pass to return to Caernarfon. In November, the hills to the east of here shriek with the engine notes of WRC (World Rally Championship) cars thundering through the pine forests – a plus or minus point, depending on your interest in motorsports. **SA**

❶ View of the Snowdon range.

Bwlch y Groes
Gwynedd, Wales

Start Bala
End Llanwddyn
Distance 32km (20 miles)
Type Culture
Map goo.gl/2XPAXM

On the south shore of Lake Bala in Snowdonia National Park in North Wales, an almost forgotten, single-lane track leads up to what English visitors once called Hellfire Pass. Bwlch y Groes (Pass of the Cross) is a steep, scree-strewn mountain road, which was originally part of a medieval pilgrims' trail to St David's. This period in its history is commemorated by an iron cross near the summit.

Between the wars, these valleys (or *cwms*) boomed with the products of Britain's biggest motor manufacturers, including Austin, MG and Triumph, which tested their newest models to destruction on these treacherous inclines. Today, the route is the scenic way to reach Lake Vyrnwy, a reservoir that flooded a small Welsh community to supply the city of Liverpool with drinking water.

The road, cut into the side of an almost treeless, V-shaped valley, heads up through rugged sheep-farming country to a small gravel car park at 545m (1,788ft). Few cars come this way other than the occasional farmer's Land Rover, but it is popular with cyclists. The next stretch weaves through boggy upland towards the reservoir's spectacular northern shore. A short hop across the top of the Victorian dam brings you to the village of Llanwddyn, where tea shops will undoubtedly be serving local specialties such as cawl (lamb stew) and the teacake bara brith. Delicious. **DIS**

❶ Hellfire Pass climbs up from Lake Bala in Snowdonia National Park.

The Evo Triangle
Denbighshire, Wales

Start Cerrigydrudion
End Cerrigydrudion
Distance 32km (20 miles)
Type Scenic
Info goo.gl/O2UHz9

This fabled 32-km- (20-mile) long, three-corner section of wild Welsh countryside is a relatively new phenomenon, which only really came to the attention of car enthusiasts in the early part of the 21st century.

Forming an almost perfect isosceles triangle, the route is named after a popular British motoring magazine dedicated to 'The Thrill of Driving', as it's the favourite location for the publication's road testers when they are assessing the latest performance automobiles.

The route itself is a simple one, and can be tackled in either direction. The road testers' preference is clockwise, and starts by heading out of Cerrigydrudion along the A5, getting the least interesting section out of the way first. Turn north onto the A543, signposted Dinbych/Denbigh, and the first stretch is narrow, with dry-stone walls either side. Soon enough this clears, though, and the moorland opens out, with tight, twisty turns providing a test to car and driver. Watch out for the bumpy road surfaces; *Evo*'s bravest journalists often get some 'air time' along here.

Turn hard right at the top of the triangle and join the B4501. This section is smoother and more flowing than the previous arm, but it has its own challenges, most notably a tight, twisting section just after a sharp plunge downhill. **TW**

Cambrian Mountains
Ceredigion/Powys, Wales

Start Aberystwyth, Ceredigion
End Rhayader, Powys
Distance 49.7km (30.9 miles)
Type Scenic
Map goo.gl/I3CJrC

For a small country, Wales packs in plenty of dramatic scenery, and this drive from the coast into the Cambrian Mountains samples some of its finest. It begins in the holiday resort and university town of Aberystwyth, then heads inland on the A4120, climbing slowly upwards, past farmers' fields and tucked-away cottages. As you get higher, there are views down into sheep-filled valleys to the sides of the road.

Just beyond the village of Pontarfynachis is Devil's Bridge, a local beauty spot and the upper terminus of the Vale of Rheidol Railway, a preserved narrow-gauge steam line that is headquartered in Aberystwyth. Pause at the viewpoint near the Mynach Falls to appreciate the three bridges built on top of each other; according to legend, the design was so complex that only the Devil could have built it. Beyond here, the B4574 road climbs into the Cambrian Mountains and through the old lead-mining village of Cwmystwyth. Now the views become increasingly impressive as the road gets narrower, cutting through valleys and past villages with tongue-twisting names (for non-Welsh people) such as Llansantffraed-Cwmdeuddwr, before dropping down into the historic market town of Rhayader, on the banks of the Wye River. If you've been blessed with good weather, the drive will stay with you forever. **MG**

The Elan Valley

Powys, Wales

Start Rhayader
End Rhayader
Distance 60km (37.2 miles)
Type Scenic
Map goo.gl/41oIN3

In the late 19th century, a series of dams and reservoirs was built in the Elan Valley in mid-Wales to provide water to the densely populated West Midlands, in England. In order to build the complex and flood the valley, all the buildings standing in the way of progress were demolished, including two old manor houses, 18 farms, a school, and a church. More than 100 people were moved out of their homes. Today, there is little evidence of this rural upheaval, just an attractive network of artificial lakes, ornate dams and rolling mountains linked by this scenic circular drive.

Leaving Rhayader, head southwest, following a spur up the Claerwen Valley. On the way, you will get a superb overview of the entire system of dams and reservoirs, and can pick up background information at the visitor centre in Elan village.

From there, skirt the lakeshore to Craig Goch Dam before heading on to the reservoir's shallow northern tip. Here the route picks up the old road along the Afon Elan valley floor to bring you back to the start point.

The roads throughout this trip are well-surfaced but narrow, with only a smattering of passing places. Rising and falling between sweeping bends, it's a thoroughly rewarding drivers' road, albeit not a fast one, amid upland vistas that are both natural and artificial, but which are all of equal beauty. **SA**

The Elan Valley's 19th-century pumphouse stands on the retaining wall of the dam.

Gospel Pass

Powys, Wales

Start Abergavenny
End Hay-on-Wye
Distance 32km (20 miles)
Type Scenic
Map goo.gl/QYIqvT

The highest road pass in Wales, the Gospel Pass rises 549m (1,801ft) above sea level, squeezing between the Twmpa mountain to the south and Hay Bluff in the Black Mountains to the north. The origin of its name is thought to be linked to the 12th-century Crusaders who swept through these parts, recruiting volunteers for the third armed expedition to the Holy Land (1189–92).

The best approach to the pass is through the Vale of Ewyas from Abergavenny in the south. The road is largely single track, although there are some passing places. After 14km (8.7 miles), the road reaches the ruins of Llanthony Priory, a 12th-century Augustinian monastery, which was dissolved by King Henry VIII in 1538. The top of the pass affords views over the hills, as well as of Offa's Dyke, the ancient earthwork that marks part of the border between England and Wales.

Should you need to read up about these places, Hay-on-Wye is the book capital of Britain and home to a justly famous literary festival at the end of May. In 2014, *Top Gear Magazine* listed Gospel Pass as one of the five best driving roads in Wales, urging its readers to explore beyond the industrialized heartland of South Wales: 'To get your driving kicks in Wales, you've got to go farther afield. Get a road atlas, mind the sheep and aim for the bits beyond the trees.' **SA**

The Devil's Staircase

Powys/Dyfed, Wales

Start Abergwesyn, Powys
End Tregaron, Dyfed
Distance 22.5km (14 miles)
Type Scenic
Map goo.gl/8uVjze

In centuries gone by, the hill farmers of the Cambrian Mountains in mid-Wales drove their livestock to market through the Abergwesyn Pass. Today, the old drover's track has turned into a narrow and twisting road, with sharp hairpin bends and 25 per cent gradients rising from the small hamlet of Abergwesyn, contortions that have earned it the nickname the Devil's Staircase.

This is not a road to tackle when the weather is wet or icy, for the turns are abrupt and the gradients steep. This is wild Wales at its magnificent best, the rugged uplands known as the Elenydd, the least populated region in the country.

Heading east to west, the road begins in tiny Abergwesyn and initially rises for 5km (3.1 miles) alongside the Irfon River, passing through dense conifer forests. At the summit, the road straightens out and rolls through a wide and isolated valley flanked by sheep-dotted moorland and occasional patches of woodland. Below, the Irfon tumbles over boulders, creating deep and hidden pools that are perfect for wild swimming. After 10km (6 miles), the road begins a steep 13-km- (8-mile) long descent through small fields to the ancient market town of Tregaron. This welcoming town has a number of inns but you might not understand everything that is being said here – 67 per cent of the townsfolk are native Welsh speakers. **SA**

Black Mountain Pass
Carmarthenshire, Wales

Start Upper Brynamman
End Llangadog
Distance 19km (12 miles)
Type Scenic
Map goo.gl/7Fvyo3

An exhilarating drivers' road through the uplands of the Brecon Beacons National Park, the Black Mountain Pass between Brynamman and Llangadog redefines the term 'joyride'. Jeremy Clarkson famously flew along it in a Mercedes CLK for an episode of the UK television series *Top Gear*.

From the old Welsh mining village of Upper Brynamman (although going north to south from Llangadog is just as rewarding), the double-lane road soars into the Beacons. Its big, languorous loops are interspersed with tighter sections, short straight stretches that allow overtaking and sudden drops to old stone bridges over streams. While drivers negotiate the switchbacks, passengers are treated to a succession of huge views, each more spectacular than the last. Parking spots allow more time to drink in the scenery, and the Mountain Road Viewpoint has picnic tables, information boards on the old lime quarries of the area and a seasonal refreshment kiosk.

The road and views are magnificent on clear sunny days, but providing it isn't actually raining, dark skies of rolling cumulus pump up the drama; just watch out for sheep that spring out of nowhere, clusters of wild ponies and for the tight hairpin bend on a sheer-sided ravine as you start the descent to the wooded valley of the River Sawdde and the village of Llangadog. **DS**

❶ Although Black Mountain Pass is a challenging drive, there are plenty of clear stretches where visibility is good.

Carmarthenshire and Pembrokeshire Coast
Carmarthenshire/Pembrokeshire, Wales

Start St Clears, Carmarthenshire
End St Davids, Pembrokeshire
Distance 103km (64 miles)
Type Scenic
Map goo.gl/WWhD68

Dylan Thomas, Wales's most celebrated literary figure, referred to Carmarthenshire as his 'fields of praise'. Its landscapes were a constant source of inspiration, and in his final, and most productive, years, he lived in Laugharne, 'a timeless, beautiful, barmy (both spellings) town, in this far, forgetful, important place'. A visit to the Dylan Thomas boathouse, with its wondrous views over the 'heron priested'"Taf estuary, is a must. Thomas's favourite watering hole, Brown's Hotel, is a short stagger from here.

Through a warren of narrow hedgerow-lined country lanes, drive towards Pendine Sands, catching glimpses of Carmarthen Bay as the road bucks and weaves westwards. In 1924, Sir Malcolm Campbell set a land speed record on this 11.3-km- (7-mile) long beach, reaching 235.22 kph (146.16 mph) in his Sunbeam 350HP Blue Bird. The Vintage Hot Rod Association still holds amateur drag races on the sands every September. For the next few miles, the coast road rises and falls over rugged headlands to Tenby, a charming Victorian seaside resort with narrow cobbled streets winding down to a pretty marina and golden beaches. The final leg cuts northwest via the spectacular natural harbour at Solva to Britain's smallest city, St Davids. With its ruined Bishop's Palace and grand cathedral, St Davids has been a site of religious pilgrimage since the 12th century. **DIS**

❶ Pendine Sands, where Sir Malcolm Campbell set a land speed record in 1924.

The Gower Peninsula West Glamorgan, Wales

Start Swansea   **End** The Mumbles   **Distance** 80km (49.7 miles)
Type Scenic   **Map** goo.gl/y6sAaQ

In 1956, the Gower Peninsula in South Wales became the first area in the United Kingdom to be designated an Area of Outstanding Natural Beauty. Deservedly so, for this stubby finger of land jutting into the Bristol Channel has miles of spectacular coastal scenery.

The best springboard for this Welsh wonder is the city of Swansea. Formerly a key centre of the copper industry, and known as Copperopolis in its 19th-century heyday, it's now a bustling university town. From Swansea, you head west onto the peninsula. To the north, the sparsely populated saltmarshes and mudflats are home to the cockle-beds of Penclawdd. A fast coast road meanders to the westerly tip and the beaches at Llangennith and Rhossili. Known for their warm currents and great surf, the sands stretch south to Worm's Head, a serpent-shaped promontory.

Refuel at any of the fine country pubs that pepper these parts before setting off back along the southern coastline, which has some fabulous sandy beaches, including Oxwich, Caswell and Three Cliffs. Sticking to the tortuous A4118, you eventually return to 'that ugly lovely town' of Swansea, the boyhood home of Dylan Thomas, and its Victorian seafront along The Mumbles. **DIS**

❶ Three Cliffs Bay on the Gower Coast.

Mid-Wales Roller Coaster South Glamorgan to Clwyd, Wales

Start Cardiff, South Glamorgan **End** Llandudno, Clwyd **Distance** 314km (195 miles)
Type Adventure **Map** goo.gl/VrsKXq

Wales's mountainous geography makes it relatively easy to travel along the river valleys from east to west but more difficult to navigate across the rocky core of the country from south to north. One road that manages to complete that journey is the A470, also known as the Glan Conwy Trunk Road.

Starting in the national capital of Cardiff, in the south, the road heads quickly up through Taff Vale to Merthyr Tydfil and then into the Brecon Beacons. On into the mountains of central Wales, it climbs steeply around the eastern foothills of Cadair Idris, the second-highest mountain in Wales after Snowdon, before dropping sharply down to Dolgellau. From there, it heads back up into the hills and, after Ffestiniog, into the high mountains of Snowdonia before cruising gently down the Vale of Conwy. It finally arrives at Llandudno on the north Welsh coast.

Now a primary trunk road, and in its southern sections a high-quality dual carriageway, the A470 was once a slow-moving twister. Students using the road to commute from Cardiff to the university town of Aberystwyth called it the Mid-Wales Roller Coaster. The road is still a rewarding drivers' road, cutting through both the Brecon Beacons and Snowdonia National Park. **SA**

➊ Going around and around on the A470.

Industrial Revolution Cradle Monmouthshire/Torfaen, Wales

Start Abergavenny, Monmouthshire   **End** Abergavenny, Monmouthshire   **Distance** 31km (19 miles)
Type Culture   **Map** goo.gl/ITgQwP

This World Heritage area in the Black Mountains of South Wales changed the world – literally. In 1878, in the furnaces of the Blaenavon Ironworks, the Gilchrist brothers perfected a technique that allowed the mass production of high-quality steel.

This drive exploring this industrial heritage begins in Llanfoist on the outskirts of Abergavenny, a town popular with foodies. A short walk uphill from the car park leads to the picturesque wharf on the Monmouthshire and Brecon Canal, from which Blaenavon's iron was transported. Walk through the tunnel to see the 19th-century tramway.

Driving on to Blaenavon, the ascent of the Blorenge mountain is spectacular, a hairpin route

used for cycling road races. Keeper's Pond at the summit has fine views over the Brecon Beacons National Park. In Blaenavon, you can visit the 19th-century ironworks, a heritage railway and the Big Pit National Mining Museum, where you can descend deep underground to a former working coal mine (entry is free, but places are limited – avoid rainy public holidays).

The return leg to Abergavenny follows a steeper single-track route (fork right about 1.6km/1 mile from Blaenavon); three parking spots along the route offer fine views. **DK**

❶ Blaenavon Ironworks in Wales's industrial heartland.

Discover Jersey Loop Jersey, Channel Islands

Start St Helier **End** St Helier **Distance** 68km (42.2 miles)
Type Culture **Map** goo.gl/JuM8XY

On the map, Jersey's circumference measures less than 80km (50 miles) but it seems a lot longer when you drive or ride around the coast. That's because progress is slow. Narrow country lanes wiggle around headlands and inlets and over roller-coaster inclines and dips.

Heading out anticlockwise from the capital of St Helier, you'll pass a glorious sequence of sandy coves, heather-covered cliff tops, ruined castles, lighthouses, wartime relics and sleepy villages. You can't get lost if you keep the sea on your right. Don't be afraid to dive off the route prescribed here; tourist honeypots and places of interest are well signposted. You'll soon discover that Jersey is a friendly place, with one foot still in the past (the 1950s, to be precise).

Jersey's spectacular coastline varies from the gentle seafront promenades in the south to the 120-m- (400-ft) high cliffs of the north. The west has windy sand dunes. while in the east Mont Orgueil Castle towers over Gorey's quaint harbour. With one of the world's biggest tidal ranges, the island grows by one-third twice a day. Park up and study the shoreline. You'll see that in some places the tide goes out for more than 3km (2 miles), revealing weird and wonderful reefs and rock gullies. **SH**

❶ Mont Orgueil Castle at Gorey.

Normandy Cider Route Normandy, France

Start Beuvron en-Auge **End** Beuvron en-Auge **Distance** 40km (25 miles)
Type Culture **Info** goo.gl/suKNLz

The Route du Cidre links the main cider-making villages of Normandy's Pays d'Auge – Beuvron en-Auge, Bonnebosq, Saint Ouen-le-Pin and Cambremer – and many smaller places in between. An enjoyable ramble along the backroads of some of Normandy's prettiest countryside, the route can be joined at any point; it is signposted by a big red apple.

The drive can easily be completed in a morning, but you'll need a day to include tastings, visits to farm shops (cheeses also a speciality) and lunch (crêperies abound), and then a night to sleep it all off. For the best experience, come in spring to see the orchards decked in pink and white blossom, or October, when it seems the entire population of this small patch of Normandy is busy bottling fall.

Signs saying 'Cru de Cambremer' signal producers. While grander estates such as Manoir de Grandouet may centre on a half-timbered manor house, basic operations are likely to be a barn or two around a higgledy-piggledy yard. As well as fine ciders and *cidre fermier* (farm cider), there are *poiré* (pear cider), *pommeau* (apple juice zhooshed up with Calvados) and vintage Calvados (apple brandy), a heady digestif, often slipped into coffee, which is around 40 per cent proof. **DS**

❶ Beuvron en-Auge in the heart of Normandy.

The Norman Abbeys Route Normandy, France

Start Le Havre   End Mont-Saint-Michel   Distance 357km (222 miles)
Type Culture   Info goo.gl/grw8n2

Norman architecture transformed Europe. This drive through the seat of the Norman dukes is a lesson in how that architecture developed, from the restrained style of Romanesque, with its rounded arches and clean lines, to the flying buttresses, pointed arches and rose windows of Gothic.

The 50 notable abbeys identified by the tourist board would take the best part of a month to see, so it is best to be selective. This drive east of Le Havre focuses on the Seine Valley, peeling off the A131 (E5) to take the D982 backroad to Rouen. The ruins of Jumièges Abbey, enclosed in a loop of the Seine, has the tallest Romanesque nave in Normandy, while Saint-Georges de Boscherville

Abbey in Saint-Martin-de-Boscherville is a Romanesque gem. By contrast, Rouen's cathedral, 30km (19 miles) from Jumièges, spans 400 years of French Gothic; among its treasure is the tomb of England's Richard the Lionheart.

To extend the tour, head west on the A13 to Caen (129km/80 miles) for the Abbey of Sainte-Trinité and the Abbey of Saint-Étienne, founded by William the Conqueror. About 120km (75 miles) farther along the A84 from Caen is Mont-Saint-Michel, a spectacular Norman monastery piled on a rocky island on the flats of the Couesnon estuary. **DS**

❶ The Norman monastery of Mont-Saint-Michel.

Passage du Gois
Pays de la Loire, France

Start Beauvoir-sur-Mer
End Barbâtre
Distance 12km (7.5 miles)
Type Adventure
Info goo.gl/i3Fwpi

Search for this route on the Internet and you'll probably find a photo showing what appears to be the sea with the forlorn roof of a new luxury saloon car just poking up above the waves.

After seeing that, dare you try to tackle this narrow tidal causeway? It links the island of Noirmoutier with the mainland of western France. Twice a day the tide goes out far enough to permit vehicles to reach the island along the 4.5-km- (7.2-mile) long causeway. Depending on the time of year, the causeway is clear for between one hour and two hours.

Sounds quite doable, doesn't it? But there are other factors to consider: the tide comes in very quickly because of the shallow nature of the Bay of Bourgneuf. There's little margin for error. Secondly, the old cobbled causeway is very slippery, unsurprisingly in view of the fact that it spends most of the day under water. And thirdly it can get jammed up with pedestrians, runners, cyclists and other tourist traffic.

Still fancy a go? Your reward will be reaching the 19 x 6-km (12 x 4-mile) island of salt marshes, sandbanks and sand dunes. You'll feel pretty intrepid. What about getting back again? Oh, sorry, didn't anyone mention it? They've also built a nice new road bridge as a boring – but dry – alternative way of getting to and from the island. **SH**

Le Mans
Pays de la Loire, France

Start Mulsanne Straight
End Mulsanne Straight
Distance 16km (9.9 miles)
Type Culture
Map goo.gl/OTkgB1

There are more glamorous motorsport venues there are many more challenging and technica circuits; there are even a few that cover a greater distance. But no other race in history has captured the hearts of motorsport enthusiasts quite like the Le Mans 24 Hours.

The first Le Mans was held in 1923 on public roads that made up a 17.4-km- (10.8-mile) long course – a circuit dominated by the fabulou Bentley Boys. Slowly, through the 1950s and 1960s as Le Mans' reputation grew and speeds increased purpose-built sections were added to create a safer and faster, 13.5-km- (8.5-mile) long race circuit. The good news today is that many of the circuit's original bends, chicanes and straights have been absorbed into the French road network.

This road trip begins at the Tertre Rouge corner on the N138, then heads on to the famous 6-km- (3.7-mile) long Mulsanne Straight and through its two modern chicanes; triple-height Armco hints at the dangers drivers face as they exceed 338 kph (210 mph) along here. A sharp right on a roundabout leads toward Indianapolis, one of Le Mans' most technical sections. After Porschekurven your road trip runs parallel to the modern racetrack, along the street that was until 1932 the circuit. **DIS**

➲ Drive in the tracks of motorsports heroes.

Circuit des Remparts
Nouvelle-Aquitaine, France

Start Angoulême
End Angoulême
Distance 167km (104 miles)
Type Scenic
Info goo.gl/PmpoAQ **Map** goo.gl/CgQThW

Each year in mid-September, hundreds of vintage and classic cars arrive in Angoulême to compete in the Circuit des Remparts. Over the three-day event there is first a civilized day's drive around the medieval villages of the surrounding Charente region, and then two days of serious racing around a tight circuit on the ramparts of the old town. The highlight is the race for vintage Bugattis, whose leather-helmet-and-goggles-wearing owners really go for it, chucking their priceless motors around the course. There are many other races, and anyone with a vaguely classic car can enter. Thousands come to watch. However, both routes – the country drive and the old-town circuit – are public roads. So, outside of the dates of the event, anyone can drive them. You may even be able to sneak a go around the prepared circuit in the days immediately before the races. The clockwise routes of both the day tour and the race circuit are shown in the maps. On the day tour, the traditional lunch stop is at Chalais, but there are many other places to choose from, nearly all of which are attractive sleepy villages with Romanesque churches. A detour to Aubeterre-sur-Dronne and its 7th-century subterranean monolithic church, hewn out of a rock face, is also highly recommended. **DK**

◐ Vintage and classic cars muster at the starting line.

Biarritz to Bordeaux
Nouvelle-Aquitaine, France

Start Biarritz
End Bordeaux
Distance 254km (158 miles)
Type Scenic
Map goo.gl/X2mJVk

The surf will be pounding on the sands of La Grande Plage as you drive away from the elegant seafront of Biarritz, but you won't be leaving the sea behind.

The coast heading north is a continuous sequence of sandy beaches backed by thick pine forests. These aren't beaches for paddling. Instead, the Atlantic breakers roll in from the west in a thunder of white water and sea spray.

The main A63 is available to whisk you up to Bordeaux in just 150 minutes, but it's best to try exploring the small roads through the forests, popping out to the small towns and beaches as often as you want.

The Aquitaine coastal strip is flat and the roads are smooth. Apart from a few summer jams around the resorts, driving is easy and relaxed. Look out for the best family-friendly beaches like Messanges, Vielle-Saint-Girons and Mimizan. You'll be passing through the protected countryside of the Gascony Natural Park.

As you get close to Bordeaux, it's worth making the diversion to Arcachon, a grand old town looking out into its own seawater lagoon. Take advantage of its reputation for fine oysters before looping back round to Bordeaux, one of France's best undiscovered urban treasures, with a wonderful intact historic centre that is as good for shoppers and gourmets as it is for sightseers. **SH**

Circuit de Pau-Ville Nouvelle-Aquitaine, France

Start Pau   End Pau   Distance 2.7km (1.7 miles)
Type Culture   Info goo.gl/C3eZZT

The handsome city of Pau, nestling in the foothills of the Pyrenees between Biarritz and Toulouse, is steeped in motorsport history. In 1901, it hosted the first motor race to be called a Grand Prix, and it was the home until the 1980s of France's top-flight races. Pau still hosts lower formula events but the highlight of the calendar is the Grand Prix Historique in late May, in which cars from the circuit's golden years return to do battle along its narrow streets.

In 1963, Jim Clark famously won the Pau Grand Prix in his Lotus 25, setting a fastest lap of just 1:35.5. Unfortunately, you will be driving under the beady eye of the local gendarmes (but you'll want to slow down anyway to appreciate the wonderfully ornate architecture and manicured parklands of this affluent tourist town). Even at sedate speeds, you can soak up the circuit's high-octane heritage as you navigate its painted curbstones, starting grid and ominous Armco barriers.

For an authentic lap, start on Avenue Gaston Lacoste, swinging right through Garage Hairpin to the fast straight on Boulevard des Pyrénées and the tricky left-hander at Point Oscar; after another mile of fast, sweeping bends, you will appreciate why Pau was once considered the ultimate barometer of a racing driver's talents. DIS

❶ Taking a bend on the Circuit de Pau-Ville.

Côte d'Opale Hauts-de-France, France

Start Bray-Dunes   End Berck   Distance 121km (75 miles)
Type Scenic   Map goo.gl/be6SQy

The coast between Bray-Dunes on the Belgium border and Berck in the Marquenterre bird reserve is one of long, dune-backed beaches washed by rolling surf. With the exception of fashionable Le Touquet (aka 'Paris by the Sea'), and the busy cross-Channel ports of Calais and Boulogne, the coast is low-key and calming, a place to breathe deeply. J.M.W. Turner painted seascapes here. A little later, French artist Édouard Lévêque named it *Le Côte d'Opale* (The Opal Coast) for the quality of its light.

The D940 runs along the coast, sometimes next to it but mainly leaving a generous margin of marshes or marram grass, with lanes leading off to seaside villages and nature reserves. Villages such as Wissant, Audresselles, Ambleteuse and Wimereux offer good eateries; if you are self-catering, look out for fishermen selling crabs, oysters and lobsters from roadside pop-ups. Around Calais, you will see signposts for Les Deux Caps, two promontories that mirror the white cliffs of Dover, the nearest point in England. Branch off the D940 near Escalles for Cap Blanc Nez, and turn left onto the D191 just north of Audresselles for Cap Gris Nez. An obelisk topping Cap Blanc Nez commemorates the Dover Patrol, which kept the Channel free from German U-boats during World War II. **DS**

❶ The coast looks out on a busy shipping lane.

Battlefields of the Somme – A Circuit of Remembrance
Hauts-de-France, France

Start Museum of the Great War, Péronne, Somme
End Museum of the Great War, Péronne, Somme
Distance 124km (77 miles)
Type Culture
Map goo.gl/FzHyNZ

The Battle of the Somme in World War I commenced on 1 July 1916, and lasted for five months. It was one of the war's bloodiest engagements, with more than a million casualties on both sides. Some 19,000 British soldiers died on the first day.

The numbers defy comprehension. A century on, the best way to understand the enormity of the sacrifice and slaughter is to see the sites for ourselves. This route – the Remembrance Trail – begins and ends at the Museum of the Great War at Péronne and takes in the main memorials and museums dedicated to the battle – the Memorial Chappelle de Rancourt; the South African Museum and Memorial at Delville Wood; the Memorial ANZAC at Pozières; the Ulster Tower and the Beaumont Hamel Newfoundland Memorial near Thiepval; the Thiepval Memorial to British and South African forces; the Welsh monument at Mametz Wood; and the Australian Military Cemetery at Villers-Bretonneux. The German Military Cemetery at Fricourt is also included.

The route also takes in the Lochnagar Crater, created by a British mine on the first day of the battle, the Somme 1916 Museum at Albert and the Froissy Dompierre Military and Industrial Railways Museum at Froissy. This is a sombre and deeply disquieting tour, but perhaps one that everyone should consider making. **DK**

❶ The Thiepval Memorial to British and South African forces lost in the Battle of the Somme.

Bourne Identity Paris Car Chase Île-de-France, France

Start Gare du Nord, 97 Rue de Maubeuge
End Hotel de la Paix, Rue de l'Orillon.
Distance 32km (19.8 miles)
Type Culture
Map goo.gl/dIKWjM

Rogue CIA assassin Jason Bourne is in Paris and has just been spotted by police at the wheel of a battered old Mini parked outside the Gare du Nord. Desperate to avoid capture, Bourne flees in the direction of the Place Vendôme. Police cars and motorcycles swarm off in pursuit. One of cinema's great car chases has begun.

Unfortunately, after a lot of editing plus a *soupçon* of artistic licence, the route that you see on the big screen is not what one would call a route. Just moments into the pursuit, the Mini makes a right turn off the rue de Transvaal – which is actually 5km (3 miles) to the east – and careers into the impossibly narrow Passage Plantin. Bourne then exits down a set of stairs and on to the rue des Couronnes. Seconds later, however, he emerges near Pont Mirabeau on the western side of Paris, roaring down Quai Louis-Bleriot on the banks of the River Seine.

However, a good approximation of this epic movie sequence can be driven at sensible speeds in little over an hour (leaving out Bourne's shortcut down the steps) if you follow the map link included here. Clearly, in 2002, Doug Liman, the director of *The Bourne Identity*, didn't feel quite so constrained by the real-world geography of Paris: his scene lasts three minutes and 35 seconds. Not even Jason Bourne is that good behind the wheel. **BDS**

C'était un rendez-vous Île-de-France, France

Start Bois de Boulogne
End Sacré-Coeur, Montmartre
Distance 13km (8 miles)
Type Culture
Map goo.gl/LOWaQw

The French movie *C'était un rendez-vous* (1976, *It was a Date*) lasts just eight minutes. But this low-budget, single-take short directed by Claude Lelouch has become a cult classic among keen driving enthusiasts around the world.

It features a man driving to meet his blonde girlfriend at dawn on the steps on the Sacré-Coeur church in Montmartre, Paris. The journey he takes is an outrageous, high-speed drive in a high-performance car around the main streets of the French capital. The camera appears to be positioned on the front bumper, capturing every twist, turn and acceleration as the car screeches around the Eiffel Tower and the Opéra and roars along the Champs Élysées and across Place de la Concorde without stopping.

The driver ploughs through red lights, goes on the wrong side of the road and even mounts the pavement at one point. The vehicle was believed to be Lelouch's own Mercedes 450SEL, although the more inspiring soundtrack of a Ferrari 275GTB was later added.

No sane driver would tackle the route at the same speed today, but a similar journey through the heart of Paris is possible (with the odd detour around new one-way systems). You should certainly allow rather more than the movie's eight minutes to complete it. **SH**

Route des Crêtes
Alsace, France

Start Sainte-Marie-aux-Mines
End Cernay
Distance 92km (57.2 miles)
Type Scenic
Map goo.gl/cIrPVr

The little-known French mountains of the Vosges, in the Alsace region to the west of Strasbourg, are completely overshadowed by the Alps, a short way to the east. But, peaking at 1.424m (4,672ft), the Vosges are high enough to look impressive . . . and higher than any mountains in countries such as the UK, Finland or Ireland.

The best way to appreciate this range is by travelling along the 88.5-km- (55-mile) long Route des Crêtes or 'Crest Road'. This landmark route, which begins on the D148, follows ridges that once formed the border between France and Germany. The road reaches 1,340m (4,400ft) in places, and big, wide views spread out below. Snow sometimes causes closures between December and March, but in summer, you can see glorious green slopes marching away to the horizon.

The locals call these peaks *ballons* (balloons), because they are round and smooth. The road passes directly under the summit of the highest peak, Grand Ballon, which can be recognized by the telecommunications dome on top. On clear days, you will be able gaze across the Rhine River into Germany and towards the Alps. On exceptional days, locals say you can see Mont Blanc. Even if the weather is glum, expect to see pretty villages, lofty castles, sparkling lakes, dark forests . . . and lots of lovely hairpin bends. **SH**

❶ The Route des Crêtes is a largely undiscovered driving gem in the Vosges Mountains.

Alsatian Wine Route
Grand-Est, France

Start Marlenheim
End Thann
Distance 129km (80 miles)
Type Culture
Info goo.gl/biJ8nE

There are some 100 wine-producing villages on the Route des Vins between Marlenheim and Thann. Some operate as cooperatives, with up to 200 families contributing to the *vendange*; others centre on exclusive wine estates belonging to noble dynasties. The starting point, Marlenheim, is just 16km (10 miles) from Strasbourg international airport, where you can rent suitably stylish wheels for this epicurean jaunt.

Driving the route is predictably stop-start, with many diversions, from tasting cellars to Romanesque churches and castles. Among the highlights are the medieval towns of Bergheim, Ribeauvillé, Riquewihr and Eguisheim, all clustered around Colmar. Eating well is as important as tasting the wine. In addition to having enough Michelin-starred restaurants to last you a month without having to visit the same place twice, the route has excellent inns and artisan bakeries, charcuteries and cheesemongers oozing from half-timbered buildings.

Visiting during the grape harvest (September to November) is fun – every village holds its own festival – but you may find you spend too much time in traffic jams and other bottlenecks. Early summer is more likely to fulfill expectations of leisurely drives through rolling vineyards, with stops for tastings, and to stash a case or two of *grand cru* in the boot. **DS**

❶ The cobbled streets and half-timbered buildings of Eguisheim, a typical town on the Route des Vins.

Reims Circuit Grand-Est, France

Start Reims Circuit pit lane   End Reims Circuit pit lane   Distance 7.8km (4.9 miles)
Type Culture   Map goo.gl/otIbsz

Even those with only a passing interest in motorsport can't fail to be awestruck by the ghostly remains of the Reims Circuit's grandstands, pit lanes and control towers. Just 7.3km (4.5 miles) outside the city, in the heart of France's Champagne region, these windowless, crumbling relics loom over the start-finish straight, which last hosted the French Formula One Grand Prix in 1966. Slowly falling out of favour with the FIA, and rapidly falling into disrepair, the circuit has now been rescued by a local conservation group, and is once again a mecca for road-tripping motor enthusiasts.

Comprising a simple triangle in its earliest configuration, from 1926 to 1951, this was a fast and dangerous circuit that pushed its racers ever harder with tempting prize funds. To complete your own lap in honour of the racing greats who competed (and perished) here, head out clockwise from the pits into Gueux village centre. Here, between a long-gone grocer's shop and a duck pond, the original road swung north to Virage de la Garenne before the fastest leg along the Thillois straight. The last F1 winner here, Ferrari's Lorenzo Bandini, completed the circuit at an average of 228.62 kph (142.09 mph). Today, the police will take a very dim view of you doing it at half that speed. **DIS**

❶ The period charm of the Reims Circuit.

Route des Grands Crus Bourgogne-Franche-Comté, France

Start Dijon **End** Santenay **Distance** 60km (37 miles)
Type Culture **Info** goo.gl/LQZmsm

Apart from choosing the right variety of grape, winemaking is all about the *terroir* – where the fruit is grown, the soil type and the climate. It turns out that the ideal *terroir* is found in only a few small areas, which is why the best Burgundy winemakers are crammed cheek by jowl into a narrow strip of land just 110km (70 miles) long and little more than 3km (2 miles) wide. Here you will find Nuits-St-Georges, Volnay, Montrachet, Mercurey, Pommard, Meursault, Pouilly-Fuissé and many more.

This road trip through the northern section is particularly lovely – pretty villages, a surfeit of great places to dine and, of course, wineries to visit (more than 40 vineyards on this route offer tours). In addition to the wineries, there are wine-tasting courses, specialist wine sellers and, in Beaune, a museum devoted to Burgundy wine. When ou tire of the fermented grape – as if that's ever likely – there are imposing châteaux and ancient abbeys to explore.

Food figures big, too, with cookery courses and invitations to eat truffles or sample the local *escargots* (snails). And since this is a tourist region, that's not all. There are classic Citroën 2CV car tours, horse-drawn carts, ballooning, helicopter rides, and tranquil cruises down the mighty River Saône. **DK**

➊ The vine-clad hills around Beaune.

The Pilgrims' Trail Bourgogne-Franche-Comté, France

Start Vézelay **End** Montbard **Distance** 121km (75.2 miles)
Type Culture **Map** goo.gl/t3JDz6

This charming day's drive around pilgrimage sites in Burgundy, eastern France, begins in the hill town of Vézelay in the Regional Park of Morvan. The imposing 11th-century Romanesque basilica of Sainte-Marie-Madeleine is a World Heritage Site; it once housed relics believed to belong to Mary Magdalene.

A short drive south are the beautiful Gothic church of Saint-Père and the Roman baths of Les Fontaines-Salées, built around hot springs said to cure rheumatism. The pretty little hamlet of Bazoches clusters around its squat church. Look out for a turreted castle among the trees. Château de Bazoches was the home of the celebrated 17th-century military engineer Vauban.

Follow narrow country roads east to the working monastery at Quarré-les-Tombes, a good place to buy hand-made cheese. From here, continue to the town of Saulieu. Biblical scenes have been carved into the pillars of its 12th-century basilica.

Semur-en-Auxois stands on a raised bank above the River Armançon. A medieval gatehouse leads to a gorgeous old centre gathered around another fine church. Farther north, at Montbard, allow time to explore the dormitory, cloisters, chapter house, and refectory of the ancient Fontenay Abbey – another World Heritage Site. **SH**

❶ The sleepy town of Semur-en-Auxois.

Col de la Croix-Morand Auvergne-Rhône-Alpes, France

Start Le Mont-Dore   **End** Chambon-sur-Lac   **Distance** 16km (10 miles)
Type Scenic   **Map** goo.gl/uNEE6r

This remote and steep mountain pass lies deep in the Massif Central of southern mid-France. Its scribbled route follows the twisting trail of the little D996 country road through thick woods and up over the pass at 1,401m (4,596ft).

There are plenty of severe bends and gradients, interspersed with gentler sections where you can enjoy views across the soft green peaks of the Massif. There's a neat little café with a sunny terrace opposite the car park at the Col itself, although the views from the bleak grassy plateau aren't as good as those on the way up and down. Just a mile farther on, for example, there's a turnout with a gasp-inducing panorama across rolling hills.

The road surface is generally smooth and wide and the traffic usually light, so it's a favourite among bikers and fast drivers who want to enjoy the short straights and open flowing corners when the weather is good. Often, though, it's wet or very cold – so don't underestimate the dangers just because it's not in the Alps.

And spare a thought for the cyclists who often tackle this climb. The pass has featured many times in the Tour de France and is regarded as one of the toughest challenges in the most demanding bike race in the world. **SH**

❶　Le Mont-Dore and the Sancy mountain range.

Route de Presles
Auvergne-Rhône-Alpes, France

Start Metrière
End Ruisseau de Presles
Distance 9km (5.6 miles)
Type Adventure
Map goo.gl/aZv2h7

When it comes to road genres, few provide the primeval sense of adventure that you feel as you approach a 'balcony road', a road chiselled into the side of a mountain. They are often sprinkled with tunnels and sometimes strung with bridges. Balcony road are not new concepts. The Chinese were building them in the 4th century BCE, as were Caesar and Napoleon later. The only down side? They are often just too short; you're through them too quickly, and then comes the let-down: When you emerge, mountain roads just don't seem so exciting any more.

The breathtaking Route de Presles (D292) in southeast France is one such road. It offers 7km (4.5 miles) of pure balcony heaven, complete with all the usual exhilarating hazards, such as blind corners, single lanes, potential landslides, drop-offs so vertical you could base jump off them. The views over the Hauts Plateaux du Vercors will stay with you a long time, as will the fear of facing an oncoming vehicle as you drive the single-lane section towards the Gorges du Nan. Don't attempt the drive if you can't reverse.

Popular with road cyclists and boasting one of the finest rock-climbing cliffs in Europe, the Presles escarpment is a magnet for adventure lovers, whether they are on four wheels, two wheels – or no wheels at all. **BDS**

❶ This section of the route is daunting, even with the retaining walls.

La Grande Boucle Motorcycle Tour
Auvergne-Rhône-Alpes, France

Start Clermont-Ferrand
End Clermont-Ferrand
Distance 1,100km (683 miles)
Type Adventure
Info goo.gl/RpeUy3

France's Auvergne region has long been a favourite destination for bikers, who are drawn to the twisty, challenging roads and stupendous panoramas of this ancient volcanic region. This week-long compendium route starts at Clermont-Ferrand and racks up some serious mileage, back and forth between Vichy and Saint-Flour and from Salers to Amber. The idea is not just to zoom along brilliant roads – though that, of course, is excellent fun – but also to take time to sample good regional cooking, visit ancient towns and gaze at the many breathtaking views on the way.

La Grande Boucle Moto is an umbrella title for up to 21 shorter routes, which join up to form one circuit, so you can decide how much or how little of the route to complete. The highlight of the drive itself is the ascent through the four peaks of the Cantal in the Parc Naturel Régional des Volcans d'Auvergne – Le Mont Dore, La Bourboule, La Godivelle and Pas de Peyrol.

It's worth stopping to explore the famous spa town of Vichy and the medieval architecture of Salers, Le Puy-en-Velay and Saint-Flour. The route also includes several attractions that will particularly appeal to motorcyclists – including the Baster Motorcycle Museum in Riom, which has an extensive collection of classic Springfield-made Indian motorbikes. **DK**

❶ The road through the Mandailles Valley is one of the most enchanting parts of this trip.

Col de l'Iseran
Auvergne-Rhône-Alpes, France

Start Bonneval-sur-Arc
End Val d'Isère
Distance 30km (18.6 miles)
Type Adventure
Map goo.gl/pg74G1

The French Alps are blessed with an amazing array of brilliant driving roads, but there seems little point adventuring into this picturesque region and then not tackling the highest road in France while you are here. To stick this road-tripping feather in your cap, head to the Col de l'Iseran in the Savoie department, close to the Italian border. Known as the King of the Alps, this mountain pass rises to over 2,700m (9,000ft) above sea level.

The pass links the valley of the Arc River with the valley of the Isère and can be reached in a number of ways. One popular route starts at the rustic village of Bonneval-sur-Arc, but you can also do it in the other direction by beginning in the popular ski resort of Val d'Isère.

Both routes offer a tarmac route to the summit of the pass, with looping bends stitched seamlessly together. The road snakes from left to right, doubling back and looping around as it winds its way up the mountain. In places, you are hemmed in by rock walls; in others, gentle slopes tease up your speed.

Because of ice and snow, the pass is only open in summer. It's popular with cyclists, so watch out for wobbling riders as their legs begin to tire. Otherwise the road is generally safe, but pay close attention to your speedometer as the flowing bends start to weave their spell. **JI**

❶ The Lac du Chevril near Val d'Isère serves as a reservoir for the Tignes Dam.

Route des Grande Alpes
Auvergne to Provence, France

Start Thonon-les-Bains, Auvergne-Rhône-Alpes
End Menton, Provence-Alpes-Côte d'Azur
Distance 684km (425 miles)
Type Adventure
Info goo.gl/toABoc

In the early 20th century, the Touring Club de France, originally set up to encourage tourism by bicycle, joined ranks with the growing band of motorists to campaign for better roads, signposting and roadside amenities. They also promoted epic road-trip itineraries, including, in 1911, the Route des Grande Alpes.

There's a majesty and vastness to the French Alps that is both romantic and intimidating. This is big scenery: twisty mountain roads with high summits, offering tantalizing glimpses of the valley floor laid out below, then quick descents to the foot of the next climb.

This famous route – infamous if you are a cyclist – runs north to south through the whole of the French Alps, beginning at Thonon-les-Bains on the shores of Lake Geneva and ending at Menton on the Côte d'Azur – the Mediterranean coast. It's a blast of a ride. Just the names of the places along the route – Bourg-Saint-Maurice, Mont Blanc, Val d'Isère, Les Ecrins, Briançon, Col d'Izoard and Col de Castillon – send shivers of happy anticipation down one's spine, as does the excellent food and drink available at rest stops

The route threads through 16 high-altitude alpine passes, so the weather will be a big factor in when you do this magnificent trip; the best time is between early June and late September. **DK**

Col du Chaussy
Auvergne-Rhône-Alpes, France

Start Pontamafrey-Montpascal
End Col du Chaussy
Distance 14km (8.7 miles)
Type Adventure
Map goo.gl/7OHLcl

When you first plot your journey to Col du Chaussy, using an old-fashioned paper road map, you'll be convinced there must have been an accident at the printers. With 17 savagely tight hairpin bends draped on top of one another, it's almost impossible to make out the roadway. These are the aptly named Lacets de Montvernier (Bootlaces of Montvernier) – a gear-grinding serpentine ascent on the first leg to the top of this amazing pass.

Heading out from Pontamafrey-Montpascal, the road climbs and quickly narrows until it's barely wide enough for two cars to pass. The general rule is vehicles going up have priority, which requires an uphill slalom for the unlucky road tripper coming in the opposite direction. The flimsy iron railings along the roadside appear to be for decoration more than protection, but at least they don't block the view. The road surfaces are generally good lower down, but are a little weathered and ragged at the higher altitudes.

After the hairpin bends, it's a lovely climb through alpine meadows at a leisurely gradient, passing through the little villages of Le Noirey, Montbrunal and Montpascal.

The mountain pass sits at 1,553m (5,029ft) surrounded by fashionable French ski resorts. As you finally crest this magnificent road, the smart mountaintop restaurant is a welcome sight. **DIS**

Combe Laval Balcony Road
Auvergne-Rhône-Alpes, France

Start Saint-Jean-en-Royans
End Vassieux-en-Vercours
Distance 32km (20 miles)
Type Adventure
Map goo.gl/iffGRO

The European Alps have always been a significant natural barrier to transportation. These days, using sophisticated rock-boring machines, it is possible to tunnel long distances through whole mountains. Such an option was not available to earlier generations of road builders. Engineers followed the contours of the mountains wherever possible, and if that was not an option, they created 'balconies' – narrow ledges blasted from the external surface of the rock.

This route – the Combe Laval Balcony – is the finest example of this type of construction in the French Alps. It was built in stages over forty years in the late 19th century to carry timber from the high alpine forests to the woodworking factories at Saint-Jean-en-Royans.

Today, tourists drive the road for the views of the dramatic Vercors Massif mountain range. The most spectacular section is the first 13km (8 miles) from Saint-Jean-en-Royans to Col de la Machine, the highest road col in the Vercours region. Along this stretch, the road alternates between ledges and tunnels, with memorable panoramic vistas out across the surrounding National Park. At Col de la Machine there is a restaurant, which is a good place to take a breather and drink in the views. **DK**

● An 'eye' in the rockface of the balcony road.

Circuit d'Auvergne
Auvergne-Rhône-Alpes, France

Start Clermont-Ferrand
End Clermont-Ferrand
Distance 137km (85 miles)
Type Culture
Map goo.gl/eqSog7

The Gordon Bennett Cup races, held across Europe from 1900 to 1905, were sponsored by Bennett, a flamboyant American media mogul, to create content for the sports pages of his newspapers. Bennett, who brought the world's greatest motor manufacturers together for the first time, is said to be the godfather of modern Formula One.

In 1905, France hosted the sixth Gordon Bennett Cup. To gain the home advantage, the French officials looked for a new, technically demanding road circuit. They found exactly what they were looking for at Puy-de-Dôme, in the volcanic foothills of the Auvergne Mountains.

With big elevation changes, steep drop-offs and nearly 3,000 corners, the Circuit d'Auvergne (Auvergne Circuit) is still an exhilarating road trip, although modern road building has blunted some of its tightest curves. Beginning at the home of Michelin tyres in Clermont-Ferrand, the D943 heads north before turning east towards Pontaumur. A fast approximation of the old roads then runs south towards Gimard before tracking back to the start-finish line. In recognition of his contribution to motorsport the circuit is now a designated scenic drive, with brown 'Coupe Gordon Bennett 1905' signage. Ironically, Bennett never owned a car himself – but he did like to drive his coach and horses in the dead of night, stark naked. **DIS**

Millau Viaduct Loop Occitanie, France

Start Millau   End Millau   Distance 64km (40 miles)
Type Adventure   Map goo.gl/W0GC76

In the mountainous Cevennes region of southern France, the A75 highway crosses the Tarn River via the world's tallest bridge. This figure-of-eight itinerary crosses the bridge and passes beneath it.

Start in Millau, whose residents still marvel at the reduction in road traffic since the bridge bypassed them in 2004. Now you can explore the pretty little traditional French market town largely untroubled by other tourists. Then loop around to join the A75 heading south over the bridge. Slow down, enjoy the view and try not to be distracted – even though the highest part of the bridge is 343m (1,125ft) above the ground. Most of the support towers are taller than the Eiffel Tower in Paris. The

roadway is so high that at certain times you can be driving along it and be above the clouds in the valley below.

Designed by British architect Norman Foster and French structural engineer Michel Virlogeux, the Millau Viaduct is regarded as one of the world's best-looking bridges. So you need to see it from every possible vantage point. Take a scenic loop off the main road through the sleepy villages of Saint-Rome-de-Cernon and Saint-Rome-de-Tarn. You'll end up travelling along the river valley directly underneath the structure. SH

❶ The Millau Viaduct should be seen from all angles.

Gorges de l'Aude Occitanie, France

Start Axat   **End** Quillan   **Distance** 13km (8 miles)
Type Adventure   **Map** goo.gl/lRsCjU

Many sections of this route are too narrow for converging vehicles to pass each other. So be prepared to back up for considerable distances, often around blind bends with unguarded drops. But apart from that, the road is lovely.

The Aude River has carved a series of marvellous deep gorges and ravines through the rocky landscape in this corner of southwest France. The area has become popular with climbers, white-water rafters, cavers and hikers, but has traditionally been less attractive to drivers and bikers.

The roads are certainly dramatic, though, curving along 200-m- (700-ft) high limestone cliffs with raging torrents below and overhanging rocks above. You'll have to negotiate narrow, unlit tunnels blasted through the cliffs, and sections of very old, rough-edged tarmac. There is often no more than token crash protection along the sides with dangerous drops, while on the other side of the road are sheer cliffs of bare rock.

This is obviously a route for proceeding slowly and carefully. Sadly no one seems to have told that to some of the local residents, who often drive at inappropriately high speeds. They are doubtless frustrated with streams of terrified tourists who dare not back up to let them pass. **SH**

❶ The Hermitage of Galamus in Quillan.

The Knights Templar Circuit Occitanie, France

Start Millau   **End** Sainte-Eulalie-de-Cernon   **Distance** 85km (53 miles)
Type Culture   **Info** goo.gl/EUTpaE

This route provides a circuit of impressive medieval sites connected with the Knights Templar. For 200 years, around the time of the Crusades, the prosperous order of knights was based in this small rural area. The six fortified settlements they left behind create a fascinating historical road trip through the rugged hills of Larzac.

The Templar soldier-monks were drawn from the nobility and accrued massive wealth, so you'll find that their buildings are beautifully built and opulently decorated.

It's all easy to reach from the north, via the A75 and the spectacular Millau Viaduct. Continue south to La Cavalerie, with its imposing gateway and fortified ramparts. At La Couvertoirade you'll find an intact Templar hilltop village inside a mighty perimeter wall, while at Saint-Jean d'Alcas you'll see rows of small, identical cottages protected by four great stone towers. Nearby, Viala-du-Pas-de-Jaux has just one enormous fortified tower.

The route ends at the local headquarters of the Templars at Saint-Eulalie-de-Cernon, where you will find a fortified church overlooking a pretty square with an ancient fountain surrounded by medieval ramparts and towers. In the summer, the tour guides dress in period crusader costumes. **SH**

❶ The fortified village of La Cavalerie.

Côte d'Azur Provence-Alpes-Côte d'Azur, France

Start Nice   **End** Saint-Tropez   **Distance** 122km (76 miles)
Type Scenic   **Map** goo.gl/H3A5UE

Anyone who cares what others think will wonder whether a budget rental car is good enough for this drive along the Mediterranean coast, on an auto route where Ferraris and Lamborghinis soon become as unremarkable as Chryslers and Toyotas elsewhere.

Before heading west from Nice, don't miss the Parc de la Colline du Château or the Matisse Museum. Leave the city along the Promenade des Anglais and join the A8, a toll road.

Antibes, the first town along the road, was, according to British novelist Graham Greene, the only place on the French Riviera that had retained its soul. See the Picasso Museum, and, if the spirit moves you, take a side trip out to Cap d'Antibes to marvel at the mansions where movie stars stay during the celebrated film festival held every May at the next stop – Cannes, which gets glitzier every year, especially around La Croisette beach.

The next town, Sainte-Maxime, is a timely reminder that life can be lived at less than breakneck speed, and it's a good place to gather strength before hitting Saint-Tropez, which was a hangout for artists and bohemians from the end of the 19th century but became a jet-set favourite only after Roger Vadim used it as a location in his movie *And God Created Woman* (1956). **JP**

❶ **Overlooking the Mediterranean in Nice.**

Route de Gentelly Provence-Alpes-Côte d'Azur, France

Start Vence   End Gréolières-les-Neiges   Distance 60km (37.2 miles)
Type Scenic   Map goo.gl/KZvSvA

This road trip delivers much within a short distance. It starts in the medieval walled village of Vence, 32km (20 miles) inland from the coast at Nice. Looking back downhill from here, there are striking views of the Mediterranean.

The road onwards into the Alpes Maritimes is a driver's treat, with wooden fences on both sides of a twisting path with plenty of banked corners, and rocky scenery along the top of a breathtaking valley that is green almost year round.

The next settlement is Gréolières, a village with four restaurants – almost one for every hundred permanent residents. Beyond that, there's an even more circuitous and demanding final section that

leads to the end point of this unforgettable trip. Gréolières-les-Neiges is only 1,000m (3,250ft) above sea level, but it is nevertheless good for skiing between Christmas and March because it lies on a north-facing slope. Above a huddle of chalets, the road goes around in a little loop to save nine-point turns before the descent back to Gréolières.

Film buffs might recognize some stretches of this dramatic road from the 1995 Bond film *Goldeneye*, where 007 duels his DB5 against a Ferrari 355 through the road's rock pinnacles and arches. It also appears in the chase scenes of the cult classic *Ronin* (1998). **JP**

❶ A rock arch outside Gréolières.

Mont Ventoux Provence-Alpes-Côte d'Azur, France

Start Les Bruns **End** Malaucène **Distance** 39km (24.2 miles)
Type Adventure **Map** goo.gl/CuvwaW

Known by many cyclists as the 'Beast of Provence', this 1,903-m- (6,263-ft) high extinct volcano looms over the picturesque Rhône Valley. The road that ascends its slopes is both tortuous and steep, and has earned, since its first inclusion in the Tour de France in 1951, a fearsome reputation as the most gruelling mountain stage of the race.

Between 1902 and 1971, Mont Ventoux also drew motorsport fans to watch cars and motorcycles compete in hill climbs – in the 1930s, hill climbing was as big as today's Formula One, and Ventoux was the highlight of the calendar. The unrivalled master of this mountain was the German Hans Stuck who, in 1934, slid his 550-bhp V16 Grand Prix car up the course to one of the most spectacular victories in the history of the sport. The green-and-white curbstones from those days are still visible in places.

Today, the D974 ascends smooth, well-maintained tarmac, with barriers in all the places you'd want, but it's still an exhilarating drive. Mixing fast straights, sweeping corners and savage switchbacks, this route is a magnet for Europe's most enthusiastic drivers and bikers.

Chalet Reynard, the famous cyclists' hangout, is halfway up and a handy stop-off if you don't mind hordes of sweaty men in Lycra. **DIS**

❶ The summit of Mont Ventoux.

Gorges du Cians Provence-Alpes-Côte d'Azur, France

Start Touët-sur-Var
End Beuil
Distance 24km (15 miles)
Type Adventure
Map goo.gl/dK2CNK

Driving the D28 through the Gorges du Cians in the south of France is not for the timid. One of France's aptly named Routes des Balcons – engineering feats carved into the sides of mountains – it climbs suddenly and rapidly from Touët-sur-Var, threading in and out of tunnels that look like giant mouse holes. Tight turns and steep drops demand total concentration, but if you heed all the 'Don't look down!' cries that your passengers are likely to shriek, you will miss impressive views of the tree-filled gorge and the Cians River running below. The section around the village of Rigaud, 10km (6 miles) into the drive, has daunting views of the switchbacks still to come.

If, at Beuil, you don't want to return the way you came, extend the trip by continuing on the D28 an additional 20km (12 miles) to Guillaumes, passing through the local ski area, and then turning down the Var Valley via the D2202 and the D902 to Entrevaux, an additional 25km (15 miles). The section between Guillaumes and Entrevaux passes through the Gorges de Daluis, a thrilling ravine with perched villages and perilously positioned bridges. It's no surprise that the gorge is known locally as a mini Grand Canyon: if you want to get closer to the magnificent nature, park at one of the places provided and strike out on one of the many well-signed hiking trails. **DS**

Gorges du Verdon Provence-Alpes-Côte d'Azur, France

Start Moustiers-Sainte-Marie
End Castellane
Distance 45km (28 miles)
Type Adventure
Info goo.gl/MOrl1P

Like a secret valley at the end of Lac de Sainte-Croix in the Alpes-de-Haute-Provence, the Gorges du Verdon is the deepest canyon in France. It plunges 700m (2,300ft) in places, a magnificent limestone setting for the turquoise ribbon of the Verdon River. Adventure seekers love it; climbers cling to the sheer walls; whitewater canoeists wrestle the turbulent river below.

Motorists can drive the rim of the gorge, accessing either the north side (D952: Route des Gorges) or the south bank (D957 and D71: Route de la Corniche Sublime) from Moustiers-Sainte-Marie. To extend the route, take a detour north and connect to the Route des Crêtes (D23) just past the village of La Palud-sur-Verdon. This self-contained, long-distance circuit takes you to the very roof of the gorge, with views over the massif. The route is closed between November and mid-April.

Back on the Route des Gorges, the road continues to the aptly named Point Sublime lookout, beyond which it hugs the gorge all the way to Castellane. The traffic – caravans, RVs, coaches and view-admiring pedestrians – means the going is careful rather than carefree. Nonetheless, it's a thrilling drive. Stop for refreshment at one of the tiny villages crammed into the rocky outcrops – preferably one not already overrun by the cyclists who swarm here in summer. **DS**

Col d'Izoard
Provence-Alpes-Côte d'Azur, France

Start Briançon
End Col d'Izoard
Distance 20km (12.4 miles)
Type Adventure
Map goo.gl/QoCPt2

Whenever you think you've discovered a great new driving road in the Alps, you'll often find that cyclists have beaten you to it. The Col d'Izoard in the Hautes-Alpes region of France is a magnet for competitive and recreational pedallers; one of the most formidable climbs here is to 2,360m (7,750ft) above sea level.

The D902, part of the famous Routes des Grandes Alpes, runs up into the mountains from the town of Briançon. It's played a key role in the Tour de France over the decades, and blurry, black-and-white photos show brave cyclists making the punishing ascent when the road was little more than compacted gravel.

These days it's smooth tarmac and there is a dedicated cycle lane (marked with a dashed white line) at the side of the road. It's an incredible Alpine driving experience, with the succession of bends becoming almost hypnotic. The road doubles back on itself so many times that you'll be able to see other traffic directly above or below you. The terrain itself varies from forests at the low levels to barren scree and boulder fields at the summit.

There are switchbacks and tight corners to test your driving skill, and short straights that dare you to put your foot down. The route is open only in the summer months, and is generally safe, but do keep an eye out for exhausted wayward pedal pushers. JI

❶ A long exposure time makes the Col d'Izoard into a fiery thread across the Alps.

Col de la Bonette Mountain Pass
Provence-Alpes-Côte d'Azur, France

Start Saint-Étienne-de-Tinée
End Col de la Bonette, Saint-Dalmas-le-Selvage
Distance 25km (15.5 miles)
Type Adventure
Map goo.gl/WAh2Pz

Close to the French–Italian border is the Col de la Bonette mountain pass. It's an Alpine road that takes you to an elevation of 2,700m (8,900ft) above sea level and is often quoted as the highest road in Europe. While that's not technically true – the title goes to Veleta in the Sierra Nevada, Spain – this is still an amazing drive to dizzying heights.

If you start from the town of Saint-Étienne-de-Tinée, you'll climb around 1,650m (5,000ft) to the peak, with gradients of up to 10 per cent in places. But the tarmac surface is good (although the road is open only during the summer months), and the numerous switchbacks are a joy to conquer. The vistas at every turn are incredible, with the kind of views usually reserved for chocolate-box lids and jigsaw puzzles.

It rewards the keen driver, with bends flowing into each other and hairpin sections that bring you down to a first-gear crawl. There aren't many safety barriers in some parts, and the run-off can be minimal, but you can at least see traffic travelling in the opposite direction.

This is not a fast drive, but it's one to test the concentration, and rewards motorists and riders with some amazing views as they weave their way to the summit through avenues of snow poles under the inquisitive gaze of the Alpine marmots that thrive on these slopes. **JI**

This is a road that has almost everything: challenging twists and turns, and stunning Alpine scenery.

Clue de Barles
Provence-Alpes-Côte d'Azur, France

Start Digne-les-Bains
End Verdaches
Distance 29km (18 miles)
Type Adventure
Map goo.gl/hq5kUk

Most of this route is a very attractive saunter through the valley of the Bes River in the foothills of the Alps. The leafy tarmac country road curves around green hills stretching out in all directions.

You'll wonder what all the fuss is about until, around 24km (15 miles) from Digne, you'll see what seems to be the road disappearing into a solid wall of rock. A road sign announces 'Clue de Barles', which means 'the Barles impasse'. But over the millennia the Bes has carved a way through this mountainous limestone barricade . . . and you're going to drive along it.

The next stretch of road is certainly memorable. The D900A winds through a ridiculously narrow gorge alongside the river. At points the huge vertical rock faces are just 10m (30ft) apart. The road and the river have to squeeze through that gap, side by side.

The road is worryingly thin, and at several points it curves under vast overhangs of rock. One car can just fit. Two cars meeting will require significant reversing. And in some sections the headroom is only 2.8m (9ft). Don't try this route in either a super-wide Hummer or a double-decker bus.

You'll also see signs warning of avalanches and rock falls, although there are no suggestions about precisely what action you are expected to take if they occur. **SH**

❶ One of the few passing places for drivers on this narrow and demanding road.

Col de Turini Provence-Alpes-Côte d'Azur, France

Start Sospel
End La Bollène-Vésubie
Distance 36km (22.4 miles)
Type Culture
Map goo.gl/VyioON

The original Monte Carlo Rally of 1911 was a bizarre affair, designed to draw wealthy French car owners into Monaco's expensive hotels, restaurants and casinos. Chauffeur-driven in many cases, owners scored points for vehicle comfort, presentation and number of passengers carried as much as for speed and reliability. It wasn't until 1961 that the Monte was transformed into the navigational and 'flat-out' closed-road special stages you see in modern World Rally Championships.

There are many renowned stages in these mountains above Monaco, but perhaps the most famous of all is the Col de Turini.

Running from the medieval town of Sospel, it begins with a series of short, fast straights until you hit your first mass of hairpin bends near Notre-Dame de la Menour, climbing into a deep, dark pine forest. Passing wooden chalets, picnic areas and neat cafés full of motorcyclists, the rally stage weaves its way to the summit.

At the summit is a hotel (often fully booked by visiting car clubs) and a small restaurant decorated with photographs of rallying legends. Perhaps the most famous were the plucky Mini Coopers that dominated this stage in the mid-1960s. As a possible homage to those golden years, you could drive on this magical road in a modern Mini rented at Nice Airport. **DIS**

Roman Roads and Ruins
Provence-Alpes-Côte d'Azur, France

Start Saint-Gilles
End Saint-Gilles
Distance 246km (153 miles)
Type Culture
Map goo.gl/zuKiQV

This circular tour links up the very best Roman archaeological sites in southern France – but it is also an excuse for a scenic meander through the river delta of the Camargue and the best of Provence.

The Via Domitia was the key transport route built by the Romans in the 1st century CE to link Italy to Spain – and nearly all of the Roman archaeological sites on this trip are located along this ancient route. The starting point, Saint-Gilles, has some of the finest examples. At Ambrussum you can see excellently preserved paved sections of the road itself. Nîmes has probably the best-preserved Roman amphitheatre outside Italy, as well as the Maison Carrée, a beautiful 1st-century Corinthian temple. The photographers' favourite, the Pont du Gard, is the finest example of a Roman aqueduct in Europe, and Glanum has a spectacular Roman mausoleum and triumphal arch. At Barbegal there is a Roman mill and aqueduct and, finally, Arles has the remains of a Roman theatre, as well as its own beautiful Roman arena.

But this road trip is also about the landscape – the beauty of Provence, the small villages, the flat wetlands of the Camargue with its famous white horses and flocks of flamingos, and, of course, the food and wine. If you make this a two-day trip, then it is well worth spending a night in the regional capital, Nîmes. **DK**

Route Napoléon
Provence-Alpes-Côte d'Azur/Auvergne-Rhône-Alpes, France

Start Golfe-Juan, Provence-Alpes-Côte d'Azur
End Grenoble, Auvergne-Rhône-Alpes
Distance 322km (200 miles)
Type Culture
Info goo.gl/Y5a5od

The Route Napoléon is a drivers' drive par excellence: it's fast, with some challenging sections and great scenery throughout.

It was the path taken by the Emperor on his return in March 1815 from exile on the island of Elba to overthrow French King Louis XVIII. This was the start of the Hundred Days – his last attempt to regain power, which ended in defeat at the Battle of Waterloo in June of the same year.

The Route was opened in its present form in 1932, with many cambered bends and marked along its course with gilded statues of the French imperial eagle. Starting at Golfe-Juan, it goes east along the Côte d'Azur to Antibes, then bends inland through Grasse and Saint-Vallier-de-Thiey, around which are numerous ancient dolmens and Bronze Age relics.

North of Castellane the road becomes steeper as it crosses the Col des Lèques, 1,146m (3,760ft) above sea level. From Digne-les-Bains, it runs along the banks of the Bléone River to Malijai, where Napoleon spent a night.

Next is Sisteron, a town in the narrow gap eaten through two mountain ridges by the Durance River. North of Gap, the Route traverses the Col Bayard at 1,248m (4,094ft) before descending through the towns of Corps and La Mure to end at Grenoble, 500m (1,640ft) above sea level. **JP**

❶ This twisting stretch of the Route Napoléon is enlivened by a rock arch on a blind curve.

Bentley's Blue Train Races France to England

Start Carlton Hotel, Cannes, France   End St James's Club, London, England   Distance 1,378km (856 miles)
Type Adventure   Map goo.gl/jVQuCy

Bentley chairman Woolf Barnato bet his fellow diners at the Carlton Hotel in Cannes that his Speed Six sports saloon could reach his club in St James's in London faster than the Blue Train rail express could travel from the French Riviera to Calais.

It was March 1930, and the following afternoon, as the Blue Train left Cannes, Barnato set off from the Carlton bar to prove his claim. Despite a burst tyre, heavy rain, getting lost and having to be loaded onto a packet ship to cross the English Channel, the Bentley arrived in St James's four minutes before the train reached Calais.

Barnato won his £100 bet, but was later heavily fined by French authorities for racing on their roads.

In 2004 BBC Television's *Top Gear* recreated the race, with one of the three presenters driving an Aston Martin DB9 while the other two used public transport. Unsurprisingly, the car won.

The route still makes an enjoyable road trip between the French Riviera and London. Barnato did it in 21 hours 35 minutes, but he ignored the speed limits. Today, on modern French highways, it's still a challenge to beat the express at legal speeds. If you attempted to do it following Barnato's original 1930 backroads route, then that really would be an adventure. **SH**

❶ The 1929 Speed Six Coupe Blue Train Bentley.

Col de Tende France/Italy

Start Tende, Provence-Alpes-Côte d'Azur, France   End Limone Piemonte, Piedmont, Italy   Distance 32km (19.9 miles)
Type Adventure   Map goo.gl/gpbqkC

There are two kinds of hairpin-bend-rich mountain roads in the European Alps: those that are paved, which can be scary enough, and those that are not paved, which are just plain terrifying. The gravel road of the 1,870-m- (6,135-ft) high Col de Tende on the French–Italian border was described by 19th-century journalist George Sala as 'precisely the kind of agony I should like my worst enemy to experience'.

This ancient pass, used by the Romans, the Greeks and the Phoenicians before them, is still a viable crossing between the Maritime and the Ligurian Alps, even though it was bypassed in 1882 by the 3.18-km- (1.98-mile) long Col de Tende Road

Tunnel, which is also worth a trip if you have time. Closed in winter, the Col de Tende is not particularly steep, with an average grade of only 3 to 4 per cent, but it is the relentless switchbacks and the unstable surface that give it its edginess.

Although the road is gradually being updated with tarmac, at the time of publication of the present volume it was still dominated by loose gravel. It's a little steeper on the Italian side, but from whatever direction you approach it, the 48 hairpin bends you'll negotiate in just 6km (4 miles) will make sure you never forget it. **BDS**

❶ This view makes the road irresistible to daring drivers.

Monaco GP Street Circuit
Monaco

Start Port de Monaco
End Port de Monaco
Distance 3.4km (2.1 miles)
Type Culture
Map goo.gl/r9TyBN

The traffic is horrendous, the hotel prices are exorbitant and you will struggle to get up to third gear anywhere on this tiny loop – but who cares?

This legendary Formula One street circuit has remained virtually unchanged since its 1928 debut, squeezed onto the manicured avenues running parallel to Port de Monaco. You can begin your own hot lap from the marina car park through the Swimming Pool chicane before turning hard right through Rascasse and Virage. Driving along the finish straight, over the painted starting grid, you swing right and uphill past designer boutiques and around the half-abandoned hypercars that litter Casino Square, and into the Grand Hotel Hairpin. You'll still be pondering how a cumbersome F1 car can negotiate these ridiculously tight switchbacks as you drop downhill through the famous Monaco tunnel and emerge, blinking into the sunlight, alongside a flotilla of super-yachts.

Lewis Hamilton can lap this street circuit in just 1 minute 50 seconds. After battling the swarms of reckless moped riders and slow-moving tourist buses, you'll be lucky to do it in less than five times as long. Nevertheless, after just one lap you will be smitten by Monaco, and see why this billionaires' playground is the jewel of the F1 calendar. **DIS**

➲ The 2014 Monaco Grand Prix.

Gorges de la Restonica
Corsica, France

Start Corte
End Bergeries de Grotelle
Distance 16km (10 miles)
Type Scenic
Map goo.gl/FgjVFL

After exploring the old Corsican capital of Corte, with its dramatic citadel perched on a rocky outcrop high above the town, you head southwest up the forested foothills of the massif of Monte Rotondo.

Popular with local bikers, hikers and cyclists, the Gorges de la Restonica is one of the most scenic stretches of road on this French island in the Mediterranean. The long, winding climb along the D623 ascends 960m (3,150ft) through thick pine and birch woodland peppered in spring with pink, white and green native flowers. The gorge road is narrow in places, with occasional potholes and off-camber bends that should be treated with caution. The paucity of guardrails is a mixed blessing – there's nothing but your judgment to prevent a fall over the precipice, but equally nothing to obstruct the views. Overall it's wise to take your time.

This pretty, winding stretch of road can get very busy in the peak holiday season – the area's glaciated landscapes, crystal-clear lakes and spectacular panoramas make it a popular tourist attraction for nature lovers.

At the head of the Restonica Valley you arrive at the large car park at Bergeries de Grotelle. From there most hikers then head off into the wilds or up the short climb to the Lac de Mélo, which has plentiful trout for anglers and cool, clear waters for swimmers. **DIS**

Calanques de Piana
Corsica, France

Start Ota
End Piana
Distance 11.8km (7.3 miles)
Type Adventure
Map goo.gl/9xYsdA

Perched high above the Gulf of Porto, the D81 from Ota to Piana traverses this Corsican balcony road to deliver breathtaking panoramas and hair-raising terror in almost equal measure. With long sections of steep and dusty single-track tarmac winding through jagged rock outcrops, you'll need to be a confident driver or rider to tackle this one, and be capable of backing up for a mile or so if you do happen to meet another motorist coming in the opposite direction.

What is really terrifying is that the Calanques de Piana was once part of the Tour de Corse, in which high-powered rally cars would charge along these roads at full chat with only a shin-high stone wall to stop them plunging 400m (1,30ft) into the azure waters below.

However, there is no dispute that the rewards are worth the effort. The area is a designated UNESCO World Heritage Site thanks to its outstanding natural beauty, rich ecology and unique geology; late afternoon is said to be the best time to visit, when the setting sun casts dramatic long shadows and bathes the granite cliffs in a deep, red glow.

There will be no desire to rush this road trip. Thankfully there is a terraced bar along the route where you can linger, sip an espresso and drink in the wonderful views for just a little longer. **DIS**

Col de Vergio
Corsica, France

Start Porto
End Ponte Castirla
Distance 76km (47 miles)
Type Adventure
Map goo.gl/MKGQLp

Col de Vergio, known as Bocca Verghju in Corsican, is the highest mountain pass in Corsica, rising to 1,468m (4,816ft) over the 38-km- (23.6-mile) long drive from Porto's marina to the summit, with a maximum gradient of 13 per cent and an average of 4 per cent. Traversed by the D84 – a decent tarmac road – the climb presents the usual challenges for automotive adventurers on the less-travelled back roads of Corsica, such as the rock debris, the narrow single-track sections and the worrying shortage of safety barriers. But crossing Col de Vergio presents an added hazard from wild pigs, which have scant regard for other road users and roam the local area causing mischief.

Winding its way through the Regional Natural Park of Corsica, the road is lined with larch, beech and dwarf juniper until the final few miles over the barren windswept pass at 1,478m (4,849ft) above sea level. The summit itself is dominated by a 9.5-m- (31-ft) high pink granite statue of Christ the King; in the summer months, a roadside café gets good trade from the road cyclists who come to conquer this climb.

The descent to the east drops gently below the tree line and finishes at the pretty mountain village of Ponte Castirla – an ideal pit stop for a spot of lunch. Unsurprisingly perhaps, *civet de sanglier* (wild boar stew) is a popular local dish. **DIS**

❶ One of the few stretches of the road that has safety walls: imagine the scene without them.

Tour de Corse
Corsica, France

Start Vico
End Bastelica
Distance 106km (66 miles)
Type Culture
Info goo.gl/ME1f86

Nicknamed the Rally of 10,000 Corners, the inaugural 1956 Tour de Corse was a punishing week-long circuit of the French Mediterranean island. Even on modern, well-surfaced roads, this 966-km- (600-mile) long loop around Corsica's flowing coastal highways is a challenging, but extremely rewarding, road trip in its own right.

Armies of bikers and motorsport fanatics come every year to sample for themselves certain sections of the fabulous driving roads that play a part in the island's infamous World Rally Championship (WRC) stages. Perhaps the most celebrated is the 34.2-km- (21.2-mile) long stage that heads out from the hills near Vico downhill to Plage di Liamone, a beach just north of the island's capital, Ajaccio. Clinging to the red cliffs, the road is perilously narrow and twisty as it threads its way through a succession of pretty mountain villages before opening up onto the flatter coastal plains. This is a seriously testing drive: rally cars usually finish the route with their brake pads and tyres in tatters. To sample more delights from the Tour de Corse, head east to pick up the 26-km- (16-mile) long Ucciani–Bastelica stage, which climbs to 1,193m (3,913ft) over the spectacular Col de Scalella.

If possible, time your visit to late September when the WRC arrives and you can see how professional drivers tackle these roads. **DIS**

○ A Mercedes 350SLC roars along a backroad during the 2016 Tour de Corse Historique.

Romantic Tour of Belgium
Brussels and more, Belgium

Start Brussels
End Durbuy
Distance 291km (181 miles)
Type Scenic
Map goo.gl/cAOgJB

Delicious chocolate, inimitable beer, beautiful scenery and historic architecture – Belgium packs a lot into a small area around the size of the US state of Maryland. This proposed itinerary is intended as a two-day trip.

Fly, get the train or drive to Brussels before setting off on the E411 to the historic city of Namur, where the Sambre and Meuse Rivers meet. The history of the city stretches right back to the Middle Ages, with the Citadel of Namur– the fortress that sits at the confluence of the riversdating from 937. If you're hungry, then pause at Galler Chocolat-Thé, which specializes in Belgium's most delicious confectionery products.

From Namur, head east along the Meuse to Dinant, another small city on the banks of the river. The large rocky cliff face that looms over the centre is home to another ancient citadel, or castle, while the town itself is notable for its 13th-century Gothic-style church, the Collégiale Notre Dame de Dinant. There should still be time on day one to get to the village of Habaye la Neuve, where you can stay overnight in old and beautiful buildings such as the Château de Pont d'Oye.

Next day, head on to Durbuy, where the temptation might be to linger to sample the town's beers, which are widely regarded as some of the finest in all of Belgium. **TW**

Ardennes Scenic Drive
Belgium/France

Start Dinant, Namur, Belgium
End Rochehaut, Luxembourg, Belgium
Distance 79km (49 miles)
Type Scenic
Map goo.gl/AD3LqB

In the heart of one of the most densely populated parts of Europe – the Paris–Amsterdam–Cologne triangle – lie the Ardennes, a largely deserted expanse of rolling hills and forests through which the navigable Meuse River cuts a deep channel on its journey from central France to the North Sea.

If the road is clear (and it usually is; it's well maintained and fast), you can drive this route in not much more than 90 minutes, but it merits at least half a day to take in the scenic highlights. The road trip starts at Dinant, a pretty town on both banks of the river and hemmed in by steep cliffs. From here the route south follows the Meuse upstream through thick woods as far as Hierges, where there is a medieval castle whose 11th-century occupants took part in the First Crusade. (It's not open to visitors, but it's impressive enough from the outside.)

In the meantime, the road has crossed the frontier into France, but the border is marked only with signs; there are no barriers or customs officers to detain you.

At Vireux-Molhain the route leaves the Meuse and heads east, back into Belgium across another frontier that won't require even a touch of the brake pedal, to journey's end at Rochehaut, a traditionally agricultural town that caters well for road trippers with hotels and restaurants for all budgets. **JP**

Battle of the Bulge
Liège, Belgium

Start Henri-Chapelle American Cemetery
End Bastogne
Distance 113km (70 miles)
Type Culture
Map goo.gl/z9za6y

This itinerary runs north–south along the line of the celebrated battle in the final stages of World War II, when the Nazis tried to repel the Allied advance towards Germany.

The journey starts at Henri-Chapelle American Cemetery in which 8,000 US servicemen lie buried. The next stop is Spa, which has given its name to health-giving mineral springs the world over.

In La Gleize, which was close to the heart of the German counteroffensive, the December 1944 Museum counts among its prize exhibits an American Willys jeep and a Wehrmacht Panzer tank. The town's 12th-century Romanesque stone church, badly damaged in the war but now fully restored, is also not to be missed.

Most of the 7,000 graves in the German war cemetery at Recogne belong to casualties in the fight for the next town on the road – Foy, which was liberated by the US 101st Airborne Division. The momentous events here in December 1944 and January 1945 feature in the HBO drama series *Band of Brothers* (2001).

The American war memorial at Mardasson is built in the shape of a five-pointed star with the names of what were then all 48 states of the Union inscribed around the outer perimeter. At the end of the trip in Bastogne is a museum dedicated to the 101st Airborne. **JP**

❶ A German Panzer tank stands alongside the route in the town of Houffalize.

Spa-Francorchamps
Liège, Belgium

Start Virage de Malmedy
End Blanchimont
Distance 13km (8 miles)
Type Culture
Map goo.gl/mdyGih

The modern race circuit of Spa-Francorchamps, nestled in the picturesque Ardennes region, is longer than any other venue on the current Formula One calendar, and is perhaps the last of F1's truly great endurance circuits. However, the original track on which races were held between 1921 and 1970 – a rough triangle of mixed public roads – dwarfed this current one and included terrifyingly tight corners, tricky chicanes and long, fast straights that claimed numerous lives over those years.

You can rediscover these historic roads by heading away from the new circuit's chain-link fences on the N62 Route de Spa in a looping arc towards the fast straight heading west from Malmedy to the notorious Masta Kink. This left–right chicane was a test of raw nerve and is still discernible by the old circuit curbstones that now fringe a roadside parking area. Charging down to Stavelot is a banked right turn that takes you north towards Blanchimont on a ragged stretch of neglected tarmac to the edge of the new circuit, which would have then continued up the fast curves to the Clubhouse turn.

If you're determined to link up this historic circuit tour with a lap of the current GP circuit, then join one of the many trackdays, or the much tamer Public Driving Experiences that take place here regularly throughout the year. **DIS**

Liège–Brescia Rally
Belgium and more

Start Liège, Belgium
End Liège, Belgium
Distance 3,219km (2,000 miles)
Type Culture
Map goo.gl/COdEk4

The world's first international rally for microcars took this challenging route across Europe from Belgium to Italy. It was held in 1958, two years after the Suez Crisis, when interest in tiny-engined, fuel-efficient cars peaked.

Twenty-seven tiny 'bubble' cars set off from Liège, determined to show that cars with engines of no more than 500 cc could tackle such a demanding itinerary. The competitors, including minuscule Messerschmitts, Fiats and Citroëns, traveled nonstop through Germany, then crossed the Alps in Austria, tackled the Dolomites in what was then Yugoslavia, and looped back to Brescia in Italy via the notorious Stelvio Pass. Then the crews had eight hours' rest before returning the same way.

The whole round trip was a total of more than 3,200km (2,000 miles) flat out in tiny cramped vehicles over three days and nights. Only 13 of the cars completed the route.

Since then, several classic car rallies have recreated the event using roughly the same marathon route. And it is presented here because it's available for anyone to drive in any vehicle.

Today you'll find that all the roads are better than they were in 1958, the border crossings are quicker and easier, and the tricky Yugoslav section now falls into Slovenia. But will you be able to complete the return trip in just three days? **SH**

Bollenstreek Route – The Flower Route
South Holland to North Holland, Netherlands

Start Naaldwijk
End Haarlem
Distance 72km (45 miles)
Type Scenic
Map goo.gl/ZWol9b

The Netherlands is the centre of the world flower trade and this kaleidoscopic jaunt – which for best effect must be undertaken around mid-April – passes through the huge expanse of flower fields in the west of the country.

Start off in the business centre of the trade, Naaldwijk, where the world's blooms go under the hammer – around $5 billion-worth annually. Some auction houses offer tours. Then head out into the fields, through the main greenhouse district. After a quick zip on the A4 past Delft and The Hague, the route enters the main outdoor growing region: vast numbers of crocuses, daffodils, roses and tulips. At Leiden, go to the Hortus Botanicus, the country's oldest botanical garden. It's a short hop to Lisse, and the real star of this trip, the Keukenhof Gardens. Just in numbers, this public garden is staggering: every year, seven million bulbs are planted in 28 hectares (70 acres) of grounds with 14km (9 miles) of paths, which are walked by three-quarters of a million visitors. It's a blockbuster spectacle. After this, there are yet more geometrically multi-coloured landscapes (remember to keep the windows down – this trip is about scent as well as sight) before you reach Haarlem, with its quaint canals and waterfront buildings. This city bore the brunt of the 17th-century tulip-bubble financial crash, but remains the hub of the tulip trade today. DK

❶ In spring every year, the greater part of the western Netherlands looks just like this.

Oyster Dam
Zeeland, Netherlands

Start Tholen
End Rilland
Distance 23km (14 miles)
Type Scenic
Map goo.gl/AGzzle

This is a chance to drive across the heart of the Delta Works – a vast area of dams, sluices, canals and locks designed to manage water in the low-lying landscape of Holland, the southwestern region of the Netherlands. The Delta Works are the biggest flood prevention system in the world, and protect a country in which more than one-quarter of the land lies below sea level.

The whole project is a marvel of civil engineering that took around 50 years to complete. You can drive around much of it and see various visitor centres and barrier gates in operation. The Eastern Scheldt Storm Surge Barrier that can cut off a complete river mouth is particularly impressive.

The Oesterdam (Oyster Dam) is your driving route because it is the longest structure in the Delta Works complex – and you can drive right across the top of it. The dam was finished in 1986 and measures 11km (6.8 miles) long. Your road trip connects the villages of Tholen to the north and Rilland to the south via the N659.

Driving across the dam is easy: it's a long, smooth, straight, two-lane highway. After so many years, the shoulders now have grass and undergrowth. You'll see the sea close by on both sides, and far-reaching views of wind turbines and freight barges. And being in the Netherlands, of course, the route is completely flat. **SH**

Hamaland Route
Netherlands/Germany

Start Aalten, Gelderland, Netherlands
End Aalten, Gelderland, Netherlands
Distance 253km (157 miles)
Type Scenic
Info goo.gl/KTiOhp

Hamaland is the name given to the flat expanse of land that stretches across the border between western Germany and the eastern Netherlands. It probably got its name from the Chamavi tribe who lived here during the time of the Roman Empire. Their lands later became part of Charlemagne's vast empire, and were organized as a duchy during the 800s. The family's estates included much of what is now the eastern Netherlands, as well as lands in German Münsterland. After the line of Hamaland counts died out, the territory became part of the Dutch Duchy of Guelders.

Today this divided realm can be explored along the Hamaland Route, a picturesque circular tour of culture and history that takes you past moated palaces and romantic castles, along tree-lined avenues and through a long succession of picturesque villages.

Since the route is circular, you can start and finish at any point you like and go round in either direction, although Aalten in the Netherlands and Ahaus in Germany are both good places to set out from. With so much to see along the route, this is not a road trip to rush, and it is particularly worth stopping in the Merfelder Bruch area west of Dülmen in Germany, where the Duke of Croy owns and breeds around 250 wild horses that may be seen grazing in the meadows. **SH**

Baltic Coast Road Schleswig-Holstein, Germany

Start Kiel   **End** Usedom   **Distance** 599km (372 miles)
Type Scenic   **Map** goo.gl/Fcbz8Q

This long stretch of sandy beaches, islands and historic towns has never attracted many foreign tourists, maybe because they face north. You have to have a certain pain threshold to enjoy swimming in the Baltic. But on this fascinating scenic drive, you don't have to leave the comfort of your car.

Start in the lively port of Kiel, where the world's busiest canal reaches the Baltic. The Kiel festival at the end of June is one of Europe's biggest and best-attended parties, but don't even try to drive into the city in that week. Most roads are closed.

Head west to Lübeck to see the merchants' houses and Gothic churches in the picturesque medieval centre of the city.

Keep close to the coast for the best views from the road, particularly as you head towards Germany's largest island, Rügen. At the end of a causeway road linking to the mainland, you'll discover this is holiday territory for northern Germans. The sea is shallow and calm, so the resorts are geared towards families. Expect long sandy beaches, white cliffs and the protected green landscapes of Jasmund National Park.

Finally, swing down towards the Polish border and the island of Usedom, dotted with period resorts dating from the time of Kaiser Wilhelm. **SH**

❶ Chalk cliffs on Rügen.

Eifel Range North Rhine-Westphalia/Rhineland-Palatinate, Germany

Start Aachen, North Rhine-Westphalia   End Mayen, Rhineland-Palatinate   Distance 137km (85 miles)
Type Scenic   Map goo.gl/3lQit3

Few people outside the state of Rhineland-Palatinate, in the southwest corner of Germany, are aware of the wonderfully scenic roads that cut through the dark pine forests of the Eifel Mountains; most visiting drivers are so excited about getting to the legendary Nürburgring race circuit nestled in the middle of the region that they forget that the perfect road trip is as much about the journey as the arrival. This stretch of road is a treat for any keen motorist or motorcyclist.

Bundesstrasse 258 runs from the city of Aachen, along the Belgian border heading southeast towards Monschau, before turning east towards Blankenheim along the stunning Ahr Valley, famed for its red wines. From Müsch the next stop is the Nürburgring where, for a modest fee, the brave can venture out on to the old Nordschleife (North Loop) and the new Grand Prix circuit to the south. From shopping arcades to motorsport-themed eateries and museums, there's plenty to do and see.

From here it's a scenic, undulating, and gently winding cruise to Mayen. Take it easy, enjoy the scenery and watch your mirrors for over-eager bikers and speeding Ring-bound sports cars ... and meanwhile, keep scanning the road ahead for lurking traffic cops trying to catch them. DIS

🛈 A winding road through the scenic countryside.

Industrial Heritage Route North Rhine-Westphalia, Germany

Start Zollverein Coal Mine, Essen   End Lake Dortmund   Distance 402km (250 miles)
Type Culture   Info goo.gl/4eqkyb

The Ruhr area in Germany is famous as the home of the country's industrial heritage: giant steel works, deep coal mining and massive smelting plants. The Industrial Heritage Route takes you on a journey through this region, running along fast, smooth tarmac in a loop from Essen to Dortmund and back, with key stops all marked by brown tourist signs.

Along the 400km (250 miles) of tarmac you'll drive past former gas works, coking plants and mining towns, many of which have been transformed into historical attractions. The keenest industrial archaeologists will want to cover the whole route, but for visitors with less commitment and only limited time, it is best to set out from the coal mine and coke oven at Zollverein, near Essen, which is now a UNESCO World Heritage Site. It was decommissioned in 1993, and the gigantic industrial buildings now house several museums, restaurants and cafés, as well as a design centre.

The German Mining Museum at Bochum welcomes 400,000 visitors every year. It comes complete with a replica mine, so you get a taste of what it was like underground for miners.

It's not a route to be taken in one sweep; you'll want to stop and soak up some of the 150 years of history that surrounds you. JI

❶ A preserved mining tower near Dortmund.

Bergstrasse Hesse/Baden-Württemberg, Germany

Start Darmstadt, Hesse   End Wiesloch, Baden-Württemberg   Distance 76km (47 miles)
Type Scenic   Map goo.gl/UmeQP4

It was once a trade route skirting the wetlands of the Rhine River. Today the little B3 road between Darmstadt and Wiesloch trickles through appealing countryside at the edge of the Rhine plain and the foothills of the Odenwald forests and mountains.

This quiet north–south country road is a specially marked tourist route through vineyards, old market towns, sleepy villages and pretty orchards and woods. Bergstrasse – sometimes alternatively known as Strata Montana – follows the course of an ancient Roman road, traces of which can still be seen in Heppenheim.

The highlights of this relaxing road trip include the castle at Heidelberg, which magnificently overlooks the intact Baroque Old Town squeezed alongside the River Neckar. You'll also discover the acclaimed medieval town centre and cathedral of Heppenheim and the wonderful 1,200-year-old Lorsch Abbey. Learn about the local culture in quirky spots like the Darmstadt Artists' Colony, Heidelberg's Philosophers' Walk and the Gerberbach Quarter in Weinheim.

This route is also a chance to immerse yourself in a traditional German rustic landscape. Be sure to make frequent stops to explore the shops, churches and cafés that line the route. **SH**

❶ The market square in Heppenheim.

Frankfurt–Darmstadt Autobahn Hesse, Germany

Start Frankfurt Airport
End Weiterstadt
Distance 16km (10 miles)
Type Culture
Map goo.gl/4whTRi

Germany is the only country in the world with no national speed limit; the general rule is that, if no upper limit is displayed at the roadside, then it's legal to drive as fast as you wish as long as it's within the limits of the driver and the vehicle. This applies to about half the country's autobahns, a network of high-speed roads originally designed in the 1930s.

German motoring groups have lobbied hard to keep the legal right to v-max cars and bikes, and every year people come from all over Europe just to test their mettle and machines to their limits.

This itinerary runs along a poker-straight section of the A5 that has now been bypassed by more modern highways but which remains a draw for motorists because of its interesting past.

In 1938 Mercedes and Auto Union were locked in a fierce motorsport rivalry that spilled over into land-speed record attempts on what was then the newly completed Frankfurt to Darmstadt autobahn. It was on this short stretch that Bernd Rosemeyer, Auto Union's rising star, was approaching 435 kph (270 mph) in his 6.3-litre V16 Silver Arrow when a gust of wind blew him off course; he span the car, hit a bridge embankment and later died from his injuries. Today a memorial near the A5's southbound Bernd-Rosemayer-Parkplatz serves as a poignant reminder of this tragedy and a wise warning to visiting speed freaks. **DIS**

The Fairy Tale Route Hesse, Germany

Start Hanau
End Hamelin
Distance 595km (370 miles)
Type Culture
Info goo.gl/C8KCOt

The Deutsche Märchenstrasse (German Fairy Tale Route) was devised in 1975 to bring to life the places associated with the Brothers Grimm, authors of the scariest stories in the history of children's literature. It fulfills the brief. Driving through half-timbered villages with crooked chimneys, past castles topped by turrets shaped like witches' hats and through miles of deep dark forests (some with big bad wolves), you might well think you've jumped into the pages of a story book.

The drive, on highways and backroads, takes in 70 towns and villages of Hesse and Lower Saxony, beginning in Hanau, birthplace of the brothers, and ending in Hamelin, where the Pied Piper famously expelled a plague of rats and then kidnapped the children (a tale based on fact and brilliantly told by the town's tourist industry). Among the highlights en route are the Brüder-Grimm-Haus museum in Steinau; Marburg with its 'Cinderella's castle'; Snow White's House in Bergfreiheit; and Sababurg Castle in the thickly wooded Reinhardswald, devoted to Sleeping Beauty.

Tracing the career of the Grimms and the folktales that inspired their work, the route intertwines history, legend and fantasy with straightforward commercial exploitation. You'll find 'characters' at many of the stops – expect to bump into a prince or two in most of the wayside towns. **DS**

Volcano Street
Rhineland-Palatinate, Germany

Start Laacher See
End Manderscheid
Distance 280km (174 miles)
Type Scenic
Info goo.gl/L4A7g9

You'll start this route in the gentle, leafy countryside of the Eifel region of western Germany alongside what appears to be a pretty lake. In fact, you'll soon discover that the Laacher See is the flooded crater of an extinct volcano . . . and that you're about to tackle the daunting-sounding Vulkanstrasse (Volcano Street).

It's a marked tourist route around the Eifel district, taking in the relics and sites of what was once an area of monstrous volcanic activity. There's nothing to worry about today, though; this is Germany at its most relaxed and appealing.

Between volcano museums and visitor centres you'll pass ordinary tourist sights, too, including the grand old multi-towered Benedictine abbey at Glees and the 12th-century pilgrims' church at Arensberg. And there are lots of pretty little villages to pass through, too.

But it's evidence of lava, magma and violent eruptions that you'll mostly be looking for, and there's plenty of that sort of thing along the winding, S-shaped route. You'll see volcanic underground tunnels, a quarry of volcanic ash, a volcanic cone and even a natural geyser pumping water out of the ground like a stately fountain in Wallenborn. You'll also get to see geological marvels such as sinkholes, walls of pumice, carbonated springs and hot spots in the ground. **SH**

❶ Andernach Geyser spouts to heights of up to 60m (200ft), higher than any cold-water geyser in the world.

Nürburgring Nordschleife
Rhineland-Palatinate, Germany

Start Nürburg
End Nürburg
Distance 20.8km (12.9 miles)
Type Adventure
Info goo.gl/ax6ObV

Snaking through the thick pine forests of Germany's Eifel mountain range lies the infamous Nordschleife, a track conceived in the 1920s to rival the beauty, challenges and character of Italy's Targa Florio road race but with onsite facilities and infrastructure to equal England's Brooklands circuit. With more than 100 turns, huge changes in elevation and damp road surfaces in the deeply wooded sections, it was dubbed the 'Green Hell' by Formula One world champion Jackie Stewart. It was also the home of the German Grand Prix until Austrian world champion Niki Lauda's horrific crash in 1976 finally saw it removed from the Formula One calendar.

Today, it still plays host to German touring car races and is hugely popular with car manufacturers, who use this punishing circuit to test their sportiest models to their absolute limits. However, at other times the Nordschleife technically becomes a derestricted toll road, allowing any member of the public to blast around its hallowed ribbon of graffiti-plastered tarmac for a reasonable entry charge. At peak times, the track is swarming with high-performance cars and bikes; it is a truly terrifying adventure for the uninitiated. Perhaps the best way to experience the circuit in relative safety is to board one of the official BMW Ring-Taxis, often piloted by professional racing drivers, for a ride like nothing you have ever known before. **DIS**

❶ A 24-hour touring car race is held every year in May.
❷ Aerial view of the track and the Eifel mountain range.

German Wine Road Rhineland-Palatinate, Germany

Start Schweigen-Rechtenbach   End Kirzenheim   Distance 84km (52 miles)
Type Culture   Info goo.gl/WBYXLN

Created in 1935, the Deutsche Weinstrasse (German Wine Road) through the Pfalz is the oldest wine route in Germany. Rather like a temple for the worship of Riesling, the start of the route has its own monumental entrance (Deutsche Weintor) in Schweigen-Rechtenbach on the border between Germany and France. Passing through the gate, head north along the B38 to Bad Bergzabern and then take the B48, looking out for yellow signposts depicting bunches of grapes. The meandering route takes to the backroads after Eschbach, linking chocolate-box wine villages like St Martin and notable estates such as those of Bassermann Jordan in Deidesheim and Bürklin-Wolf in Wachenheim.

There are lots of opportunities to quaff the lip-smacking Rieslings; look for signs saying *Weinprobe* (wine tasting) and *Weinverkauf* (wine sales).

Each month has its own attractions. Highlights are March, when almond blossom festoons the route, and September, when the harvest festivals are in full swing (check out the Durkheimer Wurstmarkt, the biggest, in Bad Durkheim). In October, *neuer Wein* (new wine) is sold from roadside stalls; drunk within two days of being bottled, it is deceptively potent, so go easy if you are behind the wheel. **DS**

❶ The gateway to the trip in Schweigen-Rechtenbach.

Black Forest High Road Baden-Württemberg, Germany

Start Freudenstadt   **End** Baden-Baden   **Distance** 61km (38 miles)
Type Scenic   **Map** goo.gl/DLb9gt

Opened in 1930, the Schwarzwaldhochstrasse (Black Forest High Road) was the first of Germany's Panorama Roads' through areas of outstanding beauty. It is now part of the B500 federal highway. The high mountain scenery is consistently spectacular, and the road itself is a perfect run of smooth tarmac. It's a lovely, graceful, curving ride.

From the start in the market town of Freudenstadt, after a short climb, the next two-thirds of the route on this high granite ridge are relatively flat, offering glorious vistas to both left and right – although at times you may be too busy enjoying the flow of the road to notice. At the halfway mark you reach Mummelsee, an almost circular glacial lake, and shortly beyond that, the Hornisgrinde, the highest point. Here there is a car park where you can breathe in the pine-scented woodland air and, in good weather, see as far as the Vosges Mountains.

After this, the tempo of the road changes; the descent becomes steep and twists sharply through dense woodland before arriving in the famous spa town of Baden-Baden, where you can recuperate and be pampered. This route gets busy, so if it's the drive rather than the scenery that you are after, you may need to be up early. **DK**

❶ The road is open year round, even in weather like this.

Titisee to Bad Krozingen
Baden-Württemberg, Germany

Start Titisee-Neustadt
End Bad Krozingen
Distance 64km (39.5 miles)
Type Scenic
Map goo.gl/nanoZk

This is the kind of road trip where you need to keep your eyes on the road, but will want to let them feast on the Black Forest scenery, too. For couples the answer may be to do the short but spectacular journey in both directions, with a different driver each way.

The Black Forest is renowned as one of the most beautiful parts of Germany, with its thickly wooded mountain slopes, its rivers and its lakes. This short drive through just a small part of it adds to the drama by throwing in section after section of hairpin bends and blind corners.

It starts in the town of Titisee-Neustadt, and the road immediately takes you past Lake Titisee before winding its way through alternate stretches of dense forest and rural farmland. About halfway along, the laid-back town of Todtnau makes a convenient place for a pit stop, with the Todtnau Waterfalls a popular and photogenic draw.

From here the road continues its twisting way through more forests past the former Benedictine Monastery of St Trudpert's Abbey (the Kloster St Trudpert), which is well worth a visit. The journey ends on the banks of the Neumagen River in the smart resort of Bad Krozingen, a decent-sized spa town whose world-famous thermal baths are the perfect way to unwind after a hard day at the wheel or in the saddle. **MG**

O The beautiful valley near Todtnau in the heart of the Black Forest.

German Clock Route
Baden-Württemberg, Germany

Start Villingen-Schwenningen
End Lake Titisee
Distance 320km (199 miles)
Type Culture
Info goo.gl/fuObmo

If you want a novel take on Germany's Black Forest, with some great distractions thrown in for good measure, then this is almost certainly the trip for you. The German Clock Route is a semi-circular tour through the southwest of the country, from the central Black Forest to the Baar region. As its name suggests, it goes through the heart of the nation's clock-making industry.

You'll learn more than you can ever have imagined about the history of German clock-making – for one thing, that the cuckoo clock is the symbol of the Black Forest. They've been making clocks of all shapes and sizes in this part of the world since at least 1667.

On the way there are plenty of places to stop if you want to learn even more about this intricate craft, with museums and factories along the length of the route. There are also workshops and retail outlets from which you can buy your own timepieces. How about stopping off in Triberg, near Schönberg, to see what *Guinness World Records* has confirmed as the world's biggest clock, which stands 15m (49ft) high.

Between each town you'll be passing traditional southern German timber-built villages and isolated farmhouses, and traversing dense forests. You'll want time itself to slow down, to give you chance to enjoy it all. **JI**

❶ Every tourist should make time for a visit to the House of Clocks in Triberg.

Bertha Benz Memorial
Baden-Württemberg, Germany

Start Mannhein
End Pforzheim
Distance 103km (64 miles)
Type Culture
Info goo.gl/TmbvJK

In 1888 Bertha Benz undertook the world's very first road trip from her home in Mannheim to her mother's house in Pforzheim in Germany's Black Forest. Just two years earlier her husband, the celebrated engineer Karl Benz, had patented the very first self-propelled automobile, and Bertha saw an opportunity to market the fantastic new invention. With her two sons in tow, she took the Benz Patent-Motorwagen on its first long-distance jolly – until this point, the fragile prototypes had only been on short, controlled test runs.

Producing less than two horsepower, the three-wheeled carriage needed constant fettling and improvised repairs along the way. In Wiesloch, Bertha bought solvent from the village chemist to use as fuel, and in Bruchsal the blacksmith had to fix the drive-chain. When the block brakes wore away, a cobbler in Neulingen attached leather pads, inadvertently creating the very first brake linings.

After the three-day road trip, Bertha and her boys returned to Mannheim and, just as she'd hoped, their adventure caught the media's attention and resulted in the car's first sales.

In 2008 the Bertha Benz Memorial Route was officially opened, waymarked with brown tourist signs and calling at the same towns she did; it's a fitting, and pleasantly scenic, tribute to Mercedes-Benz's very first marketing maven. **DIS**

Burgenstrasse
Baden-Württemberg, Germany

Start Mannheim
End Bayreuth
Distance 344km (214 miles)
Type Culture
Map goo.gl/kK3SkC

Germany is great for castles. Bristling with turrets and pinnacles, they rise grandly from hills and cliff tops, guarding valleys and dominating towns. Some are ancient seats of nobles, while others are 19th-century extravaganzas inspired by the Romantic Movement.

There are several 'castle routes', but the Burgenstrasse, running east–west in southern Germany, is particularly well endowed, with some 65 castles on its list. The route, on minor highways and freeways, is divided into six sections, with a seventh, comprising another 15 castles, extending to Prague in the Czech Republic; signs with a castle symbol point the way.

Among the must-sees is Schloss Heidelberg – once the seat of the Wittelsbach dynasty, now a vast ruin towering over the town – and the 85-km (52-mile) stretch along the Necker River valley, where the castles come thick and fast. Between Eberbach and Gundelsheim, visit Mosbach, just off the valley, to see its extravagantly half-timbered centre.

Bayreuth – Rococo architecture, opera festival, thermal baths and four schlosses – ends the German section of the drive. As an alternative to Prague, head north to Eisenach, where Wartburg Castle perches on a 410-m (1,230-ft) precipice. It was here, in 1522, that Martin Luther translated the New Testament into German. **DS**

Hohenzollern Route
Baden-Württemberg, Germany

Start Glatt
End Glatt
Distance 300km (186 miles)
Type Culture
Info goo.gl/qoFD8I

With roots that can be traced back to the 11th century, the House of Hohenzollern was an important dynastic family in this part of Germany. Throughout its long history it always had a fondness for building fortifications. The family seat, Hohenzollern Castle, is just one of the historic castles and other sites to be seen on this circular tour through the beautiful scenery of Baden-Württemberg in southwest Germany. Baden-Württemberg is where you'll find the Black Forest, and is also where the Danube River rises.

This popular drive starts and ends in the village of Glatt, and kicks off with a visit to Glatt Castle itself, which dates from the 13th century and is one of the few water castles (castles with moats) that is still standing in Germany. The route then takes you east through farmland and woodland to the town of Haigerloch with its medieval houses, 18th-century church and infamous atomic cellar, where the Germans worked on nuclear fission near the end of World War II.

Farther east is Hohenzollern Castle, which was founded in around 1000 CE. Hechingen, the town in its shadow, is also full of interest, so you may want to plan a longer break there. In fact, German history enthusiasts could happily loop around this route again and again, and discover something new on every circuit. **MG**

❶ Hohenzollern Castle stands above the morning fog that conceals the town of Hechingen below.

Pan-Germania Motorbike Route
Berlin and more, Germany

Start Berlin
End Berlin
Distance 9,978km (6,200 miles)
Type Adventure
Info goo.gl/Ackrao

Germany is a great destination for any biker – the roads are sweeping and fluid, and the scenery is varied and marvellous. This complicated and, let's be fair, extremely lengthy route – dreamed up by the German tourist boffins – is basically made up of all the best non-autobahn motorcycling roads in Germany gathered up and placed end to end. There's something for everyone – mountain climbs in the Bavarian Alps, picturesque valleys, the northern coast, the Mosel winemaking region, plus pretty much every historic town there is. And loads of famous motorcycling-related sites: racetracks, motorcycle museums, works factories, plus a comprehensive selection of biker-friendly refreshment and accommodation halts.

This route is an amazing creation – a one-stop-shop for all things biker in almost every part of Germany. It's quite an achievement. However, even if you don't fancy undertaking the whole lot, this Pan-Germania itinerary is broken up into bite-sized chunks, each with its own detailed route map. Highlights include the Freiburg-Schauinsland hill climb, the Kyffhäuser mountain ascent, the BMW Museum in Munich, the motorcycle museum at Ibbenbüren and the historic Schottenring racetrack, one of Germany's oldest and most famous motorcycle grand prix circuits, once home to the World Championships. **DK**

❶ Harley-Davidsons take part in the 2016 annual parade through the centre of Hamburg.

Bad Schandau to Hohnstein
Saxony-Anhalt, Germany

Start Bad Schandau
End Hohnstein
Distance 14.5km (9 miles)
Type Adventure
Map goo.gl/L6FDbr

Saxony, in landlocked central Germany, is drenched in history going back to Roman times and beyond. It is also an exceptionally pretty part of the country. This road trip begins from the banks of the River Elbe and heads upwards through testing twisty sections and tricky hairpin bends; it is a route, especially in the final mile, where drivers and riders will need to err on the side of caution.

The journey starts in the popular spa town of Bad Schandau. It slowly leaves buildings behind and the scenery gets better as the road cuts through thick native woodland, the kind that once covered much of Europe, following the route of the Lachsbach, one of the major tributaries of the Elbe. As you reach the pretty little village of Porschdorf, instead of continuing north – the quickest way to Hohnstein – take the fork heading west, which is a little longer but far more dramatic. After some straight stretches through farmland and more rural communities, a right turn sends you twisting down through more forests before emerging in the historic town of Hohnstein, famous for the castle that dominates the local landscape.

The structure dates back to 1200 CE, and in the past it has been a prison, a concentration camp and a youth hostel. Today it provides accommodation, through the Friends of Nature organization, should you wish to stay overnight. **MG**

❶ These traditional half-timbered buildings in the village of Bad Schandau are typical of the region.

Romanesque Road
Saxony-Anhalt, Germany

Start Magdeburg
End Hecklingen
Distance 1,200km (745 miles)
Type Culture
Info goo.gl/KDw8qo

In the 11th century, Germany was flourishing. Trade was booming, cities were expanding and the church and nobility were commissioning buildings on an unprecedented scale.

Romanesque, with its monumental walls, semi-circular arches and vaults, was the dominant architectural style. Gothic did not gain hold until well into the 13th century.

Tracing a large figure of eight through Saxony-Anhalt, inside the old Cold War east–west border, the Romanesque Road identifies 80 buildings worth seeing, beginning in Magdeburg, home of Germany's first Gothic cathedral.

Leaving Magdeburg, the route proceeds through unspoiled countryside past castles, cathedrals and sweet village churches. Don't miss the church of St Thomas in Pretzien, which has late-Romanesque wall paintings, or Stephanikirche, a gem in the half-timbered town of Osterwieck. However, the real jewel in the Romanesque crown is Stiftskirche St Servatius in Quedlinburg. The church crypt has cross vaults, tombs, exquisitely carved capitals and murals.

As a break from medieval architecture, consider taking the 55-km- (34-mile) long Harz Mountain Trail, accessed near Quedlinburg. It's an enjoyable drive through wooded hills, with stops for caves and hikes, and a string of sleepy villages. **DS**

❶ There are many worthwhile sights on this road trip, but this church in Quedlinburg is the one not to miss.

German Alpine Road
Bavaria, Germany

Start Lindau, Lake Constance
End Schönau, Lake Königssee
Distance 451km (280 miles)
Type Scenic
Info goo.gl/f9cM3B

From the Riviera atmosphere of Lindau's waterfront restaurants to the classic views from the Königssee mountain lakeside, this long west–east road trip goes through Germany's best Alpine scenery.

The big sights are all included, with the route linking beautiful Lake Constance, the religious wood-carving village of Oberammergau and the dreamlike, fairytale 19th-century castles of Neuschwanstein and Hohenschwangau. You'll cross the Oberjoch Pass, with its 106 bends, drive to Lake Chiemsee and its popular islands, and reach the famous landscapes of Berchtesgadener. There are at least 25 castles, palaces and monasteries along the route.

But the best of all the sights may just be a pretty farming village surrounded by lush green pastures in a deep valley between snowcapped mountains or a small sparkling lake surrounded by dark forests.

A road trip through the mountains south of Munich was a favourite of wealthy visitors over 100 years ago, but these paved roads linking Constance and Königssee were not completed until 1960.

Today it's well signed, mapped and lined with all the necessary service amenities, from garages to guesthouses. Local companies rent out classic German cars in which to do the route in style, including Mercedes SL Pagodas, Porsche 911s and 356 Speedsters. **SH**

❶ This is a typical section of the German Alpine Road, with Hoher Göll Mountain in the background.

Rossfeldpanoramastrasse Toll Road Germany/Austria

Start Unterau, Germany
End Rossfeldpanoramastrasse, Germany
Distance 13km (8 miles)
Type Scenic
Map goo.gl/UinhvO

Built in the late 1930s by the Nazis, this road was originally intended as a section of the Alpenstrasse, a continuous scenic route through the Bavarian Alps between Oberau and Königssee.

The link was never completed in the way the Third Reich envisaged, partly because of the outbreak of World War II and partly because some of the road goes through Austrian territory. The latter was not a problem for Adolf Hitler, who assimilated Austria into Germany in the Anschluss of 1938, but at the end of the conflict the nations readopted their separate identities. Although today the border is not controlled, and passage is unrestricted in both directions, tourist maps often reference alternative routes: the full itinerary crosses and recrosses the frontier; shorter variants remain within Germany. Because the road leads nowhere, the Austrians did not want responsibility for its upkeep, so it is maintained by the German government with money raised by vehicle tolls. This trip takes you to the road's end, climbing to 1,500m (5,000ft) through an average gradient of 13 perc ent and passing the highest point on any road in Germany. If you descend via Purtschellerstrasse back to Berchtesgaden, it's even steeper, nudging 24 per cent in places. **JP**

◗ Rossfeldpanoramastrasse in winter.

Romantische Strasse Bavaria, Germany

Start Würzburg
End Füssen
Distance 370km (230 miles)
Type Culture
Info goo.gl/ZI8UYH

Loosely following old trading routes and Roman roads, the Romantische Strasse (Romantic Road) was constructed by a post-World War II Germany desperate to rebuild its infrastructure and encourage tourism. Opened in 1950 with an emphasis on nature, culture and hospitality, it has become the most beloved of the nation's numerous themed highways.

Beginning in the north on the Main River in Würzburg with its 18th-century Residenz, Germany's most lavish Baroque palace, the route bisects the Tauber Valley. This region includes the medieval gems of Rothenburg ob der Tauber, with its wealth of half-timbered houses (be sure to climb the bell tower for breathtaking views), as well as tiny Nordlingen, set within an ancient volcanic crater and encircled by ramparts.

The road then passes through Augsburg, Germany's third-oldest city, and the Pfaffenwinkel district or 'priest's corner', with its Rococo masterpiece, the Pilgrimage Church of the Scourged Saviour. The Romatic Road ends at Füssen, in the shadows of the Bavarian Alps, a stone's throw from the Austrian border and gateway to Neuschwanstein, the grand fairytale castle of King Ludwig II.

The route is well marked with brown Romantische Strasse signs, but any unintended detour here will hardly be a cause for concern. **BDS**

Kehlsteinhaus – Road to the Eagle's Nest
Bavaria, Germany

Start Berchtesgaden
End Eagle's Nest
Distance 12km (7.5 miles)
Type Culture
Map goo.gl/L27vnP

Adolf Hitler's Kehlsteinhais, his mountaintop retreat better known as the Eagle's Nest, sits atop a 1,834-m- (6,017-ft) high subpeak of the 2,522-m- (8,274-ft) high Hoher Göll range.

Approaching on the pretty Salzbergstrasse, it's difficult to convey the sense of expectation that accompanies you on this short road trip. A quick history lesson awaits you at the Documentation Centre, now a first-rate museum covering the era of the Third Reich. From here the road ascends 792m (2,600ft) in just 6.4km (4 miles); it's a treacherously steep final leg that has to be done on an Eagle's Nest shuttle bus running every 25 minutes. The 'Fuhrer's driveway' included several hairpin bends and five tunnels, all blasted from solid rock in just 13 months.

You know what's awaiting you at the end of the road. That's why you're there, after all. You know its terrible history, its significance and the kind of person for whom it was built – a present for his fiftieth birthday. Now repurposed as a neat wood-panelled restaurant, it's a strange experience drinking coffee in the same spot that Hitler, Himmler, Goebbels and the rest held banquets. Nevertheless, from the terraces, at eye level with the Alps, the extensive views over the jagged peaks of Germany and Hitler's native Austria are undeniably beautiful. **BDS**

❶ This view shows the Eagle's Nest mountaintop restaurant and the Alps beyond.

Lake Geneva Road Trip
Switzerland/France

Start Geneva, Switzerland
End Geneva, Switzerland
Distance 186km (115.6 miles)
Type Scenic
Map goo.gl/PjVOjZ

The quiet, smooth roads around the shores of Lac Léman (Lake Geneva) sweep through steep vineyards, lush green farmland and quaint medieval villages. It's one of the best circular routes in Europe for laid-back cruising and admiring the scenery.

Wherever you are on the circuit, the lake itself creates a constant glistening view, and there are always mountains rising up from the shore.

Then there's Geneva itself, a handsome, affluent city with views of Mont Blanc from the centre. Look out for the Jet d'Eau squirting a 137-m- (450-ft) high fountain from the lake.

On the southern shore you pass into France and see classy spa resorts like Évian-les-Bains and ancient waterside villages like Yvoire.

You'll also drive right through the tiny terraces of the Lavaux vineyards. These steps up the precipitous slopes were carved by 12th-century monks and are now a UNESCO World Heritage Site.

At the eastern end, the road passes the fairytale Chillon Castle perched on an island in the lake. It's Switzerland's number one tourist attraction.

Nearby is musical Montreux, where you can find Freddie Mercury's statue at the waterfront and a special museum about the band Queen. This, of course, is also where in 1972 Deep Purple famously spotted a fire across the lake . . . and promptly recorded 'Smoke on the Water.' **SH**

❶ The shores of the lake near Montreux are a productive wine-growing region.

Route de l'Hongrin
Vaud, Switzerland

Start Aigle
End Lac de l'Hongrin
Distance 35km (22 miles)
Type Adventure
Map goo.gl/53b80C

A reservoir in the Canton of Vaud to the north of Lake Geneva, Lac de l'Hongrin may not pack the sort of visual punch common to Swiss Alpine lakes like Thunersee or Oeschinensee, but one adrenaline-charged road around its southern and eastern shorelines will make you forget about notions of aesthetic appeal.

Beginning in the town of Aigle, this sealed road, barely wide enough for two cars in places, passes through vineyards and farmlands before starting its climb to the lake. A highlight is driving through the unlit (with the exception of a few cut-outs to allow in natural light) though quite exquisite single-lane Tunnel de la Sarse, built between 1938 and 1940, which operates on a strict timetable – signs at either end with passage times – to avoid any grille-to-grille encounters at its centre.

The road climbs to Les Agites, a mountain pass 1,569m (5,148ft) above sea level, and comes with some serious gradients, including a 12.8-km (8-mile) section with a 9 per cent incline, and some brief climbs at a nerve-jangling 20 per cent. Closed in winter, the road passes through a military zone too, the Petit Hongrin, and so is open to civilian traffic only on weekends. But once you've survived this demanding hill climb, the thought of driving through a shooting range may seem less daunting and perhaps even preferable. **BDS**

🅞 Lac de l'Hongrin is a pool of tranquility alongside a road of wild excitement.

Col du Pillon
Vaud, Switzerland

Start Aigle
End Les Diablerets
Distance 28km (17.4 miles)
Type Adventure
Info goo.gl/qvKwKL

The Col du Pillon is a tightly winding pass from the town of Aigle through the western Swiss Alps. Despite successive stacks of switchbacks as the pass gains height, especially around Le Sépey, Route 11 is an easy, exhilarating ride, with a well-maintained surface. There are plenty of opportunities to look at the huge alpine valleys that spread out on both sides beneath you.

The higher you climb, the more dramatic the views become. The end point, the Christmas-card village of Les Diablerets, sits in the apron of the Diablerets Massif – a 10-km- (6-mile) long chain of peaks with year-round snow. At the heart of the massif, the Tsanfleuron Glacier (cable car from the Col du Pillon summit, a 10-minute drive beyond Les Diablerets itself, forms part of the Glacier 3000 ski resort, a winter playground with views of the Matterhorn, the Eiger and Mont Blanc, as well as various attractions, such as an alpine roller coaster and an astonishing 107-m- (350-ft) high suspension bridge slung between two peaks.

From Les Diablerets, you can return down the same pass or continue another 21km (13 miles) to the opulent winter resort of Gstaad. Another possibility is to return to Aigle via the less travelled Col de la Croix (closed until late May), which has several tiny side roads leading to remote farms and quiet hamlets. **DS**

❶ The viaduct that takes the road across a valley near the village of Le Sépey.

Panoramastrasse Oberaar
Bern, Switzerland

Start Murmeltierpark Grimselpass
End Berghaus Oberaar
Distance 5.6km (3.5 miles)
Type Scenic
Map goo.gl/TzpLJS

This short, sharp shock of a road trip takes drivers and riders through the heart of the Swiss Alps. It starts 2,303m (7,556ft) above sea level, near the summit of the Grimsel Pass, which links the Hasli Valley in the Bernese Oberland with Goms in Valais. From there, the road twists and climbs steeply an additonal 185m (600ft) on gradients averaging 3.4 per cent, with sheer drops on either side. To the right of the climb is Grimselsee, an artificial lake behind a dam with a hydroelectric power plant; to the left is the imposing peak of the Sidelhorn, at 2,764m (9,068ft).

At the end of the journey, the Berghaus (hotel) looks out on the Oberaar Lake, around which a network of footpaths lead to a great glacier on the western shore. The Oberaar Dam was completed in 1953. It is drained by the Oberaarbach, which flows into Grimselsee.

The road, which is open only during the summer months, is so narrow in places that vehicles are allowed to set off in either direction only at certain times: from the Grimsel Pass to Berghaus Oberaar during the first ten minutes of every hour; from the hotel back to the pass only between half past and twenty minutes to the hour. The flow is controlled by coloured traffic signals. **JP**

➲ A broad section of the Panoramastrasse Oberaar.

Chluse Gorge Road
Bern, Switzerland

Start Chalet Basilea, Kandersteg
End Gasteretal, Kandersteg
Distance 6.4km (4 miles)
Type Adventure
Map goo.gl/GMHxOQ

The Chluse Gorge Road hugs the side of the gorge for dear life. This is a road hacked and blasted out of solid rock at the tail end of the 19th century. Over the decades, it has escaped being improved and updated and remains a narrow passage that curves and bends with the contours of the sheer rock wall.

The road cuts through the chasm carved out by the River Kander, near the ski village of Kandersteg in the Bern canton of Switzerland. The surface is tarmac but, unusually for Switzerland, it is in poor condition and littered with gravel and debris, some of which has fallen onto the road from above. You need to keep a close eye out for oncoming traffic. Dry-stone walls and parapets stop you from dropping off the edge, but they also limit passing room.

In places the walls of the gorge hang out over the road like a stone roof, albeit damp and leaking, while in some sections you pass through unlit tunnels – this is one of the reasons why Switzerland requires all motor vehicles to have their headlights on when in use at all times, day and night.

In a country famous for its efficiency, the Chluse Gorge Road is a brilliant throwback to earlier times. It's not inherently dangerous, but does need concentration and a light foot on the accelerator. Nor is it a long route, but leave plenty of time to navigate it. **JI**

Grimsel Pass
Bern/Valais, Switzerland

Start Meiringen, Bern
End Gletsch, Valais
Distance 39km (24 miles)
Type Adventure
Map goo.gl/cDNB95

One of the Alps' highest mountain passes, the Grimsel Pass, built in 1894 at a height of 2,164m (7,100ft) over the Bernese Alps, follows an ancient trading route connecting the Bernese Highlands to the Lombardy Plain. Because it can snow here even in summer, the road has a year-round edge. In winter, snowploughs get a real workout, as valiant attempts are made to keep the road open as long as possible, it being the only road connecting the cantons of Valais and Bern.

The hydroelectric stations you pass, built between the 1920s and the 1950s, would be distractions if they were almost anywhere else, but here they are almost insignificant details in a magnificent landscape. Plenty of turnouts allow you to enjoy the panoramic mountain views safely out of the traffic flow.

Begin in the north at Meiringen, stop at Handegg, home to Switzerland's steepest funicular, then climb the hairpin bends snaking to the summit. A scenic service road near the Hotel Alpenröesli takes you to the Oberaar storage lake. It's worth driving this for the views to Grimsel Pass and lovely Totensee Lake. A tyre-squealing series of switchbacks lead to Gletsch, the end point, in the upper valley of the Rhône. **BDS**

➔ The road helter-skelters through the Grimsel Pass.

Susten Pass Bern/Uri, Switzerland

Start Innertkirchen, Bern   **End** Wassen, Uri   **Distance** 43km (27 miles)
Type Scenic   **Map** goo.gl/ludVqi

When they opened the Susten Pass in 1945 it was considered a modern marvel, one of Europe's finest roads. It was the world's first new, purpose-built mountain pass for motor traffic, rather than an evolution of a medieval mule track.

Tourists come specially to drive over Susten from the foot of the Gotthard Mountain in the Reuss Valley to Hasli Valley in the Bernese Oberland, via 26 bridges and tunnels en route.

The problem is that the pass is not particularly useful. It doesn't link major routes or cities. Its traffic is mostly people who enjoy spectacular roads for their own sake. This means it's a low priority for the Swiss authorities, and one of the last on the waiting list for local snowploughs in winter. As a result, the pass is often closed from November to June; at other times, it's a magnet for motorcyclists, who enjoy the thrilling downhill portions and tightly banked curves.

There are splendid views for most of the way, including a panorama across the Steinen Glacier, but when you get towards the 2,260-m (7,415-ft) summit, the road passes through a tunnel 36m (118ft) below the peak. This means you have to stop twice – once on each side – to take in the views to east and west. **SH**

❶ The Susten Pass in summer.

Nufenen Pass Valais/Ticino, Switzerland

Start Ulrichen, Valais   End Airolo, Ticino   Distance 38km (23.5 miles)
Type Adventure   Map goo.gl/RJbGtk

The drive through Nufenen Pass takes visitors along the second-highest paved mountain road in Switzerland. On its ascent to 2,478m (8,130ft), the road's initially easy sections lull visitors into a false sense of security; more challenging segments await higher up. However, at all stages this road trip rewards its brave riders and drivers with the most marvellous Swiss mountain scenery.

The journey starts in the village of Ulrichen, where you are already at a height of 1,346m (4,416ft). From here, it goes southeast, with some testing switchbacks to warm you up, and into dark pine forests. As the road clears the trees and heads upwards towards the pass, on your left you can see the Bernese Alps, and their highest point, Finsteraarhorn. At 4,274m (14,022ft), it is one of the most prominent peaks in the country.

It can be hard to realize just how high you are climbing, as the ascent is gentle, but gradually you will notice the air getting thinner. At the top of the pass, there is a restaurant where you can take a break, grab a warming drink and enjoy the views over Gries Glacier and the jagged, snowcapped peaks. The descent has equally handsome scenery, but is considerably less difficult to drive, concluding in the pretty historic village of Airolo. MG

ℹ Nufenen Pass is a relatively quiet scenic drive.

Furka Pass – *Goldfinger* Car Chase Valais, Switzerland

Start Gletsch   **End** Furka Pass   **Distance** 10km (6.2 miles)
Type Culture   **Map** goo.gl/jKPv5K

One of Switzerland's highest passes, at 2,431m (7,975ft), the Furka Pass twists up sharply from the hamlet of Gletsch, in the upper Rhône Valley. A couple of very tight bends straighten out to trace a lovely sweeping line through the valley. The road, its surface maintained to the usual immaculate standards of the Swiss, then turns back upon itself to ascend in a breathtaking series of switchbacks to the grand old Hotel Belvedere. This is a popular starting point for hikes up to the Rhône Glacier, though sadly the glacier is not as impressive as it was in Auric Goldfinger's day.

In 1964, the year *Goldfinger* was released, moviegoers everywhere must have recognized a match made in heaven: an Aston Martin DB5, the world's most coveted motor car, with James Bond (played by Sean Connery) at the wheel, in a car chase along one of Europe's most beautiful mountain roads. Pursued by Tilly Masterson (Tania Mallet), doing her best to outmanoeuvre 007 in her cream-white Ford Mustang convertible, the chase came to a premature end thanks to Bond's timely deployment of the Aston's tyre-shredder. A pity, really. Not because it brought to an end a good car chase, but because audiences all wanted to see what was around the next bend. **BDS**

❶ The Furka Pass, one of the highest roads in the Alps.

Great St Bernard Pass Switzerland/Italy

Start Martigny, Valais, Switzerland   **End** Aosta, Italy   **Distance** 82km (51 miles)
Type Scenic   **Map** goo.gl/602aY4

The Great St Bernard is the third-highest road pass in Switzerland and the oldest pass through the Alps. It is the route taken by both Julius Caesar and Napoleon Bonaparte on their way to conquer Gaul and Italy respectively.

At the summit you'll find the Hospice du Grand-Saint-Bernard, at a dizzy 2,469m (8,691ft) and a few metres from the border with Italy. This is a hostel that has been offering rest and sustenance to travellers for more than one thousand years.

It was here that St Bernard dogs were specially bred and trained to sniff out travellers stranded in deep snow. Sadly, that thing about them carrying little barrels of booze is probably a Victorian myth.

This is a great route for a road trip, offering a wide range of driving challenges and magnificent vistas: hairpin bends, steep climbs, waterfalls, bell-clanging cattle, the Rhône River deep in its valley and all the mountain views your camera can hold.

You'll enjoy the super-smooth Swiss road snaking around well-guarded drops, but note that after dark and in harsh conditions it can become treacherous. The lake at the pass summit is frozen solid for 265 days a year, and up to 10m (30ft) of snow can block the road, which is closed from November to June. **SH**

❶ View from the Great St Bernard Pass.

Simplon Pass Switzerland/Italy

Start Brig, Valais, Switzerland   **End** Domodossola, Piedmont, Italy   **Distance** 79km (49 miles)
Type Scenic   **Info** goo.gl/4yc697

No matter how timid a driver or biker you may be, here is a chance to enjoy one of the greatest European mountain pass routes. It's such an easy, gentle, wide highway that some locals call it 'the mountain freeway'.

That's exaggerating – it's mostly a two-lane highway with a few three-lane stretches – but the gradient never exceeds 9 per cent and the bends are easy enough for articulated trucks to negotiate. The road is open in all but the worst weather.

Your reward for tackling this softest of Alpine passes is a series of fabulous views. The pass reaches a giddy 2,005m (6,578ft) and cuts between five peaks more than 4,500m (15,000ft) high.

The original route was a narrow paved trail built by Napoleon Bonaparte's engineers to transport artillery into Italy more than 200 years ago. In the 1950s the Swiss government decided to turn Simplon into a major all-year traffic route, using extensive avalanche shelters and tunnels. It is now a popular route for truckers. They say 100,000 heavy goods vehicles use the Simplon every year.

If the Simplon seems too simple, there are a few offshoots that are decidedly more challenging, including the Zwischbergenstrasse, a winding trail that branches off south into a remote valley. **SH**

❶ The big and beautiful Simplon Pass.

The Italian Job Tour Switzerland/Italy

Start Great St Bernard Pass, Valais, Switzerland   **End** Colle del Nivolet, Piedmont, Italy   **Distance** 406km (252 miles)
Type Culture   **Map** goo.gl/OOmoqx

The original *The Italian Job* (1969) is widely acknowledged as having one of the greatest car chases of all time. And for most fans of the movie, the stars of this British crime caper – even outshining the likes of Michael Caine and Nöel Coward – were the three classic Mini Coopers in their patriotic paint jobs of red, white and blue.

This road trip attempts to follow the action in roughly chronological order, beginning with the opening credits when a Lamborghini Miura blasts through the snowcapped Great St Bernard Pass, set to Matt Monro's 'On Days Like These'.

Short detours west and south take you to where the Mafia henchmen bulldoze the Miura off the mountain (followed, later on, by Caine's convoy of classic Jaguars and his Aston Martin), before picking up the route to Turin, where the Minis feature.

Some of the sequences filmed in Turin, including the Minis' escape down the steps of the Gran Madre di Dio Church and through the Galleria Subalpina and San Federico shopping arcades, are best covered on foot. After a must-see diversion to the old test track on the roof of the former Lingotto Fiat factory, head back to the Alps for the final cliffhanger scene at Colle del Nivolet. Don't forget to pack your Quincy Jones soundtrack. **DIS**

❶ Drive a Lamborghini Miura like in the movie.

Axenstrasse
Schwyz/Uri, Switzerland

Start Brunnen, Schwyz
End Flüelen, Uri
Distance 14km (8.7 miles)
Type Adventure
Map goo.gl/78X1G4

Chiselled into steep cliffs on the eastern shore of Lake Lucerne, the Axenstrasse links Switzerland's A2 and A4 freeways. The particularly impressive section between Flüelen and the lakeside village of Sisikon cuts into a 609-m- (2,000-ft) high wall of sheer rock. The Axenstrasse is a new incarnation of the Old Axenstrasse, built in 1860 to allow land passage across the Urnersee, the lower section of the lake. Much of the old road has been converted to a walkway/cycle route.

There are no major junctions to slow you down, and the endless sweeping bends can cast a hypnotic spell. The highway is characterized by a seemingly endless succession of tunnels and rock overhangs, with supports creating windows onto the shimmering lake. The drive is best made from north to south; that way you'll be on the lake side of the road with uninterrupted views. You will also be able to access the turnouts more easily and take the little roads leading down to the water's edge, where a number of hotels offer accommodation and refreshment.

Now a part of European Route 41, the 'old' Axenstrasse might now be 'new', but it its function is the same: to transport motorists up and down Lake Lucerne as spectacularly as possible. **BDS**

➲ The Axenstrasse's 'windows' onto Lake Lucerne.

Klausen Pass
Glarus, Switzerland

Start Linthal
End Klausen Pass
Distance 23km (14.3 miles)
Type Culture
Info goo.gl/6M3Jq1

Thanks to a blanket ban on all forms of motor racing since 1955, 'speed' and 'Switzerland' are two words you rarely find in the same sentence. However, between 1922 and 1934, this road played host to the Klausenrennen, a fiercely competitive long-distance hill climb. With 136 corners (including 35 savagely tight switchbacks) and a perilous unlit tunnel, it was once considered Europe's toughest test of man and machine.

Racing fans keep the Klausenrennen's legend alive with crudely repainted start and finish lines, the first of which is on the fringes of Linthal, a village at the foot of the pass. As you pull away on smooth modern tarmac, bewitching views of the mountain course fill your windscreen. Bypassing the now-abandoned tunnel, you reach the first wall of hairpin bends. Above this comes Urner Boden, a fast straight through thinning pine forest and Alpine meadow, where racers could hit 258 kph (160 mph) in the glory days.

A final clutch of arm-wrenching switchbacks eventually brings you to the road's summit at 1,947m (6,403ft) and over the scrawled yellow finish line. From here, filled with self-satisfaction and a new-found respect for those pre-war racing drivers, you can enjoy wonderful views across the valley, with the legendary hill climb course unravelling below like a discarded grey bootlace. **DIS**

Gotthard Pass Ticino/Uri, Switzerland

Start Airolo, Ticino   **End** Andermatt, Uri   **Distance** 27km (17 miles)
Type Adventure   **Map** goo.gl/QJtbMz

Switzerland's 2,091-m- (6,860-ft) high Gotthard Pass has everything you've ever wished for in a Swiss mountain road. It's wide, it's fast and it has panoramic views. It will also test your driving skills and your vehicle's braking and handling. It has less traffic (thanks mainly to the opening of the Gotthard Road Tunnel in 1980) than other hairpin-rich mountain drives, though it can still get clogged in summer. It has fewer blind spots, too, and it even has sections where you can pass should you encounter an RV or tortoise-like tourists.

After negotiating the many switchbacks north of Airolo, you'll encounter a fabulously long, flat 5-km- (3.2-mile) long section of cobbled road that takes you to the summit of the pass and the must-visit National Gotthard Museum, chronicling the pass's considerable history.

From here, it's over the top and downhill to Andermatt, where you'll fly through the sort of variations that every great road should have: a mix of hairpins, straights and fast corners. Driving here can be a nightmare in the dark or when there's fog or mist, but it is worth it, if only to see the famous Devil's Bridge, now disused, but forever a triumph of engineering. It was painted by Brtish artist J. M. W. Turner on a visit to the Alps in 1802. **BDS**

❶ Sweeping through the Gotthard Pass.

Lago del Sambuco and Lago del Narèt Ticino, Switzerland

Start Locarno   End Lago del Narèt   Distance 61km (38 miles)
Type Adventure   Map goo.gl/CGtU69

This beautiful jaunt in the Lepontine Alps begins at Locarno, on the Swiss end of Lake Maggiore, and then climbs into the mountains, hugging the side of Val Sambuco and a necklace of unfeasibly pretty lakes. Higher and higher the road goes, eventually reaching Lago del Narèt at an elevation of over 2,310m (7,500ft). The going is steady and you'll need to be a confident driver, with a good head for heights. The road was built as an occasional access road for the hydroelectric scheme in the valley and the ragged tarmac is not designed for heavy traffic.

The road leads to a really special place, totally peaceful, with only the odd passing road tripper or a roadside waterfall to break the silence. Every so often you will come across a mountain goat reluctant to let you by. Snow remains on the ground until quite late in the year, and the views of the white-dappled mountains are superb.

On the plateau beyond Lago del Sambuco, the road snakes elegantly back and forth along the glaciated valley floor, totally encircled by snowy peaks, before dropping down towards the still blue waters of Lago del Narèt, the end of the road. Literally. There is nowhere to go from here, but turn around and do this pretty Alpine road trip in reverse. DK

🔾 Lago del Narèt, in the Lepontine Alps.

Flüela Pass
Graubünden, Switzerland

Start Davos
End Susch
Distance 27km (17 miles)
Type Scenic
Map goo.gl/FTFyr2

Of course, you could choose to put your vehicle on the shuttle train through the Vereina Tunnel. It's open all year round, and runs in a straight line under the Graubünden Alps. You'll be in Susch before you know it, and can then whizz off to join the highway traffic. But what's the point of that?

The railroad through the mountain was built for those who believe that it is better to arrive than to travel hopefully. For those who enjoy spectacular road journeys, this drive is unmissable.

The proposed itinerary covers one of eastern Switzerland's most dramatic stretches of tarmac. The ascent to the pass features 37 bends, of which 19 are sharp hairpins. At the summit you'll be 2,383m (7,818ft) above sea level.

You have to work to get to there, though: you'll be tackling some severe cornering on demanding gradients. This high in the Alps there is a constant danger of avalanches, and the road is often closed in winter or at times of high risk of snow or rock fall. It is important to check the weather conditions before setting out.

But as you're sweeping along those smooth Swiss curves, past Lake Davorsee, with rocky mountain peaks all around you and the sun illuminating the forest below, you'll be in no doubt about the reasons for recommending this route rather than the tunnel. **SH**

The steep ascent to the Flüela Pass has 19 tight hairpin bends.

Ofen Pass

Graubünden, Switzerland

Start Zernez
End Val Müstair
Distance 35km (22 miles)
Type Scenic
Map goo.gl/jSOiuf

The Ofen Pass, also known as Fuorn Pass or Passo del Forno, gets its name from the primitive Iron Age ovens built by metalworkers who once inhabited the region. Some of this ancient archaeology can still be seen, though you'll have to get out of the car and hike on to some of the Alpine trails.

This itinerary goes along Route 28 through Switzerland's only national park, and starts in the town of Zernez, location of the park headquarters and a good place to learn a little more about the area before heading off.

The pass climbs through cool pine forests to a height of 2,149m (7,051ft) above sea level before opening up above the tree line onto a rugged landscape of gray, white and rust-red rock formations. In the distance, tree-covered mountain slopes rise up all around, with yet higher mountain peaks in the distance, providing glorious vistas whatever the season. The Ofen Pass is usually open all year round, although it can be closed if there's excessive snow in winter.

The picturesque Val Müstair is part of a UNESCO Biosphere Reserve. It is formed by the Rom River, a short tributary of the Adige River. The final stretch of road has some entertaining bends for the keener rider and driver, although the legendary Umbrail Pass and Stelvio Pass are just to the south if you fancy a real challenge. **MG**

❶ The smooth roads are undemanding and make it easier to take in the Alpine scenery.

San Bernadino Pass
Graubünden/Ticino, Switzerland

Start Hinterrhein, Graubünden
End Arbedo-Castione, Ticino
Distance 54km (33.5 miles)
Type Scenic
Info goo.gl/xASw4k

This may be a high pass through the Alps but it's Swiss, so it's one of the smoothest mountain roads in this book. It offers a really picturesque, if slower, alternative to the 6.6-km- (4.1-mile) long San Bernadino road tunnel.

While most of the traffic speeds under the mountains with its lights on, you can climb past several ruined castles to a bleak, tundra-like environment dotted with sparkling lakes and scattered rocks of glacial debris.

The carefully maintained tarmac of Highway 13 is smooth, but the summit of the pass is still a lofty location, standing at 2,066m (6,778ft) above sea level. The road is open only in the summer, and then only if there's no snow.

San Bernadino is one of the quieter, prettier Alpine passes. It's the sort of spot where you will suddenly come across convoys of classic cars or motorbikes charging along, enjoying the challenge and the scenery.

There are demanding bends along the way to help the road climb, but the maximum gradient is a comparatively gentle 9 per cent. You'll have to steer a bit, but you'll still have time to glance up at the impressive scenery. In places the road is helpfully wide and the corners surprisingly mild – but don't relax too much, since it can suddenly get narrow and hit a series of blind hairpin bends. **SH**

❶ There are several Alpine lakes along the way through the mountain pass.

Oberalp Pass
Graubünden/Uri, Switzerland

Start Andermatt, Graubünden
End Disentis, Uri
Distance 32km (20 miles)
Type Adventure
Map goo.gl/KLRmo2

It may not come with daunting Alpine gradients, and might not be as high as Switzerland's more celebrated passes, but some might argue lower gradients allow you to go faster, and the lower the pass, the more you can look up. Make no mistake, there are plenty of upsides to driving the 2,044-m (6,706-ft) Oberalp Pass.

Beginning at Andermatt, a succession of hairpins are upon you in no time, as you more or less follow the Furka Oberalp, a narrow-gauge mountain railway, to the summit. The railway then disappears into a tunnel, but the views stay with you, opening up over huge Alpine valleys and across to the 2,431-m- (7,976-ft) high Furka Pass. At the summit of the pass, take a pit stop at Gasthaus Piz Calmot on the shore of Oberalpsee. Tucked into the mountains to the south of here is Lake Toma, the source of the Rhine River, which drains 70 per cent of Switzerland's entire land mass. It is marked by, of all things, the world's highest lighthouse.

Once over the pass, the route descends via another brace of hairpin bends towards the ski resort of Disentis. From here, you can return the same way or take a right turn and eventually climb the famous Gotthard Pass back to Andermatt, thus completing an enviable 'three passes' traverse – a road trip that can easily be done in a day but will be talked about long after. **BDS**

❶ Long, broad loops rather than steep ascents allow you to go faster.

Albula Pass
Graubünden, Switzerland

Start Thusis
End La Punt-Chamues
Distance 53km (33 miles)
Type Adventure
Map goo.gl/Kot8wn

This little-known high Alpine pass heads south from the small town of Thusis across the mountains and down into the Engadin Valley region at La Punt. It comprises a tough combination of narrow sections, severe gradients, uncertain road surfaces, crumbling edges, blind hairpin bends and confusing place names.

As with many Alpine journeys, you will find different spellings and pronunciations for everywhere along the route. Even the pass itself is known as Passo dell'Albula in Italian or Pass da l'Alvra in local Swiss. Whatever you call this beautiful route, however, you will find it creeps over the summit at a lofty 2,315m (7,595ft), between the spectacular snowy peaks of Piz Calderas and Alplihorn in eastern Switzerland. The journey follows a railroad track for much of the way. This winds up towards the pass but disappears into a tunnel just after Preda, thereby avoiding the full height of the road trip.

The pass is closed in winter but the road is not abandoned entirely. Adventurous Swiss locals often take the train up to Preda, then toboggan down the route of the road back to Bergun. In summer there is a bar, hotel and shop at the summit. Traffic is light, but tourists often stop for refreshments on the sunny terrace and gaze at the snowcapped mountains in all directions. **SH**

Splügen Pass
Switzerland/Italy

Start Splügen, Graubünden, Switzerland
End Chiavenna, Lombardy, Italy
Distance 124km (77 miles)
Type Adventure
Info goo.gl/o1txfS

Once a vital link between the Valle Spluga in the Italian province of Sondrio and the Hinterrhein Valley in Switzerland, the Splügen Pass (2,115m/6,939 ft) sits on the boundary of the Lepontine and Rhaetian Alps, a watershed feeding the Po and Rhine Rivers. First trudged by the Romans, and an important mule track during the Middle Ages, the pass was upgraded to a road by the rulers of the Kingdom of Lombardy-Venetia in the 1820s. Mary Shelley, the author of *Frankenstein*, who walked it in 1840, described it as a 'most marvellous road'.

One of the Alps' most famous hairpin drives, the pass demands caution. The hairpins – which have an average gradient of 8 per cent – are not flagged. The avalanche gallery, running alongside the road at one point, was one of the first (1824) in the Alps.

Once over the pass, if coming from the Swiss side, the hairpins give way to a fast and truly thrilling 30-km- (19-mile) long descent to Chiavenna, an Italian mountain village on the banks of the Mera River. The construction of the San Bernardino Tunnel in 1967 means this is very much a tourist route now. *Top Gear* visited the pass in 2007 and declared it one of the best driving roads in Europe. Its newfound reputation, especially among touring motorcyclists, means you'll rarely get this wonderful road to yourself in high summer. And in winter, the pass is closed by snow. **BDS**

Arlberg Pass
Vorarlberg/Tyrol, Austria

Start Bludenz, Vorarlberg
End Strengen, Tyrol
Distance 61km (37.9 miles)
Type Scenic
Map goo.gl/ZzeAsV

The Arlberg Road has long been a primary link through the Arlberg Mountains between the town of Bludenz to the south of Lake Constance on the German/Swiss/Austrian border and the city of Innsbruck. This route still exists, of course, but for those who are in a hurry and don't want to waste time driving over the 1,793-m- (5,883-ft) high Arlberg Pass, there's a time-saving detour: the Arlberg Road Tunnel, opened in 1978.

This is undoubtedly an impressive feat of civil engineering, but of course it does not provide the greatest – or indeed any – vistas. So if you're looking to cross the Arlberg massif but want to enjoy stunning Alpine views in the process (plus do it toll free), the old road over the Arlberg Pass still beckons. Popular with motorcyclists in the summer months, the road is in excellent condition as it meanders through the village of St Anton, and follows the flowing curves of the Rosanne River as it heads down to Strengen.

The Arlberg Road has its origins as an old mule trail used by salt traders in the 14th century, and survives today as Federal Highway B197, by far the most exhilarating crossing of the Arlberg. It is well serviced with fine hotels and upmarket restaurants along the route, catering for the winter sports tourists who flock to Austria's largest contiguous ski area. **BDS**

❶ The Arlberg Pass takes in the striking Alpine scenery and is in an area noted for winter sports.

Flexen Pass
Vorarlberg, Austria

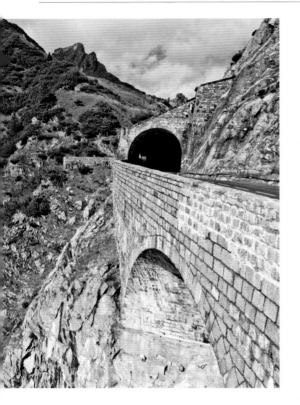

Start Warth
End Stuben
Distance 17km (10.5 miles)
Type Adventure
Map goo.gl/tTRdWB

Deep in the west Austrian Alps, just north of the world-famous Tyrol peaks, there is the lesser-known Arlberg mountain range and a challenging little road that leads right through its heart. Flexen Pass runs north to south to cross the Arlberg Mountains via a pass at 1,793m (5,883ft) above sea level. The poor old road is basically a tarmac version of a 14th-century drovers' track, which has to wind up steeply from the forests of the Lech river valley to gasp its way over the saddle of this challenging mountain range.

In winter the road is packed with serious skiers heading for the slopes. In summer, however, it is traversed by a select bunch of bikers and sports car enthusiasts who wish to discover what this narrow, winding jewel of a road has to offer. Stupendous mountain panoramas greet them at every turn. At the numerous village cafés near the twin ski resorts of Lech and Zürs, there is the opportunity to take a break, grab some refreshment and gaze up at the snowy peaks as your hard-pressed engine ticks cool.

Note that there are a number of avalanche tunnels along the route, the longest of which is a single-lane, scarily dilapidated road, which is managed by traffic lights that seem to take forever to change. If this road trip has not fully sated your thirst for adventure, pick up the scenic Arlberg Pass near Stuben. **SH**

❶ The stone-block tunnels provide necessary protection from avalanches.

Silvretta High Alpine Road
Vorarlberg/Tyrol, Austria

Start Partenen, Vorarlberg
End Galtür, Tyrol
Distance 26km (16.1 miles)
Type Adventure
Map goo.gl/2zmpdS

Long considered one of Europe's premier Alpine roads, the Silvretta High Alpine Road in Austria's Central Eastern Alps takes you through a region packed with some 70 peaks of at least 3,00m (9,800ft). In the 1920s, the hydroelectric power company Voralberger Illwerke saw the region's potential for power generation and got to work building the infrastructure you see today – man-made reservoirs, storage dams, hydroelectric power plants, water tunnels and power lines .

Leaving Partenen, the road enters a series of uphill hairpins through rich farmland and deep forests. Emerging on a small plateau above the tree line, it passes the Vermunt storage lake and continues to Bielerhöhe Pass (2.034m/6,673ft), where you will probably want to stop to marvel at the grandeur of the 3,312-m- (10,866-ft) high Piz Buin on the Austrian/Swiss border and the panorama of accompanying peaks encircling the 2-km- (1.3-mile) long Silvretta storage lake. If you come up here in winter via the cable car (the road will be closed from November), you will find the lake frozen over and perfect for skating.

Leaving the Bielerhöhe Pass, the route follows the Vermuntbach River down into the Paznauntal Valley, passing through several tunnels. Opened to the public in 1954, the road has provided access to the beauty of the Montafon ever since. **BDS**

Hahntennjoch High Mountain Pass Tyrol, Austria

Start Elmen
End Imst
Distance 30km (18.6 miles)
Type Scenic
Map goo.gl/sTMMVD

Connecting Elmen in the Lech Valley with Imst on the Inn River, with a summit at 1,884m (6,181 ft) above sea level, the Hahntennjoch High Mountain Pass is not as high as some of its more fancied Alpine cousins, but it's high enough. The surrounding peaks are just as spectacular, and its surface is as smooth as an airport runway. No wonder, then, that it has become a firm favourite with motorcyclists from all over the world.

The ascent begins in the town of Elmen on the banks of the Lech River, a tributary of the Danube. Almost immediately, you are confronted with a series of 180-degree hairpin bends, but then the road opens up to hug the side of the broad valley below. This may be one of the lower-altitude Tyrolean road trips, but you should nevertheless be wary of rock and mudslides spilling onto the tarmac; such debris can tumble down at any time of the year.

On the other side of the pass, the landscape becomes more desolate, but a thrilling descent to the pretty Alpine village of Imst awaits you. A mix of broad, sweeping curves takes you along a section of road chiselled out of the rock face, followed by 20 right-angle bends in the course of less than 3km (2 miles). This grand finale to a thrilling road trip will test not only your frazzled nerves, but also your brakes. **BDS**

Staller Saddle Austria/Italy

Start St Jakob in Defereggen, Tyrol, Austria   End Arbusti, South Tyrol, Italy   Distance 23km (14.3 miles)
Type Scenic   Map goo.gl/QtGlG1

One-way streets with slow-changing traffic lights do not sound like the ingredients for a memorable road trip, but in reality itineraries don't come any better than this one through the Staller Saddle in the Alps.

At the top of the pass, there is surely one of the most isolated and idyllically located set of traffic lights on any road in the world. They are there because of the tight, twisty, narrow road on the Italian side of the mountain – it is so narrow that it is far too dangerous even to attempt to pass another vehicle, so the road effectively becomes a one-way street while cars and motorcycles head up, or down, the mountain in alternate single file.

For this reason, if you are driving the road for pleasure, it is best to approach from the Austrian side. If you want to arrive in time for the traffic lights to let you down to Italy immediately, then the one-way system switches to 'down' on the hour, and remains green for fifteen minutes. If you miss this slot, though, you can soak up the stunning views over the Antholz Valley in the South Tyrol, with the Obersee Lake and the Villgraten Mountains some of the highlights.

The pass is open only from 5:30am to 10:15pm between May and October. **TW**

❶ The Defereggen Valley.

Fern Pass Tyrol, Austria

Start Lermoos, Lechtal Alps   **End** Wiesenmühle   **Distance** 23km (14.5 miles)

Type Scenic   **Map** goo.gl/pWev6p

If you're looking for a fairly quick and easy route into the wonderful Tyrolean Alps, then Fern Pass might be for you. It's a major route on modern, smooth tarmac that weaves and cuts its way through the mountains between Germany and Austria.

It begins near the village of Lermoos and takes you around the Zugspitze mountain, which towers above the landscape. This section can be very busy in high summer season, with coaches, campervans, and trucks. Combine that with tight bends and you have what can be a challenging and patience-testing drive at times.

The Fern Pass itself reaches an elevation of 1,200m (4,000ft), and at its peak is the Zugsplitzblick

viewing-point that overlooks Blindsee, the largest lake in the region.

From there the road runs in a succession of swift, smooth and mostly safe curves. It is one lane in each direction, but if traffic is light you can enjoy bend after bend. That said, traffic can be busy in winter; this is a major route through the Alps to the numerous ski resorts.

Fern Pass is a route that drivers love or loathe. It takes you right into the heart of the Austrian Alps, but you may have to share those stunning views with many other road trippers. **JI**

❶ **Blindsee framed by the Tyrolean Alps.**

Kaunertal Glacier Road
Tyrol, Austria

Start Feichten im Kaunertal
End Weisseeferner
Distance 27km (17 miles)
Type Scenic
Map goo.gl/OzftQU

This relatively little-known route through the Austrian Tyrol near the Italian frontier starts at 1,273m (4,176ft) above sea level and rises in a short distance via 29 hairpin bends to 2,750m (9,022ft). The start point, in Feichten im Kaunertal, is reached most easily from Innsbruck or Munich.

At the upper level, the ice cover is permanent, but the road is passable year round: from 7:00am to 7:30pm in June, July and August, and between 7:00am and 5:00pm the rest of the year. Even in the finest weather, the road is never less than challenging, but most travellers agree that the outstanding views are worth the stress. In addition to the magnificent mountains, highlights include the Gepatsch Reservoir (created in the 1960s to power a hydroelectric generator at Prutz) and, in spring and early summer, carpets of wildflowers that are among the finest in the Alps.

The road ends at Weisseeferner, on the edge of the Kaunertal Glacier, from where a cable car carries on to a height of 3,108m (10,197ft). At the top, there are spectacular views of three countries – Austria, Italy and Switzerland. Between September and June, the area is thronged with skiers and snowboarders. There are nursery slopes near Falginjoch ridge and a black run from Karlesspitze to Ochsenalm that includes a 140-m- (153-yard) long floodlit tunnel. **JP**

Zillertaler Höhenstrasse
Tyrol, Austria

Start Strass im Zillertal
End Hippach
Distance 27km (17 miles)
Type Scenic
Info goo.gl/RgFj7D

Built in the 1960s to give local farmers access to the Alpine meadows, this short route through the pretty Ziller Valley was later opened up to toll-paying members of the public. The Höhenstrasse (High Road) begins on the banks of the Inn River and follows the valley of its tributary, the Ziller, almost to its source. The road then descends the southern side of the mountain.

The start point, Strass im Zillertal, is a pretty village next to Zell am Ziller, an intermediate stop on the Zillertalbahn, a narrow-gauge railway that links Jenbach and Mayrhofen. The scenery along the valley is simply breathtaking, and so too is the air at the top. On reaching the summit, travellers will have climbed almost 1,500m (5,000ft) from their starting point to a height of 2,020m (6,627ft) above sea level.

After pausing to take in the bird's-eye view of the mountains, proceed through the villages of Ried, Kaltenbach and Aschau to the place that some regard as the best-looking of them all – Hippach. In spring and summer, the village is set off by a sea of wildflowers, while in winter it is one of Austria's top centres for winter sports, with toboggan runs, a skating rink and the country's steepest ski slope. If the Höhenstrasse is closed because of snow, you can still reach Hippach by taking the low road through the valley instead. **JP**

Ötztal Glacier Road
Tyrol, Austria

Start Sölden
End Ötztal Glacier ski lifts
Distance 16km (10 miles)
Type Scenic
Map goo.gl/Nzw3wI

At 2,830m (9,285ft) above sea level, the Ötztal Glacier Road is Europe's second-highest paved road. Built in 1972 as a spur off the Hochsölden road near Sölden, it ascends the Rettenbach Valley to the cold, shaded Rettenbach Glacier, before entering the dimly lit 1.7-km- (1-mile) long Rosi Mittermaier Tunnel, Europe's highest road tunnel, and emerging at the base of the sunnier, east-facing Tiefenbach Glacier at 3,250m (10,662ft). That's a lot of road trip to squash into just 16km (10 miles).

Open from June to October each year, but only when considered to be free from the threat of avalanches, the road has 11 to 14 per cent inclines and a number of adrenaline-inducing switchbacks. Snow chains are always advisable, even in early summer, since the region is notorious, even by Alpine standards, for sudden and dramatic drops in temperature.

Non-skiers are required to pay a small toll to use this route. Because it isn't a through road, it has been utilized for all sorts of special purposes, including cycle races and even a movie location. In early 2015, a 500-strong crew from the James Bond movie *Spectre* came here for 15 days to film a thrilling car and plane chase sequence on the Ötztal Glacier Road – a claim to fame that should guarantee the road's popularity for several decades to come. **BDS**

❶ The isolated church outside Sölden village on the Ötztal Glacier Road.

Passo del Rombo
Austria/Italy

Start Obergurgl, Tyrol, Austria
End San Leonardo in Passiria, South Tyrol, Italy
Distance 43km (27 miles)
Type Adventure
Map goo.gl/ZkkjS7

Although the pass is steep in parts, the road is in good condition and there are places to stop to enjoy the view.

Sitting some 2,509m (8,231ft) above sea level, Passo del Rombo, also known to locals as the Timmelsjoch, is one of the highest mountain passes in the Alps. It is also one of the quieter Alpine routes, with the nearby Brenner Pass and Reschen Pass, which are both easier to drive, sharing the load of mountain-crossing traffic.

Crossing the border from Austria to Italy, the narrow, twisty road runs for 43km (27 miles) as it bridges the saddle point between the Jochköpfl at 3,141m (10,305ft) and Wurmkogel at 3,082m (10,112ft). It offers stunning views over the snowcapped Ötztal Alps that separate the two countries, assuming that the weather is in your favour. Sudden changes in conditions are a major hazard at this kind of altitude; patchy stretches of shin-high guard wall do not offer much protection if you fail to treat this Alpine road with the respect it deserves. The gradient is steep and there are at least 60 extreme bends to negotiate. Pick your time carefully if you plan to traverse Passo del Rombo: it is usually only open from the first half of June to the second half of October, between 7:00am and 8:00pm. Approach from the Austrian side and there is a small toll to pay, but it is worth every penny. In addition to the views, you get to enjoy a spectacular driving challenge on this quiet, hidden gem of the Eastern Alps. **TW**

Strubklamm Strasse
Salzburg, Austria

Start Faistenau
End Ebenau
Distance 6.9km (4.3 miles)
Type Adventure
Map goo.gl/xKOpI6

Sometimes roads have little choice but to conform to the landscapes through which they pass, and there are few places in the world where this is more evident than along a section of Austria's Strubklamm Strasse. The eye of the needle is the impressive Almbach Gorge, as the road threads through the small rural towns of Faistenau and Ebenau. The segment that bisects the gorge is west of Faistenau, and as you emerge from it, heading farther west, the views broaden into forest and then open farmland, before entering Ebenau.

One of Austria's narrowest roads, the Strubklamm Strasse runs, in part, alongside the Almbach River, with the gorge towering almost vertically above it. In places it is so narrow that there is barely room for protective guardrails, much less a footpath. The descent from the top of the gorge to the river has all the usual hairpin bends, and the gorge is a popular spot for hikers, who come to walk trails first cut by pioneers in the 1890s. One of the prettiest and longest gorges in the Eastern Alps, at 700m (2,300ft), Almbach is at a deceptively high elevation, and in winter it can be made hazardous by snowfalls and avalanches. The road trip can be treacherous, too, even in summer, with an unforgiving gorge right outside your car window, so it is best to keep your eyes fixed on the straight and narrow, however tempting the views. **BDS**

❶ Along the Almbach Gorge there are numerous hiking paths of varying degrees of difficulty.

Grossglockner High Alpine Road Salzburg/Styria, Austria

Start Fusch, Salzburg
End Hochtor, Styria
Distance 26km (16.2 miles)
Type Adventure
Map goo.gl/2NtjJY

At one time, this mountain wonderland was the preserve of skilled alpinists, but in 1930 work began to create a high mountain passage between Austria and Italy. It took 3,200 labourers five years to blast the 1.5 million tons of rock required to create cuttings, embankments and the 67 bridges that form Grossglockner High Alpine Road. To celebrate this triumph of engineering, an international hill-climb event was hosted, drawing the world's greatest racing drivers.

Although the tightest of its 37 turns have been slightly blunted to accommodate today's tourist buses, it is still a thrilling drive. Fast, sweeping bends head south from Fusch, before a tangle of switchbacks up to Fuscher Törl and a serpentine descent from the pass to Hochtor. Today, the road is clad in smooth gray tarmac (completely rebuilt after tanks ripped its surface to shreds during World War II), but to catch a glimpse of what it was like during the inaugural hill climb of 1935, take the cobbled spur road to Edelweissspitze just before the summit, which snakes to a breathtaking viewpoint at an ear-popping 2,564m (8,433ft). In short, Grossglockner has everything: superb driving roads, a rich and varied history and incredible panoramas over the High Tauern National Park. **DIS**

➲ The tortuous ascent up Austria's highest paved road.

Goldeck Panorama Road Carinthia, Austria

Start Zlan
End Seetal
Distance 14.5km (9 miles)
Type Scenic
Info goo.gl/T3ORfU

Most local traffic sticks to the fast, shady roads in the wooded depths of the Drava River valley near Stockenboi in the Carinthian Mountains of Austria. However, most road trippers to the area would much prefer to be thousands of feet higher up on the open sunny slopes of Goldeck Mountain. Luckily their preferences have been accommodated by an intrepid team of ingenious Austrian road builders who have created the perfect road for drivers and sightseers alike.

You'll have to pay a small toll to enter the Goldeck Panorama Road, but it's worth it. This is a smoothly paved highway rising very steeply up the side of the valley in a series of switchback hairpin bends. You'll find sections with a gradient as steep as 10 per cent as it climbs to 1,895m (6,217ft) above sea level in a breathtakingly short distance. Note that the road is open only in the summer months, weather permitting.

The road was designed because the views from the top are particularly brilliant. How good? Well, even locals take this road regularly just to sit at the top and gaze lovingly at the surrounding peaks with lakes, forests and farmland in the valleys between. There's a car park and a café with a sun terrace at the top. But that's not enough for the more energetic visitors; they take a 45-minute hike from here to the summit of the mountain. **SH**

The Maltatal

Carinthia, Austria

Start Gmünd
End Maltatal
Distance 29km (18 miles)
Type Scenic
Map goo.gl/jRsf3c

The Maltatal is a steep-sided valley that had nothing in it but the river after which it is named until the 1970s, when it was flooded following the construction of the 200-m- (656-ft) high Kölnbrein Dam. Removal of the earthworks required a service access road, which has since become one of the most scenic tourist routes in Europe. It is also one of the most diverse and satisfying routes to drive, with numerous challenging bends and six tunnels.

The road is open in daylight between the first week of May and the last week of October, and the best time to ride it is near the start of the season, when the sides of the valley are covered with Alpine flowers and punctuated by seasonal waterfalls fed by the snowmelt.

The journey begins at Gmünd, the birthplace of the Porsche motor company in central Austria, and climbs 1,450m (4,750ft) in 29km (18 miles), bringing you on to the top of the dam wall. Almost 2,000m (6,600ft) above sea level, the area around the dam has become a popular attraction, with a hotel and an exhibition centre. There are guided tours of the power plant, bungee jumping off the semi-circular dam wall and a horseshoe-shaped cantilever platform that sticks out over the abyss to create a skywalk. The turquoise waters of the reservoir below are used by Austria's Olympic rowers for altitude training. **JP**

Grosser Oscheniksee

Carinthia, Austria

Start Innerfragant
End Grosser Oscheniksee
Distance 10km (6.2 miles)
Type Adventure
Map goo.gl/MuESxr

Although this road trip takes less than half-hour to complete, it is still quite an adventure. It starts on a seemingly innocent country road leading through a pleasant wooded valley in the mid-Austrian region of Carinthia. However, when you turn off onto a small backroad after less than 1km (half a mile), everything changes.

The road rises into the mountains like an elevator through the trees. Over the course of 11.2km (7 miles), there is a gain of 1,429m (4,688ft), which is an average gradient of almost 12 per cent, and often more like 20 per cent. In addition, this gruelling stretch of road is stupidly narrow, has very few safety barriers and includes 40 hairpin bends. Don't even think about tackling the route between September and June, when snow may be present – it would be madness.

The road emerges from the tree line into a desolate and rocky mountain landscape. At the top, you can drive on to the dam of the Oscheniksee Reservoir at 72,394m (,854ft). The 360-degree panoramas will distract you from the thought of the brake-burning descent to come.

Once you have driven this route, one of the most severely ascending roads in the Alps, don't expect any congratulations. The ones who deserve real praise are those who regularly attempt the climb, not in motorized vehicles but on bicycles. **SH**

Grosser Speikkogel
Carinthia/Styria, Austria

Start Wolfsberg, Carinthia
End Deutschlandsberg, Styria
Distance 47km (29 miles)
Type Scenic
Map goo.gl/pFpL81

This short scenic road trip is an ideal introduction to the imposing Koralpe mountain range of southern Austria and the upper slopes of its highest peak, Grosser Speikkogel, 2,140m (7,021ft) above sea level.

Wolfsberg stands on the Lavant River, a tributary of the Drava. The nearby village of Priel was the site of Stalag XVIII-A, a notorious prisoner-of-war camp in World War II.

Leaving town in a northerly direction, the road swings east and passes through Frantschach-Sankt Gertraud. The next section of the L148 is mainly straight until a hairpin bend marks the beginning of a twisting and sharply undulating stretch of highway with plenty of parking areas where travellers can picnic or set off on foot to the peak.

Beyond Weinebene, the road leaves one Austrian province, Carinthia, and enters another, Styria. The village of Trahütten may seem unremarkable, but it was here that Austrian composer Alban Berg wrote the operas *Wozzeck* (1922) and *Lulu* (1935).

Deutschlandsberg has a medieval castle and long-established trade links with Slovenia, the frontier of which is only 10km (6 miles) to the south. The town did much to help that state of the former Yugoslavia to achieve independence in 1991, and thus avoid the long wars that blighted other parts of the region at the end of the 20th century. **JP**

❶ Low morning cloud covers the Lavant River valley below the main road.

Tragoess to Birkfeld
Styria, Austria

Start Tragoess
End Birkfeld
Distance 84km (52.2 miles)
Type Scenic
Map goo.gl/YoiqZN

This fast, winding mountain journey through the Austrian state of Styria is a favourite among motorbikers. It starts near the remote village of Tragoess, in the foothills of some big Alpine peaks and just to the south of the Grüner See (Green Lake), which is renowned for growing and shrinking with the seasons. In some autumns it disappears completely, and in some springs it is so full of melted snow that divers explore it to spot the submerged footpaths and benches.

Follow the smooth, quiet country road south through the forest-covered valley of the Laming River until it meets the Mürz, then continue along its banks to the bustling country town of Mürzhofen, from where a side road goes off through rolling farmland and woods.

After passing several sleepy rural villages and farmsteads, the road reaches the prosperous town of Fischbach, with its luxurious spa hotels sheltering under the 1,498-m- (4,195-ft) high Teufelstein Mountain. The views from the road around here are well worth stopping for.

A few miles farther on, you'll drop down into the pretty market town of Birkfeld, which is dominated by its huge church on a hill. In the woods above the town is its unlikely main attraction: a sombre set of gallows where criminals were publicly hanged until the end of the 17th century. **SH**

❶ A diver explores a path below the Grüner See, a seasonal body of water.

Neusiedler See Loop
Austria/Hungary

Start Rust, Burgenland, Austria
End Rust, Burgenland, Austria
Distance 126km (78 miles)
Type Scenic
Map goo.gl/6mD2sp

Straddling the border between Austria and Hungary, Lake Neusiedl – 36km (22 miles) long, 12km (7.5 miles) across at its widest point and nowhere more than 2m (6ft) deep – is a popular outdoor leisure resort for locals and, increasingly, foreign visitors. Austrians call it the 'Sea of the Viennese' because so many city dwellers go there for day trips.

The proposed itinerary here runs right around the lake, through both countries. As it's a circuit, you can start where you like. This trip starts in Rust, a pleasant historic Austrian town surrounded by vineyards, with a harbour on the lakeside, good restaurants and an unmissable *Buschenschank* (wine tavern).

The journey will take you around the attractive shores and give you plenty of chances to stop. Note that the landscape is pretty flat, so you can't always see the lake from the road.

Generally you'll find that the best beaches are on the eastern shore. The western side is covered with thick reed beds, which are perfect for ornithologists – more than 300 different species of bird breed here.

Because the lake is so shallow, it heats up very quickly in the 300 days of sunshine that it enjoys every year. So, along with windsurfing, camping, sailing, fishing and cycling, swimming is very popular here. **SH**

Port d'Envalira
Andorra

Start El Tarter
End El Pas de la Casa
Distance 33km (20.5 miles)
Type Adventure
Map goo.gl/rvmVlJ

There are some roads that you look at on a map and instantly think, 'I want to go there. I have to go there!' Many people regard Port d'Envalira in Andorra as a good example of this type. Technically, Port d'Envalira is not the actual name of this road but that of a mountain pass crossing the Pyrenees, but such details seem insignificant when you are busy at the steering wheel. In the route's final section, switchback follows switchback, bend follows bend, as you fight your way up to the border with France. It is an intricate piece of road that fills your sat-nav's tiny screen with little more than a spidery doodle.

On the plus side, there are sturdy guardrails throughout and the tarmace surface is runway-smooth, which is no surprise in view of the fact that this is Andorra, a tiny but wealthy principality tucked in between Spain and France. It is also the highest paved road in the Pyrenees, and the highest in Europe to stay open all year round, thus providing access to its popular ski areas.

At its highest point, Port d'Envalira is almost 2,400m (8,000ft) above sea level, and from the starting point of this trip the elevation gain is 1,400m (4,600ft). A road tunnel opened in 2002 takes away the heavy local traffic, leaving road trippers to enjoy a long, steady climb that has featured in the Tour de France. **JI**

Discover El Hierro
El Hierro, Spain

Start Valverde
End Valverde
Distance 127km (79 miles)
Type Scenic
Map goo.gl/tAkGsb

The boomerang-shaped island of El Hierro is the smallest and most southerly of the Canaries and a popular destination for nature lovers, hikers and scuba divers. The airport has several car rental companies vying for trade, and from there you can begin this recommended clockwise circuit. Rent the smallest runabout you can; when you hit the island's narrow coastal roads you'll be glad you weren't tempted by a cut-price limousine.

Keep the sea to your left, and you won't get lost – the island is only 269 sq km (104 square miles) in area. The spectacular highway passes the black volcanic beaches at Timijiraque, before climbing the tortuous backroad to Isora and the Biosphere Reserve Interpretation Centere where you can learn about El Hierro's designation as a UNESCO Geopark. Continue south to the colourful fishing port of Restinga. Along this section of the route, you'll pass purple laurels, thick pine forest and juniper groves, interspersed by lumpy lava fields laid down during a major eruption in 1793. The viewpoint at El Mirador de las Playas, a huge natural amphitheatre towering 1,500m (5,000ft) over the bay, is not to be missed.

Arguably, the best drivers' roads are the western stretches; a squiggle on your map announces a tortuous stretch that is followed by a loop back along the north shore to Valverde. **DIS**

Carretera al Roque de los Muchachos La Palma, Spain

Start Santa Cruz de la Palma
End Roque de Santa Domingo de Garafia
Distance 74km (46 miles)
Type Adventure
Map goo.gl/qIMz7q

La Palma – the fifth-largest island in the Canaries – is basically a pair of volcanoes, jutting out of the sea. The island is something of a hidden gem. Its lack of golden beaches has enabled it to retain some traditional charm, rather than, like some of its neighbours, succumb to high-rise hotels and timeshare developments.

This exciting road cuts through the island's central mountainous region, skirting the rim of the oldest volcano, the steep-sided 2,423-m- (7,949-ft) high Caldera Taburiente.

The route begins in the island's elegant capital, Santa Cruz de la Palma. Leaving its cobbled streets, you quickly gain elevation on a challenging, hairpin-packed climb into uninterrupted temperate cloud forest. Eventually, after a 90-minute climb, the road reaches the island's highest point, the Roque de los Muchachos, which has terrific views over the island. Here, too, is the Roque de los Muchachos Observatory, an impressive cluster of structures for star-gazing.

It is all downhill to the less-visited and wilder northwestern coast. Here, there are pretty villages such as Las Tricias, Don Pedro, El Castillo and Franceses, as well as the larger town of Santo Domingo de Garafia, a good spot for some well-deserved refreshment – perhaps some Luna de Awara goat cheese, washed down with wine. **DK**

TF-21 – Where the Earth Holds up the Sky
Tenerife, Spain

Start La Orotava
End Vilaflor
Distance 60km (37 miles)
Type Scenic
Map goo.gl/kTN8EH

The grand hillside town of La Orotava stands among the old colonial plantations of northern Tenerife. The island's most elegant town is the gateway to a spectacular road trip, either by car or scooter, along one of the most impressive roads in Europe.

This Spanish holiday island is a favourite for winter sun-seekers who flock to the south coast resorts. Many of them do not realize that their destination is built on the relic of a volcanic cone, with the peak of 13,718-m- (2.198-ft) high Mt Teide in the centere known in local folklore as 'where the earth holds up the sky'.

From La Orotava's lush valley, follow a winding road up into steep pine forests. Views back down over the town and coast are fabulous here, but there is more to come: the highway emerges from the forest into an extraordinary volcanic moonscape. Spot bright orange rock formations, lava trails and piles of dark basalt in the lifeless landscape that has been formed by eruptions over hundreds of thousands of years. Then loop around the base of the mountain where you can stop for a cable car ride almost to the top. Finally, follow the road winding back down to Vilaflor, and then on, if you like, to a completely different world of black-sand beaches, tourist bars and cafés at purpose-built resorts such as Playa de las Américas on the popular south coast. **SH**

❶ This might be mistaken for an airport runway, but it is in fact a part of this unusual road itinerary.

Masca to Santiago del Teide Tenerife, Spain

Start Masca
End Santiago del Teide
Distance 6km (3.7 miles)
Type Adventure
Map goo.gl/OrvPI1

The short, steep road from tiny Masca – in the view of many, Tenerife's loveliest village – to the town of Santiago del Teide is what they call 'two-lane narrow' – wide enough for two cars to pass, but not so wide that you won't instinctively place your foot over the brake when confronted by an oncoming vehicle. Concrete barriers line the route, so there's no need to worry about plunging over the vertiginous edges.

Well paved, with lovely old stone walls to guard against landslides, this drive is routinely rated as one of Europe's most exhilarating road trips. Thanks to the average 16 per cent gradient of the road, high-altitude vantage points are reached in no time all. As you gain height– 308m (1,010ft) in just 5km (3.2 miles – the views over the Atlantic Ocean leap out to greet you.

Keeping your eyes on the road when the scenery demands your immediate attention is the most difficult part of the drive. Fortunately, there are plenty of turnouts in which to stop and take a longer look. Contemplate the massive bulk of El Teide, the 3,718-m- (12,198-ft) high cone of a volcano (still active) whose eruption raised the island of Tenerife out of the sea. You are now driving along the volcano's lower western flank to reach Santiago del Teide, a thought that may lend a little frisson to the trip. **BDS**

TF-28 – The Forgotten Road Tenerife, Spain

Start San Cristóbal de La Laguna
End Playa de las Américas
Distance 103km (64 miles)
Type Adventure
Map goo.gl/fc4KpC

San Cristóbal de La Laguna is a UNESCO World Heritage Site contiguous with the city of Santa Cruz de Tenerife, the capital of the island and the joint capital (with Las Palmas) of the whole Canary Islands group.

The shortest and quickest way between this beautiful old town and the main holiday resorts in the south of the island is along the TF-1 coastal road, a smooth and comfortable highway that has plenty of heavy traffic and some excellent views over the Atlantic Ocean.

By contrast, the TF-28 that runs parallel to this main road for part of the way has very few trucks or buses (because it is so narrow and has so many twists and turns), and even better views, because it is built on much higher ground. Consequently the TF-28 is the route that will be preferred by adventurous road trippers; plenty of cyclists ride it, so car drivers will often be slowed down behind groups of super-fit pedallers.

The northern section of the route is wild and barren, and characterized by spectacular volcanic rock formations. Farther south, the density of holiday homes increases. A little way beyond Chayofa – the most attractive of these building developments, which is marketed, mainly to Britons and Germans, as 'the green garden city' – the road rejoins the TF-1 on the outskirts of Playa de las Américas. **SH**

Fast & Furious 6 – Tenerife Movie Tour
Tenerife, Spain

Start Adeje
End Punta de Teno
Distance 55km (34.2 miles)
Type Culture
Map goo.gl/2EEz5k

When it comes to blowing up cars on freeways, England's law enforcement officials have no sense of humour. This is why the makers of *Fast & Furious 6*, a stunt-packed action movie set in England, filmed the car chases on Tenerife, in the Canary Islands. Other locations were scouted, but the combination of gorgeous weather, overly generous tax credits and a government that allowed the makers to blow up pretty much what they liked made Tenerife the obvious choice.

From September to November 2012, the moviemakers crashed and detonated virtually everything in sight. Sections of highway were left blackened, including an unfinished section of the highway between Adeje and Guía de Isora in the island's southwest, used for the scene featuring a souped-up 70-ton Chieftain tank. The longest freeway in the archipelago, the TF-1 runs from the capital of Santa Cruz to Santiago del Teide.

However, it's the TF-445 from Buenavista del Norte to Punta de Teno, the island's most westerly point, that is the undisputed highlight of this road trip. The road was used for the opening chase scene between O'Conner's Nissan GT-R R35 and Dom's modified Dodge Challenger along a narrow coastal balcony road that threads its way through rock-cut tunnels above the crashing surf. Slow and Cautious are the watchwords here. **BDS**

❶ A rock-cut tunnel on the road to Punta de Teno: scenery like this greatly enhanced the movie.

Carretera GC-60 to Roque Nublo Gran Canaria, Spain

Start Maspalomas   **End** Roque Nublo   **Distance** 38km (23.6 miles)
Type Adventure   **Map** goo.gl/OHPYVm

Popular with masochistic cyclists, the GC-60 heads due north from the town of Maspalomas, famed for its sprawling sand dunes, up into the heart of this volcanic island that rose from the sea 10 million years ago. It's a relentless climb on crazed gray tarmac into the rocky, arid interior.

For those looking for a real challenge, the GC-602 branches off to the west just before Fataga, and offers a testing and tortuous alternative route for your return leg to Maspalomas. For those with a more relaxed approach, grab a coffee at Bar el Labrador and drink in the dramatic landscape.

Beyond here the first real greenery appears – pine trees that survive on high-altitude cloud vapour – and temperatures start to drop a little. Weaving along the sides of V-shaped valleys, between rock pinnacles, the GC-60 continues to climb towards San Bartolomé. Beyond here the road squeezes through a narrow gap between the rocks to the next valley, presenting a vista of jagged mountains specked with cacti and spiky shrubs.

In Ayacata a trio of bars are usually littered with cyclists refuelling themselves before the final push to Roque Nublo (Cloud Rock), an imposing remnant of the volcano's lava dome and arguably the finest panorama in the Canary Islands. **DIS**

❶ A fantastic view on a truly crazy drive near Fataga.

Pico de las Nieves Gran Canaria, Spain

Start La Pasadilla   **End** Cruz de Tejeda   **Distance** 23km (14.3 miles)
Type Scenic   **Map** goo.gl/PvnuuN

A day trip to Gran Canaria's highest peak is a popular excursion from the bustling resorts on the south and east coasts. There are a number of fantastic routes into the island's volcanic hinterland, but try the less-travelled GC-120, starting in La Pasadilla, to avoid the convoys of tourist coaches.

Hill climb competitions take place along a 7.1-km- (4.4-mile) section of this road. The Subida La Pasadilla is one of the longest and toughest climbs in Spain, a charge over smooth tarmac, through scrubby, sun-baked hillsides, with lengths of modern Armco above precipitous drops.

Merging with the GC-130, the road winds its way upwards past the tiny lake of Presa de Cuevas Blancas. A left turn onto the GC-134 takes you the short distance to the summit. It might be hard to believe in the parched summer months, but the mountain's name means 'Peak of the Snows', a reference to the snow that was once trapped in the human-made pits near here for making ice cream and for medical purposes.

A military radar installation shaped like a football dominates the mountaintop plateau. On clear days, the public viewing platform below the base of this structure offers wonderful panoramas over half the island. **DIS**

🢂 The dramatic contours of Gran Canaria.

Carretera GC-210 Gran Canaria, Spain

Start Los Cardones **End** El Majuelo **Distance** 35km (22 miles)
Type Adventure **Map** goo.gl/7Bszut

This route is essentially the twin of the notorious cliff-hugging traverse that collapsed into the sea in 2016. While that road featured sheer drops, highway GC-210 takes you steeply into the central mountainous region of the island. Several scenes from the action movie *Fast & Furious 6* (2013) were shot on this road. It is often called the loneliest road on the island, because it goes from pretty much nowhere to very much nowhere.

It does this very dangerously. The road climbs relentlessly for its whole length; it includes 32 hairpin bends and eventually passes through Artenara, the island's highest village, piled against a rocky peak at an altitude of more than 1,250m

(4,000ft) above sea level. If you are foolhardy enough to run the road the other way, make sure your brake pads are in good shape because you will be stamping on the stop pedal for an absurdly long period of time.

Avalanches and landslides are commonplace, so check before setting off that the route is open. The road is notoriously slippery when wet. Even if the weather looks good when you set off, it can change fast in this mountainous terrain; unexpected torrential downpours can turn this dangerous road into something unimaginably nasty. **DK**

❶ Many find the risky nature of the route an attraction.

Ruta de los Volcanes Lanzarote, Spain

Start Islote de Hilario   End Islote de Hilario   Distance 10km (6 miles)
Type Adventure   Map goo.gl/G3TGu9

The volcano park at Timanfaya is easily the number one tourist attraction of the Spanish island of Lanzarote. At least one million people a year visit the landscape of lava, craters and cones. Most of them are on guided bus tours, but the little road that loops through the park is a great drive if you have your own rental car. Start at the car park at Islote de Hilario, where the roads lead up from the coastal resorts. Ruta de los Volcanes is a 10-km (6-mile) circuit from here through the heart of what remains from a thunderous series of eruptions 300 years ago. The road was planned by the island's ubiquitous artist/figurehead César Manrique, who chose the best possible route through the craters for optimum views of this barren, alien terrain. You will see the cones of the volcanoes, craters, colourful sand, strange lava formations and piles of volcanic pebbles.

When you return to Islote de Hilario, it is worth popping into the restaurant. The chefs use the heat from a fissure in the earth's crust here to cook meat. Local guides pour water down cracks in the ground outside to demonstrate how it fountains back up like a hot geyser. They also love passing visitors a handful of sand to prove how stingingly hot it is. **SH**

❶ Looping through the volcanic landscape is the fun bit.

Picos de Europa Circuit
Asturias, Spain

Start Cangas de Onís
End Cangas de Onís
Distance 254km (158 miles)
Type Adventure
Map goo.gl/pn1lko

One of the advantages of Spain's Picos de Europa (Peaks of Europe) is that you can enjoy short bursts through selected highlights or do a grand tour, such as this circular route. If you are going for the whole shebang, start in the town of Cangas de Onís, not far from the major ferry port of Santander, and head to Beyos Gorge and the snaking River Sella. This is a picturesque drive through villages and farmland. Around you, snowcapped mountains soar more than 800m (half a mile) above the gorge.

If you are looking for adventure, there are plenty of bends and twists to test your driving skills. The route also crosses the valley floor over several bridges. It then climbs to Oseja de Sajambre, a remote village with only 300 inhabitants. From here, head to Panderruedas Pass, which sits 1,450m (just under a mile) above sea level, and then on to the spectacular pass of San Glorio, which is even higher.

The tortuous N-621 is a real drivers' road, weaving northeast through stunning forested mountains to the town of Ojedo. From here, you can continue on the N-621 for a scenic shortcut through the dramatic La Hermida Gorge. Or, if you are eager for yet more testing driving, take the extended loop through Sierra de Peña Sagra and the mountain village of Puentenansa, which will bring you back to the start point. JI

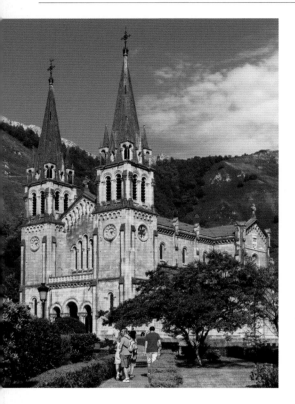

➊ The basilica at Covadonga, just off the route.
➔ The jagged peaks of the Picos de Europa.

Alto de l'Angliru Asturias, Spain

Start La Vega, Riosa   **End** Alto de l'Angliru   **Distance** 12.2km (7.6 miles)
Type Culture   **Map** goo.gl/th4FpO

Professional racing cyclists are a tough bunch, used to punishing training regimes, harsh conditions out on the road and fearsome climbs. But even in the world of road racing, the Alto de l'Angliru ranks as one of the most challenging courses. It runs for 12.2km (7.6 miles) in Asturias in northern Spain and is often used in the Vuelta a España race.

From La Vega, there's an elevation gain of around 1,200m (4,000ft) over the course of the route, with an average incline of nearly 10 per cent and an incredible 23.5 per cent as you near the top. The peak sits 1.5km (5,100ft) above sea level.

The punishment meted out by the climb has led some riders to refuse to tackle this stage. It goes without saying that it's an engine-straining challenge for cars and motorbikes, too. In fact, during one rain-soaked cycle race several support cars stalled on the climb and struggled for traction due to slogans painted on the tarmac by race fans. The surface may technically be 'sealed', but it's broken in places and rough overall.

The road itself is also very narrow and incredibly twisty; the run-off on either side is either unyielding rock or simply not there at all. At any time of year, snow tyres may be needed, along with a strong head for heights. JI

❶ Rounding a corner on the Alto de l'Angliru.

Desfiladero de La Hermida Cantabria, Spain

Start Panes   End Ojedo   Distance 27km (16.5 miles)
Type Adventure   Map goo.gl/XDHv7M

This astonishing route cuts north to south, through the dominant range of mountains in northern Spain known as the Picos de Europa. These 'peaks of Europe' are a national park: a wild wilderness characterized by deep valleys and jagged pinnacles of more than 2,600m (8,500ft) in height. On this road, the drama of the landscape is all about you as it follows the Deva River south from the sea towards its source above Ojedo. This landscape is part of the largest single lump of mountain limestone in Europe, and it is this geology that has allowed the river to cut a series of deep, near-vertical ravines. Everywhere you look, there are sharp-toothed mountains and precipitous drops. However, this is not some little-travelled mountain road. It is the N-621, a busy national route carrying a considerable amount of commercial traffic. At places, the route is extremely narrow and, unfortunately, passing on a blind bend is not completely unknown. This has given this stretch of road a reputation as one of the most dangerous in Europe. There is simply nowhere to go if anything unexpected should happen: the choice is either up a vertical cliff or through the barrier and into the ravine. Towards the end of the trip, the 10th-century Mozarabic church of Santa María de Lebeña is well worth a look. **DK**

❶ The Deva River gorge.

Basque Country Coastal Road Basque Country, Spain

Start Zumaia   **End** Zarautz   **Distance** 12km (7.5 miles)
Type Scenic   **Map** goo.gl/x2Bpl1

This drive along the N-634 road between the seaside villages of Zumaia and Zarautz promises to be a short but interesting trip along the rugged coast of the Basque Country. On one side, there are spectacular views of the cliffs down to the sea, and on the other vineyards scattered across rolling hills. Not only will drivers get to look out at the Bay of Biscay, this is a road that will test motoring skills, taking in 22 turns along the way. The surface is good, but this is a two-lane rural road so drivers also need to be aware of cyclists and slow-moving trucks lingering behind blind bends. However, there are plenty of opportunities to stop en route. Some of the road has a pavement along the sea wall; this is especially popular among hikers who are travelling along the Camino del Norte northern route of the Camino de Santiago pilgrimage trail to Santiago de Compostela.

If time is not an issue, the best place to stop is at Getaría, which has a small harbour. Otherwise, keep going until Zarautz, which has a sandy beach that is the longest in the Basque Country. If your driving is over for the day, take the opportunity to try the local white wine, Txakolí. Slightly sparkling, and very dry, it is the perfect companion for a sunny day lazing by the sea. **CK**

❶ The beach at Zarautz is great for surfing.

Basque Circuit Spain/France

Start Bilbao, Spain   **End** Biarritz, France   **Distance** 303km (188 miles)
Type Scenic   **Map** goo.gl/Og4gtV

It is considered one of the great road trips of Europe, but there is no definitive route for the Basque Circuit. You simply make a rough loop south from Bilbao through the Pyrenees and up to Biarritz. The route can be as fast or as slow as you like, depending on the roads you follow. For example, the toll road will whisk you south from Bilbao to Vitoria-Gasteiz on a pretty route through the mountains. It is not as memorable, however, as the smaller BI-623, which will take you three times as long as it wiggles through a tiny mountain pass. And there is also the scenic route via Durango.

Whichever journey you take, Vitoria-Gasteiz is an undiscovered gem: a classic grand Spanish city in the hills with a medieval heart and broad, tree-lined boulevards. When heading east from here to the mountain city of Pamplona, you have a similar choice of freeways, rural highways or winding mountain roads through the Sierra de Urbasa. After that, cross the Pyrenees via the old border town of Roncesvalles on a spectacular twisting road that will satisfy all except the most impatient traveller. Finally, wind down from the mountains towards the Bay of Biscay and the elegant beach resort of Biarritz, where the huge waves pound on a long sandy stretch in front of a period promenade. **SH**

❶ An historic cliff-top villa on the rocky coast of Biarritz.

Along the Atlantic Coast Basque Country, Spain

Start San Sebastián, Guipúzcoa   **End** Vigo, Pontevedra   **Distance** 810km (503 miles)
Type Culture   **Map** goo.gl/A86jna

This is a marathon road trip across the top of Spain, taking in the Bay of Biscay coast and heading around the corner to face the Atlantic. It's a chance to explore the quieter, greener side of Spain, well away from the tourist-jammed Costas.

Start your Iberian adventure close to the French border in the classy resort of San Sebastián, with its long, sandy beach and atmospheric old quarter. Head west to the busy port city of Bilbao to see the modern Guggenheim Museum and continue on to the dramatic bay at Santander to visit the beaches and old town.

Farther west you'll cross into the old kingdom of Asturias, a distinctive region where the green mountains of the Picos de Europa sweep down to the sea. Explore the fascinating coastal towns of Llanes, Ribadesella and Gijon, and enjoy the local ice cream, seafood and cider.

In the wild Celtic province of Galicia, big estuaries punctuate a rugged rocky coastline. It's essential to see the ancient lighthouse and elegant harbour at A Coruña and Santiago de Compostela's cathedral, a destination for pilgrims for over a thousand years.

Finish in the grand old port of Vigo. From there, take a short boat trip to the Islas Cies, whose beaches have been voted the best in Europe. **SH**

❶ The sandy, crescent-shaped bay of San Sebastián.

Rioja Balcony Road Basque Country, Spain

Start Vitoria-Gasteiz **End** Rioja Alavesa **Distance** 51km (31.7 miles)
Type Culture **Map** goo.gl/NOvrHd

The Rioja region of northern Spain is best known for its bold red wines, but there are also some great drives, the finest of which is along this road, which ascends to the top of the Puerto de Herrera mountain pass at 1,000m (3,300ft).

From the town of Vitoria-Gasteiz, head south on the A-2124, a main road through open farmland and vineyards. There's only one lane in each direction but it's swift and flat, with the odd kink to liven things up; the most interesting stuff comes as you go deeper into the Basque region. You begin to climb into the mountains, but the route here is more a succession of ascents and descents with switchbacks and tight turns.

There are barriers to protect you from the drop on one side, but fortunately little to stop you from enjoying the view across the Ebro River valley to the Sierra de la Demanda mountains, a patchwork of vineyards, wheat fields and pretty little villages awaiting your discovery. There are plenty of observation points, so there's no need to stop at the side of the rather narrow road.

On to journey's end at Rioja Alavesa, there to catch your breath before turning around and heading back to base where, almost certainly, a nice glass of red wine awaits. JI

❶ The Ebro River valley near Logroño.

Fiscal to Escalona
Aragon/Castile-La Mancha, Spain

Start Fiscal, Aragon
End Escalona, Castile-La Mancha
Distance 46km (28.6 miles)
Type Scenic
Map goo.gl/S167Df

The province of Huesca in northeastern Spain nestles below the Pyrenees, where every slice of tarmac takes visitors through impressive mountain scenery. This trip, though, is a little special and one of the most delightful mountain drives in Spain. It is not the longest road trip, but, given the nature of the road in some places, drivers and riders might regard this as a blessing in disguise.

The first part of the route from Fiscal is on a well-surfaced main road as it follows the Río Ara up towards its source in the mountains. On one side are tree-lined mountain slopes, on the other wooded valleys. In the mountain town of Sarvisé, the route leaves the main road. Although the views remain equally spectacular, the road narrows and within a few minutes you will be driving slowly around 90-degree bends, followed by others that twist back around a full 360 degrees as they climb. In some places, there are steep ascents, in others barely space for two cars to get past one another, although this is an exhilarating adventure rather than a white-knuckle drive. The landscape opens out so that you have views over several valleys towards distant mountains, and eventually, 73 bends later, you descend into the smart mountain village of Escalona, a delightful journey's end. **MG**

○ The picturesque Monte Perdido National Park.

Pyrenees Heights – Vielha to Aigüestortes National Park
Catalonia, Spain

Start Vielha
End Espot
Distance 55km (34 miles)
Type Scenic
Map goo.gl/QdJIH6

High in the Pyrenees mountains on the Spanish side of the border with France, you'll find this wonderful winding road trip.

It connects the remote town of Vielha with an old mountain village called Espot. You'll get there by crossing the Port de la Bonaigua pass on the C28 road along the Aran and Aneu Valleys. This is a paved, twisting mountain road that is among Spain's highest. It reaches 2,072m (6,798ft) at its summit. It is often impassable in winter.

You'll find Spain's most popular ski resort, Baqueira-Beret, near the summit of the pass. It offers 146km (91 miles) of marked ski trails and 35 ski lifts. In the summer it's also popular for hunting, fishing, hiking and kayaking.

Whether you are driving or motorbiking, this is a good road for a day trip, combining great mountain vistas with challenging switchbacks and steep gradients. You'll see pine forests, high mountain lakes, waterfalls and long, deep valleys as you rev your way up to the pass and pick your way down the other side.

The route ends up at Espot in the Aigüestortes National Park. You'll discover how this remote farming community is gradually embracing tourism and winter sports. So in the summer you'll see cattle grazing on grass outside the village; in winter the fields will be ski runs. **SH**

❶ This stream in the Aran Valley is a headwater of the Garonne, one of the great rivers of France.

La Ruta Minera
Catalonia, Spain

Start Berga
End Berga
Distance 166km (103 miles)
Type Scenic
Map goo.gl/Gb8Zbq

This is a route that is quite well known within the cycling fraternity as a popular time trialists' circuit. It is high in the Pyrenees, around 100km (60 miles) north of Barcelona. Mountain cyclists, of course, are prepared for a lot more pain than the average pedalpusher, so for most visitors it is advisable to regard this road trip as a scenic journey to be made by motorized transport. It certainly involves a spectacular amount of ups and downs, with seven peaks of more than 1,000m (3,280ft) and a combined ascent of 14,150m (3,615ft).

Along La Ruta Minera, be prepared for plenty of arm-twirling corners and rapid gear changes. The road itself winds in a circuit through attractive pine forests on good-quality smooth road surfaces beneath towering rocky faces and distant peaks. It also offers the opportunity to stop and explore hilltop villages, wooded gorges, sparkling lakes and high mountain passes. The area around Berga was once renowned for its coal-mining industry; today it is a little-visited mountain area with quiet roads. A few abandoned mine workings and visitor centres hint at the old industrial heritage. However, the highlight of the trip is Coll de Pradell, which has a very steep approach of 23 per cent gradient. As you enjoy the far-reaching views, having revved your way to the top, you will be glad that you made the trip by car. SH

East Pyrenees Scenic Drive
Catalonia, Spain

Start Ribes de Freser
End Puigcerdà
Distance 47km (29 miles)
Type Scenic
Map goo.gl/RNE4lr

The road from Barcelona up to the French border at Puigcerda is enduringly popular with bikers looking for the ultimate ride through the Pyrenees. It's a good route for car drivers, too, as Jeremy Clarkson discovered during his time as one of the hosts of BBC TV's *Top Gear*: at the end of his road trip through the mountains, he promptly declared that the route was among his all-time favourites.

This route is the final and best section of the journey, as the N260 winds up from Ribes de Freser in a sequence of classic mountain twists and turns.

This is a good-quality road with a proper tarmac surface and good visibility, too, even with severe bends and rocky cliffs on one side of the road for almost its whole length. It's certainly helpful to know whether there are sheep, cattle or horses on the road ahead, which there often are along these remote rural stretches.

Look out for the intriguing road sign just after the start that warns of 'bends for the next 45 km'. On the way up, you climb through the Col de Toses mountain pass where you'll find a handy café to stop for a while to get your breath back. The views from this summit are fabulous.

Want some more action? The roads descending on the French side of the Pyrenees are pretty good, too. Try the N116 to Prades or the little D618 to Mont-Louis. SH

The Road of a Thousand Bends

Catalonia, Spain

Start Sant Feliu de Guixols
End Tossa de Mar
Distance 23km (14 miles)
Type Scenic
Map goo.gl/zHHRCc

Think the Costa Brava is nothing but an over-developed stretch of family beach resorts? Think again. This little stretch of the GI-682 between two of the main resorts on the Costa is nicknamed 'The Road of a Thousand Bends' by locals.

Sant Feliu and Tossa de Mar are internationally famous modern resorts that are often excessively crowded, but the little scenic road along the cliff tops that links them is a taste of this part of northeast Spain before the Costas. It's undeveloped, wild and beautifully raw.

The GI-682 winds along the mountainous cliffs with the sparkling Mediterranean far below. You'll lose count of the number of hairpin bends, and there are few chances to get out of low gear. It's hard to look at the coastal views and negotiate the curves and gradients simultaneously, so take photo stops regularly.

The sheer drops are well guarded by safety barriers, but it's still a challenging section of road. On Sunday mornings you'll find plenty of local bikers testing themselves along the GI-682. At other times, you'll probably have the road to yourself.

If you don't fancy it, there's a safer, easier inland route that is half as long again. Without all those bends, you may even do the journey quicker. But you will likely enjoy the prettier, and bendier, coastal road trip a lot more. **SH**

❶ There's a fast modern highway along the Costa Brava, but who needs it when there's this road, too?

La Carretera del Vi—The Wine Road Catalonia, Spain

Start Sant Marti Sarroca
End Sitges
Distance 40km (24.9 miles)
Type Culture
Info goo.gl/9h7BB8

La Carretera del Vi, Spain's first official 'wine road', began as an initiative by 12 local wine producers who wanted to establish a route that linked not only their wineries but also various points of historical and cultural interest. It begins at the medieval Castillo de Sant Marti Sarroca and its adjacent Romanesque–Norman church, then heads southeast towards the coastal town of Sitges. You can make as many or as few stops as you like on this well-surfaced highway, following your nose along local roads not so much for the thrill of the drive, but more for the love of the grape.

Wineries include: Pares Balta, family-owned since 1790, with wines of 'personality' made from vines grown in their organic and biodynamic soils; and Colet, family-owned for centuries and specializing in Xarel-lo, wine made from white-skinned grapes, a Catalonian specialty. At Bodegas Torre del Veguer, the vines surround a 14th-century country estate that houses original artworks by the Surrealist painter Salvador Dalí, a close friend of this wine-making family. The wines at Finca Viladellops in the town of Viladellops exhibit the characteristics of its chalky limestone soil, with ingredients such as iodine and gypsum, as well as thyme, rosemary and fennel. Distinctive wines that speak with a Catalonian tongue, growing along a distinctive Catalonian road. **BDS**

Benidorm to Guadalest Valencia, Spain

Start Benidorm
End Guadalest
Distance 23km (14 miles)
Type Scenic
Map goo.gl/2HRrze

Benidorm grew from a small fishing village in the 1960s into one of the biggest holiday resorts in Europe. At one stage it was the single most popular attraction for British holidaymakers, and still boasts the largest number of skyscrapers per head of population in the world, one of which is the tallest hotel in Europe.

So why would you pick this as the starting point for one of the world's great drives? Start cruising north along the CV-70 from the busy, modern, city centre and you'll soon find out. You'll cross under the E-15 highway in a few minutes and already you'll be in semi-desert landscapes with mountains looming up in front.

After the village of Polop, the road starts rising through a series of gentle hairpin bends. The gradual gradients do nothing to deter the scores of tour buses that head this way carrying the more adventurous of Benidorm's visitors.

You'll pass whitewashed, terra-cotta-roofed Alicante farms with terraced groves of olives. Finally climb up into Guadalest to find what has become another major tourist attraction. Excuse the gift shops and cafés, because it's certainly worth exploring the old village and castle perched on steep crags. The views of neighbouring mountains and the reservoir below will soon make you forget all about Benidorm's tower blocks. **SH**

Puerto de Velefique Andalusia, Spain

Start Camino de Bacares a Tahal   **End** Velefique   **Distance** 12km (7.5 miles)
Type Scenic   **Map** goo.gl/wfhFSg

This convoluted mountain road climbs through the dry slopes of the jagged Sierra de los Filabres, through the Velefique Pass, and down to the village of Velefique itself. In order to reach the Pass of Velefique, at 1,820m (5,971ft), it is necessary to negotiate a dramatic series of hairpin bends slicing up through the slopes. On the other side of the pass, there are more severe bends descending to the village. It is, however, a simple route: all you do is follow the smooth, tarmac AL-3102 road from its junction with the Camino de Bacares a Tahal. There is little traffic and the road is in excellent condition.

The scenery is a dry landscape with bare rocks dotted with prickly pears and clumps of yellow grass. It is often very hot and hazy here. The highlights are distant views across the mountain wilderness, vineyards and desert plain of Tabernas beyond. Look out for wildlife such as wild boar and ibex here, too; in the summer, local hunters venture out in the peaks trying to track them down.

The village of Velefique was an important retreat in Moorish times, when it was considered a remote hideaway for poets and religious extremists. Thanks to the road, it is not so remote any more, and if you explore the area you will see that many of the old homes date from this period. **SH**

❶ Perfect for cyclists, there is little traffic on the pass.

Cabo de Gata-Níjar National Park Andalusia, Spain

Start Agua Amarga   End San Miguel de Cabo de Gata   Distance 61km (38 miles)
Type Scenic   Map goo.gl/fVB6am

Almería's Mediterranean coastline remains some of the most unspoiled in Spain, and this stretch in the National Park is particularly lovely. The route begins in Agua Amarga, a charming beach-front village with a few restaurants directly overlooking the water. From there, it twists inland for a stretch before regaining the coast. Pass Las Negras and La Isleta del Moro (both delightful fishing villages) to San José. Despite its marina and newer apartments, this is still very laid back, and a great place to overnight before the highlight of the trip: the road between San José and San Miguel de Cabo de Gata.

Note that the road quality is poor and access may be restricted during the summer months unless you are up very early. It is worth the effort, though, because the beach at Mónsul is one of the most beautiful in Spain. This is partly because there is no human intervention at all – not even a café – but also because of the huge slug of volcanic lava that once flowed across part of the beach and solidified into strange shapes, thereby making a great backdrop for Harrison Ford in *Indiana Jones and the Last Crusade* (1989). Beyond Mónsul, the road clings to the cliffs to reach the point of the cape and the lighthouse, before dropping down to an area of salt flats and journey's end at San Miguel. DK

❶ The road with Cabo de Gata in the distance.

Puerto de las Palomas
Andalusia, Spain

Start Grazalema
End Zahara de la Sierra
Distance 16km (10 miles)
Type Adventure
Map goo.gl/Ohzw9N

This is a road trip dedicated to those who mistakenly believe that Spain's southern Andalusia region is nothing but golf resorts, nightlife and all-inclusive holiday clubs. Just inland from the coast, there is an abundance of wild, awe-inspiring mountain scenery, and this road trip runs right through the middle of it.

Puerto de las Palomas (Dove Pass) leads through Sierra de Grazalema Natural Park, a UNESCO Biosphere Reserve, high over a rugged pass with long views to the north and south. It is a very narrow, steep and winding road. The section close to Zahara de la Sierra is a nonstop series of hairpin bends with unguarded, steep, roadside drops. It is somehow appropriate that the highlights of the local wildlife are the vultures that you may spot circling overhead. The route sets off from the village of Grazalema, surrounded by the foothills of the mountains. It is a sleepy, dusty and remote spot that is worth exploring for its taste of old rural Spain. The unlikely tourist highlight is a Museum of Cloaks.

On the approach to Zahara, you will realize why it is better to travel from south to north: the views of this whitewashed village clinging to a rocky pinnacle are sensational. The quaint village itself is one of the sights of southern Spain and well worth a visit to relax at one of the cafés shaded by orange trees in the tiny village square. **SH**

❶ Zahara de la Sierra is one of the *pueblos blancos* (white towns) of Andalusia.

Pico del Veleta
Andalusia, Spain

Start Granada
End Pico del Veleta
Distance 45km (28 miles)
Type Adventure
Map goo.gl/zMp4rq

For adventurous cyclists, an ascent of this mountain, on the highest paved road in Europe, is an essential bucket-list challenge. On any given weekend before the snows start falling, its slopes are littered with panting Lycra-clad masochists, left gasping and shivering at the roadsides with a combination of exhaustion and oxygen starvation as they approach its summit at 3,384m (11,102ft) in temperatures that can be as much as 20°C (36°F) lower than at sea level. On one cycling website's list of the world's hardest climbs, Veleta was ranked number 16, just behind a mountain pass in the Himalayas. Not that this should bother automotive adventurers too much, but if you are renting a car for this road trip, rent something with plenty of muscle: budget vehicles just won't cut it.

Veleta translates as 'weather vane', a nod to the mountain's odd-shaped peak, which is the second-highest in the Sierra Nevada. Its ski station access road stops just a short distance from the summit – it is not open to general traffic, but it still merits its place in the record books. As you might expect, guardrails here are sparse and hairpin bends are numerous. Also, the road surface deteriorates rapidly with altitude; it is so rutted and broken in the last kilometre that cyclists often carry their fragile race bikes up the final stretch. Perhaps a rental car is a good idea for this one. **DIS**

Ruta de la Plata
Andalusia/Asturias, Spain

Start Seville, Andalusia
End Gijón, Asturias
Distance 861km (535 miles)
Type Culture
Map goo.gl/17JLwy

Even as far back as the Bronze Age, the Guadalquivir River in southern Spain – easily navigable inland as far as Seville – was a crucial gateway to trade for the Iberian Peninsula. And when the Romans arrived, their ambitious infrastructure building program upgraded the existing transport links and created the Ruta de la Plata (Silver Route) – the ancient overland trade route to Spain's northern coast, which for centuries was an important path for military, commercial and religious communication.

Today the Ruta de la Plata has largely lost this significance, but it still makes a great trip through the much less tourist-travelled western regions of Spain. If time is short, the E-803 expressway can help. You will still see the scenery, but will miss out on much of the history. It is far better to meander, sticking to the old roads and taking time to explore the magnificent historic centres of Mérida, Cáceres, Salamanca and Astorga. Each of these cities was originally a staging post along the ancient route, and each today is steeped in history with old fortifications and grand cathedrals. Of particular note are: the Roman antiquities in Mérida, Rome's former Iberian capital; the Gothic and Renaissance architecture at Cáceres; the ancient university at Salamanca; the walled city of Zamora, and the Romanesque and Gothic architectural gems at both Astorga and León. **DK**

The Best of Andalusia
Andalusia, Spain

Start Malaga
End Malaga
Distance 748km (465 miles)
Type Culture
Map goo.gl/AhtRcR

This road trip has everything: ancient sites, grand arid scenery, terrific regional food and the characteristic music of the region – flamenco. This is all about the legacy left by the Moors, who came from North Africa and conquered the region of Andalusia beginning in 711. Their rule continued until the 15th century.

There is almost too much to see: the hilltop *pueblo blanco* (white town) of Ronda, with its handsome bullring and spectacular bridge over the gorge that famously separates the two halves of the community; Seville, with its 16th-century Gothic cathedral together with the surviving Islamic minaret, the Giralda, and also the Alcázar, a 14th-century Moorish palace; Córdoba, with its unique Mesquita – a huge mosque complex with a medieval Christian cathedral dropped into its centre. And, finally, the Alhambra in Granada – the extraordinary 14th-century Moorish palace and gardens.

As well as all this, the road itself is spectacular. The route winds into the hills towards Ronda and on to Seville. Even though much of the trip from then on is taken on major highways, the dusty semi-desert scenery remains beautiful and unforgettable. To conclude the route takes in a short section of Mediterranean coast, including Almuñécar, with its appealing old town. **DK**

Discover Gibraltar
Gibraltar

Start Winston Churchill Avenue
End North Mole Road
Distance 18km (11 miles)
Type Culture
Map goo.gl/pv1oTJ

The tiny British territory of Gibraltar, at the southern tip of Spain, covers only 6.7 sq km (2.6 square miles). This road trip through its heart will last approximately two hours, during which time it will take in winding streets, spectacular viewpoints and interesting historical landmarks.

This route starts from the Spanish border post on Winston Churchill Avenue, after which you have the unique experience of driving across the main runway of the international airport to reach the rest of the town. You'll loop around the east of the Rock on the impressive road that clings to the cliffs, and through a tunnel to emerge at Europa Point at the southern end of Gibraltar, where you'll find a lighthouse and the mosque of the local Muslim community. Look out for views of North Africa on the horizon.

You'll turn back towards the tower blocks of the main part of the town on the west of the Rock. Take the steep twisting road up to the summit at 426m (1,398ft). Amid old fortifications and artillery, it's a great spot to stop for the views and the resident monkeys. You can also visit old military tunnels here that once formed bombproof shelters and ammunition stores.

Other Gibraltar highlights include the Moorish castle, the cosmopolitan harbourside cafés and the impressive array of shops. **SH**

Discover Formentera
Formentera, Spain

Start La Savina
End Far de la Mola
Distance 23km (14.3 miles)
Type Culture
Map goo.gl/GOEhfi

At first sight, the smallest of Spain's Balearic Islands may seem an odd choice for a road trip. The tiny Mediterranean outcrop is, after all, only 19km (12 miles) long and 6km (4 miles) across at its widest point. In places you could walk from one side of the island to the other in a few minutes. But this sunny, unspoiled beach paradise has an excellent road system, and it would be negligent to make no mention of it in the present volume.

The only way to get to Formentera is by boat from Ibiza. You can take a car over on a ferry, or go on foot and rent a car or bike when you arrive.

The roads are quiet, of course, like the island. And that's part of the joy as you cruise around the flat, sandy landscape dotted with palm trees and beaches. The island is so small that you can see the sea from any part of it. The population is small, too, and that creates a relaxed vibe – which may be why Formenterans have the longest life expectancy in Spain.

The main routes are smoothly paved, but the smaller country roads are rougher and less forgiving. Nevertheless, you should be able to have a good adventure whether you're using a four-wheel-drive or a moped. The proposed itinerary is a simple route down to the magnificent lighthouse Far de la Mola, but go wherever you want. On Formentera it's hard to get lost. **SH**

ⓘ Formentera is renowned for its beaches, and this one at Iletas is widely regarded as the finest of them all.

Carretera de Sa Calobra Majorca, Spain

Start Escorca
End Port de Sa Calobra
Distance 24km (14.9 miles)
Type Scenic
Map goo.gl/3lM89Q

Large swathes of Majorca do not conform to the popular image of a cheap holiday resort. These areas, mostly along the north coast of the island, are wild, sparsely inhabited places, dramatic and rocky, with precipitous drops to perfect blue seas. It is here that you will find the narrow route Carretera de Sa Calobra. Designed in 1932 by Italian engineer Antonio Paretti, this is Majorca's most famous road. Two sections are particularly notable. One is the Nus de Sa Calobra ('necktie') – a curve of more than three-quarters of a circle, so that the road turns continuously, going under itself as it descends from the high Serra de Tramuntana mountain range to the Mediterranean coast. The other is a short but extremely pinched cleft that has been cut through the rock and is almost, but not quite, a tunnel. Because the route was constructed entirely by hand, the road snakes around and between the contours of the mountains. The panoramas, looking down on its twisty route with views out to the sea beyond, are wonderful.

At Sa Calobra there is a popular short walk through tunnels to a beach on a freshwater lake and a spectacular narrow gorge, the Torrent de Pareis. It can get quite busy in high season, so if you are looking for quiet, take the left fork near the end to Cala Tuent where there is a medieval church, a tranquil cove and an attractive restaurant. **DK**

Carretera Ma-1131 Majorca, Spain

Start Valldemossa
End Port de Valldemossa
Distance 7km (4.3 miles)
Type Adventure
Map goo.gl/4ngW8G

At first glance, a road trip on the Ma-1131 doesn't sound too promising. But it might pique your interest to know that in some tourist literature it is also referred to as the 'world's most wiggly road . . . to almost nearly nowhere'. Buckle up road trippers, it's going to be a bumpy ride.

In addition to being a bit peculiar, the road is even today, rather dangerous: it is one of the narrowest mountain roads in Europe and lacks such new-fangled accoutrements as safety barriers in many sections. The route includes nine hairpin bends, some of which are extraordinarily tight. Buses, if their drivers are foolhardy enough to attempt this trip – and, almost unbelievably, a few are – have to take turns to get around each of them. In a car, there is often no room to pass any type of vehicle, and precious few passing places.

On the steep descent, there are fabulous views out to sea. Every so often, there are also glimpses of the destination – the relatively tourist-free Port de Valldemossa – and it appears an unfeasibly long way down: a preview of the gruelling test of your car's brakes that is yet to come. This is not a road to drive angrily. Calm is needed. Perhaps a handy tip to help you relax might be to listen to one of Chopin's *Preludes*, which he finished while holed up in the nearby monastery of Valldemossa – the museum is a must-see for music lovers. **DK**

Road to Cap de Formentor Lighthouse
Majorca, Spain

Start Port de Pollença
End Cap Formentor
Distance 18km (11.2 miles)
Type Adventure
Map goo.gl/xj2FsN

Majorca's northeastern coast is a wild and unforgiving place, a brutal termination of the Tramuntana mountain range with a series of limestone cliffs jutting sharply out into the Mediterranean. It is great for views and even better for driving. The road trip begins in the attractive inland town of Pollença and quickly becomes a test of motoring skill. It is one of two famous roads engineered in the 1930s by the Italian Antonio Paretti (the other is Sa Calobra). The route was hand-cut to follow the contours, and the result is an exceptional drive.

After 1.6km (a mile or so), when the journey reaches the northern coast, make a stop at the parking lot adjacent to Mirador Es Colomer, easily the most spectacular viewing point on the island. After that, the road winds and twists all the way to the end of the peninsula at Cap de Formentor. This is a singularly barren headland, with an imposing lighthouse and, depending on the weather, fine views as far as the neighbouring island of Menorca. On the return leg, stop for refreshments at Playa de Formentor, where the grand Formentor Hotel is an old-school oasis of luxury with terraced formal gardens leading down to a crescent bay. In the 1950s this was a notable retreat for the rich and famous, and today it can serve you some of the best cocktails in Europe. **DK**

❶ The final approach to the lighthouse: wherever the climb was too steep, Paretti added a bend.

Pico do Arieiro Madeira, Portugal

Start Funchal **End** Pico do Arieiro **Distance** 19km (12 miles)
Type Scenic **Map** goo.gl/pwPzre

The balmy, humid Portuguese holiday island of Madeira stands in the Atlantic, 1,000km (560 miles) southwest of mainland Europe. It has a lush, damp landscape with jagged volcanic peaks in the centre. Time this road trip right and you will travel from sea level, up through the clouds, to emerge into a heavenly world of cotton-wool panoramas punctured by occasional rocky peaks. Time it wrong and you will see a lot of drizzly clouds.

Pico do Arieiro is Madeira's third-highest mountain and, unusually, there is a good road to the summit. Start in the capital, Funchal, and take the steep twisting road to the quaint village of Monte. Keep climbing through overhanging forest until you break out of the trees where, if the weather is good, the dramatic 360-degree views will have you wondering which way to look. It is one of the most popular outings on the island, so avoid the crowds by doing the route before or after the tour buses. If there is snow at the summitcar park, it is traditional to drive back down into the sunshine with a small snowman on your bonnet. One tip: don't make the common mistake of setting off in summer clothing. It may be perfect for hanging out at sea level, but 1,818m (5,965ft) up in the sky you will be shuddering with cold. **SH**

❶ Pico do Arieiro from the road to its summit.

ER101 Coast Road Madeira, Portugal

Start Funchal   End Funchal   Distance 185km (115 miles)
Type Adventure   Info goo.gl/VocXql

Madeira is perhaps more noted for its hiking routes and subtropical botanical gardens than for its driving possibilities. That's a pity, because this old route – the Antigo Traçado – is terrific. It's a complete and rather excellently squiggly coastal circuit – keep driving and eventually you will end up back where you began. If you are planning to run the whole route, then you must go round it anticlockwise. One of the best sections of the original coast road – the ER101 – in the northeast has now been bypassed. You will want to still follow the old road – indeed, this section draws tourists for its cliff-hugging twistiness – but it is now drivable only in this one direction.

There are numerous highlights en route. At the start, the cable car to Monte from the capital Funchal; to the east, the Caniçal Peninsula, a wild and windy volcanic headland with several fine viewing points. Ribeira de Janela, in the north, is an attractive seaside village surrounded by vineyards. Nearby, at Porto Moniz, there are several natural saltwater bathing pools. From Ponta di Parco – the westernmost point – there are superb clifftop views from near the lighthouse. When you stop for lunch, you may want to try the local delicacies of grilled limpets and rich honey cake. DK

➊ The road near Seixtal, to the east of Porto Moniz.

Peso da Régua to Pinhão
Porto, Portugal

Start Peso da Régua
End Pinhão
Distance 28km (17.5 miles)
Type Scenic
Map goo.gl/uSROGj

In 2015 this short stretch of road running through Portugal's wine region in the north of the country was voted the best driving road in the world in an online survey, beating off stiff competition from the likes of California's Pacific Coastal Highway, Stelvio Pass in northern Italy and the Amalfi Coast Road in Italy's Campania region.

Running for a tortuous 28.2km (17.5 miles) through the Douro Valley, itself a UNESCO World Heritage Site, Estrada Nacional 222 weaves around 93 corners cut into the schist hillsides, with farmland and terraced vineyards rising above it like the many layers on a wedding cake. This is a proper drivers' road that just begs to be driven; choose your transport carefully to extract maximum satisfaction. The views along the way are truly captivating, with the valley floor stretching down to the broad Douro River. But the land is more than just pretty – it is farmed and maintained by proud local families who have been here for centuries.

The road trip ends in the sleepy town of Pinhão, home to Porto wine producers and pretty blue-tiled civic buildings. To really enjoy the charms of this spectacular region, it is best to slow down, give your motorbike or car a well-earned rest and join one of the many guided wine tours that head out from here. JI

❶ Vineyards are plentiful along the riverbank.
● The scenic route winds its way alongside the Douro River.

Estremoz to Évora to Sines Alentejo, Portugal

Start Estremoz **End** Sines **Distance** 182km (113 miles)
Type Culture **Map** goo.gl/plkdIJ

Here's a chance to take a trip through the timeless plains of Portugal's Alentejo region. This route starts at the pretty hilltop town of Estremoz. Within the 13th-century ramparts, the town is full of grand old whitewashed houses topped with terracotta roofs. Estremoz is famous for its marble quarries, so expect to see that stone used everywhere – in roads, buildings and monuments.

Ignore the main highway and head southwest through the flat, dry, olive groves on the quiet N18. You'll pass the old royal castle at Evoramonte and reach Evora itself, another ancient walled outpost. This is one of Portugal's prized historic cities, which has been awarded UNESCO World Heritage status.

Spend some time exploring the narrow streets of the old centre to find a Roman temple, a Gothic cathedral and another impressive royal palace.

Stick to the small roads as you head from there toward the coast. Sines is a busy port today but it's easy to find the old fishing harbour, castle and town centre. Relax on the long, sandy São Torpes Beach just outside the town or discover the town's monument to an explorer even more intrepid than you. Sines is the birthplace of the 15th-century explorer Vasco da Gama – the first European to sail around the Cape of Good Hope. **SH**

❶ **Evoramonte Castle is worth a short detour.**

Western Algarve Alentejo/Algarve, Portugal

Start Vila Nova de Milfontes, Alentejo **End** Sagres, Algarve **Distance** 113km (70 miles)
Type Scenic **Map** goo.gl/1MM7Yx

The Algarve usually refers to the busy highly developed tourist strip along the southern coast of Portugal. But there is much more to it. If you journey around the Cape St Vincent at the bottom corner of Portugal and head north, you can explore the marvellous western Algarve. It is a completely different area.

For almost 161km (100 miles), this western coast is a protected natural park with hardly a town or village. Instead, there are scores of huge, empty, sandy beaches facing into the Atlantic breakers. There is only one road to take, which wiggles prettily through green rolling hills and woods a short way inland. In order to get down to the sea,

take any of the numerous little lanes that head west. Each one is an adventure and usually ends at a gorgeous seascape amid huge cliffs, dunes and sea spray. For example, the enormous sands at Odeceixe are framed by tree-covered cliffs, and remote beaches such as those at Bordeira and Amado can often be deserted. Sometimes there is a little shack or caravan selling seafood snacks, occasionally a few surfers strumming guitars around a makeshift bonfire. If you are not too keen on timeshare resorts and mini-golf, the wilds of the Vicentina Coast are the perfect solution. **SH**

ⓘ View from Torre de Aspa to the Vicentina Coast.

High Sierras to the Coast Centro, Portugal

Start Guarda   End Lisbon   Distance 460km (286 miles)
Type Culture   Map goo.gl/5oE1sb

This is the Portuguese leg of a popular road trip east to west from Madrid to Lisbon. It begins in Guarda, Portugal's highest city, and ends at sea level in the capital, Lisbon.

After looking at Guarda's fine cathedral, head west through the Parque Natural da Serra de Estrela, an impressive granite ridge and the country's highest point. Then follow the dramatic crags and gorges down through the forests to the medieval city of Coimbra. This riverfront former capital sports Roman ruins and a 13th-century university. Onwards through the Parque Natural das Serras de Aire e Candeeiros – noted for its limestone caves – to the coast at Peniche. This traditional fishing port

is a jumping-off point for marine tourism. From here the route follows the coast south to Sintra, one of Portugal's top tourist attractions. Don't be put off by the crowds – this multi-coloured town of romantic fairytale castles is something special. Sintra is full of delights – the National Palace, the Castelo dos Mouros and the Pena National Palace. Finally, as the route loops around the coast towards Lisbon, it runs alongside sandy beaches at the resort towns of Cascais and Estoril, before arriving in the heart of the capital via the waterfront along the banks of the Tagus River. DK

❶ Coimbra is home to the oldest university in Portugal.

Torre, Serra da Estrela Centro, Portugal

Start Covilha   End Torre   Distance 23km (14 miles)
Type Scenic   Map goo.gl/gAh5Qs

You will find this high rocky plateau in Serra da Estrela Natural Park in the centre of Portugal. The road from Covilha to the east offers an impressive sequence of hairpin bends to climb up into the highlands, but you could equally make the trip from the Coimbra direction in the west. Either way, your GPS will probably inform you that it is only a 40-minute drive. It is better to allow a full morning to discover all its delights. Along the route, there are the usual attractions of the best European mountain journeys: views, hairpin bends, rugged scenery, lakes and sleepy hotels in remote spots. In summer you will have a good chance of a clear view; in winter it is snowy and often busy with skiers.

The route is an ordinary provincial country road that passes along the highest point in Portugal. It occurs, rather bizarrely, in the centre of a roundabout where a geographer's trig point marks the extreme spot at 1,993m (6,539ft). Alongside the country's highest-altitude roundabout, there is a deserted military base with quirky domed towers, some gift shops and cafés. You will see a rough track leading off into the wilderness. Don't fret about whether you can get along it – the track does not lead anywhere interesting and peters out after a few hundred metres. SH

❶ Covão Dam near Serra da Estrela.

Lisbon and the Estoril Coast Lisbon, Portugal

Start Lisbon   **End** Cascais   **Distance** 34km (21.1 miles)
Type Scenic   **Map** goo.gl/aEapx6

Lisbon is said to be Western Europe's most delightful capital for a short break, and this simple road trip along the northern shore of the River Tagus provides a snapshot of all that is good about the city. The highways are good, drivers are well behaved and even the traffic police are friendly, usually.

Start in the heart of Lisbon on the grand 18th-century Rossio Square. Watch out for rickety old trams and head west along the historic waterfront. Pass under the massive Ponte 25 de Abril suspension bridge across the river, named to celebrate the ousting of Portugal's dictator in the 1960s. The ornate facade of Jerónimos Monastery appears on your right, and almost next door is

Pastéis de Belém café, an unmissable Lisbon institution that makes and serves more than 14,000 delicious egg-custard tarts each day. Along the road is Belém Tower, a pretty little castle standing in the river itself, and the Monument to the Navigators, a striking modern landmark commemorating Portuguese explorers of the Middle Ages.

As you cruise along this coast road, the estuary widens into the sea and the city suburbs become dominated by leafy retreats. In stylish Estoril and the beach resort of Cascais, you'll be weaving between millionaires' mansions overlooking the sea. **SH**

❶ Cosmopolitan Cascais was once a fishing village.

Sintra to Praia das Maçãs Lisbon, Portugal

Start Sintra   End Praia das Maçãs   Distance 12km (7.5 miles)
Type Scenic   Map goo.gl/D9Ctje

A drive to the sea is always fun. The expectation of your first glimpse of glinting waves adds something to the journey. That is definitely the case with this road trip: the run from Sintra to the seaside town of Praia das Maçãs on the Atlantic coast. It starts in the beautiful town of Sintra, sufficiently historic and well preserved to be a UNESCO World Heritage Site. In times past, this mountain retreat is where Portuguese royalty spent their summers, at Pena Palace, completed in 1854.

Head out of town to the west; the road curves and twists as it leaves Sintra behind, eventually opening out into fast, open sweeps with only the occasional hairpin bend thrown in to keep drivers on their toes. Accompanying you along the way is a local tram line. The rails occasionally disappear behind trees and buildings but reappear farther down the track.

The route heads up into the mountains and towards the sea, so expect plenty of steep gradients. Above you are farms and terraced fields, gripping on to the slopes. When you arrive in Praia das Maçãs, a seaside town popular with surfers and body-boarders, you have to decide whether to stop for a long, cool drink at one of the seafront bars or do the journey all over again in reverse. It's a tough call. JI

❶ Pena Palace in the Sintra Mountains above the town.

Lagos to Cape St Vincent
Algarve, Portugal

Start Lagos
End Cape St. Vincent
Distance 39km (24 miles)
Type Scenic
Map goo.gl/jTv72I

Explore the extreme southwest corner of the European mainland by taking a winding route through a surprisingly unspoiled and charming part of Portugal. Start in the seaside resort of Lagos, at the gentler western end of the Algarve tourist strip. Lagos is not yet overrun and retains the charm of an old, whitewashed, fishing town, with cobbled alleys and makeshift restaurants around the marina, where the day's catch is on sale.

The roads heading west regularly loop down to the shore to deliver amazing seascapes of orange rock formations and sea-stacks framing empty sandy bays. Inland, there is little hint of the tourism to the east, as you pass through sleepy villages among the rolling farmland. Stop at one of the cafés to try traditional homemade egg-custard tarts. Towards the end of the journey, you are heading for the impressive cliff-top fort at Sagres. Wander the intact fortifications to learn intrepid historical tales of Henry the Navigator, a 15th-century Portuguese prince, and Francis Drake. From here, simply keep driving west until the land runs out. This is Cape St Vincent, the rugged headland topped by a stumpy lighthouse, café, visitor centre and colourful souvenir stalls. The Romans thought this spot was the end of the world – and looking at the Atlantic rollers breaking against formidable cliffs marching off to the north, you can see why. **SH**

São Marcos da Serra to Monchique Algarve, Portugal

Start São Marcos da Serra
End Monchique
Distance 35km (21.7 miles)
Type Scenic
Map goo.gl/Bck6Bp

It may be only a relatively short road trip, through the rugged hills of the northern Algarve, but the road is both a challenge and a delight to drive as it rises and falls along the entire length, from an elevation of approximately 100m (328ft) to a maximum height of 450m (1,476ft). Climbing up and over four increasingly high mountain passes, drivers also have to navigate more than 80 twists and turns.

In addition to the fun gained from steering serious bends on a well-maintained road surface, you will thoroughly enjoy the scenery in this rural area of the country. There are plenty of places to stop along the way, including small wooded rest areas, and traditional Algarve farming villages to visit, such as Alferce with its rustic church and ruinous traditional buildings.

The road itself may be twisty, but there are barriers along its length to prevent vehicles dropping off the edge. The bends link up, drawing you along through sweep after sweep. On either side, the countryside is a treat, too: a mix of native woodland, scrub and arid mountainous terrain. Your final destination, Monchique, is a market town with plenty of cafés and restaurants. The town is also famous for its Roman baths and modern hydrotherapy spas – a perfect way to unwind after an afternoon behind the wheel. **JI**

Portimão to Fóia
Algarve, Portugal

Start Portimão
End Fóia
Distance 31km (19.3 miles)
Type Scenic
Map goo.gl/geh2N6

Portugal has some mighty fine roads, and this one is a prime example. Heading north from the coastal town of Portimão, drive inland towards the mountains. The initial section is fairly straight, with some wide sweeps and the odd tight bend thrown in for good measure.

At Caldas de Monchique, you will find a spa town that was popular with the Romans, who came to take the waters that could, apparently, cure all ills. Sceptics might like to try alternative medication in the form of the local spirit, Medronho, which is made from strawberry tree berries. After the town, the road becomes not only twistier but also hillier, as you head farther north. It straightens again around Gil Bordalo and stretches up to Monchique. This is a traditional village of the Algarve, with whitewashed houses and yet more Roman influences. It is also known for its traditional furniture makers. From Monchique, there are some amazing sections of road, with hairpin bends and virtual 180-degree turns that flow from one to another. Short bursts of straight tarmac lead to yet more tight bends. Sadly, you won't have time to take your eyes off the road to look at the terraced farms and vineyards around you. Instead, wait until you reach Fóia. Looking back from the Serra de Monchique mountains towards the sea, you will feel that you have really earned that view. JI

❶ Take a detour to one of the many cork tree forests traditionally found in this region of southern Portugal.

Colle Fauniera
Piedmont, Italy

Start Pradleves
End Colle Fauniera
Distance 23km (14 miles)
Type Adventure
Map goo.gl/9z7PKL

Look one way from the village of Pradleves, the so-called 'village of cheeses', and all you see is a slice of the beautiful Pianura Padana, the Po Valley, that vast, sediment-filled trough filled with irrigation works, farms and all the stuff of rural Italian life. Then turn around, and look west at what awaits you – the SP23, the SP112 and the SP333, which together comprise an unrelenting ascent over a 7.5 per-cent gradient. The 'slow food' phenomenon was born hereabouts. You might say the same about the driving, too.

Also known as the Colle dei Morti ('Hill of the Dead'), the Colle Fauniera is a pass in the Cottian Alps on the French–Italian border with a summit at 2,511m (8,238ft) above sea level. Starting at Pradleves (you can also begin at Ponte Marmora or Demonte), you gain an impressive 1,689m (5,541ft) in elevation over the whole length of the journey.

A favourite of cyclists on the Giro d'Italia since it was paved in 1999, whenever you drive this route you're likely to encounter cyclists inching their way towards the statue of the great cyclist Marco Pantani that awaits you at the summit. One of the most beautiful passes in the Alps, it is also one of its narrowest – built, you might think, more for bicycles than for cars as it takes you through a land of Alpine flowers and marmots on Piedmont's little-known 'cyclist's road'. **BDS**

❶ The statue of Italian racing cyclist Marco Pantani at the Colle Fauniera pass.

Assietta High Altitude Road Piedmont, Italy

Start Sestriere
End Colle delle Finestre
Distance 39km (24 miles)
Type Adventure
Map goo.gl/5EU6Tf

Tucked up in a far northern corner of Italy, close to the French border, Strada Provinciale (SP) 173 is a breathtaking mountain road officially designated as a military highway but open to the public annually between early June and the end of October. It is mostly unfinished, with gravel and rocky debris under your wheels as you climb along a steep mountain ridge.

SP 173 is a challenge, even for an off-roader. The greater part of its length lies at more than 2,000m (6,500ft) above sea level, so you can expect to be in the clouds. It starts at Sestriere, one of Italy's biggest ski resorts, which is surrounded by four great peaks: Monte Fraiteve, 2,701m (8,862ft); Monte Sises, 2,658m (8,720ft); Punta Rognosa di Sestriere, 3,280m (10,761ft); and Monte Motta, 2,850m (9,350ft). On the road to Colle delle Finestre there are no safety barriers and a rocky slope rolling away to one side of you. Even where there is some form of protection, it might only be a low stone wall between you and a long drop.

As well as the road being closed over winter and for much of spring, there are other traffic restrictions. Large vehicles are banned and overtaking is forbidden since the road is so narrow. There are also signs warning of rock falls, drops and even roaming wildlife. But the rewards are great, with the views of the Alps as stunning as you can imagine. **JI**

The Wine Road from Alba to Barolo Piedmont, Italy

Start Alba
End Barolo
Distance 20km (12.4 miles)
Type Culture
Map goo.gl/3Fnjxa

This gentle wine trail through Italy's Piedmont links Alba, 62km (38 miles) south of Turin, with the town of Barolo, a small gem with a big name thanks to its much-admired red wine. The journey can be completed in 15 minutes without stops, but that would be to bypass the many red-roofed villages and rush past the gorgeous views of checkerboard hills set against snowcapped Alps: if you hurry, you'll miss it all.

From Alba, an elegant town with a superb covered food market, head south on Strada Provinciale (SP) 3. Several wine villages, producing Barbaresco as well as Barolo, lie on either side of this route: quiet backroads, some no more than tracks, join the terracotta dots. Among the most romantic villages are Grinzane Cavour, Serralunga d'Alba and La Morra, each tightly wound around a castle (almost every village in this once disputed region has one). Barolo's castle, off the SP 3 a few miles farther south, is now the Enetoca Regionale del Barolo, where you can taste the full gamut of regional wines.

Piedmont is a bastion of gastronomy, with food to match the excellent wine. Specialties include white truffles, Gorgonzola, game and fungi, not to mention hazelnuts, which supply the Ferrero Rocher chocolate factory in Alba. Don't miss the candied chestnuts. **DS**

Riviera dei Fiori – Ligurian Coast Drive
Liguria, Italy

● The skyline of Imperia is dominated by the
late-18th-century Cathedral of San Maurizio.

Start Ventimiglia
End Savona
Distance 122km (76 miles)
Type Scenic
Map goo.gl/58snbl

The opulence of the French Riviera is well known
– prowling Ferraris, super-yachts, celebrity villas,
casinos. Keep heading east over the border into
Italy, however, and you'll discover a far less famous
stretch of Mediterranean coastline – the Riviera dei
Fiori (Riviera of Flowers), most of which faces east
on to the Ligurian Sea.

The important thing is that it offers a great scenic
road trip. You'll start just inside Italy at the frontier
town of Ventimiglia, and from there wind along the
SS1 to Savona, hugging the coast, twisting around
cliffs and headlands, looking down on bypassed
beaches and marinas.

It's an area sheltered from northern weather by
the Alps, and which gets the same amount of
sunshine as the French Riviera. Little wonder it's
known for its colourful flora, which you'll see
tumbling from window boxes, climbing up walls
and blooming in terracotta pots wherever you go.

This is a route to discover a series of classic
Victorian resorts, such as San Remo and Finale. The
highlights include the fortified port of Imperia,
Savona's old fortified harbour and Cervo's colourfully
painted houses perched on a hill overlooking the
sea. If you have time for just one detour, take the SP
64 a short distance inland to the village of
Dolceaqua, one of the most photogenic spots in
the region. SH

Strada Provinciale 227 di Portofino Liguria, Italy

Start Rapallo
End Portofino
Distance 8.1km (5 miles)
Type Scenic
Map goo.gl/JNP18n

At a pricey sidewalk café on Rapallo's glamorous waterfront, you will think that there could not be anything more typical of the jet set than this jewel of the Italian Riviera. There is a palm-fringed promenade between two lovely restored castle towers and everyone else seems to have a better ride than you. But wait . . . you haven't been to Portofino yet. This 'fishing village' just around the headland is off the scale. Take the narrow winding road south, via Santa Margherita Ligure and Paraggi, along the shore-front mansions, castles, top-notch restaurants, manicured private beaches, bustling marinas and five-star hotels; just be careful not to scrape any of the Ferraris coming the other way.

It is difficult to get into the pastel-painted heart of Portofino. There may well be a fashion magazine photo shoot or a visiting celebrity's entourage blocking the highway. Eventually, though, you enter a fantasy world of super-yachts, supermodels and supercars that has completely taken over what was once a quaint little village on a picturesque wooded inlet. Wisteria-covered villas overlooking the water now belong to European presidents, racing drivers and fashion icons. The Splendido Hotel is a good spot for coffee, with or without a small bowl of caviar, if you have the means. Just try not to park in the space by the entrance that is reserved for George Clooney's motorbike. **SH**

Circuito di Ospedaletti Liguria, Italy

Start Ospedaletti
End Ospedaletti
Distance 3.4km (2.1 miles)
Type Culture
Info goo.gl/9HvVrI

The Ospedaletti Circuit road race in the Italian town of the same name may have ended in 1972, but you can still experience the same route, if perhaps not at quite the speeds of the original competitors. Situated on the northwest coast of Italy, less than an hour's drive east from its glamorous neighbour Monaco, the course was once another highlight of the motorsport calendar.

The race began in 1937 as the San Remo Grand Prix and was held, not surprisingly, in San Remo, 6km (3.7 miles) east of Ospedaletti. In 1947, though, the circuit at San Remo was no longer good enough for the ever-evolving Grand Prix cars, and the race was moved to the streets of Ospedaletti. It was still called the San Remo Grand Prix until that race ended in 1951, but a road race around the tight and undulating Ospedaletti Circuit continued to be held annually until 1972.

The circuit was continually modified, but ended up being 3.38km (2.1 miles) around the streets of this holiday town, with the lap record being set at an average speed of 105.53 kph (65.57 mph) by Alberto Ascari in his Ferrari 375. If you want to sample the route at more sedate speeds, take the map and drive anticlockwise around the seven famous turns (still identifiable by their black-and-white painted apexes) of this once revered F1 street circuit. **MG**

Passo del Bocco
Liguria/Emilia-Romagna, Italy

Start Borgonovo Ligure, Liguria
End Santa Maria del Taro, Emilia-Romagna
Distance 23km (14 miles)
Type Scenic
Map goo.gl/TDou1R

As the Giro d'Italia of 2011 weaved through the woods that characterize this region, the cyclists climbed over the Passo del Bocco and were hurtling down the far side, when young professional rider, Wouter Weylandt, took up a promising position. Suddenly, however, the Belgian lost control at 80 kph (50 mph), crashed into a wall and died instantly. The road has been notorious ever since. Car drivers can only wonder at the effort, courage and skill cyclists need to race at high speed over roads like this, which are tough enough when you are piloting a powered machine.

Begin in Borgonovo Ligure, a village high above the Italian Riviera between Genoa and La Spezia. The proposed itinerary takes you from Liguria into the neighbouring province of Emilia-Romagna. Keep heading east on small country roads and there is a day's worth of exploring ahead. Alternatively, simply turn around to head back through the pass and down to the coast again. The pass itself rises to 956m (3,136ft) above sea level. From the west, it is an inexorable climb with an average gradient of 5.6 per cent over the first 15km (9 miles). It is a beautifully leafy route, twisting up and down green mountains, through villages and farmsteads that almost spill across the road. When the trees take a step back, there are glorious views of forests in all directions to the horizon. **SH**

Umbrailpass
Italy/Switzerland

Start Strada del Passo dello Stelvio, Lombardy, Italy
End Santa Maria Val Müstair, Graubünden, Switzerland
Distance 13km (8 miles)
Type Adventure
Map goo.gl/qNSW3b

Of all the mountain pass roads in the European Alps, this southern gateway between Switzerland and Italy is particularly nerve-wracking. Its summit of 2,501m (8,205ft) above sea level makes it the highest metalled road in Switzerland. And that's only been true since 2015 – before that, sections of the route remained a compacted gravel track.

Due to snow, the road is only open from May to December. It begins just below the summit of the Stelvio Pass in Italy. Just a minute or so after turning onto the Umbrail from the Stelvio, you arrive at the Swiss border. It's not always manned, but cars are regularly stopped. Coming from the Italian side, the route is deceptive. It doesn't seem that steep. That's because most of the climb has already been done by the time the route begins. Once over the summit, in the shadow of Piz Umbrail, things start to get tricky. Between here and the end point, the road drops more than 1,100m (3,700ft).

As the road falls away into the Val Müstair, there are 34 hairpin turns, some with well-placed turnouts offering spectacular views north to the Sesvenna Alps. Set in lush green meadows at the foot of the pass is the hamlet of Santa Maria Val Müstair, which is an ideal spot for lunch and a chance to let the brakes cool off. Afterwards, drive 3km (2 miles) north of town to see the Benedictine monastery of St John, a World Heritage Site. **DK**

Strada della Forra
Lombardy, Italy

Start Campione
End Tremosine
Distance 13km (8 miles)
Type Scenic
Map goo.gl/Hyrarw

Winding up from the beautiful western shore of Lake Garda, this twisted spaghetti of a route turns a distance of a little under 4km (3 miles) as the crow flies into a tangled road that is more than three times that length.

Of course, the reason for all the twists is the crazy terrain. The road has to concertina up the mountainous sides of the lake, wind through a deep narrow gorge and twist around huge rocky cliffs. The result is an amazingly scenic route, but one that demands full concentration from the driver. Use a motorbike or small car; wide vehicles will end up with battered wings or stuck fast in a thin rock tunnel wondering how to get home. It's mostly very narrow, so if you meet someone on one of the blind hairpins or tunnels one of you will have to reverse to a passing place.

The highway squeezes through jagged clefts in the rock, through holes blasted through mountains and under arches carved from cliffs. It was built more than 100 years ago and the unlikely driving adventurer Sir Winston Churchill once tackled it. The British statesman declared that the road was 'the eighth wonder of the world'.

James Bond's Aston Martin tackled part of this route at high speed in the opening car chase of the film *Quantum of Solace* (2008). But don't attempt to replicate that feat. **SH**

❶ This winding road along the western shore of Lake Garda is formidably challenging.

Gavia Pass
Lombardy, Italy

Start Bormio
End Ponte di Legno
Distance 43km (26.7 miles)
Type Scenic
Map goo.gl/Awp1Pi

The Gavia Pass is a firm favourite among keen Alpine road trippers. However, in the summer months visitors must share this winding strip of tarmac – some of it single track – with swarms of cyclists who descend on the route from all across Europe, thanks to its reputation as one of the most gruelling stages of the Giro d'Italia.

From Bormio, a Lombard ski resort with thermal waters, the route runs along the banks of first the Adda River and then its tributary, the Torrente Frigidolfo, into Stelvio National Park. Climbing all the time, travellers pass into the shadow of two Alpine peaks: on the right, Monte Gavia (3,223m/10,574ft) and on the left, Monte Corno dei Tre Signori (3,360m/11,023ft).

At the edge of the next landmark, Lago Bianco, a glacial lake, stands a large crucifix erected in gratitude by a man who, with his wife and mother, survived a night stranded in a blizzard there in 1929. Beyond the lake, the ascent continues in a series of hairpin bends past Lago Nero to the summit at 2,545m (8,350ft) above sea level, where there is an Alpine lodge and a pyramidal memorial to victims of the World War I Battle of San Matteo (1918), one of the highest battles in history. The steep descent into the province of Brescia is punctuated by an 800-m- (2,625-ft) long tunnel, which is dank, dark and narrow. **JP**

Passo del Maloja
Italy/Switzerland

Start Chiavenna, Lombardy, Italy
End Silvaplana, Graubünden, Switzerland
Distance 43km (26.7 miles)
Type Scenic
Map goo.gl/xfClqR

A clump of jagged mountain peaks stands between Chiavenna in northern Italy and the Engadin Valley and resort of St Moritz in Switzerland. There is no conventional neat gap through the mountains to use as a pass here. However, hundreds of years ago someone must have decided this was a good route. So the road drives quite easily from Chiavenna for 20km (12 miles), without bends or hills. Then suddenly it climbs 800m (2,625ft) in a couple of miles via a seemingly endless series of hairpin bends to reach Maloja, at 1,815m (5,955 ft). After that, the route stays at the same altitude to reach Silvaplana, 11km (7 miles) farther on. Because of this brutal geography, the road has acquired the nickname 'the pass that never was'. They could have called it 'the staircase with one step' instead, because of its one stretch of steep gradient.

Of course, it makes a memorable road trip. For cars, the severe switchback serpentine leading up to Maloja involves prodigious arm-twirling. Meanwhile, bikers will start to feel seasick with all the swaying to and fro. When you reach the small village of Maloja at the top, there is a café where you can stop and get your breath back. Everyone takes panoramic photographs to celebrate. From there, continue along an attractive stretch of smooth Swiss road by the shore of Lake Silvaplana – and there is barely a gradient along the way. **SH**

ⓘ This well-maintained serpentine route through forests and mountains is fun to drive.

Anfo Ridge Road
Lombardy, Italy

Start Anfo
End Maniva Ski Resort, Giogo del Maniva
Distance 27km (16.5 miles)
Type Adventure
Map goo.gl/s9wvFe

This may be a relatively short road trip, but it is one for which you will need nerves of steel if you are going to risk driving it. Not for nothing has it been called one of the most dangerous roads in the world.

The drive starts pleasantly enough in the little town of Anfo on the shores of Lake Idro, which is 368m (1,207ft) above sea level. The road runs parallel to the lakeshore, with mountain views all around, until you approach the northern end of the lake when a left turn on to the SP669 gives you a chance to head into the Bergamo Alps and climb up through several ever-higher mountain passes. By the time you reach Passo del Dosso Alto (also called Passo delle Portole), you will be at an altitude of 1,727m (5,666ft).

The old military road twists and turns and the surface worsens, with some stretches weathered to loose gravel. In places, it is so narrow that there is only room for one car, and drivers have to be prepared to reverse around corners until they reach a suitable passing place. The flimsy railings between your vehicle and a sheer drop of several hundred feet do not inspire confidence. Although the route has a fearsome reputation, you will at least be privileged to see some spectacular Alpine views as you drive it. Be aware that rockfalls are an ever-present danger. **MG**

Passo del Mortirolo
Lombardy, Italy

Start Mazzo di Valtellina
End Mortirolo Pass
Distance 11km (6.8 miles)
Type Adventure
Map goo.gl/4DDCVl

They sweat profusely, they gasp for air, their legs almost burst with effort – but in a car you'll be able to cruise gently past the cyclists as they turn purple attempting the holy grail of pedalling.

This Alpine mountain pass is known to cyclists as the 'Queen Climb of Europe', many professionals describe it as the toughest ride they ever did, but as a car driver or motorbike rider you may wonder what all the fuss is about. Yes, it's steep and has a few hairpin bends, but they will seem like a small price to pay for the mesmerizing views across the surrounding mountains.

Admittedly, climbing up from the pretty Lombardy village of Mazzo di Valtellina, this long, narrow, steep ascent has an average gradient of 11 per cent and reaches the summit of the pass at a lofty 1,852m (6,076ft) above sea level. The steepest section of road has a daunting gradient of 18 per cent. Little wonder, then, that when it is used as part of the classic annual Giro d'Italia cycle race the first rider to the top wins a special prize. You'll also see that the route has cycling monuments and graffiti all along its length.

So spare a thought for your non-motorized friends as they struggle up this beautifully scenic route. You'll be appreciating the leafy views, the smooth tarmac and the old buildings dotted along the roadside. The cyclists probably won't. **SH**

Sondrio to Campo Moro
Lombardy, Italy

Start Sondrio
End Campo Moro
Distance 35km (22 miles)
Type Adventure
Map goo.gl/cAe289

From the pleasant bustling Alpine town of Sondrio, the surrounding peaks look like a landscape scene from a jigsaw puzzle. Attempt to drive north into the heart of the mountains, however, and the environment begins to take on a darker nature. The route to this remote lake starts by climbing out of Sondrio and twists gracefully through the terraced gardens of grand houses. But mile by mile the road seems to get narrower and trees appear to overhang a little more. Bends become harder work and gradients more noticeable. When the road opens out, you will see that the mountains are much closer, looming over the tarmac.

By the time the route is climbing through villages such as Tornadri and Lanzada, high gears are a distant memory. This is when the hairpin bends begin. Don't be alarmed by vicious skid marks on the tarmac or unguarded drops to the valley below. Instead, prepare yourself for an extraordinary sequence of narrow tunnels carved through the mountain faces. You will be surrounded by jagged rock and driving on cobbles. These amazing tunnels include 'windows' blasted through the sides to reveal unbelievable mountain vistas.

Reaching the genteel hotels and cafés around the lakeside car park is almost an anticlimax, but don't relax too much, because you have still got the return journey to face. **SH**

❶ This tower is one of several defensive installations along the route once used by the Italian army.

Mille Miglia South Tyrol, Italy

Start Brescia   **End** Brescia   **Distance** 1,609km (1,000 miles)
Type Culture   **Info** goo.gl/2yWAAH

The Mille Miglia (Thousand Miles) was one of the world's most famous road races. Like the Le Mans 24 Hours race, it was a gruelling endurance test of driver and machine. It was first held in 1927, travelling south from Brescia through the mountains of northern Italy, all the way to Rome and then back to the start point. Apart from an interruption during World War II, it continued as the Mille Miglia until 1957 when, following two deaths in that year's race, it changed format to the Rally 1000 Miglia.

It's easy enough to get hold of a map of the route and to enjoy the drive at a more leisurely pace, as it goes through many famous places that are well worth stopping off in rather than racing through

– the record average speed recorded for the race was an astonishing 157.65 kph (97.96 mph). Yes, that's just over ten hours of driving at that average speed from Brescia to Rome and back.

Brescia itself is worth lingering in, with several monuments on UNESCO's World Heritage List, while the route also goes through towns like Ravenna and Modena (home to Ferrari, Lamborghini and Maserati), the Republic of San Marino and Florence. In particular, the second half of the journey from Rome to Brescia goes through some classic Italian hill scenery. **MG**

❶ Old cars still retrace the famous course.

Passo Gardena South Tyrol, Italy

Start Selva-Wolkenstein   End Corvara In Badia   Distance 18km (11.2 miles)
Type Scenic   Map goo.gl/oTGOiM

This pass in northern Italy's exceptionally scenic South Tyrol region attains a height of 2,136m (7,008ft), and rather than simply driving through it visitors might want to take advantage of the accommodation that is up there and stay overnight to enjoy some of the hiking and other activities available. However, if you prefer to stay on the road, it is still one of the most dramatic drives in the region.

Also known as Grödner Joch, the pass is well surfaced, which it needs to be because it is a very popular drive and you are unlikely to have the road to yourself in the summer months. There are some thrill-making ascents and descents en route,

and it is better, if you can, to drive it at quieter times of year when you can enjoy the roads at your own pace. You will also want to be able to stop and take in the scenery, as the mountain slopes are covered in Alpine meadows, at their colourful best in the spring. The endless switchbacks mean that you will not always be able to stop exactly where you want, but there are many places where you can pull over and see across distant valleys to mountains and yet more mountains receding into the distance. It is, perhaps, the best scenic road trip through the Dolomites. MG

❶ The unique shape of the Dolomites adds to the charm.

Passo di Costalunga South Tyrol, Italy

Start Bolzano   **End** Vigo di Fassa   **Distance** 39km (24 miles)
Type Scenic   **Map** goo.gl/fMpZRV

It might not be the highest Alpine pass – at a good to middling 1,754m (5,755ft) above sea level – and it may not be the most challenging to drive, as the road is generally smooth, wide and well signed, with fairly relaxed bends and gradients. However, Passo di Costalunga, or Karerpass in German, is certainly one of the most scenic. The route through the Eggental and Welschnofen Valleys is mostly a gentle climb and descent, punctuated with a sequence of jaw-dropping panoramas of distant snowy peaks and closer wooded slopes.

Karersee, or Lago di Carezza, is the highlight. This small turquoise lake stands in an idyllic location, surrounded by steep slopes of evergreen forest.

Jagged mountains and trees are beautifully reflected in the water, making it one of the favourite spots in the Dolomites for photographers. The footpaths around the shore are worth exploring, too, if you have time. Karersee is a couple of miles from the summit of the pass. You'll find this is a gentle grassy plateau with a collection of mountain hotels, lodges and cafés in which to sit and admire the scenery. It is a popular place with tourist buses in the height of summer; overall, you will find the driving experience much more fun in the shoulder seasons of spring and autumn. **SH**

❶ The Catinaccio massif is popular with climbers.

Passo delle Palade South Tyrol, Italy

Start Fondo   End Lana   Distance 33km (20.5 miles)
Type Scenic   Map goo.gl/wz97Wt

As far back as the Middle Ages, the local counts of Tyrol realized how useful this route through the mountains of northeast Italy was to travellers, so they employed toll keepers to stay high up on the pass and collect money from all the merchants using the path between the Adige and Non River valleys. Thankfully, today you won't meet anyone waving a list of charges at the top. Instead, you will find an unexpected sight: an underground museum and gallery. A major complex of underground tunnels was built here by the Italians as a defence against possible German attack before World War II. It was never used, and the multi-level Gampen Bunker has been restored. It is now open as an exhibition centre, curated by mountaineering hero Reinhold Messner. Subterranean galleries include elegant educational displays of the geology and geography of the mountains and their inhabitants.

The rest of the route is a classic drive through the wooded mountains of the southern Alps. The two-lane paved road rises and falls steeply to the pass at 1,518m (4,980ft), mostly through attractive forested slopes. There are a few hairpin bends, but the road is always wide and smooth enough. The best bits are the far-reaching views into the green valleys on either side of the pass. SH

🛈 The snowcapped Dolomites blend into the clouds.

Monte Martello
South Tyrol, Italy

Start Coldrano
End Lake Gioveretto
Distance 21km (13 miles)
Type Scenic
Map goo.gl/gcVo5d

This testing climb into the mountains of Italy's South Tyrol is just a few miles to the east of the the Stelvio Pass, so if the latter – widely regarded as the toughest drive of all – leaves you unsatisfied, this is a conveniently located source of additional thrills. It cannot compete with Stelvio for glamour and fame, but this little mountain route is far quieter, nearly as demanding and just as pretty.

Pick up the trail in the little village of Coldrano in the Adige River valley, heading toward Bolzano. It is a sheltered area of fruit farms and vineyards, but surrounded by some hard-core mountain terrain. At first, you will drive through meadows with scattered farmhouses before the road rises in leisurely loops between steep forested slopes. There are small villages, mountain hotels and places to stop offering fabulous photo opportunities. In the last couple of miles you have to concentrate, as the road narrows and begins to bend its way steeply up through the trees.

Finally, you will reach a dam and Lago Gioveretto. The highlight of the trip is when the road snakes around the shore of this picturesque lake. You can continue a few miles farther to reach a small turning point before heading back down. Here, the smooth tarmac ends; there are rough tracks leading even higher into the mountains, but the official signs warn you: 'This is the end of the road.' **SH**

🄾 This road trip is demanding, but this view from the summit makes it well worth the effort.

Passo di Lavazè
South Tyrol, Italy

Start Bolzano
End Varena
Distance 31km (19 miles)
Type Scenic
Map goo.gl/X2Yhn3

Start this road trip at the charming old city of Bolzano, deep in a valley in the Italian Tyrolean Alps. It is a place full of markets, grand buildings, monuments and well-tended parks. Even in the heart of the city though, you can spot jagged snowy peaks in all directions. First, head east along the Adige River valley, cross the highway and turn south. Before long, there is a lengthy tunnel, from which you will emerge into a mountainous world. It is still a wide paved road, but now it passes rocky gorges, steep wooded valleys and avalanche protection defences. Enjoy some pleasant fast straight sections, too. Drivers should be able to pass dawdling trucks easily.

After Birchabruck, the climb becomes a little more serious, gradually rising through the pine forest towards Lavazè Pass. There are a couple of hairpin bends to negotiate, but this is a popular route for tourists, so gradients are quite relaxed and civilized. You will emerge onto a grassy plateau with good views and a few cafés. The pass is a broad saddle rather than a sudden ridge, so it is a pleasant spot to stop for a meal and a stroll.

The road down the other side is just as gradual and easy. There are a couple of narrower sections, but few sudden bends. Generally, this is one of the least stressful ways to experience the stunning scenery of a high Alpine pass. **SH**

❶ Unlike most other beautiful Italian cities, Bolzano remains removed from the usual tourist routes.

Rifugio Fodara Vedla
South Tyrol, Italy

Start San Martino in Badia
End Rifugio Fodara Vedla, Mareo
Distance 24km (15 miles)
Type Adventure
Map goo.gl/ibzfIe

Not only is this a really exciting, spectacular mountain road, but it also finishes its climb in an area well known for its beautiful summer Alpine walking trails. It's a fun drive, and at the end there are great panoramic views across the Dolomite Mountains in the Italian South Tyrol. In winter, snow will make this journey difficult, if not impossible. The best time to go is in late spring, when the sun is shining and the meadows are in full bloom.

Leaving the charming little town of San Martino in Badia, the route climbs steeply through the pretty village of San Vigilio – access point for the extensive Kronplatz ski and hiking area – then carries on up into the high Alps. The going is relatively easy until Rifugio Pederù, but the final ascent includes a testing staircase of tarmac, linking more than 20 consecutive switchbacks. From the top, the views are stunning. Rifugio Fodara Vedla is within the Fanes-Sennes-Prags Nature Park, and in spring the Alpine meadows here are in bloom with anemones, ox-eye daisies, campanulas and gentians. If you do the trip in the morning, then from the parking spot at the end it is a scenic 3-km- (2-mile) long walk across the high alpine pasture to the Rifugio Munt de Sennes – a mountain refuge and restaurant at 2,176m (7,139ft) in altitude, with a spectacular view out across the Croda Rossa and the Monte Cristallo Mountains. **DK**

❶ The Rifugio Fodara Vedla is situated in the heart of the Fanes-Sennes-Prags Nature Park.

South Tyrolean Wine Road
South Tyrol, Italy

Start Bolzano
End Bolzano
Distance 137km (85 miles)
Type Culture
Info goo.gl/mVnOL1

The wines of the South Tyrol region of Italy are perhaps not quite as well known as the more robust Italian reds from farther south, but this drive through the impressive Tyrolean landscape will help you to discover just how good the northern grapes can be. The proposed itinerary also takes you through what must be one of the most scenic wine regions in the world, bordering as it does the foothills of the Alps.

Although Bolzano makes a good base, the trip can start anywhere and can also be adapted by taking in other vineyards not included on the official route. Bolzano, the capital of South Tyrol, has a marvellous medieval centre and a Museum of Archaeology in which is housed the mummy of Ötzi the Iceman, who lay undiscovered in the mountains between around 3300 BCE and 1991.

From here you head north to Andriano, where you'll find the oldest wine cellar in the Adige Valley, the heart of the wine country. You'll soon be sampling delicious Gewürztraminers and Rieslings: these are probably familiar, so try some of the less common grapes, such as Silvaner and Veltline.

The drive north to Merano and then back south again in an anticlockwise circle takes you past picturesque hillside vineyards and into towns like Vadena, with its medieval castle. It's a delightful drive that blends scenery, history – and wine. **MG**

❶ Between the rocky peaks of the European Alps lie verdant valleys full of vines.

Stelvio Pass
South Tyrol, Italy

Start Prato allo Stelvio
End Bormio
Distance 47km (29 miles)
Type Adventure
Map goo.gl/cBkuSJ

Championed by the presenters of BBC's *Top Gear* as one of 'the greatest driving roads in the world', Italy's Stelvio Pass – the third-highest public road in the Alps – ascends to 2,757m (9,045ft) above sea level through a relentless series of tight hairpin bends snaking up its northern flank.

It was built in the 1820s by the occupying Austrian Empire and was a marvel of civil engineering in its day, climbing 1,871m (6,138ft). Closed for half of the year due to snow, the Stelvio Pass today is primarily a tourist attraction and a mecca for adventurous motorists and motorcyclists from across Europe. When approaching from Prato in the north, the road sweeps up through the cool Alpine forests in the heart of the Stelvio National Park, before the steep climb begins above the tree line. It is often sited in various 'top tens' of the world's most treacherous roads, and the pass's 48 tortuous switchbacks are a tough test of both driver and machine. However, the spectacular vistas from the summit looking over Ortler Glacier and the Eastern Alps are a just reward for your efforts as you, and your engine, take a well-earned breather.

There are another 27 hairpin bends and several rock tunnels to enjoy on the southerly descent to Bormio. There you will find thermal baths, which offer a perfect way to unwind after a demanding day's road tripping. **DIS**

❶ The road viewed from the summit.
❷ Low concrete barriers protect drivers from the edge.

Great Dolomites Road
South Tyrol/Veneto, Italy

Start Bolzano, South Tyrol
End Cortina d'Ampezzo, Veneto
Distance 111km (69 miles)
Type Adventure
Map goo.gl/noHTPC

With a name like Great Dolomites Road, or Grande Strada delle Dolomiti in Italian, this route sets itself up to be quite a road trip – and it is. The road is steep, narrow and in places a little daunting, but visitors will want to allow as much time as possible to stop and take photographs or simply to soak up the views and breath in the fresh mountain air.

The route starts in the South Tyrol capital city of Bolzano, at a modest 262m (862ft) above sea level, and heads east into the most marvellous mountain scenery. You will see the peaks of the Dolomites rising up all around you, except when you are plunging through the tunnels that take you underneath them. The road twists through dense pine forests and across bridges, with some fierce hairpin bends and narrow stretches where there is room for only one car. Before long, it reaches Lago di Carezza, a lake that was popular with Empress Elisabeth of Austria and remains a favourite with visitors today. Even when crowded, it is a good place to take a break.

The road continues to provide dramatic views and experiences, and after going through Passo Pordoi at 2,239m (7,346ft) above sea level, it descends into the Veneto region. With a final twisting flourish offering glorious open valley and mountain views, Great Dolomites Road delivers you to the ski resort of Cortina d'Ampezzo. **MG**

❶ The Lago di Carezza is a perfect place to stop and enjoy views of the Latemar Group.

Passo San Boldo
Veneto, Italy

Start Trichiana
End Tovena
Distance 16.3km (10.1 miles)
Type Adventure
Map goo.gl/hkKw14

Passo San Boldo in the Veneto region of northeastern Italy lies at the southern end of the Alps. It may not be the highest mountain pass in this part of the world – reaching a height of only 706m (2,316ft) – but with its tunnels and serpentine twists, it offers a road trip that you will never forget.

From the starting point in Trichiana, surrounded by soaring mountains, it is hard to believe that you are only 69.2km (43 miles) from the tourist crowds of Venice. However, the route begins delightfully, rising gently as it heads through villages and past farms, with no hint at all of the dramas that lie ahead. Very gradually, though, the bends get a little sharper and the ascent a little steeper until you reach the entrance to the pass itself.

There follows a series of tunnels through the mountainside, with six hairpin turns actually inside them. On the far side of the pass there are seven consecutive steep switchbacks, where the road loses height rapidly and the drama of the drive continues. Remarkably, when it opened in June 1918, this road was called 'the Road of 100 Days' because that is approximately how long it took some 7,000 people to construct it.

Should you be tempted to tackle the Passo San Boldo in your RV or similar, be aware that there is a height limit of 10.5 feet (3.2 m) because of those tortuous tunnels. **MG**

❶ The unique series of single-lane tunnels on Passo San Boldo is controlled by traffic lights.

Forcella Lavardet
Veneto/Friuli-Venezia Giulia, Italy

Start Campolongo, Veneto
End Comeglians, Friuli-Venezia Giulia
Distance 23km (14.3 miles)
Type Adventure
Map goo.gl/lUWxTT

The Dolomites of northern Italy provide many fabulous road trips through spectacular scenery. However, this particular adventure is about the challenge of the ascent.

The Strada Statale (State Road) 465 through the Forcella Lavardet pass consists of 14 hairpin bends, one piled tightly on top of another. Photographs do not do justice to this wonderful road. It snakes up a series of verdant embankments, with a dry watercourse to the left and a cascading, rock-strewn, Alpine stream to the right. The original road was hastily constructed by the military to take heavy artillery over the pass, hence the low gradients and tightly packed bends. While the hairpin bends themselves are now tarmacked, much of the rest of the road is compacted gravel.

The best way to approach this monster is from the north, heading south along the SS 465 from Campolongo. As you approach the switchbacks, you cross a bridge and then begin your ascent to the summit. By the time you reach 1,542m (5,000ft) above sea level, you are enclosed by mountains. From then on, the road wanders south and then east until you drop down into the rustic village of Comeglians, set on a widening of the Degano River. Be aware that this road is frequently closed due to landslides, so check current conditions before starting out. **SA**

❶ The spectacular Forcella Lavardet is a high mountain pass in the Dolomites range.

Quantum of Solace Car Chase
Veneto to Tuscany, Italy

Start Malcesine, Veneto
End Siena, Tuscany
Distance 518km (322 miles)
Type Culture
Map goo.gl/bFwlqH

Whether it's planes, snowmobiles, motorbikes, helicopters, powerboats or gadget-laden Aston Martins, there's nothing better in a James Bond movie than a chase, and the choreographed car chase of 2008's *Quantum of Solace* was excellent, even by Bond standards.

Don't expect to do this drive through Italy in the same amount of time, though. The director took a few liberties with geography to fast-forward 007, at one point covering a couple of hundred miles in a few seconds. And this is not a landscape you want to fast-forward through: it is a part of Italy to savour slowly.

The chase begins in the town of Malcesine, topped by the white stone tower of its ancient castle on the shores of Lake Garda. From here Bond's DBS V12 races around the lake before heading south through the wooded hills of Verona, emerging on the Mediterranean coast near Carrara. Hopefully, you'll avoid the fate of the pursuing Alfa Romeo, which plunged off the mountainside near here in spectacular fashion.

After travelling down the coast for a while, the route heads through the Tuscan countryside, passing more rolling hills, woods and vineyards, and the cities of Lucca and Florence. The road trip ends in enchanting Siena – the perfect place to unwind with a Vesper Martini. **MG**

❶ At the start of the route, the road hugs the beautiful shores of Lake Garda.

Trieste to the Dolomites
Friuli-Venezia Giulia/Veneto, Italy

Start Trieste, Friuli-Venezia Giulia
End Cortina d'Ampezzo, Veneto
Distance 241km (150 miles)
Type Adventure
Map goo.gl/bLJncO

This route across Italy's northeastern corner is an adventure through an historic landscape that is not overwhelmed by tourism. Start in the romantic outpost of Trieste, a grand port with an elegant waterfront and medieval town centre. Take the coastal road north along the Gulf of Trieste, passing the fairytale sight of Miramare Castle – the seaside home of a 19th-century Austrian archduke – jutting into the sea. At Palmanova, stop to explore the citadel built in the shape of a nine-pointed star, which contains an intact Renaissance town. From there the flat, tree-lined roads lead towards Udine, with more ancient fortifications and Renaissance palaces. It is a university city, so the restaurants and nightlife can be lively.

The jagged peaks of the Dolomites grow on the horizon as you head towards Maniago, with its wonderful grand central square, the Piazza d'Italia. From there the road climbs into the foothills and winds through thick forests, crossing fast mountain rivers and running through tunnels in the rock. Soon the mountains are looming over you. This stretch of road is renowned for its views of the sawtooth skyline of this southern Alpine range. You are twisting through the gorges and passes up to the old 1960s jet-set ski resort of Cortina d'Ampezzo. Recognize anything? The city is full of locations from the James Bond film *For Your Eyes Only* (1981). **SH**

Passo del Cason di Lanza
Friuli-Venezia Giulia, Italy

Start Pontebba
End Paularo
Distance 30km (18.6 miles)
Type Scenic
Map goo.gl/d4gdYM

If you are in the mountainous northernmost part of Italy, near the border with Austria, and you decide to make a trip from Pontebba to Paularo, two possible routes will spring to your attention: an easy but roundabout 65-km- (40-mile) long trip via Tolmezzo, which any vehicle should be able to do without difficulty, and a shorter but more demanding road, best suited to automotive adventurers who like a bit of a challenge.

Be warned: the latter route is tough in several ways. High in the Italian Alps, you might expect it to be steep: Pontebba is 600m (nearly 2,000ft) lower than Paularo, and the mean gradient between the two villages on this route is 6.4 per cent. This road is also so narrow in parts that only the smallest, most agile vehicles can dependably get through: two-wheelers are fine, with or without motors (the route has been used by the Giro d'Italia), but it would be unwise to undertake this journey in any car bigger than the narrowest two-seater: passing places are few; smart thinking may be required.

There is something almost illicit about the stolen views from this Lilliputian road trip. Its tiny proportions make you feel fully immersed in the landscape as you scoot across its thickly forested slopes, weave around craggy outcrops and pause at its vertiginous overlooks. Certainly, it is one of Italy's hidden gems. **JP**

Strade del Monte San Simeone
Friuli-Venezia Giulia, Italy

Start Bordano
End Monte San Simeone
Distance 13km (8 miles)
Type Adventure
Map goo.gl/XRNnfa

In the leafy, tranquil setting of Bordano, northern Italy's 'Butterfly Town', it is difficult to believe what automotive horrors are waiting for you just up the road known as Strada del Monte San Simeone. The town was destroyed in an earthquake in 1976 and has been prettily rebuilt, with butterflies painted on all the houses and a popular butterfly garden tourist attraction. Yet this does not disguise the fact that one of the country's most notorious stretches of tarmac tarts on the town's outskirts – a frantic squiggle of Z-bends and tunnels up the side of Monte Simeone.

The route climbs 1,204m (3,950ft) on a road that is roughly paved and alarmingly steep. Look out for potholes, large cracks and crumbling shoulders. Even more dangerous are the roadside drops of hundreds of feet with nothing to protect you. Keep your eyes on the road and do not be distracted by the scenery, however glorious. There are stretches that are too narrow for vehicles to pass, so be prepared to stop and reverse, perhaps around a blind hairpin bend.

Let your heart rate return to normal at the top of the route by appreciating the magnificent view. When you have recovered, you can trek the extra 300m (1,000ft) to the summit, a 45-minute climb. It is hard work, but worth it for the 360-degree view of the Dolomites. SH

❶ There are few better ways of seeing the mighty Dolomites than from the Strada del Monte San Simeone.

Panoramica delle Vette
Friuli-Venezia Giulia, Italy

Start Ravascletto
End Ravascletto
Distance 33.5km (20.8 miles)
Type Adventure
Map goo.gl/l9z4K6

This is no road trip for the foolhardy, fainthearted or inexperienced. It was once under consideration as a section of the annual Giro d'Italia cycling race, but the riders convinced the organizers and sponsors that it was just too dangerous.

It is a short but demanding circuit high in the Italian Alps, 1,982m (6,500ft) above sea level in the shadow of Monte Crostis, close to the Austrian frontier and around 64km (40 miles) north of Udine. Most of the course is paved, but that is about the only comfort available here on the mountain slopes. The rest of the track is gravel, which is slippery and treacherous. Furthermore, there is almost no straight section worthy of the description, and no flat stretch: the average gradient is 11 per cent, and the most severe inclines are almost twice as steep. There is a 1,400-m (4,600-ft) difference in altitude between the lowest and the highest points on the course.

The circuit starts and finishes in the skiing village of Ravascletto, from where the brave proceed anticlockwise along a switchback course that often has big drops on one or both sides, but seldom any safety barriers. As a further indication of the Panoramica delle Vette's degree of difficulty, it takes experienced motorcyclists around 45 minutes to complete the loop – an average speed of less than 348 kph (30 mkph). JP

Discover Rome by Classic Fiat 500 Lazio, Italy

Start Via Ostilia 48, Rome
End Piazzale Giuseppe Garibaldi, Rome
Distance 16km (9.9 miles) approx.
Type Culture
Info goo.gl/BzwEGr

This is not quite *The Italian Job*, but it is just as good. Instead of classic Minis in Turin, it offers a true Italian icon, the original Fiat 500, on the streets of Rome. If you're not quite brave enough to face the fast-moving traffic by taking the wheel yourself, you can travel as a passenger and let a local drive you, which may be even more fun.

In 1957 the first Fiat 500 was produced. It had a tiny 479cc engine and few creature comforts and it could seat four people, although that could be a challenge for the taller driver.

You could simply rent a Cinquecento and tour Rome yourself, of course, but the company Rome 500 EXP offers fully restored cars, as well as routes to give you the best possible experience of the Eternal City. Setting off in a convoy, the guided tour begins at the company garage, close to the Colosseum, and takes in the Square of the Knights of Malta, the Orange Garden, the Pyramid of Cestius, the alleys of Trastevere and the terraces of the Janiculum Hill.

There are other options available, some focusing on food and wine, others aimed at history buffs, and there's an off-the-beaten-path tour called Seven Hidden Gems of Rome. Whichever one you choose, it's the only way to road-trip Rome. MG

⮞ A flock of Cinquecentos in Rome.

State Road 64 Porrettana
Tuscany/Emilia-Romagna, Italy

Start Pistoia, Tuscany
End Sasso Marconi, Emilia-Romagna
Distance 77km (48 miles)
Type Scenic
Map goo.gl/2Oy8Jh

The Apennine Mountains run down the length of Italy like a backbone, creating a formidable barrier between the east and west coasts. It's a volatile region, with earthquakes regularly disrupting towns and villages along the range.

Road and rail links have been forced through the mountain barrier. One of the most impressive routes is the State Road 64 Porrettana, linking Tuscany and Emilia-Romagna. Established in 1928, it has undergone several modifications. Its current incarnation begins in the picturesque Roman city of Pistoia and heads north through Il Signorino and over the Passo della Porretta, a 932-m- (3,057-ft) high pass across the Apennines, through which Hannibal might have marched with his elephants.

Once in Emilia-Romagna, the road continues down the valley of the (Italian) Rhine, through Porretta Terme and Vergato to Sasso Marconi, 17km (11 miles) southwest of Bologna. *Sasso* means 'rock' in Italian, but the Marconi bit of the name is in honour of Guglielmo Marconi, the radio pioneer born in 1902 in Bologna.

This is a drivers' road, mirroring the meandering watercourse below the pretty wooded slopes of Parco Storico di Monte Sole. It is especially popular with the lucky owners of this region's famous automotive exports – Ferrari, Ducati and Pagani, among others. **SA**

Via Chiantigiana
Tuscany, Italy

Start Florence
End Siena
Distance 82km (51 miles)
Type Scenic
Map goo.gl/XbftkX

Regarded by many as Tuscany's finest driving route, the 'Chianti Road' cuts through one of the most prized regions of central Italy, renowned worldwide for its vineyards; it is a place Britons and other northern Europeans have flocked to buy second homes. Despite this, it remains largely unspoiled. From Florence, an easy 31-km- (19-mile) long stretch of highway leads to Greve in Chianti, an old town with a Franciscan monastery, triangular main square and annual wine festival in September. Halfway along the route, Panzano in Chianti stands on a tall ridge from which its castle surveys the surrounding landscape it once dominated. The butcher here is renowned and the most popular eaterie is Solociccia, a restaurant with communal tables.

Castellina in Chianti stands on another hilltop. The architectural highlights here are a 14th-century fortress; a 16th-century church; and Via delle Volte, a medieval arched passageway. On the outskirts are pre-Roman Etruscan burial tombs on Monte Calvario and the necropolis of Poggino.

This relaxing scenic road trip ends at Siena, a city famous for its art, architecture, horse race (the Palio, held on July 2 and August 16 every year) around the central Piazza del Campo, cuisine and – of course – its fine wines. **JP**

⊃ One of the world's greatest wine-growing districts.

The Monti Sibillini Loop
Umbria/Le Marche, Italy

Start Spoleto, Umbria
End Monte Sibilla, Le Marche
Distance 124km (77 miles)
Type Scenic
Map goo.gl/DAoBau

❶ Il Ponte delle Torri (Bridge of Towers) in Spoleto is 230m (750ft) long and 76m (267ft) high.

The limestone Sibillini Mountains form part of the central Apennines. They lie between eastern Umbria and Le Marche in eastern Italy, an area whose beauty has afforded it, since 1993, national park status. A good way to explore this part of Umbria is on the road from Spoleto to Monte Sibilla.

Your starting point is the ancient town of Spoleto, commanding the head of a wide valley, surrounded by mountains. Rich in history, the town was attacked by the Carthaginian general Hannibal in 217 BCE, flourished during the Roman Empire, became a powerful duchy in 570 and in 1809 was the short-lived capital of a French department under Napoleon Bonaparte.

Heading out of the town on the twisty Strada Statale (State Road) 395, the road heads up the steep-sided Valnerina and across a fertile upland to the town of Norcia, renowned for gastronomy (sausages and truffles) and a Benedictine monastery, though the 14th-century basilica was destroyed in 2016 in an earthquake. From Norcia a scenic route snakes out of town, taking you deeper into the Parco Nazionale dei Monti Sibillini and the Piano Grande uplands – a picture-perfect landscape dominated by U-shaped valleys. If you come in late May or June, the crocuses, fritillaries and lentils will be in flower, but still be prepared for some snow, since the road tops out at 1,452m (4,763ft). **SA**

Pescara Circuit
Abruzzo, Italy

Start Pescara
End Pescara
Distance 25.7km (16 miles)
Type Culture
Map goo.gl/JgD9yO

From 1927, the city of Pescara, a popular beach resort on the Adriatic Sea, provided an attractive backdrop to what was considered to be one of the most dangerous road races of them all, the Pescara Circuit. Races of various kinds continued to be held on this roughly triangular circuit until 1961, when it was retired from motor racing. Today, you can still follow the twists and turns of the route and enjoy the scenery rather more than race drivers were ever able to do.

The scenery is pleasant rather than spectacular, as the route takes you out of Pescara and up into the surrounding hills, through farmland and rural villages, before dropping back down to the coast and finally heading south through Pescara's beachfront suburbs to the finish. At 25.75km (16 miles) per lap, it is the longest Formula One circuit ever put to use.

Driven at a leisurely pace, the route presents few technical challenges to motorcyclists or drivers, so to understand the risks, you have to imagine it being raced through at breakneck speed. The fastest lap ever recorded at Pescara was by the British racing driver Stirling Moss, who completed the circuit in 9 minutes 44.6 seconds, at the 1957 Grand Prix. Enzo Ferrari would not let any members of his race team enter the race because he was so concerned for their safety. **MG**

❶ The 1957 Grand Prix recorded the fastest-ever time for the Pescara Circuit.

Amalfi Coast Road
Campania, Italy

Start Salerno
End Sorrento
Distance 76km (47 miles)
Type Scenic
Map goo.gl/HWCCS8

One of the most famous highways in the world, the Amalfi Coast Road has been used as a location in numerous movies, including John Huston's *Beat the Devil* (1953), starring Humphrey Bogart. It twists and turns alongside the Tyrrhenian Sea, by the shoreline and along the cliff tops, sometimes with protective barriers along the edge, often without. Cautious drivers prefer this proposed westerly route; daredevils like it better in the opposite direction, where they are nearer the abyss.

Leaving Salerno, the road hits the coast at Vietri sul Mare. The first stop is Ravello, which stands on a headland above the road. Apart from its inherent beauty and sea views, the town's main claim to fame is as the home, at various times, of composer Richard Wagner and authors D. H. Lawrence, Virginia Woolf and Gore Vidal. Head on to Amalfi, which 1,000 years ago was a major maritime republic; today, it is little more than an extensive pizzeria, but pretty enough. The western section of the road passes Grotta dello Smeraldo (worth an excursion into the marine cave), the stunning Vallone di Furore gorge and the exquisite villages of Praiano and Positano before arriving at Sorrento. This coastal town overlooks the Bay of Naples. It is a busy package resort but has plenty of places of historical interest and fine collections of classical and medieval paintings and sculptures. JP

❶ Sorrento overlooks the Bay of Naples.
❍ The road to Positano is spectacular.

Pompeii, Herculaneum and Paestum Campania, Italy

Start Naples   End Paestum   Distance 183km (114 miles)
Type Culture   Map goo.gl/Avq7Qd

The eruption of Mt Vesuvius in 79 CE engulfed the Roman cities of Pompeii and Herculaneum in lava and ash, entombing them as time capsules. The towns are the best-preserved Roman archaeological sites in the world.

This tour begins in Naples and covers 11 attractions. There's a lot to see – Pompeii alone covers 40 hectares (100 acres) – so it will take a few days to see them all. The National Museum of Archaeology of Naples provides excellent context for what you are about to see. It's also the place to pick up your multi-site museum discount ticket.

From Naples the ancient Roman sites come thick and fast, beginning west of the city with the Flavian Amphitheatre and the Temple of Serapis in Pozzuoli, and the Phlegraean Fields. From there the route loops back to the coast east of Naples along the Passeggiata Archeologica, to Herculaneum, the Villa Poppaea, the Boscoreale Antiquarium, Pompeii and Stabiae, with its exquisite Roman villas of St Marco, Arianna and Dei Cesari.

The trip then continues farther along the coast to something a little different: the ancient Greek city of Paestum. To get there, it is worth taking the longer but more scenic coastal route via Sorrento and Amalfi. DK

❶ The Temple of Apollo at Pompeii.

Historic Puglia Puglia, Italy

Start Manfredonia   End Brindisi   Distance 282km (175 miles)
Type Culture   Map goo.gl/HQkq16

For decades, Puglia was a neglected backwater. While tourists flocked to Tuscany, the ancient province of Puglia was forgotten. This route will take you through the best of this memorable landscape of hill towns and olive groves at the heel of Italy.

Start at the seaside resort of Manfredonia, in the Gargano National Park, with its deep beech woods and rocky coastline. Head south along the beaches towards the old town of Andria and its 13th-century Castel del Monte. A World Heritage Site, this intact, hilltop stronghold was built by the Holy Roman Emperor Frederick II employing a motif of 'eight'. It is octagonal and has eight towers, each containing eight rooms. Nobody knows why.

Explore the old fortified port of Bari, its labyrinth of tiny streets in the old town, and the stone chapel holding the remains of St Nicholas, known now as Santa Claus. Farther south, the route arrives at Alberobello, a dusty country town famous for its conical *trulli* houses.

Ostuni, the 'White City', dazzles as the sun bounces off its whitewashed buildings. It's great for a relaxing wander through its shady squares and cobblestoned alleyways. For a fitting finale, follow the Appian Way, the old Roman highway from the capital, into the old harbourside at Brindisi. SH

❶ The conical houses known as *trulli* in Alberobello.

Strada Cristo Redentore di Maratea
Basilicata/Lazio, Italy

Start Maratea, Basilicata
End Monte San Biagio, Lazio
Distance 7km (4.3 miles)
Type Scenic
Map goo.gl/lkjEX3

Are you ready to tackle one of the most extraordinary stretches of road in the Mediterranean? This short route from the coastal resort of Maratea in southern Italy climbs up a ridiculous pinnacle of rock overlooking the town, thanks to a daring sequence of 18 hairpin bends supported on concrete pillars. It involves an exhausting amount of steering or bike leaning and terrifying, exposed drops on each of the corners. Adventurous as this drive may be, it is the unrivalled views of the coast that set this route apart.

Where the road runs out, there is a short paved walkway to the point of the rocky pinnacle of Monte San Biagio. Right on the summit of the cliff face is a huge white figure of Christ the Redeemer, with arms outstretched, like an Italian version of the renowned statue in Rio de Janeiro. It was carved in 1965 from marble by sculptor Bruno Innocenti. The figure is 21m (69ft) tall and stares out to sea.

From here, at a height of 592m (1,942ft), you can see the town and shoreline below and the mountainous Basilicata coastline leading off to the north and south. And looking back down the sheer face of the rock you are standing on, you can contemplate the amazing concertina of road that you now have to tackle to return to the safety of the world below. **SH**

❶ One of the crazy hairpin bends jutting out to sea, viewed from another identical curve directly above it.

Griffons Route
Sardinia, Italy

Start Alghero
End Bosa Marina
Distance 45km (27.8 miles)
Type Scenic
Map goo.gl/QTMaFd

This hour-long route hugs the western coast of Sardinia, heading north from the city of Alghero along well-maintained highways to arrive at Bosa Marina. It is the ideal trip to take on a sunny day in a cabriolet, which affords the opportunity to look at the open road ahead, the glistening Mediterranean Sea on one side, and on the other, rocky hills covered with maquis and olive trees. Going topless also increases the likelihood of seeing the griffon vulture (*Gyps fulvus*) bird of prey, after which the route is named.

The Bosa area is home to the island's two remaining griffon vulture colonies, and this route has several dedicated spots where you can pause to scan the cliffs below. In summer, there is a good chance that you will catch sight of the majestic white-and-buff-coloured bird, which has a wingspan of up to 3m (9ft).

In order to make the most of the scenery, and to avoid the crowds on what is a narrow, twisting road only two lanes wide, hit the tarmac early. That way, you should also have time to stop for a dip in the sea. It is best to wait until after Capo Marrargiu, when there will be opportunities to take a path down to a beach on one of the many inlets. Alternatively, drive on until you reach the sandy beach at Bosa Marina, which is said to be one of the cleanest in Italy. **CK**

Orientale Sarda
Sardinia, Italy

Start Santa Maria Navarrese
End Dorgali
Distance 57km (35.4 miles)
Type Scenic
Map goo.gl/KIkLuT

Tucked away on the east coast of the island of Sardinia is a mesmerizing stretch of twisting highway. Some call it one of Europe's most beautiful roads; others describe it as dangerous. *Lonely Planet* referred to it as 'hair-raising'. Certainly, this road trip makes an impression on all who drive it.

The Orientale Sarda is a wild roller coaster of hairpin bends, gorges, climbs and unguarded drops through the little-known Gennargentu National Park. This area may not be what you expect from a sunny Mediterranean holiday island, but the park covers 730 sq km (280 square miles) of serious snowcapped mountains that swoop down to the sea or into thick-forested canyons. It is the sort of place where you can look out for eagles, vultures and wildcats. However, not all wildlife is welcomed by the visiting road tripper: at dawn and dusk, tribes of wild pigs and goats are renowned for suddenly wandering across the highway. Apart from that, your only hazards are regular rockfalls from above.

The road itself is well paved and well signed, but it has to cope with some hard-core terrain. Most of this stretch is uninhabited by humans. It has to pick its way across the park, through tunnels and around rocky outcrops, clinging to rock faces. The reward is discovering some stupendous viewpoints, and the feeling of having overcome another fantastic motoring challenge. **SH**

Mt Etna Scenic Drive Sicily, Italy

Start Taormina, Messina **End** Funicular Etna, Catania **Distance** 68km (42 miles)
Type Scenic **Map** goo.gl/kCIids

The best time to take this road trip in Sicily is out of peak season, since the route from the island's top tourist resort at Taormina can get very busy when resident Italians are heading to the beach during the scorching hot days of summer. Most of the route is a straightforward drive along the A18 freeway, which is one of the few toll roads on the island. However, the rewards are well worth the fee, with views from Etna and across the strange, black volcanic environment.

It is best to check if there is any volcanic activity at Mt Etna before setting out, because when there is the nearby roads are closed. And it is not only lava that drivers need to be careful to avoid: when there is an eruption, the surrounding area can be covered with black volcanic ash for many miles, and the roads close to Etna become very slippery.

The ascent up Mt Etna is truly memorable. Via a series of twists and turns, the Sicilian terrain of olive groves and stone houses gives way to a bleak and black landscape that seems more akin to the moon. Etna is a live volcano and the most active in Europe. Passing by the remains of buildings that jut out from the jagged black rock is a reminder that nature, rather than humankind, holds sway on this part of the island. **CK**

❶ The route snakes across the volcanic landcape.

Targa Florio and the Piccolo Madonie Circuit Sicily, Italy

Start Cerda   End Cerda   Distance 75km (46.6 miles)
Type Culture   Map goo.gl/OgP9tJ

Hailed by many motorsport aficionados as the greatest road race of all time, the Targa Florio can trace its origins back to 1906, when Sicilian car fanatic Vincenzo Florio first hosted a nine-hour endurance race around Sicily's rugged interior.

By the 1950s 'the Targa' had become the highlight of the World Sportscar Championship calendar, attracting the racing greats, including Stirling Moss, Tazio Nuvolari and Juan Manuel Fangio. From 1951 to 1977 (before several fatalities saw its demise), the shorter Piccolo Madonie Circuit was used; with some 700 corners crammed into just 72km (45 miles) of mountain road, it was the ultimate test of man and machine.

To follow in the tracks of legends, start at the ghostly old pit lanes, with their crumbling paint-peeled grandstands, just north of Cerda, and then head in an anticlockwise loop to the mountain town of Caltavuturo. At Collesano, you'll find it hard to believe that 500-brake horsepower Ferraris once thundered through its narrow shop-lined streets.

Since its racing heyday the tarmac of the Targa Florio's mountain sections has deteriorated badly. Take your time, watch out for potholes and enjoy the wonderful Sicilian scenery as you wind down to the coast. **DIS**

❶ Action in 1970 on the Piccolo Madonie Circuit.

Giro di Sicilia
Sicily, Italy

Start Palermo
End Palermo
Distance 956km (594 miles)
Type Culture
Map goo.gl/neM4rJ

In 1898 wealthy Sicilian wine merchant Vincenzo Florio was bitten by the motoring bug after spotting a De Dion motor tricycle in a Paris showroom. In a flurry of excitement, he bought the vehicle and had it shipped back to Palermo. On unpacking the crate at the docks, Vincenzo faced two problems: Sicily had no petrol and no drivable roads.

Yet such was Florio's passion for motorsport that eight years later the first Sicilian road race was held on a prepared mountain circuit, with a large silver platter (*targa*) as the winner's trophy. In 1912, in a political move to encourage the authorities to improve Sicily's highways, the annual Targa Florio became a full circuit of the island's perimeter. Twenty-six cars started this gruelling race, which was won by British driver Cyril Snipe, in a mind-boggling 24 hours 37 minutes 19 seconds.

Despite today's smooth coastal roads, you'll be hard pressed to complete this road trip much quicker than Snipe a century before you. However, retracing this historic route, which later became known as the Giro di Sicilia, is a great excuse for a week-long exploration of the island's hidden gems. Among these are the cliff-top village of Erice and the unspoiled beaches of the south, including Foce del Fiume Belice, close to the quaint fishing village of Porto Palo. Nearby Sciacca is the perfect spot for the first of many *al fresco* lunch stops. **DIS**

Discover Malta
Malta

Start Valetta
End Valetta
Distance 69km (43 miles)
Type Culture
Map goo.gl/Sq3YKV

Malta is not a big place – the main island is just 30km (20 miles) long – but there is lots to see on this circular tour. Poised between North Africa and Europe, Malta has attracted armies for centuries. They have left medieval castles, Knights Templar churches and World War II defences, adding to a rich legacy of megalithic monuments. This trip combines all this history with a good snapshot of the rest of what the island has to offer.

Once you have left Valetta, the roads are poor and it takes a surprising time to get anywhere, so allocate two days for the drive. On the threshold of the capital is one of the island's top historical sites, the Neolithic Ħal-Saflieni Hypogeum, a huge underground burial chamber dating from 4000 BCE (reserve tickets well in advance). A little farther south are three megalithic sites, the Tarxien, Ħaġar Qim and Mnajdra temple complexes. On the coast take in the pretty fishing harbor of Marsaxlokk and the resorts of St Julian's and Sliema.

The best place to overnight is the island's former capital, Mdina. While Valetta feels European, Mdina's medieval walls enclose something altogether Moorish. Try to stay in the old centre of town, where cars are prohibited – it's only a short walk from the parking. **DK**

⊜ The Mnajdra temple complex, Malta.

Road to the Wolf's Lair
Warmia-Masuria, Poland

Start Kętrzyn
End Wolf's Lair
Distance 9km (5.6 miles)
Type Culture
Map goo.gl/jIRYuE

In the Masurian region of northern Poland, a land famous for endless forests and more than 2,000 lakes, lies one of World War II's great relics. Just 9km (5.6 miles) to the east of Kętrzyn, in the Masurian woods, are the ruins of Adolf Hitler's Wolfsschanze, or Wolf's Lair. Built between 1940 and 1941, the site contains more than 80 buildings, including Hitler's personal bunker, all destroyed by the Germans in January 1945, in the face of an unstoppable Red Army offensive.

The rural roads that take you there from nearby Kętrzyn are typical of the region. Leaving Kętrzyn on Route 592, you turn left onto a paved two-lane road at the town of Karolewo. After a few miles driving through farmland, the road plunges into the Masurian forest, an area once protected by some 10,000 land mines. Turning into the narrow entrance road – still clad in the same cobbles that the Führer's Mercedes car trundled over – it's only a short drive up to the compound itself.

Hitler spent more than 800 days here, overseeing operations on the Russian front. He famously survived a 20 July 1944 assassination attempt by Colonel Claus von Stauffenberg at the Wolfsschanze. Touring the bunkers, the air raid shelters and the administrative buildings – some just rubble, others almost intact – can easily fill an entire day. It's a fascinating site. **BDS**

Giant Mountains
Lower Silesia, Poland

Start Wrocław
End Kłodzko
Distance 241km (150 miles)
Type Scenic
Map goo.gl/MbfPev

This trip through Lower Silesia begins on the banks of the Oder River in Wrocław, an ancient city that was almost completely destroyed in World War II but has since been restored to something like its pristine state. The Rynek (Old Market Square) has a special charm.

The route as far as Kostomloty is along a section of the longest highway in Europe, which extends from Calais in France to Ridder in Kazakhstan near the Chinese frontier. Having turned onto a quieter road, after some 112km (70 miles) you reach Jelenia Góra. This city, which lies among four mountain ranges, makes a good base for excursions into Karkonosze National Park, but before diverting, be sure to visit the Baroque main square. Continuing south, the itinerary passes through the ski resort of Karpacz before ending in Kłodzko.

This town is something of an anomaly: it's Polish but with a strong influence from the Czech Republic, which closely surrounds it on three sides. Among the main tourist attractions are the old fortress on a high rock, the Gothic bridge across the Nysa Kłodzka (Eastern Neisse) and the network of tunnels beneath the town centre. From Kłodzko, travellers could continue into the Czech Republic to Prague, 196km (123 miles) to the west. **JP**

⊃ Stunning vista across Karkonosze National Park.

Przełęcz Przysłup Pass
Lesser Poland, Poland

Start Tyrawa Wołoska
End Solina
Distance 40km (25 miles)
Type Culture
Map goo.gl/SUOxSt

Deep in Central Europe, a little less than 400km (250 miles) south of Warsaw, this handsome but challenging road passes through the heart of the Beskid Mountains, in a wedge of Polish territory between Slovakia and Ukraine.

The Beskid form part of the mighty Carpathian range. The first third of the proposed north to south route is uphill – an average gradient of 6 per cent, with the steepest sections 13 per cent. This is easy enough for motorized vehicles, but sweat-raising for cyclists, many of whom come to pedal the pass. By the time the road reaches its highest point, the elevation has increased by 298m (978ft) to 2626m (2,054ft) above sea level. From the top, on a clear day, views over the mountains stretch to the horizon.

The second third of the journey consists of sweeping curves and nine hairpin bends on the descent into the valley of the San River, where the Przełęcz Przysłup Pass ends at a ruined castle built between 1333 and 1370 during the reign of Casimir III (the Great), king of Poland.

The final part of the trip runs parallel to the river to the shores of Lake Solina, which was created in 1968 by the completion of a dam to power the Zapora Wodna hydroelectric plant. The lake is a major tourist attraction and popular with watersports enthusiasts. **JP**

Niedzica to Kamienka
Poland/Slovakia

Start Niedzica
End Kamienka
Distance 29km (18 miles)
Type Scenic
Map goo.gl/Y4T3yp

This international route is well maintained, mainly straight and reasonably easy throughout its length. Consequently, it has become a firm favourite among Eastern European bikers and cyclists.

The starting point, Niedzica, is a popular resort on the shores of Lake Czorsztyn, a large artificial expanse of freshwater created in 1995 by a dam built to prevent flooding on the Dunajec river and to power a hydroelectric plant. It's worth climbing up to the medieval castle crowning a promontory on the waterfront.

From Niedzica, set off eastwards into Slovakia across a frontier marked, at the time of writing, by nothing more than some roadside signs. Almost immediately, the road enters Pieniny National Park, where the Dunajec forms a magnificent gorge. Also worth seeing in these parts is Červený Kláštor, a 14th-century monastery with terracotta-tiled roofs. The complex has served many purposes in its history. In 1563, after the Reformation, it became a nobleman's residence, and in the 20th century it served as a retreat for the Communists' top brass. Today it is a museum of local history.

This road trip ends in the traditional village of Kamienka, historically the westernmost settlement of the diasporic Rusyn Ukrainian peoples, a minority who were suppressed during the Soviet domination of Poland. **JP**

Discover Czech Republic
Central Bohemia, Czech Republic

Start Prague
End Prague
Distance 668km (415 miles)
Type Culture
Map goo.gl/45Il2o

This Bohemian rhapsody through the southwest of the Czech Republic is great for culture vultures, wine lovers and history buffs. To do it properly will take at least a week because there are so many medieval castles, Renaissance châteaux and historic towns to visit.

About three hours' drive from Prague brings you to the first of the grand châteaux – the Baroque Valtice (which has a wine museum) and the neo-Gothic Lednice, both sitting in country estates. Their associated villages, or nearby Mikulov, are good places to take a break. Next comes Znojmo in the heart of the Moravian wine region. Farther on, Slavonice and Telč are Renaissance gems that are UNESCO World Heritage Sites.

The medieval spa town of Třeboň, set among picturesque fishponds, is a good place to overnight, before traveling on to Český Krumlov. After Prague, this is the most visited destination in the Czech Republic. Its slightly out-of-the-way location near the Austrian border isolated it from the architectural changes that took place elsewhere, thus preserving its medieval and Baroque character. It is crowned by a huge 13th-century castle containing the Gothic St Vitus Church and a Baroque theatre, which are both must-sees. The road trip ends with a visit to Tábor, the focus of the 15th-century Hussite Reformation. **DK**

❶ The Old Town Square in Prague, the start and end of this circular tour.

Mt Luční
Hradec Králové, Czech Republic

Start Pec Pod Sněžkou
End Hotel Luční Bouda
Distance 8km (5 miles)
Type Scenic
Map goo.gl/Hfz9mW

High in the Krkonoše (Giant Mountains), on the border of the Czech Republic and Poland, a narrow mountain trail snakes up from the small ski resort of Pec Pod Sněžkou. The Czech Republic's highest mountain, Sněžka (1,603m/5,529ft), rises just to the north, but this route heads west, up through lush meadows and pine forest into Krkonoše National Park. The lane loops up the slopes of Mt Luční, which at 1,555m/5,102ft) high is the country's second highest peak.

In good weather this is a scenic drive, but it quickly becomes more challenging if conditions deteriorate. The serpentine turns and sheer drops assume more menace as the road surface becomes slippery. Whatever the weather, you will be climbing into the heart of the mountain range and will soon be surrounded by a sea of impressive peaks. Near the top is a windswept area of treeless tundra. The environment here is considered so special that it has been designated a UNESCO Biosphere Reserve. It is also the source of the great River Elbe, which flows via Germany into the North Sea, some 1,091lm (678 miles) away.

You can park near the summit of the mountain and walk the last few hundred yards to its peak. Unexpectedly, there is a hotel alone on the far side, where you can stop for a meal in the highest restaurant in the Czech Republic. **SH**

Masaryk F1 Street Circuit
South Moravia, Czech Republic

Start Nový Lískovec
End Nový Lískovec
Distance 31km (19 miles)
Type Culture
Map goo.gl/aBrJVO

The Masaryk Circuit (more widely known as the Brno Circuit, after the Czech Republic's second-largest city), is about 200km (124 miles) southeast of Prague. The circuit was created in 1930 and then constantly tweaked over six decades in an effort to make it faster, safer and better to spectate. Run on the main public roads along the fringes of an ever-growing Brno, it was eventually replaced in 1987 by the purpose-built racetrack of the same name located nearby.

Once considered one of the most beautiful racetracks in the Formula One stable, the circuit offers few clues to its illustrious past, apart from the shabby, repurposed pit lanes and the odd length of rusting Armco safety barrier. Nevertheless, it's still possible to enjoy a drive around the original 1930–37 route, when the race was driven anticlockwise from the Brno suburb of Nový Lískovec. Smooth tarmac then takes you north through wooded hills, a little more built-up now than it was in the 1930s but still pleasantly rural in parts. The old circuit then heads west through more suburbs before reaching beautiful tree-lined avenues that lead to the pretty little town of Brno-Žebětín. The route extends as far as the historic town of Otrokovice before returning to Nový Lískovec along even more delightful tree-lined roads virtually unchanged since the circuit's heyday. **MG**

Orava Castle Scenic Drive
Zilina, Slovakia

Start Oravský Podzámok
End Oravský Podzámok
Distance 14km (8.7 miles)
Type Scenic
Map goo.gl/x2KsFN

The area of Slovakia on the border with Poland has some fabulous scenic mountain roads that twist and turn, rise and fall. The region also offers wild rivers, unspoiled lakes, historic bridges and pretty villages. There are some grand buildings, too, including Orava Castle.

One of the largest castles in Slovakia, it sits high on a rocky outcrop above the village of Oravský Podzámok. Like something from a *Harry Potter* movie or the lair of a Bond supervillain (it was actually used for the filming of the 1922 horror classic *Nosferatu*), the fortification looms over you from above and creates a great centrepiece for a short but challenging drive. Orava Castle was built in the 14th century, burned down in 1800 and restored after World War II. It is named after the Orava River, which you will cross nine times as you make this road trip.

Listed in Slovakia's top five scenic drives, the route is along roads that are smooth, broad and maintained to a high standard, with fast straights and sweeping corners on the R3 section. However, the scenery is like something from a fairy tale, and all the while you have the mighty castle jutting out from the cliffs above. If you are staying in the area, join one of the night tours or attend an evening theatre performance to see this magnificent citadel at its most atmospheric. **JI**

❶ The castle buildings – palaces, courtyards, towers and chapels – are arranged over three levels.

Lake Balaton
Transdanubia, Hungary

Start Budapest Airport
End Budapest Airport
Distance 338km (210 miles)
Type Scenic
Map goo.gl/VgHdJI

Fly into Budapest; pick up a rental car; drive to the holiday resort of Siófok, 133km (83 miles) to the west, and you are on the shores of the largest expanse of freshwater between Switzerland and the Russia–Finland border. It is a popular trip because there is always plenty to do on Lake Balaton: swimming and sailing in the summer; iceboating in the winter; fishing year round. From Siófok, the road is relatively straight and flat and fast to Keszthely, an old market town. From here it is recommended to take an 8-km- (5-mile) long detour to Hévíz, where the world's second-largest thermal lake (the biggest such formation is the Frying Pan Lake in New Zealand) promises a cure for skin ailments. There are also vineyards in the vicinity, and you will discover that there is more to Hungarian wine than Bull's Blood. Drivers must not touch a drop, however; there is zero tolerance for alcohol in the bloodstream of motorists.

On the north side of Balaton, the road runs between the waterfront and the slopes of the low-lying Bakony Mountains. There are many beachside tourist resorts along this stretch before the main town, Balatonfüred, which is the nightclub mecca of this part of Hungary – the north-bank equivalent of Siófok. And it's to Siófok that you then return to complete the circuit, before you fork left and return the car to Budapest Ferenc Liszt International. **JP**

Discover Hungary
Budapest, Hungary

Start Budapest
End Budapest
Distance 1,254km (779 miles)
Type Culture
Map goo.gl/xV4b00

Budapest is a fashionable weekend destination for Europeans, but most visitors don't venture much beyond the capital. This week-long circuit through the Hungarian countryside shows how much they are missing. Following the flow of the great Danube River, it stops in lakeside villages untouched by time, meanders through the wine region and passes through forests with spectacular waterfalls.

From Budapest, drive west through Szentendre and Visegrád to the basilica at Esztergom and Komarom Castle in Komárno. Continue to the medieval town of Sopron and Lake Fertő (German: Neusiedler See) on the Austrian border and then turn south to overnight at Körmend. From there to Tapolka, the route meanders through idyllic villages on Lake Balaton and then heads cross-country to the town of Kecskemét. The landscape flattens as the road crosses the central plain, following the winding Tisza River. Turning north it enters Hungary's wine-growing region. It's worth buying a bottle of the honey-coloured Tokaji dessert wine.

The return to Budapest takes in the castle at Szerencs and then travels through the heart of the Matra Mountains and the Bükki National Park, before arriving at the medieval town of Eger. Lastly, to the World Heritage Site of Hollókő, a Palóc village whose wooden buildings typify rural settlements before industrialization. **DK**

Mangart Road
Slovene Littoral, Slovenia

Start Bovec
End Mangart Saddle
Distance 26 km (16.2 miles)
Type Adventure
Map goo.gl/MpzyW5

Built in 1938 at a time when this mountainous region of Slovenia was a part of Italy, Mangart Road has stood the test of time. It remains the country's highest-lying road, but despite being sealed over its entire length, some sections are currently in a poor state of repair. Precipitous drop-offs are uncomfortably close to the driving surface and there are few guardrails to provide a buffer, although locally cut stones do line the roadside. (The large ones will save you; the small ones are more likely to accompany you over the edge.) The road is unnervingly narrow in places, too, with only occasional places for passing. The primitive-looking tunnels through which it passes are hacked through granite and are not lit.

All of these shortcomings, of course, contribute significantly to the adrenaline rush experienced on this dead-end, out-and-back road that takes you up to an altitude of 2,055m (6,742ft). From the summit, Mangart Saddle, there are stunning views across the western Julian Alps and the trailhead frequented by climbers eager to begin their ascent to the 2,679-m- (8,789-ft) high summit of Mangart, the mountain that looms above. You will feel refreshingly alone driving the one-way loop near the saddle. The absence of head-on traffic means that you can enjoy a road that seems to have been put there just for you. **BDS**

❶ Mangart Road is still thought of as one of Slovenia's most beautiful Alpine roads.

Solčava Panoramic Road Solčava, Slovenia

Start Solčava   **End** Solčava   **Distance** 37km (23 miles)
Type Scenic   **Info** goo.gl/myeBAU

Following in the footsteps of Austria and Italy and their fine driving roads, Slovenia has begun to promote its own tarmac-clad playground for keen motorists and bikers. There are many highlights, including all the usual desirables, from ancient castles and soaring peaks to dairy farms and highland homesteads. But the Solčava Panoramic Road's unique selling point is the incomparable Logar Valley, one of three parallel glacial valleys that rate among Europe's finest.

The area is famous in local folklore: tales involve fiery dragons and shepherd boys looking for lost sheep. Here, legend and landscape are connected by the Solčava Panoramic Road. It offers a road trip experience not only of nature, but also of culture. Passing through traditional, high-altitude subsistence farms, which preserve a precious ethnological heritage, it is home to a people who cling to their roots through fairy tales, dance and music.

Eighty per cent of the Solčava region is protected, and this wonderful road, with its gentle cambers and effortless gradients, can be driven easily in a single day. There are no tolls, either, unlike the Grossglockner or Nockalmstrasse, and not a great deal of traffic in this stunning corner of Slovenia's Kamnik-Savinja Alps. **BDS**

❶ Perhaps the most beautiful Alpine valley in Slovenia.

Mt Vojak Istria, Croatia

Start Vela Učka   **End** Vojak   **Distance** 7km (4.3 miles)
Type Scenic   **Info** goo.gl/u8kG3a

This short, sharp, and immensely rewarding climb takes the you from 955m (3,133ft) to 1,369m (4,491ft) above sea level, over gradients averaging 7 per cent but as much as 23 per cent in places. Clearly this is not a road trip for those in bigger vehicles. There is a well-signed speed limit –30 kph (19 mph) –but that is just about the only rule: drivers are at liberty to take their vehicles off road and across the shrub-covered mountain slopes, though all but the most experienced would be ill-advised to try.

The proposed itinerary passes through Učka Nature Park, one of only a few places in Europe frequented by griffon vultures and golden eagles.

The wayside scenery is beautiful, but it pales into insignificance in comparison with the view from the top of Mt Vojak, at 1,401m (4,596ft), the highest point on the Istrian peninsula. At the summit, there is a lookout and a stone tower from which the Adriatic islands of Krk, Lošinj and Cres are visible in the middle distance. On the clearest days Switzerland, the Dolomites,and Venice can also be seen from here.

The start point at Vela Učka is reachable via a turnoff from the E751, the highway between Rijeka and Pula, the two main cities of the region. **JP**

➊ View over the Adriatic islands from Mt Vojak.

Krk Highway
Krk Island, Croatia

Start D8 highway intersection at Šmrika
End Baska
Distance 48km (29.9 miles)
Type Scenic
Map goo.gl/oL8Hxd

Krk – the most populous and one of the largest islands in the Adriatic Sea – teems with sun worshippers from all over Europe during its parched summer months. However, out of season, its easy access, mild climate and rugged beauty make it the ideal destination for a winter road trip.

The island has been continuously inhabited since Neolithic times, and boasts numerous Iron and Bronze Age earthworks and Roman ruins. Variously occupied by Venetians, Austrians and Italians, it became part of Yugoslavia in 1921, and since 1991 has formed part of independent Croatia. Since 1980 the island has been connected to the Balkan mainland via the 1,430-m- (4,690-ft) long Krk Bridge, a magnificent structure made from reinforced concrete, which includes the second-longest concrete arch in the world. A small toll is payable by vehicles crossing the bridge.

Running south across the bridge and then down the length of the island to its southern tip at Baska is the D102, the Krk Highway, which is parallel to the northwest coast of the island and then turns south to Krk, a thriving port since Roman times. From there the road heads southeast to the popular resort town of Baska, famous for its 1,800-m- (5,904-ft) long Vela Plaža (Great Beach); this is a good stopping-off point for refuelling both vehicle and driver. **SA**

Adriatic Highway
Croatia/Bosnia and Herzegovina

Start Rijeka, Croatia
End Dubrovnik, Croatia
Distance 533km (331 miles)
Type Scenic
Map goo.gl/dZyZXT

Whether twisting around sea cliffs with a panorama of islands stretching to the horizon or skirting beautiful forests hanging above glittering sandy beaches, the Adriatic Highway is one of the Mediterranean's finest driving routes. The full highway runs from the Italian border near Trieste, along the length of Croatia's coast, including a short stretch in Bosnia, and continues into Montenegro.

This is the finest section, from the elegant northern beach resort of Rijeka to the World Heritage Site of Dubrovnik, mostly following the E65. It's a sequence of sunny villages and towns full of old stone houses topped with terracotta tiles. Amid rocky gorges and lush valleys, heading to the sea, you'll find farmers selling fresh oranges on the roadside, and seafood restaurants serving whatever has been caught that day.

The small stretch through Bosnia adds little delay; border checks are minimal, if they happen at all. The road is of good quality, although be prepared for lots of wiggling in and out along Croatia's jagged coastline. Take it easy on the bends: safety barriers alongside vertical drops may not be as secure as you would wish.

The finale is Dubrovnik, one of the great sights of Europe. This intact walled city contains a labyrinth of atmospheric stone alleys lined with fine palaces and Baroque churches. **SH**

Sveti Jure
Split–Dalmatia, Croatia

Start Podgora
End Sveti Jure
Distance 26km (16.2 miles)
Type Adventure
Info goo.gl/eTBVUQ

Reaching a height of 1,762m (5,780ft), this is the highest mountain road in Croatia. It takes you from the deep blue waters of the Adriatic on the Dalmatian Coast to the highest point in the Biokovo Mountains, the second-tallest mountain range in the country. The journey is dramatic.

Heading inland from the small resort of Podgora, the road immediately starts to rise as it zigzags through thick woods. You very quickly get good views back down to the coast and across to the large islands of Brač and Hvar, which lie just offshore. In places, sea views extend into the distance on one side, and the karst cliffs of the Biokovo Mountains rise sheer on the other. Elsewhere on the route, the road plunges through tunnels, forcing its way up and around the mountain barrier.

At first the road is well surfaced and wide, but be prepared for it to narrow and be ready to back up, sometimes for a considerable distance, if a car comes towards you – there are not always safety barriers in place, so don't rush. It is a spectacular drive, but not recommended if conditions are wet or slippery.

Once you reach the top of Sveti Jure (St George), what then? Well, you enjoy the views, bask in a sense of achievement and then turn around and go down. This time, however, it will be someone else's turn to do the reversing. MG

❶ The rugged karst of the Biokovo Mountains is riddled with sinkholes and caves in the limestone.

Pitve-Zavala Fire Road and Tunnel
Split–Dalmatia, Croatia

Start Zavala
End Zavala
Distance 18km (11.2 miles)
Type Adventure
Map goo.gl/qYatT5

The Croatian island of Hvar regularly tops lists of the most beautiful islands in the Adriatic, and Hvar is sometimes described as the new St Tropez. Less well known is that Hvar also offers one of the most feared road trips in Europe – a circular roller coaster starting and ending in the village of Zavala on the south coast.

Access to Zavala and its beaches was once only possible through a scary 1.4-km- (0.87-mile) long tunnel, carved out of solid rock to carry water pipes in 1962, and later converted into a public road. However, the Pitve Tunnel's potholed surface, leaking roof, deep puddles and total darkness – not to mention its lack of places to pass – is too much for many road-tripping tourists, no matter good those beaches.

Luckily, a fire road over the hills bypasses the tunnel. It is accessed to the right of the tunnel entrance. However, this road brings new terrors: there are no guardrails and the loose-surfaced road often teeters on the edge of sheer drops to the valley lying hundreds of feet below. The views from up here, and the air quality, are certainly much better, though.

This road trip gives you a taste of both routes, underground and over mountain, before ending in Zavala, where you can calm your nerves in one of the resort's many bars and cafés. **SA**

❶ Nearly a mile long, the Pitve Tunnel is not recommended for nervous drivers.

Piva Canyon Road
Bosnia and Herzegovina/Montenegro

Start Vučevo, Bosnia and Herzegovina
End Pluzine, Montenegro
Distance 27km (17 miles)
Type Scenic
Map goo.gl/G3HYmb

This itinerary covers a short section of the E762, a major highway that links three European capitals: Sarajevo (Bosnia and Herzegovina) and Tirana (Albania) via Podgorica (Montenegro). The inherent challenges of this stretch of the road – only two lanes, tight corners, steep sides above and below the road, narrow bridges and tunnels with severely restricted width and headroom – are complicated by heavy traffic, including big passenger buses and long-distance trucks.

For those undeterred by that warning, the views along the route are more than ample reward for the stresses of driving it. Piva Canyon is an amazing part of this astonishingly beautiful part of the Balkans. As one reviewer on TripAdvisor remarked: 'This seriously would be a highlight attraction at most [US] National Parks, and it's just another gorge in Montenegro.'

From the Bosnia border at Vučevo, much of the road runs alongside the Piva River, which trickled far below the highway until 1975, when the completion of the Mratinje Dam inundated the steep-sided valley to create an area of outstanding, if not entirely natural, beauty.

The southern end of this road trip, the town of Pluzine, previously perched on the banks of the original watercourse, but was moved in its entirety up the hillside before the waters rose. **JP**

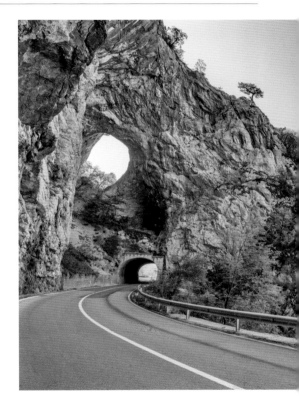

❶ An 'eye' in the cliffs on the Piva Canyon Road that provides some stunning views.

M5 Srpska/FBIH, Bosnia and Herzegovina

Start Pale   End Ustiprača   Distance 60km (37 miles)
Type Adventure   Map goo.gl/x8QMiw

After the end of the Bosnian War of 1995, some of the country's railways were earmarked for 'adaptive reuse'. One of the best examples of this trend is the Eastern Narrow Gauge Railway, a section of railroad from Pale to the southeast of Sarajevo that was turned into a road, the M5.

Although some sections near the major towns are now smooth, modern roadway, the interesting bit is the 20-km- (12.4-mile) long section from the Rakitnica River to Hrenovica through the picturesque Praca Canyon. This poorly graded gravel track, once part of the Sarajevo to Pale railroad, takes you through 40 roughly hewn tunnels built for steam trains that will test the

nerves of even the most ardent of tunnel lovers. The distance between some tunnels is just a few metres, so blink and you'll miss the slivers of daylight between the darkness. In other places, especially when rounding rocky outcrops, there are terrifying drop-offs to the side of the road.

The route is mostly a single lane, but with just enough of a shoulder to allow the safe passage of two vehicles. The longest tunnel is 852m (2,795ft) with two internal bends, creating a pitch-black central section that is a much-loved habitat for bats. **BDS**

❶ One of the many narrow tunnels on the route.

Jerma River Canyon Road Pirot, Serbia

Start Petačinci   End Vlasi   Distance 18km (11.2 miles)
Type Adventure   Map goo.gl/LsR4Zl

The Jerma River in southeast Serbia is only 74km (46 miles) long, yet it twice crosses the border with Bulgaria, where it is known as the Erma, before heading north and emptying into the Nišava River. This road trip follows the Jerma as it winds through a spectacular gorge carved out of the bedrock by its own eroding forces.

Entry to the gorge is on the 223 road north of Petačinci, a small village divided between Serbia and Bulgaria, although the Serbian half has a population of only 19 people. From here the river gorge winds through the hills. The road itself is narrow, and single file in places, although there are places to pass. Cliffs towering up to 230m

(600ft) line the sides of the route, sometimes enclosing the road entirely to form tunnels. Falls of rock, and snow in winter, often result in the road's closure, so it's best to check that it is open before setting out.

The road is quite a recent structure, since the gorge was completely impassable until a narrow-gauge railroad was built in 1927 to service the Rakita coal mine. When the mine closed in the 1960s, the railroad was removed and the route resurfaced to create one of the most dramatic driving experiences in Serbia. It's not to be missed. SA

❶ The Jerma River Canyon Road, a scenic adventure.

Kotor to Sveti Stefan
Kotor, Montenegro

Start Kotor
End Sveti Stefan
Distance 44km (27.3 miles)
Type Adventure
Map goo.gl/RjBUFM

Kotor lies on the bay to which it gives its name – one of the world's most beautiful sheltered marine inlets. The walled town is well worth a visit, but it is best avoided when one of the many passing Mediterranean cruise liners is in port.

Heading south from Kotor, the first section of the drive is through pleasant Balkan countryside before heading on to the more scenic but challenging Donjogrbaljski Put (take the E65 if you want a faster, easier alternative). However, the real thrills begin on the outskirts of Budva, a popular holiday resort; from here the road hugs the coast in a series of tight curves that lead to Sveti Stefan, a small islet in the Adriatic Sea, connected to the mainland by a walkway over a narrow isthmus.

This is one of rugged Montenegro's more relaxing drives. Travellers who want a tougher challenge between the two towns should take the minor road around the bay: between Kotor and the airport at Tivat, much of the way is so narrow that reversing and pulling into the driveways of houses is often the only way to avoid oncoming traffic, which includes big trucks and buses. On the right-hand side, there is usually a barrier between road and sea, but not always – what looks like a turnoff may turn out to be a flight of steps to the water's edge – and the lack of street lighting can make this a dangerous place at night. **JP**

❶ View over the exclusive island village of Sveti Stefan, a playground for the very wealthy.

Kotor Serpentine
Kotor, Montenegro

Start Kotor
End Cetinje
Distance 46.7km (29 miles)
Type Adventure
Info goo.gl/PhmCLW Map goo.gl/H5hXYC

The main appeal of this road trip lies in its views of the Bay of Kotor, which become increasingly spectacular with every loop of the ascent – 25 numbered hairpin bends that rise from sea level to 881m (2,890ft) in less than 8km (5 miles). And there are plenty of opportunities to appreciate the vista: not even the most devil-may-care driver will get much above 24 kph (15 mph) at any point because it is simply too dangerous. The road is perfectly well surfaced and maintained, but it rises so steeply – the shallowest gradient is a little over 5 per cent – and has so few barriers that constant care and vigilance are essential.

At the summit the bay disappears from view as the road enters Lovćen National Park. Here you can take a break to visit the impressive mausoleum of ruler Petar II Petrovic-Njegos. The 461 steps up to the national hero's monument may seem forbidding from thecar park, but the effort is rewarded by even more fabulous views – this time of almost the whole of Montenegro and beyond, from the capital, Podgorica, to the Adriatic Sea, and from Bosnia to Albania.

From here the road descends through less spectacular but pretty countryside to Cetinje, the old capital. The historic sights include a Serbian Orthodox monastery and the 15th-century Vlaskan church. **JP**

❶ Near the highest point on the road, where sea views give way to a panorama of the nation.

Jezerski Vrh Mountain
Budva/Cetinje, Montenegro

Start Budva, Budva
End Mausoleum of Petar II Petrovic-Njegos, Cetinje
Distance 53km (33 miles)
Type Scenic
Map goo.gl/jrzd5q

Petar II Petrovic-Njegos was very particular about where he should be interred. The 19th-century poet, prince-bishop and all-around Montenegrin hero decreed that he wanted to be laid to rest at the top of Mt Lovćen, an imposing mountain close to the coast. Petar's body was transferred to what may be the highest mausoleum in the world – at 1,749m (5,738ft) – in 1855, a few years after his death. Today, the mausoleum makes an unusual goal for a brilliant road trip from the coast.

Start on the waterfront in the Adriatic resort of Budva. Overlooked by mountains, ancient Venetian fortifications and blocks of luxury apartments, it forms an elegant contrast to what is to come. Head east to pick up the M2.3. (Note that 'M' stands for 'Montenegro', not 'motorway'.)

Within a couple of miles you'll be twisting into the mountains, one moment thrilled by huge views over the bay and the next alarmed by the hairy roadside drops.

The road itself isn't in bad condition and has an extra lane for overtaking trucks struggling to make the climb. After Cetinje, it enters Lovcen National Park and becomes more like a country lane. Still very scenic, it winds up through the Jezerski Vrh Pass to a tiny car park. From there you can walk through a tunnel and up a staircase to Petar's mausoleum at the summit. **SH**

Shores of Lake Skadar
Bar/Ulcinj, Montenegro

Start Virpazar, Bar
End Vladimir, Ulcinj
Distance 52km (32.5 miles)
Type Scenic
Map goo.gl/wtsNZc

This road is not for the fainthearted or for anyone with vertigo. It starts off innocuously enough at the village of Virpaza on the water's edge of Lake Skadar, which is the largest lake in southern Europe. Montenegrins regard the vast freshwater lake as the heart of their nation, and it was on these rocky shores that the country's former royal family would reside for the summer.

However, the route doesn't linger at this level for very long and soon rises to ear-popping heights along an unrelentingly scary narrow road, with only occasional passing places and almost invariably soaring mountainsides to the right and a sheer drop to the left.

The fear of meeting a big oncoming vehicle is unceasing; meanwhile, it is wise to beware of flocks and herds being shepherded across and along the road from hill to field – they tend to congregate around blind corners and farmers make few concessions to motorized traffic.

Just as the driver starts to fear that the road may rise for ever, it makes a sharp right at the border with Albania and starts a gradual descent into the village of Vladimir, which is the first rest stop on the route.

Many people prefer to push on 20km (12 miles) along the E851 to Ulcinj, a cosmopolitan coastal town in which Western nightclub music mingles with the cries of muezzins from the minarets. **JP**

Žabljak to Suvodo
Žabljak, Montenegro

Start Žabljak
End Suvodo
Distance 41 km (25.5 miles)
Type Adventure
Map goo.gl/9dwSOl

This short but menacing road trip up and over a mountain in northern Montenegro is paved throughout its whole length, but that is just about the only creature comfort it has to offer. The route is a relentless succession of twists and turns and undulations, a warren of narrow rocky tunnels and perilous drops on either side that you will only ever fall down once.

It starts 1,456m (4,777ft) above sea level at Žabljak. This pretty village was twice razed to the ground, first in the Balkan Wars of 1912–13 and then again in World War II, but rose both times from the ashes and is currently being developed as a winter sports resort. The route climbs through Prevoj Sedlo, a high pass in the Durmitor massif, and peaks at an elevation of 1,907m (6,256ft) before easing off downhill into Suvodo, a small settlement in a valley. Not far from here, and well worth an excursion, is Pivsko jezero (Lake Piva), a beautiful reservoir that, at 675m (2,215ft) above sea level, claims to be the highest artificial lake in the world.

The road trip from Žabljak to Suvodo is a spectacular and exhilarating excursion for visitors in this region, and it should not be missed. However, the locals, quite understandably, are looking forward to the opening of the freeway, which will bypass this incredible road. JP

❶ The road heads into the craggy heights of the Durmitor National Park.

Tara River Canyon
Mojkovac, Montenegro

Start Mojkovac
End Đurđevića Tara Bridge
Distance 47km (29.2 miles)
Type Adventure
Map goo.gl/e3q6Tm

Tara River Canyon, the second-longest geological formation of its kind in the world, after the Grand Canyon, is a World Heritage Site. Heading north, as the canyon walls close in, the road matches the meanders in the Tara River bend for bend, until the two are virtually indistinguishable on the map. The ragged tarmac cuts through the rock walls in a series of tunnels, the only protection from the rapids below provided by an occasional knee-high barrier. The road is narrow and twisty, but the jaw-dropping views are well worth the demands it makes on drivers.

Spectacular as the ride through the canyon is, the whole trip is merely a gentle preparation for its climax – Đurđevića Tara Bridge. Opened in 1940, this concrete structure has five arches that extend 365m (1,200ft) across the river, 172m (564ft) below. The memorial at one end honours Božidar Žugić, a lieutenant of the Yugoslav army who was killed in 1941 while defending the bridge against Italian invaders. The structure was fully restored in 1946, and since then has formed part of a major transportation artery. It has also been a magnet for road-tripping tourists and even starred in the action movie *Force 10 from Navarone* (1978). The bridge is a popular site for bungee jumping and the starting point for white-water rafting trips back down the river. **JP**

Morača River Canyon Road
Podgorica, Montenegro

Start Podgorica
End Kolašin
Distance 71km (44 miles)
Type Adventure
Map goo.gl/AOhDD9

The more challenging driving routes in this book tend to be secret little backroads winding through narrow mountain passes that locals no longer use. This one, however, is different. The E65 and E80 along the Morača River Canyon are two of the main roads in Montenegro.

The two roads form the principal artery between the coast and the capital, Podgorica, and beyond to the Serbian border. Some people claim the roads form one of Europe's most dangerous routes, and it's certainly among the most scenic. Shadowing the course of the Morača Canyon, the road plunges through tunnels and rock arches and curls around rugged spurs, with only the flimsiest of barriers to protect you from sheer drops. You'll see a lot of rock very close up, and there are occasional blue-green glimpses of the fast-flowing river below.

In 2013 the danger of the road was demonstrated by a bus crash that killed or injured 47 Romanians after it plunged from the road into the ravine during a rainstorm. Afterwards, both the Romanian and Montenegrin governments held periods of mourning. Today, the British Foreign and Commonwealth Office takes the unusual step of specifically warning British visitors about the dangers of the Morača River Canyon Road. **SH**

➲ A bird's-eye view of the Morača River Canyon Road.

Rugova Gorge Road
Peć, Kosovo

Start Peja
End Kuqishtë
Distance 22km (13.6 miles)
Type Adventure
Map goo.gl/0vfvvu

A tributary of the Drin, the Peć Bistrica – known as the Lumbardhi i Pejës in the local Albanian language – rises on the eastern slopes of the Mokra mountain on the border of Kosovo and Montenegro and first flows south before turning east. At this point, what has thus far been a fairly undistinguished river takes on a completely new guise, for along the next 25km (16 miles) of its length it flows through the majestic Rugova Gorge. With a depth of up to 1,000m (3,280ft), this is one of Europe's longest and deepest canyons. The gorge has been formed by a combination of water erosion and the retreat of the Peć glacier at the end of the last Ice Age, carving through not just the top layers of limestone and slate but also the underlying, harder layers of marble and serpentine to create a geological structure of stunning magnificence.

The best way to approach this great wonder is from its eastern end in Peja. From there the M9 ascends west through the gorge before ending abruptly near the border with Montenegro.

On the way, the road passes through several single-track rock tunnels, over the delightful Autumn Bridge and round some sharp hairpin bends. Waterfalls crash down the rocky canyon sides, while vast and often unexplored caves disappear into the mountains, some of which were once home to ancient peoples. **SA**

❶ The road hugs the side of the Rugova Gorge, one of Europe's longest canyons.

Negovanu Lake
Transylvania, Romania

Start Tălmaciu
End Negovanu Lake
Distance 39km (24.2 miles)
Type Adventure
Map goo.gl/lICuYO

Nothing about the small and ancient town of Tălmaciu in central Romania prepares you for this thrilling road trip on its doorstep. The sleepy town lies on one of the main roads between Wallachia in the south and Transylvania to the northwest. It has thread manufacturing and spinning industries and a factory that bottles the local spring water.

From Tălmaciu the cross-country road heads to Negovanu Lake, a zigzagging journey into the Southern Carpathians, a heavily wooded region with wolves and brown bears. This human-made body of water, at 1,150m (3,772ft) above sea level, was created by the damming of the Sadu River. It is a scenic and deeply peaceful spot.

A 4x4 is the best bet for this trip, even though the lake isn't that far from Tălmaciu. The road is so remote that it is not marked on many printed maps and there are no signposts; it is easy to take the wrong track and become lost, stuck or both. Even when you are on the right road, the tarmac soon gives way to gravel and sand, and you'll find yourself bumping around blind curves and hairpin bends with no guardrails to protect you. In places the road is only just wide enough for one vehicle, so a slow pace is best. On your way up to the lake, you will pass through some of Romania's poorest villages, a reminder that this is somewhere the modern age has yet to reach. **SA**

❶ Negovanu Lake, in the Southern Carpathians, a remote corner of Romania.

Transfăgărășan Highway Transylvania/Muntenia, Romania

Start Cârțișoara, Transylvania   End Albestii de Arges, Muntenia   Distance 106km (66 miles)
Type Adventure   Map goo.gl/zyWyai

This road trip skirts Dracula's castle, tackles a 2,042-m-(6,699-ft) high mountain pass and crosses the top of one of Europe's tallest dams. Amazingly, none of these features is its main claim to fame.

Instead, the highway became famous in 2009 when BBC TV's *Top Gear* pronounced it 'the best road in the world', with 'every great corner from every great racetrack lined up one after the other'. It certainly has corners. On the map, the road dangles like an infuriatingly twisted and knotted cable strung across the Carpathian Mountains. The Transfăgărășan features five unlit tunnels, countless hairpin bends, precipitous viaducts and huge unguarded drops.

It's a sensational bit of tarmac. Along this short stretch you'll see Bâlea Lake and Waterfall, Dracula's Poenari Fortress and Lake Vidraru and its huge dam, as well as some of Romania's highest mountains and most rugged landscapes.

The road was a pet project of Communist dictator Nicolae Ceaușescu in the 1970s. The self-styled 'Genius of the Carpathians' ordered the Romanian army to build a road through ridiculously inhospitable terrain. Many workers died during its construction – perhaps more than 100 – and today locals still call it Ceaușescu's Folly. **SH**

❶ One of the easier stretches of the route.

Transalpina Oltenia to Transylvania, Romania

Start Sebeş, Oltenia   **End** Novaci, Transylvania   **Distance** 82 miles (132 km)
Type Adventure   **Map** goo.gl/LOoHia

Called the Devil's Pathway by locals and one of the highest roads in the Southern Carpathians, Romania's Transalpina may have been used by the Romans to reach the outpost of Sarmizegetusa during the Dacian Wars. In a state of disrepair prior to World War II, the road was rebuilt by German troops, but it wasn't until 2012 that a resurfacing project turned it from a gravelly, narrow track through an Alpine wasteland into the thrill ride it is today.

Drivable in an ordinary car, the highest road in a country renowned for its many excellent mountain drives, the 67C's highest point is the Urdele Pass, at 2,145m (7,037ft). The pass crosses the Parâng

Mountains on a north-to-south line, following ridge lines, plateaux and the mountainsides above the Olt and Jiu Valleys. Along the way, it provides access to three glacial lakes and passes through a still vibrant pastoral culture of herding and farming.

On the return journey take advantage of the adrenaline-pumping 29-km- (18-mile) long section from Rânca to Obârşia Lotrului, a joyous drive over sweeping uplands. The road closes at the first hint of snow, so the driving season here is a short one. Next-to-no guardrails and icy conditions don't play well together. **BDS**

❶ High above the clouds on the Transalpina.

Transrarau Moldova, Romania

Start Chiril End Pojorâta Distance 27km (17 miles)
Type Scenic Map goo.gl/ii5XWB

For many years, only the bravest or the most foolhardy travellers would have contemplated this route through the Rarau Mountains in the eastern part of the Carpathian range. In 2014, however, the Romanian government completed a comprehensive improvement programme that brought the Transrarau up to international standards; it is now a pleasure to drive, with runway-smooth tarmac all the way and memorable vistas on all sides.

At the summit of the route, 1,400m (4,600ft) above sea level, is a budget chalet near the celebrated natural formation known as The Lady's Rocks. It is to somewhere near here that, according to legend, King Peter IV (Petru Rares) retreated in 1541 with his wife and son to take refuge from invading Tatars. The hotel is a popular base for hikers exploring the heavily forested surrounding area.

On the farther, northern, side of the mountain pass, the road zigzags down a series of sweeping straights and viciously tight hairpin bends to the banks of the Moldova River and terminates at Pojorâta, a small village with mainly Alpine-style buildings and, perhaps a little incongruously, a 1,000-seater soccer stadium – the home ground of ACS Bucovina Pojorâta from 1950 until the club collapsed financially and was disbanded in 2016. JP

◐ A typical view from the Transrarau route.

Bicaz Gorge – The Neck of Hell Moldova/Transylvania, Romania

Start Bicaz, Moldova   End Gheorgheni, Transylvania   Distance 60km (37.2 miles)
Type Adventure   Map goo.gl/KbKrdc

Spotting a road called 'The Neck of Hell' might be enough to put you off heading in that direction. But with the Bicaz Gorge you would be missing something rather special.

The gorge runs between the Romanian regions of Transylvania and Moldova, and was cut by the Bicaz River. As you drive along, ragged stone walls loom way up above you. But more than their height, it's their proximity to the road that is most striking and unnerving. In some sections, the cliffs sprout from the side of the road, while in others they actually lean inwards over you. It gives the impression that you're driving through the rock itself – hence the ominous nickname.

About two-thirds of the way along the route is the mysterious Lacul Roşu ('Red Lake'). With its forest of decaying tree stumps jutting at strange angles out of the murky rust-red waters, it's a popular spot for weekend picnickers.

The DN12C road itself is in a decent condition, but there are a number of severe switchbacks and blind bends. The sheer rock to one side of you limits your view into the corners, while on the other side you're faced with a long drop; taken at a sensible speed, though, the route is more breathtaking than it is dangerous. JI

❶ The road seems to disappear into the rock.

Bran Pass
Muntenia, Romania

Start Râşnov
End Câmpulung
Distance 69km (43 miles)
Type Scenic
Map goo.gl/yssTph

This road is a little-known gem that runs through countless obscure corners to reach a series of high-altitude passes in central Romania.

You'll travel through quiet country towns and pretty villages, through unspoiled forests and farmland, and over rounded green mountains with views of rolling hills and distant rocky peaks. The DJ73 road, part of the European E574 route, runs from Brasov to Pitesti, but this concentrates on the most scenic stretch between the two cities.

Highlights along this impressive route include the Bran or Giuvala Pass at 1,275m (4,183ft) and the Posada Pass at 836m (2,743ft). Locals boast that the views from the Bran Pass are the best in Romania. The highest point on this stretch of road is 1,300m (4,265ft) above sea level.

Moieciu village is renowned for its walks and waterfalls, and Cheile has become a popular local ski resort in the winter.

At the village of Bran itself you'll pass the grand hilltop castle, a Romanian National Monument often called 'Dracula's Castle'. It has all the Gothic turrets and dark corridors required for fictional vampire aristocrats – but is actually little to do with the Dracula legend. Nevertheless, it's open to visitors and makes an intriguing stop along the route. **SH**

◉ View from near the road over the Făgăraş Mountains.

Transbucegi
Muntenia, Romania

Start Sinaia
End Cabana Piatra Arsa
Distance 36km (22.5 miles)
Type Scenic
Info goo.gl/lLj2fz

The Bucegi Mountains are part of the Southern Carpathian range. 'Transbucegi' is something of a misnomer: there is no 'trans' about it; it goes nowhere; it is a cul-de-sac; the only way out is the way in. But the scenery is so great, and the DJ-713 is such fun to drive, that a second go at it is always welcome, at least for as long as the weather allows.

The starting point, Sinaia, is a summer holiday and skiing resort that sprang up around the 17th-century monastery of the same name. The must-sees here are the Peles Museum, formerly a summer residence of the Romanian royal family, and the nearby Pelisor Palace.

The road up the mountainside goes through a long series of hairpin bends into Bucegi Natural Park. Among the points of interest on or near the highway are the Babele (Old Dames) and Sfinxul (Sphinx) rock formations, and the 2,384-m- (7,821-ft) high Caraiman Peak, on top of which stands the Heroes' Cross, a memorial to the Romanian dead of World War I.

The road then passes through the shadow of two other mountains – Costila, 2,491m (8,173 ft), and Omu, 2,508m (8,229ft) – before reaching Cabana Piatra Arsa, at a height of 1,925m (6,316ft). Here is a Romanian National Sports Complex, where athletes of many disciplines come for intensive training. JP

❶ The Bucegi Mountains form one-quarter of the Carpathian range; their highest point is Mt Omu.

Bucharest Street Circuit
Bucharest, Romania

Start Bulevardui Liberatii
End Bulevardui Liberatii
Distance 3.2km (2 miles)
Type Culture
Map goo.gl/OxWYpv

Street racing circuits have a particular draw to them, with their unique blend of the ordinary – white lines, signs, traffic lights – and the high-octane heroics of past motor-racing spectacles. They are also a wonderful excuse for a themed urban road trip through some of the world's greatest cities.

This road trip is a loop of inner city road that once formed the Bucharestring (Bucharest Ring). Shaped roughly like a rectangle with a corner lopped off, the course incorporated 14 turns (seven left-handers and seven right-handers) and five fast straights.

At the centre of the Bucharest Street Circuit is the Romanian Palace of the Parliament, built in the 1980s by former dictator Nicolae Ceauşescu. It's the heaviest building in the world and the second-largest administrative structure, after The Pentagon in the United States.

The circuit was laid out by German track designer Hermann Tilke, and it's held several events, including two FIA GT meetings in 2007 and 2008. In recent years, though, it hasn't seen much action. Naturally, if you do follow the route you'll be restricted to speed limits, but at least you can get a flavour of what it must be like to compete on a top-level street circuit, while also admiring the city's elegant neo-classical and Art Deco architecture, which once earned it the byname 'the Paris of Eastern Europe'. JI

Discover Albania
Shkodër, Albania

Start Shkodër
End Gjirokastër
Distance 373km (232 miles)
Type Culture
Map goo.gl/CzYfUu

Albania was hidden behind the Iron Curtain for much of the 20th century, but it has much to offer the foreign tourist, with its castles, UNESCO World Heritage Sites and genuinely engaging towns and villages. A great way to get to know the country is on a road trip. Try starting in the north, in the town of Shkodër. It sits at the meeting point of the rivers Bojana and Drin and was a military stronghold as far back as 300 BCE.

Head south towards Kruja. The road is modern tarmac, a sign of the improvements in Albania's infrastructure post Communism. In places, though, the roads and bridges are still less than perfect.

Kruja itself is home to museums and a grand castle on the top of a hill. Once you've had a mooch around, get back on the road and keep going south to Berat – the 'town of a thousand windows' that spreads up the steep slopes on either side of the Osumi River.

You can keep going south to Gjirokastër, a rare and well-preserved Ottoman town and UNESCO World Heritage Site. The road climbs into the centre, where you'll find yet another castle and a museum in what was once the home of the country's Communist leader, Enver Hoxha.

There are plenty of fuel stops, the locals are friendly and the signage to Albania's less-hidden gems is generally good. JI

SH8 – The Albanian Riviera Vlorë, Albania

Start Vlorë   **End** Sarandë   **Distance** 230km (143 miles)
Type Scenic   **Map** goo.gl/5vtEkK

The SH8 highway links Albania's second-largest port with its biggest tourist resort along the coast of the Adriatic Sea. The route has been in regular use since antiquity, notably by Julius Caesar, but it has been paved and suitable for motor vehicles only since the fall of Communism in the 1990s.

Heading south from the commercial docks of Vlorë, the road hugs the coast as far the town of Orikum, then turns inland, with the sea on the right and Mt Cika on the left, and rises steeply and circuitously to its highest point of 1,043m (3,422ft) in the Llogara Pass. Travellers should pause here for spectacular views of the Ionian Islands and the Italian coast of Apulia.

The road comes back down to the beaches at Himarë, then rises again, but not so high this time, before easing into Sarandë, which is within sight of the Greek island of Corfu.

The SH8 is a challenge: drivers will need to stop to appreciate any of the magnificent scenery, because for as long as they're moving they will need to keep their eyes glued on the road ahead, which is twisty, not very wide and often without barriers along the edge of dizzying precipices. And in the southbound direction, the vehicle is always closest to the drop. **JP**

❶ The Llogara Pass in high summer.

Lake Prespa to Lake Ohrid Resen to Struga, Macedonia

Start Krani, Resen   End Struga, Struga   Distance 101km (62.7 miles)
Type Scenic   Map goo.gl/SP3bRj

This road trip through southern Macedonia covers a demanding and picturesque route between the two highest tectonic lakes in the Balkans. The starting point, Krani, near the border with Greece, is a village that houses a fishing community that has been here since the 4th century BCE.

From there, the road goes inland along the western slopes of Baba Mountain – at 2,601m (8,533ft), the third-highest peak in Macedonia – to Kozjak, a town with a population of under 10,000.

After negotiating many tight corners through sylvan terrain, the traveller descends to the banks of Lake Prespa, then crosses Galichica National Park to Lake Ohrid, the deepest lake in the Balkans.

Next comes the town of Ohrid, sometimes known as 'the Jerusalem of the Balkans' because of its numerous churches – a 17th-century travel writer famously claimed that it has one for every day of the year. This was probably never true, and is certainly not the case today. There are still plenty of ecclesiastical structures to see, however, notably St Panteleimon's.

The journey ends at Struga, a town of around 17,000 inhabitants, 55 per cent of whom are Orthodox Christians, 43 per cent Muslim. On the other side of the lake is Albania. **JP**

❶ Lake Ohrid, a shining pearl of the Balkans.

Shipka Pass Gabrovo, Bulgaria

Start South of Gabrovo   End North of Kazanlak   Distance 13km (8 miles)
Type Scenic   Map goo.gl/k3iVaf

This section of road carries the E85, the highway that links Lithuania and Greece, through the Balkan Mountains of Bulgaria. The pass is part of the Bulgarka Nature Park, which is noted for its flora and fauna, particularly the Eurasian brown bear.

The tree-lined highway is broad, with sweeping bends, and is generally in a good state of repair with guardrails throughout. Snowfall in winter can present problems so check ahead. The highest point on the drive, 1,150m (3,820ft) above sea level, is in the shadow of the peak of Buzludzha, a 1,441-m- (4,728-ft) high mountain with a brutalist Communist monument on top that can be reached on a 12-km (7.5-mile) detour from the main drag.

As the only viable route through the mountains, the Shipka Pass was of great historical significance, particularly during the Russo-Turkish War of 1877 to 1878, when Bulgarians sought, with the help of their Russian allies, to break away from the Ottoman Empire. The greatest human-made scenic highlight is the memorial to those who died in this conflict – a 31.5-m (98-ft) flat-top stone pyramid with, above its entrance, a giant bronze lion, 8m (26ft) long and 4m (13ft) high, and the figure of a woman symbolizing victory. The top of the Shipka Memorial, 900 steps up, gives the best views of the area. JP

❶ This monument on the route honours Communism.

Buynovo Gorge Smolyan, Bulgaria

Start Yagodina   End Teshel   Distance 16km (10 miles)
Type Adventure   Map goo.gl/ckDOej

Around 104km (65 miles) south of Plovdiv, near the border with Greece in the Rhodope mountain range, lies Yagodina, the site of one of the world's most spectacular cave systems, a complex that extends over several levels for more than 8km (5 miles) and which was carved out of solid rock by the Buynovska River. Inhabited by humans in Neolithic times, today one of the great halls is equipped for marriage ceremonies.

This short but challenging itinerary follows the course of the Buynovska when it re-emerges from the limestone. Even on the widest sections of the road, cars struggle to pass each other in opposite directions, so drivers should be prepared for a lot of

reversing – no minor task when there are no shoulders, only low stone walls or precipices.

There are also hazards overhead at Vuclhi Skok ((Wolf Jump), where cliffs rise above both sides of the road and lean over towards each other, almost touching at a height of less than 3m (10ft) above the tarmac – this is no place for Winnebagos.

At the end of the trip, the road opens out into the village of Teshel, built next to an artificial lake that backs up behind a dam with a hydroelectric power station. Nearby is Kastrakliy Nature Reserve, which is renowned for its butterflies. JP

❶ The wild Rhodope Mountains.

Scenic Southern Corfu Corfu, Greece

Start Corfu Town End Corfu Town Distance 66km (41 miles)
Type Scenic Map goo.gl/mOdIoD

Corfu Town is one of the most European of Greek island capitals, thanks to its proximity to Italy and a fascinating history that has seen it run by Normans, Britons and Venetians, among others, but never conquered by the Turks. This drive around the south and east of the island takes in some of that history, as well as the delightful rural scenery of the interior.

The first major stop is the Achilleion Palace. Built in 1890 as a summer palace by Elisabeth of Bavaria, Empress of Austria, it has had a checkered history including being a military hospital, a museum, a popular movie location and a casino. Today the palace and gardens have been fully restored as visitor attractions.

Beyond the palace the road winds down to the busy holiday resort of Benitses, and then heads south along the coast towards two adjoining busy resorts, Moraitika and Messonghi. After them, the road is quieter until it arrives at the pretty little seaside town of Boukari, whose fish tavernas are a popular weekend spot for islanders.

Here the main road swings inland, and you can return north to Corfu Town through the wooded hills and villages of the island interior, a rural area that seems a world away from the busy beaches of the coast. MG

❶ Statue of dying Achilles in Achilleion Palace gardens.

Corfu Town to Mt Pantokrator Circuit Corfu, Greece

Start Corfu Town   End Corfu Town   Distance 90km (56 miles)
Type Adventure   Map goo.gl/EMnXEj

Who needs to lounge on the beautiful beaches of Corfu when you could be exploring the backroads in a car or on a motorbike? Here's an excellent road trip around the northeast of the island, starting and finishing in Corfu Town.

Take the coast road around the eastern and northern resorts to Acharavi, then cut across the wild, rugged interior. The road gets much narrower here, and you will twist through olive farms in the mountain foothills before branching off on a steep climbing detour to Mt Pantokrator.

The mountain is well worth the challenging trail to the top. It's Corfu's highest peak, at 906m (2,972ft) above sea level, and from the top you can see the whole of the island and as far as the coast of Albania.

On this route you'll leave tarmac for only a short stretch at the top of Mt Pantokrator. The coast road in particular is well maintained and relaxing to travel on. But before you can get back on it there is a hairy sequence of 25 switchback bends in just 4km (2.5 miles) down from the mountains to Ipsos. This section of often unguarded mountain highway descending through the olive terraces is a scenic delight – if you dare to take your eyes off the road for a second. SH

❶ The fortress and marina of Corfu Town.

Karavomylos Road
Cephalonia, Greece

Start Agia Effimia
End Karavomylos
Distance 7km (4.5 miles)
Type Scenic
Map goo.gl/DSLGeS

The largest of the Ionian Islands of Greece, Cephalonia lies off the western entrance to the Gulf of Patras. Its highest point is Mt Ainos, 1,628m (5,341ft) above sea level, and its main population centres are Argostoli, the capital, and Lixouri.

This road trip along the eastern coast of the island starts in a settlement that was traditionally a fishing village but was largely rebuilt after a major earthquake in 1953. Since then, the smart little town of Agia Effimia has largely given itself over to holidaymakers, especially those on yachts.

The road hugs the shore all the way, twisting and turning and rising and falling – the paucity of barriers is a potential concern at beach level and a positive worry along the cliff-top sections; also alarming is the width of the tarmac, which is in parts too small for vehicles to pass each other in opposite directions – shunting and reversing en route are more than likely.

Apart from the amazing views that the route affords across the sound to other, smaller islands and the Greek mainland, the main point of interest is the watermarks along the cliff edges, which are higher than the tide ever seems to rise – that's not a seasonal variation, but a consequence of the fact that the aforementioned seismic tremor raised the whole of Cephalonia almost 60cm (2ft) above its previous height. **JP**

❶ Agia Paraskevi is just one of the beautiful and largely unspoiled beaches along this route.

Aristi–Papingo Road
Epirus, Greece

Start Aristi
End Papingo
Distance 11km (7 miles)
Type Scenic
Map goo.gl/4KmIWe

There is one particular view near the end of this itinerary that it is absolutely compulsory to photograph – it really is that good.

As your road trip approaches its conclusion, get out of the car and capture this: the road twists between trees into dozens of hairpin bends ahead of you, with a steep, sudden drop beyond the guardrail and then a sweeping, dark green wooded mountain slope across the chasm, and behind that a monstrous flat topped rocky peak that locals call 'The Towers'.

Apart from that inspirational vista, the rest of the Eparchiaki Odos route through the Vikos-Aoos National Park is rather special, too. Don't be put off by the terrifying scribble of road filling your sat-nav display; the road surfaces are generally good, although they can hit gradients of as much as 10 per cent in places.

This is the only way to reach the remote tavernas of Papingo. You'll have to negotiate 23 switchbacks on the way up this ridge of pink rock, covered in dense green vegetation overlooking the rushing Voidomatis River.

And there's another gorgeous bit, where you cross the river under a thick canopy of trees on a sweet little single-track bridge. Sorry, you may have to stop to photograph that bit, too. It's best in spring, but great all year round SH

① Even the least spectacular sections of this route are beautiful and appeal to photographers and drivers.

Ioannina to Metéora
Epirus/Thessaly, Greece

Start Ioannina, Epirus
End Metéora, Thessaly
Distance 103km (64 miles)
Type Scenic
Map goo.gl/7X8SJO

Ioannina is the historic capital of the Greek region of Epirus, and has a beautiful location on the shores of Lake Pamvotis. From here a road winds up into the Pindus Mountains and crosses through them to emerge on the Plain of Thessaly.

Heading north from Ioannina leads you to the small town of Perama, where the Perama Cave is a popular attraction, extending up to 5km (3.1 miles) underground. Beyond there the road skirts the northern shore of Lake Pamvotis before it starts to snake its way up into the mountains. The road can be closed during the winter, and you should always check weather conditions before setting off – and make sure you have a full tank of petrol.

The only major town en route is Metsovo, where you should stop to see its museums and merchants' mansions and perhaps have lunch somewhere with a mountain view and serving the local speciality, Metsovo cheese.

Beyond Metsovo there is little to distract you other than more Pindus Mountains scenery. The route continues on towards the town of Kalabaka, the gateway to the unique and marvelous monasteries of Metéora, which cling to and perch on top of the startling rock formations that rise from the Thessaly Plain. **MG**

⦿ An Eastern Orthodox retreat on a rocky promontory.

Perdikaki to Patiopoulo
Central Greece, Greece

Start Perdikaki
End Patiopoulo
Distance 24.3km (15.1 miles)
Type Adventure
Map goo.gl/kBG1dr

Driving in Greece can be daunting at the best of times, but nowhere more so than on this twisting mountain road that regularly appears on lists of the most dangerous drives in the world. One look up at the steeply zigzagging road from the base of Mt Patiopoulo, and you know you're in for a challenge. It is not for anyone who's nervous of heights and who doesn't like looking out of the car window and seeing a long drop below them. There is a 30 kph (19 mph) speed limit in place; stick to it, if only because the feeble-looking, knee-high barriers won't offer much protection if you do make an error of judgment.

The route begins in the picturesque mountain village of Perdikaki, where just a few hundred people live. You're already at an altitude of about 750m (2,460ft) before you set off, and by the time you've finished you will have ascended to 1,160m (3,806ft) above sea level.

In addition to its vertigo-inducing drop-offs, the road is very narrow, and being mostly gravel it does not offer road tyres a great deal of grip. To make matters worse, it is also littered with potholes that require circumnavigation. You will also have to watch out for pedestrians and livestock, and hope that you meet nothing coming in the opposite direction. Other than that, it's a wonderful road trip with fabulous views. **MG**

Mt Parnassus Central Greece, Greece

Start Delphi   **End** Liakoura   **Distance** 45km (27.7 miles)
Type Culture   **Map** goo.gl/OebiSF

Visiting the ancient site of Delphi is a popular day trip from Athens, giving visitors a chance to see not only the site of the ancient oracle but also the glorious scenery that surrounds it. Below it a valley filled with olive trees falls away to the sea, and behind it rise the peaks of the Parnassus mountain range. This drive heads farther into the mountains and to the top of the highest peak, Parnassus itself.

The route first follows the main road back towards Athens, but just before entering the characterful mountain village of Arachova it begins a twisting route to the north, around sharp bends up into the mountains. It passes through the Arachova Wildlife Refuge, part of the Parnassus

National Park, where you should watch out for eagles and vultures in the skies; if you're very lucky you might see the bears, wild boar, badgers, foxes and other creatures that live here. Watch the road ahead for crossing tortoises and lizards.

The road finally zigzags its way to the peak of Mt Parnassus itself, 2,457m (8,061ft) above sea level. From here there are naturally views that surpass even those from Delphi itself, making you realize why this was a sacred mountain and home to the Muses, the goddesses who inspired humans in their creative endeavours. **MG**

❶ The Temple of Athena at Delphi.

Langada Pass Peloponnese, Greece

Start Kalamata   **End** New Sparta   **Distance** 58km (36 miles)
Type Adventure   **Map** goo.gl/duploq

The southern Peloponnese has some of the finest mountain landscapes in Greece, and this road trip through the Taÿgetos range is one of the most exhilarating and beautiful drives in the region.

Leaving Kalamata, you'll soon be driving through the olive groves that have made the town's name famous throughout the world. On and on they go, like a pale green carpet heading to the distant mountains. Route 82 climbs gently at first, before steepening and eventually resorting to a series of sharp switchbacks to make progress up the pass's punishing middle reaches.

But it's only when the road reaches the Langada Gorge that the fun really begins. The tarmac clings to the steep side of the overhanging gorge, and for a short way it seems to be nothing but hairpin bends till it gets to the highest point, 1,524m (5,000ft) above sea level. The ancient olive trees have now been replaced by pine forests.

From here the descent is equally dramatic, in some places the road corkscrewing around on itself as you quickly lose the height you had so rapidly gained and head towards journey's end – New Sparta, the adjective adopted to differentiate the modern town from the ancient city of which few traces now remain. MG

 An overhang on the pass through the Langada Gorge.

Discover Ancient Greece
Peloponnese, Greece

Start Corinth
End Corinth
Distance 167km (104 miles)
Type Culture
Map goo.gl/rKufPd

This two-day Homeric odyssey heads out east across the Corinth Canal – a wonder of engineering when it was opened in 1893, but so narrow that it is all but useless for modern shipping. After an hour's splendid driving overlooking the turquoise-blue waters of the Saronic Gulf, you arrive at Epidaurus. The open-air theatre here was built in the 4th century BCE by Polykleitos the Younger, who knew a thing or two about acoustics – be sure to stand on the stage and send your companions to the outer reaches of the seating. Even when you whisper they will hear you.

Nafplion is the place to rest up for the night. This coastal town was once part of the Venetian empire and is home to the impressive fortress of Palamidi, with its famous 999-step staircase to the castle battlements and some amazing views over the Argolic Gulf.

Next morning, a 30-minute drive leads to another jewel – the altogether older acropolis of Mycenae. Although inhabited from Early Neolithic times, most of what there is today was built in around 1300 BCE. It's something really special, huge blocks of stone being somehow manoeuvred into place to create the citadel, and at its entrance the intriguing Lion Gate. Inside are the Treasury of Atreus and the Tomb of Clytemnestra, according to legend the slayer of her husband, Agamemnon. **DK**

Kastoria to the Prespa Lakes
Macedonia, Greece

Start Kastoria
End Agios Germanos
Distance 59km (36.4 miles)
Type Scenic
Map goo.gl/sSjrdn

Those who visit only the main cities and the islands of Greece are missing out on some of the nation's greatest attractions: its northern mountains. Lakeside towns such as Kastoria, with their wealth of history, have picture-postcard settings; one of the few reasons ever to leave is to take a road trip north, where even more dramatically located lakes await, right on the border with Albania.

This proposed itinerary takes little more than an hour to complete, and not many years ago no one could head into this border territory for security reasons. However, it was open as the present volume went to press. The road heading north from Kastoria runs along the forested slopes of the Pindus Mountains, whose highest point, the 2,637-m- (8,652-ft) high Mt Smolikas, is the second-highest peak in Greece after Mt Olympus.

After an easily missed left turn, the road weaves its way through more woodland until the Small Prespa Lake comes into view. A spit of land separates this from the Great Prespa Lake, in the middle of which is the point where the borders of Greece, Albania and the former Yugoslav Republic of Macedonia intersect. A few miles from the border is the little town of Agios Germanos, with a population of under 200. Rest here and enjoy the peace, the breathtaking lake and the wondrous mountain views. **MG**

Black Sea Silk Road Corridor
Greece/Armenia

Start Thessaloníki, Macedonia, Greece
End Meghri, Syunik, Armenia
Distance 3,058km (1,900 miles)
Type Culture
Info goo.gl/nFg6vF

The Silk Road was a historic network of trading routes between Europe and Asia, so named because it allowed the transportation of exotic goods and produce between the two continents, notably Chinese silk.

The Black Sea Silk Road Corridor is a modern update on this ancient thoroughfare, aimed at linking Armenia, Georgia, Turkey and Greece. The new road will run for around 3,000km (1,900 miles) across varied terrain and is designed to boost industry and commerce, rather than a being a great drive in itself. It is also envisioned to link in future through Azerbaijan and Turkmenistan, and thence on again to China.

For the truly adventurous, what could be more challenging than a journey from the fringes of Europe into a part of Asia that a lot of Westerners never visit? Billions of dollars are being invested in the development of the new road, with the United States and the European Union among the major investors. One part of the scheme that should appeal to drivers is to create a tourist trail from Thessaloníki in Greece to Meghri in Armenia.

The aim is for drivers to be able to access information on the route via a range of different digital platforms. It's a hugely ambitious project, but one that should see the opening up of a major new route between the two continents. JI

❶ The road through the Meghri Pass in Armenia is scheduled for upgrade to a major highway.

Thirty-Three-Beach Island
Thasos, Greece

Start Thasos Town
End Thasos Town
Distance 132km (82 miles)
Type Adventure
Map goo.gl/u39QCr

Thasos is rare among Greek islands in that it has the perfect size, shape and topography for an all-day circular road trip without losing sight of the sea. Most other islands are either too big or too small, or have large, inaccessible regions protected by fierce cliffs. Whether you go clockwise or anticlockwise around Thasos, you're blessed with stunning sea views on one side and an ever-changing landscape of pine-filled hills on the other. But the main appeal of the Aegean island is its 33 golden beaches that any sun-worshipping road tripper can spend a week hopping between in a hire car or on a rented scooter.

Among the most prized stretches of sand are Paradise Beach, Makriamos and Potos, while the pebbled beach at Livadi is in a particularly scenic cove nestled between two scrubby headlands.

If beaches aren't your thing, then a leisurely cruise on the coastal ring road can be completed in a day, diverting inland to drive to mountains and monasteries, or pretty hill villages where fewer holidaymakers venture. If you make only one stop on your island circuit, make it in Limenaria, on the south coast. The island's second-largest settlement, after Thasos Town on the north coast, this is a relaxed place that has managed to retain its local culture and is the best place to seek out authentic Greek dishes. **MG**

Vrontados Mountain Road
Chios, Greece

Start Vrontados
End Mesta
Distance 72km (45 miles)
Type Scenic
Map goo.gl/WoODCf

Chios is a Greek island in the Aegean Sea only 8km (5 miles) off the west coast of Turkey. It is rich in legend: the poet Homer is said to have been born here, and Christopher Columbus reputedly dropped by to pick up sailing tips from local mariners before setting off to discover the New World.

Volcanic in origin, the island has a mountainous spine running north–south along most of its 50-km (30-mile) length. There is a flat, low-lying littoral belt around the perimeter, and it is from here that this exhilarating road trip commences.

From the harbour the road rises steeply into the hills through eight sharp switchbacks. Historic sights en route include the Greek Orthodox chapel near the cave that was the home of St Macarius, a 4th-century hermit.

At the summit of this trip is Mt Epos, around 450m (1,500ft) above sea level. From here the views are spectacular: back down over the sound to the Turkish coastal town of Çesme, and up towards the centre of the island, which is dominated by its highest peak, Mt Pelinaíon. From here, head on over to the west coast to the ornate mastic villages of Elata, Olimpi and Mesta (which have produced the medicinal gum since Roman times) to explore their labyrinths of narrow streets and fortified gates originally installed to protect the islanders against marauding pirates. **JP**

Kamiros Skala Coastal Road
Rhodes, Greece

Start Rhodes Town
End Kamiros Skala
Distance 50km (31 miles)
Type Scenic
Map goo.gl/xqlNbx

Rhodes is the largest of the Dodecanese, a large group of Greek islands in the Aegean Sea. Its capital, Rhodes Town, situated at the northern tip, is within sight of mainland Turkey across the Strait of Marmara. Among the essential sites to see before heading off are the medieval perimeter walls, the 15th-century Grand Master's Palace, the 16th-century Mosque of Suleiman the Magnificent and the 20th-century Roman Catholic Cathedral of St Francis of Assisi.

Heading south along the coast, the road runs first through two holiday resorts – Ialysos, which markets itself mainly to windsurfers, and Vagies, which attracts sun worshippers. Beyond Theologos, where the outstanding landmark is the white bell tower of the church of Agios Spironidas, comes Fanes, a small town with a yacht port in its harbour.

From here onwards, there is less tourism and more traditional life in two farming villages – Kalavarda (a good stopping place for those who want to hike into the island's wooded interior) and Mandriko, which produces around one-third of all the island's vegetables.

The town of Kamiros Skala is relatively tourist free, because its beach is one of the least attractive on Rhodes. However, it thrives as a fishing port and a terminal for ferries to and from Halki Island, 6km (4 miles) offshore. **JP**

❶ Kritinia Castle, near Kamiros Skala, was built in the 15th century to protect Rhodes from the Ottomans.

Ancient Thera Road
Santorini, Greece

Start Kamari
End Ancient Thera
Distance 3.5km (2.2 miles)
Type Culture
Map goo.gl/f28yEv

This short but thrilling road trip begins at sea level near the site of a 2,500-year-old necropolis in the town of Kamari and ends at Ancient Thera, an abandoned Minoan city 360m (1,180 ft) above it, strung out along a ridge on Santorini's Mesa Vouno mountain, overlooking the island's southeast coast. Once a thriving centre of Minoan life and culture, ancient Thera was devastated by the great volcanic eruption that laid waste to the island in 1630 BCE, an event that led to the eventual demise of the Minoan way of life. The history here is heady. So is this road.

The coastal highway from Kamari up to Ancient Thera is dizzying and intimidating as a result of the presence of the so-called Kamari Serpentines, a sequence of 22 hairpin bends in a tortuous 2.3-km (1.4-mile) section, with a 198-m (650-ft) elevation gain and an average 8.6 per cent gradient.

The road follows an ancient trail that was first laid down by the Minoans themselves, then maintained by the Greeks, and then the Romans after them. Once you reach the top, the ruins of Ancient Thera (not open on Mondays) await, with their mix of Minoan, Greek and Roman cemeteries and temples, together with a royal portico, an agora and a 1,500-seat theatre dating from the 2nd century BCE, all beautifully constructed from the local limestone. **BDS**

🛈 Some of the remnants of the Minoan civilization along the top of Mesa Vouno.

Chania to Palaiochora
Crete, Greece

Start Chania
End Palaiochora
Distance 71km (44 miles)
Type Scenic
Map goo.gl/eYwSiO

Crete is Greece's largest island, and although it is quite narrow – only 59.5km (37 miles) at its widest point – its mountainous interior means that it can be a challenge to get from the north coast to the less populated south. The road that leads across the western part of the island to the busy southern resort of Palaiochora is one of the easiest and most scenic travel options.

This proposed itinerary begins in one of Crete's most charming towns, Chania, whose Venetian harbour is one of the prettiest spots on the island. The main highway west out of Chania isn't anything special at first, but that all changes almost as soon as you switch to the main road south. The road climbs gently into the hills, passing groves of olive trees, and soon offers wonderfully open views across fertile valleys towards distant mountains on either side.

It's a well-surfaced, two-lane road, and generally an easy drive, although allowances may have to be made for the occasional wandering animal (or hiker) in the road. The route passes through several hill villages, any one of which is worth a stop for coffee or a typical Cretan snack of fried snails. As the route descends, the scenery softens and the switchbacks peter out; distant glimpses of the Libyan Sea tell you that the journey's end at Palaiochora is not too far away. **MG**

Kallikratis to Kapsodasos
Crete, Greece

Start Kallikratis
End Kapsodasos
Distance 11km (7 miles)
Type Adventure
Map goo.gl/SydZDx

Connecting the villages of Kallikratis on the Askifou Plateau and Kapsodasos at sea level near the base of the White Mountains is a challenging stretch of road with some pretty impressive vital statistics: 27 hairpin turns, an elevation gain of 800m (2,620ft), including a scary 2.1-km (1.5-mile) section with seven hairpin bends on an almost 9 per cent gradient. It's a road trip that cannot be rushed – the speed limit for the most part is 30 kph (less than 20 mph), which will see you take a whopping 25 minutes to drive just 11km (7 miles). On aerial photographs, this squiggle of tarmac looks like icing on the side of a cake-like mountain.

On the way up, the views over Crete's broad Frangokastello coastal plain and out to the Libyan Sea are simply stupendous – but you need to be wary. In between hairpin bends, the road narrows appreciably, and sheer drop-offs accompany you for much of the way. If you want to take in the views, pull over first, preferably in one of the gravel patches off the outer edge of a bend. Do not consider driving this route at night.

One of the world's most famous zigzag thoroughfares, this road was first tarmacked as recently as 2006. It must have been an expensive undertaking – or at least it looks that way, because they evidently did not have any money left over for the installation of a single guardrail. **BDS**

Kotsifou Canyon Road Crete, Greece

Start Kanevos   End Sellia   Distance 4.3km (2.7 miles)
Type Adventure   Map goo.gl/KoDQMq

Between Krioneritis – 1,312m (4,304ft) above sea level – and Kouroupa – 984m (3,228ft) – in southern Crete, the Kotsifou Canyon road offers a brief but memorable drive through the narrowest of the gorges on an island that is renowned for such topographical features. Although well sealed, and for the most part wide enough to accommodate two vehicles, this route is in some places so narrow that you'll be backing up considerable distances if you encounter an oncoming vehicle.

As deep as 600m (1,970ft) in places, the near-vertical walls of the gorge tower menacingly above you. There are numerous blind bends, around one of which is the small but picturesque Greek Orthodox chapel of Agios Nikolaos, built into a rock overhang. The canyon's slot-like configuration acts as a wind tunnel that 'could blow the ears off a donkey', according to one traditional saying.

The gorge contains a high concentration of endemic plants, and keep your eyes out for an abandoned watermill and an old stone bridge. This road trip is a respite from crowded beaches during blisteringly hot Mediterranean summers, and good for waterfall-spotting in winter and spring. Mostly, though, it's refreshing just to find an unspoilt Cretan gorge that is so accessible by car or motorbike. **BDS**

❶ Kotsifou Canyon road near the village of Armenoi.

Hora Sfakion–Anopolis Road Crete, Greece

Start Hora Sfakion   End Anopolis   Distance 12km (7.5 miles)
Type Adventure   Map goo.gl/PFnE14

If you ever decide to book a villa and rental car holiday on the south coast of Crete, it might be best to check the local roads first. There are plenty of isolated little houses with nice pools looking down to the sea along this stretch. They say there are very nice walks along the mountainous coast in this area. The villas around here would look lovely in a brochure. But a word of warning: unless you are a fanatical switchback enthusiast or a WRC rally-driver looking for somewhere to practise, the daily commute to the beach and back could give you serious pause for a pre-booking rethink.

This tarmac road concertinas down to the town of Hora Sfakion via a stupendous series of extremely steep and twisting bends. The maximum gradient is a hefty 10 per cent, and there are 19 switchbacks to negotiate. Yes, the views are lovely, and you will reach the sea eventually – but there is always the danger of reaching the sea much quicker than you wanted.

And don't think you can head off in the other direction. The road leads up into a sleepy farming village and then comes to a dead end high in the hills. So if you forgot to get a loaf of bread from the shop before setting off, there's no alternative to going back through all those bends again. SH

❶ Heading toward Anopolis.

Panagia to Skoulli Paphos, Cyprus

Start Panagia **End** Skoulli **Distance** 149km (92.6 miles)
Type Adventure **Map** goo.gl/ZF9bz1

The village of Panagia gets its name from the many churches and monasteries in the area that are named after the Virgin Mary, who in Greek is called Panayia. The surrounding area is noted for its rare wildlife, including the mouflon wild sheep, one of the two ancestors of all modern sheep breeds. If you are not into sheep, the local wine is considered to be the best on the island.

But perhaps the main attraction, for the visiting motoring enthusiast, is the roads –said to be the most technically demanding and twisty pieces of tarmac on the whole of Cyprus. A left turn in the village marks the start of the mountainous road to Skoulli, 55km (34 miles) of sharp corners, twists and turns up through the Koilada ton Kedron (Cedar Valley). After about 20km (12 miles), a right turn takes you across country to the Kykkos Monastery and the Troodos mountain range. A wide loop via Kalopanayiotis brings you back west to the forestry station of Stavros tis Psokas and its welcome coffee shop, and from then on stay on the B7 road as it heads north to Skoulli. All sections of the road are a pleasure to drive, not least because it is unlikely that you will encounter any other car on the road. The mountainous scenery is dramatic and spectacular, so take your time to stop and stare. **SA**

❶ The monastery at Panagia.

Road to Fontana Amoroza Paphos, Cyprus

Start Baths of Aphrodite (Venus Bath)   **End** Fontana Amoroza   **Distance** 6km (3.7 miles)
Type Adventure   **Map** goo.gl/8bIjjo

In the far northwest corner of Cyprus is the rugged, inaccessible and unspoiled Akamas Peninsula National Park. It's a beautiful protected area of forests, mountains and wild coastline that contrasts with most of the highly developed tourist resorts throughout the rest of the island.

There are no paved roads on this peninsula, so reaching any of the sights is tricky. The track from the resort of Latsi to the Baths of Aphrodite (Venus Bath) – a rocky spring where the goddess is said to have bathed – is rough enough. But if you want to go farther along the north coast of Akamas you'll either have to rent a boat or tackle this hard-core stretch of coastal track.

It's a dusty, bumpy, dirt road that climbs steeply and twists severely. The road is narrow, with loose rocks and crumbling edges, and it skirts around cliffs and gorges with unguarded deadly drops to one side. The views are amazing, of course. You'll look down on the secluded bay known as The Blue Lagoon, and discover Amoroza itself – a sandy bay that, unusually for the Mediterranean, is almost completely undeveloped.

This route is clearly marked on local maps, but a sign at the start says: 'Do not enter. Dangerous road.' Decide for yourself. **SH**

❶ The Mediterranean from the Akamas Peninsula.

Churches of Cyprus Circuit
Nicosia, Cyprus

○ Part of the Agios Ioannis Lampadistis Monastery in the village of Kalopanayiotis.

Start Beginning of A9, outside Nicosia
End Beginning of A9, outside Nicosia
Distance 183km (114 miles)
Type Culture
Map goo.gl/lZna9B

This trip may seem a bit Byzantine. And it is. This is a dramatic cultural road trip in the Republic of Cyprus (the Greek part) up into the central Troodos Mountains. Here, in these foothills tucked out of harm's way and all built in the Byzantine style, is an astonishing collection of ten beautifully preserved medieval churches, each with colourful painted interiors, murals, frescoes and religious portraits.

This trip begins somewhat arbitrarily at the start of Route A9 in easy reach of the capital, Nicosia, and the main airport. From here it takes a contorted route up through the hills to these religious monuments. Collect the set in order: Panagia Forviotissa in the village of Nikitari; Agios Ioannis Lampadistis in Kalopanayiotis; Panagia tou Moutoulla (Moutoullas); Archangelos Michaelis (Pedoulas); Pangia tis Podithou (Galata); Agios Nikolaos tis Stegis (Kakopetria); Timios Stavros (Pelentri); Panagia tou Arakou (Lagoudera); Stavros Ayiasmati (Platanistasa); and Metamorfosis tou Sotiros Soteros (Palaichori). All the churches date from between the 11th and 16th centuries. The stars are the monastic buildings at Kalopanayiotis and the church at Palaichori, which has the most complete and detailed set of wall paintings. Note that you must dress conservatively to enter the churches – no shorts or sleeveless tops, and flash photography is not allowed. **DK**

Rohuküla–Heltermaa Ice Road Lääne, Estonia

Start Rohuküla
End Heltermaa
Distance 27km (16.5 miles)
Type Adventure
Map goo.gl/JufPBz

If walking on water is a miracle, then driving over it as part of a 26.5-km (16.5-mile) road trip is little less awe-inspiring. It may take you only around half an hour to make this crossing from the Estonian mainland to the island of Hiiuma, but they'll be minutes that are hard to match when it comes to driving experiences crossing the longest ice road in Europe.

The Rohuküla–Heltermaa Ice Road becomes safe for traffic only when it reaches a thickness of 22cm (8.6in). It seems remarkably little to support the weight of a modern automobile, but it does help you to appreciate the enormous strength of the ice. The Baltic Sea isn't particularly deep here – no more than around 10m (32ft) – but it's still a rather nervous feeling to entrust yourself and your vehicle to the ice.

To enjoy this unique experience, you must first get yourself to the small western Estonian seaport of Rohuküla, after confirming that the road is actually open; increasingly, in recent years, the ice has not been thick enough for the crossing to be safe. After swallowing your brave pills you then drive out, between the snow poles on the two-lane ice road, to the island of Heltermaa. You are advised to keep above 40 kph (25 mph) in order to minimize vibrations, and seatbelts should be left unclipped for rapid escapes should the worst happen. **MG**

Estonian Road Trip Harju, Estonia

Start Tallinn
End Tallinn
Distance 908km (564 miles)
Type Scenic
Map goo.gl/oHE82t

In many places, the little Baltic country of Estonia appears untouched by time, and driving through it can seem like a return to a more rural and peaceful past. This long, circular drive (allow a good week to do it comfortably) takes in much of this rural idyll, but begins and ends in the capital and passes throught the nation's two other major cities.

Tallinn is one of Europe's oldest capitals, and you'll want to allow time to explore its old town, which is a UNESCO World Heritage Site, before heading east out of the city through woodland and flat, open farmland – Estonia's highest point is only 318m (1,043ft) above sea level.

Narva is the country's third city, sitting right on the border with Russia and overlooked by a 15th-century castle. From there, the proposed route proceeds south through forests and past Lake Peipus to the second city, Tartu, then west along a pine-lined road to Pärnu. The next stop is Virtsu, from where a 30-minute ferry ride takes you to the island of Muhu, which is linked by a bridge to Saaremaa. The largest of Estonia's islands and islets – there are an estimated 2,222 of them – Saaremaa is the perfect place to chill out for several days. With more than 40 per cent of the island covered in forest, it's a haven for wildlife and wildlife lovers, and a place to unwind before taking the final drive back through more pine forests to Tallinn. **MG**

Gulf of Riga Coast and Cape Kolka Riga, Latvia

Start Riga   End Cape Kolka   Distance 158km (98 miles)
Type Scenic   Map goo.gl/6NSnl3

This route along the coast of the Gulf of Riga offers some wonderful scenery, much of which is designated national park. There are fishing villages to explore, too, but the focus here is on the unique habitats of the region and the wildlife they support.

Riga is near the sea, and the proposed route hits the coast only 4km (2.5 miles) out of town. The first big human settlement is the city of Jermala, where there are long beaches and pretty Art Nouveau houses. In Soviet times, both Brezhnev and Khrushchev liked to holiday here. Beyond the city, the route enters the Kermeru National Park. Here the fishing village of Lapmežciems has an interesting local market. In the park itself, there is a

boardwalk and bird observation tower at Kaniera Lake, and a photogenic rocky beach at Keltene. Farther on, the route becomes deeply wooded. Just inland at the village of Pliencciems, you come to the nature reserve at Plienciema White Dune, an extraordinary 20-m (65-ft) sand deposit more than 6,000 years old. The journey ends in the Slitere National Park, at the viewpoint at Cape Kolka – the point where the Baltic Sea and the Gulf of Riga meet. Often the sea on one side of the Cape is as still as a millpond, while on the other there can be a raging storm. **DK**

❶ **Riga stands on the mouth of the Daugava River.**

Cold War Latvia – Guided Military Truck Tour Vidzeme, Latvia

Start Riga   End Riga   Distance 32km (20 miles)
Type Culture   Info goo.gl/ObWQDs

When the Soviet Union collapsed in 1991, many Russians left Latvia, taking most of what was portable with them. Among the things that they could not repatriate was this military city.

Aboard the Russian-built GAZ66 military truck this road trip goes right to the secret heart of the Cold War, with a guided tour of a formerly prohibited military area – the huge, abandoned Soviet military complex once dubbed 'The Starlet'. Imagine a mini Chernobyl-style ghost town, only without the radiation. After an hour's car journey from the capital into North Kurzeme, the trip switches to a chunky ex-military truck for the onward journey into the top-secret Soviet complex, now largely abandoned and quietly crumbling. Built on Latvia's Baltic coast, the vast facility was full of surveillance equipment to spy on NATO communications. The tour of the mysterious espionage facility, hidden deep in the Slītere Forest, includes an exploration of the former Soviet radio telescope array at Ventspils and the secret army town – apartment blocks, barracks, even schools – built to service it. The tour also visits the eighth-largest radio telescope in the world, now repaired and returned to operation. Finally, at day's end, a restorative and much-needed mug of soup, back at base camp. **DK**

❶ The trip also takes in fortifications from the Tsarist era.

Palaces of Zemgale Vidzeme, Latvia

Start Riga   End Mežotne   Distance 103km (64 miles)
Type Culture   Info goo.gl/mKE4yp

The road trip ahead offers three of Latvia's grandest palaces to explore. But like all the best adventures, the getting there is just as good as the arriving. For more than an hour, the route takes you south from the capital on a leisurely meander through Zemgale – the rich agricultural heartland of Latvia. Peaceful summer pastures and lazy rivers. It's an idyllic drive. The first stop is the castle at Bauska, established on a strategic confluence of rivers by Knights of the Livonian Order in the 15th century, then greatly extended in the late 16th century. This imposing castle defended the important trade route from Lithuania to Riga. From here the itinerary splits, offering a few minutes' drive along either bank of the Lielupe River, where two very different grand stately homes face each other across the water. The mid-18th-century Rundāle Palace on the north bank is a masterpiece of Baroque and Rococo architecture, with French-style formal gardens. On the other bank, Mežotne Palace is late-18th-century neoclassical, with English-style landscape gardens. Rundāle Palace is regarded as one of the finest buildings in Latvia and has been the subject of an ambitious restoration programme. Part of Mežotne Palace is now a posh hotel, so it could be a good choice as the final stop. DK

❶ Rundāle Palace and grounds.

Lithuanian Coast and the Curonian Spit Klaipėda, Lithuania

Start Palanga   End Nida   Distance 78km (48.4 miles)
Type Scenic   Map goo.gl/7HVOuH

This delightful journey explores the Lithuanian Baltic coast. The trip begins with the popular beaches, bars and restaurants of Palanga, then heads south into an altogether wilder sort of landscape of shifting dunes and pretty fishing villages. After an initial 33km (20-mile) run south from Palanga through densely wooded coastline, the trip reaches Lithuania's third city, the port of Klaipėda, the old town of which has German and Scandinavian architecture. From here it's a bracing 15-minute ferry crossing on to the Curonian Spit – a giant linear sand dune, 100km (60 miles) long and 1.5km (1 mile) wide. On one side of it is the Baltic, on the other a giant freshwater lagoon. Halfway along it is the frontier between Lithuania and the Kaliningrad Russian Oblast.

Known as the 'Lithuanian Sahara', the Spit is noted for its extraordinary windswept dunes and quaint wooden houses. In the 19th century, the town of Nida was a haven for artists. Now it is a charming upmarket resort, with modern galleries, a summerhouse built by German novelist Thomas Mann and an electronica music festival. From Nida it may be possible to continue your journey into Kaliningrad, but the border is hard to cross, so it is more likely that you will retrace your steps. DK

❶ Boats in the harbour at Nida.

Panemunė Road
Kaunas, Lithuania

O Raudoné Castle has been rebuilt many times and its neo-Gothic tower dates to the 19th century.

Start Kaunas
End Klaipėda
Distance 216 km (134 miles)
Type Scenic
Map goo.gl/IM7ORm

This road trip follows the lower course of the Nemunas River, which is shallow and slow flowing but nevertheless one of the most important water courses in central-eastern Europe.

The starting point, Kaunas, the second-largest city in Lithuania, is rich in relics of several different traditions – not only those of the native people, but also those of settlers and occupiers, including Teutonic knights, Germans and Russians.

Among the highlights en route are two great historic buildings. The first is Raudondvaris Castle, which resembles a manor house rather than a traditional fortification, but is no less impressive for that. It is now a museum.

The second major landmark is Raudoné Castle, which, in spite of its 33,5-m- (110-ft) tall crenelated neo-Gothic tower, is still not quite what one might expect from a structure with such a name: it was founded in the 16th century by Teutonic knights, and is now a public school.

The road then passes through a succession of picturesque villages before reaching the Baltic Sea coast at Klaipėda, which was developed under Soviet rule (1944–91) into a major fishing port and shipyard but retains a Germanic atmosphere from its time under Prussian occupation. The city is a gateway to the Curonian Lagoon, which is separated from the main Baltic by a narrow sandspit. **JP**

The Four Capitals Route

Vilnius, Lithuania

Start Vilnius
End Kaunas
Distance 161km (100 miles)
Type Culture
Map goo.gl/Q1uP3S

This short, pleasant and informative journey from Lithuania's present capital, Vilnius, visits three former capitals through the unspoiled southeastern part of the country. Vilnius has been the capital since the early 14th century, and the route heads out of the city past its largest park, Vingis Park, which itself has a distinguished history going back several centuries.

Although the route takes you along the busy A16 and A107, it is pleasantly tree lined for much of the way as it slices through the countryside to medieval Trakai, whose castle is one of the most visited tourist spots in the country. The castle was built by Grand Duke Gediminas, who made Trakai the capital of the Grand Duchy of Lithuania, but when he moved to Vilnius the capital moved, too.

Heading north from Trakai the road passes between two of the 200 or so lakes that surround the city, taking you eventually, with a detour, to ancient Kernavė. This grand town was the capital of this region in the late 13th century. Returning north then heading west along the Neris River, the trip takes you through flat farmlands and forests to Kaunas, the ancient city that was the temporary capital of Lithuania from 1920 to 1939, while Vilnius was under Polish control. This fascinating road trip takes in sights of great natural beauty and helps to clarify Lithuania's complicated political history. **MG**

Baidarsky Pass

Crimean Peninsula, Ukraine

Start Honcharne
End Alupka
Distance 39km (24 miles)
Type Scenic
Map goo.gl/I7nke8

The authorities in Tsarist Russia certainly knew how to make a road seem special. They built this great twisting route along the beautiful mountainous coast between Yalta and Sebastopol in 1848. With an admirable sense of grandeur, at the highest point of the Bairdarsky Pass, they built a huge neoclassical covered gateway.

It's still there. You climb up to 1,650 feet (503 m) above sea level on this scruffy old road, then celebrate reaching the summit by driving right through what looks like a magnificent colonnaded Greek temple known as the Baydar Gate. From there you can see the domed 19th-century church on a precipitous rocky outcrop at Foros once visited by the Tsar.

Nowadays most traffic uses the modern road through the Laspi Pass while this old T2709 is a quirky scenic route for tourists. The best section is the short stretch over the mountains into the Baydar Valley. It links the Black Sea resort of Alupka, down on the new Yalta road, to the small town of Honcharne via the Baydar Gate.

When you finally get there you'll see that Honcharne stands in a secluded plain to the east of the fortified naval dockyard city of Sebastopol. This strategic area was once the site of the Battle of Balaclava in the Crimean War and the tragic Charge of the Light Brigade. **SH**

Bakhchysarai Highway
Crimean Peninsula, Ukraine

Start Yalta
End Bakhchysarai
Distance 84km (52 miles)
Type Scenic
Map goo.gl/ssxsXX

The Crimean Peninsula has long been Russia's favourite holiday destination. Tsars and Communist dictators built beautiful waterfront palaces along its coast, and Yalta became one of the nation's main beach resorts. Territorial disputes between independent Ukraine and Russia have muddied the water somewhat, but the area still offers magnificent scenery . . . and, most importantly, roads.

The T0117, the Bakhchysarai Highway, is one of the most spectacular – and more than a little challenging. It links Yalta with the old Tatar capital in the central mountains. The highway features more hairpin bends than almost any equivalent-length route in this book – more than 50 of them. Along with those you'll get all the near-death experiences you require, like vertical unguarded drops from crumbling road edges and blind narrow bends with the chance of oncoming traffic.

Yet the views across forested slopes down to a twinkling Black Sea make it all worthwhile. Once you're up on the high plateau, you'll travel through wide green plains dotted with old villages and farms, with rocky cliffs and peaks always in the distance. Then you'll wind along monumental rocky valleys until you reach Bakhchysarai. Your reward will be the chance to explore the city and its glorious 16th-century Islamic palace and gardens, which rival the Alhambra in Granada, Spain. **SH**

Belarus Motorcycle Tour
Minsk, Belarus

Start Minsk
End Minsk
Distance 1,207km (750 miles)
Type Culture
Map goo.gl/k6yUAW

If you were planning a motorcycling road trip through the heart of Europe, you might first think of a blast through southern France or an extended exploration of the Italian Alps. But if you're after something a little different, how about an Eastern European country that, decades after the end of the Cold War, is still unknown to many tourists?

This popular itinerary is a great way to see the best of Belarus. To avoid confusion this trip kicks off in Minsk, but many bikers prefer to start and end in Vilnius, in neighbouring Lithuania, which has better transport connections with the rest of Europe.

From the Belarus capital, you head southwest and begin what is a roughly circular loop. Along the way are medieval castles, UNESCO World Heritage Sites and a lot of places with connections to World War II – Belarus was in the middle of the Eastern Front. In Minsk, you can visit a museum dedicated to the 'Stalin Line', a chain of defensive installations built to hold back the Nazis. If you're lucky, you'll get to ride on a tank. In the city itself is the massive former KGB headquarters from the Soviet era. While the architecture can be austere, Belarus's rolling farmlands, dense forests, 3,000 rivers and 4,000 lakes are a joy to behold. The roads are generally flat and in a decent condition, but be aware that Belarusian winters can be cold, with temperatures reaching as low as -6°C (21°F). **JI**

The Turquoise Coast
Aegean Region/Mediterranean Region, Turkey

Start Datça, Aegean Region
End Antalya, Mediterranean Region
Distance 483km (300 miles)
Type Scenic
Map goo.gl/H4KaFx

The long, winding D400 road runs from Turkey's Aegean Coast in the west all the way to the border with Iran in the east, 2,057km (1,278 miles) away. Aside from the security fears of travelling in far eastern Turkey, this concentrates on the most scenic stretch, which also happens to be the safer western portion of the road.

This part of the D400 provides a gorgeous road trip curving around the jagged Turquoise Coast of Turkey, visiting all the major resorts and sights.

You'll start among the bougainvillea-covered cottages and Greek ruins at the pretty little seaside town of Datça and simply head east. Pass through Marmaris with its busy nightlife and cafés, Dalyan with its mud baths, rock tombs and spectacular beaches, and Fethiye, which offers more boat trips, beaches and ancient Lycian remains.

Other tourist centres along the route include Kemer, where cable cars run up to the top of Tahtali Mountain, and the strange Yanartas natural burning gas vents.

Between all the beach resorts you'll see a more rural Turkey. There will be quiet areas where mountains plunge down to the sea amid pine forests. By the roadside you can spot farmers selling tempting fresh produce, semi-overgrown ancient ruins, empty sandy coves and rest areas with wonderful views along the coast. **SH**

❶ Another way to see the Turquoise Coast is to charter one of the many gulets (two- or three-masted yachts).

Bayburt State Road D915
Black Sea Region, Turkey

Start Of
End Bayburt
Distance 56km (35 miles)
Type Adventure
Map goo.gl/xPRp2Z

There's a good chance you might want to strap yourself in before even reading about this road, let alone driving it. It is one of the most perilous highways you'll encounter anywhere on the planet. Put simply, one mistake and you'll be tasting fresh air as you drop off the side of a mountain on a one-way shortcut to the bottom.

The D915, the Bayburt State Road, runs north to south in the Trabzon province in northeastern Turkey, close to the Black Sea. It was built during World War I by Russian troops and reaches 2,035m (6,677 ft) above sea level. For much of the road's 56km (35 miles) there are no guardrails, just dirty snowdrifts year round and relentless switchbacks scribbled onto the mountain's flank.

One of the problems (apart from the absence of guardrails) is that the road looks like it hasn't seen much maintenance since the Russians finished working on it. The surface is badly worn, and in some parts the tarmac gives way to gravel. There are also places where there isn't room for two vehicles to pass, meaning a slow and terrifying reverse for one driver.

Throw in the risk of avalanches, fog, snow and landslides and you have a road that only expert drivers or the crazy would consider. But just as you cannot put a lion off his leap, this will not discourage the determined road tripper. JI

❶ Part of this road's terrifying course passes through the Coruh Valley.

Kuş Yuvasi Pass
Central Anatolia, Turkey

Start Alanya
End Karapinar Köyü
Distance 58km (36 miles)
Type Adventure
Map goo.gl/WRauge

The Kuş Yuvasi Pass – otherwise known as the Karapınar–Gumuskavak road – is a notoriously dangerous mountain route in Central Anatolia that lifts you up, in short order, from sea level to more than 1,400m (4,500ft). If you need to reach Karapinar, then you have no choice but to attempt this daft ascent. But very few people need to get there – they go because the road to it is a thrilling, adrenaline-pumping automotive challenge.

It's a perilous trip because of the loose surface of the road, the back-to-back hairpin bends, the totally-without-guardrails drop-offs and, worst of all – or best, depending on your perspective – the highly unpredictable violent crosswinds. And that's when conditions are good. Depending on the time of year, you may also have to contend with avalanches, landslides, blizzards and sheet ice. Most normal folk might wonder why you would subject yourself and your vehicle to all these indignities, but every year many hundreds come here just to experience one of Turkey's greatest roads.

If this all sounds a bit much, the lower section of the route in the Dim Valley as far as the Dim Dam hydroelectric project is a popular destination for hiking and walking.

After a hard day's adventuring, the beach back at Alanya is a great place to unwind with an Efes beer or two. **DK**

❶ The Dim Dam lies in a valley between some of the highest peaks in central Anatolia.

Kemaliye Taş Yolu Eastern Anatolia, Turkey

Start Ergü   **End** Divriği   **Distance** 80km (50 miles)
Type Adventure   **Map** goo.gl/WEyS2w

Kemaliye Taş Yolu (The Stone Road) is a gravel-and-dirt track that follows a canyon through steep rock faces along the course of the Euphrates River in the remote mountains of eastern Turkey.

The road is said to have taken more than 100 years to build, with Turkish workmen cutting a slot along the cliff faces and tunne;ling through 5km (3 miles) of mountainsides by hand. You'll pass a memorial to those who died in the process.

The narrow stony track traverses what locals call 'The Dark Canyon', where the rock walls are so high that they block the sunlight from the river below.

The track links the town of Kemaliye in the picturesque Munzur Mountains and Divriği, which boasts a fabulous 13th-century mosque. The journey between the two places is daunting, whether by car or motorbike. It features all the usual hazards familiar from similar dangerous routes around the world: blind hairpin bends, narrow widths and unguarded drops with crumbling edges. There are also bridges and fords that become hazardous in heavy rain.

Nevertheless, this track has somehow become a tourist attraction –so expect to face coaches and even cyclists coming the other way towards you around the corners. **SH**

❶ The town of Kemaliye on the Euphrates River.

Mt Nemrut Southeast Anatolia, Turkey

Start Cendere Köprüsü **End** Karadut **Distance** 38km (23.6 miles)
Type Culture **Map** goo.gl/q5L1Cs

The remote and ancient landscape of eastern Turkey is where the Hellenistic and Persian worlds converged, littering the high plateau with temples and tombs. Among these ancient sites is Mt Nemrut, which contains the mausoleum of Antiochus I, king of Commagene (part of modern Armenia) in the 1st century BCE.

Approach the site from the west on smooth, broad tarmac. The Roman bridge over the Cendere River at the foot of the mountain has three Doric columns and a dedication to the Emperor Severus. From here, a cobbled road ascends 8km (5 miles) to Mt Nemrut's car park. For an interesting detour, turn left after 5km (3 miles) to see Eski Kale, a 13th-century castle that is crumbling into its craggy perch. From the car park, a stepped path leads to the mausoleum's terraces, where two sets of five heads, of Antiochus and four gods, gaze out, toppled from their bodies (which sit behind), by earthquakes, ice or iconoclasts. Reliefs elsewhere on the site show Antiochus shaking hands with Apollo, Zeus and Hercules before journeying into the afterlife.

From Nemrut Dagi National Park, head south to the village of Karadut on the Euphrates plain and on towards the western edge of Lake Atatürk. **DS**

❶ A great but little-known ancient burial place.

Tusheti Road over Abano Pass Kakheti, Georgia

Start Pshaveli   End Omalo   Distance 84.5km (52.5 miles)
Type Adventure   Map goo.gl/Jyi33V

Built in 1978, this treacherous trail is the main access route to the village of Omalo high on the northern slopes of the Greater Caucasus mountain range. It is accessible only during the summer months by 4x4, and at 2,950m (9,680ft) above sea level the Abano Pass is among the highest motorable roads in Europe.

In 2014 the Tusheti Road was featured in BBC TV's *World's Most Dangerous Roads* series; it was terrifying to watch as the celebrity drivers tackled the single-track mud-and-gravel track snaking up the mountainside through mist, rain and hail. The road can take even experienced off-road drivers more than six hours to traverse.

Frequent roadside shrines along the route are hardly a glowing endorsement of this route's safety record. On the way up there is a ramshackle spa that local Tushetiens believe is a revitalizing cure-all for a long list of ailments . . . but sadly not vertigo.

Although drivers won't dare to take their eyes off the track in front, the views from the Tusheti Road are truly breathtaking. Deep gorges, snowcapped peaks, cascading rivers and lush rolling pastures teeming with wildflowers – together with the Georgians' famously warm hospitality – make this a road trip well worth the challenge. **DIS**

➊ Near the summit of the Abano Pass.

David Gareja Monastery Road Kakheti, Georgia

Start Sagarejo   End David Gareja Monastery   Distance 45km (28 miles)
Type Culture   Map goo.gl/ecbDDY

In the 6th century CE, 13 Assyrian monks arrived in Georgia. One of them, St David Gareja, founded a monastery that became one of the major centres of the Georgian Orthodox Church. However, part of its lands are in neighbouring Azerbaijan, and the subject of a bitter border dispute. The stalemate continues today, but it is usually safe to visit the monastery from the Georgian side of the border.

Starting in the national capital, Tbilisi, the S5 highway will take you east to Sagarejo, from where you head south down the B172 through Udabno to the monastery. The loose gravel road here is in a poor state of repair, and deteriorates rapidly after heavy rainfall. A sturdy 4x4 is the wise choice.

Moreover, although the drop-offs to the side of the road are mostly gentle grassy slopes, there is the added danger of venomous snakes that thrive in this region.

In the parched Georgian summers it's a dusty, sun-baked lunar landscape; better to visit here in late spring when the steppe is greener and its wildflowers bloom. This isn't an easy road trip, but the monastery will make up for any discomforts. Many of the frescoes are of great beauty, while the stone buildings with their terracotta roofs are simply wonderful. SA

❶ The monastery at journey's end.

Aragats Cosmic Ray Station Road
Aragatsotn, Armenia

Start Agarak
End Agarats Cosmic Ray Station
Distance 31.5km (19.6 miles)
Type Adventure
Map goo.gl/CjEE7q

Perched on the slopes of Mt Aragats in Armenia is a group of scientists studying the heavens. The Aragats Cosmic Ray Research Station, founded in 1943, carries out research into astroparticle physics, solar–terrestrial connections, space weather and geophysics – which will all probably be of great interest to you as you slip and slide your way up the H20 road that links the Cosmic Ray Station with the rest of the world.

In summer the drive is challenging but breathtaking. The station sits 3.2km (2 miles) above sea level, close to the peak of Mt Agarats, at the end of a narrow, steep, asphalt road that's riddled with switchbacks. The rise in elevation from the town of Agarak is 1.3 miles (2.1 km). On a plateau on the mountain top there's even a lake – Kari Lij (Stone Lake).

But there's a catch. There's snow on the ground for 250 days a year, and during winter the researchers are sealed off for weeks at a time, with temperatures down to -40°C (-40°C). To clear the road involves the deployment of huge bulldozers, and even they can fail in the task.

Once the job is done, the road is bordered by sheer walls of snow; you should also be wary of mist and high winds. But at the top, you'll have unrivalled views of Armenia below you and the cosmos above your head. **JI**

❶ Lake Kari, on the slopes of Mt Aragats, is formed mainly by melting ice and snow.

Vardenyats Pass and Lake Sevan
Aragatsotn, Armenia

Start Shatin
End Sevan
Distance 114km (71 miles)
Type Culture
Map goo.gl/TxExp6

Approximately halfway along the M10 between Yeghegnadzor and Sevan – a distance of 129km (80 miles) – the highway leaves the marshy plateau that has formed most of the scenery thus far and carves its way through the Vardenis mountain range until it reaches Orbelian's Caravanserai (formerly Selim Caravanserai), a rest house for travellers since at least the 14th century, when it was a stop on one of the busiest Silk Roads between Europe and China. The surrounding countryside is particularly rich in bird life – among the species that can be seen here at various times of year are eagles, hoopoes and shrikes.

Not far beyond this great historic site – which, after years of neglect under Soviet rule, has now been fully restored to its pristine glory – the modern road plunges nearly 2,400m (8,000 ft) in a series of switchbacks to the shores of Lake Sevan, the largest expanse of freshwater in the Caucasus and a popular beach resort for Armenian holidaymakers.

The views from the mountains are magnificent, and the contrast between the rocky, arid, almost treeless terrain at the summit and the verdant waterfront is unforgettable – from steppe to solarium in less than an hour's drive. Having negotiated the downhill run, stop at the town of Martuni and check out the Iron Age fortifications before proceeding along the side of the lake. JP

❶ The Hayravank Monastery lies between the road and Lake Sevan.

Meghri Pass
Syunik, Armenia

❶ The 10th-century Surp Hovhannes Church lies deep in the Meghri Valley.

Start Kapan
End Meghri
Distance 89km (55 miles)
Type Scenic
Map goo.gl/TMi5oc

In 1810 British Army officer William Monteith described the Meghri Valley in Armenia as 'one of the most beautiful in any country'. What struck him were the spectacular mountains, with their heavily forested slopes, and the human-made structures dotted among the trees, including a large number of churches. Nothing much has changed.

The Meghri Pass takes you through the valley at a height of 2,500m (8,300ft) above sea level. It's an asphalt road which is known as the Kapan–Meghri Motorway, or the M17. It's only one lane in each direction, but it is the main route linking southern Armenia and Iran with the Armenian capital, Yerevan.

It's a meandering route, with fast-flowing sections and good lines of sight of the road ahead. In its middle stretches, the switchbacks chop back and forth on the mountain slopes around the side of the Shikahogh State Reserve. On either side of the road are rising mountain peaks stretching into the distance towards Iran and Azerbaijan.

The M17 is relatively safe, with barriers and run-offs where necessary, but in winter there's a high chance that the road may be blocked by snow as it crosses a region prone to avalanches. Throw in some high winds, fog, ice and a dash of falling scree and it begins to makes this road trip a lot more challenging . . . but it's still worth it. JI

Trans-Siberian Highway
Northwestern FD to Far Eastern FD, Russia

Start St Petersburg, Northwestern Federal District
End Vladivostok, Far Eastern Federal District
Distance 10,944km (6,800 miles)
Type Adventure
Info goo.gl/aOAhmG

More a network of federal roads than a single, purpose-built freeway, the Trans-Siberian Highway spans eight time zones, was built largely by the inmates and political prisoners of countless gulags, and passes through some of the most inhospitable terrain on Earth.

The surface is an alternating mix of concrete, tarmac and (in some places still) gravel. As a general rule, the farther east you drive, the worse the highway becomes. This is one road trip that will require an immense amount of forward planning – and make sure you begin and end your trip between June and September, otherwise blizzards, snowstorms and ice will bring a premature end to this once-in-a-lifetime drive.

The general itinerary starts in St Petersburg, from where you take the M10 to Moscow, the M5 to Chelyabinsk, the M55 to Chita and finally the M60 into Vladivostok. The Ural Mountains, a brief dip south into Kazakhstan, Lake Baikal and the immense taiga forests – the sheer amount and variety of scenery can be overwhelming.

The highway, however, is not without its critics. Even Russian President Vladimir Putin, who drove a 350-km (218-mile) section between Chita and Khabarovsk in 2010 in a yellow Lada Kalina, later described it as 'a dependable, modern farm road, but not the Autobahn'. **BDS**

❶ The Trans-Siberian Highway is used by locals, who travel by bus as well as by car.

Moscow's Golden Ring Moscow, Russia

Start Vladimir   **End** Sergiev Posad   **Distance** 499km (310 miles)
Type Culture   **Info** goo.gl/VLfF6v

If you can successfully negotiate the mind-boggling tangle of traffic that routinely clogs Moscow's exit roads, something wonderful awaits you. Long before there was ever a Soviet Union, the Russian Orthodox Church held sway over a religious people whose faith has outlasted the theories of Marxism Leninism. A ring of eight cities around Moscow – Vladimir, Suzdal, Ivanovo, Kostroma, Yaroslavl, Rostov, Pereslavl-Zalessky and Sergiev Posad – are home to some of Russia's finest concentrations of monasteries, cathedrals and churches. A throng of onion domes and cloisters, these buildings and the tradition-laden rural communities that surround them are the reason for the construction, in the 1960s, of a road that takes you to them all as it immerses you in the colourful, opulent heart of pre-Soviet Russia – the famous Golden Ring.

The trip can be made by train or by bus, and many tour companies have four-day itineraries to see the main sights, but it is easy nowadays to rent a car in Moscow and do the driving yourself. Going anticlockwise, you follow the M7 out of Moscow to Vladimir and return from Sergiev Posad on the M8. The route is well signposted throughout and, in addition to the ecclesiastical sights, takes in some of Europe's finest open-air museums. **BDS**

❶ Every Russian city has a Kremlin: this is Rostov's.

Caucasian Riviera North Caucasus, Russia

Start Sochi   End Novorossiysk   Distance 285km (177 miles)
Type Scenic   Map goo.gl/9lajK8

This road traverses the coastal fringe of a region known to the ancient Greeks as Colchis, which was the destination of the Argonauts and a land of riches 'beyond the dreams of avarice'. The reality is a little more prosaic, but no less surprising for anyone who pictures Russia as a country in the depth of perpetual winter: this section of the Black Sea littoral has a humid, subtropical climate that in 1896 inspired the foundation of Sochi, which has remained a popular holiday destination ever since. The city's year-round warmth and proximity to the Caucasus mountain range inspired its selection as the venue for the 2014 Winter Olympic and Paralympic Games. The Alpine and Nordic events were held in the nearby ski resort of Krasnaya Polyana, 68km (42 miles) inland.

Heading northwest on A147, Greater Sochi – a ribbon-development of hotels, health spas and other leisure amenities – stretches out for almost 150km (90 miles). Beyond this section, the coast is clear and the drive quite easy until Gelendzhik, a spa town with sandy beaches.

Novorossiysk is a major commercial and naval port, a big cement producer and an oil-pipeline terminal. But don't let that discourage you: it's a spacious and attractively laid-out city. JP

❶ Elevated section through woods near Sochi.

Chegem Canyon and Waterfalls North Caucasus, Russia

Start Nalchik   **End** Chegem Waterfalls   **Distance** 46km (28.6 miles)
Type Scenic   **Map** goo.gl/w3Chft

Nalchik is the capital of the Kabardino-Balkaria region of the Caucasus in southwestern Russia, near the frontier with Georgia. Founded as a fortress in the early 19th century, it is now an important industrial city and a popular holiday resort that markets itself as a climbing centre and health spa.

This road trip along a narrow, twisting and often slippery road heads up the side of the Chegem River through a deep and winding canyon, past the village of Khushto-Syrt (Hushtosyrt) to the Chegem Waterfalls, which tumble down a 300-m (1,000-ft) cliff into the river on the right.

The local name for the falls is Su-Auzu, which means 'water from the throat' in the local Balkar language. This is an apt term for a torrent that appears to spout from nowhere, and makes loud, gurgling noises as it hurls itself over the precipice. Depending on the time of year, the falls are 30–50m) (100–150ft) wide at the top. The cascade bounces off protruding rocks, creating beautiful rainbows in sunny weather and freezing in winter into ice sculptures of pillars and arcs.

Archaeological research shows that the valley has been inhabited by humans since prehistory. It is now popular for its mineral waters. There are numerous cafés and gift shops around the falls. **JP**

❶ Ancient tombs in the Chegem Canyon.

Tsoi-Pede North Caucasus, Russia

Start Grozny   End Tsoi-Pede   Distance 111km (69 miles)
Type Adventure   Map goo.gl/IwFmYh

This is a perilous journey to a remote city of the dead. And there is a distinct risk that you could join them, so dangerous is the route. First, the destination: Tsoi-Pede is an ancient necropolis, located on an isolated mountainside in Chechnya, close to the border with Georgia. A historic monument, it is one of the largest medieval cemeteries in the Caucasus. A walled enclosure and a guard tower surround 40 or so ancient burial crypts. This is a lonely, bleak place, far from anywhere. One has to say that, unless you are an archaeologist, it is difficult to see the attraction. And then there is the route itself, for which you will need a vehicle with off-road capabilities. It starts out easily enough, heading south from the regional capital, Grozny. However, after the crossroads at the junction with E50 at Krasnodar-Baku, things take a considerable turn for the worse. The surface is loose, and as the track winds up the steep Argun Gorge there are unprotected sheer drops that have recently claimed the lives of travellers. There is a memorial, part way, to some of these victims. It is a journey that seems to go on forever – 90km (55 miles) of unmetalled road before you reach your destination. Additionally, this is currently outlaw country and there is a risk of ambush. **DK**

❶ The road through the gorge of the Argun River.

Cherek Gorge Road to Blue Lakes North Caucasus, Russia

Start Babugent
End Verkhnyaya Balkariya
Distance 21km (13 miles)
Type Adventure
Map goo.gl/p2Yqmk

It's a torment for many keen drivers and travellers that some of most stunning places on Earth are accessible only via roads that threaten to kill them at every opportunity. The Cherek Gorge Road in Russia is one good example.

The gorge, in the foothills of the Caucasus Mountains, is eye-poppingly beautiful. It contains the Bezengi Wall, a 12-km- (7-mile) long ridge, covered year round in snow and ice. Farther down into the valley there are lush forests, vast waterfalls and the Blue Lake – one of the deepest in the world, with a maximum depth of 258m (850ft). It is fed from underground streams, with water flowing out of it via a single river on the surface, and it is teeming with life.

So far, so beautiful. But the drive there is an absolute nightmare. The Cherek Gorge Road is carved into the side of the mountains – much of its course resembles a tunnel with one side removed. There are no run-offs, merely rock on one side and fresh air on the other. There are stone barriers in places, but they are not very high and would put up only token resistance before you'd be in free-fall to the gorge bottom.

Passing places are scant, so you need to be familiar with reverse gear, and when the weather closes in it gets even worse. Overall, it's a piece of heaven at the end of a road from hell. JI

Georgian Military Road Russia/Georgia

Start Vladikavkaz, North Caucasus, Russia
End Tbilisi, Georgia
Distance 198km (123 miles)
Type Adventure
Map goo.gl/YHrvJ2

A trade path through the Jvari Pass in the South Caucasus Mountains has existed since the 1st century BCE; an extensive Russian works programme in the late 1700s expanded it into a paved highway.

The Georgian Military Road, part of the E117, is a wide, flowing, well-surfaced highway in its lower reaches, but the harsh mountain climate has weathered some of the upper stretches into narrow gravel tracks. Despite frequent rock falls, road subsidence and occasional avalanches, the road stays open for much of the year. It remains a busy artery between the two countries, with three million vehicles crossing the border each year.

Rising to 2,379m (7,815ft) through the Terek Valley, the road passes close to the 14th-century Gergeti Trinity Church (an interesting short detour to the west) up to the Jvari Pass, marked by a large, red stone cross near the summit. From there the dramatic views across the Caucasus are simply breathtaking, but it's best not to linger – this is one of the highest paved roads in Europe and there are potential risks of altitude sickness.

When first constructed, the highway was considered an engineering masterpiece. Today the Georgian Military Road seems quaint and dated, but it offers challenge and adventure. DIS

➲ This little road links Georgia and Russia.

Africa

◓ Twist and turn on the Leba
mountain road in Angola.

Monte Verde Mountain Road
São Vicente, Cape Verde

Start Mindelo
End Monte Verde
Distance 12km (7.5 miles)
Type Adventure
Map goo.gl/zrQ5TA

São Vicente – one of the Barlavento Islands of the Cape Verde archipelago – is largely desertified, with only a smattering of the natural vegetation that once flourished. Its most prominent landform, 750-m- (2,460-ft) high Monte Verde (Green Mountain), is inaccurately named – the extinct volcano is predominantly a sandy brown colour – but its prominence makes it a magnet for all who come to this part of West Africa.

The road to the summit is usually windy, often cold and not infrequently shrouded in mist. That should not deter the traveller: weather permitting, there are great views from the summit, and to leave the island without having made this trip would be a matter of regret.

Most sealed roads inspire confidence, but this highway does not quite manage that; the road is more cobbled, really – a mix of rock and shale. And, of course, it is narrow and winding, with several switchbacks. At the summit, space is so tight that you will have to make a three-point turn before starting your descent.

Go early in the morning if you can, having checked the weather forecast the previous day. The entire island should be laid out before you, with views to neighbouring islands. Road signs are in short supply on São Vicente, so make sure you bring a good map with you from home. **BDS**

❶ Drive to the top of Monte Verde for outstanding views over the Cape Verde archipelago.

Ain-Diab Street Circuit
Casablanca-Settat, Morocco

Start Casablanca Coastal Road
End Casablanca Coastal Road
Distance 7.6km (4.7 miles)
Type Culture
Info goo.gl/t1IPYd

Motorsport historians and Formula One aficionados may know of this short-lived street circuit as the final showdown in the fiercely contested 1958 F1 season. It was here that Sir Stirling Moss, the greatest racing driver never to win an F1 championship, was pipped to the post by his friend and rival, Mike Hawthorn, after a gruelling 53-lap race. Hastily constructed over just six weeks, the oblong-shaped Ain Diab circuit utilized the Atlantic coast highway and the parallel road to Azemmour. It can still be driven today.

Few remnants of Morocco's one and only F1 venue are visible today. Nevertheless, to the uninitiated visitor retracing its route, the streets of downtown Casablanca are an experience you'll not forget. Caution and courtesy are considered signs of weakness by most Moroccan commuters; traffic signals and road markings are similarly seen as suggestions rather than law. It's truly terrifying.

With jangled nerves and the blare of car horns and screeching tyres still ringing in your ears, you'll want to conclude this road trip somewhere calm and civilized. Rick's Café, developed by a former American diplomat, is a wonderful re-creation of the bar made famous by Humphrey Bogart and Ingrid Bergman in the movie classic *Casablanca* (1942). Issam, the resident pianist, claims he got this gig on the strength of his name alone. **DIS**

Tizi n'Test Road Marrakesh-Safi/Drâa-Tafilalet, Morocco

Start Marrakesh, Marrakesh-Safi
End Taroudant, Drâa-Tafilalet
Distance 227 km (141 miles)
Type Adventure
Map goo.gl/UcU4eO

This route through Morocco's Atlas Mountains – formally known as the R203 – is dangerous. Its surface is poor, there are no road markings, it carries a considerable number of commercial trucks and there are sheer drops at points on the route where there is no retaining barrier. It's not wise to attempt it in the dark or if it is raining, due to frequent rockslides. At other times of year it is impassable because of snow.

Such considerations may deter some people, but if you are still game, this is one of the most spectacular drives in North Africa. The best section of the road is the middle third, on the steep and winding climb through the High Atlas Mountains – a 1240km- (77-mile) long stretch between Tahanaout and the junction with the N10 near Oulad Berhil. The high point, the Tizi n'Test Pass, is 2,100m (7,000ft) above sea level. When you get there, you may feel a bit frazzled and be grateful that there is a small café right at the top; less than 1km (half a mile) farther on there is a hotel and restaurant with outside terraces. In good weather, both offer amazing views down into the Souss Valley and south even as far as the Anti-Atlas mountain range. After this point the road drops quickly via an exhilarating series of hairpin bends, until arriving in the interesting and untouristy walled market town of Taroudant. **DK**

Tizi n'Tichka Pass
Marrakesh-Safi/Drâa-Tafilalet, Morocco

Start Marrakesh, Marrakesh-Safi
End Ouarzazate, Drâa-Tafilalet
Distance 196km (122 miles)
Type Adventure
Map goo.gl/prVdvF

The Atlas Mountains is one of the great ranges in Africa, standing high between the Mediterranean and Atlantic coasts and the Sahara Desert farther south. The mountains stretch for approximately 2,575km (1,600 miles) across Algeria, Morocco and Tunisia and, while there are easier ways to traverse them, the Tizi n'Tichka Pass is by far the most exciting way to appreciate their grandeur.

The route is well maintained and relatively easy to drive. Make sure you have a full tank of petrol when you set off, as well as a fully charged mobile phone and five good tyres. As you leave Marrakesh the landscape is surprisingly green, a reminder of how fertile northern African countries can be.

Emerging from the Toufliht forest, where the road will start to weave a little more, you head for the mountains. Here, the N9 begins its infamous, tyre-squealing switchbacks, rising up to the summit of the pass at 2,260m (7,415 ft). These dramatically angular, sun-parched corners are frequently seen in motoring magazines and were shortlisted in BBC *Top Gear*'s 'Drives of a Lifetime'.

Beyond there, the descent begins through barren heights topped by *ksour* (the sand castle architecture of southern Morocco). You are left in no doubt that, if you kept going, you would be heading into the world's largest desert. Better to stop in Ouarzazate, the gateway to the Sahara. **MG**

➊ The distinctive *ksour* architecture near the pass.
➋ The Tizi n'Tichka Pass through the Atlas Mountains.

Dadès and Todra Gorges Circuit Drâa-Tafilalet, Morocco

Start Tinghir   **End** Tinghir   **Distance** 264km (164 miles)
Type Adventure   **Map** goo.gl/zBw4Dy

This remote route through the High Atlas Mountains often features in lists of the world's most dangerous roads. Undoubtedly, the roads are precipitous and very risky, yet the route also features on lists of the most scenic, and the Dadès and Todra Gorges are definitely worth making the effort to see. It is a very beautiful, if inhospitable, red-hued desert landscape, punctuated by lush oases and dotted with hundreds of ancient crenellated Berber forts or casbahs. The regional capital, the oasis town of Tinghir, makes a good base from which to explore.

On a clockwise loop, the N10 to Boumalne Dadès provides a gentle warm-up before you hit the angular, staccato switchbacks of the Dadès Gorge.

The first 63km (39 miles) are a drivers' road *par excellence*; on a surface of smooth, black tarmac, the road snakes up the gorge walls with only a crumbling knee-high wall to stop you from falling off in dramatic fashion. The overlook near the top offers amazing views back down the tangle of hairpin bends you've just climbed. However, the road's nature changes dramatically in the northern section; rather than a low-slung sports car, you'll now wish you had a decent off-road vehicle. If you do not fancy the ragged northern part, then just enjoy the crazy zigzags of the surfaced southern sections. **DK**

❶ **The winding road through the rugged Dadès Gorge.**

Drâa Valley – Agdz to Mhamid   Drâa-Tafilalet, Morocco

Start Ouarzazate   **End** Mhamid   **Distance** 261km (162 miles)
Type Adventure   **Map** goo.gl/AnEDtY

This is a journey to the very edge of the Sahara Desert. Mhamid, the destination, is one of only two easy-to-access places in Morocco that are actually in the desert proper. And the other – Merzouga – is arguably more touristy and less authentic. So, if you want to experience golden sand and shifting dunes as far as the eye can see – the Sahara of popular imagination – then this is the place to go. Without stopping, Mhamid is about a five-hour car ride from Ouarzazate, itself around four hours from Marrakesh. The N9 road is good, easily possible in an ordinary car. The trip is unforgettable; passing through small villages as far as Agdz, the archetypal caravansarai oasis, with its mud-brick casbahs and palm grove still

intact. Beyond that is Zagora, a provincial capital on the edge of the Sahara. Here, you will see a famous sign indicating that it's a 52-day camel ride from there to Timbuktu.

Beyond this point the road ascends a pass into the open desert and then, after about another hour-and-a-half's run, your journey – and the road itself – ends at Mhamid. Once this was the point where huge trade caravans of up to 5,000 camels would gather before setting off into the greater Sahara; it is now a place from which to make organized camping and trekking trips into the desert. **DK**

❶ The classic oasis of Agdz, which means 'resting place'.

Trans-Sahara Highway
Algeria to Nigeria

Start Algiers, Algeria
End Lagos, Nigeria
Distance 4,506km (2,800 miles)
Type Adventure
Map goo.gl/lk1uo5

The Trans-Sahara Highway is always near the top of most 'World's Most Dangerous Roads' lists, despite now being almost entirely paved after more than four decades of continuous construction. Yet even its paved sections can disappear for days on end under persistent sand drifts, while bureaucratic entanglements at border crossings and security concerns are ever present.

You need to be self-sufficient with fuel, food and water, all of which can be unobtainable for long periods; sandstorms can reduce visibility to zero, and potholes and surface cracking are regular obstacles in the baking Saharan sun. On top of this, there are often reports of bandits along the way.

The quality of the road surface varies from country to country. In Nigeria it is entirely paved, with some 480km (300 miles) a divided four-lane highway; in Algeria's south, some sections are prone to flooding; and in Niger, while mostly paved, much is still in poor condition.

First proposed in the early 1960s with a view to increasing trade and bringing together the world's least-integrated continent, it spans the planet's largest desert, from the Mediterranean Sea in the north to the Gulf of Guinea in the south, and continues to attract adventure-lovers for whom road signs with red skulls and crossbones are little more than lures. **BDS**

❶ This barren landscape in Tamanrasset, Algeria, gives an idea of how deserted parts of the route are.

Tikjda Pass
Bouïra, Algeria

Start Bouïra
End Tikjda
Distance 32km (20 miles)
Type Adventure
Map goo.gl/tXuL5j

This road trip explores the Djurdjura Mountains in northern Algeria, a small range just 60km (37 miles) long, spiked with jagged rocky summits that rise impressively above cedar-clad hillsides and green alpine meadows. The key mountain pass is bisected by a circuitous, winding road, the condition of which tends to vary as a consequence of rockfalls, fluctuations in temperature and a general lack of maintenance or safety features. But don't let that stop you from coming here.

This is the N33, the Tikjda Pass, a potentially nerve-jangling mountain road at an elevation of 1,600m (5,250ft), which is high enough to offer glimpses of the Mediterranean on a clear day. The village of Tikjda is a good place to wrap up your tour across the Massif Central Kabylie to explore its traditional Berber dwellings. It's also a popular ski resort between December and March, so bring your chains or snow tyres. Why, a 3.2-km- (2-mile) long detour even takes you to a small glacier – the Takouatz Guerissene in Djurdjura National Park.

There is plenty to see along this route, but drivers must concentrate throughout. Expanses of broken tarmac or unmelted snow can turn this two-lane road into little more than a narrow, ragged trail. A general absence of guardrails and the sheer drops immediately beyond the edge of the tarmac are strong incentives to remain focused. **BDS**

ⓘ This road is dangerous and far from hospitals and amenities. But it is a great adventure.

Star Wars Desert Road Trip
Medenine to Gafsa, Tunisia

Start Djerba, Medenine
End Sidi Bouhlel, Gafsa
Distance 512km (318 miles)
Type Culture
Map goo.gl/lMRRvY

As *Star Wars* fans know, many of the landscapes that doubled for planets in galaxies far, far away were, in reality, just a short hop across the Mediterranean Sea in the deserts of Tunisia. This is a sci-fi lover's dream road trip to amazing film locations. It begins in Djerba, where Obi-Wan Kenobi lived during his exile, and also has the famous cantina exterior. Nearby is Ajim, where the sandtroopers stopped Luke and the droids and where the *Millennium Falcon* blasts off from the Mos Eisley spaceport.

Next stop is Medenine, one of three locations used in *The Phantom Menace* (1999) for the Slave Quarters Row, and then Tataouine, an obvious source for the planet's name although not actually a film location. Hard-core aficionados might also like to call at Sidi Jemour, which doubled as Anchorhead and Tosche Station in some deleted scenes. In Matmata you can stay in the Hotel Sidi Driss, where the interior scenes of the Lars homestead were filmed, while outside Sidi Bouhlel at Tozeur is what is now known as the Star Wars Canyon, as so many location shots were filmed there. These and a dozen more iconic movie backdrops await your discovery, but the deserts of Tunisia can be inhospitable and it's easy to get lost. You could use the Force; far wiser to employ the services of a trusty local guide. **SA**

● *Star Wars* scenery in the Tunisian desert at Tozeur.

Libyan Coastal Highway
Nuqat al Khams to Butnan, Libya

Start Ras Ajdir, Nuqat al Khams
End Musaid, Butnan
Distance 1,778km (1,105 miles)
Type Culture
Map goo.gl/onklEz

Built by Italian governor-general Italo Balbo in the 1930s as a means to further Italy's expansion throughout North Africa, and opened by Benito Mussolini in March 1937, the Libyan Coastal Highway is part of the longer Cairo to Dakar Highway. It is the only major road that runs the entire length of the country's Mediterranean coast; heavily damaged during World War II, it lay unrepaired for decades until 1967, when it was fully repaved by an independent Libya.

From the border with Tunisia in the west to the border with Egypt in the east, it is the nation's primary artery for transport and communication, linking the capital, Tripoli, to the port city of Benghazi and all of Libya's coastal communities. It provides access to some of the finest Roman ruins in the world, too, at Leptis Magna, and the ruins of Greek Cyrene outside the city of Al Bayda in the foothills of the Jebel Akhdar. It also crosses several road junctions that can take you south into the deserts and dry valleys of the Fezzan region and to the vastness of the Sahara Desert itself.

A dozen new bridges are soon to be built in a continuing effort to maintain and improve Libya's most vital stretch of highway, the road that the famous German Field Marshal Erwin Rommel (also known as Desert Fox) once coveted as the 'Via Balbia' – the Road to Egypt. **BDS**

Four Oases Desert Route
Cairo/Asyut, Egypt

Start Cairo
End Asyut
Distance 1,334km (829 miles)
Type Adventure
Map goo.gl/r6qdji

The Sahara Desert extends between the west bank of the Nile River and the Atlantic Ocean, 5,000km (3,000 miles) away, continually changing from vast tracts of stony scrub to billowing sand dunes. But the great sand sea is not entirely barren. Oases dot the desert, fed by an underground aquifer thought to be an ancient branch of the Nile, which has supported lively communities since antiquity. Four of these oases in Egypt's Western Desert – Bahariya, Farafra, Dakhla and Kharga – are accessed and linked by fast, paved roads, and driving the full circuit makes an exhilarating change from the well-trodden Nile Valley.

It is always advisable to join an organized tour (which will include necessary permissions from the military and security), with four-wheel drive vehicles if you want to see the ancient sites around the oases, go dune-bashing or sleep under the stars.

There is plenty to see along the way, from the hills of black quartz around Bahariya and the wind-sculpted chalk of the White Desert near Farafra, to the golden mummies in Bawiti museum, Bahariya. If time is tight, focus on these two oases alone. Factor in time for simply soaking up the life of the oases – sampling the hot springs, buying freshly picked dates and pomegranates, or just sitting in cafés and watching the hems of the women's abayas make lacy patterns in the sand. **DS**

❶ The limestone rock formations of the White Desert near Farafra are a major attraction of this route.

Luxor–Hurghada Highway

Luxor/Red Sea, Egypt

Start Luxor
End Hurghada, Red Sea
Distance 294km (182.7 miles)
Type Adventure
Map goo.gl/ZJOZkR

This trip begins on the Nile River at Luxor, which is built around the site of Thebes, the capital of Egypt in the time of the pharaohs. The tombs of most of those who ruled between 1500 and 1000 BCE may be seen here in the Valley of the Kings.

The road is well built, but its beauty is only tarmac-deep: the desert that it crosses has no amenities, so breaking down or running out of petrol could be catastrophic. Worse, this is bandit country; the outlaws operate at night, so in order to avoid getting robbed, or worse, many people drive without lights, which explains why this is often billed as one of the most dangerous roads in the world. If you do this trip, do it by day, but take night-vision goggles with you in case of delay.

At the end of the eastbound stretch, the Red Sea comes into view at Safaga, an interesting little town whose economy depends on phosphate mining and holidaymakers who come for the beach and the reputedly health-giving mineral springs. Safaga is also the terminus for ferries to and from Duba in Saudi Arabia.

At the start of the 20th century, Hurghada was scarcely a dot on even the most detailed maps; by the millennium it had outstripped Sharm el-Sheikh as Egypt's biggest holiday destination. Much of its current prosperity is thanks to tourists visiting from Russia. **JP**

Aswan to Abu Simbel Road

Aswan, Egypt

Start Aswan
End Abu Simbel
Distance 288km (179 miles)
Type Adventure
Map goo.gl/M7GPBo

There was a time when the Aswan to Abu Simbel Road was a trackless byway that had been forged mostly by locals. Then came the construction of Egypt's Aswan High Dam in the 1960s, and the need to relocate the Great Temple of Ramses II and the Temple of Nefertari 200m (656ft) back from and 60m (197ft) higher than the high watermark of the soon-to-arrive Lake Nasser. The cutting into sections and precise relocating of these temples overseen by UNESCO is perhaps the greatest feat of archaeological salvage ever attempted.

Today, the road out of Aswan south to the shoreline of Lake Nasser, where these majestic temples now sit, is not a particularly demanding drive, and if you want to go there, you can either rent a car or a driver. Convoys used to leave Aswan every day with a police escort for the three-hour, one-way trip, but the road is now deemed safe and no convoys are necessary. If you leave at 4:00am, the sunrise is spectacular and the road is sealed and well maintained.

And although there's a supposed dearth of highlights, one can argue the desert itself is the main attraction. Not to mention the great Nubian monuments that patiently await you, forgotten and half buried by sand until 1813, when they were rediscovered. Never has a six-hour-return road trip been so worth the effort. **BDS**

Ethiopian Highlands Tigray, Ethiopia

Start Adigrat   **End** Axum   **Distance** 126km (78.3 miles)
Type Scenic   **Map** goo.gl/apXAQO

The Ethiopian Ministry of Transport has invested heavily in the national road network that has made it the envy of Eastern Africa. This 2.5-hour point–to-point drive along Route 2 in the country's most northernmost region is an absolute delight that begins in the university town of Adigrat at 2,438m (8,000ft) above sea level in the Ethiopian Highlands. The road climbs quickly for the next 12km (7.5 miles) up into the mountains towards the summit in Mugulat, as the landscape changes from leafy green to spiky browns and rocky greys.

The roads themselves are modern and smooth, making them popular with keen European cyclists looking for warm, high-altitude training, and are unfettered with intrusive crash barriers that would otherwise spoil the fabulous views. The descent past Bizet towards Enticho, via a sweeping complex of hairpin bends, is a particularly scenic stretch of road as dramatic views of the towering Adwa Mountains fill your windscreen. From here the road weaves and bucks up a series of short, sharp climbs to the old town of Adwa, before the final ascent towards Axum. A UNESCO World Heritage Site, this ancient city is believed to be the oldest continuously inhabited places in Africa and, according to legend, was once home to the Queen of Sheba. **DIS**

❶ Drivers will enjoy the view on the road to Axum.

Djibouti City to Lake Assal Djibouti to Tadjourah, Djibouti

Start Djibouti City, Djibouti End Lake Assal, Tadjourah Distance 114km (71 miles)
Type Adventure Map goo.gl/xTQ26i

It takes only an hour and 45 minutes to drive south from Djibouti City across the arid Danakil Depression to the western shoreline of Lake Assal – at 155m (508ft) below sea level, the lowest point in Africa. Nicknamed 'Hell' by local Djiboutis, the RN9 road to the lake was recently upgraded by the Chinese and is generally considered, without hyperbole, to be 'pretty good' – barely two lanes wide, but thankfully sealed. The drive may remind motorists of the highway through Death Valley in California – it is every bit as hot and forbidding, and potentially life-threatening. However, it lacks the US infrastructure and emergency services and has far fewer passersby.

On the approach to the lake, Earth's crust thins as you pass roadside thermal pools. There are fumaroles and lava tunnels, too. Assal is a crater lake ringed by dormant volcanoes and lava fields; its water is saltier than that of the Dead Sea and so dense that it is impossible to sink. Temperatures can hit 50°C (120°F) in spring and autumn (don't come in summer), so bring plenty of water. Its salt flats resemble a beach, and if you take a 4x4 you can drive on them while watching Afar camel herders cut salt bricks from the shimmering white rim of the lake. **BDS**

❶ Local men harvest salt crystals at Lake Assal.

Serra da Leba Pass
Huíla/Namibe, Angola

Start Humpata, Huíla
End Caraculo, Namibe
Distance 97km (60 miles)
Type Adventure
Map goo.gl/LpVzGW

The EN280 is the main highway built in the 1970s by the Chinese between Lubango and Namibe, a total distance of 185km (115 miles). Its middle section traverses the side of the Serra da Leba, a steep, 1,000-m- (3,300-ft) high mountain. A national landmark, the pass is part of the Great Escarpment that runs parallel to the coast around much of southern Africa.

This short but intense stretch of tarmac road twists through 95 curves, seven of which are consecutive hairpin bends, over a distance of only 1.7km (just over 1 mile). The summit – the *plano alto* – is 1,845m (6,000ft) high; between there and the valley floor, which is almost at sea level, the traveller passes through between three and four different climate zones.

Driving west from the Angolan interior towards the Atlantic coast, you reach a toll booth, near which are telecoms masts and a viewing point over the valley below. Beyond the barrier the fun really starts. At least, it's fun in good weather, but on wet or windy days it may be wise not to attempt the journey at all – not all of the curves have crash barriers and heavy commercial trucks hog the road regardless of weather conditions. It is also advisable not to make the trip in the dark –to miss the view would be unfortunate; to miss one of the bends might be lethal. **JP**

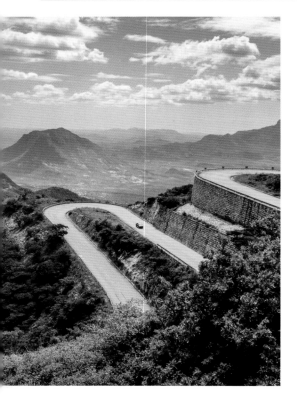

❶ Two of the seven consecutive hairpin bends of the breathtaking mountain pass of Serra da Leba.

Kigali to Musanze
Kigali City/Northern Province, Rwanda

Start Kigali, Kigali City
End Musanze, Northern Province
Distance 109km (68 miles)
Type Scenic
Map goo.gl/y3XetV

Some people call it a scenic wonder, others say it's a scary challenge. One thing's for sure: you won't be bored on the RN4 from Kigali to Musanze.

The fact that there's a maximum speed limit of 60 kph (37 mph) for the whole stretch gives you a hint of what the road is like. Don't expect a smooth western motorway.

Most foreign visitors arrive in Rwanda at Kigali International Airport. You'll take RN 4 as it heads northwest, through the jungle to Ruhengeri, which is more often called Musanze these days. It's a popular route with tourists because Musanze stands in the foothills of Volcanoes National Park.

The whole road is now paved but does pass through very hilly terrain. Expect sharp bends, occasional potholes and unpredictable behaviour by other drivers. The few settlements along the route, like Tare and Nyarutovu, are small and rural.

You'll find that Musanze is larger, the third-biggest city in Rwanda, and has grown up around a lively market square. So it makes a good base to explore the park, which was the setting for the movie *Gorillas in the Mist* (1988). The park is a densely forested wildlife sanctuary set among five extinct volcanoes. Visitors can take hikes up the volcanoes and enjoy wildlife tours, spotting not only the famous gorillas but also golden monkeys, buffalo and spotted hyenas. **SH**

❶ Rwandan women walking to work near Musanze, where this road trip ends.

Lake Malawi Central Region/ Northern Region, Malawi

Start Senga Bay, Central Region
End Mzuzu, Northern Region
Distance 365km (227 miles)
Type Scenic
Map goo.gl/CvkOmY

Malawi is sometimes known as the 'warm heart of Africa' – and a drive through its attractive countryside and along the shores of Lake Malawi is the best way to get to know it. This small country is one of the world's least developed nations, with a still overwhelmingly rural population.

The trip begins by the sandy beaches at Senga Bay, then heads west past pretty farming villages to pick up the M5, a good – if narrow – tarmac road that runs the length of the country. Driving conditions are easy. Traffic is sparse, though when motor vehicles appear, local children may play chicken with them to see who bails first onto the dirt hard shoulder.

The first third of the proposed itinerary is mostly through farmland. Near Nkhotakota is a newly established national park, an area of untouched wilderness with elephants and an extraordinary profusion of exotic birds. After that the route runs close along the shores of Lake Malawi. At the end of this stretch is Nkhata Bay – a relaxing lakeside stop. Here you can dine on fish from the lake – chambo, usipa or mpasa. After Nkhata the route begins a long climb into more hilly terrain before arrival at Mzuzu, the country's third-largest city. All along the trip it is easy to find places to stay, and there are plenty of rest stops on the M5 for fuel, food and refrigerated drinks. **DK**

M1 – Malawi's Highway Central Region, Malawi

Start Lilongwe
End Dedza
Distance 89km (55 miles)
Type Culture
Map goo.gl/JE26ld

The landlocked country of Malawi in southern Africa is a long, thin sliver of land squashed between the shores of Lake Malawi to its east and Zambia to its west. Its main north-to-south road is the M1, a 1,100-km- (680-mile) long artery for the nation. It is worth an entire trip to explore the country along this road, but for those with limited time, a short hop from the capital of Lilongwe to the high-altitude town of Dedza gives a good snapshot of this magnificent country.

Once a sleepy fishing village on the Lilongwe River, Lilongwe rapidly grew in size and importance, becoming a properly recognized town in 1947; since 1975 it has been the new nation's capital. From here the M1 heads east through rolling hills to Dedza, the traffic decreasing as you leave the capital behind. A loop of the M1 then connects you to the town. At 1,590m (5,215ft) above sea level, Dedza is Malawi's highest town, making it chilly in the mornings and evenings of June and July. A short walk out of town up a maintenance road for communication aerials takes you up to Dedza Mountain, its 12,198-m- (7,209-ft) high summit affording magnificent views over the surrounding countryside. Among the places to stay is the Dedza Pottery, which sells a range of ceramics. **SA**

⊃ Fishing in Lake Malawi.

Foothills of Kilimanjaro
Mara/Arusha, Tanzania

Start Seronera, Mara
End Arusha, Arusha
Distance 306km (190 miles)
Type Adventure
Map goo.gl/XEfdwW

This route starts in the Serengeti – 14,763 sq km (5,700 square miles) of grassland and woodland savanna and the only place on Earth where mass animal migrations still regularly take place.

Leaving the park, the road enters the Ngorongoro Conservation Area, which is named after the vast volcanic caldera at its heart. It is in the Olduvai Gorge in this region that archaeologists have discovered the remains of early humans who lived there more than three million years ago.

The road then skirts the northern shore of Lake Manyara, 50km (30 miles) long and 16km (10 miles) wide, which, as the principal source of water in the region, is a magnet for a wide range of animals, including lions, leopards, elephants, rhinoceros and buffalo. The lake is sometimes so densely populated with flamingoes that its surface looks pink from a distance.

This itinerary ends 100km (60 miles) to the northeast at Arusha, a city at the heart of an important coffee-producing area that lies within sight and easy reach of Mt Kilimanjaro, at 5,895m (19,341ft), the highest peak in Africa.

Most people who travel this route do so in tour groups, but among the provisions for road trippers are rental cars and 4x4s equipped with double petrol tanks to compensate for the absence of petrol stations in the region. **JP**

❶ At Lake Manyara you can enjoy diverse flora and fauna, including flamingoes and tree-climbing lions.

Moshi to Marangu Gate

Kilimanjaro, Tanzania

Start Moshi
End Mandara Huts
Distance 53km (33 miles)
Type Adventure
Map goo.gl/nybvNT

The highest mountain in Africa, Mt Kilimanjaro, rises up to 5,895m (19,341ft) above sea level. This dormant volcano last erupted around 200,000 years ago. The origin of its name is unclear, although it is likely a Swahili name meaning 'mountain of greatness'. Today, the mountain is a major destination for climbers who seek a challenge.

The road from Moshi starts off well, but soon deteriorates to rutted and dusty tracks that climb steeply through thick forests towards the gates of Kilimanjaro National Park. This is the start of the Marangu Route, the most popular trekking trail to the mountain peak towering above you. The first recorded ascent on foot was by two Germans with a local guide in 1889; in 1974 eight Spanish motorcyclists beat the world altitude record by climbing Kilimanjaro on modified Bultaco trials bikes. The highest most 4x4s can ascend to is Marangu Gate, from where it's then a short hike to Mandara Huts, a cluster of wooden A-frame buildings in a forest clearing, at 2,743m (8,999ft) above sea level. Here there's accommodation, hosted in relative luxury, with a resident cook, solar-generated lighting and running water. If you're not joining the climbers, then there's lots to explore within a short drive from here, including Lake Chala, Arusha National Park, several coffee and banana plantations and organized day safaris. **DIS**

Pangani Coastal Road

Tanga, Tanzania

Start Pangani
End Ushongo
Distance 35km (21.7 miles)
Type Scenic
Map goo.gl/OR3DmN

Visitors often neglect the Indian Ocean coastline of Tanzania in favour of its inland safaris, but this long coastline is remarkably beautiful and unspoiled. The sands are golden, the Indian Ocean surprisingly warm and the beaches are lined with forests of tall palms, spreading baobab trees and vibrantly colourful bougainvillea.

An ideal place to enjoy all this luxury is Pangani, a small Swahili town north of Dar es Salaam. The town was once an important trading centre, the terminus for caravan routes from the interior and the slave route to Tanzania's large sugar plantations. Today, Pangani is a sleepy resort, with walking tours organized around its historic centre. Almost-deserted beaches run on either side of the town, connected by good tarmac roadways, with a particularly beautiful beach 20km (12.4 miles) to the north. About 15km (9.3 miles) to the south is the idyllic palm-fringed Ushongo Bay, which can only be reached by taking the (quaint but irregular) car ferry across the river. This beach is even wider and longer than its partner to the north, and as the tides are not strong, you can swim all day. Both beaches have lodges and small resorts in which to stay, as well as small bars and restaurants to enjoy. Go on, indulge yourself with this easy, laid-back and spectacularly scenic road trip before everyone else discovers it. **SA**

Indian Ocean Road Trip Dar es Salaam/Lindi, Tanzania

Start Dar es Salaam **End** Kilwa, Lindi **Distance** 323km (201 miles)
Type Adventure **Map** goo.gl/hFcbTg

Most visitors to Tanzania head inland on safari and then move offshore to Zanzibar and its beautiful beaches. But there is more to Tanzania than wild animals and beaches: there's a history that can be enjoyed on a road trip south from Dar es Salaam. The city, whose name means 'the abode of peace', is Tanzania's largest city and, until 1974, its capital. From here, the main B2 road heads south along the coast, past the interestingly named Mafia Island.

The entire coast was once controlled by the Kilwa Sultanate, a Muslim trading empire founded by a Persian prince in the 10th century, and the Swahili language of this coastal region still contains many Arabic words. Remains of this rich empire can be seen in Kilwa, a collective name given to three places: a Swahili ruined fort, a mosque and other historic buildings, some dating to the 11th century on Kilwa Kisiwani island, now a UNESCO World Heritage Site. Visitors can stay in the small coastal port of Kilwa Masoko, or visit Kilwa Kivinje, now a peaceful fishing village but once the capital for the region when Tanganyika, as the country was previously called, was a German colony. If you're simply looking to kick back after this hot and dusty road trip, you can head straight for the pale, white sands of neighbouring Jimbizi Beach. **SA**

❶ A ruined castle at Kilwa Kisiwani.

Skeleton Coast Freeway Ohangwena, Namibia

Start Swakopmund   **End** Terrace Bay   **Distance** 459km (285 miles)
Type Adventure   **Info** goo.gl/hfyEeF

Namibia is like nowhere else in Africa, and this drive along its northwestern coast is like no other road journey on Earth. In places you'll wonder if you still are on the same planet, since the landscapes and seascapes take on otherworldly appearances. This feeling is enhanced by the changing nature of the C34's road surface, which switches from desert sand to sea salt for half its length, the rest being gravel. Be warned that on wet or misty days the sand stretches can be slick and more like driving on ice.

Set out from the German colonial town of Swakopmund, a seaside resort with a backdrop of the Namib Desert. Heading north from there, you have endless vistas of desert on your right and the South Atlantic Ocean on your left; the roadside is largely devoid of landmarks or amenities. The feelings of adventure are enhanced by the very name of the place: the Skeleton Coast. The term was coined in 1944 by John Henry Marsh, who used it as the title of his book about a shipwreck along here. The name stuck, although in the more distant past this coast has also been called 'The Land God Made in Anger' by Namibian Bushmen.

You will see many shipwrecks along the way, which enhance the eerie beauty of a coastline that is unlike any other. **MG**

❶ Shipwrecks bring a haunting beauty to this coastline.

Sossusvlei Sand Dunes
Hardap, Namibia

Start Sesriem Campsite, Sesriem
End Dune 45, Hardap
Distance 45km (28 miles)
Type Adventure
Map goo.gl/6nIf85

The vast and spectacular country of Namibia is renowned for the dramatic scenery of the Namib Desert, home to the Namib-Naukluft National Park, the largest game park in Africa and the fourth largest in the world. Most people who visit the park head to the Sossusvlei, a white-salt and clay pan, named from *sossus*, which is Namib for 'no return' and *vlei*, which is Afrikaans for 'marsh'.

The Sossusvlei is renowned for its towering pink-to-orange sand dunes, some more than 400m (1,400ft) in height, and also for its remarkably straight road. This highway starts at the Sesriem Campsite off the C27, the main access to the park and the Sossusvlei itself. Head south and then west along the flat saltpan between the towering dunes. Dune 45 looms up on your left, so called because it is 45 km (28 miles) in from Sesriem.

As you approach the village of Sossusvlei, the tarmac runs out, and the road returns to sand for the last 6km (3.7 miles); only four-wheeled vehicles or capable off-road motorbikes should proceed on to this deeply rutted final leg of the itinerary.

Finally, a few words of advice: don't get lost wandering in the desert; always cover your head; remember that Namibia is a very dry country, so carry lots of water; watch out for scorpions and snakes; and, perhaps most important of all, don't forget your camera. **SA**

❶ Spectacular red sand dunes dominate the scenery on the road to Sossusvlei.

Spreetshoogte Pass
Khomas/Hardap, Namibia

Start Solitaire, Khomas
End Rehoboth, Hardap
Distance 161km (100 miles)
Type Adventure
Map goo.gl/ltEMZu

During the 1940s, farmer Nicolaas Spreeth faced a problem. His farm stood at the foot of the Great Escarpment – a monumental stretch of geology that runs around the bottom edge of southern Africa's Central Plateau. Deliveries to his farm in what is now Namibia were dropped at a bus stop on top of the escarpment. To retrieve them he either had to travel via the distant Remhoogte Pass to the south or trek uphill along zebra paths. He chose the latter, slowly fortifying the path with quartzite rocks every time he went for his parcels. Gradually, his path took shape, the bright white rocks lining the route with dynamite employed to remove the most stubborn obstacles.

Today the Spreetshoogte Pass is a popular road trip, and part of the D1275 district road connecting the Namib Desert with the Khomas Highland of the Great Escarpment. The pass is the steepest in Namibia – at one point ascending almost 1,000m (3,300ft) within 4km (2.5 miles). Only vehicles without trailers can use the pass, which is forbidden to trucks and caravans. Namibia's Road Authority's heavy vehicles can only drive uphill to maintain it due to its steepness. The route takes you up from Solitaire through the pass to Rehoboth, but it is possible to double your fun by returning to Solitaire down the M47 and the D1274 and via the Remhoogte Pass. **SA**

❶ View from the Rantberg Mountains into the Namib Desert on the Spreetshoogte Pass.

Classic Botswana Safari Drive Botswana/Zambia

Start Nxai Pan, Botswana **End** Victoria Falls, Zambia **Distance** 917km (570 miles)
Type Adventure **Info** goo.gl/C21tUn

There's nothing like a road trip to northern Botswana. Ease your vehicle around rocky hillocks, inch up steep ridges in low range, plunge through sandy canyons and there are surprises at every turn – perhaps a pride of lions lying under a tree, a zebra at a waterhole or a stunning view of the African plain.

Today, many safari companies ply the country, but the independence of a self-driven tour takes the experience up a notch or two. Some companies will help you to get started (organize flights, routes, vehicles and accommodation), but it is easy enough to devise and execute your own itinerary, especially if you are an experienced off-road driver. In two weeks you can take in the grasslands and salt flats of Nxai Pan; Chobe National Park, known for its large herds of elephants; and Moremi Game Reserve, on the edge of the Okavango Delta, where you can observe the diverse birdlife and the 'big five' mammals – lion, elephant, buffalo, rhino and leopard. With a flash of your passport you can be over the border into Zambia, where the Zambezi River crashes down 100m (330ft) at Victoria Falls.

It is important to reserve campgrounds or lodges well in advance. A four-wheel-drive vehicle is essential, preferably with traction tracks and a roof tent, as is a GPS. **DS**

❶ Up close and personal with an African bush elephant.

Namaqua Flower Route Northern Cape, South Africa

Start Nieuwoudtville   End Springbok   Distance 270km (168 miles)
Type Scenic   Info goo.gl/SjTWA7

If you are in South Africa in August or September, drive the Namaqua Flower Route in the Northern Cape. Winter rains give this coastal desert a gown of many colours. Flowers in neon pink and purple, bright orange and blazing yellow turn Namaqua into the ultimate jewel garden, as some 4,000 species of plant compete for the attention of pollinators.

The annual flower show covers several national parks, including Richtersveld (4x4s only), rich in succulents; the Goegap Nature Reserve; and Namaqua National Park, near Springbok. Goegap includes the Hester Malan Wildflower Garden, from where a 16-km- (10-mile) long loop takes in the best displays as well as the aptly named quiver trees.

Focusing on the northern section of the region, begin in Nieuwoudtville and follow the N7 south for 272km (170 miles) to Springbok (the floral reveal gets later as you travel south, so it is best to drive this way around). Displays vary according to season, and so it is wise to ask the staff at tourist offices to point you in the direction of the best blooms at the time of your visit. Pink and purple vygies, yellow daisies, blue sporries and orange gazanias are a given, but many other flowers are featured. Don't set off too early; blooms don't open until the sun has warmed the veld, generally by around10:00am. **DS**

❶ The brilliant orange flowers of Namaqua.

Swartberg Pass
Western Cape, South Africa

Start Oudtshoorn
End Prince Albert
Distance 27km (16.7 miles)
Type Scenic
Info goo.gl/dWWexb

The Swartberg ('black mountain') range runs roughly from east to west along the northern edge of the arid Little Karoo region of the Western Cape. For the geologists among you, the range is a superb example of mountain folding, the rocks tilted every which way. Bizarrely, quartzite in the rock gives the mountains every colour except the black of their name. The mountains were once a major barrier to accessing the interior, and in the 1880s, the prolific road engineer Thomas Bain used convict labour to construct a pass that looped with the landscape's contours to keep gradients as low as possible. It has been described as the 'Rubicon of gravel road passes', a feat of engineering using the most primitive of tools, and is now designated as a national monument.

The Swartberg Pass (designated the R328/P0369) runs north from Oudtshoorn, renowned as 'the ostrich capital of the world', into the Great Karoo, and ends at the small town of Prince Albert, so named in 1845 in honour of Queen Victoria's consort. In the pass itself, you drive past such evocatively named stages as Die Stalletjie (The Stall) and Skelmdraai (known in English as 'Devious Corner'), although imagination ran out near the summit, which at 1,575m (5,166ft) above sea level is prosaically named Die Top (The Top). There are four picnic sites on the way up, with more spectacular vistas the higher you climb. **SA**

❶ A solitary cyclist on the untarred road of one of the world's most spectacular mountain passes.

Clarence Drive
Western Cape, South Africa

Start Rooi-Els
End Gordon's Bay
Distance 23km (14.2 miles)
Type Scenic
Map goo.gl/EESSMJ

Around the Cape of Good Hope and across False Bay (named in the 1600s by sailors who'd missed the safe anchorage of Cape Town) lie the Hottentots Holland mountains. This majestic range forms a barrier between Cape Town and the southern Overberg coast. When the first European settlers left Cape Town in 1835 on their Great Trek northwards, they crossed these mountains: the cuts and wheel markings of their wagons can still be seen in places. No such problems exist today, for the scenic Clarence Drive swoops tight around the coastline from the hamlet of Rooi-Els in the south up to the naval town of Gordon's Bay in the north. Officially the R44, the road takes its popular name from Jack Clarence, who first laid out its beautiful course. Magnificent it really is, with excellent views across both sea and mountains. If you visit in winter, between May and October, you can watch the whales that calve in the warm and sheltered waters of False Bay.

For the most part this is a leisurely drive amid wonderful coastal landscapes, but its 77 corners (of which four are tighter than 150 degrees) do add some spice for the more keen driver. The tarmac is in great condition throughout, and as such, attracts swarms of cyclists at peak season weekends; come midweek at the crack of dawn to get the best out of Clarence Drive. **SA**

ⓘ This smooth and sinuous coastal road has a top-quality tarmac surface as well as magnificent views.

Chapman's Peak Drive
Western Cape, South Africa

Start Noordhoek
End Hout Bay
Distance 9km (5.6 miles)
Type Scenic
Info goo.gl/O39GB2

The first thing anyone should do in Cape Town is drive around Chapman's Peak, a mountain on the western side of the Cape Peninsula, about 15km (9 miles) from the centre. Nothing better reveals the staggering beauty of the Cape Peninsula.

Driving this snaking route is like being part of a theatrical performance: each of the 114 twists in the road reveals a new perspective on Cape Town's scenic wonders. For the best show, with the peaks of the Table Mountain National Park visible up ahead rather than in the rear-view mirror, travel south to north. The gently undulating ascent from Noordhoek, with long views of its spectacular white beach, give way to tight turns and rocky drops before the descent to Hout Bay, a pretty fishing community enclosed by mountains, including the anvil-shaped Sentinel.

Known to the locals as 'Chappies', this is a popular route year round, so try to avoid peak times. There are plenty of lookouts, picnic spots and start points for hikes. For the most memorable experience, drive Chapman's in the late afternoon to catch the sunset, and be sure to bring binoculars: in spring, from June to November, whales enter the waters of the Western Cape to calve. High winds or rockfalls sometimes close the road, so check the conditions before setting out; the toll booths take cash or credit cards. **DS**

➊ Hout Bay from Chapman's Peak Drive.
➋ The road at nightfall.

Garden Route Western Cape/Eastern Cape, South Africa

Start Mossel Bay, Western Cape   **End** Storms River, Eastern Cape   **Distance** 233km (145 miles)
Type Scenic   **Info** goo.gl/hnosdp

The Garden Route combines a beautiful coastline and long sandy beaches with accessible inland lakes, enchanting forests, game reserves and nature parks. The outstanding beauty of the region, and its mild climate, have long attracted artists and writers. Charming towns and villages have evolved and the region is now a major tourist destination.

The trip along the Western Cape follows the coast for much of the journey, beginning in the bustling harbour town of Mossel Bay and ending at the laid-back village at Storms River. In between, whatever your interests – beach activities, nature, history, hiking, boating, golf, wineries, even ostrich riding – there's a huge range of things to do.

Highlights (going east to west) include the Botlierskop Private Game Reserve, Outeniqua Transport Museum, Oudtshoorn Ostrich Farm, the Klein Karoo semidesert, Goukamma Nature Reserve, Knysna Lagoon, Knysna Old Gaol Museum, Robberg Nature and Marine Reserve, the Garden Route National Park and the fantastical Tsitsikamma Forest with its ferns and colorful birdlife.

You could do the route in a day, but with so much to explore you should spend a week or more. Good places to stop over or use as a base are George, Sedgefield, Knysna and Plettenberg Bay. **DK**

❶ Along the Garden Route in Cape Province.

Bainskloof Pass Western Cape, South Africa

Start Wellington   **End** Ceres   **Distance** 26.7km (16.6 miles)
Type Adventure   **Info** goo.gl/rCUQiP

There are not many roads that come with a severe warning, demarcated with a skull and crossbones on the map. But the Bainskloof Pass on the R301 regional road between Wellington and Ceres in the Western Cape is one such thoroughfare. It's not that surprising, given that it crosses the Limiet Mountains at a height of nearly 600m (2,000ft) above sea level. The narrow road bends and twists the entire way, with mountains on one side and fresh air on the other, and there's only a motley collection of rough boulders on the curbside to stop you from plunging into the river below. The R301's surface may be tarmac, but it's fallen into disrepair in some sections. Other hazards include rockfalls and overhangs, and

watch out for damp patches, too. For all its hazards, however, the route is venerated by motorcyclists, who congregate en route at the highly regarded Calabash Bush Pub.

The rugged landscape, wildlife and the sense of achievement once it is conquered make this road worth the risk. You may want to consider the history of the pass as a distraction: it was designed in the mid-19 century by a Scotsman with no real background in engineering and constructed by forced convict labourers . . . On second thought, perhaps this is not something to dwell on. **JI**

❶ View from the pass overlooking Wellington Valley.

Cape Route 62 Western Cape/Eastern Cape, South Africa

Start Cape Town, Western Cape   **End** Port Elizabeth, Eastern Cape   **Distance** 848km (527 miles)
Type Culture   **Info** goo.gl/D3wNDF

Some road trips need to be taken at full throttle to fully enjoy the thrill of travelling at high speed from points A to B. Others need to be savoured gently on the palate, like a fine wine. For this is exactly what you will be drinking on this scenic route through the beautiful vineyards of the Western and Eastern Cape provinces of South Africa. Take your time, savour the aromas and enjoy the scenery at your own pace (remembering, of course, that drunk-driving laws apply in South Africa as elsewhere). This road is long, but it does not mean you have to – or even need to – cover the whole distance. Sample a few vintages, get to know the area and come back for more the next time.

The great advantage of this road, Cape Route 62, is that it is not the heavily trafficked N2 highway that runs to the south. This special road takes its time to stop in such wonderful places as Montagu, with its thermal baths and fruit trees, the former mission stations of Zoar and Amalienstein, the South African centre of ostrich breeding at Oudtshoorn, and Calitzdorp, the hub of South African port wine production. Along the way are numerous wine tours, safari drives, museums and cultural events, as well as hiking, mountain climbing and canoeing for the more adventurous. Enjoy them all. **DS**

❶ Near Ladismith in the Klein Karoo on Cape Route 62.

Bikers' Breakfast Run Gauteng/North West Province, South Africa

Start Johannesburg, Gauteng   **End** Johannesburg, Gauteng   **Distance** 221km (137 miles)

Type Scenic   **Map** goo.gl/RR1WUF

The Magaliesburg is a mountain range to the northwest of Johannesburg that is also known as the Cashan Mountains. At their highest point at Nooitgedacht, the peaks reach to 1,852m (6,074ft) and form a natural barrier between the low-lying Bushveld to the north and the cooler Highveld plateau to the south. What better way to explore this beautiful region than to follow a popular motorbike route out of Johannesburg and let the wind blow in your face?

Start in Johannesburg and first head north on the M1, then northwest on the R511. Eventually, you will reach the Hartbeespoort Dam – popularly known as the Harties – on the meaningfully named Crocodile River, a tributary of the Limpopo. Once here, do as every biker does and make a pit stop, stretch your legs and enjoy the view. It is worth driving around the edge of the dam to look at the beautiful houses in the remote village of Kosmos, named after the pretty flowers that grow wild here. Then head west on the R560 via Hekpoort to the town of Magliesburg before driving back down the R563 and M47 to Johannesburg. Adventure-bike owners might like to know that there's also a slightly longer gravel road alternative to this popular Sunday morning jaunt. **SA**

❶ Up, up and away above the Magaliesburg.

Maloti Drakensberg Route Free State, South Africa

Start Phuthaditjhaba   End Wepener   Distance 280km (174 miles)
Type Scenic   Info goo.gl/YfX74

Squeezed along the northern border of Lesotho, the Maloti Drakensberg Route (MDR) winds along the R712, R711 and R26. It was designed to open up these remote areas to visitors so that they could better explore the spectacular countryside and enjoy its bounteous wildlife. The route gets its name from the Maloti Mountains of Lesotho and the Free State, an impressive range of peaks up to 3,400m (11,200ft) in height, part of the Drakensberg system of mountains that form the eastern edge of the Great Escarpment.

Starting at Phuthaditjhaba, the MDR soon heads into the Golden Gate Highlands National Park, distinguished by its gold- and ochre-coloured sandstone cliffs and outcrops. Many of the caves and shelters contain San rock paintings. From there the road meanders past breathtaking mountain peaks, lush valleys and the traditional homelands of the Basotho and Xhosa people, whose cultures and crafts can be seen in the villages.

This road trip will take several days to complete, so take your pick from the wide range of local accommodations, from the spartan to the luxurious. Adventurous folks will find plenty of outdoor activities en route, from fly-fishing and ballooning to white-water rafting and quad bike safaris. SA

❶ Naude's Nek Pass, the highest point on the route.

Moteng Pass Butha-Buthe/Mokhotlong, Lesotho

Start Butha-Buthe **End** Mokhotlong **Distance** 126km (78 miles)
Type Adventure **Map** goo.gl/kYpyLF

The impoverished, landlocked country of Lesotho has one odd claim to fame: it is the only independent state in the world that lies entirely above 1,000m (3,280ft). In fact, even its lowest point of 1,300m (4,593ft) is the highest lowest place of any country in the world; more than 80 per cent of Lesotho lies above 1,900m (5,905ft).

Lesotho makes its living from livestock and mining, but its mountainous terrain makes internal travel difficult: the Maloti range in the north of the country boasts Thabana Ntlenyana – 3,482m (11,424ft) – the highest peak in Africa, south of Mt Kilimanjaro. It is through this range of peaks that the Moteng Pass connects Butha-Buthe to the diamond-mining town of Mokhotlong. The approach to this high mountain pass is up a steeply inclined 25-km- (15.5-mile) long road that crosses the Maloti range at a height of 2,820m (9,252ft) above sea level. The views here are stupendous, but this is a road trip that should be attempted only by experienced drivers. The road twists and turns alarmingly, while heavy snowfalls often close the pass in winter. The most hazardous stage is the final approach to Mokhotlong, where there are numerous potholes and large patches of ice. Snow chains or snow tyres are required year round. **SA**

❶ The view over eastern Lesotho from the Moteng Pass.

Sani Pass
South Africa/Lesotho

Start Himeville, KwaZulu-Natal, South Africa
End Mokhotlong, Mokhotlong, Lesotho
Distance 9km (5.6 miles)
Type Adventure
Info goo.gl/Z7I74R

Lesotho – a constitutional monarchy that is both landlocked and completely surrounded by South Africa – has some of the loveliest highland landscapes in the world. To its west, the Drakensberg – as this part of the continent-spanning Great Escarpment is known – presents a wall of rock to the adjoining KwaZulu-Natal province of South Africa, pierced only by the notorious Sani Pass.

This is a fearsome road, starting at 1,544m (5,065ft) above sea level and climbing steeply at gradients of 33 per cent up 1,332m (4,370ft) to the top. The pass has a gravel surface, and it can be covered with snow and ice in winter, so that gives poor traction.

It opens each day between 6:00am and 6:00pm and will always be closed in bad weather. South African law at the bottom of the pass only allows 4x4s, although the Lesotho authorities at the top have less concern about what goes down. Respective border controls operate at each end of the pass, although technically the pass lies entirely within South Africa.

It goes without saying that extreme care must be exercised when tackling the Sani Pass, as the evidence of wrecked vehicles strewn down the mountainside testifies. Even in a 4x4 this is a challenging drive – not for the fainthearted, but exhilarating for everyone else. **SA**

❶ On this gravel pass a 4x4 is essential.
⮑ Dramatic scenery from the pass to the Drakensberg.

Mahé Island Tour

Mahé, Seychelles

Start Victoria
End Victoria
Distance 97km (60 miles)
Type Culture
Map goo.gl/n8lGgB

Driving around Mahé Island, which is the largest island in the Seychelles archipelago – and one of only two islands where it is possible to rent a car – can be a lot of fun, but it also comes with its own set of peculiarities. Traffic is blissfully sparse and the coastal and interior roads, while narrow and lined with a profusion of rock and mortar walls rather than curbs to keep you honest, are well maintained. Steep drop-offs are also common, and there is an annoying scarcity of both views – and, for some reason, streetlights. And because there are no pavements here beyond the former British colonial capital of Victoria, you need to keep an ever-vigilant eye out for pedestrians, too, for whom every road is a scenic footpath.

A quick island loop is about 96.5km (60 miles), but allow at least two days for a proper exploration of Mahé on steep interior roads that seem to wind and tunnel their way through lush jungle canopies, and along its coastal ring road that is a little straighter – but not much. Hairpin bends and blind corners are de rigueur here, but the breathtaking scenery more than makes up for everything.

Find time to walk the idyllic beaches at Turtle Bay, Carana Beach, Anse à la Mouche and Anse Forbans, where you can also swim and snorkel. One final piece of advice: always defer to Mahé's bus drivers. They take no prisoners. **BDS**

Avenue of the Baobabs

Menabe/Betsiboka, Madagascar

Start Morondava Airport, Menabe
End Andriamena, Betsiboka
Distance 15.8km (9.8 miles)
Type Scenic
Map goo.gl/U6Jq4F

This rough, rural dirt road has become one of the most popular sights in Madagascar. The bumpy and dusty track leads between paddy fields, sugarcane plantations and scrubby fields near Morondava on the west coast of the island.

This spectacular avenue of baobab trees helps to form such an impressive landscape that many tourists make the challenging journey to this remote spot by 4x4. Many employ local chauffeurs who are familiar with the rutted and challenging road, but the most adventurous can rent suitable vehicles to make the trip independently.

Increasing numbers of overseas visitors come to the avenue to photograph the trees at sunrise and sunset. There's no fee, but you'll find that local villagers often gather by a small car park, trying to sell their tree-shaped wood carvings. The trees are hundreds of years old, and locals call them 'upside-down trees' or 'bottle trees'.

Baobabs can be found in many parts of Africa, but these giant Madagascan baobabs are an unusually large version, with massive trunks up to 3m (10ft) across and 30m (100ft) tall. They can live for up to 800 years and have protected status. The avenue has now become an unofficial national monument. **SH**

➲ A quiet day on the avenue.

Tour of Mauritius
Port Louis to Moka, Mauritius

Start Port Louis
End Moka
Distance 235km (146 miles)
Type Scenic
Map goo.gl/srNJ9R

This straightforward circular itinerary along well-signposted and well-maintained roads is designed for visitors who are determined to resist the almost overwhelming temptation to do no more than relax by the pool or the sea in the tropical heat. After exploring the national capital and largest town, Port Louis, take the Royal Road to Cap Malheureux, a picturesque fishing village at the most northerly tip of the island. Offshore can be seen three tiny islands: Île Plate (Flat Island) has a lighthouse and is a world-renowned location where divers go to watch sharks; Île Ronde (Round Island) is an uninhabited bird sanctuary and nature reserve that is home to several species found nowhere else on Earth; and Coin de Mire has a luxury hotel and a night-diving centre.

Heading south along the east coast through the villages of Goodlands and Roches Noires, the road runs alongside a string of beaches, including Poste Lafayette, which many think is the finest on Mauritius. Beyond the developing resort of Mahébourg, the road turns inland through mangrove forests before reemerging beside the Indian Ocean at Souillac, a small town near the most southerly point of the island. The journey up the west coast passes high-end residential developments, the most notable of which are those at Flic en Flac and Moka. **JP**

◉ Trois Mamelles and Mt Rempart in west Mauritius.

Asia

⊕ Try out the Kunshan Tunnel
Road in China's Taihang Mountains.

Israeli Dead Sea Highway
Northern District to Southern District, Israel

Start Metula, Northern District
End Eilat, Southern District
Distance 468km (291 miles)
Type Scenic
Map goo.gl/eDc5o6

At 393m (1,289ft) below sea level, the Dead Sea Highway is the second-lowest road in the world, surpassed only by the thoroughfare that runs parallel to it along the Jordanian side of the water.

Driving the whole of Israel's longest road, Highway 90, between Metula and the resort of Eilat, is a rare experience through one of the Middle East's most unusual landscapes. The road starts near the border with Lebanon in the tiny town of Metula, which lies near the biblical towns of Dan and Avel Bet Ma'akha.

Before you know it, you're out in the scrubby desert. Farther south the road runs alongside the Sea of Galilee, which in spite of its name is a freshwater lake and the second-lowest lake in the world after the hypersaline Dead Sea, 120km (75 miles) to the south.

Of course, you'll want to stop off for a dip in the Dead Sea, sample the healing properties of its mud and experience the buoyancy caused by its extreme saltiness. It pays to keep refreshed and alert on this drive because with being the country's longest road, it is also one of its most dangerous. Long straight stretches through monotonous desert terrain cause some drivers to lose concentration or even to fall asleep at the wheel, and although the surface is good, as is the visibility, accidents are all too common. **MG**

❶ The western coast of the Dead Sea; on the far side of the water is Jordan.

Highway 60 – Way of the Patriarchs
Northern District to Southern District, Israel

Start Nazareth, Northern District
End Beersheba, Southern District
Distance 251km (156 miles)
Type Culture
Map goo.gl/DROl9S

Israel is replete with history, but few of its roads can boast the kind of connections to history that Highway 60 can. Also known as the Way of the Patriarchs, it traces a north-to-south line through the country's central watershed, approximating and providing access to the journeys taken in the Old Testament by Abraham, Isaac and Jacob, and later by Jesus and his apostles. Bisecting the occupied West Bank, it runs from Nazareth to Beersheba through Hebron, Bethlehem and Jerusalem, where it passes the Jaffa Gate and under Mt Zion.

Be under no illusions: travelling through the West Bank can be problematic. Check that your rental car has proper insurance and be mindful that the road is particularly narrow and winding, since it is notorious for nasty traffic accidents. From the Galilee region to Jerusalem you might even want to detour via Tel Aviv on Highway 6. It's not quite as interesting or scenic, but it is safer.

Along the way you'll pass many *trempiadas*, pickup points where hitchhikers can solicit rides in a country where the practice is still common and regarded as safe. Tunnels and bypasses have been built so that drivers can avoid driving through the heart of the strife-prone cities of Hebron and Bethlehem, but for the most part you'll find the drive an inspiring and exhilarating one through the heart of the Holy Land. **BDS**

❶ The highway runs through scrubland as well as desert; here, it passes a Palestinian village.

Highway 1 – The Roman's Ascent Tel Aviv, Israel

Start Tel Aviv
End Near Beit HaArava
Distance 93km (58 miles)
Type Culture
Map goo.gl/bOaXtA

The main road link between Tel Aviv on the coast, Ben Gurion International Airport, Jerusalem, and then eastwards into the Jordan Valley, Highway 1 is a six-lane freeway at its western end before narrowing to four lanes on the ascent through the Judean Mountains. It follows Ma'aleh HaRoma'im (Roman's Ascent), an ancient road into the city that was widened by the occupying Ottoman Turks in the 1860s. On the outskirts of Jerusalem, the road reaches its highest point at 815m (2,674ft) above sea level at Sha'ar Mizrach Junction before descending into the Jordan Valley and joining the historic Jericho Road, an ancient path to the Dead Sea rebuilt by the British in the 1920s. The highway then falls below sea level and passes near to Nabi Musa, believed by Muslims to be the burial place of Moses, and ends at Beit HaArava, a West Bank kibbutz established in 1939 near the intersection with Highway 90.

In common with almost everywhere in Israel, the history and sense of discovery when driving Highway 1 are palpable and constant. Barely a detour is dug without workers stumbling over something of great antiquity and significance. In 2015, while widening the highway near the Arab village of Abu Ghosh, a 5th-century Byzantine church was unearthed. Just another reminder of the ancient heritage of this much-trodden trail. **BDS**

Madaba to Al-Karak Road Madaba/Karak, Jordan

Start Madaba, Madaba
End Al-Karak, Karak
Distance 90km (56 miles)
Type Adventure
Map goo.gl/BDyUbT

Have you taken the camel ride into Petra? Floated on the Dead Sea? Still up for more fun in Jordan? Then try the nation's Route 35 south from Madaba to Al-Karak, constructed during the reign of King Hussein from 1952 to 1999 and following the path of the ancient King's Highway; this was a trade and pilgrimage route that once stretched from the Nile Delta north through Jordan to Damascus in Syria and on to the Euphrates River.

Madaba lies just southwest of the Jordanian capital, Amman, and is mentioned for its Moabite connections in the Old Testament of the Bible. Today the city is best known for its beautiful 6th-century mosaic map of the region, including Jerusalem, that is preserved in the floor of a Greek Orthodox church.

From Madaba, Route 35 runs south through magnificent mountains and hills along the eastern shore of the Dead Sea. There are sheer drops to either or both sides for most of the route, and enough hairpin bends to test the skills of even the most capable drivers. Near its end, the road turns sharply west and heads into Al-Karak, a roughly triangular hilltop city around 1,000m (3,300ft) above sea level, which is surrounded on three sides by a valley with startling views out west to the Dead Sea. The city is best known for its 12th-century Crusader castle, one of the finest in the region. **SA**

Jordanian Dead Sea Highway
Amman/Aqaba, Jordan

Start Amman, Amman
End Aqaba, Aqaba
Distance 333km (207 miles)
Type Adventure
Map goo.gl/BRpaQ7

It's fast, it's quiet and it's as low as you can get on four wheels: Jordan's Dead Sea Highway runs north to south along the eastern side of the great expanse of salt water and bottoms out at 430m (1,412ft) below sea level.

Here, instead of driving along a broad coastal plain as you would on the Israeli side (see page 764), you're squeezed, like sand through an hourglass, between a perennially buoyant salt-filled lake on one side and the towering, arid majesty of the Moab Mountains, rising to 1,311m (4,300ft) above you, on the other. There are even snowfalls across its vast plateau in winter and spring – a stark contrast to the pervasive aridity of the Judean Desert that lies to the west.

Driving from the capital, Amman, via Madaba involves a sharp descent from an elevation of 1,097m (3,600ft) to the lowest point on Earth on a series of fabulous switchbacks past Bedouin communities and ancient, terraced farmlands. Then down you go, into a world of copper oxides, vermilion and iron ore – a veritable painted desert on a road that accesses some of the most beautiful wadis and varied arid-zone landscapes to be found anywhere in the Middle East. One of the few things that grows around these parts is the number of tourists, who are well catered for at the Dead Sea Panoramic Complex. **BDS**

❶ The road runs along the Jordanian side of the Dead Sea; on the far shore is Israel.

Taif Escarpment
Makkah, Saudi Arabia

Start Taif
End Mecca
Distance 109km (67.7 miles)
Type Adventure
Map goo.gl/gkePK9

Far above the heat, humidity and modernity of nearby Jeddah and Mecca, the wide expanses of the Taif Escarpment are a welcome sanctuary, a respite from Saudi Arabia's relentless heat and ever-expanding cities. The route to it, the Taif–Jeddah Escarpment Road, takes you up Shafa Mountains and was built by the Saudi Binladin Construction Group. It's a fast, modern highway with two two-lane roadways looping around the mountainside.

It also is a hill climber's dream come true, with 93 drama-filled twists and a steep, short-distance elevation gain of a massive 1,981m (6,500ft). Once you reach the top of the incline, the Ramada Al-Hada Hotel and a gaggle of baboons that live along the top of the escarpment wait to greet you, as does the town of Taif, set in its rose-scented hollow surrounded by the granite and basalt hills of the Hejaz.

There is history here, too. Taif accepted Islam in 631 CE, and the Koran describes Mecca and Taif as 'the two cities'. There is everything from pre-Islamic souks to Turkish forts. But it is the climb you've come for, a dizzying ascent on a demanding drivers' road, blessed with scenic overlooks, designated U-turn areas and police cameras that help to keep the driver's mind focused on the speed limit, which is otherwise easy to forget, especially on the way back down the hill. **BDS**

Highway 10
Eastern Province, Saudi Arabia

Start Haradh
End Al Batha
Distance 261km (162 miles)
Type Adventure
Map goo.gl/Ghxy5i

If overcoming fatigue or finding interesting aspects to an endlessly repetitive landscape are not your strong points, you might want to give this road trip a miss. For others, it will be of interest for its unbending design.

Saudi Arabia's Highway 10 east of the small town of Haradh, known only for the wealth of oil and gas fields upon which it sits, is the longest, ruler-straight section of road in the world. Sure, one should always be cautious when talking up supposedly 'straight' roads because more often than not there will be a kink, a deviation, a few degrees of a course change somewhere. Highway 10 between Haradh and the border with the United Arab Emirates, however, possesses no such deviations. There is barely even a need for a steering wheel until you reach an oh-so-slight bend just prior to reaching the United Arab Emirates' border.

The speed limit in Saudi Arabia is 120 kph (80 mph), but with no frame of reference for miles around, you need to keep an eye on your speedometer, which will have a tendency to creep upwards. Highway 10 lies on a precise easterly line across a tiny patch of the Empty Quarter – the Rub' al-Khali – the world's largest unbroken sand desert, a land where fossils and meteorite fragments outnumber living things such as scorpions, snakes and, of course, humans. **BDS**

Saudi–Oman Highway
Eastern Province, Saudi Arabia

Start Salwa
End Shaybah
Distance 486km (302 miles)
Type Adventure
Map goo.gl/TgD5gX

The Rub' al-Khali desert in Saudi Arabia is better known by the atmospheric, but vaguely threatening, name of the Empty Quarter. At 1,000km (620 miles) long and about half as wide, this desert consists of reddish-orange sand dunes rising up to 250m (820ft), interspersed with gravel and gypsum plains. Other than a few local tribes, the area is uninhabited, since rain is extremely rare and daily temperatures can rise to 47°C (1247°F) and drop almost to freezing at night.

Perhaps unsurprisingly, therefore, there are few roads that cross the region, other than this divided highway that is set to connect Saudi Arabia with Oman to its east. After departing the coastal town of Salwa, on the northern border with Qatar, you pick up this new road after crossing the arrow-straight Highway 10. From here it heads due south into the Empty Quarter and then east across to the Shaybah oil field, skirting the United Arab Emirates to its north. Eventually, a new border crossing will shave 800km (500 miles) off the journey between the eponymous nations.

Comprising three legs of unswerving tarmac the road is considered an engineering marvel, built on shifting sand and requiring bridges between the tallest dunes. Car buffs should also keep an eye out along the way for camouflaged prototypes undergoing extreme weather testing. **SA**

❶ The highway is divided throughout its length by a raised median strip.

Jabal Sabir
Taiz, Yemen

Start Taiz
End Ad Dimnah
Distance 46km (28.5 miles)
Type Adventure
Map goo.gl/NQhYyZ

The mountains in the southern province of Taiz in Yemen rise up to 3,050m (10,000ft) and more, creating a barrier to transport and trade. Perhaps the most interesting route across this natural barrier is through the Jabal Sabir Pass, which rises to 2,883m (9,458ft) above sea level. Traversed by the Saber Road (official designation Highway 412), via 55 switchbacks and tight sweeping bends, the broad tarmac surface is generally smooth and well maintained. However, gradients can be steep, rising to 13 per cent in some stretches.

The road starts in Sheikh Zayeds Park to the south of the provincial capital and then heads in a roughly southerly direction over the mountains before swinging east to Ad Dimnah. The scenery is truly spectacular, with an enthralling overlook onto the walled city of Tiaz below.

Jabal Sabir has increasingly become a popular road-trip destination with its dramatic vistas and foothills dotted with bountiful fruit farms, cool mineral springs and important religious sites including the Mosque of the Seven Sleepers in the village of Mo'qab. The region's numerous fortresses hint at Tiaz's turbulent political history, which sadly continues to this day, so make sure you check your government's travel-advice website before heading off; nevertheless, it's definitely worthy of adding to your road-tripping wish list. SA

❶ The generally arid scenery along the route is punctuated by hill-hung houses such as these.

Lawdar Mountain Pass
Abyan/Al Bayda, Yemen

Start Lawdar, Abyan
End Mukayris, Al Bayda
Distance 32km (20 miles)
Type Adventure
Map goo.gl/q9f2HY

Abyan province in Yemen lies in the south of the country, just to the northeast of the port city of Aden. On any journey inland, coastal plains soon give way to mountains. The nation's tallest peak, at 3,666m (12,028ft) above sea level, is Jabal an Nabi Shu'ayb, but in the view of many its most impressive natural landmark is Lawdar Mountain, the pass over which rises to 2,267m (7,437ft).

This is a road for adventure, since it has 34 switchbacks and numerous other testing corners. The road – officially the N6 or R4234 – starts in Lawdar and heads west in a deceptively leisurely manner before turning north into the mountains, which is where the hairpin bends begin. The bends come in tight groups, giving you a short but welcome time to recover from one flurry before entering the next set. While the driver will dare not take their eyes of the tarmac ahead, passengers looking back down can catch a spectacular view of the tortuous hairpins below unravelling like an untied shoelace. The scenery is wild, with little vegetation to cover the bare and rocky mountainsides. Once up the pass, the road gently swerves along the top of a plateau in Al Bayda province via the village of Aryab to finish in Mukayris.

The military base near here hints at the high levels of unrest Yemen has experienced. Be sure to take appropriate checks before setting off. **SA**

Bahrain Old Capital
Tour Capital/Muharraq, Bahrain

Start Manama, Capital Governorate
End Muharraq, Muharraq Governorate
Distance 16km (10 miles)
Type Culture
Map goo.gl/6A6iSJ

Some cities are perfect for exploring by foot, but the temperatures in Manama, Bahrain, can reach close to a sweltering 48°C (120°F) in the height of summer, while the humidity can hit 90 per cent during the warm winter months. Moreover, in view of the fact that many of the must-see sights in Manama and the surrounding area are not right next to one another, the only sensible way to get around is in the cool confines of an air-conditioned automobile.

You can rent a car, plot your own route and set off, but Manama has a host of local guides who will take you around for a reasonable fee, which gets all the more reasonable if shared among a small group. Set off with friends to see the 15th-century Arad Fort; the Shaikh Isa Bin Ali Mosque, which is arguably Bahrain's most impressive example of Gulf Islamic architecture; and the souk at Muharraq.

Other sights within easy reach of Manama are the 25-km- (15.5-mile) long King Fahd Causeway that connects Bahrain to mainland Saudi Arabia, and of course, the Bahrain International Circuit, which first featured in 2004 on the Formula One motor-racing calendar. Lying 35km (21.7 miles) southwest of Manama, this circuit is best seen on a guided tour, which takes in the track, the control tower, the media centre and the famous Sakhir Tower VIP area. **TW**

Discover Qatar
Doha, Qatar

Start Doha
End Doha
Distance 381km (237 miles)
Type Culture
Map goo.gl/2Qt43U

The Qatari peninsula is flat and regularly swept clean by the persistent Shamal wind. Almost all its 11,610 sq km (4,483 square miles) are underlain by a vast sheet of abnormally uniform limestone – again, flat. Apart from sand dunes in the south, the terrain is almost featureless, its highways gun-barrel straight because they have no obstacles or landforms to avoid. Sealed, multi-lane highways fan out everywhere over this flat, baked landscape, and wealthy Qataris – which is almost all of them – drive very fast cars. A reason, perhaps, why there are more than 4,000 accidents a year here involving vehicles. Roads now have a safety star system, and rumble strips and crash barriers are increasingly common sights in a country where speed is an ever-present danger.

This fast-flowing loop that starts and ends in the capital first heads north to the ruins of the old fishing villages near Al Ruwais, where there are echoes of a time before the oil boom. Heading southwest brings you to the shores of Dukhan Beach before a fast leg east to the famous Singing Sand Dunes near Mesaieed. Dune-bashing in 4x4s is, of course, a must on any Qatari road trip. Back on the tarmac, it's a short blast to the historic Barzan Towers before heading back to the air-conditioned comforts of central Doha. All this can be achieved in a one-day action-packed itinerary. **BDS**

Tal Mireb Road
Abu Dhabi, United Arab Emirates

Start Liwa Oasis
End Tal Mireb
Distance 26km (16 miles)
Type Scenic
Map goo.gl/YD7diI

The smooth, dark tarmac of the Tal Mireb Road stretches for nearly 22km (14 miles) into the Rub al-Khali desert south of the Liwa Oasis. Without the usual roadside furniture or palm trees, it is appropriate that this is the main access road into the area known as the Empty Quarter.

As its name suggests, Liwa Oasis is a source of water, which is a rare and highly prized commodity in the heart of the world's largest sandy desert. Several Bedouin villages have been constructed around it, and these are generally well appointed, with shops, places to stay and filling stations.

The gently sweeping highway has surprisingly large changes in elevation as it rolls over the stark and beautiful landscape of endless sand dunes, weaving its way towards Tal Mireb (better known as Moreeb Dune, meaning 'Scary Mountain'), a dune complex whose highest points are nearly 300m (1,000ft) high.

Few people actually use this road, since it doesn't really go anywhere. Those who do drive it often go dune-bashing in powerful 4x4s, and there are regular hill-climb competitions held on Moreeb Dune's intimidatingly steep slip face. Many local companies will rent you expedition vehicles, so you can also get out and explore this wonderfully desolate automotive playground and maybe even camp under the vast desert skies. **DIS**

Jabal Hafeet Mountain Road
Abu Dhabi, United Arab Emirates

Start Green Mubazzarah Hot Streams Pools
End Jabal Hafeet summit
Distance 12km (7.5 miles)
Type Adventure
Map goo.gl/tNd2yh

This short strip of supersmooth tarmac is considered by many motoring journalists to be one of the world's greatest driving roads, attracting swarms of the Middle East's more keen drivers and bikers to tackle its 60 sweeping bends that squirm to the summit at 1,249m (4,097ft).

The barren, rock-strewn landscape permits great lines of sight that allow 'spirited' drivers to link together fast corners and anticipate changes in elevation on the wide two-lane ascent. In this wealthy, oil-producing region, Jabal Hafeet ('Empty Mountain') has become the habitual haunt of supercar owners and adrenaline-pumped bikers: always watch your mirrors for fast-approaching Bugattis, Ferraris, McLarens and Ninjas. Porsche sometimes uses this road for hot-weather testing.

The best times to visit are at dawn and dusk, when the sun casts long, ominous shadows and cliff walls glow red; after dark, 500 streetlamps light up the road like an airport runway.

At the summit sits the Mercure Grand Jebel Hafeet Al Ain Hotel alongside an impressive palace belonging to the country's rulers. That's the end of the trip; from here the only way is back down the single-lane road to the starting point, Green Mubazzarah, a popular tourist attraction at the foot of the mountain; famed for its thermal springs and natural hot tubs, it's the perfect spot to unwind. **DIS**

❶ Aerial view of the Jabal Hafeet mountain road: 'dull would he be of soul' who wouldn't want to drive it.

Jabal Jais Mountain Road Ras Al-Khaimah, United Arab Emirates

Start Wadi Bih   **End** Jabal Jais   **Distance** 58km (36 miles)
Type Scenic   **Map** goo.gl/AbOLcy

Jabal Jais – at 1,911m (6,268ft) the highest peak of the Al-Hajar Mountains – has been a magnet for enthusiastic motorists and bikers ever since it was opened just a decade ago. This magnificent scribble of tarmac was the brainchild of Sheikh Saud bin Saqr al Qasimi and is just one part of a grand plan to develop tourism in this remote corner of the United Arab Emirates. Cafés, hotels, a paragliding centre, climbing trails, a cable car and even a ski resort (temperatures drop below freezing at this altitude in the depths of the Arabian winter) are all on the drawing board.

It takes around 30 minutes to cover this spectacular climb on the perfectly smooth, three-lane (two going up, one going down) mountain road. The real fun starts at the halfway point, where the switchbacks begin.

The treeless, monochromatic gray rock, flecked with orange limestone and prickly green juniper, has a unique, rugged beauty. Sadly, you'll rarely get the place to yourself; on weekends the canyon walls echo with the wails of visiting supercars and high-powered sports bikes – some of which have come from Kuwait and Saudi Arabia simply to experience this astonishing road, which has been well described as 'a ribbon of perfection'. **DIS**

❶ The silence is broken only by cars and motorbikes.

Rustaq Loop Castles Tour Al Batinah North, Oman

Start Barka   **End** Barka   **Distance** 192km (119 miles)
Type Culture   **Map** goo.gl/r8TVr6

Castles are cool. Whether you dream of being a princess in a tower or a warrior on the battlements, who doesn't love something that big and dramatic? On the Rustaq Loop in Oman, you get to see three such fortresses, each perfectly preserved and straight out of some historic book, perhaps *The Arabian Nights* (1706).

This is a circular route on smooth, well-maintained tarmac that throws up no nasty surprises. It runs for 192km (119 miles) from Barka on the Gulf of Oman to Nakhal Fort, then to Rustaq and Al Hazm. You should allow around three hours driving time, plus stops. You could manage the journey in less time, but there's much more fun to be had if you take your time and explore. The Nakhal Fort, for example, is built into a hillside. It predates Islam but was rebuilt in the 17th century. Al Rustaq Fort is one of the largest structures of its type in Oman, with four towers and a prison. Al Hazm Castle is a maze of passageways and corridors and has a room laid out to depict life here in the 18th century.

This is very much a historical drive, but one that will capture the imagination. The roads are good and the weather is always great. All in all, it's a fabulous combination. **JI**

❶ Rustaq Fort was built in the 17th century.

Muscat to Sur

Muscat/Ash Sharqiyah, Oman

Wadi An Nakhr

Ad Dakhiliyah, Oman

Start Ruwi, Muscat
End Sur, Ash Sharqiyah
Distance 241km (150 miles)
Type Scenic
Map goo.gl/d7PByJ

Start Al Hamra
End An Nakhr
Distance 43km (27 miles)
Type Adventure
Map goo.gl/6OFGlq

Completed in the first decade of the 21st century, the Muscat–Sur Coastal Road runs from the capital of Oman to Sur, a city on the Arabian Gulf and home to the country's shipbuilding industry. As you speed along its gleaming tarmac, you have water on one side, mountains on the other and history all around you.

Along the way there are wadis – water-filled valleys – such as Wadi Al Arbeieen and Wadi Shab. They're popular places to cool off and swim, with water that is crystal clear.

If you choose to venture off the main road (though a 4x4 will be essential), you can head to the Eastern Hajar Mountains and the ancient beehive tombs at Jaylah. A must-see en route is the sinkhole at Bimmah, formed from a meteor impact and linked to the sea by an underground tunnel.

Sur itself is a picturesque, historic city where dhows (traditional wooden ships) are built. There is also a beach at Ras al Jinz, where you can observe green turtles laying their eggs in the sand.

One thing to beware of is the heat. Even in January the average temperature is approximately 22°C (71°F). But conditions are generally excellent for driving. The four-lane road is modern, safe and well signposted. There are bends and twists in the early sections, but as you near Sur it opens out and runs almost entirely straight. **JI**

Wadi An Nakhr is sometimes known as Oman's Grand Canyon – and with good reason. It's the deepest and most spectacular desert canyon in the region. Travelling on the road to Jebel Shams Resort, one can experience the canyon from above, and it's a mighty impressive view out over the giant chasm. But the best way to grasp the real scale of this natural phenomenon is to drive up the gorge at canyon-floor level. To do this, take the road northwest from Al Hamra, and after about ten minutes, when you reach Ghul, turn right. The access road to the canyon is a rough gravel track, so you will need a suitable 4x4, and it is best you also take a guide.

Not many people take the trouble to find this road, so you will not be slowed by crowds of tourists. It is used mostly by locals who live in traditional villages along the canyon floor. As you follow upstream alongside the watercourse, at first the landscape is quite open, but then, after the small hamlet of Masirat Nakhr, the cliffs begin to crowd in and the area becomes strewn with giant boulders. After about 5km (3 miles) more, the road reaches An Nakhr. Motor vehicles must park here, but one can continue to explore on foot. Even if you stay put, this is a spectacular spot to rest and take it all in – the sheer rock sides of the canyon dwarf the green palm trees in the wadi. **DK**

Lahich Yolu Mountain Road
Masally/Ismailli, Azerbaijan

Start Tazakand, Masally
End Lahich, Ismailli
Distance 20km (12.4 miles)
Type Adventure
Map goo.gl/qUJ4Uy

Do you like driving along rough gravel tracks halfway up a vertical cliff? Are you bored with smooth, fast, safe, well-maintained and signposted roads? Well, try heading immediately to Azerbaijan to tackle this alarming stretch of what can only loosely be termed a road.

Azerbaijan is a wealthy independent nation standing alongside the Caspian Sea in the Caucasus. It has many fine and boring paved highways. It also has this daunting route.

You'll leave the comfort of the R8 just outside Tasakand village and head north into the hills. The first stretch is easy. It leads up to the small village of Birinci Yeniyol, which even has a hotel, although it appears that the guests sleep in wooden sheds in the garden.

The trail continues along the side of a ravine, and the views are magnificent. There's nothing too scary so far. Gradually, however, it starts becoming a little bit medieval. The gravel-and-stone surface becomes potholed, and the road edges crumble away down unprotected vertical slopes.

By the end it's too narrow, too steep and too unreliable to be deemed a road. And yet this is the only way to reach the pretty little mountain village of Lahich, with its cobbled alleys, stone cottages and old church. Amazingly, it is an increasingly popular tourist destination. **SH**

❶ This is one of the less demanding stretches of the middle section of this route.

Baku Street Circuit
Absheron, Azerbaijan

Start Azadliq Square, Baku
End Azadliq Square, Baku
Distance 6km (3.72 miles)
Type Culture
Info goo.gl/3wcEOS

The busy race calendar of modern Formula One, jet-setting between 20 different circuits across the globe, must be disorienting, but even those with a weak grasp of geography must have been surprised to find that the inaugural Baku Grand Prix in Azerbaijan in 2016 was billed as the European Grand Prix. Azerbaijan, in Europe? A country on the Caspian Sea with Turkey and Iran among its neighbours? Surely, some mistake: you must be in Asia? Regardless of contentious geography, the Grand Prix was a great success, a street circuit that ran through the centre of this historic city providing exciting sport for drivers and spectators alike. One element that caught everyone's attention was the frighteningly narrow 7.6-m- (25-ft) long gap between an ancient tower and the buildings opposite in Aziz Aliyev Street, a thoroughfare more designed for handcarts than for 900 brake horsepower Formula One race cars. Yet the race was accident free.

Since the event takes places on public roads, anyone can drive the course. The start and finish lines are in Azadliq Square at the end of the main promenade, Neftchilar Avenue. The track then twists and turns anticlockwise around the city, with long straight drags interrupted by tight right- and left-hand corners. You might not reach Formula One speeds, but you'll get an idea of the challenges faced by inaugural event winner Nico Rosberg. **SA**

❶ Some of Baku's latest buildings are shaped like flames to symbolize the oil on which its wealth is founded.

Dizin Road
Tehran/Alborz, Iran

Start Shemshak, Tehran
End Dizin, Alborz
Distance 16km (10 miles)
Type Adventure
Map goo.gl/Ddk5XS

Just a short drive from the centre of Tehran, in the Alborz Mountains to the north of the city, lies the Dizin ski resort, the largest in Iran and a playground for the country's wealthy winter-sport enthusiasts to enjoy the slopes. The contrast between the cacophony of Tehran and the emptiness of the mountains is almost incredible, and the highway up to the resort is hugely impressive, too.

Road 425 starts at the Shemshak ski resort, itself the second largest in Iran, and then heads north. As you climb up a road that in places is 3,200m (10,500ft) above sea level, the views over the plains below are mesmerizing, but beware: altitude sickness can be a real problem; the more slowly you climb, the better your body will acclimatize.

Some of the small towns on the road are worth stopping at en route; many travellers have praised their street food as being truly awesome. But as you approach the final 5.9km (3.7 miles), the road suddenly rises up a series of 17 tight hairpin bends, climbing through the scree slopes of the mountainside. Perhaps not unexpectedly, the road is often blocked by avalanches and heavy snowfall makes the surface treacherous. Once at the top you can catch your breath and admire the wonderful panorama over the Alborz Mountains. But best of all, you can also enjoy the rare experience of skiing in the Middle East. **SA**

❶ One of the main attractions of this road trip is that it traverses the heart of the beautiful Alborz Range.

Chalus Road

Tehran/Mazandaran, Iran

Start Tehran, Tehran
End Chalus, Mazandaran
Distance 200km (124 miles)
Type Adventure
Map goo.gl/lknQFC

The Chalus Road in Iran, also known as Road 59, is a popular route for people living in the capital, Tehran, who use it to reach holiday destinations and weekend retreats. It's named after the suburb of Chalus, home to spectacular beech trees. But this is more than just a quiet drive out of the city; it's both spectacular and dangerous in places.

North of Tehran is the Alborz mountain range, and the Chalus Road cuts right through it. The landscape ranges from lush forests to ravines and rivers and, eventually, the Caspian Sea, while the mountains above you reach 4,000m (13,000ft) above sea level. The local wildlife includes bears, wolves and lynxes.

Chalus itself is a popular seaside resort, but reaching it can be a challenge. The road is narrow and twisty, and although it is tarmacked it can be hazardous, with tunnels and tight corners that offer little room for vehicles to pass. Walls of solid rock loom in over you, but there are precious few safety barriers at the roadside. But take it slowly and safely and you're rewarded with panoramic views of the Alborz Mountains and the valleys beneath them.

Feted by *BMW Magazine* as one of the most thrilling roads in Asia, the route is increasingly popular among adventurous motorcyclists. **JI**

🌀 A dramatic rockface at the side of the Chalus Road.

Shemshak Road

Tehran, Iran

Start Oshan Fasham Road
End Shemshak
Distance 29km (18 miles)
Type Scenic
Map goo.gl/pHkF8R

You start on the outskirts of the capital, Tehran, then begin a winding route into the Alborz Mountains to the north. You pass through the protected landscapes of the Varjin Protected Area, where you will see lush green valleys interspersed between harsh dry mountains, often topped with snow even through the summer.

The road is smooth and wide near the towns and villages in the valleys, but becomes narrower with steep and twisting sections as it rises through the more remote areas.

To the north of the small town of Fasham, the gradients become more severe. You ascend to 2,549m (8,363ft) above sea level through rocky gorges, alongside fast-flowing mountain rivers and under vast cliffs and overhangs.

This high up, snow can close the road at any time, and there are often huge drifts alongside the road. Eventually, you come to Iran's main ski areas. The popular resort of Dizin is a little farther on, but you're stopping at the town of Shemshak, perhaps the country's hippest winter resort.

From November to April or May, there is a wide variety of skiing and snowboarding runs here, including some of Iran's most difficult slopes. There are cross-country trails, off-piste areas and illuminated runs for night skiing, all serviced by a selection of modern ski lifts. **SH**

M32 – Aral Highway
West Kazakhstan to South Kazakhstan, Kazakhstan

Start Uralsk, West Kazakhstan
End Shymkent, South Kazakhstan
Distance 1,999km (1,242 miles)
Type Adventure
Map goo.gl/yS182q

Even the hardiest proponent of the phrase 'the good old days' would have trouble applying it with any conviction to Kazakhstan's M32. Once one of the world's most poorly maintained highways, it runs on a northwest-to-southeast line through the heart of the country, from Uralsk to Shymkent. It has come a long way in the last few years. Once a mix of gravel, sand and mud that in some sections was so potholed it looked like it had been the target of air strikes (although it had never been thus attacked), muddied stretches were so appallingly glue-like that you had to leave the road and drive parallel to it across the surrounding desert. Now, thankfully, it is paved, and what was once a 4x4-only route can be made comfortably in ordinary road vehicles.

The highway takes you, as its name suggests, past the Aral Sea, once one of the world's largest lakes, now one of the world's great environmental catastrophes after its waters were drained to feed Soviet-era irrigation projects in the 1960s. The scenery is mostly flat, the vast steppes cultivated with grain crops and populated by free-ranging cows as well as sheep and goats. One must-do stop is in the town of Aralsk, once a vibrant fishing port on the Aral Sea, now a graveyard for ships that sit, rusting, on the bed of one of the world's newest, human-made deserts. **BDS**

❶ The draining of large areas of the Aral Sea has left hundreds of ships high and dry and abandoned.

Anzob Circuit
Sughd, Tajikistan

Start Anzob
End Anzob
Distance 97km (60 miles)
Type Adventure
Map goo.gl/SB4VRQ

If you happen to be in the remote, mountainous Central Asian republic of Tajikistan and looking for an interesting day trip, this is just the thing. To the north of the capital, Dushanbe, you will find this challenging circuit using the Anzob Pass and the Anzob Tunnel.

Although it is still in regular use by local traffic, the Anzob Pass has a fearsome reputation for being one of Asia's most deadly roads. It crosses the Zarafshan Mountain range at around 3,400m (11,000ft), and is higher than any road in Europe. Avalanches and rockfalls are frequent in the depths of winter and in the heights of summer, so make sure to time your escapades wisely.

Once you've enjoyed the wild, unspoilt mountains of Tajikistan, you can return via the M34 and the Anzob Tunnel; built as a safe alternative shortcut in 2006 it fell a little short of its remit due to financial cutbacks. In fact, for several years, it was known to locals as the 'Tunnel of Death'"because the 5-km- (3-mile) long underground stretch was unlit, partially flooded and littered with axle-breaking potholes. Thankfully, it's now much improved and you no longer need to sign a waiver before entering it as it speeds you back to the mining town of Anzob for a warming bowl of *palav* (rice cooked with meat and oil); your just reward for an epic automotive adventure. **SH**

❶ In 2006 the Anzob Tunnel was draped in flags on the day of its official opening.

Song Köl
Naryn, Kyrgyzstan

Start Sarybulak
End Lake Song Köl
Distance 140km (87 miles)
Type Adventure
Map goo.gl/DQy8gj

This is an adventurous route across the heart of the Central Asian republic of Kyrgyzstan, a mountainous, landlocked and sparsely populated country. The proposed itinerary is remote, but the road is well maintained and largely safe.

You'll leave the smooth tarmac of the A365 just south of the hamlet of Sary-Bulak, where a few yurts sell snacks to passing Chinese truck drivers. Your route now climbs through a remote village and twists alongside the Tolok River.

The landscape here is dry and rugged, as you weave between rocky cliffs and big brown hills. Strange geological shapes appear amid beautifully weathered rocks. You may see locals tending their cattle and yaks. Others might be travelling on the same track as you, but on horseback.

If the weather is reasonable in the summer months, the track is quite drivable. You should be able to reach the beauty spot of the lake in about 90 minutes.

Song Köl is worth the journey. It's a large lake of about 270 sq km (100 square miles) surrounded by mountains. The protected shoreline is unspoiled: there are no developments or facilities here, although a few farmers may sell you some food or rent out a yurt for accommodation. Whatever you do at the lake, don't stray too far alone. The protected species here include wolves. **SH**

❶ The road to Lake Song Köl is slow and serpentine, but no one wants to hurry through scenery like this.

Pamir Highway
Afghanistan to Kyrgyzstan

Start Mazari Sharif, Balkh, Afghanistan
End Osh, Kyrgyzstan
Distance 1,577km (980 miles)
Type Adventure
Map goo.gl/BNfG7d

The good news is that the section of the Pamir Highway (M41) from Osh, in the Central Asia nation of Kyrgyzstan, to Khorog on the Pamir Plateau in Tajikistan, is definitely paved. The not-so-good news is that there are many sections of this semi-paved highway (the second-highest highway in the world) that are all sorts of other surfaces, including sand, gravel, rock and even mud.

The higher up you go, the more the weather deteriorates, and so does the road, which becomes increasingly pockmarked and cracked in the upper reaches. Landslides and rockfalls close sections of it at a moment's notice, and the jury's still out as to precisely where the highway's terminus is. None of which should be cause for concern. After all, you don't come to Central Asia if your goal is to remain within your comfort zone.

The Pamir Highway follows a route that was known to locals for millennia before it was crafted into something resembling a road by Soviet military engineers in the 1930s. It passes through spectacular landscapes including the Ak-Baital Pass, its highest point at 4,655m (15,270ft); the lush Wakhan Valley; and the enchanting scenery of the Hindu Kush. Something of a pilgrimage for 4x4ers and adventurous motorcyclists, the Pamir Highway is gaining a reputation as a 'last frontier' road trip. Which makes it a rare road trip indeed. **BDS**

❶ There are growing numbers of motorcyclists on the Pamir Highway, but as yet there's no risk of gridlock.

Makran Coastal Highway
Sindh/Balochistan, Pakistan

Start Karachi, Sindh
End Gwadar, Balochistan
Distance 636km (395 miles)
Type Adventure
Map goo.gl/rttXfe

Before 2004, the only way to travel between Karachi and Gwadar was by an unfinished dirt track. Journey times were measured in days, and you would need a tough off-road vehicle. Cautious drivers chose to take a much longer but safer route, where you would at least have tarmac beneath your wheels.

Then, as part of a major improvement and development programme inside the country, the Pakistan government ordered the construction of a new road – the N10/Makran Coastal Highway. Built by the Frontier Works Organization, a specialist engineering division of the army, its key aim was to help boost commerce and industry along the southern Pakistani coast.

It's an impressive feat, with tarmac now snaking along by the side of the Arabian Sea for 635km (395 miles) and through the Hingol National Park and Buzi Makola Wildlife Sanctuary. It twists and bends through canyons and rocky outcrops; barriers are few and far between, and there is the added danger of rockfalls on certain sections. It's not inherently risky, though; just a road that requires respect and attention at all times. The rewards – stunning sea, forest and mountain views – are immense.

The Makran Coastal Highway is a great source of pride in Pakistan – justifiably so, since it has turned a two-day trek into a journey that can be completed in around seven hours. JI

Karakoram Highway
Pakistan/China

Start Hassan Abdal, Punjab, Pakistan
End Kashgar, Xinjiang, China
Distance 1,624km (1,009 miles)
Type Adventure
Map goo.gl/3JPGr9

This incredible feat of civil engineering is regularly lauded as the eighth wonder of the world. Among the highest paved highways in the world, it took 20 years to construct, and cost the lives of more than 1,000 construction workers. It finally opened in 1979 and is still under constant maintenance and improvement, which recently included 24km (15 miles) of new road tunnels.

A thriving niche tourist industry has attracted adventurous bikers and motorists to take on the Karakoram Highway, also known as the China–Pakistan Friendship Highway. Most begin their journey in Hassan Abdal, at the end of the Grand Trunk Road, one of Sikhism's holiest pilgrimage sites.

As you head up along a branch of the ancient Silk Road the surfaces are, for the most part, sealed and smooth, although progress can be slow if you get caught behind an overloaded local bus or a slow-moving jingle truck (one of Pakistan's customized vehicles dripping with gaudy decorations and ornaments). Patience is needed; accidents are frequent and wrecked vehicles litter the roadsides. The safest time to travel is in spring or autumn, since summer monsoons frequently cause landslides. Plan ahead, do your research and don't forget your visas – it's going to be an amazing trip. DIS

➲ The scenery is even more wonderful than the road.

Road to Fairy Meadows
Gilgit-Baltistan, Pakistan

Start Raikot Bridge, Karakoram Highway
End South of Tattu
Distance 16km (9.9 miles)
Type Adventure
Map goo.gl/pAvG2j

It may sound innocuous, even charming, but the Road to Fairy Meadows is not somewhere to take the kids. This unpaved track branching off from the Karakoram Highway to the foot of Nanga Parbat (aka 'Killer Mountain'), the eighth highest in the Himalayas at 8,126m (26,660ft), is a gruelling grind, albeit through some of the most spectacular scenery on Earth. There are crumbling edges and long, sheer drops; patches of corrugated rock and constant clouds of dust. There is very little wriggle room.

The starting point is Raikot Bridge, where you can rent jeeps with drivers and obtain police permission if necessary (depending on the security situation). From there the track spirals heavenwards, following the glacier-fed Raikot River, a tributary of the Indus. Staggering views of lofty, snowcapped peaks unfold at every switchback, but there is little opportunity to enjoy them unless you actually stop. The road requires the full attention of driver and passengers – two eyes are nowhere near enough – with one eye always on the lookout for oncoming jeeps, laden with locals, that rattle along seemingly oblivious to other road users.

The road straightens up beyond Tattu and then stops. From there, Fairy Meadows – a lush, green amphitheatre in the lap of Nanga Parbat's north face, with camping, basic accommodations and cafés – is an additional 5-km- (2-mile) long hike. **DS**

❶ A busload of mountaineers.
❷ Fairy Meadows in the light of dawn.

Khunjerab Pass Gilgit-Baltistan, Pakistan

Start Nazimabad **End** Karakoram Highway **Distance** 89km (55 miles)
Type Adventure **Map** goo.gl/QCcxjH

Regardless of which direction you take to get there, by the time you reach the 4,693-m- (15,397-ft) long Khunjerab Pass, high in the Karakoram Range on the China–Pakistan border, you've already conquered a good portion of one of the world's great drives, the Karakoram Highway. The world's highest sealed international border, the pass is your international crossing point, the line where left-hand traffic Pakistan meets right-hand-drive China.

Completed in 1982, this long and quite flat pass on the Pamir Plateau, closed to all but large trucks from December to April because of snow and mudslides, can be done in a car, although 4x4s are preferable considering the poor condition of the

tarmac on the Chinese side and the gravel surface in Pakistan. Seasonal freezing, with temperatures of -40°C (-40°F), can also cause suspension-wrecking ripples in its surface.

Make sure you have your visa (you can't obtain one at the pass) so that you can cross as a tourist with only minor bureaucratic delays. If you carry on into China, do not pass the town of Tashkurgan without stopping at its ancient stone castle, from the top of which you can gaze over mountains and grasslands traversed for more than 2,000 years by Silk Road merchants and traders. **BDS**

❶ Near the Khunjerab Pass.

Khardung La Jammu and Kashmir, India

Start Leh   **End** Khardung La   **Distance** 40km (25 miles)
Type Adventure   **Map** goo.gl/PPTIkn

Opened in 1988, the Khardung La follows part of the ancient Silk Route tramped by traders' camel caravans heading for Central Asia; traversing the Ladakh mountain range, it connects the bustling city of Leh with the spectacular Nubra Valley, famed for its wildflowers. Winding up past glaciers and abandoned construction camps, and through a chain of barren, snowcapped mountains, intrepid adventurers are finally rewarded with black tea at the world's highest roadside café. Here, among the rock cairns and prayer flags, a battered metal road sign proudly boasts that, at 5,602m (18,380ft) above sea level, Khardung La is the 'highest motorable road in the world'.

Much of the ascent is well surfaced, only deteriorating to narrower dirt road near the summit. Despite the real dangers from altitude sickness, land slides, rockfalls and snowmelt, Khardung La is a well-trodden tourist route between May and October, which can lead to traffic jams.

Built and maintained by the Indian army, the Khardung La road is a feat of engineering. However, the surveying is a little less impressive: modern GPS shows its true altitude to be 5,359m (17,582ft), putting it at number three in today's world rankings, according to motoring website Jalopnik. **DIS**

❶ No matter its height, this is still a great drive.

Zojila Pass
Jammu and Kashmir, India

Start Sonamarg
End Dras
Distance 63km (39 miles)
Type Adventure
Map goo.gl/Zk3LTw

A vital link between Ladakh and Kashmir, the Zojila Pass in the western Himalayas comes with a sobering trio of facts: it lies 3,530m (11,580ft) above sea level on the remote Srinagar to Leh Highway; it is unnervingly narrow; and it has no guardrails. Strong winds can blow through the conically shaped gorges that lie either side of it, and 20-m- (60-ft) high snowfalls see it closed over winter. Hundreds of travellers have had to be rescued after being trapped by landslides along the way. The upside? Driving it, you've never felt so alive. Giant walls of near-vertical rock stare at you from every direction, and the road is so slow that there is plenty of time to marvel at your surroundings.

Bordered by the Kashmir and Dras Basins, there is little room for miscalculation here with drop-offs of hundreds of feet only a mistimed turn or a moment's distraction away. With its surface a mix of rocks, gravel, heavily pummelled dirt and occasional and unexpected stretches of paving, you should attempt this journey only when weather permits, between late spring and the onset of winter.

During the Indo-Pakistani War of 1947, Zojila was seized by Pakistani forces. In the following year Operation Bison, an Indian assault to regain the pass, achieved success due to the surprise use of tanks, the highest altitude at which such weapons have ever been deployed. **BDS**

❶ In April 2012 mounted porters carried goods along the highway shortly after the snows were cleared.

Keylong to Kishtwar Road
Jammu and Kashmir/Himachal Pradesh, India

Start Keylong, Jammu and Kashmir
End Kishtwar, Himachal Pradesh
Distance 219km (136 miles)
Type Adventure
Map goo.gl/YLkmGZ

The name National Highway 26 has a comfortable, reassuring sound. Don't be fooled. This stretch of it is among the most spectacularly dangerous routes in the world. The Keylong to Kishtwar Road is a route that many readers wouldn't want to walk, let alone take a motorized vehicle along.

It's a rocky dirt track at extreme altitude that cuts along the sheer face of mountains with enormous drops to one side and bare rock on the other. The mountain overhangs the roof of your vehicle so closely it seems you'll never get through the gap.

Meanwhile, the road edges crumble away into chasms that are up to around 750m (2,500ft) deep. The brave can peer over the edge to see a river winding through the canyon far below. The track reaches an altitude of 3,080m (10,100ft), where the air is very thin to breathe and the high winds can be treacherous.

As if that was not enough, the road is badly rutted, potholed and often only just wide enough for one vehicle. There are huge puddles, and in certain places seasonal waterfalls plunge onto the road from high up the mountain. Sharp bends in the rocks obscure your view of stationary and oncoming hazards. The latter are particularly alarming because in order to pass another vehicle, it may be necessary to dangle one of your wheels out over the precipice. **SH**

❶ Along the side of the Sutlej River, the crash barrier looks more like a decoration than a safeguard.

Marsimik La
Jammu and Kashmir, India

Start Pangong Lake
End Chang Chenmo
Distance 74km (46 miles)
Type Adventure
Map goo.gl/dqnSoA

It is often claimed that Khardung La in Kashmir is the 'highest motorable road in the world', but, in fact, Marsimik La, a desolate mountain track in the Chang Chenmo Range of northern India, is at least 222m (730ft) higher.

This record-breaking road trip traverses an awe-inspiring yet barren and hostile land. Built in 1983 under the supervision of an Everest guide, the trail begins at Pangong Lake, which is a five-hour drive from Leh, the nearest major city, along a rough mountain road, past small villages and several military checkpoints, before crossing Pagal Naala ('Crazy Stream') to the shores of the amazing saline Pangong Lake straddling the Indian–Chinese border. Special permits and an accredited guide are required for non-Indians to travel anywhere in this disputed region.

From here the 31-km- (19.3-mile) long ascent begins, rising by 1,290m (4,232ft) along a steady 4 per cent gradient for much of the way. However, it's the term 'motorable' that you'll start to question before too long, as the roadway deteriorates into a pair of barely decipherable tyre tracks in a barren moonscape of buff-gray boulders and screes. In this rarefied air, the engines of many trail bikes and 4x4s start to flounder near the summit, as do their occupants. Only the most intrepid automotive adventurers need apply for this one. **DIS**

National Highway 1D
Jammu and Kashmir, India

Start Dras
End Lamayuru
Distance 166km (103 miles)
Type Adventure
Map goo.gl/fouNzB

This is the safe and easy alternative to the Leh to Manali Highway for getting between the Kashmir Valley and the old home of the Dalai Lama in Ladakh. But the concept of safe and easy needs to be understood in the context of India and crossing the highest range of mountains in the world.

National Highway 1D is a more reliable route across the top of the subcontinent and offers a nonstop sequence of imperious mountains and grand valleys to enjoy. To the west it passes over the treacherous Zojila Pass, which decends to Srinagar; to the east it passes beneath Lamayuru Monastery and continues to the high desert city of Leh, once the Himalayan crossroads of the ancient Silk Road. Along this dramatic interconnecting section of the Highway you'll trace the mighty Indus River, cross frighteningly high mountain passes where both you and your engine will gasp for oxygen and see all sorts of ancient temples, monasteries and fortresses.

National Highway 1D still has all the problems of high altitude. Outside the months of June to October, even this main artery is closed. Each spring, workers are sent to clear the snow and debris and repair the road before it reopens. Then the monsoons of July can cause sudden landslides and floods that close the road once more. This one needs some forward planning. **SH**

Leh to Manali Highway

Jammu and Kashmir/Himachal Pradesh, India

Start Leh, Jammu and Kashmir
End Manali, Himachal Pradesh
Distance 473km (294 miles)
Type Adventure
Map goo.gl/vjd3kG

Welcome to one of India's best known and most feared road trips. Whether you tackle this Himalayan motoring marathon by bike or 4x4, you are undertaking a brave adventure through some of the most amazing terrain on Earth.

The summit of this trip is at Taglang La, which, at 5,328m (17,480ft) above sea level, is among the world's highest stretches of road. The most dangerous is the Rohtang Pass; in Hindi, *rohtang* means 'the ground of the corpses'.

Get used to thin air: the average altitude on this route is around 4km (2.5 miles) above sea level. You also need to get used to long, uninhabited stretches. Carry emergency supplies. The road is open only for four or five months in the summer, but even then it can get extremely wet, cold and windy.

The views will be stupendous, of course, and the heavy traffic of tourists, Indian military and local supply trucks makes it almost inevitable that you'll have all sorts of unpredictable experiences on such a primitive road in such a hostile landscape.

Expect traffic in the middle of nowhere as awkward trucks block narrow hairpin bends at the edge of unguarded vertical drops. Have your camera constantly on hand: the chances are that some impatient local biker will try to pick his way past on the outside of the truck with one leg dangling scarily over the edge. **SH**

❶ Petrol tankers make their way slowly along the narrow highway through the Rohtang Pass.

Lamayuru Monastery Road
Jammu and Kashmir, India

Start Leh
End Lamayuru
Distance 126km (78 miles)
Type Culture
Map goo.gl/f9iLzF

Even getting to this trip's start point, Leh – the former capital of the remote Himalayan kingdom of Ladakh – is something of an achievement. The journey, along a section of the Srinagar to Leh Highway, is part of the ancient trade route, the Silk Road. People have been making this high-altitude trip for thousands of years, and now you and your vehicle can join them.

Himalayan desert scenery is unforgettably extraordinary, with dramatically craggy, arid peaks, scored and shaped by millennia of ice and snow. The reason to make the trip to Lamayuru is two-fold: first, to see the otherworldly rock landscape that surrounds the village – the so-called 'Ladakh moonland', with its odd, convoluted sedimentary shapes in strong colours: golden yellows, pinks and ochres – and second, to visit the 10th-century Buddhist monastery. Perched on an outcrop, slightly apart from the village, this fascinating ancient temple with its 1,000-armed Avalokiteśvara statue and rambling ruins is home to some 150 Tibetan Buddhist monks. After visiting the monastery, the more intrepid can continue on the Srinagar to Ladakh road, over the Fotu La Pass, to Kargil and then to Srinagar in Kashmir, some 300km (190 miles) farther on. **DK**

◑ Lamayuru is well worth an overnight stay.

Shimla to Manali Road
Himachal Pradesh, India

Start Shimla
End Manali
Distance 251km (156 miles)
Type Adventure
Map goo.gl/sKR9bO

If you want an insight into the conditions of the road that links Shimla and Manali, two of the most popular hill stations in the Himalayan state of Himachal Pradesh, you have only to look at the travel times and do a little maths. Two towns, less than 256km (160 miles) apart, but with a suggested drive time of nine hours. That is an average speed of less than 29 kph (18 mph).

Such a calculation may raise concerns about what the road may be like, and one would be right to worry: there are few roads anywhere in the world that blend such a heady cocktail of beauty and peril. Just remember to make an early start from Shimla to arrive in Manali before dark. The road is not affected by winter snowfalls and is open year round, but it is a mountainous road, cut right into the gorge walls, with some truly gargantuan drop-offs. It is plied by trucks of all sizes that can slow you to a crawl if you're travelling in the same direction and force you off the road if they're coming in the opposite direction.

The treasures of this road trip come at you with a mind-blowing rapidity: the Beas River, the 2.8-km- (1.7-mile) long tunnel into Aut, the wooden castle outside Nagar and everywhere those soaring Himalayan peaks. And then you realize that it's the scenery here, not necessarily the road, that really slows you down. **BDS**

Jalori Pass
Himachal Pradesh, India

Start Luhri
End Aut
Distance 93km (58 miles)
Type Adventure
Map goo.gl/RWBDpi

Deep in Himachal Pradesh, more than 320km (200 miles) north of New Delhi, this challenging road runs at a mean height of 3,223m (10,574ft) above sea level. It is reliably passable only between March and November – for the other three months of the year, there is usually too much snow for road vehicles.

Heading north from the state capital, Shimla, it is 96km (60 miles) to Luhri, where beyond the turn-off to the pass the road changes from a relatively unremarkable Indian highway into an arduous track that cannot be hurried: both the ascent and the descent are so steep that even the toughest off-roaders struggle to get out of first gear. Occasional breaks in the tall fir trees and cedars that line the route afford spectacular views across the Himalayas. At the summit of the Jalori Pass are a Hindu temple and a restaurant.

On the descent the first human settlement after 12km (7.5 miles) is Shoja, a small town with good wooden chalet accommodation for visitors; it is here that the track joins the main Shimla–Manali Highway. Next comes the village of Jibhi. Banjar, 8km (5 miles) farther north, is larger and has several tourist shops and eateries. In the gorge of the Beas River is the human-made scenic highlight of the trip: completed in 2007, the Larji hydroelectric dam, just south of journey's end at Aut. **JP**

❶ Cyclists are increasingly in evidence in the Jalori Pass; high altitude requires a high level of physical fitness.

Kinnaur Road
Himachal Pradesh, India

Start Dakhaye
End Dubling
Distance 74km (46 miles)
Type Adventure
Map goo.gl/rDnUFK

It may be potholed, puddled, rutted and have crumbling edges, but at least the Kinnaur Road is covered with tarmac. That's some consolation as you squeeze around blind bends with terrifying drops into the ravine alongside you.

You'll find this route high in the Himalayas, in the northern Indian state of Himachal Pradesh, near the Tibetan border. You'll be amid landscape to take your breath away, and not just because of the thin air at these lofty altitudes. Panoramas of green mountains, deep lush valleys and a backdrop of misty, snowy peaks are constant. Colourful, bustling villages are a riot of overhead cables, billboards and half-built homes. The surroundings are surreal, and the only road here is like something from *The Lord of the Rings* movies (2001–03).

Some sections hang from vertical cliffs; others are carved like slots into the side of a mountain. Expect multiple corners, huge rock overhangs and arches, single-file narrow stretches and loose rocks lying around in the road.

You won't be using your highest gears very often. Instead you'll be on the alert for wobbly buses hurtling around the corners towards you and army convoys that aren't going to budge from the centre of the road. By comparison, the frequent farmers herding sheep along the road for hours are a minor hazard. **SH**

❶ The cultivated lower slopes of the Kinnaur Valley are renowned for their apple orchards.

Spiti Valley Road
Himachal Pradesh, India

Start Kaza
End Gramphu
Distance 136km (84.5 miles)
Type Adventure
Map goo.gl/uYI84h

As the NH505 enters a wide plateau between two banks of mountains, it passes beneath a makeshift arch decorated with local Buddhist carvings and paintings. Across the top it says: 'Most Welcome to Spiti Valley'.

But do not let the greeting mislead you: this is not a well-trodden tourist route but an almost constantly deserted hidden valley, deep in the northern Indian Himalayas. The main reason for its neglect is the state of the NH505.

The road through Spiti Valley is regarded as the worst in India. Almost all of it is unpaved gravel and rock, and it's 3,400m (11,000ft) high. Long stretches are formed from narrow slots carved into sheer mountain faces. Rivers have to be forded, piles of sand climbed over and narrow gaps between rocks negotiated. Deadly drops are commonplace.

After a sequence of gravelly hairpin bends, the summit of the route is the Kunzum Pass, a bleak, windswept spot at a dangerously high 4,590m (15,059ft). Very few vehicles pass this way.

After being rescued halfway along the route, one traveller wrote an online review agreeing how bad the road is. Significantly, however, he then added: 'It was still one of the most rewarding experiences of my life.' SH

● The portal of a Buddhist monastery along the route.

Jauljibi to Madkote Road
Uttarakhand, India

Start Jauljibi
End Madkote
Distance 45km (28 miles)
Type Adventure
Map goo.gl/R5SD8P

They call this Jauljibi to Madkote route a 'cliff road'. That should set any traveller's alarm bells ringing. What exactly is a 'cliff road'?

It turns out that this unpaved track runs along the edge of the Goriganga River, a rocky torrent that plunges down from Himalayan glaciers in Nepal to eventually join the Ganges and reach the Bay of Bengal hundreds of miles away.

This remote stretch in the northern Indian hill state of Uttarakhand is admittedly particularly scenic. The fast-flowing river has cut itself a deep gorge through the rocks, and there are views along the valley to the ridge of five snowcapped Panchachuli Mountains in the distance.

But it's the road that's the problem here. The narrow, winding track suffers erosion – not just from the river alongside, but from the torrents cascading down the sides of the gorge in the rainy season. At times they wash the whole road away, and reconstruction is irregular and haphazard.

Vehicles trying to pick their way along what's left often have to drive right through waterfalls tumbling from far above. No wonder that you'll find long sections of badly potholed road with the edges tumbling away into the river. And when you finally reach the steep section of hairpin bends, you'll find there are no safety barriers, even on drops of hundreds of feet. SH

India's Golden Triangle

Delhi and more, India

Start New Delhi, Delhi
End New Delhi, Delhi
Distance 750km (466 miles)
Type Culture
Map goo.gl/FVhHfq

This is the classic Indian grand tour, taking in three of the subcontinent's most famous sites. The route begins in the frenetic congestion of downtown Delhi, moves out through the countryside to Agra, and then travels west to the arid landscapes of Rajasthan and Jaipur. The trip is mostly about the historical sites built by the Mughal emperors between the 16th and 18th centuries. Of these the most famous is the Taj Mahal in Agra, a sublime marble mausoleum for the third wife of the emperor Shah Jahan.

Other major attractions along the route include Humayun's Tomb, the minaret of Qutb Minar and the Red Fort Complex in Old Delhi; the city palace – Hawa Mahal – and the extraordinary astronomical observatory Jantar Mantar in Jaipur.

But this is also about the journey itself. Here, the normal rules of the road do not apply. Delhi is gridlocked anarchy. Elsewhere on the divided highways you may be surprised to find slow-moving traffic such as elephants and oil tankers approaching in the wrong direction. Traffic often travels against the flow until it can find a break in the highway divider. Just how good a plan this is can be judged by the many burned-out cars and trucks littering the sides of the roads. **DK**

⊖ Gurudwara Bangla Sahib, a Sikh temple in New Delhi.

Mumbai to Goa Road Trip

Maharashtra/Goa, India

Start Mumbai, Maharashtra
End Bandoli, Goa
Distance 628km (390 miles)
Type Adventure
Map goo.gl/EO8UbU

With so much to see in India, it is difficult to choose: culture or nature, mountains or beaches? Or bits of everything, as on this road trip south from Mumbai to the seaside paradise of Goa? There are two possible routes. The quicker although longer itinerary goes inland along the NH48; the shorter but slower, more scenic route is down the NH66 along the coast; the latter is the preferred route of Mumbai's mobile young Indians striking out for the rural seaside.

The starting point, Mumbai, is the most populous city in India, with more than 18.4 million inhabitants; it is also the home of the Bollywood film industry. Head south out of the city, and be sure to leave very early in the morning to avoid the rush-hour traffic. The route is straightforward, passing through verdant forests and fields on either side. Ornithologists might want to spend some time at the Karnala Bird Sanctuary, while worshippers of Ganesha will definitely stop in the old port city of Pen, where huge idols of the Hindu deity are carved. Stop also at the old sea fort of Sindhudurg, built on an offshore island by the Maratha Empire in 1664, or indeed anywhere along the road to enjoy the local cuisine. From here, it is but a short distance to Bandoli, a city in the middle of Goa and thus well positioned for exploring the state's glorious beaches and temples. **SA**

Mumbai to Chennai Rickshaw Rally
Maharastra to Tamil Nadu, India

● Some people enter this rally to win it; others are there simply for the joy of taking part.

Start Mumbai, Maharashtra
End Chennai, Tamil Nadu
Distance 1,910km (1,187 miles)
Type Adventure
Info goo.gl/GRlsEF

This is the Mumbai Xpress – a crazy, two-week coast-to-coast voyage in three-wheeled Indian auto-rickshaws, vehicles that are little more than motorized shopping carts.

Organized by the Travel Scientists, this adventure is a race to some entrants, but to others, a high-octane sightseeing tour. These are not speedy contraptions, so there's plenty of time to take in the sights, but be careful not to get too distracted – Indian road traffic rules are more of a serving suggestion than something anyone actually adheres to. It is important not to take the competitive aspect of the trip too seriously – you will want to take time to stop and explore the imposing Aga Khan Palace in Pune and take in the views from the Hill Station at Wilson's Point in Mahabaleshwar. By the time you arrive at the half-way mark, you'll probably be in need of a bit of time for rest and recuperation on the region's famous sandy beaches. A visit to Panaji, the state capital, with its elegant formerly Portuguese architectural centre, is also a must. After this interlude, you will turn eastwards, cross-country, first to Mysuru, with its incredible 14th-century Indo-Saracenic Mysore Palace, and then to the tech city of Bangalore, before arriving, exhausted but one hopes happy, in the city of Chennai on the coast of the Bay of Bengal. **DK**

Muzhappilangad Drive-In Beach
Kerala, India

Start Edakkad Beach Road
End Muzhappilangad Beach Road
Distance 3.2km (2 miles)
Type Scenic
Map goo.gl/HxJfAS

Along the coast of Kerala in southwest India there are many fine beaches, but the stretch of sand at Muzhappilangad is considered unique: you're allowed to drive any vehicle onto the beach and travel its full length.

Cars often drive through the shallow waves, and motorbikes race one another along the sands. Enthusiastic drivers attempt skids and drifts, while bikers practise wheelies.

It is claimed to be India's longest drive-in beach, and it has been featured at or near the top of international surveys of the world's best places for driving on sand by the sea.

All this would count for little if Muzhappilangad were not such a picturesque spot. The firm, flat sands are backed by lush trees and vegetation. There are no big hotels or apartments. A short distance offshore is an impressive reef of jagged black rocks sheltering the beach and making beautiful silhouettes against the evening sunsets. The exotic island of Dharmadam stands off the southern end of the beach, like a dollop of thick jungle floating on the sea.

More people drive, or watch the drivers, than bother with swimming. Often there are food stands and traders catering to the crowds along the shore here. It is busy year round, but particularly crowded during the annual festival in April. **SH**

❶ Muzhappilangad Beach during one of its quieter moments: traffic can get much busier than this.

State Highway 49
Tamil Nadu, India

Start Chennai
End Puducherry
Distance 154km (96 miles)
Type Scenic
Map goo.gl/ofMTPH

Indian State Highway 49 is an excellent, modern toll road running down the east coast of the Bay of Bengal. It's a route that offers many great views and chances to stop off at scores of fishing hamlets and beach resorts.

The starting point, Chennai (formerly Madras), the capital of Tamil Nadu, is a beguiling mix of ancient, colonial and modern cultures with sights ranging from the Mamallapuram temple complex to the fabulous Marina Beach, one of the biggest beaches in the world.

The journey continues south along the East Coast Road with more temples, forts, shrines, beaches and craft villages than you'll ever have time to visit. You'll find everything from speedboats to rent to a zoo full of crocodiles.

Finally, you'll reach Puducherry, a former French colony with swaying palms on the promenade and beaches facing the Indian Ocean. Locals call it Pondy, and its French architecture and boulevards make it a popular holiday destination for locals and foreign visitors alike.

It may be overdoing it, but in the interests of safety perhaps it is best to mention that about halfway along this route, around Devaneri, there is a stretch that is said by locals to be haunted. A ghostly lady in a white sari appears, distracts drivers and has been blamed for several crashes. **SH**

Kolli Hills Road
Tamil Nadu, India

Start Kalappanaickenpatti
End Ariyurnadu
Distance 39km (24 miles)
Type Adventure
Map goo.gl/dXZc9T

Some locals call this the 'Road of Death'. They probably need to read this book thoroughly. Compared to some of the routes in this volume, even in their own country, the Kolli Hills Road seems like a gentle scenic drive.

Yes, there are approximately 70 hairpin bends in quick succession as the highway clambers steeply up the side of a mountain – but the surface is smoothly paved and wide enough to pass someone coming the other way. Admittedly, at some points you'll find potholes and rough surfaces as the route snakes through a thick forest. Longer vehicles may need several manoeuvres to get around the tightest corners. But there are plenty of turnouts, passing places and even observation points from which to look out over misty treetops extending in all directions as far as the eye can see.

The Kolli Hills Road also affords glorious views across the plains of southern India. It is usually busy with local traffic and has recently become a minor tourist attraction in its own right, with the result that there may be congestion in high season.

Search online and you'll find a video of a gang of Indian bikers who tackle Kolli Hills Road at full speed, passing a selfie stick between them like a relay baton. At the end of the ride they tell you with big grins: 'It's not the road of death – it's the road of fun!' Go see for yourself. **SH**

Puri to Konark Highway
Odisha, India

Start Puri
End Konark
Distance 37km (23 miles)
Type Scenic
Map goo.gl/a1zYtg

This route along the Bay of Bengal begins at Puri, where the 12th-century Hindu temple of Jagannatha ('Lord of the Universe') is an important site of Hindu pilgrimage. (It is from the name of this deity that the English word 'juggernaut' is derived.)

Leaving the city, the NH203 first follows a tree-lined course across an alluvial plain full of rice fields. Then, moving closer to the Indian Ocean, it cuts through the Balukhand-Konark Wildlife Sanctuary. This nature reserve of sand dunes and evergreen vegetation is home to herds of protected blackbuck (Indian antelope) and a breeding ground for olive ridley sea turtles. This route has become a tourist favourite, but while it is often busy, it is not as congested as many roads in India.

The journey ends inland at Konark, the site of another Hindu temple. Dedicated to the sun god Surya, it is built in the shape of the deity's chariot, with twelve stone wheels and seven stone horses around its base. The walls are adorned with lavish and intricate carvings, many of which are of an overtly erotic nature. The structure dominates the surrounding flatlands and is visible from the bay; early mariners used it as a navigational aid, but that did not save many of them from running aground nearby, with the result that the temple was regarded as unlucky by non-Hindus and became known by them as the Black Pagoda. **JP**

❶ The 13th-century Konark Sun Temple is a big draw for Hindus and non-Hindus alike.

Three-Level Zigzag
Sikkim, India

Start Rongli
End Lungthung
Distance 48km (29.8 miles)
Type Adventure
Map goo.gl/qNYeFH

Many Indians claim this to be the bendiest road in the world, and they may well be right. The Three-Level Zigzag has more than 100 hairpin bends in a short stretch of just 32km (20 miles). On the map, sections of the route merge into a virtually indecipherable scribble.

You'll find this bizarre sight in the Himalayan foothills of eastern Sikkim. There are special viewing points where you can look out across the beautiful green landscape crisscrossed scores of times by the same road.

The route seems to twist back on itself over and over again, up and down the steep sides of this row of mountains. It's such an odd view that the road itself has become an attraction. The landscape falls away into a hazy row of mountain ranges, but the neighbouring hills appear to be densely striped with roads: these stripes are all part of the Three-Level Zigzag.

The track is paved, but has a ridiculous number of loops with unguarded drops at either end. And the Three-Level Zigzag stands at such a high altitude – 3,414m (11,200 ft) above sea level – that it is prone to snow and floods throughout the year. And if there's ice on the surface of this particular road, you shouldn't be there. **SH**

◐ This partial view gives some idea of what's involved.

Jelep La and the Sikkim Silk Road Sikkim, India

Start Gangtok   End Gangtok   Distance 204km (127 miles)
Type Adventure   Map goo.gl/CzpeY7

The Silk Road was an ancient network of mule tracks through the mountains between the civilizations of the West and the East. In northern India it crossed difficult but spectacular mountain terrain for centuries. The tracks slowly evolved into roads, but repeated wars in these border regions mean there's no clear highway through the Himalayas today.

Instead you can take road trips like this one, along sections of the old trade route linking the former kingdom of Sikkim with remote hill stations and sights like Menmecho Lake, deep in a cleft in the mountains, or the intimidating zigzag road at Zuluk.

Gangtok, the former capital of Sikkim, makes a good base to explore the frontier region. The colourful city occupies such a steep site that one local means of transport is by cable car. Other highlights of this trip include the monasteries at Lingtum and the Thambi View Point, which offers distant views of Kanchenjunga.

It's close to the border with China, and you'll reach the old way through to Tibet, the Jelep La, at 4,267m (13,999ft) above sea level.

This was once a vital route, but has long been closed by repeated conflicts in the region. You can view this pass from the monastery at the village of Lava but will be unable to get any closer to it. SH

❶ Part of the old Silk Road on the India–China frontier.

Jaffna to Nainativu Island-Hop Northern Province, Sri Lanka

Start Jaffna   End Nainativu   Distance 37km (23 miles)
Type Scenic   Map goo.gl/BPYS2N

Here's a chance to go island hopping, starting from Jaffna, an intriguing port that has largely recovered from extensive damage during a civil war (1983–2009) to become a quirky destination in the heart of the Tamil region. Its attractions include old Dutch colonial architecture and modern shopping malls.

Jaffna also makes a great base to explore the pretty islands to the west. It's easy to drive out to them, using the chain of causeways a few feet above the waves. You can drive for miles across the sea in this manner, often alongside fishermen up to their waists in water. At some points the causeways pass through marshes so shallow that cattle are wading in them.

Thus you can explore the three main islands – Mandaitivu, Kayts and Punkudutivu – by road. Look out for relics of Arab, Dutch and Portuguese colonists among the markets, temples and fishing villages.

To go farther, to Delft Island and Nainativu, you will need to take ferries. The discomfort of the cramped sailing vessels is worth enduring in order to reach these remote outposts. Delft is a sleepy, friendly beach community where you can sample excellent fresh seafood. Nainativu is home to an important and picturesque shrine that makes it a popular place of pilgrimage for Hindus. **SH**

❶ A typical causeway near Jaffna.

Eighteen-Bend Road Central Province/Uva Province, Sri Lanka

Start Kandy, Central Province
End Mahiyanganaya, Uva Province
Distance 77km (48 miles)
Type Scenic
Map goo.gl/BZWyV6

Once this was a notorious mountain track linking the city of Kandy with the sacred Buddhist town of Mahiyanganaya. It was famous for a sequence of 18 hairpin bends twisting down the side of a thickly forested mountain. Its rough, narrow sections were feared by many travellers.

Today, the route has lost much of its challenge, but it is still a scenic driving highlight of Sri Lanka's mountainous Central Province. The new road has become a popular tourist spot, with its wide views across the hills, valley, lakes and rivers. From some vantage points you can look at the road twisting away into the distance.

The new Eighteen-Bend Road, or Daha ata Wanguwa, has been widened and surfaced with smooth tarmac. The refurbishment also removed one of the famous bends, so technically, it should be renamed the Seventeen-Bend Road. The curves and drops now have stone guard walls and safety mirrors. The whole road has been designed to be easy enough for use by 12-m- (40-ft) long trucks.

It's still a serious journey, involving ten bridges and plenty of bends and gradients, but much of the route is now divided highway and the average journey time has been halved. There are new retaining walls (covered with murals of wild animals), but drivers still have to watch out for mud and rock slides in the rainy season. **SH**

Beach Hop Western Province/ Southern Province, Sri Lanka

Start Colombo, Western Province
End Rekawa Beach, Southern Province
Distance 212km (132 miles)
Type Scenic
Map goo.gl/GqJXaM

Sri Lanka's west coast is the most developed part of the island, drawing a sun-starved European clientele to its glorious beaches and luxurious hotels.

Heading south from the capital, Colombo, on the old A2 coastal road, you pass through the upmarket package-holiday resorts of Kalutara, Beruwala and finally Bentota, with its long spit of soft, white sand sandwiched between the rolling Indian Ocean and an azure-blue lagoon.

From there, the less-travelled southern coastal road takes adventurous road trippers to some of Sri Lanka's real hidden gems, starting with Hikkaduwa. In the 1970s this was a thriving hippy hangout. Still popular with younger independent travellers, it hosts a three-day beach festival in August attracting A-list DJs from around the globe. It's also a magnet for keen surfers and divers.

Farther south lie the silver sands of Unawatuna Beach, with adjacent coral reefs and ghostly shipwrecks. For a palm-fringed tropical paradise, a short hop on the A2 brings you to Mirissa Beach.

The sleepy Dutch colonial town of Tangalla, on a stubby headland pointing east, is a great place for an overnight rest stop.

The final leg loops inland around the Rekawa Lagoon to Turtle Point, where hawksbill and leatherback turtles come ashore to lay eggs between April and September. **DIS**

The Devil's Staircase
Uva Province, Sri Lanka

Start Bambarakanda Waterfalls
End Ohiya
Distance 13km (8 miles)
Type Adventure
Map goo.gl/ZLyFoD

Fancy taking this shortcut between the southern Sri Lankan towns of Kalupahana and Ohiya? It's less than half the distance of the normal paved road, but you'll need a four-wheel-drive vehicle to tackle it. Actually, you'll need some skill and courage, too, for this notorious route lives up to its name.

You can take a winding paved road up into the hills from the A4 highway to a well-known local attraction, the Bambarakanda Waterfalls, at 263m (863ft), the tallest in Sri Lanka.

From this popular spot, a mud-and-rock track rises into the pine forests. This was once a major colonial road and will carry you over the hills to Ohiya. It takes you to viewing points overlooking the waterfalls and the plains beyond.

High in the green slopes, you'll pass through a narrow cleft in the rocks known locally as the 'V Cut'. Note the tiny altar built into the side of the road here. Amid remote tea plantations, you'll then drive across a ford that goes on to feed the Bambarakanda Waterfalls.

After a section of high plateau with great views of the surrounding countryside, the track descends a very steep series of narrow, unguarded hairpin bends – this is the Devil's Staircase. At the foot of the descent, either take a detour to the Horton Plains National Park Visitor Centre or continue to the popular tourist village of Ohiya. **SH**

❶ The Bambarakanda Waterfalls are among the highlights of this challenging excursion.

Araniko Highway
Bagmati, Nepal

Start Kathmandu
End Kodari
Distance 113km (70 miles)
Type Adventure
Map goo.gl/9Pa3dp

❶ Nepalese commuters travel on the top of the buses along Araniko Highway in Kathmandu.

It would be irresponsible to attempt to hide the fact that the Araniko Highway is one of the most dangerous roads on the planet. It was built by the Chinese in the 1960s to link Nepal with China and is a major trade route between the two countries. It winds its way through the Himalayan mountains north of the Kathmandu Valley, clinging to the edge of the slopes, and is used by a seemingly endless procession of heavy trucks and buses.

In sections there is room for only one vehicle to pass at a time, with no guardrails to stop you from slipping off the side. It's a long way down: several hundred feet before you'd hit the rocky valley floor. Fully laden buses have been known to disappear over the edge.

The steeply sloping mountainsides also cause rockfalls and landslides. In bad weather (including monsoons) the road can easily become blocked. In 2014 the highway was shut by landslides for 46 days. Then in 2015, earthquakes forced its closure once again.

But this is a vital commercial route, and when it is open you'll find it heaving with large vehicles. But it's also increasingly popular with mountain bikers, who recklessly mix in with the big boys. You'll need a 4x4 to proceed with confidence along the route, together with a great head for heights and rock-steady nerves. JI

Dhaka to Mahasthangarh
Dhaka, Bangladesh

Start Dhaka
End Mahasthangarh
Distance 204km (127 miles)
Type Culture
Map goo.gl/ArnWU1

Bangladesh is the eighth most populous country in the world, with around 160 million people in an area the size of New York State, which has only 20 million residents. With such density of population, you can expect any road trip to involve plenty of traffic. This ranges from brightly painted trucks to human-powered rickshaws, and pedestrians carrying enormous loads.

Bangladesh is a fascinating place to explore by road. Expect a mind-blowing sequence of tropical jungles, vast rivers, rambling paddy fields and chaotic cities. You'll pass markets, lakes, mosques, pineapple plantations, roadside traders and passengers travelling on the top of heavily laden commercial trucks.

This route heads to the north of the capital, Dhaka, a city of seven million who may sometimes seem to all be on the road at once – in front of you. Enjoy the eccentric bustle as part of your Bangladesh experience and keep going north on the Tangail Highway, the N4.

Soon the route curves to the west to cross the mighty Jamuna River via the 5.6-km- (3.5-mile) long Bangabandhu toll bridge. The N5 then turns north to Bogra and your final destination: the ruins of Mahasthangarh, an ancient city that ruled this whole region while Rome and Carthage were still battling for control of the Mediterranean. **SH**

❶ Traffic comes in all forms on the Mirpur Road in the Dhanmondi area of Dhaka.

Grand Trunk Road Bangladesh to Afghanistan

Start Chittagong, Bangladesh   **End** Kabul, Afghanistan   **Distance** 2,500km (1,553 miles)
Type Adventure   **Map** goo.gl/O1UPiq

One of the world's oldest and longest roads runs right across the Asian subcontinent and offers a trip like no other. You start your journey in the bustling, chaotic seaport of Chittagong on the Indian Ocean in Bangladesh and end up in Kabul, in the mountainous desert of Afghanistan.

The road is paved nearly all the way, and there are no major topographical difficulties. However, in view of the volatile political climate and nature of life in the areas through which the route passes, you are likely to encounter some major dramas along the way. This is a famous route, but its planning will require due diligence. Locals call this road the 'GT' – an allusion to Gran Turismo sports cars that is

entirely ironic: there is unlikely to be any fast cruising here. Delays are essential parts of the Grand Trunk Experience, whether a camel running wild on the highway or overloaded trucks colliding.

Rudyard Kipling called the road 'the river of life'. Thanks to Moghul emperors it has been paved since the 16th century, and today it is a busy local highway along much of its length.

The great sights along the way range from the Khyber Pass to the Golden Temple of Amritsar, India, but the greatest memories probably will be the Grand Trunk incidents that no one can predict. **SH**

❶ The road through the Khyber Pass.

Paro to Thimphu Paro/Thimphu, Bhutan

Start Paro, Paro   End Thimphu, Thimphu   Distance 50km (31 miles)
Type Scenic   Map goo.gl/Fa1LgG

The kingdom of Bhutan has few properly paved roads. The only one that traverses the whole country is the 'Lateral Road', which is usually no more than 2.5m (8ft) wide. Much of it is unpaved, unsigned and subject to severe landslides and unpredictable weather conditions.

The best constructed and maintained stretch of road is between the international airport city of Paro and the capital and largest city, Thimphu.

Leave Paro on a paved surface running parallel to the Paro Chu. On both sides of this river are wooded slopes with distinctive local houses, forts and temples. Sometimes traffic has to move onto the unmade road shoulder to pass other vehicles.

After miles of sweeping through this attractive valley, dodging overloaded freight trucks and rickety buses, you turn into the Thimphu Chu Valley. There's no letting up in the scenerym though; green mountains disappear into the clouds and deep valleys twist away into the mist.

The final section of this itinerary, between Babesa and Thimphu, is a modern divided highway with street lights, road markings and safety barriers. If possible, time your visit for September or October to catch the Tshechu, a four-day Buddhist festival in the capital. **SH**

ⓘ Bhutan is said to be the happiest nation on Earth.

Urumqi to Kanas Lake Loop
Northwest China, China

Start Urumqi, Xinjiang
End Urumqi, Xinjiang
Distance 1,679km (1,043 miles)
Type Scenic
Map goo.gl/UZePOP

Start this marathon road trip through the northern Xinjiang region at Urumqi, a major metropolis with three million residents, huge skyscrapers and an international airport. With a long list of tourist attractions, ranging from the world's biggest Islamic bazaar to a leading Chinese soccer stadium, it makes a perfect base for touring this region of mountains, glaciers and national parks.

You'll travel north on excellent highways to find the 'Heavenly Lake' in the Tian Shan, a glorious area of forested slopes around a mountain lake 2,000m (6,300ft) above sea level. The landscapes of the Bogeda Reserve here have been declared a UNESCO Biosphere Reserve and are popular visitor attractions among the Chinese.

Farther north you'll find the remote mountain city of Altay – this is the most convenient base for onward expeditions to Kanas Lake, which is close to the northern border with Russia and full of legendary monsters.

The route then leads southwest on good roads through a desert with massive rock formations. At the affluent riverside city of Karamay, don't miss the daily, lavish, coloured fountain show financed by the country's biggest oil fields nearby. And before you turn east and head back to Urumqi, China's oil capital is probably the perfect place to fill up with fuel for the journey. **SH**

❶ The Kanas River flows out of the lake of the same name; it is a tributary of the Russian Ob River.

China National Highway 219
Northwest China, China

Start Kargilik, Xinjiang
End Lhatse, Tibet
Distance 2,089km (1,298 miles)
Type Adventure
Map goo.gl/GwmuPe

If ever a highway was designed to get the adrenaline flowing and the senses tingling, this is it. One of the world's highest thoroughfares, China's National Highway 219 runs to the north of the nation's southwestern border with Nepal and India, traversing countless high mountain passes on a road that was a mix of sand, gravel and corrugated ruts until 2013, when it was fully paved. Paved or not, however, it remains one of the world's most demanding drives and one of the most invigorating adventures one can have behind a steering wheel.

Begun in 1951, the road took six years to complete. A 'secret' highway, its construction through the disputed Aksai Chin high-altitude desert of northern India was a trigger for the 1962 Sino-Indian War. The border dispute has long stopped simmering, but the snowstorms and blizzards here can still appear out of a seemingly blue sky, and winter temperatures can drop to -25°C (-13°F) or below.

The scenery is drop-dead gorgeous – something you'd expect, perhaps, on a road with an average altitude of 4,500m (14,760ft). There are wonderful views over the Takla Makan Desert, one of the planet's most inhospitable environments, but all you need do is see a picture of it snaking its way through the Bangong Lake region before you start yearning to pack your bags and get going. **BDS**

❶ A view to whet the appetite of any driver: part of the 219 through the highlands of northwest China.

Zhongnanshan Tunnel
Northwest China, China

Start Niubeiliang National Forest Park, Shaanxi
End Wangmang Residential District, Xi'an, Shaanxi
Distance 49km (30.4 miles)
Type Adventure
Map goo.gl/V1Ei1m

The 18-km- (11.2-mile) long Zhongnanshan Tunnel, which runs through the gneiss and granite interior of Zhongnan Mountains in northwest China, was part of the long-distance link between Baotou, in the Inner Mongolia Autonomous Region, and Beihai, in the Guangxi Zhuang Autonomous Region. Opened in 2007, it was the world's second-longest road tunnel. It was also the world's most colourful. Mindful of combating driver fatigue, its designers equipped it with special lighting designed to create multiple kaleidoscopic patterns, and installed artificial trees. Some sections even have images of clouds projected onto the ceiling in an effort to reduce eyestrain.

The two tubes of the tunnel each carry two lanes, with the distance between the centre lines of each being 30m (98ft). The maximum depth of the tunnel is 1,640m (5,381ft), and when completed it cost $410 million. It had the world's deepest ventilation shafts – 661m (2,169ft) – and the world's most advanced monitoring technology. The maximum speed is 80 kph (50 mph). The experience is unlike any you've ever had in a tunnel before. Forget all those familiar rock-hewn and plain concrete tunnels: here, the tunnel has been redefined, now punctuated by trees below and clouds above – a subterranean phantasmagoria of colour and light. **BDS**

Tarim Desert Highway
Northwest China, China

Start Luntai, Xinjiang
End Minfeng, Xinjiang
Distance 581km (361 miles)
Type Adventure
Map goo.gl/bUQIKK

If you look down onto China from your space station, a large sandy oval is visible in the west of the country. This is the Tarim Basin, which is bounded by the Tian Shan to the north and the Kunlun Shan on the edge of the Tibetan Plateau to the south. The Takla Makan Desert fills most of the basin, a desert of which for thousands of years there was no recorded human crossing. Traders on the Silk Road between China and the west skirted around its edges.

This isolation changed in 1993, when work began on the Tarim Desert Highway. The petroleum industry needed to ship oil quickly across the desert, hence this brand-new road. Today, you can enjoy its amazing isolation for yourself. The highway starts in Luntai and then heads due south across the desert on the S165 to Minfeng on G315. Around 446km (276 miles) of its total length crosses through shifting sand dunes, making it the longest desert highway in the world. To stop the sand dunes from covering the freeway, the Chinese constructors planted bushes and other vegetation by the side of the road and set up a massive irrigation system to keep the plants alive. Halfway along the route, there is a filling station and a few restaurants. Other than that, you totally are on your own. **SA**

❯ Much of the highway is as straight as an arrow.

Road to Heaven Northwest China, China

Start Yongding, Hunan   End Tianmen Mountain, Hunan   Distance 14km (8.7 miles)
Type Adventure   Map goo.gl/NFRZMS

The road up the 1,519-m- (4,983-ft) high Tianmen Mountain is so extreme that it has become a major tourist attraction. People visit the mountain by cable car, just to look at the road.

No such timorousness for you. You're going up this automotive helter-skelter. Prepare yourself and your vehicle for a spiral of 99 hairpin bends in close sequence. Visitors are warned not to take the journey if they get carsick.

China's Country Road 104 has many unofficial names, including 'The Avenue Towards Heaven', 'The 99 Bends' and 'Heaven's Gate'. You'll probably make up some unpublishable ones of your own on the way up.

The road surface is smooth, and there are concrete barriers protecting you from the deadly drops. At the top you'll find 999 steps up to a huge rock arch, a beautiful old temple on the summit and a glass skywalk above a yawning canyon that you may well find even scarier than the road.

The cable car is a very popular alternative for those who can't face the road. Only when they get onboard the gondola do they find that they've let themselves in for the world's longest cable car journey at 7.5km (4.6 miles), which rises at an unusually steep angle of 37 degrees. SH

❶ Snaking hairpin bends on Tianmen Mountain.

Xinduqiao to Danba Scenic Drive Southwest China, China

Start Xinduqiao, Sichuan **End** Danba, Sichuan **Distance** 146km (91 miles)
Type Scenic **Map** goo.gl/edO2Gx

This road trip through southern China offers a snapshot of classic Tibet. You'll start in the busy small town of Xinduqiao, high in the mountains. It's a modern place and set amid scenery that attracts photographers from all over China.

Note that it's about 3,300m (11,000ft) above sea level here, so breathing difficulties and altitude sickness can strike visitors. Once you've acclimatized, though, you'll find you're in an amazing landscape of rivers, woods and pastures dotted with temples and pagodas against a backdrop of snowy peaks.

You'll head north on the smooth S303 through rural areas inhabited by nomadic farmers. Look out for grazing yaks and fluttering prayer flags.

At Tagong town there's a large Buddhist temple with a golden pagoda that can be seen for miles. There are huge mantras painted on hillsides and colourful patterns of flags high on the slopes above.

You'll pass by Huiyuan Temple, a former home of the Dalai Lama, and see the holy Yala Snow Mountain at 5,820m (19,094ft) poking through the clouds before you reach journey's end at Danba, which is known as 'the village of a thousand blockhouses' for its ornate little traditional Tibetan homes. perched on terraces leading up the steep slopes on either side of a winding river. **SH**

❶ Tagong Temple is one of the highlights of this trip.

Yunnan–Tibet Highway
Southwest China, China

Start Xiaguan, Yunnan
End Markam, Tibet
Distance 753km (468 miles)
Type Scenic
Map goo.gl/MZDajS

This is a challenging adventure from southern China into Tibet across the Hengduan Mountains, home of giant pandas and the source of the Mekong and Yangtze Rivers. To call this part of the historic 'Tea Horse Road' a scenic drive is an understatement.

The road itself is excellent, with smooth tarmac and clear road markings. Transport problems arise due to frequent landslides or heavy snow in very remote regions. Check the conditions before you set off, carry supplies and be prepared for delays.

You'll be tackling some severe terrain. The highest point of the journey is the pass through Hongla Snow Mountain, at around 4,300m (14,100ft). You'll also travel close to Baima Snow Mountain, a lofty sheer-sided peak of 5,640m (18,504ft), which to date has never been climbed.

As you negotiate a seemingly endless succession of steep hairpin bends, you'll see the environment change dramatically around you. Within a relatively short distance, the road rises steeply into snowy mountains and then drops down into deep valleys, thick with humid rainforest.

Amid these spectacular landscapes you'll spot ancient Buddhist temples and monasteries, simple rural villages and bustling towns. Whether you end your journey in Markam or continue on to the capital, Lhasa, expect to end up with a head full of memories and a camera full of photographs. **SH**

🄯 A Tibetan pavilion with some of the peaks of the Hengduan Mountains in the background.

Tiger Leaping Gorge
Southwest China, China

Start Hutiaoxiazhen, Yunnan
End Deqen, Yunnan
Distance 37km (23 miles)
Type Adventure
Map goo.gl/jxX7Lg

As the Jinsha River flows down to join the upper Yangtze River in Yunnan Province, Southwest China, it runs west to east through a spectacular gorge. At a maximum depth of 3,790m (12,434ft) from river bed to mountain peak, this gorge is one of the deepest in the world. It extends for 15km (9.3 miles) between the Jade Dragon Snow Mountain to the south and the Haba Snow Mountain to the north; the river jumps over a series of rapids between the sheer cliffs.

Its name is derived from the legend that a tiger escaping a hunter jumped over the river. Since the gorge at its narrowest point is 25m (82ft) wide, it is doubtful if this account has any basis in fact – but it's a good story, anyhow. What is clear is that the gorge is almost unnavigable: four rafters went down it in the early 1980s and were never seen again, although in 1986 a successful attempt was made.

The less adventurous should stick to four wheels along the riverbank. This road starts in Hutiaoxiazhen, north of Lijiang, and runs along the northern side of the gorge, hugging the mountainside and passing through several tunnels. There are plenty of places where one can scramble down to the cascading river itself. At Yongke village the road leaves the gorge and heads north and inland, ending your amazing adventure. **SA**

❶ An arch bridge spans one of the narrowest points of the Tiger Leaping Gorge.

The Twenty-Four-Zig Road Southwest China, China

Start G320, Qinglong Xian   **End** G320, Shuangshan   **Distance** 8.9km (5.5 miles)
Type Adventure   **Map** goo.gl/InRsoQ

Here's a chance to drive on a infamous road dating back to World War II, deep in the wild mountainous jungle of southwest China. It was built to help US convoys carry war supplies to Chinese forces fighting the Japanese.

It was notorious among the army truckers, who traditionally said a prayer 'for safety' before embarking on the concertina of switchback bends that rise steeply up the side of a mountain. There are many stories of trucks full of guns, ammunition or food overturning on the 8 per cent gradients.

At the time the road was a part of a giant jungle highway from Burma to China and a symbol of Allied cooperation that was trumpeted around the world. At its peak more than 2,000 US army trucks climbed the Twenty-Four-Zig Road a day.

Today, the Chinese authorities are doing a similar thing, promoting the quiet, remote road as an example of long-standing Sino–US friendship. There is now a viewing platform on the mountain face from which you can get an overall view of the road on the other side.

If you manage to find the Twenty-Four-Zig Road, you'll see that all the zigzags are still there, completely unguarded . . . and the road surface is still a rough track of gravel. **SH**

❶ It's plain to see how this road acquired its name.

Sichuan to Tibet Highway Southwest China, China

Start Chengdu, Sichuan   **End** Lhasa, Tibet   **Distance** 2,082km (1,294 miles)
Type Adventure   **Map** goo.gl/mVR4Ht

In order to connect Tibet with the rest of China, the Chinese government constructed a new highway in 1954 from Chengdu in Sichuan Province west across the Roof of the World, to Lhasa, the Tibetan capital. The road, technically part of China National Highway G318, is one of the great thoroughfares of the world, a lengthy, and in places dangerous, course used by long-distance truckers and eager road trippers alike. Given its length, it's not surprising that both scenery and climate change considerably along its length. The road starts in the clamour of Chengdu, but soon leaves the lush scenery behind as the mountains loom up ahead. The road crosses over 14 major peaks at an average height of 4,500m

(14,760ft) above sea level, as well as traversing numerous rivers, cutting through some splendid gorges and navigating down 99 tight hairpin bends.

The road is tarmacked in places but is more usually sand or gravel, making it a mud trap in the rain. Landslides, ice and snow add to the danger, while traffic accidents are common. All of these can result in traffic lines that stretch for miles, so be patient while you wait. If you want to drive this road, be prepared for it to take around a fortnight and do prepare your vehicle well. There is no other drive like it. **SA**

❶ The road ducks and weaves through extreme terrain.

Everest Base Camp Road Southwest China, China

Start Lhasa, Tibet   End Everest Base Camp, Tibet   Distance 612km (380 miles)
Type Adventure   Map goo.gl/5gCZI6

It isn't going to quicken the pulse of purists who feel that the only way to appreciate a great trek is to walk it, but nothing can alter the fact that the Chinese have built a new road from the Tibetan capital of Lhasa all the way to Everest Base Camp (EBC). The road, which the Chinese government says has now conquered the Roof of the World, has countless switchbacks along which it takes you over multiple 5,182-m- (17,000-ft) high mountain passes, and fills your windscreen with some of the most revered and feared Himalayan peaks – Lhotse, Makalu, Cho Oyu and, of course, Everest, the 'Goddess Mother of the World'. The highway is a stunning achievement.

There's just one nagging problem. Roads bring development. As the present volume went to press, plans were in place for a visitor centre and hotel at EBC. Officially billed as a 'mountaineering complex', it is pure tourism. What environmental damage will this all bring, and to what degree will this road, and its associated infrastructure, cheapen the experience of getting there? Only time will tell.

No doubt, the lure of this new road will draw adventurous travellers from across the globe. But for many it's a question of whether they should be there in the first place. **BDS**

❶ The road to EBC, with the peak in the distance.

Over-Water Highway South Central China, China

Start Zhaojun Bridge, Hubei End Gufuzhen, Hubei Distance 13km (8 miles)
Type Scenic Map goo.gl/TRV3SC

Here, the road transport engineers have created a total one-off – a glorious, swooping, arcing highway on stilts over water. This project may have seemed strange on paper, but the result is strangely beautiful. The Over-Water Highway – officially the Guzhao Highway Link – was originally proposed to solve a chronic traffic congestion problem between Zhaojun Bridge and Guzhao in Hubei Province. Several routes up this narrow valley were proposed, all involving a huge impact on the forests and ecology of the region. Then someone proposed building the road in the river – and the rest is history. In August 2015 the 'ecological overwater road' opened for traffic.

Dubbed by many as 'Asia's Most Scenic Highway', the stretch of tarmac in the middle of the Xiangxi River has become quite a tourist attraction, drawing drivers from all over the world to stare at the audacity of the thing as they glide along at the designated 60 kph (40 mph) speed limit, taking photographs of the beautiful wooded scenery. While the highway's 'eco' credentials are somewhat questionable, any tourist revenue that it happens to generate will be very welcome in this part of China, since the project cost an estimated $70 million to construct. DK

❶ The road in the middle of the river.

Aizhai Winding Road
South Central China, China

Start Jishou, Hunan
End Jishou, Hunan
Distance 20km (12.5 miles)
Type Scenic
Map goo.gl/fqyOJZ

This road trip covers a short section of National Highway 319, which links Xiamen in Fujian with Chengdu in Sichuan, a total distance of 2,984km (1,854 miles).

The route suggested here starts near the Yangtze River and goes up the side of a steep hill in a tight series of 13 hairpin bends. At the top of the ascent, the road goes into a tunnel, then re-emerges onto the Aizhai Bridge before going straight back into another tunnel on the other side.

Commissioned in 2007 and completed at the end of 2011, the suspension bridge is 1,146m (3,760ft) long and stands 336m (1,102ft) above the Dehang Canyon. It is neither the highest nor the longest structure of its type in the world, but at the time of publication of the present volume no other bridge that is higher was longer, and no other bridge that is longer was higher.

When first opened, the Aizhai Bridge cut an hour off journey times on this part of the 319, but it has since acted as a traffic magnet – thousands of trucks and business workers cross it in both directions every day, but so too do increasing numbers of tourists, with the result that progress along this section of the route can be as slow as it was before the bridge came off the drawing board. If you are planning a visit, make it outside rush hours and weekends. **JP**

Guoliang Tunnel Road
South Central China, China

Start Shuimocun, Henan
End Guoliang Scenic Area, Henan
Distance 3km (1.9 miles)
Type Adventure
Map goo.gl/FayqSo

The Guoliang Tunnel, high in the Taihang Mountains in central China, connects the tiny village of Guoliang to the outside world. Before it was built in the 1970s, the only route in and out of the village was the 'sky ladder', a slippery, uneven staircase carved into the cliffs. Thirteen villagers cut out the tunnel by hand. They took five years to complete the colossal feat, using 4,000 hammers, bought by selling crops and goats.

Accessed from Da Ye Road, looping through the lower end of the valley (you must pay a fee to enter the scenic area), the tunnel – or corridor – snakes in and out of the cliff, and often looks more like a set for Rivendell in *The Lord of the Rings* (2001–03) movie trilogy than part of the Chinese road network. More than thirty 'windows' cut into the wall of the tunnel look over the sheer-sided gorge; external sections are edged by stone walls. Since the tunnel has become a tourist attraction, little bridges and views have been added to the rocky ensemble; one lookout at the end of the tunnel faces an impressive waterfall.

Driving the tunnel is straightforward – just follow the vehicle in front – but watch out for oncoming vehicles and wandering pedestrians. The rules are: headlights on and honk the horn. **DS**

◐ This road is used by motor vehicles and pedestrians.

Macau Driving Tour
Macau, China

Start Ferry Terminal
End The Venetian Macao, Estrada da Baia de N. Senhora
Distance 25km (15.5 miles)
Type Culture
Map goo.gl/q7kXUR

❶ Senado Square is part of the Historic Center of Macau and a UNESCO World Heritage Site.

The tiny former Portuguese colony of Macau on China's south coast is the most densely populated place on Earth, with more than 650,000 residents on islands covering 115.3 sq km (44.5 square miles). In addition, thirty million visitors come each year because it is the gambling capital of Asia. Generating six times more income than the Las Vegas Strip, it may be hard to escape the pull of the various casinos' opulent bars and roulette tables. However, it is not impossible to do so.

From the ferry terminal, your best bet for a hassle-free road trip is to rent a car with a chauffeur. Typical guided tours take about four hours and kick off with a visit to the UNESCO-designated Historic Center, where over twenty sites 'provide a unique testimony to the meeting of aesthetic, cultural, architectural and technological influences from East and West'. Highlights include the Neoclassical Moorish Barracks, Monte Fort and the imposing Ruins of St. Paul's, a 17th-century Roman Catholic foundation.

On the far side of Seac Pai Bay is historic Coloane Village, once the haunt of traders, fishermen and pirates. If you must visit a casino, try the 39-storey Venetian Macau – the largest in the world, with 800 gambling tables, 3,400 slot machines, 350 shops, 30 restaurants and 51 gondolas for rent along the complex's canal network. **DIS**

Northern Hong Kong
Hong Kong, China

Start Cheung Uk
End Pat Heung
Distance 48km (29.8 miles)
Type Scenic
Map goo.gl/43iG7L

Heading out on a horseshoe-shaped scenic tour of northern Hong Kong takes you through agricultural regions established centuries ago by the first settlers, who saw promise in the area's fertile plateau. However, as economic activity was drawn to the bustling harbours of the south, many of these farming communities were abandoned and cultivated lands were slowly reclaimed by nature.

Your starting point, near the village of Cheung Uk, is nestled below the peaks of Ping Fung Shan, Cloudy Hill and Wong Leng. It's an idyllic location and a designated Site of Special Scientific Interest as a haven for aquatic plants, fish and insects.

Picking up the Sha Lo Tung, a narrow two-way uphill climb, you head towards Plover Cove Country Park and Plover Reservoir. This popular weekend tourist spot has bikes for rent to explore the dam and the scenic overlooks at the far southern end.

From Tai Mei Tuk, continue towards Bride's Pool Road and Robin's Nest. Also known as Hung Fa Leng (Red Flower Ridge), this was once part of the restricted border area marked with guard posts and barbed wire fences between China and Hong Kong while the latter was under British rule. Today, it's a tranquil spot with fabulous views over the Pat Sin Leng Country Park, where you could easily forget you're in Hong Kong, home to one of the most densely populated cities on the planet. **DIS**

❶ A view over Hong Kong from one of the high points on this scenic route.

Hong Kong's Country Parks
Hong Kong, China

Start Clear Water Bay
End Wong Shek Pier
Distance 28km (17.4 miles)
Type Scenic
Map goo.gl/PSugY5

Take this road trip to escape the bustle of Kowloon and explore the tranquility of Sai Kung Country Park.

Head north from Kowloon's Clear Water Bay Country Park on to Hiram's Highway, which twists and turns past the luxury houses overlooking Marina Cove. See the leisure boats jostling for space in Hebe Haven and continue through leafy villages and market gardens to Sai Kung.

First, you drive into the old fishing town, with its waterfront, pier, temple and seafood restaurants on the beach. A well-known roadside monument, the Sai Kung Memorial, honours villagers who died during the Japanese occupation in World War II.

Beyond that, the road turns into the Sai Kung East Country Park, a large, protected natural area covering this hilly, forested and jagged peninsula.

The park is a popular place for a range of outdoor activities. Among its numerous attractions are marked walking trails and an easily accessed coral-diving site. Finally, at the Wong Shek area, you'll see one of the parts of Hong Kong that is least touched by human hand – an entirely unspoiled natural environment where you can quietly relax while gazing at views of beautiful islands and waterways.

The park is also a great spot to abandon the road for once, rent a small boat from one of the many quayside operators and sail off to explore the island-dotted seascape. **SH**

Tai Tam to Shek O Road
Hong Kong, China

Start American Club, Stanley
End Shek O Beach
Distance 13km (8 miles)
Type Scenic
Map goo.gl/gCVeHe

The bustling village of Stanley is a good place to start a road trip that may defy your expectations of Hong Kong. On the south of the main island, Stanley is a popular spot, thanks to its huge market, lively waterfront, sandy beaches and its ultra-cool American Club. This is where the flashiest supercar-owning road-trip enthusiasts like to start their weekend driving adventures.

Follow the sound of wailing V8s and flat-six Porsches along the Tai Tam Road, skirting the wooded shores of Tai Tam Bay and Turtle Cove Beach. The road winds through lush vegetation to Tai Tam Tuk Reservoir. Have your camera ready as you curve across the top of the dam; it's a particularly dramatic stretch of road.

Then you'll twist up into thickly wooded hills, turning right onto the Shek O Road. This takes you into the protected country park covering most of the D'Aguilar Peninsula. You'll spot glorious coastal views between the trees here at the southeastern extremes of Hong Kong Island.

Once over the hills, you descend steeply via a bendy stretch into the beachside village of Shek O. By Hong Kong standards, this is a remote spot. The old fishing village boasts a glorious sandy beach and cafés. Whether you have a supercar or not, they are favourite places to gather for breakfast at the weekend and watch the sun rise over the Pacific. **SH**

Tai Mo Shan Road
Hong Kong, China

Start Tsuen Wan
End Tai Mo Shan
Distance 13km (8 miles)
Type Adventure
Map goo.gl/0pv18c

Yes, this really is Hong Kong. It may not seem like it as you wind your way up steep hairpin bends on the slopes of an exposed mountain, but this is one of the most unexpected road trips in the densely populated and largely urbanized Chinese province.

Yet Tai Mo Shan is 957m (3,140ft) high, so it's a proper mountain and the highest peak in the area. That means your twisting drive to the summit is rewarded on clear days with all-around views across the subtropical hills of the New Territories and the high-rise urban sprawl along the coast. You'll spot smaller islands and shipping plying to and fro. This is also a great area for hiking – indeed, that's the only way to get to see Tai Mo Shan Waterfall, Hong Kong's highest cascade.

The mountain and the country park surrounding the falls are the remains of an extinct volcano. Stop almost anywhere on the way up to feel currents of warm air emerging from far below, via cracks in the rock. Locals call this geological phenomenon 'dragon's breath'.

You'll find that this route is a perfect way to see both sides of Hong Kong within a short distance. You start amid the tower blocks, street markets and milling pedestrians of Ho Pui in Tsuen Wan and end up braced against a chill wind in Hong Kong's highest, most rugged and coldest spot no more than a few minutes later. **SH**

❶ Tai Mo Shan is Hong Kong's highest peak; its summit commands magnificent views of the surrounding city.

Hangzhou Bay Bridge East China, China

Start Jiaxing Shi, Zhejiang End Ningbo Shi, Zhejiang Distance 44km (27.3 miles)
Type Scenic Map goo.gl/2f2HSG

You drive along a six-lane highway. To the sides, there's a view of flat farmland that gradually becomes marshy and finally tidal mud flats. Then the land disappears altogether – you're travelling above water.

Entering the Hangzhou Bay Bridge is much like many major highway river crossings around the world – except that the journey goes on for much, much longer.

With a strictly enforced 100 kph (62 mph) speed limit, it could take half an hour to drive across Hangzhou Bay and the Yangtze River Delta, which are notoriously rough and very tidal. At 36km (22 miles), the bridge is one of the longest in the world. That gives you plenty of time to study the design – especially since fog often obscures the sea views.

The bridge opened in 2008 to great acclaim. Most of the main sections stand on steel pillars, but there are also two short cable-stayed sections supported by elegant, wishbone-shaped towers. The deck is 33m (108ft) wide and sits 62m (203ft) above the water, allowing container ships to pass underneath the cable-stayed stretches.

In the centre of the bridge is a unique feature: a rest stop on stilts. **SH**

❶ Labourers working on the bridge in 2008.

Kunshan Tunnel Road East China, China

Start Wangmangling Scenic Area Toll Gate   **End** Kunshan Tunnel   **Distance** 2.9km (1.8 miles)
Type Adventure   **Map** goo.gl/U7B5ff

Strange things occur when nonprofessionals get involved in highway construction. Take this road, for example. Fed up with being cut off from the main road, in the 1970s farmers in the remote hilltop villages in Shanxi Province began taking matters into their own hands. Usually, to build a cliff road, you cut a step. But if you are doing this entirely by hand, and the cliff above the ledge you are building is considerable, then maybe you dig a tunnel. But then how do you know where you are? The ingenious solution reached here was to tunnel near the edge of the cliff. That way, when you hit daylight, you knew you'd gone too far. Also, when that happened, you could heft the spoils from your digging through the jagged hole and down the mountain. The result, seen from the other side of the valley, is a bizarre chain of irregular punctuations in the cliff face, through which it is just possible to glimpse the Kunshan Road. When first built, it was absolutely terrifying. Since then, things have improved somewhat. In 2009 the government added a concrete balustrade across the 'windows'. Even so, it remains a perilous journey. The road is only single-lane – who knows what you are supposed to do if you meet traffic? Snow means the route is accessible only between May and November. **DK**

❶ The tunnel with the holes in the side.

East Coast Highway Taipeh to Taitung, Taiwan

Start Keelung City, Taipeh　**End** Shoukatiemayi Station, Taitung　**Distance** 447km (278 miles)
Type Scenic　**Map** goo.gl/ap4Azo

Prepare yourself for views of sheer cliffs and green hills rolling down to turquoise-coloured ocean, cloud-covered mountain peaks, misty forested valleys, rocky headlands and long sandy beaches. Taiwan's east coast defies the stereotypes of the rest of the island – there are no overdeveloped industries or overcrowded cities here; just a marvellous, long, uninterrupted, smooth, paved road running right down the east coast.

The highlights of this journey include the Taroko National Park, with its beautiful gorge and waterfalls; the Taitung surfing beaches; and the East Coast National Scenic Area, with its rice paddy fields, water buffalo and pretty fishing villages.

A short boat ride east from here is Ludao (Green Island), a small enclave of tropical vegetation and steaming hot saltwater springs. Farther on is Lanyu (Orchid Island), an even more exotic retreat smothered in thick greenery.

Back on the main island, continue south, passing one of Taiwan's most celebrated landscapes as the Xiuguluan River and its tributaries rush down from the mountains carving twisting gorges. You can turn back west at Shoukatiemayi Station or continue south to the Kenting National Park and the southern tip of the island. **SH**

❶ Taroko National Park has spectacular water features.

Taroko Gorge Road Hualien, Taiwan

Start Taroko   End Huitouwan   Distance 19km (11.8 miles)
Type Adventure   Info goo.gl/ghsmDY

A long time ago, according to legend, some members of a Truku tribe on Taiwan walked out of a gorge and saw the beauty of the Pacific Ocean in front of them. 'Taroko', they cried, which in the Truku language means 'magnificent and splendid'. Today, this entire area on the east coast of Taiwan is a national park, one of nine in Taiwan, and renowned for the impressive gorge carved through it by the Liwu River. The road through it is truly remarkable; a narrow, twisting stretch of tarmac that hugs the mountainsides and often passes underneath them through tunnels carved out of the solid rock. As the road is technically part of the Central Cross-Island Highway, opened in 1960, it is often packed with tour buses, trucks, scooters and pedestrians, as well as road-tripping tourists, making it hazardous in the extreme. Add to all this the facts that typhoon rains often dislodge debris onto the road and cause massive landslides, while seismic activity can cause the mountainsides to collapse all around you, and you have one of the most dangerous, and most exciting, roads in the world. Start at the coastal town of Taroko and then head west inland through to Huitouwan, where the road leaves the gorge and heads west through beautiful countryside across the island. SA

❶ A bridge over Taroko Gorge near the city of Hualien.

Hengchun Peninsula Coastal Road Pintung, Taiwan

Start Hengchun   End Manzhou   Distance 40km (25 miles)
Type Scenic   Map goo.gl/kHlqxu

The 'tail' dangling from the south of Taiwan is the Hengchun Peninsula, a beautiful, sparsely populated, undeveloped, natural region. The paved highway around the coast is one of the island's best road trips.

Start at Hengchun, where the old moated city wall and four fortress gateways can still be seen. From there, head south into the hills of Kenting National Park. This is a conservation area of sandy beaches, green mountains and towering sand dunes. You'll pass two small resorts: Nanwan, with its popular watersports facilities, and Kenting, with a lively nightlife and restaurant scene.

Stop at Cape Eluanbi, the southernmost tip of the island. This coral headland is topped by a fortified 19th-century lighthouse and a park of lush tropical greenery. The thick vegetation here is one of the most prolific spots in the world for land-dwelling crabs.

Head north along the east coast with your camera at the ready. It's Taiwan's most celebrated stretch of shoreline, with views encompassing miles of rolling grassy hills and rocky shores.

You'll finish the trip at the small town of Manzhou, which is built on a maze of rivers flowing down from the mountains. It's known as a great area for exploring (and jumping into) waterfalls. **SH**

❶ **A typically unspoiled stretch of Taiwanese coast.**

Yaza Htarni Road Naypyidaw Union Territory, Myanmar

Start Thitseinbin   End Ministry Zone   Distance 16km (9.9 miles)
Type Adventure   Map goo.gl/mggfdX

At one point there are ten lanes in each direction. The Yaza Htarni Road is one of the widest expressways in the world, but it is usually empty.

Occasionally, you may spot a lone motorbike or a couple of government street sweepers lost in its vast acreage of tarmac. The mega-highway links the poor outer suburb of Thitseinbin to the official government Ministry Zone. That's a journey few people ever make.

Welcome to the weird world of Naypyidaw – since 2005 the capital of Myanmar – purpose built by the country's military dictators in the heart of a jungle 320km (200 miles) north of the old capital, Rangoon. The project cost billions in one of Asia's poorest countries. It looks like a disaster for the planners – but not quite as bad for visitors: the spectacular roads can make for some memorable driving experiences.

Yaza Htarni Road is just one of many ten-lane highways through the vast, largely deserted urban landscape that covers an area six times greater than that of New York City. You'll find multi-level, flower-bedecked roundabout systems, neatly pruned shrubbery lining the roads, impressive bridges over vast, moated government buildings and grand entrances to huge formal parks. But what you won't find is very much, or indeed any, traffic. SH

❶ The planners hope that the road will attract traffic.

Route 1249 Chiang Mai, Thailand

Start Mae Kah   **End** Doi Ang Khang Royal Agricultural Station   **Distance** 28km (17.4 miles)
Type Scenic   **Map** goo.gl/qUyfyr

Doi Ang Khang is a 1,928-m- (6,325-ft) high mountain in northern Thailand, straddling the border with Myanmar. It forms the centrepiece of a beautiful national park and a driving route that twists among its foothills.

While some guidebooks recommend an itinerary heading from the northern end, for this trip you start at Market Mae Ngon on Highway 107 in Mae Kha to the south. Locals call this area Thailand's 'Little Switzerland' because of the cooler mountain climate and appealing scenery. Using the term 'cooler' is in the context of tropical Thailand – there is nothing colder than an occasional frost in December and January.

The important road west of here is Route 1249, which is smoothly paved but involves some hard-core hairpin bends, unguarded drops and severe gradients. The steepest section has a 19-per cent slope.

If you can cope with the road, you'll see some great views across the north of Thailand. The best days will present you with forested mountains rising out of misty valleys. Your final destination is the Royal Agricultural Station, which, in spite of its name is a horticultural garden with an interesting bonsai section. Look out, too, for a marked walk among the rhododendrons to a series of waterfalls. **SH**

❶ Morning mists beneath Doi Ang Khang.

Mae Hong Son Loop Chiang Mai, Thailand

Start Chiang Mai   **End** Chiang Mai   **Distance** 694km (431 miles)
Type Culture   **Map** goo.gl/byccyl

Most visitors to Thailand head for Bangkok and the southern beaches; the mountainous north of the country remains less well known to foreigners. A circular tour starting and finishing in the large city of Chiang Mai is a good way to explore this region. This route is usually advertised by local tour companies as taking four days, but that is the minimum, since there is so much to see and do. The temples, shrines and old city walls of Chiang Mai could keep you enthralled for weeks, but at some point you should leave and head southwest down the 108, possibly getting diverted north for a trip into the Doi Inthanon National Park, home to Thailand's highest peak. Mae Sariang is a pleasantly

quiet town surrounded by mountains and well worth getting to know. From here you head north to Mae Hong Son, another tranquil town close to the border with Myanmar (Burma), hence the mix of Burmese, Thai, Shan and hill peoples living in the town. Now a little more than halfway around the loop, you head east on the 1095 to Pai, a wonderfully exciting mountainous route with, apparently, 1,864 curves along its path. Pai itself lies in a river valley and is a bohemian delight with numerous cafés, restaurants and guesthouses. Keep on heading south and soon you are back in Chiang Mai. **SA**

❶ On the loop in northern Thailand.

Mission Hills Drive
Phuket, Thailand

Start Junction of 402 and 4027
End Junction of 402 and 4027
Distance 9.7km (6 miles)
Type Scenic
Info goo.gl/59JKqW

❶ One of the highlights of this itinerary is Promthep Cape, the southernmost point on the island of Phuket.

Phuket hosts millions of visitors every year, but very few of these holidaymakers branch out to explore the island in greater detail. This short itinerary is a quick and convenient way to broaden one's horizons and to take in some of the world's loveliest coastal scenery along the way.

It's easy to find. Turn off the main island highway, the 402, just 600m (650 yards) south of the international airport and take the smaller 4027.

You'll wind through dense exotic vegetation and pass beach houses, glimpsing the shoreline and sea beyond. Some of the makeshift homes and simple living conditions here show you what life was like on Phuket before the tourism boom.

Beyond Baan Laem Srai you'll encounter additional natural seascapes, with green hills sweeping down to the shore amid lush greenery and tropical flowers. The little 4003 road loops around the shore of this largely undeveloped peninsula, twisting through a landscape with the rainforest on one side and the drop down to the sea on the other.

You'll turn back inland around the Mission Hills Phuket Golf Resort, with its renowned waterfront course and swim-up bar, then rejoin the 4027 road. Turn right, and this will lead you past the neatly tended gardens and expensive holiday homes of Mission High Village, back to your starting point. **SH**

North East Loop
Phuket, Thailand

Start Heroines Monument, Thalang
End Heroines Monument, Thalang
Distance 34km (21 miles)
Type Scenic
Map goo.gl/XBxLgM

Heroines Monument is an important local landmark, standing on Thepkasattri Road at the busiest traffic roundabout in Thalang, in the very heart of the island of Phuket.

It's a good spot to begin a road trip to see the lesser-known side of this popular holiday resort. The story behind the monument, for example, isn't known by most foreign visitors who come to Phuket's beaches each year.

The 'heroines' are the brave Lady Chan and Lady Mook, who led an army of locals, many of whom were women, to defeat Burmese invaders more than two centuries ago, like a couple of Thai Joans of Arc. It has become traditional for locals to bring gifts of flower garlands to the monument and ask for protection.

From this inspiring spot, turn off the main Route 402 and take the smaller 4027 road through the lush vegetation and plantations to the northeast. The road loops around this quieter side of the island, with wonderful views of Phang Nga Bay, its array of beautiful forested islands and the colourful local fishing boats at work.

The sleepy villages here are a sobering contrast to the hectic beach resorts of the west coast. And the swanky new yacht marina complex at Ao Po is a hint that the old rural lifestyle won't last much longer on this side of Phuket. SH

❶ Ko Panyi is one of the pretty little fishing villages along the route.

Heritage Roads Central
Region and more, Singapore

Start Arcadia Road, Central Region
End South Buona Vista Road, Central Region
Distance 67km (41.6 miles)
Type Scenic
Info goo.gl/EIflN8

Instituted in 2001 by the National Parks Board, the five thoroughfares that make up Singapore's Heritage Road network are part of a government initiative to maintain the city's connection to its natural environment in the face of ever-increasing urban development. The five roads in question – Arcadia Road, Mt Pleasant Road, Lim Chu Kang Road, South Buona Vista Road and Mandai Road – have had their adjacent treescapes preserved and enhanced, the product of more than four decades of local maintenance, now under official government protection. And while the overall length of the Heritage Road scheme is modest – a mere 6.2km (3.8 miles) put end to end – its significance can scarcely be overestimated.

Every road has its own inimitable charms. For example, the rain trees of Arcadia Road, with their umbrella-shaped canopies, and the elegant pre-war homes along Mt Pleasant Road.

Mandai Road is one of the city's oldest stretches of tarmac, constructed in 1855 to connect the area's farming villages. In the late 1800s, pepper and rubber plantations were built beneath the broad-leaf mahogany trees along Lim Chu Kang Road, and there is the hairpin-bend-rich South Buona Vista Road, known as 'the Road of Ninety-Nine Turns'.

These are more than just roads. They are Singapore's precious botanic gardens. **BDS**

Bugak Skyway
Seoul, South Korea

Start Changuimun
End Jeongneung
Distance 19km (12 miles)
Type Scenic
Info goo.gl/tkp23s

The gentle, winding curves of the Bugak Skyway make it a popular driving route for locals. The road twists up the wooded sides of Bugaksan Mountain in the northern outskirts of the capital, Seoul.

It's a short route that leads along the northeast ridge of the mountain, with impressive views across the city and the surrounding northern peaks of Bukhansan National Park. At the summit of the route there's a car park and a viewing platform where courting couples often meet to see the lights of the city.

The highlights of the road include Palgakjeong, an ornate traditional octagonal pavilion housing a café where you can stop for a meal or drink while admiring the views amid pretty seasonal gardens with exotic, colourful flowers. The altitude here is only 342m (1,122ft), but it feels higher, with the city and its skyscrapers laid out below you.

There are plenty of walking paths through the trees and gardens here. Some lead towards remains of the old Seoul defensive city walls that you can glimpse snaking around the adjoining hills.

The skyway is an all-season attraction: in winter you can see the hills covered with snow, although the road is always open; in summer the trees offer welcome shade. The flowers of spring are renowned, whereas the red leaves of the autumn attract thousands of visitors from all over the world. **SH**

Mt Jungmi to Mt Homyeong
Gyeonggi, South Korea

Start Mt Jungmi
End Homyeong Lake
Distance 45km (28 miles)
Type Adventure
Info goo.gl/3MDrMM

Described by the *Korea Times* as one of the country's finest driving roads, this point-to-point roller coaster is said to offer an 'enjoyable level of tension and thrill' as it winds along lush, green mountainside some 48km (30 miles) east of the capital, Seoul.

The first 11km (6.8 miles) are a sequence of flowing curves as the road bucks up and down in the foothills of Mt Jungmi; the final 15km (9.3 miles) of well-surfaced, two-lane tarmac have fewer elevation changes but several surprising switchbacks to keep you on your toes.

This lovely stretch of scenic road is always popular with weekend road trippers looking to escape Korea's congested cities. However, after dark its character completely changes, since the mountain's more tortuous sections become a popular haunt for tyre-shredding drifters and fans of the modified-car scene. As the following dawn breaks, many of these young auto enthusiasts can be found gathering at Loko Gallery near Mt Homyeong; with a car park filled with exotic custom machines, the restaurant often serves huge pots of steaming ramen, free of charge, to the hungry gearheads.

If high-octane motoring isn't your thing, head out east to the end of this road trip at Homyeong Lake, a pretty pumped-storage reservoir nestled into the mountain, overlooked by an ornate octagonal pavilion in traditional Korean style. **DIS**

❶ Mt Jungmi has some of the most beautiful, unspoiled scenery on the Korean Peninsula.

National Road 7

Gangwon/Yeongnam, South Korea

Start Goseong, Gangwon
End Busan, Yeongnam
Distance 349km (217 miles)
Type Scenic
Info goo.gl/JuAvIy

This road trip takes you down the length of South Korea's east coast, from Goseong near the border with the north to Busan at the southeast tip.

Start the journey at Goseong's viewing platforms, where you can climb up to look over the border into North Korea, spotting islands and mountains as well as hostile military installations. It's all part of Unification Park, which has an unusual combination of war relics, religious statues and souvenir shops among its gardens.

Head south as the road winds along the steep, lush coastline. You'll be able to explore a sequence of pretty temples. At Naksansa, for example, the Buddhist shrine perches on the cliff edge, while at Cheongganjeong, the octagonal pavilion is a popular spot for viewing the sunrise.

There are lots of good beaches along the east coast; the best is Chilpo, with an arc of pure white sand backed by lush vegetation. And the must-see fishing village is Yeongdeok, known as 'Crab Town'. There's a huge model of a crab attached to an arch over the bridge into the town here, just in order to emphasize what's on all the menus.

Finally, you'll arrive at South Korea's second city, Busan, where the highlights include Haeundae Beach, South Korea's most popular seaside resort, and the Shinsegae shop, the world's biggest department store. SH

Jeju Island Ring Road

Jeju, South Korea

Start Jeju City
End Jeju City
Distance 180km (112 miles)
Type Scenic
Info goo.gl/OsZ61f

Highway 1132, the ring road around Jeju – an oval-shaped volcanic island off the southwest coast of the Korean Peninsula – is a rare treat. It is one of the few places in the world that are blessed with UNESCO's 'Triple Crown' of designations, being simultaneously a Natural Heritage Site, a Global Geopark and a Biosphere Reserve.

South Korea's largest island is dominated by the 1,950-m- (6,400-ft) high Hallasan shield volcano. In contrast to the mountainous interior, the coastal road is on a relatively flat plain, with constant beach views past tidal flats and volcanic beaches. Two interior roads – Highway 1139 (which provides a beautiful view over the southern part of the island) and Highway 1131 – take you along Hallasan's lower flanks, connecting the ring road's northern and southern segments.

Off the main route, one popular scenic detour is to Seogwipo, where a narrow road takes you to the only waterfall in Asia that cascades directly into the ocean; another is the Mysterious Road, where objects are said to roll uphill. The 13-km- (8-mile) long lava caves of Handong-ri, and Seongsan Ilchulbong Peak (Sunrise Peak), Jeju's 5,000-year-old tuff cone, are other must-see highlights of South Korea's superseismic showcase. BDS

● Sunrise Peak on Jeju Island.

Road to Anabar
East Siberia, Russia

Start Irkutsk
End Anabar Bay
Distance 4,000km (2,485 miles)
Type Adventure
Info goo.gl/fYghIO

It has to be the world's longest dead end – 6,400km (4,000 miles) of a snow- and ice-covered track that begins near Lake Baikal, heads north and ends in a polar wilderness in a world that few people ever see. You'll pass Mirny, once home to the world's largest diamond mine and the second-largest human-made hole in the ground, and drive a 1,600-km- (1,000-mile) long stretch that has no ambulance services, no police, no mobile phone reception, no workshops and no people. So be sure you've filled up all your spare jerricans: fuel here is rare and supplies are rationed.

The beauty, though, is overwhelming as you drive through the taiga, the world's largest land biome and home to almost one-third of the world's forests. The road's 'wilder'"parts begin at Udacnyj. A sign outside the town says it's 1,050km (652 miles) to Yuryung-Khaya on Anabar Bay, with just a few mostly abandoned villages in between. After crossing the polar circle at 66° 33', just keep going, going as far north as you'll ever go in a car – 480km (300 miles) one day, 640km (400 miles) the next. Then finally, at 72° 49', you arrive at the Arctic Ocean. Forget all those other 'northernmost' roads – Nordkapp in Norway; Prudhoe Bay in Alaska; Tuktoyaktuk in Canada – this epic road to Anabar is more challenging and more northern than any of them. **BDS**

Lake Baikal Ice Run
East Siberia, Russia

Start Irkutsk
End Irkutsk
Distance 966km (600 miles)
Type Adventure
Info goo.gl/XCz1ql

The Adventurists are a team of eccentric British chaps 'fighting to make the world less boring' by organizing some truly incredible road trips across the globe. On this notorious race, in the farthest reaches of Siberia, entrants are issued worn-out Russian motorbikes and sent off on a loosely defined circuit for some 1,000km (600 miles) across the frozen lake.

Before they can enter, contestants have to raise a minimum of £1,000 ($1,200) in charity sponsorship. The event kicks off in Irkutsk in March, by which time the spring sunshine has warmed temperatures up considerably to a balmy -20°C (-4°F).

After a three-day training and acclimatization programme, it's on to your unreliable 650cc Ural and sidecar, and out onto the ice, up the length of Lake Baikal, returning via lakeside tracks and frozen rivers.

It may be springtime, but the windchill still takes the moving temperature down another 10°C (18°F). The ice is temperamental and consequently difficult to read – one minute mirror-flat, the next like a newly ploughed field – and it is vitally important to read your map accurately and not get the fuel stashes provided at intervals en route confused with the danger areas. **DK**

➲ An off-road tourist vehicle on frozen Lake Baikal.

Strait of Tartary Pacific Coast
Far Eastern FD, Russia

Start Yuzhno-Sakhalinsk
End Smirnykh
Distance 509km (316 miles)
Type Scenic
Map goo.gl/e2HyBp

Sakhalin is the largest island in Russia – 948km (589 miles) from north to south, up to 160km (100 miles) across and with an area of 76,400 sq km (29,500 square miles). It is separated from the mainland by the Strait of Tartary, a part of the Pacific Ocean; the coastal section is the most exciting part of this trip.

The starting point on the map referenced above is the hotel in which most visitors will stay: the Mira in Yuzhno-Sakhalinsk (the city is the administrative centre of Sakhalin). From there the road heads west across the island until it reaches Kholmsk, the main port for ferries to and from Vanino on the Russian mainland.

The next, longest stretch of the trip hugs the shoreline until Krasnogorsky. Farther north, the road turns back inland before passing through Uglegorsk, a seaside coal-mining town, and then turning east for Smirnykh.

Sakhalin has a harsh climate, even in the summer, which lasts only through August and September. The Russian playwright and short-story writer Anton Chekhov did not mince his words: he said the place was Hell. But it has great unspoiled beauty and an abundance of rare and endangered wildlife (including, according to some, even bigger bears than in Siberia). The west coast is particularly rewarding; intrepid travellers should not hesitate to visit and explore. **JP**

❶ Sakhalin is hard to reach and hard to live on: what better destination for the adventurous traveller?

Petropavlovsk to Klyuchi

Far Eastern FD, Russia

Start Petropavlovsk-Kamchatskiy
End Klyuchi
Distance 566km (352 miles)
Type Adventure
Map goo.gl/YEuj3V

There is hardly a landscape anywhere on the planet like Russia's Kamchatka Peninsula. Larger than Germany and Austria combined, it's an icy, untamed world with 160 volcanoes (29 of them active) and around 16,000 Kamchatkan brown bears that are as common as rabbits in the spring, and gorge themselves in the undammed, salmon-filled rivers. The whole place has a gloriously Jurassic-like feel. In fact, the human imprint is so small that outside the region's delightful capital of Petropavlovsk, the paved roads are measured only in the hundreds of miles. If you want to get anywhere here, aging Soviet MI-8 cargo helicopters are the best option – unless, of course, you're feeling particularly intrepid and have decided you're going to drive north to Klyuchi.

Klyuchi is a rambling collection of timber shacks populated by ethnic Russians at the end of a 500-km- (310-mile) long dirt track that ends within sight of Eurasia's largest, tallest and almost continually active volcano, 4,750-m- (15,580-ft) high Klyuchevskaya Sopka. A bus leaves every day at 8:00am for the ten-hour trip, but it's possible to get there by private car. The road splits after Milkovo – take the right-hand fork – and when you get to Klyuchi, look for a guesthouse owned by a vulcanologist named Yury. You wanted adventure? You've come to the right place. **BDS**

Kolyma Highway

Far Eastern FD, Russia

Start Yakutsk
End Magadan
Distance 2,005km (1,246 miles)
Type Adventure
Map goo.gl/MU4OaW

During Joseph Stalin's reign of terror, the sides of this road were littered with gold-mining camps and forced labour gulags, all of which are now rotting and abandoned. Interns included political activists, poets, generals and rocket scientists who'd fallen out of favour with the Soviet dictator.

In 1932 inmates of the Sevvostlag labour camp were diverted onto this massive road-building project. Today, the Kolyma Highway is also considered a memorial, since the bodies of the thousands who died during its construction were simply buried in the roadway.

Since the fall of Communism, Stalin's grand highway has fallen into disrepair in its middle stretches; with collapsed bridges and washouts, the road deteriorates during the warmer months into a long, linear swamp. However, the boom in adventure tourism popularized in the *Long Way Round* TV series (2004) means that hundreds of off-road motorcyclists come each year, and specialist tour companies are now offering 4x4 expeditions along the length of the 'Road of Bones'.

This is an extremely tough trip. The road is awful and there are few supply or rest stations en route. Perhaps even worse, temperatures can range from a flesh-freezing -60°C (-76°F) to a sweltering 40°C (104°F) in summer that hatches swarms of the notorious Siberian mosquito. **DIS**

Baikal to Amur Mainline (BAM) Road
Far Eastern FD to Central FD, Russia

Start Tinda, Far Eastern Federal District
End Bratskiy, Central Federal District
Distance 7,717km (4,795 miles)
Type Adventure
Map goo.gl/yed7x3

When is a road not a road? When it's a collection of gravel tracks, swollen rivers and rickety wooden bridges that are barely left standing. Welcome to the Baikal to Amur Mainline (BAM) Road. This route is a genuine challenge for drivers and their machinery. It was built as a service track to aid the construction of a mammoth railroad, and it's fair to say that it's currently not in the best of states.

You will need either a 4x4 or an off-road motorcycle to stand even a chance of making it down the BAM Road in one piece. It's a single track, but that's not really a problem because there are whole sections where you stand little chance of meeting a fellow traveller along the way. There are some settlements on the route, but many are now abandoned. Others are used purely to service the Trans-Siberian Railroad.

You need to go equipped for all eventualities, with plenty of fuel for your vehicle and supplies for yourself. In places the road all but vanishes, and you have to pick your way through the taiga. Some adventure bikers even find themselves riding along the railroad track – that's illegal, of course, but there is seldom anyone else around and the trains do not run very often. The challenges of this route will discourage some road trippers, but to other travellers the quality of a road can be judged only by its difficulty. **JI**

❶ The road was first used to aid construction of the railway, which runs parallel to it.

Lidoga to Vanino Road
Far Eastern FD, Russia

Start Lidoga
End Vanino
Distance 325km (202 miles)
Type Adventure
Map goo.gl/xp9OId

The Russian Far East deserves its reputation as the equivalent of the 19th-century North American Wild West. This largely deserted area of Siberia is sparsely populated and bitterly cold in winter, with temperatures often well below freezing, and almost unbearably hot throughout the fleeting summer of a little less than two months.

It has few road or rail connections. One road that is open to traffic, however, is the highway from Lidoga, on the Amur River, east to the seaport of Vanino, across the Strait of Tartary from Sakhalin Island. Vanino has a grim history: it was one of the main ports from which convicts were shipped to the gulags (labour camps) of Magadan during the Stalinist era. Today, it merely trades freight and oil. Surprisingly for such a remote road, most of this highway's surface is well-maintained tarmac, although there are stretches of gravel and some of the bridges have wooden planks. The road is mostly flat, passing alongside the Anyui River.

You need to take supplies for this long journey because there are no towns along the route. And, of course, this is a road for summer journeys only. In the winter, heavy snowfalls, avalanches and landslides can occur at any time, and ice makes the surface treacherous. In 2012 the road was closed when floods swept away a bridge. Don't say you haven't been warned. **SA**

Discover Hokkaido
Hokkaido, Japan

Start Hakodate
End Akan
Distance 821km (510 miles)
Type Culture
Map goo.gl/nVYTzt

Hokkaido, Japan's northernmost island, covers 20 per cent of the country's land area but is home to only 5 per cent of its population. The pace of life is slower in the north, accommodation and food costs are lower and the scenery is stunning. With a cool temperate climate, Hokkaido is a magnet for skiers and snowboarders. Road trips are therefore best undertaken in the warmer months.

Hakodate in the west is a good starting point for this long-distance road trip; allow four days to avoid feeling rushed. The city is the terminus of the bullet train and sea ferries to and from Honshu; it is also the place to rent a car. On this first leg to Sapporo, famous for its brewery and vibrant nightlife, you pass numerous *onsens* (thermal tidal rock pools), of which Mizunashi Kaihin is the most popular.

After visiting Sapporo's excellent beer museum, you have three options: the shorter and less-travelled south coastal route; a tortuous drive along Hokkaido's desolate northern fringes; or through the island's central belt on Highway 39, with its spectacular backdrop of the snowcapped Daisetsuzan volcanic peaks.

It is best to take the last of these routes, which goes through the Bihoro Pass above the sapphire-blue Kussharo-ko, Japan's largest caldera lake. Nearby tourist villages on the shores of Lake Akan have budget accommodaton. **DIS**

Bandai to Azuma Skyline
Tohoku, Japan

Start Fukushima
End Tsuchiyu By-pass, Fukushima
Distance 30km (18.6 miles)
Type Culture
Map goo.gl/LI9mpX

One of Japan's most spectacular mountain roads, the Bandai to Azuma Skyline was opened in 1959 to provide access to the spectacular volcanic world of the Azuma Mountains and Bandai-Asahi National Park. The road begins in Fukushima at the Takayu Hot Springs, and soon takes you through a landscape of fissures, craters, marshlands and ponds, to a trailhead that leads to the rim of the elegantly symmetrical crater of Mt Azuma-kofuji, the 'little' Mt Fuji, which last erupted in 1977.

Driving through the fumarolic landscape is an end-of-the-world experience, while walking around the stratovolcano's rim provides views all the way back to Fukushima City. Back in your car, be sure to drive to the five coloured lakes of Goshikinuma, created by the 1888 eruption of Mt Bandai, in which nearly 500 people were killed.

The Japanese Ministry of Construction has voted the Bandai–Azuma Skyline one of Japan's Top 100 roads, while numerous motorcycling forums have voted it No. 1 in all Japan, due in no small part to its continuous curves through this painted, mineral-rich landscape.

The best time to visit is in autumn, when the hills are draped in red and yellow. The road is closed by heavy snowfalls between mid-November and April, an irony indeed considering the hot, sulphurous subterranean world over which it passes. **BDS**

Osado Skyline Drive
Chūbu, Japan

Start Shinbogawa Dam
End Sado Gold Mine
Distance 20km (12.4 miles)
Type Culture
Map goo.gl/lMLVkn

Symmetrically shaped a little like an S, Sado is the largest offshore island in the Sea of Japan. Once a place of exile for unpopular emperors, priests and politicians, these days it is a sanctuary rich in traditional Japanese customs and with an economy dominated by agriculture and fishing.

In the north, the Osado Mountains run north to west; the Kosado Mountains in the south run east to south; and in the middle of the S the broad, rice-covered Kuninaka Plain keeps the two mountainous halves of the island apart.

Officially known as Route 463, the Osado Skyline Drive traverses the ridgelines and ranges of the Osado Mountains, close to two of Sado Island's premier ski runs – the Winter Resort on Mt Kinpoku, and Wonder Valley Snowpark on Mt Myoken. From the drive's highpoint at Hakuundai, 942m (3,090ft) above sea level, the entire island is laid out before you, from Mano and Ryotsu Bays to the Kuninaka Plain and the Kosado Mountains beyond. The island's lush vegetation can literally hem you in at times, and obscure the otherwise expansive views, but the drive's long, green tunnels of vegetation are an experience in themselves on a road where the bends are constant, the views expansive and where the fascinatingly re-created Sado Gold Mine (opened in 1601, closed in 1989) awaits you at the road trip's end. **BDS**

Hakusan Shirakawa-go White Road
Chūbu, Japan

Start Hakusan Ichirino Hot Spring Ski Resort, Ishikawa
End Shirikawa, Gifu
Distance 33.3km (20.7 miles)
Type Scenic
Info goo.gl/Z5IPG0

This impressive route through Hakusan National Park bisects the Ryohaku Mountain range and is noted for its panoramic views. It is open between June and mid-November. However, the best time to go is in the autumn. Beginning at the higher elevations in late September, the lush forests begin to change, and the breathtaking display of colours begins. The Japanese call it *koyo*. Special jaunts to view the trees are very popular during the season.

This winding toll road is something a bit special, and offers some of the most eye-popping vistas. The first half of the journey somewhat lulls you into a false sense of security. It's a straightforward climb through dense woodland, with many impressive waterfalls right next to the road. However, the real highlight on this side of the summit has to be the hot spring with a unisex outdoor hot bath (*onsen*) where you can luxuriate in soothing waters and contemplate the magnificent beauty of the adjacent Ubagataki Waterfall.

Once over the summit and on to the Gifu side of the mountain, the road dramatically changes character. Suddenly it becomes intensely twisty, and the route is packed with memorable views of the autumn colours. Note: as well as being closed in winter, on a few summer days the route is reserved exclusively for walkers; it's best to check before setting out. **DK**

❶ Shirakawa-go, a UNESCO Historic Village in one of the valleys of Hakusan National Park.

Fuji Subaru Line
Chūbu, Japan

Start Fujikawaguchiko
End Mt Fuji Fifth Station
Distance 31km (19 miles)
Type Scenic
Info goo.gl/eT2db8

How about driving to the top of one of the world's most famous peaks, Mt Fuji, 3,776m (12,388ft) above sea level? The world-famous profile of the snowcapped, still-active volcano is almost a symbol of Japan itself, and you can actually reach it by car. This toll road to within 1.5km (less than a mile) of the top of Japan's tallest peak winds up more than 2,300m (7,500 ft) from the middle slopes. The steep, 40-minute ascent through cherry trees and forest suddenly breaks the tree line to reveal classic views of the volcano. On reaching Mt Fuji Fifth Station, which is the highest drivable point, there are spectacular scenes from the viewing platform onwards to the summit, as well as restaurants and souvenir shops.

You may also want to visit the small Komitake Shrine. For Japanese people, Fuji is a sacred mountain and, fittingly in this context, Komitake is the God of the Open Road. Although the summit is walkable from this point, the strenuous round-trip hike from the Shinto shrine to the crater rim will take at least ten and more likely twelve hours, and is possible only in July and August. As for the drive, check before going: weather conditions are a factor, and the road will be closed some days during winter. And also, for several special days in the peak summer season, due to limited parking, private cars are prohibited. **DK**

● The Komitake Shrine with, in the background, an unusually snow-free summit of Mt Fuji.

Hakone Turnpike
Chūbu, Japan

Start Hayakawa Tollgate, Odawara
End The Dammtrax Café, Daikanzan
Distance 14km (8.7 miles)
Type Adventure
Map goo.gl/f8dWdN

In 2014, staff at *Motorhead Magazine* arranged for a 14-km- (8.7-mile) long stretch of the Hakone Turnpike west of Tokyo, in the shadow of Mt Fuji, to be closed to traffic. Speed limits for the day were officially waived (though its tolls still had to be paid) and, despite it being a notoriously dangerous road, invited drivers grabbed the chance to do some high-speed drifting in the inaugural Motorhead Hill Climb. For a day, the road became a tortuous white-knuckle drag strip. Somehow, nobody died. Soon after, a legend was born.

Built in 1962, the turnpike begins at the bottom of the Izu Peninsula and ascends almost 1,006m (3,300ft) through dense woodlands that are a riot of colour in autumn and filled with cherry blossom in spring. Motorists with fast cars in Japan and around the world look upon the turnpike with reverential awe, and have dubbed it the 'Japanese Nürburgring', after the famous motorsports complex in Germany. Its surface is racetrack smooth, and there are no speed cameras in its tunnels. Sweeping bends dip and swerve all the way up to the bikers' café at the summit.

The turnpike is a private toll road, which in Japan means traffic police are few and far between, and other traffic is light. Not that these incentives to speed should be listened to, of course. That would be irresponsible. **BDS**

❶ Hakone Turnpike promises cherry blossom in the spring as well as an exciting drive.

Irohazaka Winding Road – Home of the Drifters
Chūbu, Japan

Start Kiyotaki
End Kiyotaki
Distance 40km (24.9 miles)
Type Adventure
Map goo.gl/SsNPx9

This ancient mountain has long been a historic trail for Buddhist pilgrims heading for Lake Chuzenji. But since the route was upgraded to a smooth and sweeping modern road, an altogether different kind of pilgrim has been arriving – motoring fans with modified muscle cars. In recent times, they have been joined by 'drifters' – motor enthusiasts with ridiculously powerful cars, purpose built for continuous power sliding.

Driven properly, Irohazaka Winding Road is two roads, one up, one down, each with traffic that flows only in one direction (save for a small stretch). From the air, both halves of the journey look like giant squiggles, but it's the downward leg that's the more challenging, with hairpin bend after hairpin bend. There are 48 in total – each one assigned a letter from the Japanese alphabet – with hard banked cambers and white-painted apexes that seem to encourage spirited driving.

A rest stop at the top, the Akechidaira Plateau, has great views from the lookout, especially in autumn when the trees are a patchwork of colours. And there's a second pull-off on the way down, by the waters of Lake Chuzenji.

The best time to drive Irohazaka Winding Road is at the crack of dawn, before the tourists arrive in number, or just before sunset, when the drifters' sideways antics begin. DK

❶ Kegon Falls, a beauty spot just off the road.
❷ The serpentine course of the Irohazaka.

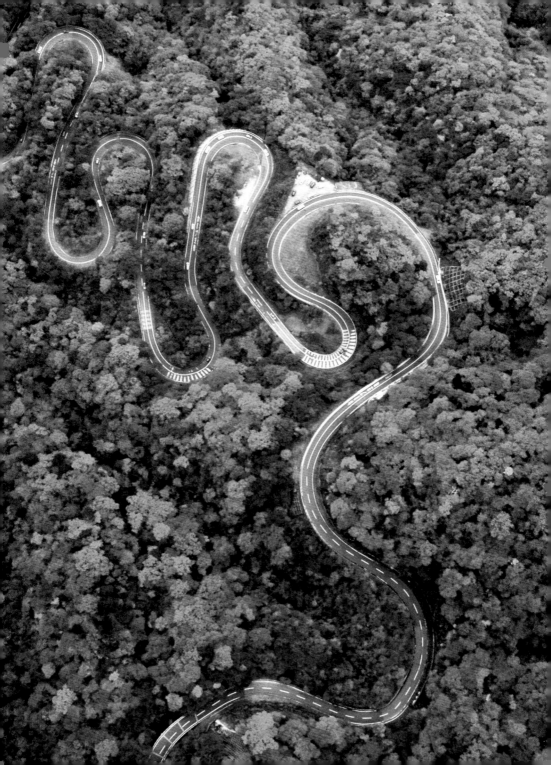

Norikura Skyline Road
Chūbu, Japan

Start Matsumoto, Nagano
End Mt Norikura, Gifu/Nagano
Distance 62km (38.5 miles)
Type Adventure
Map goo.gl/KZ3NBP

This purpose-built expressway to Mt Norikura has the distinction of being the highest road in Japan. It is so high, in fact, that the last sections soar above the clouds. Its construction is considered an engineering marvel.

Just getting to the start of the Skyline takes a bit of doing. From Matsumoto (with its must-see 16th-century castle), it's initially quite an innocuous ride. But stay on the 158 (don't take the alternative Abo Toll Road) and you will soon embark on a hill climb with fifteen tight switchbacks and some superlative views. Halfway up the hill, there is a tempting diversion – an inn with a natural hot spring baths *(onsen)*.

Past here, you arrive at the start of the Skyline Road (open May to October). Motorized access is limited these days, because of the sheer number of people who come to climb Mt Norikura, so you may have to park at Hirayukan-Takeyama Station and take a coach or taxi for the last bit. Either way, the ride is amazing. At the top, you will be nearly 2,700m (9,000ft) above sea level – high enough to notice the shortage of oxygen. On the way, you will probably pass many struggling cyclists, who love the challenge of this gruelling climb. Better, perhaps, to conserve your energy for the 40-minute hike to the summit, which begins at the end of the road. **DK**

Japan's Romance Road
Chūbu, Japan

Start Ueda City
End Utsunomiya City
Distance 274km (170 miles)
Type Culture
Info goo.gl/iFdAP5

Japan's Romance Road may be a marketing concept but it certainly captures the essence of Japan. Linking selected regional and national roads, it starts in Ueda City, northwest of Tokyo, and heads east, crossing the mountains of landlocked Gunma Prefecture, to Utsunomiya City, renowned for its early-blossoming strain of cherry trees. This is a journey through traditional Japan, a land of *onsen* (hot springs), feudal castles, active volcanoes and centuries-old *ryokan* (inns). It also takes in the UNESCO World Heritage Site of Nikko, home to Japan's most lavishly decorated shrine, and the chic mountain resort town of Karuizawa, once a favourite escape for John Lennon and Yoko Ono.

Often overlooked by foreigners, the route is largely unspoiled by development. Main streets seem frozen in time. One 48-km- (30-mile) long stretch skirts the base of Mt Asama, which is Honshu's most active volcano. It then stops at Onioshidashi Park near Karuizawa for the best views of the summit.

October is the best time to come here, not just because summers can be too hot but because autumn drenches the hills and valleys with gorgeous colour. And while you can drive it in a day, why not take three or more, hopping between *onsen* such as Kusatsu and Shima, which will slow you down in more ways than one. **BDS**

Tateyama Kurobe Alpine Highway
Chūbu, Japan

Start Bijodaira Station, Toyama
End Murodo Station, Toyama (or Omachi, Nagano)
Distance 31km (19 miles)
Type Adventure
Info goo.gl/9YBBPL

This has got to be one of the weirdest road trips you can do. High up in the Alps, it is the second-highest public road in Japan (after the Norikura Skyline), and accessible for only three months of the year because of snow. Even in high summer, the accessible sections require you to drive a 'corridor' through the snow. The walls of this corridor are typically over 15m (50ft) high, so scenic views are pretty much out of the question. It's not unlike being in a giant bobsleigh run, only going the wrong way (up instead of down).

However, the peculiarities don't stop there. If you choose the chauffeur-driven coach option, you can continue beyond Murodo Station, the terminus of this section of the road, and get to Omachi on the other side of the mountain. It's not a long journey but it is certainly a spectacular one, involving several changes of transportation. You take a trolley-bus through a long tunnel, then a short funicular, and then a cable car across a valley. After a 500-m- (500-yard) long hike around the shores of the isolated Lake Kuroyon, there's another ride through a tunnel on a trolley-bus, then it's back on a different coach for the stretch to Omachi. It's a bizarre and rather fragmented adventure, but absolutely worth it – not least for views of the Tateyama Mountains, glorious at any time of year but particularly spectacular in autumn. **DK**

❶ The road is cleared in winter, but drivers will see little other than show.

Akashi Kaikyo Bridge

Kansai, Japan

Start Sumaura Park, Honshu
End Iwaya, Awaji
Distance 30km (18.6 miles)
Type Culture
Map goo.gl/VHYida

❶ The bridge is one of the tallest in the world, as well as one of the longest.

The Akashi Strait between the main Japanese island of Honshu and its small southern neighbour, Awaji Island, was once one of the busiest and most dangerous stretches of water in the world. It is often prone to severe storms: two ferries sank here in 1955, killing 168 people. There had to be a safer way to cross the Strait.

A six-lane road bridge officially opened on 5 April 1998. Everything about Akashi Kaikyo Bridge was massive: Its central span, at 1,991m (6,532ft), is the longest span of any suspension bridge in the world, while each of the two outer spans are 960m (3,150ft). Overall, the bridge is 3.9km (2.4 miles) long.

The bridge is also in an active earthquake zone, and during its construction, the Great Hanshin earthquake in January 1995 pushed the two towers – the only parts of the bridge then in place – farther apart by 1m (1 yard), necessitating a longer span than originally planned. Severe gales mean that the bridge can withstand winds of up to 286 kph (178 mkph), while allowance has been made for the bridge to expand because of heat by up to 2m (6.6ft) a day.

For the best views of the bridge, start at Sumaura Park and drive along the coast before looping onto the bridge itself. It may be short, but this is one seriously impressive road trip. **SA**

Eshima Ohashi Bridge
Chugoku, Japan

Start Matsue, Shimane
End Sakaiminato, Tottori
Distance 1.8km (1.1 miles)
Type Adventure
Map goo.gl/frdWku

This one is more a motoring experience than a road trip. Even so, it's quite a thing. Simply to say that it is the world's third-largest rigid frame bridge doesn't do it justice.

The bridge takes vehicles from Matsue to Sakaiminato across Nakaumi Lake. The problem for the engineers was that they had to work within strict parameters: the span needed to be very high, to accommodate the passage of large cargo boats, but it also had to be short. The result looks rather like a giant roller coaster.

The bridge took nearly seven years to build. Since it opened in 2004, it has gained a certain notoriety, and is frequently voted Japan's Most Terrifying Bridge. In photographs, which regularly do the rounds on social media, it looks as though vehicles are climbing a near-vertical slope to the summit. Even if you take into account the foreshortening effects of a long lens, the ramps are certainly steep at 6.1 per cent on the Matsue side, and 5.1 per cent on the Sakaiminato side, gradients that are highly unusual for a modern bridge.

If you do take the trouble to visit this part of southwest Japan just to drive the Eshima Ohashi Bridge, be sure to drive it both ways to get the most from your efforts, though it's probably sensible to avoid the rush hour if you are nervous of doing a hill start. **DK**

❶ Once you've started, there's no going back on the Eshima Ohashi Bridge.

Mt Aso Kyushu, Japan

Start Kokonoe, Oita   **End** Aso Shinto Shrine, Kumamoto   **Distance** 137km (85 miles)
Type Culture   **Map** goo.gl/QzFBen

A bucket-list road trip for any budding vulcanologist, this single-day tour ascends Japan's most active volcano on the subtropical island of Kyushu.

Coming from Kokonoe, the tortuous Yamanami Highway leads south through the Kuju Plateau before arriving at the upper edge of an ancient caldera, an almost perfect circular ridge created by an enormous volcanic explosion 90,000 years ago. Inside the caldera, there is a patchwork of rice fields and the smouldering vents of five newer volcanoes. From here, traverse the upper edge southwest along the scenic Aso Skyline and Milk Road (so called because of the cattle that graze its slopes). Don't miss the amazing Road of Laputa near here;

also known as The Castle in the Sky, it's a short but magical detour that inspired a famous animated film by Studio Ghibli.

Once through the hairpin bends and into Akamizu town, head east between the paddy fields and on to Highway 111, known as the Aso Panorama, which loops around the volcanic cones toward Mt Aso. For a small fee, a toll road takes you to the crater's edge, which often billows with sulfurous steam. When you can stand the stench no longer, head north to the Aso Shinto Shrine to complete your cultural education. **DIS**

❶ The magical Mt Aso.

Route 13 Luang Namtha to Ventiane, Laos

Start Boten, Luang Namtha   **End** Vientiane, Vientiane   **Distance** 628km (390 miles)
Type Adventure   **Map** goo.gl/WS5Zh2

From the Chinese border to the 'City of the Moon' (the capital Vientiane) via the ancient city of Luang Prabang, Route 13 is the most important road in Laos. In addition to being the busiest route, it charts key points in the country's history – its links with China, its spiritual and cultural roots and its hopes for the future. The busiest part of this main artery, and the richest in terms of attractions, is between Luang Prabang and Vientiane. Luang Prabang, the royal capital and former seat of government, literally means 'Royal Buddha Image' and it bristles with Buddhist monasteries and temples. It is a UNESCO World Heritage Site, listed for its architectural, religious and cultural heritage.

From Luang Prabang, Route 13 continues to Vientiane, 340km (211 miles) south, a meandering journey through sleepy villages and bustling towns. While the road between the two cities is paved, it is in a poor state, and narrow with sharp bends. There are no markings or lights on the road, and people and livestock are constant hazards.

Vientiane is close to the border with Thailand, where you can pick up Highway 2 straight down to Bangkok. Alternatively Route 13 heads east, picking up the course of the Mekong River to the border with Cambodia. **SA**

❶ The Laos town of Pakse on Route 13.

Ho Chi Minh Trail
Red River Delta, Vietnam

Start Hanoi
End Ho Chi Minh City
Distance 1,609km (1,000 miles)
Type Culture
Info goo.gl/7QaHNk

The Ho Chi Minh Trail was North Vietnam's notorious route for supplying its troops and South Vietnamese allies during the Vietnam War. It was a low-tech masterpiece combining hidden paths and tunnels through the jungles of Laos, Cambodia and Vietnam. The total network comprised many parallel trails covering a total of 120,000km (12,500 miles). The trail was a major feat of military engineering that helped win the war for North Vietnam. At its most developed, trucks could drive for hundreds of miles hidden under tree canopies, while bridges were partially submerged to be invisible to American bombers.

Much of the original trail has been reclaimed by jungle, especially through Laos and Cambodia. Vietnam's government created a paved alternative for tourists: Ho Chi Minh National Highway from Hanoi to Ho Chi Minh City (the former Saigon). Many intrepid bikers want to follow a more authentic route, but for that it's best to take a local guide – there is no HCM Trail map to follow and your route will depend on the weather.

What you will see is a side to Southeast Asia that has changed little since the 1960s – wooden houses on stilts surrounded by paddy fields and forested mountains wreathed in mist. Beware of any odd metal items you find, though – the route is still peppered with unexploded bombs. **SH**

Nha Trang to Qui Nhon
South Central Coast, Vietnam

Start Nha Trang
End Qui Nhon
Distance 222km (138 miles)
Type Scenic
Map goo.gl/V5cwSf

Most guidebooks give the impression that the best way to travel between these two seaside towns is on the Reunification Express, the train that links Ho Chi Minh City with Hanoi. But unlike the railway, this road hugs the coast nearly all the way, giving the traveller easy access to some of the best beaches on the South China Sea.

The resorts have all been developed, mainly with Western and Japanese tourists in mind, but building work is less obtrusive than in many late-20th-century developments. Nha Trang, for example, caters for holidaymakers on all budgets without compromising its historical heritage. Consequently visitors can combine sun worship, diving and snorkelling with tours of 13th-century towers and temples of the Hindu Cham people. The Lonely Planet guidebook describes the town as 'brazen and brash', but it still has soul.

The northern end of the journey, Qui Nhon, was originally a fishing village. It has grown into a holiday resort, but it has enough of its traditional character to be distinctively Vietnamese rather than one of those beach resorts that could be anywhere between the Tropics. One word of caution, however: the approach roads are in a terrible state, with one travel blogger describing them as 'not so much a road as a pile of rubble'. Leave plenty of time for your journey. **JP**

Ho Chi Minh City to the DMZ
Southeast Region to North Central Coast, Vietnam

Start Ho Chi Minh City, Southeast Region
End Ben Hai River, North Central Coast
Distance 1,044km (649 miles)
Type Culture
Map goo.gl/B3saic

This journey from Ho Chi Minh City, known until 1976 as Saigon, to the former demilitarized zone (DMZ), the buffer that divided US-backed South Vietnam from Communist North Vietnam during the Vietnam War, is a fascinating way to contextualize that conflict. What was once a dirt track through a bomb alley is now the well-maintained Highway 1. The first two-thirds of this journey show few vestiges of the war, and anyone who cares to cross-reference the villages and valleys with the same locations during the conflict cannot fail to be impressed by Vietnam's recovery.

Once a US air base, the city of Da Nang, south of the horseshoe bay that bears its name, is now better known for thousand-year-old artefacts of the Hindu Cham people and the Buddhist shrines in the Marble Mountains south of town. Hue on the Huong (Perfume River), 100km (60 miles) north of Da Nang and 8km (5 miles) inland from the South China Sea, took a terrible battering during North Vietnam's 1968 Tet Offensive: the historic buildings of the imperial citadel, reduced to rubble during the battle, have been triumphantly restored.

The trip ends on the banks of the Ben Hai River at the Hien Luong Bridge. Damaged by US bombs in 1967 but preserved as a war memorial, the crossing is known as the Peace Bridge; Highway 1 crosses the river over a new structure nearby. **JP**

❶ The Imperial City walled palace within the citadel of the city of Hue, the former capital of Vietnam.

Ocean Cloud Pass Mekong River Delta, Vietnam

Start An Cu   End North of Da Nang   Distance 24km (14.9 miles)
Type Adventure   Map goo.gl/GhBezl

The Deo Hai Van (Ocean Cloud Pass) was a section of the old Highway 1 between Hanoi and Ho Chi Minh City (formerly Saigon). It has now been bypassed by a new main road and tunnel, but remains a big attraction for thrillseekers and sightseers. Jeremy Clarkson of BBC television's *Top Gear* called the road 'a deserted ribbon of perfection'. Cars can make this trip, but it's best undertaken on motorbikes.

The road rises quickly from the holiday resorts near An Cu to a maximum height of 496m (1,627ft) in the Annamite Range. The summit is often fogbound, but on clear days the view back down to the South China Sea is superb.

The road runs along what has always been a boundary: in ancient times, between two kingdoms (the Buddhist Dai Viet to the north and the Hindu Champa to the south), and now between two climatic zones (the wet and cool north and the warm and dry south).

There are many memorials to the victims of battles fought along this old frontier and to people killed in road accidents – mostly before the opening of the bypass. At the summit, local tradesmen have snack and souvenir outlets; buy from the ones who hassle the least. **JP**

❶ View of Ocean Cloud Pass.

Angkor Wat Tuk Tuk Tour Siem Reap, Cambodia

Start Siem Reap **End** Kbal Spean River **Distance** 54km (33.5 miles)
Type Culture **Map** goo.gl/ko852K

In the 1970s, the Khmer Rouge led by Pol Pot murdered more than 1.5 million Cambodians and reduced the country to famine. But Cambodia eventually rose from the ashes and has since opened up to tourism. People from across the globe come to see its immense cultural wealth, including Angkor Wat, an ancient temple complex north of the town of Siem Reap.

You can take a tour of Angkor Wat on a tuk tuk, a kind of motorized rickshaw, starting at Siem Reap. You'll need to negotiate a price with the driver. The road north towards the temples is straight and flat and the tuk tuk lets you soak in the atmosphere while also keeping cool in the breeze.

Drivers will give you time to explore each temple before taking you on to the next. Highlights include the pyramid temple at Pre Rup, built in 961, and Prasat Phnom Bok, a mountain temple from even earlier. There's also the pink-hued 'women's temple' at Banteay Srei. For a little extra money, ask your driver to take you on to Kbal Spean River to see the Hindu deities carved into the rock face.

Tuk tuks are a relatively safe way to travel. Partly thanks to the booming tourism industry, Cambodia is developing rapidly, so take advantage of this special form of transport before it disappears. JI

❶ The temple complex of Angkor Wat.

Lost Temples Motorcycle Tour
Phnom Penh, Cambodia

Start Phnom Penh
End Phnom Penh
Distance 1,012km (629 miles)
Type Adventure
Info goo.gl/eGKCDD

Most people who visit Cambodia make the trip to the world-famous 12th-century temple complex of Angkor Wat. It's a place that's on everybody's to-do list. Many join a guided minibus tour from Phnom Penh, heading out of the capital in an air-conditioned bubble.

Better perhaps to travel the way the locals do, see the country as they do and visit some off-the-beaten track historical sites. That's what this road trip is about. It's a guided motorcycle odyssey, on either a touring or an off-road bike, running the length of the country, from the capital in the south to the northern border with Thailand. Luggage is carried separately.

The route begins along the Mekong Delta, travels broken tarmac, gravel backroads and sandy tracks through remote jungle villages and wildlife sanctuaries, and ends with a ferry crossing of the Tonlé Sap Lake. You won't miss out the blockbuster sight of Angkor Wat, the largest temple complex anywhere in the world, but you will also see the Khmer Empire ruins of Preah Vihear Temple, only properly accessible since 2003, and the remote jungle archaeological site of Koh Ker, capital of the Khmer empire between 928 and 944. Koh Ker has only been reachable since 2004 and is still yielding major archaeological discoveries. The trip is a blast and one for the memory bank. **DK**

❶ Experience the soul of Cambodia by getting off the beaten track.

The Pan-Philippines Highway
Ilocos, Philippines

Start Patapat Viaduct, Luzon
End Pagudpud, Luzon
Distance 12km (7.5 miles)
Type Scenic
Map goo.gl/V1QwLX

The Pan-Philippines Highway – also known as the Maharlika (Nobility) Highway – runs north–south through the main islands of the group for 3,517km (2,185 miles), forming the nation's longest single driving route. If you can't do it all, try this short section at its very northern extreme – it's a scenic treat whether you're travelling by car or by bike.

You'll be starting on one of the most impressive pieces of road in the Philippines: the Patapat Viaduct. The two-lane highway snakes around the contours of the coastline for miles here, and for much of it the highway is raised up from the shore on 30-m- (100-ft) high concrete columns. On one side is the Pacific Ocean, on the other is a steep mountain cliff covered with lush rainforest.

From here you'll proceed into the Cordillera Mountains, twisting through a jungle of thick, exotic vegetation on either side of the road. Occasionally there are gaps in the greenery, through which you may glimpse the wonderful views across the north of Luzon Island.

Eventually the highway winds down the other side of the Cordillera into the popular resort of Pagudpud on the South China Sea. Pick your way through a few little leafy streets here to find a fabulous west-facing sandy beach backed by tall palms sheltering rows of brightly painted local fishing boats. **SH**

❶ Part of the elevated coastal section of the Pan-Philippines Highway.

Kennon Road
Ilocos/Cordillera, Philippines

Start Rosario, La Union, Ilocos, Luzon
End Baguio, Benguet, Cordillera, Luzon
Distance 37km (23 miles)
Type Adventure
Map goo.gl/w9RpLB

Originally called the Benguet Road, the route connecting Rosario on the coastal plains with Baguio in the mountains of northern Luzon was renamed in honour of its builder, Colonel Lyman Walter Vere Kennon of the US Army Corps of Engineers. Kennon and his men completed its construction in 1905. More than 2,300 local and foreign workers from 36 countries laboured on the road, many of whom died of malaria or plunged to their deaths during the course of the work.

The highway is a toll road, but the charges are not high. From Rosario, the road rises gently alongside the Bued River Canyon, affording wonderful views of the mountains and their lush vegetation on either side. As the road approaches Baguio, its course steepens and it weaves through numerous switchbacks and other tight corners. The hairpin bends were built in a similar fashion to the rice terraces that run along the local mountainsides, creating a harmonious blending of nature and human infrastructure.

The road ends in Baguio, a bustling place some 1,540m (5,050ft) above sea level and known as the summer capital of the Philippines on account of its cooler, more comfortable climate. Be aware that the Kennon Road is best avoided during the rainy season, when sections flood and accidents and landslides are common. **SA**

Halsema Highway
Cordillera, Philippines

Start Baguio, Luzon
End Bontoc, Luzon
Distance 154km (96 miles)
Type Scenic
Map goo.gl/GHNJaO

On a sunny day, the Halsema Highway, winding along the terraced slopes of the Cordillera Central Mountains in the heart of Luzon Island, feels like one of the world's great road trips. The scenery is thrilling: vast green canyons, hillside villages set in an emerald patchwork of tiny fields and mountains covered in carpets of lush rainforest disappearing into the heat haze.

On a wet day, your impression might be different. During and after the frequent downpours that occur here, the road transforms into a perilous slalom, all views blocked by rain and cloud. Under these conditions, it justifies its place on the list of the world's most dangerous, not scenic, roads. While the two-lane tarmac road is smooth and well signposted, and mostly has sturdy stone guard walls on its huge drops, the very steep, twisting highway quickly becomes flooded or obstructed by landslides of rock or mud.

This is an important route, so traffic continues regardless. Lorries and buses crawl over piles of mud and dodge crumbling road edges. Add in the tropical fogs that can strike the Philippines' highest highway and you have the recipe for a very challenging journey.

However, on the right day, in the right conditions, you will experience the road trip of a lifetime – in a good way. **SH**

Commonwealth Avenue – The Killer Highway

Metro Manila, Philippines

Start Quezon Memorial Circle, Quezon City, Luzon
End Quirino Highway, Quezon City, Luzon
Distance 14km (9 miles)
Type Adventure
Map goo.gl/XuaMNN

This book features many incredibly dangerous roads – up steep Alpine passes, along narrow canyons, across polar wasteland and volcanoes and through deep jungle and arid deserts. So you may be a little surprised to discover that, according to official statistics, the world's most dangerous road is actually bang in the middle of a capital city.

Commonwealth Avenue curves through the heart of Quezon City, the capital and biggest city in the Philippines. It forms part of the R7 ring road and is a vital daily route for hundreds of thousands of workers.

Yet the local police and media call this 14-km-(9-mile) long stretch "The Killer Highway." The problem stems from the heavy and chaotic traffic conditions. Buses, trucks, cars, motorbikes and cycles weave from lane to lane as more traffic floods in from side streets. Buses stop anywhere to collect or drop passengers, and pedestrians wander around the roadway, too. There are no traffic controls and the huge road varies in width from six lanes to an incredible 18 lanes.

In addition, Commonwealth Avenue has no streetlights, road signs or drainage, causing frequent floods and the risk of skidding. How bad is it? Official figures show that there are more than 900 casualties in traffic accidents on this short length of highway every year. Take care. **SH**

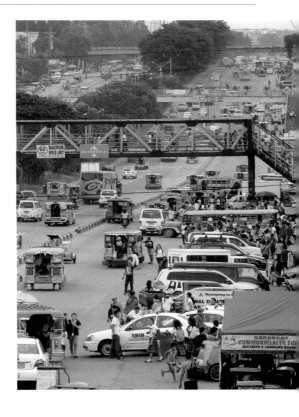

❶ Commonwealth Avenue defies the usual rules and conventions governing city highways.

Journey to Penang
East Coast, Malaysia

Start Cameron Highlands
End Penang
Distance 264km (164 miles)
Type Scenic
Info goo.gl/ONhQy

This journey from the tea plantations of the cool, damp Cameron Highlands to the island city of Penang has plenty of wayside attractions, but three stand out above all.

Kuala Kangsar is the site where Malaysia's first rubber tree was planted in the late 19th century; the nation soon became, and remains, the largest rubber producer in the world. This city's finest buildings are the Istana Iskandariah (the official residence of the Sultan of Perak, an Art Deco masterpiece) and the Ubudiah Mosque.

Taiping is the wettest place in Peninsula Malaysia, and as a consequence its public garden is a showcase for a vast array of exotic trees and plants; also worthy of a visit is the tulip farm on Bukit Larut, the nearby hill station.

Kolam Bukit Merah is the largest freshwater lake in Malaysia. There is a tourist resort here, but plenty of the rest of the area is an unspoiled habitat for a wide range of animals, plants, and birds.

Penang Island is small and round with a mountainous interior – it rises sharply from sea level to 740m (2,428ft). Its sheltered harbour at George Town has long been one of the most important ports in Asia; Batu Ferringhi on its north coast is a major global tourist destination. **JP**

● A tea plantation in the Cameron Highlands.

Kuala Lumpur to Belum Forest
Central Region, Malaysia

Start Kuala Lumpur
End Belum Forest Resort
Distance 467km (290 miles)
Type Scenic
Map goo.gl/47GugB

The greater part of this journey is along the modern six-lane North–South Expressway, which, once you get away from the metropolitan suburbs, has little traffic and plenty of fascinating scenery. Take a breather on the long haul north at the famous Cameron Highlands with its picturesque tea plantations, butterfly farms and rolling green hills. Beyond Ipoh, take the Kuala Kangsar exit towards Gerik and then join the East–West Expressway to Pulau Banding.

The final destination lies in the heart of the biggest rainforest in the Malay Peninsula and the oldest in the world, pre-dating the two largest – in the Amazon and the Congo – by millions of years. Temenggor, the lake on which Banding stands, was created by the damming of the Perak River for hydroelectricity, but the water is also good for wildlife and the island has places where humans can observe nature up close without damaging or disrupting it.

The biggest attractions are elephants and tigers: There is no guarantee of spotting either of these, but the best chances are from viewing huts concealed around the mineral deposits which the animals come to lick. The forest is also great for botanists and ornithologists – among the birds that may appear here between August and October are ten species of hornbill. **JP**

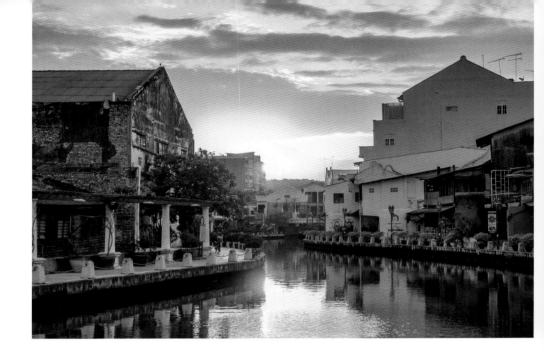

West Coast Route 5 Southern Region, Malaysia

Start Johor Bahru   End Malacca   Distance 225km (140 miles)
Type Scenic   Map goo.gl/THoLb4

Johor Bahru has much to recommend it apart from its colonial-period buildings: a rich cultural life featuring numerous museums and concert halls with programmes of international appeal. But so lovely is the tropical scenery on the main road to Kuala Lumpur – the North–South Expressway, a multi-lane highway that runs parallel to the coast of the Malacca Strait – that tourists may soon forget all about the city from which they started out.

The major settlement en route is Batu Pahat, about 100km (62 miles) from the start. This is a cosmopolitan town on a lethargic-looking river of the same name; the wealth of the inhabitants is founded on fishing and textile manufacture.

The main attraction is 54km (33 miles) farther north at Muar. This handsome place is one of Malaysia's most popular tourist destinations, especially gastronomes and connoisseurs of coffee, which is said to be better here than in South America.

With the rise of Singapore, Malacca lost much of its strategic and commercial significance, but it remains important for the export of rubber produced in the Malaysian hinterland. The harbour still bustles, but the downtown is a tranquil mix of Chinese culture with 18th- and 19th-century buildings in Dutch and Portuguese styles. JP

❶ Sunrise in Malacca.

Johor Bahru to Desaru Southern Region, Malaysia

Start Johor Bahru   **End** Desaru   **Distance** 77km (48 miles)
Type Scenic   **Map** goo.gl/CRx9vk

This road trip offers an attractive introduction to the southern tip of Peninsula Malaysia on the shores of the South China Sea.

Among the architectural highlights of the starting point, Johor Bahru, are the Istana Besar (Big Palace), the Bukit Serene Palace (the sultan's residence) and Abu Bakr Mosque.

The city is also the gateway to, and in many respects a satellite of, Singapore, which is less than a mile away across the Johor Strait. However, instead of crossing the causeway to the island republic, this route follows a four-lane highway eastwards along the coast. After the industrial town of Pasir Gudang, the Johor Strait, until now out of

sight on the right of the highway, curves inwards at the mouth of the Johor River, which motor vehicles cross on a cable-stayed bridge with a span of 1.7km (just over 1 mile).

On the eastern side of the river, the road crosses a plain and goes through the town of Bandar Penawar before reaching Desaru. This is a beach resort that during the 1980s was at risk of being ruined by unsightly tourist development, but subsequent economic recessions have restricted the architectural excesses and the place is now more of a hangout for locals than for foreign tourists. **JP**

❶ Mature oil palm trees line parts of the route.

Bintulu to Miri Sarawak, Malaysia

Start Bintulu   End Miri   Distance 203km (126 miles)
Type Scenic   Map goo.gl/3qeqCm

This interesting route along the South China Sea coast on the Malaysian part of the island of Sarawak combines nature and industry in almost equal measure. It begins at Bintulu, which is no great beauty, but of major industrial importance as a base for offshore oil and natural gas extraction.

The northern end of the road trip also owes its existence to the petroleum business: Miri was founded in 1910, when Royal Dutch Shell began drilling nearby. Over the following century, the place grew from a group of huts into a vast industrial center; it was granted city status in its centenary year.

The road from Bintulu to Miri runs between the sea on the left and dense rainforest on the right. The most commonly recurring sights in the countryside are longhouses on stilts and palm-oil plantations. There is also evidence of logging, one of Malaysia's most controversial economic activities.

Miri is a good base for exploring the six nearby national parks. The most popular of these is Gunung Mulu, which is set in heavily forested limestone terrain and has an extensive network of caves including, in the Gua Nasib Bagus complex, the largest in the world, the Sarawak Chamber, which is 700m (2,300ft) long, 396m (1,300ft) wide and nowhere less than 70m (230ft) high. **JP**

❶ An oil-palm estate on Sarawak.

Kelok Sembilan West Sumatra, Indonesia

Start Payakumbuh   **End** Harau   **Distance** 16km (10 miles)
Type Scenic   **Map** goo.gl/3TnEqt

Just north of the city of Payakumbuh, on the way to Harau, on the Indonesian island of Sumatra, there is a sensational piece of modern road – the Kelok Sembilan. The highway replaced an old Dutch colonial road of hard-core hairpin bends through a steep gorge. They say the smooth new road has chopped four hours off the journey time.

It's hard to follow the logic of the mysterious triple-S-bends and six bridges on stilts in the middle section of the gorge. Even passengers look puzzled to have entered one end of the gorge and emerged minutes later at the other.

The complex is such an extraordinarily intricate system of loops, bridges and overpasses that this remote spot in the jungle has become a tourist attraction. Visitors congregate at the top of the canyon to watch the traffic passing through the surreal array of roads. Entrepreneurial locals have set up food stalls to cater to the crowds.

Bikers and car drivers seem to enjoy flying through the 2.5-km- (1.5-mile) long stretch of swirling tarmac. Locals have dubbed the spot 'Kelok Nine' after the number of major bends. For some, this wonderful little stretch is an optical illusion; for others it's the realization of a road-builder's phantasmagoric dream. **SH**

❶ The intricate Kelok Sembilan in Sumatra.

Kintamani Coast-to-Crater Mountain Road
Bali, Indonesia

Start Singaraja City
End Mt Batur crater rim, Kintamani
Distance 55km (34 miles)
Type Scenic
Map goo.gl/mszLbi

This is rated the best biking route on the island of Bali, and it's pretty good for car drivers, too. You'll start up on the north coast at the second-largest city, Singaraja. It's worth exploring the old Dutch colonial waterfront and tree-lined streets here before setting off to the east.

Follow the busy coast road for a few miles, and then turn inland on the much quieter Jalan Gunung Batur. This wonderful road winds up towards Mt Batur through typical bustling villages spilling across the road in all directions. You'll interrupt boys playing football, pass roadside shrines and travel through the middle of clove plantations.

Each ridge seems to bring another great view across a rainforest valley with colourful houses perched at precarious angles. Every so often you'll be able to stop and catch glimpses back down to the coast.

Eventually the road twists into a pine forest and passes the important temple of Puri Penulisan, the highest on the island. You can see inside but there's a small charge for entering.

Follow the road around the rim of the volcanic crater for 7km (4.5 miles) to reach Kintamani's temple and market, from where there are amazing views right across the crater and its lake. You might not want to stay here too long, though: the volcano last erupted quite recently, in 2000. **SH**

❶ Mt Batur, the end point of this road trip, standing in splendid isolation.

Amed to Amlapura East Coast Road
Bali, Indonesia

Start Amed
End Amlapura
Distance 39km (24 miles)
Type Adventure
Map goo.gl/BoOZLo

Here's a chance to experience a colourful slice of Balinese life while taking in some of the island's finest coastal scenery. This road trip on the East Coast Road leads to Bali's eastern tip, passing through busy villages and lush jungle.

The route starts at Amed, where divers come to explore an exceptionally varied underwater landscape complete with an ancient shipwreck. The other industry here is fishing, and traditional fishing boats called *jukung* line the shore. Leaving Amed, the narrow tarmac road overflows with overladen mopeds and rickety minibuses, but the traffic eventually thins out. As the road curves around the eastern shore, it rises high above the sea, providing outstanding views of the coastline through the trees. In places, there is little between you and a long drop; thankfully, there are safety barriers on the sharpest bends.

You'll pass scores of roadside stalls selling everything from colourful shells to bottles of Bintang beer. Look out for the little island of Gili Selang; it is part of an underwater volcano and another popular dive site. Weave farther around the coast to finish in Amlapura, the biggest place in eastern Bali. The must-see sights here are the town's three former royal palaces. Their opulence reflects a time when this region was a separate kingdom from the rest of Bali. **SH**

❶ Bali's sinuous shoreline, backed by jungle and lined with fishing boats.

Oceania

⊖ Explore the Australian Outback
via the Stuart Highway.

Kokoda Track Access Road
NCD, Papua New Guinea

Start Sogeri, National Capital District
End Kokoda Track, National Capital District
Distance 21km (13 miles)
Type Adventure
Map goo.gl/SF1IyB

In the 1890s, European miners carved out a track in the Papuan forests to access the Yodda Kokoda goldfields on the far side of the Owen Stanley Range. The old track saw a different type of action in July 1942 during World War II, when invading Japanese troops landed on the north coast of New Guinea and attempted to march south across the island to seize Port Moresby in Papua. Their intention was to isolate Australia from its US allies. The two sides fought a series of battles on the old Kokoda Track, before the Japanese were forced to withdraw in November 1942.

The old track is now a recognized walking trail of some 96km (60 miles), accessed by a gravel road at its southern end. The road from Port Moresby heads north and then east, and then about 1.6km (1 mile) after Sogeri a gravel track heads off to the left. The road is easily drivable in clement weather, but can quickly become impassable after rain, so check the local weather forecast before setting out and come prepared.

Given the unpredictable conditions on the track it's best to opt for a 4x4, although the mud in the rainy season will defeat all but the most skilled off-road driver. The track finishes at the bank of the Goldie River, just before the start of the Kokoda Trail, at which point you must leave your vehicle behind and proceed on foot. SA

Boranup Drive
Western Australia, Australia

Start Boranup
End Boranup Campground
Distance 18km (11 miles)
Type Scenic
Map goo.gl/qBJXdL

Boranup Drive in Western Australia offers the chance to get off the beaten track without the need for a 4x4. It winds through the majestic Boranup Karri Forest to the Boranup Campground in Western Australia's Margaret River region.

Beneath your wheels is a track of rich, red dirt; everywhere else are the pale, straight trunks of giant karri trees, which can grow up to 50m (165ft) in height, and a rich understory of shrubs, ferns, wildflowers and fungi. The canopy above is lush and green, and stretches from Caves Road to the coast in the west.

This is a gentle drive – although you wouldn't want to pick a fight with one of those karri trees – and, apart from the occasional rut or fallen branch, the road surface is generally smooth and flat. You may have to move over to make way for oncoming vehicles, but that's no problem. Two-wheel-drive cars can easily manage the route, and it's open all year round.

For that one final photo, take the short detour up to Boranup Lookout to get a fabulous panorama over the forest and the deceptively tranquil wreck-strewn waters of Hamelin Bay in the west. The lookout is also the starting point for bushwalks through the forest. JI

● The road through Boranup Karri Forest.

Caves Road
Western Australia, Australia

● Jewel Cave outside Augusta has some of the world's finest and most easily accessible stalactites.

Start Cape Naturaliste
End Cape Leeuwin
Distance 122km (76 miles)
Type Scenic
Map goo.gl/NvqpXt

This route between two lighthouses links the southwesternmost headlands on the Australian mainland, near the point at which the Indian Ocean becomes the Southern Ocean. It passes through the Leeuwin–Naturaliste National Park, which has more visitors than any other park in Australia.

You won't see the sea from the main road, but that's no hardship because the way is lined with natural beauties of many kinds: eucalyptus forests; parrots, emus, possums, kangaroos and wallabies; and, of course, the limestone caves for which the route is named. Not all of these caves are open to the public, but the pick of those that are lie south of Margaret River: the Calgardup, Moondyne, Giants and Lakes Caves are near Redgate; Jewel Cave is outside Augusta.

If the pull of the ocean becomes irresistible, it's never far away and easily accessible at several vantage points, including Bunker Bay (an expensive beach resort), Gracetown (with spectacular if not entirely stable cliffs and some of the best surf in the region) and Hamelin Bay, which is less sheltered than its name may make it sound and is notorious for shipwrecks.

The last stop before the southern terminus is the town of Augusta, at the mouth of the Blackwood River on Flinders Bay, where humpback whales come to feed during the southern winter. **JP**

Gibb River Road
Western Australia, Australia

Start Kununurra
End Derby
Distance 660km (410 miles)
Type Adventure
Info goo.gl/8douIW

Three times the size of England or Alabama, the Kimberley region in Australia's far northwest is a world of ancient red-rock mountain ranges, sandstone gorges and 350-million-year-old limestone reefs. There are scrub-filled savannahs and monumental river systems, fed during a monsoonal wet season that dumps more than 127cm (50in) of rainfall. This landscape of desert, shaded gullies and cascading waters was once unknown to all but its Aboriginal owners. Today, it is made accessible by the Gibb River Road.

Little more than a stock route as recently as the 1960s, the road is now graded with a surface that varies from smooth tarmac to loose gravel (it is graded every year at the conclusion of the wet season). You'll see plenty of RVs, but 4x4s are recommended. Good signage gives ample warning of hazards such as soft bulldust and creek and cattle crossings. Wilderness camps and lodges offer accommodations, as do cattle stations, which are the size of small countries.

The wonders you'll see on this road trip – such as Bell Creek Gorge, with its deep pools and cascades; freshwater crocodiles in Windjana Gorge, and 40,000-year-old Aboriginal rock paintings at Tunnel Creek – leave indelible impressions. This is a journey not just through a landscape, but back through time. **BDS**

Kalamunda Zig Zag
Western Australia, Australia

Start The top of Gooseberry Hill
End The bottom of Gooseberry Hill
Distance 2.9km (1.8 miles)
Type Adventure
Map goo.gl/ZRXOwM

Western Australia's Zig Zag Scenic Drive is a roller coaster. Dropping down the side of Gooseberry Hill National Park in the Darling Range east of Perth, it is less than 3km (2 miles) long, but the forest road repeatedly loops back on itself, creating a concertina of thrilling switchbacks.

The road was originally part of a railroad, built in the 1900s to carry timber down the hill to be cut and shaped into sleepers for the growing railroad network. The switching points, where the trains changed direction, give the route its name. Due to the steep and narrow nature of the road, it is one-way only (down) and there is a 40 kph (25 mph) speed limit throughout. To get to the start, take Gooseberry Hill Road.

From the top of the hill, you can look down on the city of Perth far below. As you head down the slope, through the eucalyptus trees, the scenery changes almost from bend to bend, with views over the coastal plain and Perth airport. Not that there are many opportunities to look around safely: the tarmac is narrow and some of the turns are extremely tight. There is some run-off in most places, but frightening drops in others.

At the beginning of October, there's a Zig Zag Festival. Celebrations include measuring the longest skid mark on the hill. At other times, the hill is a popular place for picnics. **JI**

Canning Stock Route Western Australia, Australia

Start Halls Creek, Kimberley   End Wiluna   Distance 1,851km (1,150 miles)
Type Adventure   Info goo.gl/qTbRKg

At the start of the 20th century, West Kimberley cattlemen held a monopoly over the local beef trade. As a way of breaking this stranglehold on free enterprise, the government of Western Australia proposed driving a new stock road through the region and appointed Alfred Canning to survey a likely route.

From 1908 to 1910, Canning and his men sank 48 wells along the route, a course of action that antagonized Aborigines in the area, who regarded the Europeans as trespassers. The first commercial droving began in 1910. Initially, the route was unpopular. Aborigines vandalized the wells and denied the drovers access to water.

For several years the route was neglected, but in 1931 the droves started again. Around 20 droves took place between then and 1959. Today the stock route is a popular but arduous trek along what is the longest historic stock route in the world.

The sensible choice for this road trip is a sturdy and well-equipped 4x4. The route will take anything from ten to twenty days to complete. Since there are only two small settlements where fuel and other supplies can be obtained, the drive requires careful planning and should be undertaken only during the cooler months. SA

🅞 A convoy on the Canning Stock Route.

Eyre Highway Western Australia/South Australia, Australia

Start Norseman, Western Australia   End Port Augusta, South Australia   Distance 1,658km (1,030 miles)
Type Adventure   Map goo.gl/P8NfaW

In 1840 to 1841, Edward John Eyre became the first European to cross the vast Nullarbor Plain, an arid expanse to the north of the Great Australian Bight. The modern highway that crosses the plain is named after him.

In 1874 to 1877, the first trail was made across the plain, to allow the construction of the East–West Telegraph line. Nothing more advanced was put in place until the threat of war in the Pacific in 1941 forced the federal government to construct a highway, albeit still a dirt track. This highway was not fully tarmacked until 1974.

The western end of the highway is notably flat and straight: between Balladonia and Caiguna, the road stretches for 146.6km (91.1 miles), forming the longest straight road in the country and the sixth longest in the world. You will notice 'piano keys' painted on the road: These mark the runways used by the Royal Flying Doctor Service.

Look out for camels, emus and kangaroos wandering on the road, especially at dawn and dusk. All of these can do great damage to your vehicle. The biggest hazards, however, are driver fatigue, lapses in concentration and the sheer remoteness of this demanding route across one of the driest parts of Australia. SA

❶ Straight through the bush of Western Australia.

Goldfields Tourist Way Western Australia, Australia

Start Coolgardie Camel Farm   **End** Kalgoorlie   **Distance** 45km (28 miles)
Type Culture   **Map** goo.gl/q6cVvB

In 1892, gold was discovered in Western Australia. Prospectors flooded in and new towns such as Coolgardie and Kalgoorlie sprang up to house and cater to the speculators. Few of these men made their fortune, and as the deposits dwindled the towns declined.

This industrial heritage has been marked by a Tourist Way, one of 28 scenic or historic drives mapped out by the government of Western Australia during the 1990s. The route, marked with white numbers on a brown shield, travels along the eastern end of the Great Eastern Highway, from Coolgardie Camel Farm, 4km (2.5 miles) west of Coolgardie, to Kalgoorlie. Coolgardie was once a major mining community, the third-largest town in the state after Perth and Fremantle. It was founded in 1892, and Kalgoorlie was founded a year later.

Midway along the route is the Kurrawang Emu Farm, which has carved emu eggs and Aboriginal artefacts on display. The route also coincides with the easternmost section of the Golden Pipeline Heritage Trail, from Perth to Kalgoorlie, alongside the Goldfields Water Supply Scheme pipeline, serving remote communities in Western Australia's Eastern Goldfields. This new trail was introduced in 2003 to celebrate the pipeline's centenary. **SA**

❶ Gwalia ghost town.

Cossack Tourist Way Western Australia, Australia

Start Dampier **End** Cossack **Distance** 85km (52.8 miles)
Type Culture **Map** goo.gl/OfaHQ4

Dampier, the starting point of this road trip, is an important port for petrochemical, natural gas and iron-ore exports. It was an island until 1963, when a new road and rail causeway was built to link it to the mainland. The adjacent Burrup Peninsula has Aboriginal monuments, including outstanding rock carvings that date from before the last Ice Age. The surrounding 42 island archipelago, rich in coral formations and sponges, is good for sightings of dugongs and whales.

The road out of town is largely flat and straight, through scrub on reddish-brown soil. The only settlement it passes through is Roebourne, which has filling stations and grocery stores.

Cossack, journey's end, was founded in the mid-19th century as a base for gold prospecting and pearl diving. It was named for HMS *Cossack*, the wooden corvette that brought the first European settlers. The vessel had been built by the British for the Russian Navy, but the outbreak of the Crimean War between the two nations stopped its delivery.

By 1900, workable gold deposits had been exhausted, and the pearl fishers had moved to the better harbour at Broome, 800km (500 miles) up the coast. Cossack is now a ghost town, whose buildings are much as they were during the good times. **JP**

❶ Where mining has given way to tourism.

Uluru to Kings Canyon Northern Territory, Australia

Start Ayers Rock   **End** Kings Canyon   **Distance** 310km (193 miles)
Type Scenic   **Info** goo.gl/OdZFKC

Uluru, also known as Ayers Rock, is the most famous natural landmark in Australia. This impressive and isolated monolith lies in the middle of the Northern Territory's huge 'Red Centre', an area traversed by an exciting network of roads of the same name. Before getting in the car, however, stretch your legs with a walk around the great landmark's 10.6-km- (6.6-mile) long circumference.

From here, this road trip takes you through remote central Australian outback on sealed tarmac roads, unlike many others in the region. It's a relatively well-maintained and safe route to travel. However, after dark the biggest danger is the local wildlife, especially jaywalking kangaroos.

There is only one option when it comes to the route: head east on Uluru Road until you hit the Lasseter Highway. After 96km (60 miles), stop off at Curtin Springs, a family-owned cattle ranch spread over 400,000 hectares (1 million acres).

The rest of the drive can safely be completed without map or satellite navigation. At the Luritja Road, head north until you hit Watarrka National Park and the natural phenomenon that is Kings Canyon, with its red sandstone walls towering above dense palm forest, home to 600 species of native fauna and flora. **TW**

❶ Uluru: the starting point of this road trip.

The sign reads:

> **BUNTINE HIGHWAY**
> FROM 00 km TO 336 km
> **WEIGHT LIMIT**
> No. OF AXLES
> **UNSEALED SECTION**
> FROM 336 km TO 558 km
> **WEIGHT LIMIT** G.V.M. 8.0t
> No. OF AXLES
> ROAD INFORMATION 1800 246 199

Buntine Highway Northern Territory/Western Australia, Australia

Start Willeroo, Northern Territory **End** Nicolson, Western Australia **Distance** 575km (357 miles)
Type Adventure **Map** goo.gl/aTiRLO

Noel Buntine was a celebrated road-train pioneer and drover during Australia's rapid development in the second half of the 20th century. Following his death in 1994, a track crossing the existing Buchanan Highway in the Northern Territory was renamed the Buntine Highway in his honour. A granite boulder with an inlaid bronze plaque featuring a B-model road train stands as a memorial to him at the junction of the Victoria Highway and the new road. More excitingly, perhaps, a memorial handicap horse race is held in his name annually at the Alice Springs racetrack.

The road between the Victoria Highway and Kalkarindji through Top Springs is tarmacked and single track, but the remainder of this proposed itinerary is unsealed. A high-clearance, four-wheel drive vehicle is advisable. If you do get stuck, there will be few people to help you in this empty part of Australia. Kalkarindji is the only settlement, its population at the last census a sturdy 542.

That said, the road is an easy drive in good conditions. Wet weather can render the unsealed sections impassable, so check rainfall in the area before setting off. The open scenery is spectacular, with grassy plains and brown desert scrub offsetting the brick-red dust of the road. **SA**

❶ Read the signs before starting out.

Gunbarrel Highway

Northern Territory/Western Australia, Australia

Start Giles, Northern Territory
End Carnegie Station, Western Australia
Distance 1,352km (840 miles)
Type Adventure
Info goo.gl/OZO37k

Surveyor and bushman Len Beadell was one of the doyens of Australian road-building. Responsible for establishing the Gunbarrel Road Construction Party, he laid down more than 6,000km (3,730 miles) of remote outback roads, which he insisted on calling his 'highways'. The most famous, perhaps, is the Gunbarrel Highway.

Determined to make it 'as straight as a gunbarrel', Beadell created one of Australia's most rugged off-road tracks. Built on an east–west line in four stages, from 1955 to 1958, to service a now-abandoned weapon-testing facility, it links Giles in the Northern Territory to Carnegie Station in Western Australia. It represents the most extreme form of road trip, along an isolated desert road. A week might pass before you see another vehicle, and it's an unnerving 600km (372 miles) between filling stations. Don't drive between September and April, and don't leave without adequate supplies of fuel, food and water. Otherwise, Gunbarrel could be the last road trip you ever take.

All this is great for serious off-roaders. If your idea of bliss is the feel of deep corrugations beneath the wheels, of ruts and bog, deep red sand, washouts and gullies, all on a track that can simply disappear under a blanket of spinifex, this may be the road of your dreams. **BDS**

Mereenie Loop Road

Northern Territory, Australia

Start Tylers Pass
End Kings Canyon Resort
Distance 180km (112 miles)
Type Adventure
Map goo.gl/8qCvIQ

Now part of the Red Centre Way, a huge network of tourist roads that wind their way down to Uluru, the Mereenie Loop Road is an unsurfaced remnant offering a real outback experience. It is best tackled in a 4x4, especially after rain or if it hasn't been graded for a while. Standard hire cars are often banned from driving off-road.

With the right equipment, and the necessary permit (available by the day for a couple of Australian dollars), the route offers a beautiful adventure into Aboriginal country. Head southwest from Tylers Pass in the West MacDonnell Ranges and you are almost immediately on Aboriginal land. This means you're not allowed to leave the road, walk off the trail or even stop for a picnic. There is an official stop at Ginty's Lookout, from where there are great views north over the sand dunes and south to Carmichael Crag.

The corrugated surface of brick-red dirt road traverses low scrub and rocky ridges dotted with desert oaks and kurrajong trees. Attractions include car part sculptures and roadside 'tyre trees'. For those who want to explore farther in the area, Kings Canyon has red rocky walls that soar more than 100m (350ft) above the Kings Creek, where an abundance of unusual flora flourishes in the sheltered environment below. **TW**

Stuart Highway – 'The Track'

South Australia/Northern Territory,
Australia

Start Port Augusta, South Australia
End Darwin, Northern Territory
Distance 3,219km (2,000 miles)
Type Adventure
Info goo.gl/Zaigx5

There are few better ways to appreciate the sheer vastness of the Australian outback than by driving the full length of the Stuart Highway. At approximately 3,200km (2,000 miles), it is one of the most challenging road trips on the planet. Locally known as 'The Track', the road takes its official name from John McDougall Stuart, a Scottish explorer who travelled from the south of Australia to the north in 1862; it largely traces the route he took.

This is not a drive to tackle on a whim, and preparation and planning are required. There are filling stations along the route, but they are often around 200km (120 miles) apart, so stop when you can, not when you have to, and plan where you will spend the night.

Setting off from Port Augusta in the south, it is easy to lose focus after the first hundred miles of empty, shimmering, arrow-straight tarmac, but pay attention: the Flying Doctors also use this road as a landing strip. Along the route, you'll pass through the lonely, and hot, central Australian outback, and visit remote towns such as the country's opal capital, Coober Pedy. Many of the charming small towns on the road offer accommodations to break up the drive, but don't expect to see many people – places such as Kulgera and Glendambo have fewer than 50 inhabitants each. **TW**

🛈 The arrow-straight Stuart Highway connects the north and south coasts.

Moralana Scenic Drive South Australia, Australia

Start Wilpena Road   **End** Parachilna Road   **Distance** 27km (17 miles)
Type Scenic   **Info** goo.gl/hYO34T

First-time visitors to the wilds of Australia might be forgiven for assuming that every off-road adventure will require a robust 4x4 expedition vehicle. But the Moralana Scenic Drive proves that's not always the case. This route takes you on to the dirt, but it is negotiable in two-wheel-drive vehicles with reasonable ground clearance.

Efforts are rewarded with great views of the Flinders Ranges, the Black Gap Lookout and the Wilpena Pound Range. Throughout the day, the colours of the rocks change dramatically, from a sun-bleached yellow to a deep blood-red, as the sun makes its passage across the outback sky. Lining the road as it winds along the creek bed are slender cypress pines. In times past, these trees were cut down to make telegraph poles and would be carried away on carts hauled by bullocks. The Cueing Yards, where the bullocks were tended, have been restored and are open to the public.

Although the Scenic Drive is navigable with conventional cars, you will need to keep an eye on the weather – rain can change the gravel surface dramatically and may close the road. You also need to watch out for another classic Australian road hazard, the kangaroo, particularly at the start or end of the day. **JI**

❶ The Flinders Ranges from the road.

Adelaide to Barossa Valley South Australia, Australia

Start Adelaide   **End** Jacob's Creek Visitor Centre   **Distance** 78km (48.5 miles)
Type Culture   **Map** goo.gl/UqocSh

The Barossa in South Australia is a wine lover's dream. The area is home to over 150 wineries and 60 wine cellars, many of which are open to the public. There are also breweries and food producers that make the area a heaven for those who love to eat and drink. If you drive a car or ride a motorcycle, it gets even better.

Leave Adelaide, the capital of South Australia, on the A1 going north. This is a modern multi-lane highway that draws you out of the city. You then switch to the M20 Northern Expressway, out into open countryside. There is farmland on either side, a sign of things to come. This being Australia, the roads are in excellent condition.

Once you're off the main routes, it's a question of grabbing a map of the local wine producers and plotting your own course based on your personal tastes. A useful starting point might be the Barossa Information Centre.

The route concludes at one of the region's most famous wine producers, Orlando Wines, which exports its Jacob's Creek brand to more than 60 countries. Of course, you are never much more than a cork's throw from Adelaide, to which your designated driver can whisk you back once you've enjoyed the delights of the vineyard. **JI**

❶ This is a typical vineyard in the Barossa Valley.

Birdsville Track South Australia/Queensland, Australia

Start Marree, South Australia   **End** Birdsville, Queensland   **Distance** 517km (321 miles)
Type Adventure   **Info** goo.gl/EWz9vm

Opened as a stock route in the 1860s, no other road in Australia conjures up images of the outback quite like the Birdsville Track. Every Australian grows up hearing of it, though few could easily find it on a map. Fewer still will ever drive it. And that is a pity. Those who do, however, talk of it as a rite of passage, a journey through the heart of the continent.

It connects northeast South Australia to southwest Queensland, and passes through three deserts: the dune fields and small eroded knolls of the Strzelecki Desert; the compacted, glazed stones of the Sturt Stony Desert; and the salt lakes of the Tirari Desert. Although good enough to be called a 'highway' by experienced off-roaders, it remains a challenge to most, despite being navigable in well-prepared two-wheel-drive vehicles.

Its surface is dirt and gibber – compacted, interlocking angular rocks – that can provide poor traction under heavy braking and play havoc with tyres. So be sure to reduce their air pressure. And please, be self-sufficient. The only fuel/supply stop is roughly halfway at the historic Mungerannie Roadhouse, an oasis on the banks of Derwent Creek complete with its own wetland and 110-plus bird species. A pleasant sight indeed in the middle of the nation's most mythologized road. **BDS**

❶ There are few signs of human life in the outback.

Highway 1 Ring Road South Australia and more, Australia

Start Adelaide, South Australia   End Adelaide, South Australia   Distance 14,500km (9,010 miles)
Type Culture   Map goo.gl/NXhfHz

Highway 1, Australia's vast peripheral ring road, is arguably the world's longest motorable thoroughfare. While many websites say that this accolade should go to the 48,000-km- (30,000-mile) long Pan-American Highway, part of that goes through the Darién Gap, a nasty, swampy, bandit-ridden section that is virtually impassable.

Circumnavigating mainland Australia, Highway 1 mostly skirts the coastline (apart from a couple of sneaky shortcuts across the north) and passes through every state capital; there is even a short stretch that heads into Tasmania. Although it is a complete ring road, its quality varies hugely, from multi-lane tarmac to compacted gravel track.

Heading out of Adelaide, Highway 1 links with the 1,898-km- (1,179-mile) long Princes Highway before joining the arrow-straight sections of the Eyre Highway. From Perth the road heads inland through Kimberley and outback roads to Katherine. The roughest chunk of the road is between Darwin and Brisbane – especially the unpaved Savannah Way; the surface improves on the Pacific Coast Highway coming out of Cairns heading towards the Great Barrier Reef. Long, but relatively easy, hops from Brisbane to Sydney to Melbourne and Adelaide bring this trip back to its starting point. DIS

❶ A heat haze on the lengthy Highway 1.

Gold Coast Scenic Byway
Queensland, Australia

Start Surfers Paradise
End Surfers Paradise
Distance 320km (199 miles)
Type Scenic
Map goo.gl/7nNxjR

This route is a brilliant two-day snapshot of the best of Australia's Gold Coast: beaches, convoluted mountain roads and rainforest. Day One begins at Surfers Paradise, a seaside town about 40 minutes south of Brisbane. From there, follow the famous waterfront promenade along the string of coastal resorts that make up the Gold Coast Broadwater, before turning sharply inland into the mountains. Tambourine Village is an attractive first stop (there are also bush walks to Mt Tambourine). Beyond this, the road climbs deeper into rainforest. Shortly after the magnificently named Wonglepong, take the right fork, signposted O'Reilly's. What follows is one of the best drivers' roads in Queensland: single-track with loads of hairpin bends, the road ascends steeply into cooler air in Lamington National Park, part of the world's largest subtropical rainforest.

Day Two: after resting up, either here at O'Reilly's Retreat or back at Canungra, take the other fork, continuing until Springbrook Village, a good base for refreshment and to explore the Springbrook National Park. Then it's a return to the coast the long way round. Be sure to stop at Natural Arch – the name says it all. After that, its an extended winding run through delightful valleys, past waterfalls and through pretty villages to the sea and to waterfront Coolangatta, with its popular bars and restaurants to suit all budgets. **DK**

🛈 Australia's Gold Coast offers nightlife as well as beaches, surf and great views.

Great Barrier Reef Drive
Queensland, Australia

Start Cairns
End Cape Tribulation
Distance 140km (87 miles)
Type Scenic
Info goo.gl/SQgz27

The Great Barrier Reef Drive, which begins in Cairns in tropical North Queensland and takes you north to Cape Tribulation, enjoys some awfully good company. Sandwiched between two UNESCO World Heritage Sites, it has the 135-million-year-old Daintree Rainforest on one side and the Great Barrier Reef, the world's largest living organism, on the other. Its a fully sealed highway on one of Australia's premier stretches of coastline that passes through the chic coastal enclave of Port Douglas, so beloved of US President Bill Clinton, and ends in the dappled greenery of the nation's most revered rainforest. The beaches are squeaky white, the water bathtub warm.

However, the real adventure begins with the car-ferry service across the crocodile-infested Daintree River, operating every day from 6:00am to midnight. Once across, an almost primaeval world awaits you. At Cape Tribulation you'll be needing a 4x4 if you want to venture farther north on the fabulous Bloomfield Track, a dirt road built in the 1980s to connect Cape Tribulation to the remote outpost of Cooktown. Complete with unimproved creek crossings and several steep mountain ascents, the Bloomfield Track can be impassable after heavy rains, in spite or because of which it is the icing on the cake of one of the world's least spoiled and most essential tropical drives. **BDS**

❶ The Great Barrier Reef Drive at Yule Point, near Port Douglas, Queensland.

Steve Irwin Way
Queensland, Australia

Start Glenview
End Elimbah
Distance 30km (18.6 miles)
Type Scenic
Map goo.gl/yl2FA4

Australian conservationist Steve Irwin and his wife, Terri, found fame as crocodile hunters. Steve had been brought up alongside the creatures on his father's small reptile and fauna park in Queensland and had no fear of crocs, big or small. He took over management of the park in 1991 and renamed it the Australia Zoo the following year. Tragically, he was killed in 2006 by a stingray barb while filming an underwater documentary. In January 2007, the Queensland state premier announced that Glass House Mountain Road, which runs past the zoo, would be renamed Steve Irwin Way.

The greater part of this route passes through dense native woodland. Apart from providing easy access to Australia Zoo in Beerwah, the scenic road runs alongside the Glass House Mountains National Park. The unusual formations for which the region is named sit on a flat plain and consist of volcanic plugs that formed in the core of extinct volcanoes around 27 million years ago. The volcanoes have gradually eroded away, leaving the distinctive domes standing up to 556m (1,824ft) tall.

Captain James Cook named the mountains as he sailed up the Queensland coast in 1770. Their distinctive conical shape reminded him of the huge glass furnaces or glasshouses of his native Yorkshire, England. **SA**

A series of humpback ridges in the shadow of one of the Glass House peaks.

Outback Way

Queensland to Western
Australia, Australia

Start Winton, Queensland
End Laverton, Western Australia
Distance 2,800km (1,740 miles)
Type Adventure
Info goo.gl/6nrSnV

Nicknamed Australia's Longest Shortcut, the
Outback Way is a series of interconnecting roads
(two-thirds of which are currently unsealed) cutting
through the middle of the country and connecting
Winton, Queensland, with Laverton, Western
Australia. At 2,800km (1,740 miles), it's a viable
alternative to the coast roads of Highway 1, but only
if you have an adventurous spirit and a 4x4.

Despite its rugged nature it's a thoroughly
modern road trip, with its own dedicated website,
smartphone app, carbon-offset options via
PayPal, and the world's longest geocache trail. Plans
are afoot to develop its tourism potential and
completely seal its road surface – currently only
around 80 vehicles a day travel its length.

Seven major roads make up the Outback Way,
which begins in Winton with the Kennedy Highway
and includes the Donohue, Stuart and Lasseter
Highways and the Great Central Road. Along the
way you'll see vast salt lakes, indigenous art,
enormous nature reserves, waterholes, wild camels
and those famous blood-red soils. Uluru, as you
might expect, is a particular highlight en route.

Allow between four and seven days to explore
its treasures, and while decent hotels do dot the
route, you really should camp out at some point for
a true outback experience. **DIS**

Great Beach Highway

Queensland,
Australia

Start Noosa Heads
End Rainbow Beach
Distance 50km (31 miles)
Type Adventure
Info goo.gl/NFo6zY

If you want to head up Australia's Gold Coast, there
are any number of routes you can take. You could,
for example, take the M1 Pacific Motorway with
three or more lanes in each direction. But what
would be the fun in that? As a more exciting
alternative, how about driving for 50km (31 miles)
up the coast on a spectacular sandy beach?

The Beach Highway, as this route is alternatively
known, is a fully legal road that gives you the Pacific
on one side and on the other, the Great Sandy
National Park. You will need a permit and a 4x4 with
generous ground clearance, as the surface can get
rutted and has flour-soft patches that can quickly
swallow a wheel.

Ideally, you should have some experience of
driving off-road, and be prepared to take it slowly
– there is a strictly enforced speed limit of 60 kph
(about 37 mph).

If you take the Beach Highway between July and
September, you may even spot whales migrating
north in search of warmer waters. The road is
unlikely to be teeming with traffic, but beware of
the time: you only want to be driving this heavenly
stretch of sand within two hours of low tide. Should
the sea begin to cut you off, don't panic – just head
inland and loop back via Tin Can Bay and Gympie,
part of the Bruce Highway. **JI**

Lamington National Park Circuit Queensland, Australia

Start Canungra
End O'Reilly's Rainforest Retreat
Distance 50km (31 miles)
Type Adventure
Info goo.gl/9bUL7l

Lamington National Park sits on a plateau in the McPherson Range on the border of Queensland and New South Wales. It covers approximately 206 sq km (80 square miles) and contains rainforests, waterfalls and an awesome range of flora, as well as abundant wildlife.

High in the mountains is O'Reilly's Rainforest Retreat, a family-owned guesthouse and business that first opened its doors in 1926. You can get to it on a road that runs through the park. From the Gold Coast Highway, head to the town of Canungra, a small township of the Scenic Rim Region, better known as the Valley of the Owls. From here O'Reilly's is signposted along the Lamington National Park Road, which takes you out of town and up into the hills along a challenging route.

The road is tarmac and offers a great drive. There are plenty of switchbacks, blind corners and demanding elevations, with great views over the mountains. Heed the yellow warning signs about upcoming corners; the road is not very wide, so you will need to watch out for traffic coming your way and make note of the passing points. There are also plenty of places to pull over for photographs and to soak up the views of the National Park below you.

At the top is O'Reilly's, where you'll find bed and breakfast accommodation, a restaurant and a much-welcomed spa. JI

Peninsula Developmental Road Queensland, Australia

Start Lakeland
End Weipa
Distance 570km (354 miles)
Type Adventure
Info goo.gl/MftYnE

Look at a map of Australia and in the top right corner you'll see a landmass jutting up towards Papua New Guinea. That is the Cape York Peninsula in Queensland, a vast, unspoiled wilderness with a tropical climate.

Running for 571km (354 miles) from Lakeland in the southeast to Weipa in the northwest is the Peninsula Developmental Road, or PDR. This is the main route connecting the peninsula with the rest of Australia. For years this was a completely unsealed road, surfaced with the distinctive red dirt that covers the country. When it rains here, it really rains – more than 2m (70in) a year around the town of Weipa – which would frequently wash away the track.

But in recent years a major programme of works, worth more than Australian $260 million (£150 million/US $188 million), has been under way. This has included laying tarmac on the PDR in sections. The work is currently ongoing, but there are now long stretches where the road is sealed. However, this can abruptly run out, putting you back onto the dirt. In view of that, you need to check on the weather conditions before you travel.

Even on the new sections, you should remember that you are road tripping through one of the last great wilderness areas on Earth. Preparation is key – both for you and your vehicle. JI

75-Mile Beach Road
Queensland, Australia

Start Northern or southern end of beach, Fraser Island
End Northern or southern end of beach, Fraser Island
Distance 121km (75 miles)
Type Adventure
Info goo.gl/4XE2i8

Lying off the southeast coast of Queensland, Fraser Island's main claim to fame is as the world's largest sand island, measuring 120km (75 miles) long and 24km (15 miles) wide. The sand has accumulated for more than 750,000 years over volcanic bedrock, carried there by the strong offshore current that flows north up the coast. Over the years, the naturally occurring mycorrhizal fungi in the sand have released nutrients that have allowed rainforests, eucalyptus woodlands, mangrove forests, peat swamps and coastal heaths to thrive. The island is also home to a wide range of birds, amphibians and reptiles, including the occasional saltwater crocodile.

For most people, however, the beach on the eastern side of the island is the main attraction. In a 4x4, it is possible to drive along the entire length of the beach; the surface is generally smooth, with only a few bumps and dips, and the odd wandering dingo to catch out the unwary.

The beach is classified as a public highway, so speed rules and drunk-driving laws are strictly enforced by the local police. Beware, too, the state of the tide, since you cannot drive for two hours on either side of high tide and tidal flows can cut deep washouts into the beach. Otherwise, enjoy your road trip along one of the planet's more unusual official highways. **SA**

❶ In the foreground of this aerial view of the beach are cars preparing to make the journey.

Thunderbolts Way
New South Wales, Australia

Start Gloucester
End Inverell
Distance 290km (180 miles)
Type Scenic
Map goo.gl/76vocf

The story of Frederick Wordsworth Ward, aka Captain Thunderbolt, is one of those tales you simply couldn't make up. He was a 19th-century horse thief, robber, scourge of the authorities and hero of the people. Today the Thunderbolts Way between Gloucester and Inverell is named in his memory.

The first section of the route was built in the 1960s by sawmill owner Eric Carson as a logging road to access the magnificent hardwoods of the Great Divide. Now expanded and fully sealed, Thunderbolts Way runs through forested mountain areas on the east coast of Australia. This road trip passes through an area teeming with wildlife – koala, wombat and dingo can all be spotted along a route that is especially popular with Australia's motorcycling fraternity. Picnic grounds and viewing areas are dotted all along its course, and many of them offer magnificent panoramas over the forests and mountains. Carson's Lookout is a fitting memorial to the road's trailblazer and one of the most popular stopping-off points.

With a single lane in either direction, this is a safe, if not particularly fast, scenic route. Among the many bridges is Bundarra Bridge, a 204-m- (670-ft) long lattice iron construction. At Uralla, about two-thirds of the way along the drive, you can see a statue of Captain Thunderbolt himself. **JI**

Macquarie Pass
New South Wales, Australia

Start Tullimbar
End Jamberoo Mountain Road
Distance 17.7km (11 miles)
Type Scenic
Map goo.gl/oz9e2l

The Macquarie Pass is short, and a trip through it could be completed in only a few short minutes, but no matter how quickly you take the trip, it will sear pleasant visual memories in your brain that will last a lifetime. It is recommended that you drive as slowly as time allows, in order to take in as much of the scenery as possible.

The road traverses the Macquarie Pass National Park on the A48, and is part of a longer trip descending the Illawarra Escarpment between the town of Robertson and the east coast of Australia south of Sydney.

There are few signs to mark the start of the pass; those that are there warn of steep inclines and other hazards, and it does not take long for the road to become quite testing. Narrow enough not to have a centre line at some points, it also has some super-tight switchbacks which are so sharp that longer vehicles commonly have to take two attempts to get around them.

Sections are often flanked by cliff faces on one side and sheer drop-offs on the other, meaning that this is not a section to travel at high speed. However, that gives more opportunity to take in the stunning scenery. Most of the way you'll be surrounded by lush woodland, but from time to time this will break, allowing fabulous views over the wonderful landscape stretching out below. **TW**

Kosciuszko Road
New South Wales, Australia

Start Pine Valley
End Charlotte Pass ski resort
Distance 95km (59 miles)
Type Scenic
Map goo.gl/sNGp9q

There are numerous ways of reaching the Charlotte Pass Snow Resort. There are bus services that take you into the Snowy Mountain region, and if you want a truly unique trip you can take a snow tractor, complete with caterpillar tracks.

But if you want to drive the route yourself, then take the Kosciuszko Road up to Charlotte Pass from Pine Valley. The highway is named after the highest peak in Australia, Mt Kosciuszko – 2,228m (7,310ft) above sea level in the Snowy Mountains – which in turn takes its name from an 18th-century Polish national hero.

The road is a single lane in each direction; overtaking is consequently not a great idea, but this is not an inherently dangerous drive. Among its most noteworthy characteristics is its two faces. There's the friendly summer aspect: a landscape of heather moorland; smooth tarmac winds its way across the mountain slopes with safe run-offs on either side; during these months the road has an idyllic, almost hypnotic quality.

The winter aspect is altogether more challenging, especially during or after snowfall. Yet somehow the Kosciuszko Road is never hostile: it is open all the way to its summit year round, regardless of the weather conditions. Just make sure that you carry snow chains – if you're in a two-wheel drive vehicle, they are compulsory. JI

❶ The edge of the Kosciuszko Road is marked with snow poles to guide drivers in poor visibility.

Galston Gorge Road
New South Wales, Australia

Start Hornsby
End Galston
Distance 14km (8.7 miles)
Type Adventure
Map goo.gl/Tbpsxr

Somehow, people do not generally expect such highly regarded road trips to be sited so close to major cities, but the Galston Gorge Road starts in the far northwest suburbs of Sydney, just 36km (22.3 miles) from the city centre. The road is not that long, but what it lacks in length it more than makes up for in excitement.

This twisting road runs up through the Galston Gorge in the wooded Berowra Valley Regional Park. It includes five hairpin bends that are so sharp that it is forbidden to drive any vehicle longer than 6.5m (21.3ft); even cars that are shorter than this may have to back up to make some of the tightest corners. Trucks, caravans and buses are all banned. The pretty wooden bridge across Tunks Creek is one way, so you have to wait for any vehicle to clear the bridge before crossing; in wet weather, the waterfalls and streams that run alongside the road forget their manners and cascade across the highway in dramatic fashion.

In view of all these problems, this is clearly not a road for speed freaks. Traffic jams on the tight corners are inevitable, and cyclists add to the congestion. With long stretches hugging close to the rock face on one side while teetering on the edge of the gorge on the other, the highway is spectacularly scenic, but it does not make a road trip for those of a nervous disposition. **SA**

Glow Worm Tunnel Road
New South Wales, Australia

Start Lithgow
End Glow Worm Tunnel
Distance 36km (22.4 miles)
Type Adventure
Map goo.gl/hV5Tb4

In 1906 engineers constructed a 400-m- (1,312-ft) long tunnel through sandstone for the Newnes railroad, which served the oil shale mines that operated in this part of New South Wales. Closed in 1932, the rails were later removed from the tunnel and the new residents – blue, bioluminescent larvae of the fungus gnat – moved into an environment in which they effortlessly thrived.

The tunnel is in the Wollemi National Park, a popular tourist destination featuring caves, gorges and outstanding scenery. It can be reached by a rough dirt track along the former railway heading out from Lithgow. Opting for a 4x4 is strongly recommended, especially after rainfall, and keep a keen eye out for errant wildlife, especially kangaroo and wombats, and returning traffic coming head on. Slicing its way through narrow red-rock cuttings, thick vegetation and elevated embankments, the road leads through an initial tunnel before stopping short of the Glow Worm Tunnel entrance. The large gap in the road is there to keep cars and motorbikes out, as exhaust fumes would kill the sensitive glowworms. Near here is a small parking area where you can pick up the walking trail through the tunnel and witness the natural light show of these amazing little creatures for yourself. **SA**

➥ The road to the mouth of the Glow Worm Tunnel.

Wakehurst Parkway
New South Wales, Australia

Start North Narrabeen
End Balgowlah
Distance 18km (11 miles)
Type Adventure
Map goo.gl/weh9KE

During the day, Wakehurst Parkway is an innocuous stretch of single highway between North Narrabeen and Balgowlah – it's a clear and fast passage often used as a scenic shortcut between the two places. Although it winds its way through forests to the east of Garigal National Park, it is not Wakehurst Parkway's outstanding aesthetic qualities that have earned it a place in the present volume. It is because of its chilling reputation, because many people claim that after dark it plays host to more than just drivers looking for a clear run between two suburban spots.

Not only is the Parkway notorious for being a dumping ground for murder victims, but it is also rumoured to be one of the most haunted stretches of road in the world. Drivers have reported seeing several ghostly figures en route, including a wraithlike nun in her habit and a young girl known as Kelly, dressed in white. According to legend, Kelly has been known to appear in drivers' cars, joining them for part of the journey and telekinetically forcing the vehicle off the road unless she's told that her presence isn't wanted.

Other ghostly figures include a horse and cart that career along this route at great speed and a ghostlike young woman that appears on the Middle Creek Bridge. This is not so much a road trip as an automotive ghost ride. TW

Mt Panorama Circuit
New South Wales, Australia

Start Panorama Avenue, Bathurst
End Panorama Avenue, Bathurst
Distance 6.3km (3.9 miles)
Type Culture
Info goo.gl/ukNjht

Home to the legendary Bathurst 1000 V8 Supercar Championship, the Mt Panorama Racing circuit is a big draw for Australian motorsport fans who flock here each October to witness the ferocious wheel-to-wheel battles between Ford and Holden at this short, but exceptionally demanding racetrack, 203km (126 miles) west of Sydney.

Originally conceived as a scenic road and an employment-generating works programme during the Great Depression of the 1930s, it was soon commandeered for motor racing and hosted the Australian Grand Prix in 1938.

It's not a hard place to find, snaking around the wooded slopes of the Bald Hills above the city, and between races the track is a two-way public highway. Tiptoeing off the access road onto this hallowed ribbon of tarmac is a little disconcerting at first as you sail past sponsors' hoardings, painted apexes, crash barriers and pit-lane buildings. Despite appearances, you should quickly forget any fancy ideas of hot-lap heroics; a strict 60 kph (approx. 37 mph) speed limit is in force throughout. But even at sensible speeds it doesn't take long to appreciate the technical nature of this circuit, with its heady mix of fast straights, constantly changing elevation and deceptively tight corners. DIS

◉ A Ford Mustang leans into a Bathurst bend.

Hunter Valley Wine Region Loop New South Wales, Australia

Start Cessnock **End** Cessnock **Distance** 36km (22.4 miles)
Type Culture **Map** goo.gl/b8j2Q2

In view of the fact that you'll be sampling the delights of some of the best wine producers in Australia on this short road trip, it might be better to let someone else do the driving while you relax in the passenger seat.

It's a circular route (well, more of a square), starting in the town of Cessnock, New South Wales. Head north up the fabulously named Wine Country Drive until you reach the Hunter Valley Wine Society. Here you can start your tasting off by sampling a range of wines from different vineyards. Little more than a cork's throw away is Peterson House, a champagne specialist, where you can grab a taste of the sparkling stuff.

Next comes Broke Road, with a number of wine producers and restaurants to tempt you in. Then hook a left, south down McDonalds Road to McGuigan Cellars and the Hunter Valley Cheese Company. It's always good to have some cheese to wash down the wine.

The route then joins Marrowbone Road and Mount View, heading back to Cessnock. The road is all well-maintained tarmac. There are plenty of signposts and it's generally safe. You'll be passing through great Australian countryside, but it's not the scenery you're after, is it? **JI**

❶ The Hunter Valley is full of vineyards.

Sydney's Grand Pacific Drive New South Wales, Australia

Start Royal National Park   End Shoalhaven   Distance 140km (87 miles)
Type Culture   Info goo.gl/a7JML

This is so much more than a coastal drive with a stunning seascape on one side – it's a whistle-stop tour of some of the greatest experiences Australia has to offer. It takes in rainforests, beautiful beaches, small townships and the great city of Sydney.

The natural attractions are reason enough to do this drive, but it's a human-made spectacle that kicks it off: the magnificent 670-m- (2,200-ft) high Sea Cliff Bridge that snakes along the ragged coastline. From there you have endless options: visit the bustling city of Wollongong; head into the Symbio Wildlife Park; make time for some surfing on one of Wollongong's 17 beaches; or stop off at Kiama Blowhole.

The road starts high up, and its elevation provides plenty of viewing spots with glorious sea vistas – the Sapphire Coast and the Hyams Coast are two particular highlights. The latter sits in Shoalhaven, a popular holiday spot, complete with award-winning vineyards, award-winning restaurants and lush scenery.

The Grand Pacific Drive has a great website to help plan your visit (see above); its tagline – 'One drive. One ocean. Endless experiences' – neatly summarizes the attraction of this epic Australian road trip. TW

❶ The Sea Cliff Bridge is near the starting point.

Sydney to Alice Springs NSW to Northern Territory, Australia

Start Sydney, New South Wales   **End** Alice Springs, Northern Territory   **Distance** 3,314km (2,059 miles)
Type Culture   **Map** goo.gl/18wsOv

If you could somehow drive constantly without pausing for fuel, food, restroom breaks or sleep, you could make it from Sydney to Alice Springs in around 30 hours. But in the real world it's going to take a lot longer. A quick search online throws up plenty of people asking questions relating to a planned trip along this route: vehicle choice, route, time needed, and so on.

Let's assume you want to take your time and enjoy this drive into the very heart of Australia, then it would be easy to take ten days. If you follow the more southerly of the two most popular routes, you could stop at Nyngan, Broken Hill, Port Augusta and Coober Pedy, and then turn left to Uluru. From there

you can choose the easy or the hard route through the Red Centre of Australia to Alice Springs. City slickers, however, may prefer to swing south via Canberra and Adelaide.

This may not be the most exciting drive in itself: most tarmac sections are generally straight, and the view on either side of farmland, bush and acres of red dirt can get a bit repetitive. But it's about the places and people you meet along the way, and being able to say, once you've reached Alice Springs, that you've taken a road trip that many others only dream of. **JI**

❶ The road sign is inscribed in stone.

Great Alpine Road Victoria, Australia

Start Wangaratta   End Bairnsdale   Distance 303km (188 miles)
Type Scenic   Map goo.gl/o3UvTv

Victoria is famous for the Great Ocean Road that winds dramatically along its windswept southern coast. So famous, indeed, that when an even lengthier road through the Victorian Alps was officially opened in 1998, it was competitively named the Great Alpine Road. Technically, this new road bears the route number B500 and includes the former Ovens Highway and parts of the Omeo Highway. Its main star billing is that it is Australia's highest, year-round accessible road, the section between Harrietville and Omeo over Mt Hotham rising to 1,840m (6,040ft). Here the road is usually covered with snow during the winter months, and is swept free daily. Severe weather can close this section completely, so all drivers at this point are required to carry diamond-pattern snow chains during the declared snowy months.

The scenery along this road varies considerably, with rich farmland and vineyards, lush forests, steep valleys and, of course, some dramatic mountainous peaks. The route around the northern slopes of Mt Hotham and then on across the Dinner Plain is particularly fine. The entire route can be covered in one day, although there are plenty of excellent restaurants and cafés along the way to divert you should you wish to break up your journey. SA

❶ The Great Alpine Road passes near Mt Hotham.

Great Ocean Road
Victoria, Australia

Start Torquay
End Allansford
Distance 243km (151 miles)
Type Scenic
Info goo.gl/mc2r8

To give some idea of just how big a challenge the Great Ocean Road really can be, the Victoria state police once used it to train rookie highway patrol cops in advanced driving techniques.

It was built by Australian soldiers returning from World War I as a tribute to compatriots they had buried in Flanders and at Gallipoli: it is the longest war memorial on Earth.

But that's by no means its only claim to fame. It skirts sandy surfing beaches and subtropical rainforests, and twists along crumbly cliff tops – a section of the road at Princetown was washed away in 1960. Sadly, further erosion is a constant hazard, as are rock falls from the hills above the highway, so drivers need to be careful.

Among the greatest natural wonders to be seen en route in Port Campbell National Park are the Twelve Apostles, which is now a bit of a misnomer for the line of limestone stacks offshore by the roadside, because at the time of publication of the present volume wind and water erosion had reduced their number to eight. But they're still a great sight – the tallest of them towers 50m (165ft) above the water.

At Tower Hill, koalas, kangaroos and emus hang out in the bowl of an extinct volcano. In the Otway Ranges there are organized boat trips to see wild duck-billed platypus. JP

❶ Some of the remaining Twelve Apostles that line the shore in Port Campbell National Park.

South Face Road
Victoria, Australia

Start Rawson
End Mt Baw Baw Village
Distance 30km (18.6 miles)
Type Adventure
Map goo.gl/ITI9Jq

The controversial South Face Road in the Australian State of Victoria cuts through forests on the side of Mt Baw Baw. It was built in the 1990s to open up previously inaccessible areas to commercial logging, and has come in for intense criticism due to the negative environmental impacts of its construction. It is an unsealed road, and the soil in the area is susceptible to erosion, which means that the road can be damaged not only by bad weather but also by local rivers in spate.

As a drivers' road, it is challenging. The 30-km (18.6-mile) long route climbs to a height above sea level of 1,500m (5,000ft), and the weather on the mountain can change rapidly. When the road is wet, some sections can become impassable even by 4x4s, and especially by conventional vehicles. The road is fairly wide, but you need to look out for debris from the forest – even branches can be big enough to write off a car if hit.

There are no fuel stops on Mt Baw Baw, so you will need to fill up before you head off. The drive itself offers fantastic views of the forest, but bear in mind that you may be sharing your journey with logging lorries and trucks, and it is essential to carry snow chains in winter. At the summit, you'll have access to the ski resort, cafés and lodges, and the option to take the easier route down via the tarmac-surfaced Mt Baw Baw Tourist Road. JI

❶ Snow-laden trees along the Mt Baw Baw Tourist Road to the ski resort.

McKillops Road Victoria, Australia

Start Wulgulmerang   End McKillops Bridge   Distance 27km (16.8 miles)
Type Adventure   Map goo.gl/DBDpRG

The McKillops Road is a formidable undertaking. Officially designated the C611, it runs through the Snowy River National Park and is considered to be one of the most dangerous roads in Australia. The surface is loose red gravel and dirt, which takes on a terrifying sheen after the all-too-regular downpours. With the added hazard of rock falls and tree branches littering the road ahead, it is probably a good idea to try to ignore the almost total absence of crash barriers stopping you from plunging into the scrubby abyss over the road's edge.

The highway twists and turns around rocky outcrops and blind bends and over flimsy wooden bridges. In most places it is wide enough for two vehicles, while in others it narrows down to a single track. A 4x4 is the sensible choice for this road trip. Other essential equipment includes axes, shovels and ropes to clear fallen trees, which can often block the route. Despite all these warnings, this itinerary is well worth the effort; the scenery is spectacular, with ash and pine forests and Mt Gelantipy rolling out before you.

After a steep descent, you will eventually reach McKillops Bridge; the campground nearby is a great place to access the Snowy River for a spot of wild swimming after a hard day's driving. JI

❶ McKillops Bridge crosses the Snowy River.

Huon Trail Tasmania, Australia

Start Hobart   End Cockle Creek   Distance 132km (82 miles)
Type Scenic   Map goo.gl/6zKc7b   Info goo.gl/AgM4Nr

This trip from the state capital of Tasmania follows the Huon River and takes in vineyards, forests and relics of both great waves of settlers – Aborigines in prehistoric times, and Europeans from the 18th century. It's an easy drive, with scenery and history in comparable and abundant measure.

Leaving Hobart on the A6, travel southwest for 40km (25 miles) through apple orchards to the banks of the river at Huonville, where some of the pine trees are older than the Common Era. Farther down the right bank is the town of Franklin, where the essential stop-off is the Wooden Boat Centre and Boat Building School. Another 18km (11 miles) south lies Geeveston, the centre of the region's fruit-growing and logging industries, and the base for excursions into the Hartz Mountains. In the National Park there is much to do, but nothing more exhilarating than the Tahune Forest Airwalk, on which you soar above the tree canopy on a 220-m-(700-ft) long cable suspended 70m (230ft) above the forest canopy and the Huon River. Dover is a pretty town near a network of giant dolomite caves; just beyond it is Cockle Creek, the southernmost point of Australia, which is normally quiet, if not deserted, and whose main attractions are Aborigine relics and views of the Southern Ocean. JP

❶ The view from the Tahune Forest Airwalk.

Gordon River Road
Tasmania, Australia

Start Rosegarland
End Gordon Dam
Distance 121km (75 miles)
Type Scenic
Map goo.gl/o4JohB

The proposal to construct the Gordon and Serpentine Dams in southwest Tasmania to provide electricity for the whole island state prompted an urgent request from the Hydro-Electric Commission of Tasmania to the Australian government to fund the necessary access roads.

The subsequent grant paid for the construction of the Gordon River Road from January 1964. Today this highway (the B61), the dams and the large reservoirs are all attractive human-made contributions to the immense natural beauty of what is a now a UNESCO World Heritage Wilderness Area. The mountainous scenery along the road is truly outstanding. The Gordon River Road begins at Rosegarland and then heads north of the headwaters of the Florentine River towards Tim Shea, a mountain which, at 952m (3,123ft) above sea level, provides excellent views of the Mt Field National Park. The road then twists and turns through the Frodsham Pass and alongside Mt Wedge and the Sentinel Range to finish at the Gordon Dam. The dam itself is particularly impressive, standing 140m (459ft) tall, and arched both horizontally and vertically. The dam holds back Lake Gordon, which provides the largest supply of freshwater in Australia and currently generates approximately one-seventh of Tasmania's total electricity requirements. **SA**

❶ At the start of the ascent, a sign of things to come: peaks and (possibly) puddles.

Jacob's Ladder
Tasmania, Australia

Start Blessington Road, Upper Blessington
End Tasmanian Rover Ski Club Lodge, Ben Lomond
Distance 50km (31 miles)
Type Adventure
Map goo.gl/ZoZLtp

In the Old Testament Book of Genesis, Jacob's Ladder is a stairway to heaven. But of those brave souls that have actually tackled its namesake, in deepest Tasmania, many conclude that this is a poor reflection of that blissful ascent.

Officially designated the C432 Ben Lomond Road, the track relentlessly climbs to 1,600m (5,150ft) above sea level via a series of switchbacks stitched together with graded gravel. There are some safety barriers, but in many places there is nothing to stop you dropping off the edge and bouncing a long way down.

Around you the sheer walls of Ben Lomond loom, while beneath your wheels the surface is loose, wet with meltwater and littered with dirty snowdrifts. You'll need a dependable 4x4 vehicle with abundant grip to tackle this route. Check the forecast before you head off: the weather can change very quickly and you'll need to be competent at putting on snow chains.

On your way up, you also need to prepare to yield to vehicles coming back down from the summit. When you get to the top you'll find a lookout and an Alpinesque skiing lodge: this is Tasmania's oldest downhill ski area. Enjoy the vistas, gulp in that clean mountain air and decide for yourself whether Jacob's Ladder was a heavenly or a hellish road trip. **JI**

Convict Trail
Tasmania, Australia

Start Hobart
End Port Arthur
Distance 116km (72 miles)
Type Culture
Map goo.gl/wTzm1Z

Many of the historic sites along this route commemorate the convicts who were transported to Australia from Britain in the 18th century.

Leave Hobart on the A3, then turn left at Cambridge to Richmond, the site of the oldest bridge still in use in Australia, as well as the country's oldest remaining Roman Catholic church, and – most significantly, in view of what's to come – its oldest prison.

From Richmond, continue east, rejoin the A3 and then the Arthur Highway (A9), which heads south to Eaglehawk Neck. This is a narrow isthmus at the northern end of the Tasman Peninsula which, in colonial times, was guarded by soldiers, mantraps and dogs to prevent convicts escaping from where you're now heading. Stop here to visit The Officers' Quarters, a painstakingly restored wooden military building, now a history museum, and marvel at the view along the shoreline from Pirates Bay. If time, take one of the speedboat trips past the 300-m- (1,000-ft) high cliffs along the coast.

Port Arthur, 24km (15 miles) from Eaglehawk Neck, lies at the outermost edge of the peninsula. Here in the historic quarter are buildings erected by convicts and maintained as they were between 1830 and 1877, when more than 12,000 were incarcerated here. Among other must-see detours are the Convict Salt Mines at Saltwater River. **JP**

Heritage Highway
Tasmania, Australia

Start Launceston
End Hobart
Distance 208km (129 miles)
Type Culture
Map goo.gl/b5UAI5

❶ Callington Mill in Oatlands has been working continuously since it was opened in 1837.

First marked out by surveyor Charles Grimes in 1807, what has been known for most of its history as the Hobart Road was built using convict road gangs. The first link between the capital, Hobart, and the riverside town of Launceston had its first mailman in 1816 and its first stagecoach in 1821. Bushrangers liked it, too, and were so common that farmers tied handguns to their ploughs.

The Heritage Highway still follows Grimes's track, and remains the primary link between the two most populous cities of Australia's smallest, most southerly state. It passes through Tasmania's – and Australia's – finest concentration of early colonial and Georgian-era communities; a region that still reminds one of the days when Tasmania was the British Crown Colony of Van Diemen's Land and a microcosm of everything English. Places like Evandale, Ross, Tunbridge and of course Oatlands – the town with the largest collection of sandstone buildings in the country and the southern hemisphere's only working Lincolnshire flour windmill – link a priceless vein of communities and architecture that still defines Tasmania today.

A two-lane sealed highway perennially scheduled for widening, the Heritage Highway provides access to all this and more – farmlands, the nation's oldest and most beautiful bridges and a rare window onto Australia's first stirrings. **BDS**

Targa Tasmania

Tasmania, Australia

Start Launceston
End Hobart
Distance 1,040km (646 miles)
Type Culture
Info goo.gl/1KPYza

Inspired by the Sicilian Targa Florio road race, the Targa Tasmania recaptures that same high-octane atmosphere as invited drivers push their machines to the absolute limit, charging around its tortuous mountain stages. It always attracts big crowds – during its inaugural race in 1992, 150,000 of Tasmania's half-million inhabitants lined the route to watch. Stirling Moss, who competed that year in his own Ford Mustang, described it as one of the greatest driving experiences of his life.

To get a taste of the Targa Tasmania yourself, you can mix and match from any of the 40 or so special stages run over this six-day, 2,011-km- (1,250-mile) long endurance road race. Highly recommended for the keen driver is the 53-km- (30-mile) long Mt Arrowsmith stage along the infamous Lyell Highway, known to locals as the 99 Bends. It is not only a wonderful snapshot of Tasmania's stunning natural beauty, but also a demanding technical challenge as fast, narrow stretches throw up blind crests and deceptive corners, and offer little room for error as the road threads through the forests of the Franklin-Gordon Wild Rivers National Park.

For a fuller experience of the Apple Isle, you can string together numerous Targa Tasmania special stages to form a 1,040-km- (646-mile) long road trip starting and finishing in Hobart. **DIS**

Efaté Ring Road

Efate, Vanuatu

Start Port Vila
End Port Vila
Distance 122km (75.6 miles)
Type Scenic
Map goo.gl/stFQKg

Vanuatu in the South Pacific is one of the few countries in the world where, in colonial days, the French and British managed to put aside their rivalries and govern the islands as a joint condominium. The islands gained their independence in 1980 and called themselves Vanuatu, derived from the islanders' words *vanua* ('home') and *tu* ('stand').

The capital, Port Vila, stands on the island of Efaté, a roughly circular affair with Mt McDonald in the centre and a ring road right around its coast. Consequently, once you have hired your car or scooter, the only decision to make is clockwise or anticlockwise. If, on the road trip, you are struck by a sense of déjà vu, it is probably because the island has been in various movies, including *The Blue Lagoon* (1980), and numerous series of *Survivor* (2000–), a reality TV show.

A tour around the island is full of delights. It was a US military base during World War II, and the wrecks of two fighter planes can still be seen in the shallows close to Baofatu on the northern tip. Taka Kastom near Taraka promotes itself as a cultural village, and if you are feeling energetic you can explore Valeva Cave by kayak. But as much as anything, this tour is about laid-back cruising around a Pacific island paradise with luxuriant scenery, fine beaches and a sky full of sun. **SA**

Queens Road Viti Levu, Fiji

Start Nadi, Western Division   **End** Suva, Central Division   **Distance** 208km (129 miles)
Type Scenic   **Map** goo.gl/DARvew

Sandwiched between soft sand beaches and rampant jungle, Queens Road hugs the south coast of Viti Levu, Fiji's largest island. Variable road conditions (prize potholes) and a speed limit of 80 kph (50 mph) – lower through the villages – make the drive between Nadi and Suva more of a three-hour amble than a blast. However, this gives more time to appreciate the scenery and see life in this South Sea paradise: fishermen bringing in their catch; children dawdling to school; piles of tropical fruits in roadside markets.

The beaches are also likely to detain you. Sigatoka, around 64km (40 miles) from Nadi, marks the start of the Coral Coast, the most scenic stretch, strung with impeccably presented five-star resorts. Natadola Beach (accessed along a gravel drive) is regularly described as one of the great beaches of the world. Don a sarong and enjoy its long sweep of sand fringed by palm trees, perhaps on horseback, followed by a Fijian massage. Other worthy stops include Sigatoka Sand Dunes National Park and Pacific Harbor market; for a taste of the interior of Viti Levu, consider taking a jet-boat safari along the Sigatoka River Valley to visit Fijian villages. From Suva, circumnavigation of the island continues on the Kings Road around the north coast. **DS**

❶ Natadola Beach is a holiday paradise.

Upolu Island Scenic Tour Upolu, Samoa

Start Apia, Tuamasaga   End Apia, Tuamasaga   Distance 114km (71 miles)
Type Scenic   Map goo.gl/04HNQ3

In 1768 French explorer Louis-Antoine de Bougainville – after whom the flowering shrub bougainvillea is named – called the Samoan Islands the Navigator Islands in recognition of the natives' seafaring skills.

Navigation today is mostly by road map or sat-nav, with Upolu, the smaller of the two Samoan islands, a dream to explore. All tours start and finish at Apia, the nation's capital on the north coast. From here, head down the northeast coast, past the dramatic Falefa Falls, and through Le Mafa Pass, which, at 518m (1,700ft) above sea level, makes for some breathtaking views over the east and south coasts of the island.

Lush forests, plantations and traditional Samoan villages line the route to To Sua, which sensibly translates as 'big hole' on account of it being a big hole in the ground filled with water in which to swim. Access is down a steep ladder. The tour then passes the white sands of Faofao Beach, excellent for both swimming and lunch, along the southwest coast, and back north across the island via the Cross Island Road, another tree-lined adventure. The Papapapaitai Falls are worth exploring, as they drop spectacularly into a dormant volcanic crater. The route then descends back into Apia. **SA**

❶ A bus takes on a shaded section of the trip.

Whangarei Scenic Drive
Northland, New Zealand

Start Dargaville
End Whangarei Heads
Distance 293km (182 miles)
Type Scenic
Map goo.gl/9G8dpM

This horseshoe-shaped road trip, on good, well-maintained tarmac, takes in the highlights of the northern tip of New Zealand's North Island. Its start point, Dargaville on the Tasman Sea coast, has two claims to fame: the nation's longest stretch of beach, and toheroa – huge shellfish, about 15cm (6 in) in diameter, that are good to eat on their own or in a hearty, greenish soup.

The next section of the route passes through Waipoua Forest, where some of the kauri conifer trees took root before the Common Era. The road climbs through the trees before bursting into the open to reveal a lovely harbour on the Hokianga, which, although known as a river, is a drowned valley full of seawater – a fjord, which is crossed by ferry before the route goes on to the seaside resort of Paihia. From here, there is a worthwhile side trip to Russell, which is now genteel but was once notorious as the place where sailors on shore leave got up to all sorts of nefarious antics after months at sea on the Pacific Ocean.

Heading back south through lush green vegetation, you reach Whangarei, a modern city with a fabulous coastline and a specially constructed road, the Heads Tourist Drive, from which to appreciate both the tranquility of the region's sheltered coves and the power of the breakers on its surfing beaches. **JP**

❶ The beauty of New Zealand is epitomized here in this quiet stretch of Whangarei Falls.

Thermal Explorer Highway
Auckland/Waikato, New Zealand

Start Auckland
End Napier, Hawkes Bay, Waikato
Distance 457km (284 miles)
Type Culture
Info goo.gl/VQdspD

New Zealand straddles the boundary between the Pacific and Indo-Australian continental plates. Geological conflict between these two plates has created the many volcanoes, geysers, hot mud and geothermal mineral pools, and the other dramatic features that are found throughout these islands.

One of the best ways to appreciate this natural extravaganza is along the Thermal Explorer Highway, prosaically known as the north end of New Zealand State Highway 1. The key to this highway is Auckland, New Zealand's largest city, with the largest Polynesian population of any place in the world. The city sits between two vast harbours dotted with 48 extinct volcano cones.

From there, you head south up the valley of the Waikato River, New Zealand's longest river, to Hamilton, New Zealand's largest inland city. After there, the Thermal Highway really heats up. Rotorua is one of the liveliest geothermal areas in the world, with the Pohutu Geyser in Te Puia erupting up to 20 times a day, its waters reaching up to 30m (100ft). Its name means 'constant splashing' in Maori. Further south is Lake Taupo, which lies in the caldera or central depression of a super-volcano that blew its top some 28,500 years ago. At the end of your geothermal road trip lie the charming Art Deco delights of Napier, with walking tours of the city for those with artistic sensibilities. **SA**

❶ The Bridal Veil Falls lie just off the road on the Pakoka River in the Waikato area.

Port Jackson Road
Waikato, New Zealand

Start Colville
End Port Jackson
Distance 26km (15.9 miles)
Type Adventure
Map goo.gl/YoxOwS

The remote Coromandel Peninsula extends for 85km (52 miles) up the western side of the Bay of Plenty on New Zealand's North Island, sheltering the Hauraki Gulf and Auckland to its west. This narrow strip of land is steep and hilly, the Coromandel Range running like a spine along its length and rising up to 900m (2,952ft) above sea level at its highest point. Temperate rainforest covers much of the area.

One of the few roads that run up the peninsula winds along the rugged west coast. The Port Jackson Road starts at Whangarei Junction at the north end of Colville Road, not far beyond the small town of Colville. From there it hugs the coastline and skirts the inland Coromandel Forest Park. The road is narrow and twisting, with few passing places, so be prepared to reverse some distance to allow oncoming vehicles to get past. The gravel surface gets very muddy and slippery after rain, and can become impassable after a downpour, even for four-wheel drives. With steep cliffs tumbling down to the sea and no guardrails, you might also want to give this road a miss on a stormy day, but in good weather it's a different story: do bring a camera for the stunning views. If you cannot face the journey back, there is a campground to enjoy at Port Jackson, as well as stunning coastal walks through the surrounding countryside. **SA**

Forgotten World Highway
Taranaki/Manawatu, New Zealand

Start Stratford, Taranaki
End Taumarunui, Manawatu-Wanganui
Distance 299km (186 miles)
Type Scenic
Info goo.gl/LJxzgV

New Zealand's Forgotten World Highway is a beautiful, rugged road that heads northeast across the Taranaki region in the southwest of the North Island into King Country in the Manawatu–Wanganui region. Starting in Stratford on the eastern slope of Mt Taranaki, an active but generally well-behaved volcano, the highway hugs the contours of the land and rides dramatically up and down four mountainous saddles. It is a 'bit upsy downsy', as one local put it.

Caution is required in the single-track, 180-m- (590-ft) long Moki Tunnel, known as Hobbit's Hole, and also in Tangarakau Gorge, with walls that reach up to 61m (200ft). The road through the gorge is unsealed, its slippery gravel surface making it one of the ten worst roads in New Zealand for traffic accidents. Running alongside much of the highway is the Stratford–Okahukura railroad, constructed in the 1920s. Several settlements built for the construction teams are now ghost towns. The town of Whangamomona is a rare exception. Outraged at the government's decision in the 1980s to close the local school and post office, the residents declared themselves the Independent Republic of Whangamomona. Try to time your visit to arrive in January, when the celebratory Republic Day is held and a new president is elected – one year it was a goat, another a poodle. **SA**

Surf Highway 45
Taranaki, New Zealand

Start New Plymouth
End Hawera
Distance 105km (65 miles)
Type Adventure
Info goo.gl/Ar3qtd

The Taranaki region of New Zealand's North Island sticks prominently westward into the Tasman Sea. Its exposed windward coasts are famous for their surfing beaches; so famous that the New Zealand State Highway 45 that runs around the coastline has acquired the new name of the Surf Highway.

The journey starts in New Plymouth, the region's main town, which makes its living from finance, agriculture, oil and natural gas production. In 2010 the city was named as a walking and cycling 'Model Community' by the New Zealand government. So being mindful of other road users, drive south out of the city and enjoy the sea views to your right.

Most adventurous road trippers are drawn to this route because they want to try out the waves for themselves. If you're a complete newbie and time is short, then try tandem surfing at Oakura Beach, where they guarantee to get you upright from the very first session or your money back.

The landscape inland from here is gentle and predominantly agricultural, and while it is not particularly challenging geography, side winds can be a problem for bikers. Cape Egmont on the westernmost tip is your next port of call, named after the Earl of Egmont, First Lord of the Admiralty, by Captain Cook when he sailed past in 1769. From here it's a gentle jaunt down to Hawera, near the coast of the South Taranaki Bight. **SA**

❶ The Sugar Loaf Islands at New Plymouth with Mt Taranaki in the distance.

Waikaremoana Road

Hawke's Bay,
New Zealand

Start Te Urewera
End Ruatahuna
Distance 39km (24.1 miles)
Type Scenic
Map goo.gl/FvYQhI

In geological terms, Lake Waikaremoana in the east of New Zealand's North Island is a very recent arrival. Approximately 2,200 years ago, a massive landslip about 250m (820ft) high blocked a local valley, eventually causing a huge lake 54 sq km (20.8 square miles) to form. Water for the lake used to flow out through the landslip until it was sealed and an overflow created in the early 1950s.

Waikaremoana means 'sea of rippling waters' in Maori. Visitors can enjoy its delights and those of the surrounding remote countryside along Waikaremoana Road, which starts at the eastern end of the lake to the north of Te Urewera. From there, State Highway 38, as it is formally known, heads west along the north shore of the lake before turning inland to Ruatahuna. The surface of the winding road – more of a track, actually – is mainly gravel and the weather there can be very windy. However, you will not meet much other traffic en route, which is just as well because passing places are not particularly common. Restrict your speed to around 30kph (19 mph), and take care on the many blind corners. Use your headlights if the light is poor, and watch out for wandering livestock. But above all, enjoy the dramatic scenery, as Te Urewera National Park, through which you pass, is simply spectacular. **SA**

Cape Palliser Road

Wellington,
New Zealand

Start Lake Ferry
End Cape Palliser
Distance 39km (24 miles)
Type Scenic
Map goo.gl/fKwI25

Cape Palliser Road is both the beauty and the beast of scenic drives. A combination of sea views, rocky cliffs and occasional landslides, it can charm visitors on the one hand and alarm them on the other.

The 39-km- (24-mile) long road is located in the south of New Zealand's North Island and it runs from Lake Ferry Road along the southernmost tip of the island to Lake Palliser lighthouse. It is a winding tarmac route that is in a generally good state, with a number of bridges. Although the road is a single carriageway and some of the bridges are narrow, the route itself is safe and well maintained. It winds its way between a series of grey beaches running down to the turquoise ocean and steep ragged cliffs that rise vertically. The cliffs are the likely cause of any potential problems en route: there are issues with erosion close to the road at Whatarangi and rock falls do happen.

As the road gets closer to the picture-perfect, red-and-white striped Cape Palliser lighthouse, which has been unmanned since 1986, the tarmac surface turns to gravel. After rainfall, this can get quite muddy and traction can be greatly reduced. Once you arrive at the lighthouse, the final challenge is to climb the 250 steps to the top viewing platform for stunning vistas over the cape and the nearby seal colony. **JI**

Paekakariki Hill Road
Wellington,
New Zealand

Start Porirua
End Paekakariki
Distance 21km (13 miles)
Type Scenic
Map goo.gl/dZhusr

Paekakariki Hill in Wellington is located to the north of Porirua Harbour, at almost the most southwesterly tip of New Zealand's North Island. The hill affords outstanding views of the adjacent peninsula and the Kapiti, or Golden, Coast to the west. A winding road running across the hill gives visitors the chance to enjoy this wonderful scenery.

Access to Paekakariki Hill Road is off Paremata Haywards Road, officially known as State Highway 58, in Porirua, just east of the harbour. As one of the four cities that make up the Wellington metropolitan area, Porirua is a bustling place. The road, which was built in 1849, then skirts Pauatahanui Park and heads north along the western edge of Battle Hill Farm Forest Park and the massive Akatarawa Forest. A lookout point at the top of the hill is a perfect place to stop for photographs.

From there, the road twists and turns down the hillside before joining State Highway 1, which runs all along the coast, by Paekakariki Station. As the majority of Paekakariki Hill Road is seriously twisty, it is important to drive slowly and carefully at all times. Luckily, it is a dual-track route, so there is no need to worry about oncoming vehicles. However, there are very few guardrails and the drops down the hillside can be very steep, so beware of the left-hand side of the road when driving north. **SA**

❶ In some places along the route, the wind has blown the bush almost flat against the hillside.

Takarau Gorge Road
Wellington, New Zealand

Start Makara Road
End Ohariu
Distance 7.7km (4.8 miles)
Type Adventure
Map goo.gl/vDXXEw

Wellington, the capital of New Zealand, lies on the southwestern tip of North Island. A rural and relatively unpopulated peninsula protects it from the worst of the winds that whip in off the Tasman Sea to the west. Running along the length of this peninsula is the narrow Takarau Gorge, one of the many hidden delights within easy reach of what has often been described as the 'coolest little capital in the world'.

To approach the gorge, start in the centre of Wellington and head west through Karori and then north through Makara. Then take the northbound Makara Road that leads to Makara Beach on the Tasman Sea coast. The Takarau Gorge Road is a turning off to your right.

Once on the road, head up the gorge alongside the Takarau River. Steep cliffs line either side of the chasm, making for unforgettably dramatic scenery. Although the road is exhilarating to drive, it is fairly safe, although heavy rainfall can cause flooding; when sections of the road are submerged, the road is naturally closed to traffic, so do monitor the local weather forecasts. And also watch out for oncoming vehicles: the road is single-track for the most part, and there are not many places to pass. At only 7.7km (4.8 miles) long, this road is not going to take you long to drive, so take your time and enjoy the ride while it lasts. **SA**

French Pass Road
Marlborough, New Zealand

Start Rai Valley
End French Pass
Distance 57km (35.4 miles)
Type Scenic
Map goo.gl/pZ44XY

French Pass is a narrow stretch of water that runs between the north of New Zealand's South Island and a small offshore landmass known as D'Urville Island. The latter acquired its name from a visiting Frenchman, the explorer Jules-Sébastien-César Dumont d'Urville, who visited the area in 1827. Between the island and the mainland is a ferocious tidal race that whips through on each tide at more than eight knots, creating fierce whirlpools and eddies along the way. The waters might once have been easily navigated by Maori canoes, but they obviously presented a challenge for d'Urville, who twice clipped undersea reefs before arriving safely in nearby Admiralty Bay.

All this remote magnificence is connected to the rest of civilization in Marlborough by a winding rural track, accessed from Opouri Road off State Highway 6 north of Rai Valley. Within a short distance, the route climbs up Ronga Road alongside the Rai River before heading into the hills. After passing through a forest, the road renames itself Croisilles Road. Eventually, a right turn onto Hope Drive takes you into the village of Okiwi Bay. At the eastern end of the bay, the road, now usefully known as the Croisilles–French Pass Road, heads roughly northeast in a drunken stagger up the peninsula to the quiet and delightful French Pass village itself. **SA**

Queen Charlotte Drive
Marlborough, New Zealand

Start Picton
End Havelock
Distance 40km (25 miles)
Type Scenic
Info goo.gl/ilAJ6q

The northern end of New Zealand's South Island ends in a confusion of inlets, islands and rugged peninsulas. The waters, collectively named the Marlborough Sounds, are geographically known as rias, river valleys flooded by the ocean as the land subsided and sea levels rose. The drive along their southern side has been well described as 'cruising the Sounds without a boat'.

Queen Charlotte Drive starts at the seaside town of Picton, Marlborough, terminus for the Interislander Cook Strait Ferry from Wellington and the North Island. From there, head west across the flat plain along the southern shore of Queen Charlotte Sound, hugging the twisting coastline through Shakespeare Bay, Whenuanui Bay, Ngakuta Bay and Momorangi Bay. The road then crosses through Linkwater, a low 5-km- (3.1-mile) long saddle of land at the head of a long isthmus that leads to Cape Jackson and the tip of South Island. Without the tarmac road, the journey by sea around this cape would be more than 100km (60 miles).

You then emerge at the head of Pelorus Sound. A few more twists and turns up and around Cullens Point, with its magnificent views, brings you to the historic coastal town of Havelock, centre of New Zealand's green-lipped mussel industry, where plenty of local restaurants serve them up in every conceivable way. **SA**

❶ This aerial view shows how closely the highway hugs the island coast.

Karamea Highway West Coast, New Zealand

Start Westport **End** Karamea **Distance** 96km (59.6 miles)
Type Scenic **Map** goo.gl/vzb87N

There are times when it is better to travel than to arrive, and this road trip is one such occasion because Karamea Highway doesn't actually go anywhere. The winding, sweeping, tarmac road snakes down the northerly tip of New Zealand's South Island, where the hard stuff gives way to a popular walking path, the Heaphy Track. Nearly 70 bends vary in severity, from smooth curves to tight hairpins, which makes it a great road for enthusiastic bikers and drivers. There are sheer drops in places, although these days there are plenty of barriers to make you feel secure.

On the straightest coastal section of Karamea Highway, the road runs parallel to the Tasman Sea, with a view that stretches for miles; heading inland there is rainforest on both sides, and in summer the indigenous rata trees bloom. After threading through the quaint old coal-mining towns of Granity, Ngakawau and Hector, the real drivers' roads begin with the 40-km- (24.8-mile) long climb over Karamea Bluffs. After stopping off at the time-warped Village Hotel in Karamea for its much-lauded whitebait and chips, pull on your walking boots to work off a few calories and see the amazing limestone rock formations in the lush rainforest at Oparara Basin. **JI**

① The road cuts through native bush.

Great Alpine Highway Canterbury/West Coast, New Zealand

Start Christchurch, Canterbury   End Greymouth, West Coast   Distance 241km (150 miles)
Type Adventure   Info goo.gl/Q9pOyj

The Southern Alps run down the western spine of New Zealand's South Island, a spectacular range of peaks that climax at 3,724m (12,218ft) on the three peaks of Mt Cook, the nation's highest mountain. Many of these peaks are perpetually covered with snow, the entire range cut through with glaciers and lakes.

One way to access this magnificent scenery is along the Great Alpine Highway, which starts in Christchurch, an attractive and vibrant city, on the east coast of South Island. From there, follow State Highway 73 west across the Canterbury Plain before rising up into the Southern Alps past the monolithic limestone formations at Castle Hill. The roads

through here are a thrilling and heady mix of fast sweeping sections, deep rock cuttings and tight hairpin corners.

The route then crosses Porters Pass and reaches its halfway point at Arthur's Pass Village in the National Park. Here the scenery is at its most dramatic, with numerous trails heading out into the mountains. Next comes the Otira Lookout, providing panoramic views across the Otira Viaduct that will shortly conduct you across the valley. From here that drops down to the Tasman Sea coast at journey's end, Greymouth. SA

❶ The highway passes through the Canterbury region.

Mt Cook Road Canterbury, New Zealand

Start Twizel **End** Mt Cook **Distance** 64km (39.8 miles)
Type Scenic **Map** goo.gl/oXlf5S

Aoraki, also known as Mt Cook, is New Zealand's highest mountain. In 2014 the highest of its three peaks was 3,724m (12,218ft), a shrinkage of 40m (131ft) since 1991 due to a rock slide and subsequent erosion. The mountain is part of the Southern Alps that run the length of the South Island and it is popular with mountaineers.

Those who prefer to transport themselves on wheels can approach the bottom of the mountain via Mt Cook Road, or State Highway 80. This delightful road starts at the small town of Twizel, Canterbury, and quickly reaches the southern end of Lake Pukaki, running 31km (19 miles) up the left-hand side of the lake. To the left of the road is first the Mackenzie Basin and then, after about 10km (6 miles), the Ben Ohau Range. Once past the head of the lake, the road runs alongside the Tasman River, which is fed from four or more glaciers, towards Mt Cook. Be warned: there is no supermarket in the village and the high price of petrol from the self-service pump reflects its isolation.

Mt Cook Road reaches its end just north of the village at the famous Hermitage Hotel, with its luxury suites overlooking the mountain. From here, adventurous road trippers can join a tour to see the Tasman Glacier up close. **SA**

❶ View across Lake Pukaki to the peaks of Mt Cook.

Haast Pass Otago/West Coast, New Zealand

Start Wanaka, Otago   **End** Haast, West Coast   **Distance** 149km (92.3 miles)
Type Scenic   **Map** goo.gl/iJwWMj

The Southern Alps of New Zealand's South Island present a fairly formidable barrier to travellers, with only three passes. One of those, and probably the finest, is Haast Pass, a rough track converted into State Highway 6 in 1966 and tarmacked only in 1995. The pass itself rises to 564m (1,850ft) – the lowest of the three Alpine passes – and it is almost entirely unpopulated, the road largely motoring through natural beech forests.

This road trip begins at Wanaka, Otago, and heads north up State Highway 6 across the Clutha River to the Lake Hawea Dam, built in the 1950s. The road then passes up the west side of the lake and across The Neck, where two glaciers once met, to the east side of Lake Wanaka. Leave the lake behind as you run up an open valley to Makarora, gateway to Mt Aspiring National Park, West Coast, formed in 1964 and now a UNESCO World Heritage Site. Beyond is Haast Pass, first crossed by the gold prospector Charles Cameron in January 1863. Close behind him was Julius von Haast, who declared that he was the first through the pass and gave it his name. Even though his claim was disproved, the moniker stuck. Once at the top of the pass, it is downhill all the way to the sea, passing two spectacular waterfalls en route. **SA**

❶ A perfect place for watersports and mountaineering.

Lindis Pass Otago, New Zealand

Start Cromwell   End Omarama   Distance 109km (68 miles)
Type Scenic   Map goo.gl/21o3jk

Lindis Pass in the centre of South Island has many claims to fame. At 971m (3,186ft), it is the highest point on the highway network of South Island and the second highest in the whole of New Zealand. Despite its height, it is not considered an Alpine pass, since it lies in the dry interior of South Island. The pass itself is a saddle between the Lindis and Ahuriri River valleys; it forms part of State Highway 8 and is thus on the main inland route from Mackenzie Basin to central Otago.

Listed as one of New Zealand's ten most scenic roads, this is a journey to savour and it is accessible to most types of vehicle. The virtually treeless mountains either side are covered with soft, yellowish-brown grassy tussocks and look particularly enchanting with a dusting of snow in winter. In spring and summer, the hills are covered with lupins and buttercups, while grey warblers, fantails and falcons fill the skies. This is an empty landscape, with few people and not many designated picnic spots. Do not expect to race through the pass: the hilly and windy road will keep your speed down to around 48kph (30 mph), so allow a good two or three hours. Needless to say, the views are panoramic and, from the top of the pass, quite awe inspiring. **SA**

❶ The dramatic mountainscape of Lindis Pass.

Queenstown to Glenorchy Road Otago, New Zealand

Start Queenstown   End Glenorchy   Distance 46km (28.7 miles)
Type Scenic   Map goo.gl/OAeasb

The S-shaped Lake Wakatipu is one of the most beautiful lakes in New Zealand, and, at 75.2km (46.7 miles) from end to end, it is also the longest. Mountains line its sides, notably The Remarkables along its southeastern edge, which have a fantastically twisty access road to their summit if you fancy a challenging detour. Interestingly for an inland lake, the surface level fluctuates wildly, with changes of up to 20cm (8 in) at Queenstown every 50 minutes. This variation is known as a seiche, caused by a combination of changing temperatures, wind speeds and atmospheric pressure, although the Maoris believed the fluctuations were caused by the breath of an underwater giant, since the lake looked like the body of a giant with his knees drawn up.

Until recently, transport along the lake was limited to a thrice-weekly ferry. The road between Queenstown in the middle of the lake and Glenorchy at its northern end was finally opened in 1962, but remained unsealed until 1998. This road is a delight to drive, a scenic route roller-coastering along the mountainsides. Queenstown is a major tourist destination, but once out of town, around the peninsula and up the Glenorchy stretch, you will usually have much of the road to yourself. SA

❶ Lake Wakatipu is bordered by mountains on all sides.

Southern Scenic Route
Otago/Southland, New Zealand

Start Queenstown, Otago
End Dunedin, Southland
Distance 608km (378 miles)
Type Scenic
Info goo.gl/pSlnJf

New Zealand's sparse population and strung-out topography meant that, at one time, few people visited the spectacular south of the country. In 1985, a public meeting in Tuatapere, right at the very southernmost point of New Zealand, decided to rectify this. They created the long-distance Southern Scenic Route, which opened up their beautiful land to welcome tourists from far and wide.

The route, which runs in a huge loop from Queenstown to the port of Dunedin, has its own signage: a brown-and-white pointer with a red triangle depicting a white snaking road. It starts on the shores of Lake Wakatipu in Otago region before heading down into Southland region. At Five Rivers, the road runs west and then south again at Te Anau, skirting the eastern boundary of Fiordland National Park. Just south of Tuatapere, the route meets the sea and heads east along the north shore of the Foveaux Strait to Invercargill, New Zealand's southernmost city. It then wanders inland through the dense rainforest of the Catlins, and finally heads north along the coast to Dunedin, one of New Zealand's main cities. This lengthy route is to be taken at leisure, for it offers mountain views, deserted beaches, grand walks, convenient campgrounds and delightful towns aplenty. **SA**

⬥ Scenic Queenstown can be both vibrant and relaxing.

Skippers Canyon Road
Otago, New Zealand

Start Skippers Canyon Road
End Skippers Bridge
Distance 22km (13.7 miles)
Type Adventure
Map goo.gl/Tbctpv

Listed as the world's third most dangerous road, the Skippers Canyon Road started out as a pack mule track, hacked from solid schist rock by Chinese labourers, during New Zealand's gold rush boom. When local miners expanded the track into a navigable road in the late 1800s, it was a major feat of engineering that allowed much better access to the gold-rich gravel beds of Shotover River.

Today the road is popular with tourists, but it is definitely not for the faint of heart. Steep inclines, loose gravel, tight bends and the constant risk of rock falls means that this is one for intrepid drivers only. A 4x4 is strongly advised, and your rental car's insurance won't be honoured if you mess up while tackling it. For long stretches it is strictly single lane – should you happen to meet another automotive adventurer coming the other way, you may have to reverse for up to 3km (2 miles) to find a spot wide enough to squeeze past.

Farther along is Skippers Point, a gold-mining ghost town, which is a good place to make a pit stop and have a bash at gold panning. However, the undoubted highlight of this route has to be Skippers Bridge, a 96-m- (315-foot) long, timber-decked, one-lane crossing suspended 100m (330ft) over the rapids below. **DIS**

◑ The Skippers Canyon Road near Queenstown.

Crown Range Road
Otago, New Zealand

Start Queenstown
End Wanaka
Distance 68km (42.3 miles)
Type Adventure
Map goo.gl/kywRF8

Between the scenic Queenstown on Lake Wakatipu and the equally scenic Lake Wanaka, there are two roads. The longer one is a stretched loop through the Kawarau Gorge and Cromwell, while the shorter and more exciting one is straight over the Crown Range. At its summit, 1,076m (3,530ft) above sea level at the Crown Saddle, is a bronze plaque that claims the road to be the highest sealed road in New Zealand. Don't be misled, for that purported 'fact' is not quite accurate. The road is, however, the highest sealed pass – a significant distinction.

To drive along this extraordinary road, start at Queenstown and head east on State Highways 6A and 6, then turn left at Arrow Junction on to Crown Range Road. Shortly afterwards you are confronted by a series of brutal hairpin bends – this is merely a foretaste of the fun to come.

On the next stage of the journey you climb up first to the fertile Crown Terrace and then on to the Crown Saddle, from where the distant views are outstanding. The road next follows the Cardrona Creek as it grows into the Cardrona River. Tarmac and water wind together down a green and fertile valley to Cardrona, scene of a major gold rush in the 1860s. Remains of gold-prospecting camps can be seen on the riverbanks. Eventually the road will take you down to the resort of Wanaka, a small town with big-city amenities and atmosphere. **SA**

The Remarkables Otago, New Zealand

Start Frankton   **End** The Remarkables Ski Area   **Distance** 18km (11.2 miles)
Type Adventure   **Map** goo.gl/VP3577

There are two schools of thought as to how The Remarkables got their marvellous moniker. One story is that in 1857 to 1858 a local explorer, Alexander Garvie, discovered that they were one of only two mountain ranges in the world to run directly north to south, while others believe it's because of the way they look in the reddening glow of a New Zealand sunset.

For those who wish to visit the mountains by car or motorbike, The Remarkables Road is off Highway 6, the Kingston Road, just south of Frankton. At first it steadily rises through a series of switchbacks before traversing to the north side of the mountain, via some sharp hairpin bends, up to the Double Cone Ski Area at 2,319m (7,606ft). At the 4 km and 6 km marks are two fabulous viewpoints over the Shotover River that should not be missed.

In summer the road surface is mostly loose gravel that can become uncomfortably corrugated; it's also steep in places, dusty and with only a smattering of safety rails in the most terrifying sections. After snowfall it gets pretty treacherous, and snow chains will need to be used. Road signs on the way up usually warn visitors if chains need to be put on two-wheel or four-wheel drive vehicles. A remarkable road trip indeed. **SA**

❶ The winding road uphill to The Remarkables.

Treble Cone Access Road Otago, New Zealand

Start Glendhu Bay　**End** Treble Cone Ski Area　**Distance** 9km (5.6 miles)
Type Adventure　**Map** goo.gl/pB7Nby

The Treble Cone Mountain in the Southern Alps of New Zealand rises to 2,088m (6,849ft) and is the largest ski area in South Island. With a total rise of 700m (2,296ft), it boasts the longest run in the area, with the world's longest rope tow hauling its skiers to the top.

For those less concerned with winter sports, there are adventures to be had on the nearby access road, one of the highest roads in New Zealand. The road starts in Glendhu Bay, at the southwest end of Lake Wanaka, and heads west along the Wanaka–Mt Aspiring Road, which curves around the south of the lake and then proceeds directly west in a straight line until it crosses the Motapu River. Heading north again, a turning to the left takes you first to the Treble Cone Ski Area and then up the side of the mountain in a series of sharp hairpin bends.

Eventually you get to a car park from where two ski lifts take skiers and snowboarders up to their runs. At this point you are 1,250m (4,101ft) up the mountainside, with glorious views over Lake Wanaka and across to the equally impressive Mt Aspiring. The road is unsealed, steep and very windy. There are few guardrails, so do be careful when taking those all-important photographs. **SA**

❶ The road is exposed and windswept.

Milford Road
Southland, New Zealand

Start Te Anau
End Milford Sound
Distance 121km (75 miles)
Type Culture
Info goo.gl/goPO56

The Fiordland region in the southwest corner of South Island is a land of snowjcapped Alps, deep lakes and ocean-flooded west-facing valleys. Its waterfalls are among the highest in the world, its lakes the deepest in New Zealand. This wild and wet region is virtually uninhabited, which makes it all the more attractive for a road trip.

A good place to start is the tiny town of Te Anau, dwarfed by the second-largest lake in New Zealand. From here State Highway 94 heads north along the eastern shore. At around 29km (18 miles), the road reaches Te Anau Downs, heads up the Eglinton Valley and on to the shores of lakes Gunn and Fergus. Passing over a saddle, the road emerges at the top of Hollyford Valley and rises to its highest point at the Homer Tunnel. This granite tunnel was opened in 1954 and at 1,270m (3,959ft) is the second-longest road tunnel in New Zealand. At its far end you emerge at the head of the Cleddau Valley and slowly descend to Milford Sound. Often judged as one of the world's top travel destinations, this stunning stretch of water was described by Rudyard Kipling as the eighth wonder of the world. Fans of the film versions of *The Lord of the Rings* (2001–03) might recognize it as Fangorn Forest, since several scenes were shot here. **SA**

⊃ Down into the clouds along the Milford Road.

Index of Drives by Distance

Index of Drives by Distance

Index of Drives by Distance

Index of Drives by Distance

Contributors

Simon Adams is a keen motorist with a passion for Formula One. He has driven many of the routes written about in this book and has plans to drive the rest as soon as possible. He lives in Brighton, England, and writes about history.

Mike Gerrard is an award-winning British travel and drinks writer. He discovered the joy of the road trip with his American wife, when they began spending half their year in the United States. They now publish a website devoted to their favourite US road trip, the Pacific Coast Highway.

Simon Heptinstall once held the road-trip world record, by driving to twelve different countries in one day. The record has since been broken, but Simon thinks they cheated. A former Top Gear writer, he writes about travel and motoring in print, online and on social media.

David Kelly is a journalist and former magazine publisher. He thinks flying misses the best bits, and is happiest settling into a rental car, with a few days or weeks of still-to-be-decided open road ahead. He has driven extensively in North America, crisscrossing the flyover states many times.

Carol King is a writer and editor who writes about travel for magazines, websites and books. She is happiest looking out of a window at the scenery ahead, whether that is a Rocky Mountains road, the ascent to Mt Etna or the Argentinian pampas.

Jerry Ibbotson is a writer, author and former BBC reporter. He has been a fan of a good road since he jumped on a moped at the age of sixteen. One of his favourite drives is across England's North York Moors towards Whitby, where the road stretches away for miles with only a massive, secret radar base to spoil the view.

Jake Primley writes extensively for encyclopedias and partworks under his own name and a host of aliases. He has driven professionally and for pleasure all over Europe and North America and, unlike many of his British compatriots abroad, never once been scared. Maybe courage is a failure to recognize danger.

Darryl Sleath has been blogging about his numerous automotive adventures for over a decade. He has written for various print magazines and produced a number of short films celebrating the derring-do of motorsport heroes,

and rediscovering Europe's forgotten race circuits. As a self-confessed Mini and MG fanatic, Darryl spends his spare time battling rust and mechanical maladies in his fleet of old British relics.

Dorothy Stannard gained a taste for road trips as a writer and editor of guidebooks during the 1990s. She says the excitement of driving through a strange land, a road map on the dash, and hot maquis-laden air blasting through the open window, is as intoxicating today as it ever was. Her favourite road trip? Driving the Tizi n' Test through the Atlas Mountains.

Barry Stone lives in Sydney, Australia. An author and travel writer, he's written books on topics as varied as military history, sporting scandals and Neolithic prehistory. A traveller to over fifty countries and counting, his favourite road? Why, Iceland's epic Ring Road, Route 1, of course.

Tom Webster is a London-based journalist, editor and presenter specializing in all things automotive. As a result, he's been lucky enough to drive a wide array of cars on some of the most interesting and enjoyable roads around Europe and beyond.

Picture Credits

2 Patrice Latron / Corbis Documentary / Getty Images **20** Edwin Verin / Alamy Stock Photo **22** Natphotos / Getty Images **23** Lucas Payne / Getty Images **24** Design Pics Inc / Alamy Stock Photo **25** Design Pics Inc / Alamy Stock Photo **26** All Canada Photos / Alamy Stock Photo **27** Design Pics Inc / Alamy Stock Photo **28** Ray Bulson / Alamy Stock Photo **30** imageBROKER / Alamy Stock Photo **31** Chris Cheadle / Alamy Stock Photo **32** mikecranephotography.com / Alamy Stock Photo **33** All Canada Photos / Alamy Stock Photo **35** Douglas Lander / Alamy Stock Photo **36** Michael Wheatley / Alamy Stock Photo **37** John E Marriott / Alamy Stock Photo **39** All Canada Photos / Alamy Stock Photo **40** Anna Gorin / Getty Images **41** All Canada Photos / Alamy Stock Photo **42** All Canada Photos / Alamy Stock Photo **44** Terrance Klassen / Alamy Stock Photo **46** Christoph Fischer / Alamy Stock Photo **47** All Canada Photos / Alamy Stock Photo **48** Newzulu / Alamy Stock Photo **50** Barrett & MacKay / Getty Images **51** Ron Erwin / Getty Images **53** Rolf Hicker Photography / Alamy Stock Photo **54** Phil Degginger / Alamy Stock Photo **56** Cliff Nietvelt / Getty Images **57** Yves Marcoux / Getty Images **58** Barrett & MacKay / Getty Images **59** All Canada Photos / Alamy Stock Photo **60** KarenMassier / Getty Images **61** Marjorie McBride / Alamy Stock Photo **62** Westend61 / Getty Images **63** Onest Mistic / Getty Images **64** Ronald Greer / Alamy Stock Photo **65** Terry Donnelly / Alamy Stock Photo **66** Glenn Van Der Knijff / Getty Images **67** Linda Lantzy / Alamy Stock Photo **68** Gaertner / Alamy Stock Photo **70** Morey Milbradt / Alamy Stock **71** Patrick Morisson / Alamy Stock Photo **72** Michael Matti / Alamy Stock Photo **73** Bruce Shippee / EyeEm / Getty Images **75** James O'Neil / Getty Images **76** David Wall / Alamy Stock Photo **78** GJGK Photography / Alamy Stock Photo **79** Sergey Borisov / Alamy Stock Photo **80** Photo 12 / Alamy Stock Photo **81** Danita Delimont / Alamy Stock Photo **82** AF archive / Alamy Stock Photo **85** Michele Falzone / Alamy Stock Photo **86** Everett Collection Inc / Alamy Stock Photo **87** Don Smith / Getty Images **88** Ian Dagnall / Alamy Stock Photo **89** trekkerimages / Alamy Stock Photo **90** armaroli stefano / Alamy Stock Photo **91** David Kelly **93** Education Images/UIG / Getty Images **94** Sky Noir Photography by Bill Dickinson / Getty Images **95** Witold Skrypczak / Getty Images **96** David R. Frazier Photolibrary, Inc. / Alamy Stock Photo **97** George Ostertag / Alamy Stock Photo **98** Yaacov Dagan / Alamy Stock Photo **99** Rowan Romeyn / Alamy Stock Photo **101** Lee Rentz / Alamy Stock Photo **102** Allan Baxter / Getty Images **103** Dan Leffel / Robert Harding **104** Witold Skrypczak / Getty Images **105** Emily Riddell / Getty Images **106** Danita Delimont / Alamy Stock Photo **107** Gary Crabbe / Enlightened Images / Alamy Stock Photo **109** Edwin Verin / Alamy Stock Photo **111** Mint Images - Paul Edmondson / Getty Images **113** Henk Meijer / Alamy Stock Photo **114** akg-images / De Agostini / L. Romano **116** Morey Milbradt / Alamy Stock Photo **117** Kerrick James / Alamy Stock Photo **118** Henk Meijer / Alamy Stock Photo **119** Planet Observer / Getty Images **120** Janice and Nolan Braud / Alamy Stock Photo **121** Atlaspix / Paramount Pictures / Alamy Stock Photo **122** Mark Miller Photos / Getty Images **123** Philippe Sainte-Laudy Photography / Getty Images **125** NiCK / Getty Images **127** Charles Wollertz / Alamy Stock Photo **128** Connie Fitzgerald / Alamy Stock Photo **129** Alan Copson / Getty Images **130** Danita Delimont / Getty Images **131** Maciej Bledowski / Alamy Stock Photo **132** Tom Uhlman / Alamy Stock Photo **133** Stock Connection Blue / Alamy Stock Photo **134** JOE KLAMAR / Staff / Getty Images **136** Buddy Mays / Alamy Stock Photo **138** Everett Collection Inc / Alamy Stock Photo **139** Rob Greebon / Alamy Stock Photo **140** RooM the Agency / Alamy Stock Photo **141** Dan Leeth / Alamy Stock Photo **142** Prisma by Dukas Presseagentur GmbH / Alamy Stock Photo **143** Posnov / Getty Images **144** Tom Bean / Alamy Stock Photo **145** RGB Ventures / SuperStock / Alamy Stock Photo **147** Matthew Richardson / Alamy Stock Photo **149** Andre Babiak / Alamy Stock Photo **151** Susan Dykstra / Design Pics / Getty Images **152** Stock Connection Blue / Alamy Stock Photo **153** Mark Miller Photos / Getty Images **155** Don Smetzer / Alamy Stock Photo **156** David R. Frazier Photolibrary, Inc. / Alamy Stock Photo **157** John Elk / Getty Images **158** Henk Meijer / Alamy Stock Photo **159** MGM/Pathe/Kobal/REX/Shutterstock **160** John Zada / Alamy Stock Photo **161** Bob Pardue - South Central / Alamy Stock Photo **163** Rhonda Stansberry / Getty Images **164** Elena Kovalevich / Getty Images **165** Ilene MacDonald / Alamy Stock Photo **167** Don Smetzer / Alamy Stock Photo **168** age fotostock / Alamy Stock Photo **169** Linda Johnsonbaugh lighthouses / Alamy Stock Photo **170** Mark Scheuern / Alamy Stock Photo **171** Cathy Melloan / Alamy Stock Photo **172** Trigger Image / Alamy Stock Photo **173** dmac / Alamy Stock Photo **174** Car Culture / Getty Images **177** Universal Images Group North America LLC / Alamy Stock Photo **178** Mark Scheuern / Alamy Stock Photo **179** David Kelly **180** Wiskerke / Alamy Stock Photo **181** Andre Jenny / Alamy Stock Photo **182** Marcus Baker / Alamy Stock Photo **183** Frank Spinelli / Getty Images **185** Cultura RM Exclusive/Christoffer Askman / Getty Images **186** Tony Shi Photography / Getty Images **187** Pictorial Press Ltd / Alamy Stock Photo **188** Stephen St. John / Getty Images **189** Moviestore collection Ltd / Alamy Stock Photo **191** Daniel Dempster Photography / Alamy Stock Photo **193** Jon Bilous / Alamy Stock Photo **194** Maremagnum / Getty Images **195** Loop Images Ltd / Alamy Stock Photo **196** Roy Rainford / robertharding / Getty Images **197** Tetra Images / Getty Images **198** Matt Anderson Photography / Getty Images **199** Colleen Miniuk-Sperry / Alamy Stock Photo **200** Michael Hudson / Alamy Stock Photo **201** Doug van Kampen, van Kampen Photography / Getty Images **203** Alan Copson / Getty Images **204** Danita Delimont / Getty Images **205** Viktor Posnov / Alamy Stock Photo **206** Dennis Govoni / Getty Images **207** Michele Burgess / Getty Images **208** Songquan Deng / Alamy Stock Photo **211** Richard T. Nowitz / Getty Images **213** Don Smetzer / Alamy Stock Photo **214** Design Pics Inc / Alamy Stock Photo **215** L. Toshio Kishiyama / Getty Images **216** Mark Reinstein / Contributor / Getty Images **217** Sean Pavone / Alamy Stock Photo **218** Dennis Cox / Alamy Stock Photo **219** Richard Ellis / Alamy Stock Photo **220** Mary Liz Austin / Alamy Stock Photo **221** Pat & Chuck Blackley / Alamy Stock Photo **223** Ellisphotos / Alamy Stock Photo **224** Amy White & Al Petteway / Getty Images **225** Natalia Ganelin / Getty Images **226** Silver Screen Collection / Contributor / Getty Images **227** NATUREWOLRD / Alamy Stock Photo **229** Blaine Harrington III / Alamy Stock Photo **231** Leigh Anne Meeks / Alamy Stock Photo **232** Steven L. Raymer / Contributor / Getty Images **233** Steven Greaves / Getty Images **234** Christopher Price / Alamy Stock Photo **235** © Sergi Reboredo / Bridgeman Images **236** Amit Basu Photography / Getty Images **237** Christopher Stewart / Alamy Stock Photo **238** Westend61 / Getty Images **239** Sunny Awazuhara- Reed / Design Pics / Getty Images **240** Chuck Pefley / Alamy Stock Photo **241** Vaughn Greg / Getty Images **242** Logan Havens / Alamy Stock Photo **243** ZUMA Press Inc / Alamy Stock Photo **245** age fotostock / Alamy Stock Photo **246** Brian Overcast / Alamy Stock Photo **247** Matt Mawson / Getty Images **249** RacingOne / Contributor / Getty Images **250** © Iztok Alf Kurnik - www.iztokkurnik.com / Getty Images **251** Simon Lowthian / Alamy Stock Photo **252** age fotostock / Alamy Stock Photo **254** Walter Bibikow / Getty Images **255** Pola Damonte via Getty Images / Getty Images **256** age fotostock / Alamy Stock Photo **257** Anthony Pidgeon / Alamy Stock Photo **258** Westend61 / Getty Images **259** Bryan Mullennix / Getty Images **260** Connie Coleman / Getty Images **261** M.Sobreira / Alamy Stock Photo **262** Hervé Champollion / akg-images **263** George H.H. Huey / Alamy Stock Photo **264** Walter Bibikow / Getty Images **265** Michael Lawrence / Getty Images **267** Folio Images / Alamy Stock Photo **268** Upperhall Ltd / robertharding / Getty Images **271** Jane Sweeney / Getty Images **273** Stefano Paterna / Alamy Stock Photo **274** David Coleman / Alamy Stock Photo **276** Judy Waytiuk / Alamy Stock Photo **277** Greg Vaughn / Alamy Stock Photo **278** Keren Su / Getty Images **279** Ricardo Ribas / Alamy Stock Photo **280** Rob Francis / Alamy Stock Photo **281** John Coletti / Getty Images **282** Alex Robinson / Getty Images **283** Mark Green / Alamy Stock Photo **284** Westend61 GmbH / Alamy Stock Photo **286** J.Enrique Molina / Alamy Stock Photo **287** Chris Pancewicz / Alamy Stock Photo **288** cicloco / Alamy Stock Photo **289** Jan Sochor / Alamy Stock Photo **290** Stock Connection Blue / Alamy Stock Photo **292** Paulo Fridman / Contributor / Getty Images **294** DircinhaSW / Getty Images **295** Micael Bergamaschi / Getty Images **296** Pulsar Images / Alamy Stock Photo **297** Michael Fritzen / Alamy Stock Photo **299** Christophe Boisvieux / Getty Images **300** George Philipas / Alamy Stock Photo **301** imageBROKER / Alamy Stock Photo **302** Ashley Cooper pics / Alamy Stock Photo **305** imageBROKER / Alamy Stock Photo **306** Simon Montgomery / robertharding / Getty Images **308** Benedicte Desrus / Alamy Stock Photo **309** Navè Orgad / Alamy Stock Photo **310** Mark Green / Alamy Stock Photo **311** Jesse Kraft / Alamy Stock Photo **313** Sara Winter / Alamy Stock Photo **315** Novarc Images / Alamy Stock Photo **316** imageBROKER / Alamy Stock Photo **317** Nilton Sergio Ramos Quoirin / Getty Images **318** Yvan Travert / akg-images **319** pura vida / Getty Images **321** Panther Media GmbH / Alamy Stock Photo **322** Blaine Harrington III / Alamy Stock Photo **323** United Archives GmbH / Alamy Stock Photo **325** Emiliano Rodriguez / Alamy Stock Photo **326** Pulsar Images / Alamy Stock Photo **328** Stelian Porojnicu / Alamy Stock Photo **330** imageBROKER / Alamy Stock Photo **331** Mummi Bjarni / Getty Images **332** incamerastock / Alamy Stock Photo **333** subtik / Getty Images **334** Arco Images GmbH / Alamy Stock Photo **335** Niall Benvie / Alamy Stock Photo **337** Yuriy Brykaylo / Alamy Stock Photo **338** ROBERTO BENZI / Alamy Stock Photo **339** Hemis / Alamy Stock Photo **341** lucapierro / Getty Images **343** Cultura Creative (RF) / Alamy Stock Photo **345** Norimages / Alamy Stock Photo **346** Westend61 GmbH / Alamy Stock Photo **347** Erlend Haarberg / Getty Images **348** Kjersti Joergensen / Alamy Stock Photo **349** David Robertson / Alamy Stock Photo **350** daitoZen / Getty Images **353** Johner Images / Alamy Stock Photo **354** Biederbick&Rumpf / Getty Images **355** Zoonar GmbH / Alamy Stock Photo **356** Hans-Peter Merten / Getty Images **357** robertharding / Alamy Stock Photo **358** Photography by David Thyberg / Getty Images **359** Agencja Fotograficzna Caro / Alamy Stock Photo **360** Cultura RM / Alamy Stock Photo **362** Esa Hiltula / Alamy Stock Photo **363** Inga Leksina / Alamy Stock Photo **365** Chris Hill/National Geographic Creative / Bridgeman Images **366** scenicireland.com / Christopher Hill Photographic / Alamy Stock Photo **367** Radharc Images / Alamy Stock Photo **369** Dennis Frates / Alamy Stock Photo **370** © Sergi Reboredo / Bridgeman Images **371** Andrea Pistolesi / Getty Images **372** Gareth Mccormack / Getty Images **373** mika / Alamy Stock Photo **375** Peter Zoeller / Getty Images **376** kevers / Alamy Stock Photo

Picture Credits

735 AfriPics.com / Alamy Stock Photo **737** travelpixs / Alamy Stock Photo **738** by Marc Guitard / Getty Images **740** F1online digitale Bildagentur GmbH / Alamy Stock Photo **741** nick baylis / Alamy Stock Photo **742** Davide Guidolin / Alamy Stock Photo **743** Manfred Gottschalk / Getty Images **744** F1online digitale Bildagentur GmbH / Alamy Stock Photo **745** Marie Jeffsell / Alamy Stock Photo **746** frans lemmens / Alamy Stock Photo **747** Gallo Images / Alamy Stock Photo **748** Jason Edwards / Getty Images **749** Siegfried Layda / Getty Images **750** robertharding / Alamy Stock Photo **751** Graham Bartholomew / Getty Images **752** Hein von Horsten / Getty Images **753** Dori Moreno / Getty Images **754** PHOTOBYTE / Alamy Stock Photo **755** Bob Gibbons / Alamy Stock Photo **756** Edwin Remsberg / Getty Images **757** Novarc Images / Alamy Stock Photo **759** Simon Hathaway / Alamy Stock Photo **761** Michele Falzone / Alamy Stock Photo **762** View Stock / Getty Images **764** Leonid Andronov / Alamy Stock Photo **765** Eddie Gerald / Alamy Stock Photo **767** Dario Bajurin / Alamy Stock Photo **769** Fedor Selivanov / Alamy Stock Photo **770** © Santiago Urquijo / Getty Images **773** Moments of Life / Getty Images **774** DEA / ARCHIVIO J. LANGE / Contributor / Getty Images **775** Patrick Dieudonne / robertharding / Getty Images **777** Kasia Nowak / Alamy Stock Photo **778** ALLSTAR Picture Library / Alamy Stock Photo **779** Tibor Bognar / Alamy Stock Photo **780** Chalus road - ninara 02, ninara, https://en.wikipedia.org/wiki/Road_59_(Iran)#/media/File:Chalus_road_-_ninara_02.jpg, https://creativecommons.org/licenses/by/2.0/ **782** robertharding / Alamy Stock Photo **783** REUTERS / Alamy Stock Photo **784** Ivan Vdovin / Alamy Stock Photo **785** Bjorn Holland / Getty Images **787** travelib asia / Alamy Stock Photo **788** National Geographic Creative / Alamy Stock Photo **789** Feng Wei Photography / Getty Images **790** Idealink Photography / Alamy Stock Photo **791** age fotostock / Alamy Stock Photo **792** TAUSEEF MUSTAFA / Stringer / Getty Images **793** Grant Dixon / Lonely Planet Images / Getty Images **795** Idris Ahmed / Alamy Stock Photo **796** Roland and Sabrina Michaud / akg-images **798** Bhaven Jani / Alamy Stock Photo **799** Vivek Sharma / Alamy Stock Photo **800** Image Source / Getty Images **802** David Clapp / Photolibrary / Getty Images **804** james cheadle / Alamy Stock Photo **805** RESOLUTION/Balan Madhavan / Alamy Stock Photo **807** Partha Pal / The Image Bank / Getty Images **808** Dinodia Photos / Alamy Stock Photo **810** Dinodia Photos / Alamy Stock Photo **811** nandana de silva / Alamy Stock Photo **813** Matthew Williams-Ellis Travel Photography / Alamy Stock Photo **814** PRAKASH MATHEMA / Stringer / Getty Images **815** Dinodia Photos / Alamy Stock Photo **816** robertharding / Alamy Stock Photo **817** Richard l'Anson / Lonely Planet Images / Getty Images **818** TAO Images Limited / Alamy Stock Photo **819** Xinhua / Alamy Stock Photo **821** wulingyun / Moment / Getty Images **822** pkul / Shutterstock.com **823** Winters Zhang / Moment / Getty Images **824** Prasit Rodphan / Alamy Stock Photo **825** Blake Kent / Design Pics / Getty Images **826** Xinhua / Alamy Stock Photo **827** Sino Images / Getty Images **828** Philip Game / Alamy Stock Photo **829** Xinhua / Alamy Stock Photo **831** yunzen liu / 360cities.net / Getty Images **832** Manfred Gottschalk / Alamy Stock Photo **833** Ian Trower / Alamy Stock Photo **835** Bob Henry / Alamy Stock Photo **836** REUTERS / Alamy Stock Photo **837** View Stock / Getty Images **838** Henry Westheim Photography / Alamy Stock Photo **839** Sean Sprague / Alamy Stock Photo **840** Sunrise@dawn Photography / Moment Open / Getty Images **841** Taylor Weidman / Stringer / Getty Images **842** Panithan Fakseemuang / Moment / Getty Images **843** Jack Barker / Alamy Stock Photo **844** RooM the Agency / Alamy Stock Photo **845** parasola.net / Alamy Stock Photo **847** Image Republic Inc. / Alamy Stock Photo **849** robertharding / Alamy Stock Photo **851** Cultura Creative (RF) / Alamy Stock Photo **852** Gribov Andrei / Alamy Stock Photo **854** Ilaxa_RUS / Shutterstock.com **857** Yoshitsugu Nishigaki/Sebun Photo / amana images / Getty Images **858** Chris Willson / Alamy Stock Photo **859** Hakone Turnpike 20140412-1, PekePON, https://commons.wikimedia.org/wiki/File:Hakone_Turnpike_20140412-1.jpg, https://creativecommons.org/licenses/by/4.0/ **860** Christopher Kei Baron Moriyama, CK Photography / Moment / Getty Images **861** The Asahi Shimbun / Getty Images **863** The Ashasi Shimbun / Getty Images **864** Sean Pavone / Alamy Stock Photo **865** The Ashasi Shimbun / Getty Images **866** JTB Photo / Universal Images Group / Getty Images **867** Julian Nieman / Alamy Stock Photo **869** Ivan Vdovin / Alamy Stock Photo **870** Leonid Serebrennikov / Alamy Stock Photo **871** Ashit Desai / Moment / Getty Images **872** Santi Sukarnjanaprai / Moment / Getty Images **873** Carlo Caseserano / EyeEm / Getty Images **875** Friedrich Stark / Alamy Stock Photo **876** akg-images / Pictures From History **878** Chaichan Ingkawaranon / Alamy Stock Photo **879** Green Stock Media / Alamy Stock Photo **880** age fotostock / Alamy Stock Photo **881** Robertus Pudyanto / Stringer / Getty Images **882** foodfolio / Alamy Stock Photo **883** robertharding / Alamy Stock Photo **884** Andrew Jones / Getty Images **887** Australian Scenics / Photolibrary / Getty Images **888** domonabike / Alamy Stock Photo **890** John Hay / Lonely Planet Images / Getty Images **891** Taras Vyshnya / Alamy Stock Photo **892** © HADI ZAHER / Moment Open / Getty Images **893** Australian Scenics / Photolibrary / Getty Images **894** Hans-Peter Merten / The Image Bank / Getty Images **895** David Wall / Alamy Stock Photo **897** Andrew Jones / Moment / Getty Images **898** David Foster / Alamy Stock Photo **899** Mark A. Johnson / Alamy Stock Photo **900** Ingo Oeland / Alamy Stock Photo **901** LOOK Die Bildagentur der Fotografen GmbH / **902** redbrickstock.com / Alamy Stock Photo **903** David Wall / Alamy Stock Photo **904** Travel Pictures / Alamy Stock Photo **907** Michael Runkel / robertharding / Getty Images **909** Iconsinternational.Com / Alamy Stock Photo **911** Stephanie Jackson / Alamy Stock Photo **913** graham jepson / Alamy Stock Photo **914** Australian Scenics / Photographer's Choice RF / Getty Images **915** Mike Berceanu / Photolibrary / Getty Images **916** Eric Nathan / Alamy Stock Photo **917** Bernard van Dierendonck/ LOOK-foto / Getty Images **918** David Noton Photography / Alamy Stock Photo **919** Australian Scenics / Photolibrary / Getty Images **920** Iconsinternational.Com / Alamy Stock Photo **921** Ray Warren Australia / Alamy Stock Photo **922** JONATHAN AYRES / Alamy Stock Photo **924** jackie ellis / Alamy Stock Photo **926** vario images GmbH & Co.KG / Alamy Stock Photo **927** Peter Hendrie / Lonely Planet Images / Getty Images **928** Hardyuno / Alamy Stock Photo **929** Danita Delimont / Gallo Images / Getty Images **931** David Wall / Alamy Stock Photo **933** David Wall / Alamy Stock Photo **935** David Wall / Alamy Stock Photo **936** Tim Cuff / Alamy Stock Photo **937** Matthew Micah Wright / Lonely Planet Images / Getty Images **938** Zoonar GmbH / Alamy Stock Photo **939** Manon van Os / Alamy Stock Photo **940** Tom Blachford / Cultura Creative (RF) / Alamy Stock Photo **941** Rachel Stewart - rsnz photography / Getty Images **943** Ramiro Torrents / Getty Images **944** Tim Gerard Barker / Lonely Planet Images / Getty Images **946** Peter Lenk / Alamy Stock Photo **947** Matthew Scott / Alamy Stock Photo **949** Rolf_52 / Alamy Stock Photo

Acknowledgements

Firstly, I would like to thank Philip Cooper and Ruth Patrick at Quintessence for having faith in my abilities to manage this book project, and Carol King for her patience, encouragement and eagle-eyed attention to detail in putting the final proofs together.

I must also thank the team of talented writers that contributed road trips from across the globe, especially veteran *1001* General Editors Barry Stone and Simon Heptinstall for their support and assistance. But most importantly, I need to thank my wife, Jennifer, and children, Anwen and Harry, for putting up with my grumpiness during those late-night editing marathons and keeping me hydrated with an endless supply of tea.